Dr Jenny Carlyon and Dr Diana Morrow are prominent New Zealand historians. They are the authors of *Urban Village: The Story of Ponsonby, Freemans Bay and St Mary's Bay* (2008) and *A Fine Prospect: A History of Remuera, Meadowbank and St Johns* (2011). Carlyon has a PhD in History from the University of Auckland and the French qualification Licence d'histoire (equivalent to a BA). Since returning to New Zealand she has worked as a teacher and a researcher/writer for major corporates, run a small business and is now a professional historian. Morrow was born in Canada, came to New Zealand in 1980 and gained her PhD in History from Victoria University of Wellington in 1997. She has worked as an archivist, an interpretive consultant/researcher/writer for museums, a tutor and part-time lecturer and a professional historian for the Waitangi Tribunal and the Office of Treaty Settlements. She is also the co-editor of the books *City of Enterprise: Perspectives on Auckland Business History* (2006) and *Jewish Lives in New Zealand* (2012).

CHANGING TIMES

NEW ZEALAND SINCE 1945

JENNY CARLYON
& DIANA MORROW

AUCKLAND
UNIVERSITY
PRESS

First published 2013

Auckland University Press
University of Auckland
Private Bag 92019
Auckland 1142
New Zealand
www.press.auckland.ac.nz

ISBN 978 1 86940 782 7

Publication is kindly assisted by

ARTS COUNCIL OF NEW ZEALAND TOI AOTEAROA

National Library of New Zealand Cataloguing-in-Publication Data
Carlyon, Jenny, 1951-
Changing times : New Zealand since 1945 / Jenny Carlyon and
Diana Morrow.
Includes bibliographical references and index.
ISBN 978-1-86940-782-7
1. New Zealand—History—1945-1984. 2. New Zealand—History
—1984- 3. New Zealand—Social conditions—20th century.
4. New Zealand—Economic conditions—20th century.
I. Morrow, Diana. II. Title.
993.035—dc 23

Cover design: Keely O'Shannessy

Front cover: New Zealanders at a political street-corner meeting in 1969. *Marti Friedlander*
Back cover: A Wellington street scene, 1957. *EP/1957/4783-F, Evening Post Collection,*
Alexander Turnbull Library, courtesy of Fairfax Media

Printed by Everbest Printing Co., China

CONTENTS

ACKNOWLEDGEMENTS

We are grateful to Auckland University Press for suggesting the idea of a New Zealand history focusing on the post-1945 period. While this seemed a daunting prospect at the outset, Sam Elworthy, Anna Hodge, Christine O'Brien and Katrina Duncan have, through their respective expertise, eased the task considerably. We are grateful, too, to Mike Wagg for his meticulous copy-editing, Claire Gummer for proofreading and Diane Lowther for indexing.

We are indebted to a great many historians, past and present, whose work we have drawn on in this book. Thanks also to Geoff Ricketts, Rina van Bohemen, Rhys Harrison and Daniel Morrow, who read chapters at various stages of completion; Cathy Marr, Principal Research Analyst, Waitangi Tribunal, for fielding queries; Redmer Yska for helping us with bodgies and widgies; Robin Congreve, Peter Simpson, Linda Bryder, Peter Graham, Bryce Wilkinson and Brian Gaynor for advice and assistance; Steve Heap for solving Jenny's computer glitches; and research librarians at the University of Auckland, Auckland City Libraries, Alexander Turnbull Library, Archives New Zealand, Canterbury Museum and Puke Ariki, New Plymouth, for their assistance.

We are also grateful for permission to include copyright material in the book. Thank you to photographers Peter Bush, Marti Friedlander, Gil Hanly, John Miller and Ans Westra and to Dinah Morrison for the use of Robin Morrison photographs. Many thanks also to those who granted us permission to use other visuals. Natalie Marshall and Heather Mathie at the Alexander Turnbull Library and Keith Giles at Sir George Grey Special Collections, Auckland City Libraries, were helpful with image assistance, as well as forbearing. Thanks also go to Paul Millar and John Baxter, Charles Brasch literary executor Alan Roddick, Rob Campbell, Rupert Glover and Pia Glover, Alexandra Smithyman and Rob Tuwhare (honetuwharepoetry@gmail) for permission to reproduce lines from the work of James K. Baxter, Charles Brasch, Alistair Te Ariki Campbell, Denis Glover, Mary Stanley and Hone Tuwhare.

Finally, as always, we are especially grateful to our husbands, Rick Carlyon and John Morrow, for their ongoing encouragement and support.

Jenny Carlyon and Diana Morrow

Unforeseen Directions

AFTER 1945

Should you wish to erect a factory, import materials or manufactures from overseas, or send money abroad, you must obtain the state's permission . . . If you are a farmer, it offers the assistance of its agricultural experts, buys certain of your products at prices it guarantees, and markets them . . . It plants timber at its own sawmill, and sells it . . . Whenever you visit a doctor, it contributes a portion of the medical fees: and if you are unemployed, widowed, orphaned, aged or totally invalided it pays you a benefit . . . Leviathan in New Zealand is a well-nigh universal provider.
— Leslie Lipson, 1948[1]

During World War II, Leslie Lipson, an American professor of political science employed at Victoria University College in Wellington, began work on a study of New Zealand democracy. Published in 1948, *The Politics of Equality* described a small, geographically remote country and the society that had coalesced there after little more than a hundred years of formal European settlement. New Zealand, in Lipson's view, was fiercely loyal to Britain, ethnically homogenous and socially conservative. As a political community its most notable characteristics were a reputation for advanced social legislation and an unusually pronounced expectation that the state would provide. In fact, the country was 'one of the most elaborately governed democracies in the world'.[2]

Since the late nineteenth century, numerous foreign observers had extolled the degree of state intervention that Lipson found so remarkable. New Zealanders wore this distinction as a badge of national pride. Between 1939 and 1946, when Lipson lived and worked in the country, the exigencies of war prompted the state to widen its already extensive embrace. While continuing to furnish citizens with myriad protections and benefits — from insurance, to farming advice, to dental clinics — the first Labour government imposed rationing and set in place firm controls on the economy.

Lipson admired the country's 'equalitarianism', a neologism he coined to describe the state's 'levelling down and levelling up'. Yet he warned that a tendency in the national identity toward the flattening of social differences might see talent sacrificed to 'the worship of averages' and encourage dull conformity. 'In their thinking, as in their methods of living,' Lipson wrote, 'New Zealanders tend to conform to type. The same convictions, prejudices and stock symbols predominate throughout the country. There is not enough internal diversity to produce a clash of opinion.'[3] While New Zealand society held fairness and equality at a premium, he feared too tight an embrace of these very values could stifle talent, initiative and originality.

From 1946, the New Zealand state continued on its interventionist path, shaping and directing not only the economic but also, to a considerable degree, the social and cultural life of the nation. Labour and National, the major political parties, continued to accept the state's central role in managing the economy and providing social services.[4] The post-war dream of healthy, well-housed, hard-working parents, whose children flourished in a green suburban idyll, answered a need for security. This public longing for stability was not unique to New Zealand. After 1945, war-weary people and governments around the globe looked hopefully forward rather than back. New Zealanders were keen to usher in a less tumultuous and more prosperous world despite, or perhaps as a way of coping with, pronounced fears of a new economic depression and escalating geopolitical conflict in the shape of the Cold War. Having experienced so much tragedy and upheaval, New Zealand citizens, like those of other advanced democracies, warmed to a vision of ordered, comfortable domesticity.[5]

Governments in post-war Britain and Western Europe, as in New Zealand, introduced welfare benefits and social services designed to assist young couples with children. Both in terms of national defence and economic capabilities, policy-makers believed it made sense to invest in the future and in youth.[6] As an industrialising new nation rich in marketable primary produce, New

Zealand's living standards had rivalled or exceeded those of Western Europe since the late nineteenth century. Geographical isolation and American intervention, moreover, had shielded the country from the physical and economic devastation the Second World War visited on Europe. But the conflict in the Pacific increased New Zealand's awareness of its defence vulnerability. Nurturing a growing population of healthy, hard-working citizens (and potential military recruits) made eminent sense. Post-war governments saw security and prosperity for young families as an investment in future defence and economic growth.

In many respects, the New Zealand government's vision of a post-war suburban idyll was realised in the 1950s and early 1960s. The country basked in a long spell of 'golden weather',[7] with full employment, economic prosperity and a high standard of living. The government maintained a protectionist economic policy (import controls introduced during the war remained in place until the mid-1980s) that was costly and resulted in high taxes. Economic growth in terms of real per capita income was slow by international standards. By 1950, state spending accounted for nearly 30 per cent of the country's gross domestic product (GDP) each year. But most New Zealanders appreciated both the fairness and the security provided by an insulated economy and generous public welfare provisions.[8]

Over time, however, the apparent certainties of this vision of post-war progress, articulated by politicians and held dear by ordinary New Zealanders, began to erode. Some of the causes were international. New Zealand's loyalty to the Mother Country remained strong during and after the war. As the writer John Mulgan observed: 'The kind of loyalty that New Zealanders possess is stupid, irrational, and, in some melancholy way, satisfying to the heart.'[9] But Britain's weakened post-war status necessitated new defence and trading alliances, which introduced New Zealand to unfamiliar markets and cultural influences. Eventually, those new alliances would undermine the post-war foreign policy consensus as New Zealanders argued over involvement in the Vietnam War. Although international ideas and events had long played a crucial role in the country's history, global influences on ordinary New Zealanders increased rapidly after the war as new technology lessened geographical distance and facilitated faster and more frequent travel.

Other transformations were domestic in origin. The post-war proliferation of young families, encouraged by government policies, sowed the seeds of weakening government control. Urbanisation, consumerism, the advent of teen culture, wives leaving the domestic sphere to resume paid work, Maori and Pacific Islanders migrating to cities in search of greater opportunities: all had unforeseen long-term impacts that transformed New Zealand life. Paradoxically, state policy, driven by economic imperatives, encouraged many of the developments that ultimately proved most corrosive to the post-war domestic ideology.

By the late twentieth century, most of what Lipson perceived as the country's key characteristics — its remarkable state paternalism, its cultural and ethnic homogeneity, its loyal dependence on the Mother Country — had, if not vanished altogether, altered beyond recognition. New Zealand had moved away from its former dependence on Britain and developed a more independent national identity — albeit one deeply indebted to overseas ideas, events and movements. As the rest of this book attests, the process of transformation from the complacent, statist, socially conservative and loyal dominion that Lipson observed in the late 1940s into New Zealand's present incarnation was not without pain and conflict. Nor was it some Whiggish progression, moving inexorably away from dependence toward national identity and a later transnational 'independence': there was considerable loss along the way. New Zealanders no longer enjoy the security bestowed 'from the cradle to the grave' by a generous state. Lipson, in the concluding pages of his study, expressed the hope that a future New Zealand would 'continue to build on those foundations that are well and truly laid — on its hatred of privilege, its passion for social justice, and its eradication of poverty'.[10] But a recent OECD report suggests that in fact New Zealand's once relatively narrow income gap is widening faster than that of any other country in the developed world.[11] As the Global Financial Crisis made clear, the country's open economy is vulnerable to international forces beyond its control.

In 1945, the altered balance of power after the war forced New Zealand's leaders, albeit with initial reluctance, to emerge from the 'insulated cocoon' of empire.[12] This book examines the key events and beliefs that propelled the country's economic and cultural transformations, from the wake of the Second World War to the beginning of the twenty-first century. In doing so, it measures the distance and traces the continuities that separate and link the inhabitants of New Zealand in 1945 with those of the present day. It also assesses the degree to which identity — national, community and individual — was shaped and altered by overseas influences. While the country's trajectory shared strong similarities with those of other developed countries around the globe, its experiences were filtered through a unique set of economic, political and cultural circumstances.

The book's twelve chapters, which are arranged both chronologically and thematically, span the early post-war period to the present day, and engage with the key themes, ideas, people, places and events that forged the history of New Zealand in the second half of the twentieth century. In the course of our research, we were struck by the multitude of voices we were able to recover from the written record. Where possible, we have attempted to frame the story using the experiences and views of New Zealanders themselves — from the push of those advocating change, to the pull of those striving for continuity.

CHAPTER ONE

On an Even Keel?

PEACE, PROSPERITY, CONSENSUS

If the old world ends now with this war, as well it may, I have had visions and dreamed dreams of another New Zealand that might grow into the future on the foundations of the old. This country would have more people to share it. They would be hard-working peasants from Europe that know good land, craftsmen that love making things with their own hands, and all men who want the freedom that comes from an ordered, just community. There would be more children in the sands and sunshine, more small farms, gardens and cottages. Girls would wear bright dresses, men would talk quietly together. Few would be rich, none would be poor. They would fill the land and make it a nation. — John Mulgan, 1945[1]

You get up at a regular hour, go to work, you marry and have a family, a house and a garden, and you live on an even keel till you draw a pension and they bury you decently. The New Zealand way of life is ordained but who ordains it?
— Bill Pearson, 1952[2]

On 8 May 1945, New Zealanders greeted the news of the Allies' victory in Europe with jubilation. People danced in the streets, embraced passing strangers and gathered happily in pubs to toast the historic occasion. Newspapers praised the Mother Country's fortitude and stressed the urgency of ensuring that 'never again will the world be plunged into the maelstrom of total war'.[3]

Celebrations continued for days. In Wellington, on 9 May, residents woke to screaming sirens and pealing bells, and poured into the city for the official ceremonies, promenading with patriotic streamers and rosettes. No buses or trams ran during the national thanksgiving service at noon, or the citizen's service in the afternoon. Later, 'laughing, cheering crowds took complete charge of the streets. Bands played in relays. People danced to their music and generally behaved with good humoured but unrestrained exuberance' as 'a spirit of increasing abandon' took hold, culminating in 'scenes of revelry unprecedented in the history of the city'.[4] In New Plymouth:

> pent-up feelings after 5½ years of war were let loose when it was decided to 'lift the lid' and let the people give spontaneous expression to their feelings of thankfulness ... And when the sirens gave the symbol, bells and whistles took up the great chorus of rejoicing, and every noise-making device, designed and improvised, was brought into play and pandemonium, which reigned for some minutes, broke out again spasmodically at intervals afterwards.[5]

These revelries, which occurred on a smaller but no less enthusiastic scale in rural towns and communities throughout the country, marked the end of the European conflict. The war in the Pacific continued for another three months. Only after the Japanese surrender on 15 August could Prime Minister Peter Fraser finally announce that 'six long anxious, worrying, dangerous, tragic years' were over.[6]

The logistics of getting thousands of troops home meant that many loved ones did not return before late 1945 or 1946. Homecomings brought joy but frequently also sadness. Some families welcomed sons and brothers down the gangplank; others remained at home, attempting to come to terms with grief. A total of 11,928 New Zealanders lost their lives in the conflict.[7] For Flo Small, whose American husband died in the war:

> It didn't worry me that the war was over — war meant nothing to me then. It just became a thing, like you had three meals a day. I had no interest in war because everyone said we were going to win in any case. But I thought the cost was too great.
>
> The war changed our family. Somehow it changed from a nice happy family to a kind of remorseful family. There wasn't the happiness. There wasn't the laughter. There wasn't the birthday parties. When we, the family all got together, uncles, and aunts and everybody, there were too many cousins missing. Too many friends missing.[8]

Feelings of happiness and pride, but also of loss, accompanied the ceremonies to welcome home the 800-strong 28th (Maori) Battalion to Wellington on 23 January 1946. Chiefs, elders and other tribal representatives assembled in a purpose-built marae on Aotea Quay, where a feast for 1500 guests awaited. The *Dominion* newspaper described the scene:

> For six hours the people waited, and at last, just before 2 o-clock in the afternoon, the men of the Maori Battalion appeared . . . At the gate of the marae they were met and challenged by Sergeant Anania Te Amohau, brother of the paramount chief of the Arawa tribe . . .
>
> The wero completed . . . they were admitted to the marae. The kuias, the elderly women, greeted the men with the karanga, crying in unison in the traditional manner. Then the maidens and young warriors gave the powhiri, or welcome, and for some time afterward there followed the most solemn part of the ceremony, the tangihanga, or wailing for the soldiers who did not return but lay dead in other lands.[9]

Mihipeka Edwards, who attended this event, later recalled:

> I gazed at the serious men, no longer boys. I wondered to myself what terrible tragedies they had locked away in their minds. I looked at the sorrow, the tears, and the pain of many kuia, women, girls, wives, mothers, and sweethearts. They wept for sons, husbands and mokopuna who would never return to them. They mourned, broken and racked with pain. I saw young mothers with one or two little children clinging to their skirts. Maybe they would be the lucky ones, there to meet their daddies. But I looked at a lot of the others, and my heart filled with sorrow because they would have no one coming home to them.[10]

The New Zealand soldiers fortunate enough to return home needed to reacquaint themselves with wives and children, and vice versa. The process was not always easy; the shadow of war darkened relationships and lives. Many men suffered physical disabilities, ranging from minor ailments to amputation and paralysis; others returned home physically unharmed but with invisible injuries. Some veterans readjusted quickly to civilian life; others found returning to the daily round of work and family responsibilities painful and fraught. Many ex-soldiers simply never talked about their emotional or psychological problems, even with their wives. As the author and war veteran Les Cleveland later observed: 'The problem is that the stiff upper lip business and the manliness and all that prevents you from facing up to this difficulty. So you don't go around airing your problems or asking anybody for assistance."[11] Alcohol provided an 'emotional anaesthetic', but drinking frequently exacerbated marital strains and had a negative impact on family life. Some veterans suffered years of depression and withdrawal, and many found it impossible to cope with working life. By 1985, 10,070 New Zealand World War II veterans received pensions for psychiatric disorders.[12] During the hopeful, expansive post-war years, when individuals and governments looked determinedly forward, making plans for an era of peace and prosperity, a great many veterans and their families were still fighting the physical and psychic legacies of a debilitating war, engaged in a daily struggle to pretend that things were 'normal'.

Tank driver Tom May, for example, suffered numerous small breakdowns which he initially hid from medical authorities. Following a major breakdown, however, he was hospitalised. Feeling hopeless and suicidal, he 'couldn't explain to anybody what it was. I just went down to it properly. Of course you turn on your best friend. I turned on my wife with a lot of verbal abuse. And I couldn't explain it to myself, but I know very well it was the after-effects of the war.' Nightmares continued to plague him 50 years later. His wife Toni found it increasingly difficult to wake him from these persistent, terrifying dreams: 'The other night . . . he starts to scream. I had him by both shoulders shaking him and yelling back. And he gives one big yell, and then another one, and he gets louder and louder and louder until he's really at screaming point, quite piercing . . . It's very disturbing and I think, gosh, at seventy-two and you're still having these horrible things.'[13]

Medical orderly Peter Fairlie was sent home in 1944 due to uncontrollable anxiety. After his return, his first marriage failed because of continuing anxiety and unpredictable outbursts of anger and irritability. Beth Fairlie, his second wife, whom he married in 1965, although angry and bitter at his irrational treatment of her and their daughter, was powerless to stop it: 'all of a sudden he'll go off pop about something he's just thought of . . . anything out of the blue. He'd start bellowing about something perhaps [that] happened a week before.' Peter, aware of the negative effect his behaviour had, could not control it: 'You open up and then you realise what a mistake you've made. And once you've done the damage you have a job to repair it . . . you think well, I won't do that again. But, it goes on and on and on, each day.'[14]

Although for many veterans these sorts of problems made adjusting to peacetime far from peaceful, either for themselves or their families, from a practical perspective, state support helped to ease the transition to civilian life. The New Zealand government planned and worked hard to ensure that its positive vision for the future — wage-earning fathers and comfortably housed stay-at-home mothers and children — became a reality. Aware that returned soldiers deserved particular care and assistance, politicians lost no time introducing a raft of policies designed to help veterans enjoy a prosperous, productive post-war lifestyle.

Rehabilitation

After World War I, many New Zealand soldiers had returned from active service only to face unemployment and financial hardship.[15] To prevent this from reoccurring, state planning began shortly after the outbreak of war. A newly created Rehabilitation Department aimed to match manpower and training with national needs. In 1941, anticipating the demand for houses, it set up training schools for carpentry. By 1948, 24 New Zealand towns and cities contained training centres, which now taught other skills such as bricklaying, joinery, painting and plastering.

The Rehabilitation Department also offered loans for houses, tools, businesses, farms and education. By March 1946, it had helped 1640 ex-servicemen and women into small and medium-sized businesses. The Department allocated 50 per cent of all state rental houses to returned servicemen, or lent money at 2 per cent to help them buy an existing state house or build a new one. By 1948, 8242 ex-servicemen lived in state houses, but 14,137 remained on the waiting list. By March 1955, 17,905 ex-servicemen were settled in state houses; 27,225 had received loans for purchase, and another 21,960 for building.[16]

Many New Zealand veterans had struggled after World War I to farm marginal, often useless, land acquired through government loans. The Rehabilitation Department, determined not to repeat this scenario, granted suitable land and offered ongoing advice and assistance. It also stipulated that those who took up the offer to farm must have some knowledge of farm life or training.[17] By 1955, the Department had settled 12,236 ex-soldiers on farms, and 1464 remained on the waiting list.[18] When the journalist Nell Hartley visited a new farm settlement for former servicemen at Whangapoua in the Coromandel in the early 1950s, she found that:

> The 12 ex-servicemen and their families could not believe their luck . . . The balloted farms had been carved out of 2000 acres of scrubland, previously owned by three local farmers. Properties varied from a 111 acre dairy holding to a 350 acre mixed farm . . . the settlers looked out onto gentle undulating land that sloped to

the distant Whangapoua Harbour. Each valley, although still rough at the edges, was alive with industry . . . while families watched the progress from temporary pre-fabricated huts.[19]

When she returned several years later, the bush was gone and:

The valleys running back to the range were now shiny green, like fresh paint. For all I knew, Whangapoua could have been the most fertile spot in New Zealand. The farmhouses which had replaced the prefabs suggested it was. They were substantial, middle-class dwellings, the earlier ones having been demolished or refurbished for farm hands.[20]

Although the combined impact of various government policies made the rehabilitation effort after World War II a success, returning to a comfortable life of plenty was not immediate, for either veterans or the general populace. Contrary to expectations, controls introduced during the war remained on almost everything — imports, foreign exchange, land sales, rents, retail prices, marketing, building and petrol.[21] Shortages continued; electricity was rationed, as was clothing, sugar, tea, meat, butter and cream. Houses continued to be in short supply. In 1941 the state curtailed house building to divert building resources to the war effort. In 1944, when construction recommenced, 47,000 applications for state houses remained unsatisfied; 15,000 in Auckland alone, including more than 2000 from returned servicemen supposedly receiving priority.[22] Consequently these people crowded into substandard central-city housing in slum conditions, or were housed in transit camps in Victoria Park and the Domain.

By the late 1940s, the public's post-war optimism had given way to disillusionment. Consumer goods remained scarce and retail prices rose. Unions, disgruntled with economic stabilisation and compulsory arbitration, undertook seemingly endless stoppages and go-slows. The public, disenchanted with the industrial unrest, accused the Labour government of prevaricating and kowtowing to unions' ceaseless demands. As the global Cold War grew warmer, Prime Minister Peter Fraser's fear of the threat posed by communist Russia caused him to reintroduce conscription in 1949.[23] The peace so joyously welcomed in 1945 looked shaky and possibly short-lived. National's election slogan: 'Make the pound go further'[24] attracted voters alienated by Labour's austere policies. National promised to increase freedom of choice, lift restrictions and import controls, reduce bureaucracy and state interference, tame militant unions and end compulsory unionism. This agenda obviously struck a responsive chord as the party won a twelve-seat majority in 1949.[25] For the next 35 years (with the exception of two brief three-year intervals) National dominated New Zealand politics.

Despite the rhetoric, there was little difference between the two parties. Ormond Wilson, a former Labour MP, joked in 1953 about the parties' respective leaders: 'Q. What is the difference between Walter and Sid? A. Sid is a paler pink.'[26] Both parties formed governments that were essentially conservative in the business of 'managing the economy'.[27] National accused Labour of socialism when it introduced social welfare and vowed to reduce it, but once in power accepted and even added to it. Similarly, National won the 1949 election with promises of lifting controls and regulations. It did indeed start to deregulate, but reality (in the form of balance of payments deficits, inflation and the incipient threat of economic woes) saw it pull back and quickly reimpose some controls and taxes. Both National and Labour kept a tight grip on production and distribution. Keith Sinclair has noted that 'Under National, New Zealand was not noticeably nearer to free enterprise; the benefits of competition were not much in evidence . . .'[28] Most National politicians extolled 'free enterprise' on the hustings but were no less prepared to bestow the state's largesse on those they deemed deserving. Farmers and businessmen, for example, received help from the successive National ministries of Massey, Coates, Holyoake and Muldoon, all of which continued with state ownership and management of the many trading enterprises they inherited.[29]

Both parties espoused the ideology of the nuclear family with a stay-at-home mother and breadwinning father and enacted legislation to ensure the ideal. Early in its colonial history, the economic and social intervention of the New Zealand state took an upward trajectory: although state spending as a proportion of GDP grew slowly at first — in 1924 it made up 14 per cent — by the end of World War II this figure had doubled, to 28 per cent. The role of the state in almost every aspect of life, from social welfare, to media, to regulation of production, was immense and growing throughout the late 1940s and 1950s, a time when New Zealanders put great faith in the state's ability to improve people's lives. During elections, the two major parties engaged in rival bidding, each trying to outdo the other with promises about how they would spend taxpayers' money.[30]

The man who became the country's new National Prime Minister following the 1949 election was Sidney Holland, a tough decisive leader, who advocated a minimum of bureaucratic intervention, government restrictions and regulations.[31] One senior official described him as 'an Empire man' who 'shaked [sic] with patriotic fervour every time he got within 50 miles of Buckingham Palace'.[32] But he also prized his New Zealandness, and aimed to build a 'new and distinguished thing' — namely, 'the New Zealand way of life'.[33]

True to its election promises, National immediately started lifting restrictions — freeing up petrol and food prices, gradually relaxing some import controls, lifting controls on the sale of land and housing, and encouraging home ownership by the sale of state houses to tenants and making cheap loans available. But despite their rhetoric, National politicians quickly realised that to maintain full employment and a stable prosperous economy, certain controls had to remain — namely price controls, import licensing and fair rents.[34]

National's huge majority decreased in the 1954 election, as the electorate began to feel the effects of rising living costs. During this election the Social Credit Political League (a party representing small farming and business interests and advocating credit reform) first emerged as a political force, winning 122,573 votes or 11 per cent of the total count, but no seats. For the next few years, inflation continued to plague the economy. National battled it by cutting government expenditure, raising interest rates, tightening the supply of credit and reinstating some import controls.[35] Overseas prices for butter, wool and cheese started to collapse after the boom years of the Korean War, while domestic food prices rose.

In 1957, illness forced Holland to resign just ten weeks before the election. His successor Keith Holyoake was virtually unknown to most electors, particularly the crucial urban electorate: 'Many voters did not have time to see beyond the short, stout physical appearance and what one journalist described as "the mannered facade, the fruity voice, the booming bonhomie"'.[36] A relatively unknown and underestimated leader, combined with a tightening economic climate and Labour's promises of more generous family benefits, easier access to housing finance, increased pensions and free schoolbooks, and a proposed £100 rebate on the new PAYE tax, all contributed to a National defeat. The most critical factor in Labour's favour, however, was Walter Nash.

Aged 75 when he became Prime Minister, Nash was a deeply Christian humanitarian and pacifist, with a long and accomplished political career behind him. As Minister of Finance during the first Labour government (1935–49), he was largely responsible for restimulating the economy. As Minister of Social Security, he implemented the popular and comprehensive Social Security Act of 1938. From 1942, he served as New Zealand's first ambassador in the United States. After the war, and during his time as Prime

Minister, he continued to travel extensively, his greatest political interest now being international affairs.[37]

The new government faced a massive balance of payments deficit caused by falling export prices — a grim situation National had successfully concealed from the electorate.[38] Labour quickly reimposed import controls but at the same time honoured its election promises by making money available for housing at 3 per cent, and introducing a tax rebate of £100. These measures further fuelled inflation.[39] In an attempt to control the situation, in June 1958 the Minister of Finance, Arnold Nordmeyer, produced what was quickly dubbed the 'Black Budget'. This substantially increased income tax, doubled duties on beer, spirits, tobacco and cars, and increased taxes on petrol along with gift and estate duties. Some positive aspects of the budget — namely, larger benefits and pensions — went unnoticed due to the voluble public outcry over the tax hikes. National had a heyday, branding Nordmeyer as a smash-and-grab axeman who 'taxed high, taxed hard and taxed savagely'.[40] Although the 'Black Budget' helped to restore economic equilibrium, it was a political disaster. Labour resoundingly lost the 1960 election. For the next twelve years, National ran the country: for eleven and a half of them, Keith Holyoake was Prime Minister.

Holyoake, born in 1904, first entered politics in 1931 when he became MP for Motueka. He lost that seat in 1938 but returned to Parliament in 1943 as the member for Pahiatua. From 1949 until 1957, as Minister of Agriculture and Marketing, he successfully negotiated minimum prices for New Zealand primary produce into Britain, winning a reputation as 'the most successful Minister of Agriculture in the country's history'.[41] He became deputy leader and then leader of National in 1957. Politically and personally conservative, he was a skilful consensus politician who worked hard to avoid dissension within the party. He disliked radical policies, or rapid change, preferring moderation and gradual progress.[42] According to the political scientist Robert Chapman, 'his greatest feat as a Prime Minister was the slowing down of every process which, if speedily dealt with, might have represented change and political harm'.[43] His biographer Barry Gustafson summarised his aims: 'to advance his personal career, keep the National party in office, maintain New Zealand's security and prosperity and growth and gradually improve its economy and society'.[44] In keeping with a 1963 National campaign slogan, Holyoake had a 'Steady Does It' approach to politics.[45] Holyoake was also 'this country's first self-consciously and openly nationalist Prime Minister', believing firmly that New Zealanders should retain the means of production, distribution, exchange and communications: 'New Zealanders should have adequate opportunity to run their own affairs . . . I do not want to see

New Zealand continue to grow as an appendage or satellite of Britain, Australia or the United States. We are growing up . . . New Zealand should not be the plaything of multimillionaires from overseas.'[46] Determined that New Zealand should retain control of its national media, in 1965, when Lord Thomson was trying to take over Wellington's *Dominion* newspaper, Holyoake legislated against overseas media ownership. Ralph Hanan, the Minister of Justice, initiated and pushed into law much of the social liberalisation that occurred during this quintessentially conservative Prime Minister's rule. Under Hanan's guiding hand, National abolished the death penalty in 1961, liberalised divorce law, gave rights to illegitimate children and created both the office of Ombudsman in 1962 (the first in the Commonwealth) and the Indecent Publications Tribunal, which liberalised book censorship, in 1963.

Dissension

The great 1951 strike/lockout, which lasted 151 days, rocked the nation and threatened to upset the status quo and the continuing existence of a harmonious, consensual New Zealand. In April 1950, the Watersiders, along with several other unions, split from the moderate Federation of Labour (FOL) to form the more radical Trade Union Congress (TUC). The latter opposed compulsory arbitration and was committed to 'practical militancy'.[47] From May onwards, stoppages, overtime bans, wage claims and strikes on the wharves multiplied, alienating the public and pushing the government toward confrontation.[48] This came in February 1951 over a wage dispute between the Watersiders and their employers. To combat rising prices and inflation, the Arbitration Court had in January awarded a 15 per cent general pay increase. The employers offered the Watersiders 9 per cent, and argued they could work overtime to make up the extra. In response, the Watersiders stopped working overtime and were locked out. Government stepped in, declared a state of emergency, suspended civil liberties (such as free speech and a free press), deregistered the union and sent troops to load and unload the boats. The strike spread. Miners, freezing workers, harbour board employees, seamen and some hydro-construction workers joined. Railway men and most drivers refused to handle goods unloaded by non-union labour. At its height, 20,000 workers were on strike or locked out.[49]

New Zealand became a virtual police state — newspapers could not print the Watersiders' story, nor was radio allowed to air speeches critical of government. The government prohibited the display of posters and placards sympathetic to the workers. Offenders, as well as anybody involved in picketing, could be arrested without warrant. The police, their powers almost unlimited, raided underground presses and wielded batons against street marchers. Offering assistance to the Watersiders (supplying food to their families, for example) was banned. Many ignored this last injunction and organised a relief network. With wives now the sole breadwinners, numerous families struggled and grew more desperate as the dispute dragged on. Doreen Hewitt, whose husband Jim was a Watersider, remembered:

> We lived in a flat, upstairs from Jim's parents. I would walk up Collingwood Street, to the top, get a tram to Upper Queen Street, another tram to Newmarket, where I worked in a factory. I would return home exhausted . . . Later I got sick and lost the baby I was carrying. When I got out of hospital I went back to work. I thought the blue would never end.[50]

The Watersiders enjoyed little apparent public support outside of union circles, but whether this is because government controlled the media and precluded any pro-Watersider views from appearing is unclear. The press and government portrayed the strikers as part of a left-wing communist-inspired conspiracy, even as agents of the Cominform.[51] Newspapers throughout the land labelled strikers traitors to their country, and denounced them as pawns controlled by foreign communist powers.

Prime Minister Holland declared the Watersiders to be 'the enemies within'. The communist at home was 'just as unscrupulous, poisonous, treacherous and unyielding as the enemy without. He works day and night; he never lets up. He gnaws away at the very vitals of our economy just as the codlin moth enters and gnaws away at the "innards" of an apple while everything on the outside looks shiny and rosy. This government is alive to the danger that besets us and is determined to ensure that he does not succeed.'[52] The strike was 'a very determined effort . . . to overthrow orderly government by force'[53] and the work of foreign agents: 'This is part and parcel of the desperate cold war which has come to our shores in which life and limb are now constantly in danger.'[54] Minister of Labour Bill Sullivan described the dispute as 'part of the cold war, engineered by Communists to advance their cause and the cause of Russia', and asked: 'Can we tolerate law-breaking by an organization dominated by Communist international instructions, or do we stand firm in our belief in genuine differences of opinion under our democratic way of life?'[55] Jock Barnes, head of the Watersiders' Union and the TUC, was accused of being a 'puppet of the communist-controlled World Federation of Trade Unions'.[56]

In fact, neither Barnes, nor the Watersiders' Union secretary Toby Hill, had any communist affiliations. Under headlines such as 'Reign of Terror grips the whole of New Zealand', the press inveighed against 'a communist inspired wages strike [where] dock workers have begun a campaign of unrestricted violence, dynamiting railway installations, threatening to blow up the homes of cabinet Ministers and battering into insensibility men who have gone back to work'.[57]

The strikers for their part maintained that the Prime Minister was an American puppet and that the whole dispute was orchestrated from America as part of the war against communism.[58] They dubbed Holland 'the senator for Fendalton' and Auckland strikers composed a special song in his honour:

> Sing a song of Holland
> Pockets full of cash
> All in Yankee dollars,
> Out to cut a dash,
> When he got his orders,
> Sid began to yell:
> 'Bash the dirty workers,
> Give the bastards hell.'[59]

By the end of March, the Watersiders were isolated. A crucial turning point occurred when the FOL entered the dispute on the government's side and persuaded the other unions to go back to work. As Holland's successor Keith Holyoake acknowledged some years later: 'the National party . . . was fortunate in that the Federation of Labour, the responsible workers' leaders, stood firmly with the Government. The task would have been impossible without the Federation's aid'.[60] The FOL leader Fintan Patrick Walsh, a ruthless ex-communist turned government supporter (once described as 'the nearest thing to an American-style industrial gangster that New Zealand has seen'),[61] used the strike to get rid of the rival TUC. By May, he had appealed to the government for more intensive retributions against wreckers and lawbreakers 'menacing the public'.[62]

Without the support of other unions, the Watersiders fought a losing battle. On 11 July, after 151 days, they called off the strike. Their once powerful national union was smashed, replaced by 26 small separate unions in each port in the country. With militant unionism crushed, industrial relations remained relatively calm until the late 1960s.

Holland, capitalising on the massive public support for his government's stance against the union, called a snap election for 1 September. The party's promotional material during the election campaign depicted the recent struggles as 'the People versus the Wreckers'.[63] Voters who wanted to keep the communist menace at bay were exhorted to vote National. That party returned to power with an overwhelming majority (which included an extra four seats in port electorates). While Holland was seen as a preserver of law and order who cracked down on a pernicious communist influence, Labour's Walter Nash was criticised for being either a fence sitter or a supporter of 'the enemy within'.

National, riding a wave of popularity, promptly introduced new repressive legislation. The Industrial Conciliation and Arbitration Act, amended on 12 October 1951, redefined strikes and lockouts by making picketing illegal, forced unions to hold secret ballots before going on strike, imposed the election of union officials by secret ballot and set tough penalties for breaking any of the provisions. The Police Offences Amendment Bill, introduced in the same year, was so draconian that there was a widespread outcry from the press and public. Nevertheless, after amendments, it passed on 5 December 1951. This legislation widened the definition of sedition, introduced summary trial without jury, and outlawed street marches, demonstrations and poster displays during strikes. Nash described it as 'a complete negation of the basic principles of democracy',[64] and promptly repealed it during Labour's brief return to power in 1957.[65]

Enhancing the family

The ideal of the nuclear family — dear to politicians regardless of their party affiliation — was underpinned by the introduction of affordable state housing, universal benefits and free maternity care along with wage policies. Free maternity care, introduced in 1939, covered both ante- and post-natal treatment. From 1946, the universal family benefit, paid directly to mothers, covered every child from newborn to sixteen years, and went to 485,000 children in the first year, out of a total population of less than two million.[66] At 10 shillings per week per child, it was extremely generous, boosting the average net income in a three-child family by one third (its impact was eroded by inflation, however, from 1958).[67] Hilda Ross, National's Minister for the Welfare of Women and Children, noted approvingly: 'A well man in an everyday job, and with the child benefit of 10s per week per child, should be able to keep his wife in her home so that she may look after their children.'[68] Many New Zealand women greatly valued the independence the family benefit offered. As one recipient later recalled:

> The big thing was that women had an income — we were the last generation that didn't work. I was fortunate, and able to save it. For my cousin, it was her saviour: they had five children and things weren't easy at all: she had money of her own she could spend on herself and the children. Men drink in a lot of families and mothers are left without much. It gave mothers money![69]

New Zealand, in common with many other countries after the war, experienced a massive baby boom. Although this growth was an international phenomenon, New Zealand's population explosion — from 1.7 million in 1945 to just over 3 million by 1975 — was one of the most spectacular in the western world. In 1946, the Pakeha birth rate rose to over 26 per thousand (up from 16 per thousand in the mid-1930s) and the average family size doubled from two to four children — a level sustained until 1961.[70] The Maori birth rate expanded at an even greater rate, to just over 46 per thousand in 1961 — a rise related to falls in infant mortality.[71] Pakeha families grew larger, but remained smaller than those of Maori. Marriages and births delayed by the Depression and world war resulted in the initial burst of births. There were 20,000 weddings in 1946 — a number only surpassed again in 1964.[72] The economy grew, as did the number of jobs. These factors fostered a sense of security and enabled more people to marry younger. The average age at marriage fell from 25 to 21 between 1945 and 1971.[73] Couples also produced children straight away: 45 per cent of babies were born during the first twelve months of marriage and the average age at a woman's first birth decreased from nearly 26 years in 1948 to 24 years in 1958.[74] Expanding numbers of children led to an explosion in the number and size of all educational institutions from pre-school through to tertiary. By the end of the 1960s, primary school rolls had doubled while, because of the increase in the school-leaving age, secondary school numbers more than trebled. At the same time, spending on education doubled. Since Holyoake, who had regretted not going to university himself, believed that 'everybody must have the right to go to university if they wished', high priority was given to universities. Consequently, encouraged by numerous grants, bursaries and scholarships, the numbers attending tertiary institutions exploded from 'just under 20,000 to over 50,000'.[75]

Politicians realised that the ideal of the comfortable nuclear family could only become reality through the provision of affordable secure housing.

A sound home meant a contented family. Nash looked upon the family 'as the foundation of the nation' and believed that 'no nation can prosper or progress whose people lack the conditions of a "home" or "home life" . . . It is by the toil of their hands that men live, and the strength of the family that the race will continue.'[76] The journalist and author Mary Ratley, writing in the late 1950s, endorsed the view that home was central to family health and happiness: 'It is difficult to express what this word "home" really means but it conjures up thoughts of security, protection, comfort, beach, happy family relationships and activities. Perhaps it is best described as a background and setting for happy family life.'[77]

During the war, Labour formulated a comprehensive state housing policy. Although 37,000 houses had been built by 1949,[78] the housing shortage remained acute with 45,370 outstanding applicants for state houses in 1950. Applicants with children were favoured. By 1948, the number of one-bedroom units being built decreased from 5.8 per cent of all state units to less than 1 per cent, in favour of three-bedroom houses to accommodate larger families.[79] The government's preferred tenants consisted of the conventional nuclear family, keen to embrace a particular way of suburban life. They did not include single people, young or old, single-parent families, or families not considered respectable.

Because the housing policy was geared to single nuclear families and the belief that a green suburban open environment was best for children, the government did not opt for flats and apartments in problematic inner-city neighbourhoods. Instead it built houses in garden suburbs with planned shops, community centres and schools. Rationalising this policy, the Labour MP Mark Fagan explained that

> flats do not provide sufficient light or sufficient ventilation, and, generally speaking, they are undesirable for the housing of growing families. I much prefer the method of the Government building houses in the outer suburbs where a family has some privacy, where the father can have a garden and grow some vegetables, and where the children can play, instead of having to play on city streets or remain indoors all day long as they have to when living in flats.[80]

With increased car ownership, enhanced public transport and the opportunity to leave crowded inner-city tenements, families rushed to fill the new state house suburbs mushrooming in Wellington's Hutt Valley and around Auckland. These communities, so full of young families, were soon collectively dubbed 'Nappy Valley'.

The new National government of 1949 preferred home ownership to state rentals, and so started to encourage families to buy, providing inexpensive loans and long-term mortgages. At the same time, it offered cheap loans for house construction.[81] According to Prime Minister Sid Holland, home owner-ship was both a panacea and a sound basis for social stability: 'home building and home ownership develop initiative, self-reliance, thrift, and other good qualities which go to make up the moral strength of the nation . . . Above all, home ownership promotes responsible citizenship. To the community it gives stability, and to the home owner it gives a constant sense of security, pride, and well-being.'[82] This was certainly the case with F. W. Carr of One Tree Hill in Auckland who proclaimed: 'For the first time in my life since I've been married, I am independent, and I like it. Buying my state house was the best thing I have done and I can recommend anyone to do the same. Anyone will be a more substantial citizen because of it.'[83]

Eligibility for a state house became limited to those on low incomes, and tenants were given the opportunity to purchase. The second Labour govern-ment of 1957–60 continued National's policy, allowing families to capitalise their family allowance in order to get the deposit, and introduced 3 per cent loans for those earning less than £1,000 a year. The number of houses financed by state loans consequently rose to 33.6 per cent of all new construction by 1954, up from 19 per cent in 1950. By 1961, 52 per cent of all residential build-ings were funded by the state.[84] As a result of these policies, home ownership burgeoned from 56 per cent to 71 per cent of householders between 1945 and 1971.[85] Previously, home ownership seemed unattainable for many: now it was possible. According to Gael Ferguson, 'between 1950 and 1970 the symbol of the family home in the suburbs became thoroughly entrenched in the minds of New Zealanders as people took advantage of the state's generous lending programmes.'[86]

Suburban harmony?

Cities throughout the country soon began to grow around the periphery as new suburbs, often made up of a mix of state and private housing, took root and flourished. Urban growth was not a new phenomenon in New Zealand: the proportion of the population resident in cities and boroughs (as opposed to counties) was 58.3 per cent in 1926, 62.9 per cent by 1945 and 68.6 per cent by 1966.[87] After World War II, towns and cities continued to attract those seeking work in the growing manufacturing sector, new service industries and vari-ous white-collar occupations. The North Island experienced the major urban increase, with provincial centres such as Hamilton, Whangarei, Rotorua and Tauranga expanding into big towns or cities. In 1954, the *New Zealand Herald* wrote: 'An astonishing commercial boom, bigger than anything it has known before, has brought Tauranga 7,500 new residents in the past five years, increasing the population by over 60 percent.'[88]

The phenomenal growth of Auckland, which expanded from 329,000 people in 1951 to 548,300 in 1966 and to more than three quarters of a million by the end of 1975, overshadowed even this however.[89] The city's increase of 200 per cent was more than twice the rate of growth (81 per cent) of the total New Zealand population in the same period and almost twice that of the urban population (108 per cent).[90] New suburbs sprang up everywhere as housing gobbled up farmland. Auckland became a sprawling metropolis — a conglomeration of small centres that by the early 1970s stretched some '40 kilometres south from Torbay to Papakura, and some 25 kilometres east from Massey to Howick'.[91] The nature of the city's expansion was affected by the decision to make motorways its core means of transport. These were constructed to facilitate connections between suburbs; Point Chevalier was linked to Henderson by motorway, for example, and Mt Wellington to Wiri.

'Outward sprawl', the distinctive feature of urban growth in the 1950s and early 1960s, involved moving away from central-city areas to the new outer suburbs; a trend encouraged by cheap state loans and affordable state rental properties. The government planned and built whole new suburban communities. The towns of Naenae and Taita in the Hutt Valley near Wellington, for example, were intended as model suburbs, housing 20,000 people, and including all the necessary community facilities. But housing shortages after 1945 meant facilities had to wait. New residents were often startled by the barren environment and lack of basic amenities. Shirley Redpath, who shifted with her family to a new state house in Naenae aged twelve, remembered: 'My first impression of Naenae as we drove up the main street, Seddon Street, was one of shock and disbelief, hardly a tree, shrub, plant, lawn in sight, no footpaths even! What had we come to? The car pulled up at No. 61 and we all stepped out onto slightly muddy ground.'[92] The absence of footpaths and unpaved streets meant dust got everywhere, soiling the washing drying on the line. Front gardens remained unfenced and unsafe for children, while public transport was sporadic, with crowded buses and drivers who could (and did) refuse to carry prams after four o'clock.[93]

Instead of facilitating a suburban idyll, as intended, many of the new housing communities' lack of services and amenities proved problematic. In 1955,

Professor Kenneth Cumberland warned of future problems when he told a group of architecture students: 'It is proposed to build more Tamakis at Otara and Mangere Central — to condemn rich market gardens and smiling dairy lands and to replace them with more treeless deserts of tiles — inadequately roaded, sewered and lighted and unprovided with community services . . . At one and the same time, we are creating slums of different kinds both at the heart, and on the ever-expanding outer periphery of the metropolitan area.'[94] Indeed, Cumberland's prediction did eventuate in some new outer suburbs. Because low-income and young families received first priority for state houses in suburbs such as Otara and Mangere in Auckland, and Porirua in Wellington, mainly low-income families moved there. Many of these families were hit by the rising unemployment of the 1970s and 1980s. Consequently, social problems, gang violence and racism increased, a situation that provoked 'white flight'. When Otara was first developed, 66 per cent of residents were Pakeha families. In 2006, only 15 per cent remained.[95] Despite ongoing problems of violence, poverty and unemployment, and despite outsiders' perceptions of dysfunction, strong urban-based Maori and Pacific Islands communities have developed in Otara, along with numerous thriving community cultural and health facilities — churches, urban marae, sports clubs, and health clinics.[96]

Porirua suffered the same problems — white flight, large Maori and Polynesian families crowding into small state houses, gangs and violence. The largest single state housing community in the country, this new suburb was an ambitious government project that initially included plans for community centres and shopping malls.[97] These facilities lagged well behind the building of houses however. Janet Tomuri, who lived in Cannons Creek in Porirua East throughout the 1960s, remembered: 'There was nothing in Porirua in those days for kids so you made your own fun. We used to go shopping at the tip, we'd look for pram wheels so we could make trolleys and race them down our street.'[98] Rob Olsen, editor of the *Kapi-Mana News*, who grew up in Porirua at the same time, described it as 'a huge version of Nappy Valley, heaps of young kids, no entertainment, no halls, no theatres, and as a consequence you had a whole lot of people stuck out here, some kilometres from Wellington, wandering around aimlessly looking for things to do'.[99] In 'Living on the Fringe', a 1966 radio documentary about Porirua East, the poet Peter Bland condemned the absence of community feeling: '[The] houses are built on the idea of everybody having their own half acre of three-bedroom independence, you see. There's no communal sense. One's left with this terrible feeling of human poverty; of human monotony.'[100]

As unemployment escalated in the 1970s, parts of Porirua, in particular Cannons Creek, were beset by gang and racial problems. Rob Olsen recalls: 'There were parts of the community that were completely off limits, when we were kids we wouldn't even walk through Cannons Creek because of the gangs.'[101] As in Otara and Mangere, white flight increased: in the early 1960s Porirua was a largely Pakeha, blue-collar community, but large numbers of Maori and Pacific Islanders moved in to fill jobs in local factories, so that by 1991 their numbers exceeded those of Pakeha.[102] Cliff Irving, a Pakeha who moved to a house in Porirua East in the early 1970s, found it a fraught experience: 'We were there a short miserable time. Our eldest daughter had just started school and was picked on something terribly by other pupils and both my wife and I felt ostracised by the fact that we were the only "whites" in the street. My wife's health deteriorated rapidly and so did my daughter's school work. We had to get out.'[103] Although in ensuing decades unemployment in Porirua remained high and social problems persisted, as in Otara and Mangere, the community has a rich foundation of cultural and community networks, and enjoys a neighbourliness not often found in wealthier suburbs.[104]

When new state house tenants were able to integrate into an already established community the social situation was both less uncomfortable and less alienating. For example, Johnsonville, a prosperous small town not far from Wellington with a population of about 1800, was transformed between 1938 and 1956 by the construction of 329 state houses in the area. The population suddenly jumped to 3000, as young families occupied most of the new state houses. Existing voluntary and sporting associations flourished while new ones proliferated.[105] In some state housing communities, locals took matters into their own hands and formed progressive associations to push for better facilities. Auckland's Meadowbank Progressive Association, for example, proactively petitioned government for a community hall in 1946, and received an ex-army building. Local men then volunteered their services on weekends, doing plumbing, roofing and painting, while women provided afternoon teas and organised fundraising drives. The resulting community facility became a much-used centre of community life.[106]

The proliferation of new suburbs on the outer peripheries of urban centres had an impact on city centres. In Auckland, for example, Maori started migrating towards cities in large numbers during and following World War II, and initially concentrated in inexpensive inner-city areas such as Freemans Bay. But by the early 1960s, they were moving into newly developed, largely state housing suburbs such as Mangere and Otara in South Auckland. The number of people living in inner-city suburbs throughout the country declined as outward sprawl continued. In Wellington, the number of residents in the central city fell while Taita, Naenae and later Porirua experienced explosive growth. The Hutt Valley area almost doubled, from 55,786 in 1945 to 98,988 in 1961; Porirua went from a township of about 500 people in the 1930s to a large town in the early 1960s with 2800 new houses, a shopping centre, light industry and transport networks, and a population of over 20,000, and over 50,000 by the 1990s.[107] Greater Wellington, which included the Hutt Valley and the new coastal suburbs, burgeoned to 290,000 in 1966, from 200,000 in 1951.[108]

South Island towns and cities generally experienced much smaller growth. The major exception was Christchurch where the population rose from 150,000 in 1936 to 247,200 in 1966.[109] Migration from rural areas and secondary centres accelerated as large new state housing suburbs such as Aranui were created and privately developed housing estates grew up around the city. Invercargill, too, almost doubled its population, from 21,500 to 43,600 in the same period due to the opening of new fertiliser and meat freezing works along with the development of a new harbour at Bluff.[110] A state housing suburb built at Corstorphine, Dunedin, to meet the post-war housing shortage experienced comparatively small growth, expanding from 82,000 in 1936 to 108,700 in 1966.

Suburban life and cars went hand in hand. Because more people now owned cars, they could afford to live in suburbs and commute to work. By the late 1940s, New Zealand, with one car to every six people, ranked second in car ownership only to the United States, where there was one car to every four people.[111] In 1945, there were 198,158 private cars on the roads; a figure that almost quadrupled to 765,842 by 1966.[112] Roads and motorways proliferated; in 1965, there were 19,108 miles of tarsealed roads compared to only 5851 miles in 1942.[113] In 1959, the Harbour Bridge opened, linking the North Shore to central Auckland. This greatly boosted the development of North Shore suburbs such as Takapuna, Northcote and Birkenhead; and new suburbs such as Birkdale, Beachhaven and Glenfield sprang up. T. G. McGee pointed out in 1968 that 'The ownership of his own car has given the New Zealander a flexibility of movement which has counteracted the spatial isolation from his place of work, from his relatives, and from his playgrounds which residence in suburbia had often imposed on him. The motor car has become an extension of the home, on which almost as much pride and time is lavished.'[114]

Because of import restrictions, most New Zealand cars were very old. In 1953, of the 318,000 cars in the country, 186,000 were over ten years old, 101,000 over fifteen, and 45,000 over 20. Waiting lists for new cars grew so long that many dealers simply closed them.[115] New Zealand became a 'used car society'[116] with a booming market in second-hand cars. Moreover, to support British industry, any new cars that did come into the country were British. As Paul Smith has observed: 'During the 1950s when Detroit embarked on the "Great Sales Blitz" which saw its cars painted in symphonies of pink as their fins became more outlandish, we meanwhile trundled along in Austins, Vauxhall Veloxes and Wyverns, Consuls and Zephyrs.'[117] Australian cars, particularly Holdens, and large American cars only began to be available from the early 1960s.

Motorways, supermarkets and large suburban malls sprang up to serve the suburban sprawl. In 1958, New Zealand's first supermarket opened in Otahuhu, with ample parking space so that families could go and stock up on the week's groceries. The first shopping mall, LynnMall in West Auckland, opened in 1963. Industry, too, started to move away from city centres. For example, during the 1950s, Auckland's Penrose–Mt Wellington industrial zone developed, with a network of roads and motorways to enable easy access to the city. Levin, located on the main road and railway routes north of Wellington, expanded as light industry became established there.[118]

A booming economy

Residents in both the inner city and the many new outer suburbs found employment because the economy, like the population, kept expanding. During the 1950s, New Zealand enjoyed one of the highest living standards in the world. A prolonged period of prosperity was spurred by increased farm output, with productivity doubling between 1945 and 1970. Aerial top dressing, which became commonplace in the 1950s, not only significantly increased the land's stock-carrying capacity, but also allowed previously uneconomic areas to be farmed.[119]

Sheep numbers rose from 33,975,000 in 1945 to over 60,473,000 in 1968. Electrification, more efficient farm management, stock improvement, the shift to motor transport, as well as technical and mechanical developments, all contributed to this 'grasslands revolution'.[120] The number of farm tractors rose from 19,000 in 1946 to 91,000 in 1966,[121] and electric shearing and milking plants became commonplace. The export of primary produce remained an economic mainstay, with lamb, wool and dairy products sent to Britain under renegotiated duty-free guaranteed-access agreements throughout the 1950s. By 1965, 51 per cent of New Zealand's exports still went to Britain, down from 80 per cent prior to World War II.[122] The Korean War (1950–53) brought an increased demand for wool and boom times for New Zealand wool exports, which soared from £74 million in 1950 to £128 million in 1951. Wool accounted for over half the total value of all exports in that year.[123] Toward the end of the 1950s, the main market for the increasing beef export trade switched from Britain to America, as the latter paid higher prices.[124]

The notion that farmers were the 'backbone of the country' remained firmly in place throughout the 1950s and early 1960s; the national sense of identity was still linked to the long colonial heritage as 'an English farm in the Pacific'.[125] But whereas in 1936 one third of the population was rural, by 1966, only one in six lived in the country.[126] An example of how mechanisation and increased efficiency replaced people in the countryside is provided by H. C. D. Somerset's investigations of Littledene in Canterbury. In 1938, he published a study describing this typical rural area: its people, farms, population, livestock and crops, as well as the township of the same name. Between 1948 and 1952, he revisited and found significant changes. In 1938, 600 people farmed sheep and 520 were involved in dairying. By 1952, only about 350 men assisted by their wives and older children farmed in the area in total. Somerset noted: 'The fact that so much land can be farmed by so few people would be unbelievable were it not for two factors, the rapid mechanization of farming and the emergence in New Zealand of highly organized services to farmers.'[127] Tractors had replaced horses, milking machines had electrified, electrical shearing machines had been introduced, and above all, the pastures had improved because of top dressing and much more scientific methods of farming — for example, crop and stock rotation and certified seeds.

By contrast, manufacturing experienced a steep rise in numbers employed. In 1926, 13 per cent of males and 15 per cent of females worked in manufacturing: in 1966, the figures rose to 28 per cent of the male workforce and 23 per cent of the female. Manufacturing establishments increased from 5391 in 1936 to 7659 in 1966.[128] New manufacturing industries proliferated, initially spurred by wartime import restrictions, then by rising consumer demand for cars, domestic appliances and mechanical farm equipment. After the war, import licensing and controls continued to protect the nascent manufacturing sector from overseas competition. Manufacturing primarily involved processing and assembling imported components to produce items for the home market; manufactured exports remained insignificant until the 1970s.[129] The exceptions were in areas related to traditional primary produce production. New techniques for wool processing, for example, saw an emerging carpet manufacturing industry spearheaded by firms such as Feltex and Kensington Carpets.

The freezing and canning of vegetables, led by Wattie's, also became a major industry after the war. A forestry industry was built up to process pine forests planted in the 1930s. In 1953, New Zealand Forest Products erected a mill at Kinleith, in the centre of the North Island, to pulp wood, and a town, Tokoroa, to house its workers.[130] Tasman Pulp and Paper soon followed suit, establishing the mill-town of Kawerau in 1955 and a town called Murupara. At the same time, the white-collar service sector rapidly expanded. In 1955, employment in these 'tertiary' industries — in transport, commerce, government and local body service, and in the professions — increased by 200 per cent.[131] Women constituted the majority of employees in this sector. By 1971, two thirds of the female labour force had white-collar jobs as opposed to one third of the male workforce. Because of increased spending in education, health, housing and welfare, the state sector alone grew from 16 per cent to 29 per cent of the total workforce by 1966. By 1971, 41 per cent of New Zealanders were working in white-collar jobs in an increasingly white-collar society.[132]

Government undertook public works on a massive scale during the 1950s and early 1960s. It built hydro dams and the Wairakei geothermal power station to meet the increasing demand for domestic and industrial electricity. The Waikato River, for example, 'was transformed into a chain of lakes governed by dams generating electricity',[133] and the Waitaki and Clutha rivers in the South Island were dammed and hydro lakes developed. The building industry boomed, as houses, schools, universities and public buildings proliferated, keeping pace with the population explosion. Public works and domestic construction accounted for a large share of total investment in the years following the Second World War.[134]

Government policies and regulations through consumer boards, subsidies and import controls played a significant part in all this sustained economic prosperity. In agriculture, for example, semi-governmental dairy, meat and wool boards helped guarantee prices to farmers. Government subsidies bridged short-term shortfalls. Government-owned research and advisory bodies encouraged productivity and growth. In industry and manufacturing, import restrictions protected New Zealand industries and allowed them to develop strong domestic markets.[135] By regulating, subsidising and insulating, both National and Labour governments supported policies that promoted full employment, protecting the national economy from the worst global economic trends and helping increase production.

'Of European race and colour'

Predictably, the state played an important role in directing what kinds of people were allowed to settle in the country. Post-war, immigration surged, with a net migration of 225,000 between 1947 and 1968. Seventeen per cent of these new-comers were government assisted.[136] In 1947 the government had introduced an immigration scheme in response to serious labour shortages caused by the combined impact of a declining birth rate during the war, a higher school-leaving age (raised to fifteen in 1944), and a rapidly expanding manufacturing sector. Initially, young single British men and women between 20 and 35 years old and, for reasons of assimilation, 'of European race and colour',[137] were allocated employment in areas where shortages were worst. Men went into skilled and unskilled industrial labouring jobs, coal mines and hydro schemes, and women into nursing (particularly psychiatric), commercial domestic work, clerical work and work in the clothing industry. The newcomers were bonded for two years. From 1950, the scheme was extended to married people with up to two children (later four) and the age limit increased. At the same time, it was opened to include other Western European countries.

Not just any immigrant would do. New Zealand in 1945 was one of the most ethnically homogenous of all European settler societies, with 93.57 per cent of the total population originating from Great Britain.[138] As Leslie Lipson pointed out in 1948: 'The overwhelming numerical predominance of Europeans over Maoris and Orientals, of persons of British descent over those from Continental countries, of those with English and Scottish origins over the Irish, of Protestants over Catholics . . . [has] formed the mould in which is cast the character of New Zealand. The prevalence of a single national, racial, and cultural tradition — that of Britain — must enter into the final recapitulation . . . People who live alike tend to think alike.'[139]

A committee set up during the war to consider population increase deemed this monoculturalism a source of national strength and cultural harmony:

We think it important to comment that, if it is proposed to encourage the immigration of other European types, they should be of such character as will, within
a relatively short time, become completely assimilated with the New Zealand
population and have a distinctly New Zealand point of view. Quite apart from any
question of allegiance to the King's enemies, the emergence of racial islands in such
a small country as New Zealand must inevitably lead to serious maladjustments . . .
We therefore feel that if any positive steps are taken to encourage immigrants other
than from Great Britain they should be found in Northern European countries.[140]

The government believed that Southern Europeans and Jews would not assimilate easily. One official commented: '[T]he most suitable types are likely to be found amongst races other than Jews or Slavs.'[141] The Dutch were believed to be more ethnically close to the British and therefore appropriate as potential New Zealanders. Consequently, between 1950 and 1968, a net total of approximately 25,540 Dutch immigrants (6261 assisted) arrived both from Holland and from the former Dutch colony of Indonesia.[142]

Despite its reluctance to accept other nationalities, the government was pressured to take about 1100 Jews fleeing from Nazism before the outbreak of the war. But as one New Zealand Jew later wrote with some bitterness, it refused thousands more: 'We made valiant efforts to try and get as many of our brethren out of that hell as was possible. There was much lip service to the ideal of help by those in authority, but it is sad to report that results in terms of numbers were pitifully small.'[143] The mainly German-speaking, middle-class cultured professionals and business people who did manage to come made an impact on New Zealand social and cultural life that belied their small number. Viennese philosopher Karl Popper, for example, who became a lecturer in philosophy at Canterbury University College in 1937, had an impact 'on academic life [that] was greater than that of any person before or since'. Despite his influence, he wasn't encouraged to stay and in 1945 left Canterbury for the London School of Economics.[144] After professional success as an insurance broker, Denis Adam and his wife Verna became art patrons, founding the Adam Gallery at Victoria University of Wellington and the Adam Foundation; fellow émigré Harry Seresin opened some of the first cafés and restaurants in Wellington.[145] Following the war, government accepted 4584 displaced persons from European refugee camps, all carefully vetted on racial, national and economic grounds. After 1956, a further 1100 refugees fleeing the Hungarian uprising gained entry.

During a similar period immigration authorities also allowed a very small number of Chinese and Indians into the country. About 500 Chinese women and children refugees who arrived in 1939 gained permanent residence in 1947 and the authorities allowed another 1400 Chinese immigrants between 1950 and 1960.[146] Slightly relaxed restrictions also resulted in the arrival of approximately 2000 Indian immigrants between 1945 and 1963.[147] Entry still remained difficult, however, and was restricted to those with high qualifications or close family connections. Legally, discrimination relaxed; in practice, it remained. An internal memorandum written by the Department of External Affairs in 1953 acknowledged: 'Our immigration is based firmly on the principle that we are and intend to remain a country of European development. It is inevitably discriminatory against Asians — indeed against all persons who are not wholly of European race and colour. Whereas we have done much to encourage immigration from Europe, we do everything to discourage it from Asia.'[148]

Despite the desire to maintain a predominantly white and European populace, by the 1960s, Pacific migration into New Zealand gained momentum. Encouraged by government and business, young Polynesians on assistance schemes moved to the country, particularly Auckland, to fill growing vacancies for unskilled workers. Originally, the scheme organisers anticipated that young men and women would only stay temporarily, in a 'guest worker' capacity, but families soon followed. Women took up domestic work in hospitals or low-paid unskilled factory work, while a large number of men went into unskilled labouring jobs in meat works or forestry.[149] In 1956, the total population of people from islands in the Pacific in New Zealand was 8000; that number rose to 26,271 by 1966 and 61,354 by 1976. Some 47 per cent of these immigrants came from the Cook Islands, Tokelau and Niue, and therefore as New Zealand citizens had unrestricted right of entry. Over 48 per cent came from Western Samoa, which New Zealand administered from 1914 to 1962. This gave them entry on a negotiated quota system; there were also temporary work visas for both Samoans and Tongans. The latter, along with Fijians, made up some 5 per cent of the migrants. In contrast to Dutch immigrants, who spread throughout the country, Pacific Islanders settled in the main urban centres, with 60 per cent going to Auckland alone.[150]

In inner-city neighbourhoods such as Freemans Bay, they crowded into cheap run-down old villas, and added some vibrancy to the monochromatic community: 'In a Friday shopping crowd in Karangahape Road in Auckland or in Newtown in Wellington, the women in particular stand out with the bright patterns and distinctive cut of their dresses.'[151] The influx of migrants from the Pacific Islands made Auckland, by 1961, the largest Polynesian city in the world, a trend that intensified during the next years. Nonetheless, despite this slight loosening up of the immigration policy, the New Zealand population remained predominantly white and British in origin. In 1961, European residents of New Zealand from non-British stock constituted less than 2 per cent of the total population, one third of those being Dutch, while Asian and Pacific Island immigrants remained under 1 per cent.[152]

Urban Maori

New Zealand cities also became home to an ever-growing Maori population.

The inter-war trickle of rural Maori towards the cities, in particular Auckland, accelerated to a flow during World War II as young Maori found work in essential industries. More followed after the war in search of 'the big three': work, money and pleasure.[153] Pressure on land resources, and lack of work in the rural areas, spurred this migration. The Maori population more than doubled from 82,326 in 1936 to 167,086 in 1961. Because of a high birth rate, it was a young population, with over 62 per cent under 20 by 1966.[154] By the mid-1950s, whole families, not only young people, were moving into cities. From 1960, the Department of Maori Affairs urban relocation programme encouraged this process, exhorting rural families to leave the 'subsistence economy of the "pipi bed"' for urban centres, where they were helped to find work and accommodation.[155] In the decade before the war, 90 per cent of the Maori population was rural; by 1956, 35 per cent was urban; this rose to 62 per cent by 1966.[156] Auckland was home to 34 per cent of all urban Maori in 1966; its Maori population was five times larger than that of Rotorua and three times more than the combined Maori populations of Wellington and the Hutt urban areas.[157]

Many Maori were ill prepared for urban life. They suffered discrimination; some employers (the Bank of New Zealand, for example) would not employ them; clubs and restaurants often denied them entry and some cinemas made them sit in specially designated areas. Landlords frequently refused to rent to them. Mihipeka Edwards, who moved to Wellington at the beginning of the war, later recalled how difficult it was to find accommodation:

> It was very hard, very embarrassing, trying to get a place to stay. Because I was a Maori they just looked at me and shut the door. They said they were full up (while the vacancy sign was still in the window). So I pretended I was a Pakeha and tried to make myself white with make-up, but I didn't know how to use it properly. With this white powder all over my face I looked like a clown, I suppose — but I forgot about my neck. Well people still thought I was a Maori. Worse still, they must've thought I had a dirty neck.[158]

Unequipped to deal with the new freedoms afforded by the city, many fell foul of the law. Pita Sharples remembered the social problems among many Maori who migrated to Auckland in the 1940s, 1950s and 1960s: 'The change from the rural to an urban way of life was a huge culture shock. So many families were soon run down and the children were in trouble. They were broke, they had their power and water cut off, they owed rates and stuff like this. The discipline of the city was totally different from the discipline of the country. So there were huge problems.'[159] The Maori offending rate in 1958 was almost three and a half times higher than that of Pakeha.[160] Debt problems were not unusual as migrants struggled to come to grips with a cash economy.

The transition from rural to urban life continued to present many challenges, but Maori succeeded in keeping their culture and values alive in the new environment by creating voluntary associations. As Ranginui Walker has explained: 'Maori come together in groups to meet their needs for fellowship, mutual aid, the assertion of group norms and the expression of Maori values.'[161] Although the nuclear family replaced whanau as the household unit in the urban environment, larger whanau or family clubs patterned on rural models were established for mutual support.[162] Family gathered for meetings, to socialise, and to celebrate special occasions, usually at the home of a senior member. Kin-based mutual aid organisations were formed to help in the event of bereavement or emergencies caused by ill health. Melissa Matutina Williams' recent study of Maori migration from Panguru in Northland to Auckland examines how, in the 1950s, newcomers from Panguru negotiated the alien Auckland landscape by developing a range of home, church, leisure and workplace community sites specific to Panguru migrants, but 'not necessarily exclusive of the wider Auckland population'.[163] They nurtured family ties and maintained ongoing connections with their tribal homeland.[164] Karora Thomas recalled a trip home to Panguru with his mother:

> I didn't drive much, but I thought, get a car and drive home — go and see the old people . . . It's a long way from here to Panguru and I don't know where we're going. I had only gone on trains. And away we went. I think we were going through red lights in Auckland . . . Carry on, oh hell. Those days you had to catch the ferry on the car. No harbour bridge . . . We got onto the ferry and off at Devonport and see the sign 'north' . . . I don't [know] why and how, but we got home.[165]

Urban Maori also formed and participated in a range of cultural clubs, leisure associations, youth and sports clubs, and religious groups. The Catholic Church in Auckland enabled Maori to congregate and engage with each other through schools, hostels, sports teams, and dances at the Catholic Centre in Pitt Street.[166] Religious associations helped foster links between iwi: the Otara Maori Catholic Society, for example, included Maori from several tribes. Its sports teams, cultural groups and fundraising committees provided a 'social cohesion to replace the kinship system which was left behind in the rural marae'.[167] A mammoth inter-tribal fundraising effort resulted in the creation of the Auckland Maori Catholic Centre (Te Unga Waka) in Epsom in 1966.[168]

In 1959, *Te Ao Hou* (the journal established by the Department of Maori Affairs in 1952) noted that the most numerous urban Maori groups were those to do with sports and recreation. Some were attached to church or kinship organisations; others were set up by adults concerned to provide entertainment for the young. By 1963, Auckland had 36 Maori youth groups or clubs, with a collective membership of 1910.[169] Many did not last long, however, and youth clubs (other than those run by churches) and haka clubs were known to have a short life span.[170] Sports clubs, which often ran social activities and organised matches to coincide with hui on country marae, proved more enduring and successful.[171] But by the mid-1960s, when 60 per cent of the Maori population, and 75 per cent of Maori aged sixteen to nineteen, lived in cities, culture clubs started to proliferate and to survive long term.[172]

In the absence of marae, the Auckland Maori Community Centre in Freemans Bay, which began operating in 1948, and the Ngati Poneke Hall in Wellington, which opened in 1928, were the venues for important Maori ceremonies and gatherings. They had limitations however. Numbers were restricted; sleeping overnight for tangi was proscribed; and by the early 1960s, when many Auckland Maori were living in the newly created outer suburbs of Otara, Mangere, Te Atatu, Onehunga and Owairaka, Freemans Bay was a considerable distance. Nevertheless, through the 1950s and early 1960s, the Maori Community Centre was the most popular entertainment and meeting place for young Maori in Auckland.[173] Various groups based there also offered health and budgeting advice and workshops in Maori culture. In Wellington, the 'non-tribal, non-sectarian, non-political' Ngati Poneke club organised sports clubs, dances, and cultural and language classes, and generally, as one long-time member later remarked, helped young urban Maori 'hold on to our mana'.[174]

By the mid-1960s, purpose-built urban tribal and pan-tribal marae began to appear. In addition to kinship and tribal associations, wider urban Maori associations had developed during the preceding decade as numbers increased. Pan-tribalism was symbolised by names such as '"Wellington Tribe" (Ngati Poneke) and "Otara Tribe" (Ngati Otara) for the new quasi tribes of the city'.[175] In many instances, these organisations formed marae-building associations to raise funds and promote a local marae. Although the first urban marae, Te Puea, which opened in Mangere in 1965, was a traditional kin-based marae belonging to the Tainui confederation, other iwi donated money and time, giving them a stake in it.[176] By the mid-1970s, the Auckland region had more than 36 marae: church based, tribal and pan-tribal.[177]

In recognition of the increasingly pan-tribal nature of urban Maori communities, the tribal committees created under the Maori Social and Economic Advancement Act of 1945 became multi-tribal committees in 1962. Leadership was now based less on age and descent and more on merit. The committees oversaw local community issues such as delinquency, drunkenness and indebtedness. They appointed Maori wardens to act as their 'eyes and ears' by patrolling streets and hotels and generally addressing neighbourhood problems. Under the Act, the committee could assume the functions of a court and had the power to deal with petty offenders, thus avoiding the main courts.[178] By the 1970s, there were more than 36 Maori committees in the Auckland region. Collectively, they constituted the Auckland District Maori Council, which negotiated with local bodies and government on cultural and social issues pertaining to Maori.[179]

The Maori Women's Welfare League, created in the 1950s and one of the most enduring, effective Maori groups, arose out of the women's welfare committees established under the auspices of Rangi Royal, the Controller of Maori Social and Economic Advancement. At the end of the 1940s, Royal realised that the tribal committees which dealt with local issues were entirely male, and because women were not allowed to speak on marae, their voices and concerns were not being heard. He therefore encouraged the nation-wide formation of welfare committees composed of Maori women to work alongside the tribal committees. In September 1951, a national conference of Maori welfare committees was called in Wellington, and the national Maori Women's Welfare League was created.[180] With Whina Cooper as its first president, Mira Petricevich[181] as secretary and Princess Te Puea as patroness, the League aimed 'to promote fellowship and understanding between Maori and Maori and Maori and European; to take an active interest in matters concerning the health and general well-being of Maori women and children; to preserve, revive and maintain the teaching of Maori arts and crafts and to perpetuate the Maori culture'.[182]

Sponsored and given administrative support by the Department of Maori Affairs, this was the first national Maori forum and pressure group. As Aroha Harris has noted, it was also the first instance of Maori women appointing their own representatives at a national level.[183] Driven by Whina Cooper's tireless energy (she was made an MBE for her work in 1954), and supported by an able executive, the League initially focused on the difficulties facing new migrants to cities — from housing, health, welfare and education, to crime and discrimination. Local branch committees worked within communities to encourage social activities, organised weaving classes and established cultural groups and pre-schools. They sought support for a range of projects from 'the establishment of school bus services to marae-building projects' and assisted needy families, providing support and budgeting advice.[184]

At a national level, the League lobbied government to get better conditions for Maori. Initially, the most urgent problem was housing, particularly in inner-city Auckland, where many Maori lived in grossly overcrowded, substandard and insanitary dwellings.[185] In 1952, the League undertook a systematic four-month house-to-house survey of central Auckland and suburbs such as Pukekohe, where Maori worked on the market gardens and lived in substandard shacks provided by their employers.[186] A report chronicling this dire situation was presented to the Auckland City Council, the Department of Maori Affairs and the State Advances Corporation. But despite obvious need, and constant League pressure on government, change was slow. Maori continued to live in crowded, substandard conditions in the inner cities and to wait inordinately long times for state rental homes.[187]

This lengthy wait was the result of government policies concerning Maori state housing allocation. In 1949, from a total of over 30,000 state houses allocated nationwide, Maori received only 100.[188] Government believed Maori could not afford the houses and that their inferior living standards would have a detrimental effect on the area and surrounding Pakeha residents.[189] However, after pressure from the Department of Maori Affairs (as the Native Department was renamed in 1947), government agreed to allocate a certain number of houses for Maori in 1949. When it did so, it adopted a policy of 'pepperpotting' — dispersing Maori families amongst Pakeha — to avoid large concentrations of Maori in one area, and to encourage them to live as Pakeha: 'In the selection of tenants to occupy the houses set aside for Maoris the Allocation Committee . . . will, in addition to the over-riding consideration of housing hardship suffered by the applicants, have regard to the ability of the families to fit into the industrial and economic life of the community and to adjust themselves generally to the pakeha way of living.'[190]

But the number of Maori state tenants only increased slightly, the allocation committees believing that Maori would make bad tenants and the authorities fearful of building up a concentration of them in one area.[191] It took many more years for Maori to be allocated state housing on the same basis as Pakeha. Pepperpotting, popular with neither Maori nor Pakeha, was not completely abandoned until the 1970s.[192] But by the late 1950s, when the Auckland City Council began to redevelop the inner-city suburb of Freemans Bay where many Maori lived, the State Advances Corporation had allocated a large number of houses in its new housing areas of Otara and Manukau City for Maori. By 1966, only 12.4 per cent of the Auckland Maori population remained in central Auckland.[193] By 1966, there were 12,876 Maori in Manukau City, and about 6000 in Otara.[194] The total Maori population of Auckland was 33,926 at that time.[195]

In these largely Maori South Auckland suburbs, the Maori Women's Welfare League proactively addressed Maori socio-economic problems and directed government attention to finding solutions. A well-respected pressure group with more than 300 branches, 88 district councils and over 4000 members nationwide by 1955,[196] it continued to focus on welfare, health, and the preservation and teaching of te reo me ona tikanga.[197]

The transition to urban living, despite its challenges, brought considerable improvements in Maori living standards and wages. Nevertheless, inequities relative to Pakeha persisted: the Hunn Report of 1961 provided statistical evidence of considerable Maori disadvantage relative to Pakeha and offered policies aimed at both redressing this imbalance and integrating Maori into Pakeha society.[198] The prevalence of Maori (and Pacific Island peoples) in unskilled manual labour left them potentially vulnerable to economic downturns. This became all too evident from the early 1970s, when the golden economic weather turned black. In the early 1960s, though, there was no sense that Maori inequality constituted a threat to social harmony, and New Zealand race relations were a source of not a little complacent pride.[199] The more obvious threat to the post-war suburban dream at this time came, surprisingly, from its key component, the happy housewife.

Stay-at-home mothers?

A domestic idyll based on the traditional nuclear family was central to post-war government policy. A falling inter-war birth rate and the war itself (notably fear of these remote, relatively unpopulated islands being easily overrun by Japanese) gave the cult of domesticity a new lease of life. The state, concerned at the drop in the number of babies born, appointed a ten-member Population Committee in 1941 to consider 'ways and means of increasing the population of the Dominion'.[200] One of their conclusions was:

> We feel that unless respect for motherhood is inculcated, particularly in the rising generation, there will be a definite disincentive to rear families . . . Practically

all witnesses who appeared before us . . . were agreed that the basic factor in the present lack of appreciation of national responsibilities was definitely associated with a lack of a proper appreciation of the place which the home and family should have in the nation.[201]

The state encouraged women to recognise their patriotic duty as home-makers and mothers, and reminded them that national security and the future strength of the nation depended on it. This rhetoric continued in peacetime. Labour's Minister of Internal Affairs, William Parry, declared in 1945: 'We have to create such enthusiasm for the service the mother renders, that it will be lifted to the highest pinnacles of service in the nation.'[202] Magazine articles, advertising, political campaigns and radio all reinforced the message. A series of articles in the *New Zealand Woman's Weekly* on rehabilitating returned soldiers warned that the role of women 'will be an extremely delicate and self-abnegating one to be sure, but when it seems to her that she is doing all the work, bearing all the blame, she will remember those who never came back, and will throw herself into the trying tasks that confront her with renewed energy that springs from a thankful heart'.[203] Government obliged married women who had worked during the war to step aside for returning soldiers and exhorted them to remember: 'Wives are perhaps the pivot upon which the happiness and well-being of a family will turn.'[204] The Minister of Labour, for example, advised in 1945 that in the baking industry, '75 per cent of the women [packing and wrapping bread] are married and can be easily dispensed with as the men are ready to return to their employment'.[205]

Both state and church viewed working mothers censoriously. The Mazengarb Report of 1954 into juvenile delinquency (prompted by allegations that teenagers in Lower Hutt were not only hanging around milk bars but having premarital sex) highlighted the fact that a third of juvenile delinquents came from homes with working mothers. Reverend Carr, a Methodist min-ister, told the *Dominion* newspaper in the same year: 'Neglected families and a nation's loose morals are the price we pay for women's selfishness.'[206] Hilda Ross, National's Minister of Social Welfare, denounced married women who coveted independent incomes as selfish and misguided: 'The Country is today enjoying so much prosperity that married women with children should wake up to their responsibilities in the home and stay at home.'[207]

This idealisation of domesticity, and accompanying government policies designed to foster the nuclear family presided over by a male breadwinner, enjoyed considerable success initially. At the close of the war, social pressure, family expectations and public policy, combined with an acceptance that 'home duties' should take priority over paid work,[208] did result in some women (in particular, married women) returning to 'domestic duties'. The result was a drop in the percentage of women in paid employment from 25.2 per cent in 1945 to 23.2 per cent in 1951.[209]

But thereafter women, and in particular a high percentage of married women, started re-entering the workforce in ever-increasing numbers. This was not just a New Zealand phenomenon. One American writer commented: 'women returned momentarily to their home after the war out of deference to returning heroes, they did not remain in the kitchen long'.[210] A labour shortage combined with new employment opportunities and discontent at being confined to domestic duties meant that, as the 1950s progressed, women no longer saw marriage and work as mutually exclusive. One commentator observed in 1958: 'Indeed, since 1945, the labour shortage, cupidity, and the rising cost of living, interest in work and boredom with domestic routine have brought far more women, both single and married out of their homes than ever before in our history.'[211]

The use of the word 'cupidity' reflected a critical response to a growing consumer culture. During the 1950s, as elsewhere throughout the developed world, New Zealand homes increasingly boasted a range of electric appliances such as toasters, vacuum cleaners, washing machines, fridges and freezers. These sought-after items cost money, and people were prepared to borrow to get them. By 1956, New Zealanders owed £8 million in hire-purchase debt, double the figure from 20 years before; by 1965, the figure had soared to £30 million. Ironically, the new consumer items helped to relieve women's domestic burdens but at the same time freed them up for other employment. Many wives and mothers may have been obliged to seek paid work to help service the family debt.[212]

Women continued to be primarily employed in low-status, low-pay occupations such as factory, clerical, retail and receptionist work.[213] The number of single working women was rising long before the war, so the post-war increase represented a continuation of an existing trend. What was now different was the great increase in married women taking up paid employment. Whereas in 1945, just under 8 per cent of Pakeha married women worked outside the home, by 1966, 20 per cent were in paid work, comprising 41 per cent of the total female workforce.[214] These figures probably underestimate the actual number, however, for they excluded people who worked between one and nineteen hours per week. Married women, who favoured part-time employment, probably entered the workforce in greater numbers than statistics indicate.[215] Maori women followed a similar trajectory. Although their participation rate was lower in 1945, by 1961, they were employed in paid labour at a rate similar to Pakeha women, although in different areas — mainly non-skilled and seasonal work.[216]

As well as filling gaps in the growing industrial sector, married women began returning to professions previously closed to them after marriage. As the 'baby boomers' reached school age, New Zealand suddenly faced a chronic shortage of teachers, nurses and public servants. Trained women previously forced to leave those professions on marriage were now begged to return. In 1947, the Public Service Commission revoked a 1913 regulation that required women to resign upon marriage and a year later introduced maternity leave — six months without pay. The Education Department, too, made efforts to attract and keep women in teaching. Married students were allowed to remain in courses; refresher courses were created; special courses for female mathematics teachers instituted; and married women offered part-time employment. Prime Minister Nash warned, however, that this was not to interfere with the primary maternal role: '[The government] should assist the married women without young children to go back into some of the professions such as teaching. The country needs teachers and there are many qualified teachers who are married and whose children have grown up . . . That will be a most helpful provision provided those married women do not neglect their children.'[217] Recruitment policies were successful: by 1961, married women constituted 12.5 per cent of the country's teachers;[218] by 1968, 61 per cent of primary school teachers were women, up from 50 per cent in 1958.[219]

In nursing too, students who married had formerly been obliged to leave their courses. But in 1960 a nationwide advertising campaign for nurses asked: 'Married? Is your time fully occupied? Why not rejoin those of your profession now?'[220] The number of married nurses gradually rose; by the 1961 census they comprised 11.6 per cent of the profession.[221] A study in the late 1960s found that large numbers of student nurses expected to continue their profession after marriage.[222] Paradoxically, on one hand political rhetoric and government benefits promoted the domestic ideal; on the other hand married women were enticed back to work because the country needed them.[223]

The battle for equal pay also gained momentum in the 1950s, when working women began to question the accepted wisdom that men deserved a higher wage because they had a family to support. The fight commenced in the public service, where the proportion of women dramatically increased during the war and continued to grow afterward.[224] But despite their numbers, qualifications and work experience, women only received 70 per cent of the male wage. Promotion remained extremely difficult. Joyce McBeath, an equal pay activist of the time, remarked later: 'All these cadets of 18 and 19 were coming in and rising above women who had worked for years and given all their loyalty to the service. It was all wrong. To get promotion you had to be so much better than the men.'[225]

As early as 1943, a women's advisory committee of the Public Service Association (PSA) was formed and commenced lobbying for equal pay and opportunities. But it made no progress until 1956. In that year, Jean Parker, a long-term Inland Revenue Department employee and section head, successfully appealed to the Supreme Court against the classification of a newly appointed male cadet that would automatically entitle him to a faster promotion track and larger maximum salary than she currently enjoyed. The Public Service Commission (PSC) responded by demoting her and reducing her salary. An immediate and nationwide outcry forced the PSC to reverse its decision. Dan Long, general secretary of the PSA from 1960, believed that 'The Parker Case was undoubtedly a turning point in the campaign for equal pay, and at that time the support obtained by the PSA from various women's organisations, particularly the National Council of Women, would have been important in persuading Government that the issue was one which could not be placed on one side.'[226]

Consequently, Prime Minister Sid Holland, after meeting delegates from women's organisations and the PSA in October 1956, announced: 'Times have changed. Men used to be the breadwinners, but now I know that thousands of women have dependants and these women should be getting as much pay as men.'[227] He had not intended to take this stand, but the strength of feeling evidenced during the meeting caused him to modify his position. He emphasised, however, that the principle of equal pay could not be introduced in the public service until it was applied generally. Both National and Labour made equal pay one of their election platforms the next year. Whether they actually intended to act on the issue is, as Margaret Corner has noted, another matter. National's 1957 election manifesto, for example, while endorsing 'equal pay for equal work in some instances', noted that its general application involved 'complicated questions' and recommended setting up that most effective of bureaucratic delay tactics, a committee of inquiry.[228] After winning the election, Labour continued to avoid the issue. But pressure intensified, as the Council for Equal Pay and Opportunity (established in 1957 and comprised of representatives from trade unions, the New Zealand Educational Institute and women's organisations) persistently lobbied politicians and made sure equal pay for state employees remained in the public eye. Finally, in 1960, the Government Service Equal Pay Act passed, phasing in equal pay in the public service over three years. In the private sector, however, equal pay remained elusive until 1972.

Around the time equal pay was implemented in the public service, scepticism about the unpaid domestic idyll increased. The experiences of the war gave many women a new sense of independence and confidence: returning to domesticity no longer seemed the only means of fulfilment. Throughout the 1950s, questions began to be asked about conventional gender roles, with some women frankly expressing their reservations. Margot Roth, in a hard-hitting 1959 *New Zealand Listener* article entitled 'Housewives or Human Beings', condemned society's attitudes, and criticised women for being 'content to be regarded as second-class citizens', dissipating their energies 'in the trivial and the superficial' and casting 'a false glamour over what's called "the creative role" of wife and mother'. She exhorted them to look beyond domesticity and develop more satisfying activities: 'Quite obviously our society's out of plumb somewhere. And I am suggesting that one way of helping to correct it is to get nearly half of it — the women — out of the mould of inferiority in which they're settling themselves more and more firmly.'[229]

While most New Zealand women, in contrast to Roth, accepted the traditional woman's domestic role, they did take advantage of opportunities not available in earlier decades, such as employment after marriage. Many found that working part-time did not interfere with domestic duties, especially once children grew older. Even conservative magazines such as the *New Zealand Woman's Weekly*, while generally endorsing the message of unpaid domesticity, on occasion expressed reservations about its constrictions. One article, for example, inveighed: 'What a waste of woman power there is in this country that is crying for production and more production.'[230] Others commented on the loneliness and emptiness of a housewife's 'job': 'I am sure that few husbands ever understand the loneliness endured by some of their wives . . . Young brides often suffer deeply.'[231]

Sandra Coney has described the 1950s as an era when the voice of women was barely audible: 'hardly an event of significance for women ruffled the placid face of the post-war years . . . the cause of women advanced very little and even took a few steps backwards'.[232] While the radical ideology and indignation that characterised 1970s-style feminism was certainly absent in the 1950s and early 1960s, women's causes did not move backwards. Women were making changes, but most did so without challenging traditional gender roles. When married women moved into work, for example, they often did so part-time so as not to upset the balance within the family. They started to organise changes and improvements in areas that most immediately affected them — notably, childbearing and motherhood. They agitated for the rights to visit children in hospitals, for new childbirth techniques, for kindergartens, playgrounds and community facilities.[233] Organisations created during the 1950s, such as the Playcentre movement, Parents Centres, the Family Planning Association and the New Zealand Free Kindergarten Teachers' Association, all gave voice to women and their concerns. They also provided opportunities for interaction and support while allowing women to improve certain aspects of their lives. This slowly growing independence, and the idea that women could have choices and make meaningful contributions to the world outside the home, was an 'essential forerunner' to the challenges made by feminist groups in the 1970s.[234]

The return of mothers to the workforce during the 1950s and early 1960s was one of several factors that combined to weaken and ultimately transform the post-war suburban dream. Ironically, the state itself played a role in removing the contented female lynchpin from her domestic idyll, by enticing women back into professions such as nursing and teaching where they were sorely needed. When, in the immediate post-war years, the state had pursued a settled domestic idyll of young suburban families, that vision accorded with the wishes of much of the population. It reflected a consensus about what New Zealanders wanted and how they envisioned the future. For a number of prosperous, expansive years, that consensus remained intact. But tensions kept mounting: between, on the one hand, an aspirational ideal based on hard-working, happy nuclear families in a culturally homogenous dominion still deeply loyal to Britain and, on the other, the more complex reality of post-war economic and diplomatic imperatives. The 'New Zealand way of life' after 1945 was largely shaped and directed by the state, but as the years wore on, maintaining the degree of state control that existed in the immediate aftermath of the war became more and more challenging. In fact, the state itself frequently set in motion policies that undermined the post-war suburban dream and added to a list of changes that threatened to alter the culturally homogenous little dominion almost beyond recognition.

CHAPTER TWO

Loosening the Bonds

NEW FRIENDS, NEW ENEMIES

The basic fact remains that New Zealand as an organised community has always looked with pleasure on its links with Britain, and that it took a genuine delight in being 'the most British of Dominions', an outlying agricultural dependency that was an enthusiastically dutiful daughter-community. Filial sentiment for Britain, which at some times and places became unruly and irrational, has been fundamental in New Zealand life. — F. L. W. Wood, 1958[1]

Before World War II, New Zealand possessed neither an independent foreign policy nor a national intelligence organisation. Heavily reliant on Great Britain for security and trade, she expected the cloak of empire to protect her from aggressive bullies. As the diplomat George Laking observed, prior to 1939 New Zealand conducted international relations 'through the eyes and the agency of the British Government'.[2] The imperial network system mediated New Zealand's official links with the rest of the world, including Australia and Asia, and handled foreign relations. Economically, too, the Empire ruled: Britain took more than 80 per cent of New Zealand's exports.[3]

Emotional ties to Britain remained intact after the war. On 8 May 1945, the *Evening Post* responded to the advent of peace in Europe by asking: 'What has the war shown us?' and confidently answered: 'that the future destiny of this country lies with the British family of nations'.[4] But the Mother Country

— enervated after six years of conflict — shed much of her empire in ensuing decades, and long-standing economic and cultural bonds with New Zealand loosened. Defence imperatives, rather than any decrease in filial devotion by 'the most British of Dominions',[5] precipitated this protracted process. New Zealand's links with Britain and the Commonwealth remained, but old loyalties needed juggling with new economic, military and strategic considerations. Ormond Wilson, Labour MP for Palmerston North, warned in 1947:

> We must realise that we are entering on a new era and a new period of world history . . . I believe that the war has created for us a revolution which we have not yet appreciated . . . We must recognise the fact that Britain is not a Power in the East or in the Pacific today. There is no power in the Pacific today outside the United States of America . . . That is not a reason why we should break allegiance with the Commonwealth, but it is a reason that we must think again about our position in the world. Today we cannot hide behind our mother's skirts.'[6]

Between 1945 and 1965, New Zealand — reluctantly at first and then with growing confidence — moved away from the maternal folds. The altered balance of power after the war caused New Zealand to reassess both her responsibilities and vulnerabilities as a small nation in the south-west Pacific. The transformed international order after 1945, and growing Cold War fears, altered former expectations and certainties: the dutiful daughter became more aware of her geographical location, and of potential communist enemies. Seeking out new external relationships and alliances, she became over time an increasingly independent actor on a global stage. While not abandoning traditional cultural and economic ties to Britain and the Empire, she needed to cultivate new allies. First and foremost, national security was a pressing priority.

In search of security

As part of the vast, powerful British Empire, New Zealand had long felt protected from hostile invaders. That sense of security vanished in 1940 when, despite previous assurances to the contrary, the British government indicated that it would not be able to send ships to defend Singapore in the event of a Japanese attack. Moreover, Britain herself would have to rely on the American navy to safeguard her own interests in the Far East and the Pacific:

> In the unlikely event of Japan, in spite of the restraining influence of the United States of America, taking the opportunity to alter the status quo in the Far East . . .

it is most improbable that we could send adequate reinforcement to the Far East. We should therefore have to rely on the United States of America to safeguard our interests there.[7]

New Zealand was just absorbing that alarming message when German mines in the Hauraki Gulf sank the British ocean liner *Niagara* and German forces attacked and sank the New Zealand passenger liner *Rangitane* 300 miles off the East Coast, with the loss of five lives. The fall of Singapore and the destruction of the British naval base there in February 1942 provided further conclusive evidence that Britain could no longer guarantee New Zealand's security.

Historian David McIntyre has argued that the fate of Singapore 'marked the greatest turning point of New Zealand's external affairs, giving birth to a new foreign policy, directed towards the U.S.A.'[8] In 1941, the Labour government established New Zealand's first ever diplomatic post with a foreign country — in Washington. The fact that it sent the experienced and highly respected Deputy Prime Minister Walter Nash to man it reflected the importance it attached to this new venture. George Laking, a diplomat who eventually served as secretary of Foreign Affairs, believed that the appointment marked 'our emancipation from our historic and almost total reliance on the British as the channel through which we conveyed our views on international issues to the rest of the world and received our impressions of the way in which the views of other countries' interests impinged on our own'.[9] In 1943, New Zealand took another significant step: by establishing a Department of External Affairs, it created the institutional framework for conducting independent international relations. In the same year, the Labour government set up a second diplomatic post in Canberra.

In 1943, too, Dr H. V. Evatt, the Australian Minister of External Affairs, angered at being excluded from a conference to discuss the shape of the post-war Pacific region and afraid that Australia and New Zealand would be used as America's pawns, urged the two nations to 'stick together especially in relation to Pacific post-war policy'.[10] A conference held in Canberra early the next year provided an opportunity to discuss mutual interests. The outcome, the Canberra Pact or, as it was known in Australia, the ANZAC Pact, was signed in January 1944. Later described by Alister McIntosh, Secretary of the newly created External Affairs Department from 1943 to 1966, as 'New Zealand's first venture in partnership with Australia in an independent foreign policy',[11] this comprised the first formal collaborative arrangement signed directly by Australia and New Zealand without Great Britain as intermediary. The pact proposed that collaboration extend beyond security and defence to trade and civil aviation, and suggested setting up a South Seas regional advisory council for consultation on the welfare of the Pacific Island people and the economic and social development of the area.[12]

Apart from cooperation on the resulting South Pacific Commission, mutual cooperation remained limited. Denis McLean, a former diplomat, later remarked that 'the brief flowering of trans-Tasman togetherness represented by the Canberra Agreement of 1944 was a product of special strategic circumstances and frustrations with big-power partners, rather than a portent of things to come. It did not translate into a close political relationship.'[13] The threat of altered trade relations with Britain and Europe later in the century arguably played a more salient role in augmenting trans-Tasman ties. Nevertheless, the wartime situation, and apprehension about the possible future of the Pacific region, led New Zealand to take active steps in establishing a foreign policy that, for the first time, extended beyond the Mother Country and the Empire. Australia and New Zealand both hoped to achieve a protective defence alliance with the United States, now the dominant western superpower.

Emotional and economic ties

New Zealand took these first steps towards an independent foreign relations policy out of exigency rather than any diminished feeling toward Britain. Economic, sentimental and cultural ties remained strong. Although some policy-makers during and after the war realised that Britain was no longer a great power and that defence alliances need to be cultivated elsewhere, public sentiment remained loyal to the Mother Country. This devotion was amply demonstrated by the government-sponsored Aid for Britain campaign, when 'the ordinary people of the Dominion manifested their love and respect for the Homeland and its people'.[14] From August 1947 to August 1950, New Zealanders continued to put up with wartime rationing, food shortages and import restrictions; scrimping and saving to send food parcels to the 'Homeland'. Newspaper articles, government advertisements, radio, news reels and posters all exhorted New Zealanders to do their bit. Headlines such as 'Disaster Facing World if Britain not Helped', 'Hungry Britain Depends on You' and 'Without your Aid Britain can Starve', urged the public on to greater sacrifices.[15] These various appeals to sentiment and duty fostered a sense of identification as one nation of British people. As one Aid for Britain campaign radio script implored: 'Is it too much to ask of the farmers and the public of New Zealand in the hour of her economic danger to demonstrate that we too are British?'[16]

New Zealanders answered by entering wholeheartedly into the campaign, willingly putting up with sacrifices for Mother's sake. Feeding Britain became a national obsession.[17] Individuals, groups and entire communities made extensive food gifts, organised bottle drives, held cake stalls and saved ration coupons; even the (often notoriously un-cooperative) Watersiders agreed to work longer hours to clear the export backlog.[18] Newspapers tried to shame any shirkers, exhorting: 'Doubtless there are some unhappy folk who have the undistinguished distinction of never having sent a parcel to anyone in the Old Country. But they must be precious few.'[19] To encourage greater sacrifice and effort, editors highlighted letters of gratitude from Britons on the front page, and regularly featured articles describing the struggles of daily life in post-war Britain.[20] The press pushed people to do more. A *Herald* editorial spelled out how to squeeze higher production out of farms to expedite aid to Britain:

> Phosphate must be delivered expeditiously to the fertiliser works and the manufactured product distributed swiftly and smoothly to the farms. The producers themselves must be able to attract sufficient labour for the extra tasks of husbandry and maintenance which a drive for greater output will demand. Farm products must be processed for export without delay in airy factory or cool store, in slaughter house or freezing works. And finally the foodstuffs which will mean so much to Britain must be loaded by hands eager to speed the ships on errands of mercy.[21]

Such sentimental identification with and practical support for Britain's interests helps to explain why New Zealand was the last British dominion to adopt the 1931 Statute of Westminster. This legislation ensured that the six Empire dominions, while still owing allegiance to the British king, were in no way subordinate to Britain in any aspect of their domestic or external affairs.[22] New Zealand did not adopt it earlier because, as Frank Doidge, then MP for Tauranga (and later High Commissioner to London), told the House in 1947, it was felt that adoption would 'savour of cutting the painter with the Mother-land, and public opinion ran strongly against it . . . there is neither desire nor necessity in this Dominion for any alteration in its status, or in its relations with the United Kingdom.'[23] When in 1947 the Statute was finally adopted, Prime Minister Peter Fraser hastily assured the House: 'instead of lessening the ties, I believe it will strengthen the ties between the various parts of the Commonwealth and ourselves in New Zealand and the Mother-country'. Dr Martyn Finlay, MP for the North Shore, avowed that it would have 'no bearing whatsoever on our loyalty to Britain, and on our bonds with Britain'.[24]

These bonds were so strong that New Zealanders who had never been to Britain referred to it as 'Home'. Many persisted in considering themselves British subjects even after the passing of the Citizenship Act in 1948 conferred New Zealand citizenship.[25] During the debate on that Bill, one parliamentarian pointed out: 'If we had any option in the matter, we would have retained the common code'. Another lamented: 'I feel that once again we are giving away too much . . . We regret the need for this Bill, but I am glad to think that both sides of the House, during this debate, have seized the opportunity to reaffirm our pride, our loyalty, and our love for the Mother-land.'[26] The academic Leslie Lipson, in his classic study of New Zealand politics published in 1948, commented with some incredulity on the country's emotional links to Britain:

> The psychological dependence on Britain can still be most accurately described by the term 'colonialism'. The farm that feeds Britain and 'buys British' must think British thoughts and copy British ways. The English man or the Scot, turned Antipodean, clings to the customs of the past, and his grandson holds romantic illusions about a 'home' he has not seen. The working life of many a New Zealander has been conducted on one side of the world; his emotional life, on another.[27]

Immigration policy bolstered the homogeneity of New Zealand culture: 'Immigrants of British nationality are, of course, strongly preferred on obvious grounds — kinship, common political and constitutional forms and backgrounds, similarity of social standards and outlook, common allegiance etc.'[28] When government could not induce enough British migrants to New Zealand to fill post-war labour shortages, it countenanced immigrants from Northern Europe (notably the Dutch), believing they would assimilate more readily into New Zealand society than other 'foreigners'. With the notable exception of its indigenous Maori population and Pacific Island migrants, New Zealanders were white and predominantly British in origin. To be called 'a little Britain of the south seas'[29] was a source of national pride. Nationalism was compatible with, and indeed augmented by, the country's status as part of the British Empire. In 1953, for example, Edmund Hillary, a New Zealander, became the first man to climb Mt Everest, the world's highest mountain, as part of a British team. New Zealanders felt enormous pride in this achievement, not just for their own country but for the whole of the British people. As acting Prime Minister Keith Holyoake proclaimed: 'Hillary has put the British race and New Zealand at the top of the world. And what a magnificent coronation present for the Queen.'[30]

Elizabeth II's coronation in June 1953 caused fervour for the Mother Country to climb new heights. Distance notwithstanding, New Zealanders felt part of this auspicious event. The *New Zealand Listener* observed: 'British people are spread throughout the world, but they are not cut off from the beating of that strong heart in London. On June 2, as they gather around their receiving sets, they will feel the almost mystical sense of unity . . .'[31] Souvenirs provided a tangible memory of the occasion, and when a coronation film came out, New Zealanders flocked to it.

On 23 December 1953, a six-week royal tour — the first to New Zealand by a reigning monarch — prompted further excitement. The *New Zealand Observer*, describing the Queen's arrival in Auckland, waxed poetic: 'December 23, 1953 was the day Auckland went wild with joy. Strong men wept. Dignified businessmen and their wives ran. Brown and white men stood arm-in-arm and cheered. Traffic police laughed. Constables smiled and joked. Although fine rain wet the streets and subdued the colour of the decorations . . .'[32] The *Rotorua Post* pointed out that the Queen symbolised a Great Empire to which New Zealand proudly belonged:

> Few can have failed to see in the young Queen the embodiment of all the glories of
> England and Empire of which they read as children in their history books; of the
> seadogs, the yeomen and bowmen, the explorers and the scientists and the men
> of words and letters who made the world their oyster and tilled the cultural soil in
> which we have our roots. The Queen is the stuff of British history. December 23 was
> the best day of Auckland's history.[33]

The Queen's visit also enabled New Zealand to display its prosperity and recovery from depression and war:[34]

> The great upsurge of feeling owed something too to unexpressed feelings of relief
> from the tension of the war days when New Zealand was drawn so close to Britain
> that listening to the voices of her leaders became part of the daily routine of living.
> It had its source, also, in the common experiences of the post-war years — Britain's
> austerity years when the ordinary people of the Dominion manifested their love
> and respect for the Homeland and its people in 'food for Britain' campaigns. The
> Queen's coming to these shores was a triumphant sign that the whole nation had
> won through long years of tribulation . . .[35]

Unfortunately, tribulation was not relegated to the past. On the evening of

24 December, the crater lake at the top of Mt Ruapehu burst, hurtling a tsunami of 2 million cubic metres of water, ice, mud and rocks down the Whangaehu River. This lahar crashed into the pylons of the Tangiwai railway bridge, severely weakening it. A few hours later, as the Wellington–Auckland express crossed the bridge, it collapsed, plummeting the train into the river below and killing 151 passengers.[36] The nation was grief-stricken by the magnitude of the accident, the worst train wreck in its history. In her Christmas broadcast from Government House in Auckland, the young Queen included a special message of sympathy for those who had lost family in the tragedy, and later on the Duke of Edinburgh changed his schedule to attend a state funeral in Wellington for some of the victims.

The Tangiwai disaster, as it came to be known, was one tragic low point during a six-week period otherwise characterised by great jubilation and excitement at the Queen's visit. The royal tour evoked virtually no organised opposition; only a very few individuals protested. Historian Jock Phillips has noted that 'Even the Communist party could not bring itself to speak out against the Queen'.[37] Thousands of people wanted nothing more than to catch a glimpse of the royal couple. Some slept overnight on the route to be assured the best views; others followed the tour around the country. Schoolchildren, bussed to line the royal routes, waited for hours with flags and medallions to catch a glimpse of the Queen passing by. Loyal subjects waved Union Jacks at every opportunity; some even dyed their sheep and horses red, white and blue; others cut hedges into the shape of the royal cipher, or into an E.[38]

Dunedin, like every other town the Queen visited, spent months 'dressing' for the occasion. The *Otago Daily Times* reported:

> Flags, bunting, trees and the people's hearts are all in readiness . . . Dunedin is
> 'dressed overall' for the Royal visit . . . they will see the city at its best and brightest.
> Nothing has been left undone to make Dunedin the best of the four main centres
> in its welcome. One of the gayest displays of bunting, greenery flags, floral dec-
> orations, coats of arms, crowns and illuminations yet seen in the dominion will
> greet the Queen and the Duke . . . One of the features of the display will be the 700
> trees now lining streets along the routes about the city. Illuminated, they will give a
> fairyland effect at night.[39]

The royal party arrived in Dunedin on 25 January to a tumultuous crowd. When the Queen and Duke of Edinburgh appeared on the balcony of their hotel, 'the milling crowd below them threw all traditional restraint to the

winds. Their loyalty and affection was full-throated. They cheered and waved
. . . The thousands of people jammed uproarious into the intersection. Their
reception left no doubt that they fully appreciated how joyous an occasion it
was to have in their midst their lovely young queen and her husband . . . then,
the mass of people burst into song.'[40]

Of course, economic ties underscored all of this sentiment and identification with the Mother Country. Both during and after the war, New Zealand's
big three exports — wool, dairy products and meat — went primarily to Britain.
Helping New Zealand's biggest market helped New Zealand. In 1947, Finance
Minister Walter Nash, acutely aware that New Zealand's long-term prosperity
depended on that of Britain, reminded Parliament: 'Whilst our attachment to
Great Britain has stronger bonds than material self-interest, it is true to say that
our material interests are also bound up with our people in the Homeland.'[41]
Other politicians made the same point: J. Watts, MP for St Albans, for example,
warned: 'it is practically a matter of life and death to us that Britain recovers
. . . If Britain goes down . . . New Zealand will go down with Britain. We are
tied to her not only by ties of blood — family ties — but inextricably by ties
of trade.'[42] In 1950, 66 per cent of New Zealand's exports went to Britain: by
1965–66 that figure remained just over half.[43] To hasten Britain's post-war economic recovery and re-establish her export markets for manufactured goods,
the New Zealand government encouraged citizens to 'buy British'. As a result,
in 1950, New Zealand imports from Great Britain jumped to 61 per cent, up
from 47 per cent in 1940.[44] On government contracts, British tenders received
a 10 per cent advantage. New Zealand further aided Britain's recovery by continuing rationing, forgiving a £12.5 million debt, selling surplus meat and dairy
products to Britain below market price, and restricting dollar expenditure in
order to preserve sterling reserves.[45]

The allegiances of leading politicians augmented these vital economic
links. Labour leaders Peter Fraser and Walter Nash (both born in Britain)
thought in British Commonwealth terms, and did everything humanly possible after the war to help Britain.[46] Even allowing for the economic rationale behind this mindset, there is no doubting the sincerity of their loyalties.
National politician Sidney Holland, Prime Minister from 1949 to 1957 and a
New Zealander by birth, was even more unabashedly pro-British. In foreign
policy he rarely accepted that New Zealand might have interests different to
Britain, and was always reluctant to act without British approval. For Holland:
'foreign policy was what the British Government said it was'.[47] These views
led him to support the 1956 British–French invasion of Suez in the face of

almost unanimous international criticism, and against the counsel of his own advisors. The Suez Crisis erupted in late 1956 when Egyptian president Gamal Abdel Nasser nationalised the Suez Canal. As a result, Great Britain, France and Israel attacked Egypt. The international condemnation of this military action was immediate and only Australia and New Zealand were supportive of the invasion. Britain and France were forced to bow to international pressure and withdraw. Holland justified New Zealand's support in terms of loyalty: 'bearing in mind what our relations with the "Mother" country are, what she means to us in blood, tradition and trade, remembering what we have all said about where Britain stands we stand and where she goes we go, we reached the only conclusion we thought was open to us'.[48]

His successor, Keith Holyoake, did not share this kind of blind loyalty. A fourth-generation New Zealander, described by his biographer as this country's 'first self-consciously and openly nationalistic Prime Minister', he frankly informed the British that 'he saw New Zealand as a totally independent nation and himself solely as a New Zealander who could not — and would not — call himself British'.[49] This stance partly reflected his personal character but more importantly it was in line with the changed realities of the 1960s. By this time, New Zealand had moved a considerable distance from its former state of dependence. It now operated within a more diverse and complex web of alliances and trading partnerships on the global stage. While maintaining and fostering its relations with a changed and diminished Britain, it had, whatever its rhetoric concerning traditional cultural ties, an eye on its own safety, economic prosperity, and increasingly, its altered role in Asia and the Pacific. Ironically, this process was fostered by policies pursued during Holland's time, when the threat of communism forced New Zealand to look, not without some apprehension, towards the east.

Rethinking Asia

Strategic realities after World War II forced New Zealand to reassess her attitudes toward Asia. In the past, contacts with that part of the world were rare and Britain conducted any diplomacy deemed necessary. If New Zealanders ever thought about Asia at all, it was with fear that 'Asian hordes' might overrun their country. In the years immediately prior to World War II, the rapid rise of Japan as an industrial and military power inspired fear. It gave:

a new meaning in New Zealand minds to the so-called 'yellow' peril. Instead of importunate Chinese, the popular mind now envisaged the possible influx of surplus Japanese . . . [it] presented the nightmare of an over-populated Japan spilling its surplus millions down into the uninhabited spaces of Australia and so on to the inviting pastures of New Zealand.[50]

After the defeat of Japan in 1945, this concern transferred to the dread of Chinese communism infecting the whole of Asia and eventually pushing into Australia and New Zealand. Frank Doidge, speaking in the House in 1950, warned:

At present Asia is in the position of the greatest danger, and the fate of our neighbours — and they are neighbours — is a matter of the greatest and gravest concern to this country . . . This region contains half the population of the world — a thousand million people: and for centuries the masses of them have lived in poverty, in misery and among pestilence. They have known famine and hunger, and they have rarely known what it is to be adequately clothed or sheltered. These countries naturally provide a breeding ground for communism. We in New Zealand and Australia have only to pause and contrast our own abundant standard of living with the appalling poverty and misery that exist in Asia to understand the bitterness of Asian nationalism.[51]

By the end of the 1940s, the rise of insurgencies in many Asian countries and the fall of the Chinese Nationalist government to the communists in 1949 reawakened old fears of Asian expansionism in New Zealand. With the signing of the Sino–Soviet pact in 1950, the 'red menace' appeared to coalesce with the 'yellow peril'. Fears of communist contagion grew more intense.[52] Doidge's earlier warning in 1946 now seemed very real:

In the Pacific for our own protection, we have to prepare to meet any eventuality. It is clear that there is urgent need for such preparation. We live on the fringe of a great volcano. We see how Russia comes down to the Asiatic seaboard, and what is happening in India, China and Malaya and the East Indies, and we know that we must be prepared to accept a great responsibility. We must be prepared to spend much more money on defence than we have in the past . . .[53]

As a result, in 1949, Australia, New Zealand and Britain entered into a contingency planning arrangement for the defence of sea and air communications covering 'the eastern Indian ocean, Malaya, Indonesia and an area covering all New Zealand's Island territories and Western Samoa'.[54] Called ANZAM

(Australia New Zealand and Malaya), it also provided the framework for war-time collaboration. That same year, New Zealand agreed to supply planes and men and two frigates to keep the supply lines open between British colonies in the east in case of open hostilities with the Chinese communists.

In the event, the hostilities broke out on the Malay Peninsula. In 1948, Britain declared a state of emergency after communist terrorists killed three planters. British troops became involved in counter-insurgency operations against the terrorists and the New Zealand squadron was diverted to drop supplies to them. At the same time, 24 New Zealand soldiers attached to a Fijian battalion were sent to fight on the ground. Over the five years until 1956, when it was withdrawn, about 40 New Zealanders served in Malaya in this battalion.

The Korean War (1950) and the French defeat by the Vietnamese at Dien Bien Phu (1954) raised further alarm about communism's seemingly inexorable advance. Emphasising the strategic importance of the Malay Peninsula to New Zealand and Australia, Britain asked New Zealand to shift her defence commitments from the Middle East to South-East Asia and to be prepared to deploy land and air forces there in the event of a global war. Her help in the Malayan Emergency was expected to continue.[55] New Zealand agreed to these requests with alacrity, arguing: 'If people will consult a map, they will realise that the troubled area in the world — from Korea, to Japan . . . Indo-China, Indonesia — is a succession of steps in the direction of New Zealand and about the last place we can make a stand without coming into our own territory is Malaya.'[56]

Moreover, as Holland reminded Parliament, it was vitally important to retain a close association with the United Kingdom: 'We must earn the support of Britain by pulling our weight in the British Boat. That is a British thing to do. We have always done it, and now Britain has spoken to us and we have consulted her, and she has given us a plan that I believe is within our reach and our capacity.'[57] In 1955, the Commonwealth Strategic Reserve, made up of troops from Australia, New Zealand and Great Britain, was established to defend the Malay Peninsula from attack by communist forces. New Zealand's initial contribution, a Special Air Service (SAS) squadron, consisted of 133 men. The ground troops that replaced this unit in 1957 helped to mop up the last of the insurgents until 1960, when the Emergency was declared to be over.

By this stage, New Zealand had realised that she needed closer diplomatic relations with South-East Asia. Holland explained in the House, 'Because of the greatly increased importance of South-East Asia and because of the changed situation in international affairs, I think it is necessary that New Zealand should have closer links with that part of the world . . . I think the time has come when we are sufficiently grown up to undertake a little of our own diplomatic work'.[58] This was the start of a long-term relationship with Malaya, which became independent of Britain in 1957. Foss Shanahan was appointed High Commissioner to South-East Asia, resident in Singapore, in 1955, and in 1959 Charles Bennett became the first High Commissioner in Kuala Lumpur. That same year, Singapore became independent and a new defence agreement came into force — the Anglo–Malayan Defence Agreement (AMDA), to which New Zealand was a signatory. Under this agreement, Malaya agreed to allow Commonwealth forces to remain stationed in Malaya, but any deployments in the region depended on the approval of both the Singaporean and Malayan governments.[59] These forces were called into action once again in 1965 during the Malaysian Confrontation, when Indonesia's President Sukarno landed troops on the Malay Peninsula in an attempt to destabilise the area. Reduced numbers of British, Australian and New Zealand troops remained stationed in Singapore until the mid-1970s, when both the British and Australian ground forces withdrew. New Zealand maintained troops there until 1989. Since then, New Zealand has continued combined defence exercises with Malaysia and Singapore.[60]

New Zealand's contacts with Malaysia were not solely defensive. In January 1950, a conference of Commonwealth ministers at Colombo, Ceylon (Sri Lanka), sought other ways of stemming the communist tide:

> Communist Russia has been countered and contained in the West, and that is why Russia is now turning from the West to the East . . . Communism today, unhappily has overrun China; . . . We know that with the end of the Second World War Asia was left ripe for revolution and immense changes . . . there are a thousand million people in Asia and South-east Asia, the bulk of whom have never in their lifetimes known what it was to have a full stomach . . . it was only natural that under such conditions communism could and did thrive and that it made such remarkable headway.[61]

Economic aid, it was hoped, would allay some of the danger, for as Clifton Webb, Minister of External Affairs, later asserted: 'covert aggression cannot be defeated by military force alone . . . the belief is gaining strength as time goes on — that the only real and possible answer to the appeal of communism is to

The day before VE Day (8 May 1945), smiling women carry flags and celebratory streamers on Lambton Quay, Wellington. *F-1508-1/4, John Pascoe Collection, Alexander Turnbull Library*

VJ Day, 15 August 1945: on Willis Street, Wellington, crowds of people celebrate the end of the war in the Pacific. *PA Coll-5926-47, John Pascoe Collection, Alexander Turnbull Library*

Rehabilitation: a 1945 poster informs returning soldiers about employment support available to them. *Eph-A-EMPLOYMENT-1945-01, Alexander Turnbull Library*

To support British industry, only British cars such as this Humber Super Snipe were imported into New Zealand – and in limited numbers. The wait for a new car could thus be very long and, as a result, New Zealand became a used-car country. *The Mirror, May 1953, Sir George Grey Special Collections, Auckland Libraries*

A 'Feed Britain' Appeal receiving depot on Brougham Street, New Plymouth, c. 1947.
Between 1947 and 1950, New Zealanders scrimped to send food parcels 'home' to the
Mother Country. *Herb Mullen, PHO 2008-1830, collection of Puke Ariki, New Plymouth*

The gathering at Forbury Park, on 26 January 1954, when some 12,000 excited Dunedin schoolchildren greeted Queen Elizabeth II and Prince Philip. A sign in the background reads: 'Please Give Charles and Anne our love'. *F-429291/2, Archives New Zealand National Publicity Studios Collection, Alexander Turnbull Library*

The Tangiwai disaster, New Zealand's worst train wreck, occurred on Christmas Eve 1953, marring the mood of national jubilation the Queen's tour evoked. *D-1957_01, Archives New Zealand*

Peter Fraser's funeral procession, outside St John's Church, Wellington, 16 December 1950. The mourners include (left to right) Walter Nash, Prime Minister Sid Holland and Keith Holyoake. *114/239/08, Evening Post Collection, Alexander Turnbull Library*

Election campaign advertisements of 1949 and 1951 reveal few substantive differences between Labour's and National's policies. New Zealand Listener, *4 November 1949 and 31 August 1951*

Women cooking and entertaining in state houses in the 1950s. In common with other nations after the war, the New Zealand government aimed to foster well-housed, healthy nuclear families, with stay-at-home mothers and breadwinning fathers. *Neg. A 1665, AALF 6112, 19-8-747TIF, and AALF 6122, NA-25-1L 1026, Archives New Zealand*

Because state houses were in short supply, many New Zealand families had to live, sometimes for several years, in transit camps such as this one at Trentham, 1951.
114/395/08-G, Evening Post Collection, Alexander Turnbull Library

The suburban dream realised: a row of neat, well-tended state homes and gardens in Liberton, Dunedin, set off by a row of neat, well-tended-looking children.
R21644980.tif, Archives New Zealand

improve standards of living in the area and to assist the Governments of Asian countries to develop their economies'.[62] Consequently, the Colombo Plan for Cooperative Economic Development in South and Southeast Asia, an economic aid agreement signed by seven Commonwealth members — Australia, Britain, Ceylon, Canada, India, New Zealand and Pakistan — was born.

Along with capital aid to fund infrastructure projects such as hospitals, schools, railways and mills, the Colombo Plan sent technical experts, teachers and aid workers to the developing countries to help train and educate the local population. At the same time, it enabled large numbers of Asian students to travel to more developed member countries for tertiary education and training. In New Zealand, between 1951 and 1970, several thousand students came from Asia under the Colombo Plan to study. They made a considerable impression on New Zealanders, many of whom knew nothing about South-East Asia and had never even met an Asian before. Sri Linkan student Charmion Drieberg, who arrived in Wellington in 1951 with five other Sri Lankan girls to study dental nursing, recalled: 'Everywhere we went we were photographed and put in the paper . . . we certainly encountered a lot of curiosity from New Zealanders . . .'.[63] Dr Soedjati Djiwandono, who came to New Zealand in 1961, remembered the initial awkwardness of his host family in Invercargill, who admitted: 'We didn't know what to do with you! You're the first foreigner we've ever met in our lives, and an Asian at that.'[64]

Not least among the Plan's benefits was to foster an increased awareness of Asia amongst New Zealanders. T. L. Macdonald, the Minister of External Affairs, observed in 1955:

> Certainly we have enjoyed having them [Asian students] amongst us, and have valued the way they have broadened our understanding of other people. We New Zealanders, being 95 percent of a common stock, and being remote from other countries, inevitably tend at times to be parochial and unused to dealing with people whose backgrounds and traditions are utterly different from ours. It has been good for us to have this new experience . . .[65]

Mutually beneficial links were forged. Many students who studied in New Zealand went on to become high achievers in their own countries, retaining friendships and connections in New Zealand that smoothed the way for high-level contacts.[66] From the late 1970s, however, as the focus of New Zealand's aid programmes moved to the South Pacific, New Zealand became progressively less active and today, although still a member, it is no longer involved directly in Colombo Plan work. Nonetheless, residual impacts remain in the form of educational and economic links.

American alliance

While New Zealand's loyalties to the United Kingdom and her traditional role as a participant within the Commonwealth and its security system continued after World War II, the events of 1942 had dramatically brought home the need for American support to ensure security in the Pacific. But the United States lost interest in forming alliances in the region immediately after the war, making it clear that 'no firm and public commitment could be given . . . to protect Australia and New Zealand'.[67] Its attention was then fixed on Europe, where escalating tensions with the Soviet Union threatened to explode into a full-scale 'hot war'. The communist victory in China and the outbreak of the Korean War in 1950 redirected America's focus back to the Pacific.

The sudden invasion of South Korea by North Korea on 25 June 1950 precipitated the Korean War.[68] Two days later, when a South Korean defeat seemed imminent, an American-led United Nations force intervened. The *New Zealand Listener* wrote in 1950 that the invasion was perceived to be spearheaded by Russia, with North Korea no more than a Soviet puppet: 'Most people knew at once that Korea had been selected for a trial of strength between Russia and the Western nations. Moreover, they could scarcely doubt that Russia had taken the initiative.'[69] The UN immediately put pressure on New Zealand to contribute. But Holland, reluctant to act independently of a 'familiar and secure' British-led Commonwealth, waited for a lead from Britain.[70] Once New Zealand learned that Britain would send a naval detachment, it rapidly followed suit.[71] When, in mid-July, the call came for ground troops, Holland again hesitated, while the New Zealand press sought a commitment:

> Today the call that has been addressed to us comes not from our own kith and kin
> in the Motherland but from that still greater and larger entity, the United Nations.
> The affectionate sense of 'family', and ties of blood and tradition, may be lacking,
> but pledged friendship, pledged co-operation against acts of aggression, and a deep
> sense of gratitude for all that was done for us, particularly by the United States
> of America, when our beaches and homes were threatened by Japan after Pearl
> Harbour [sic], should make us deeply sensible that much more than words and
> heroic sentiment are expected.[72]

The Americans made it clear that they regarded New Zealand's contribution to be of the 'utmost importance': both as a demonstration of solidarity and as a boost to American morale.[73] The Department of External Affairs, too, advised that sending troops was a judicious move in view of the fact that New Zealand wanted an American commitment to defence in the Pacific. However, only news of Britain sending troops ultimately swayed Holland. On 26 July, he announced that New Zealand would immediately offer a 'special combat unit for service with other ground forces'.[74] Kayforce, a contingent of 1056 volunteers, departed in December 1950 to serve as part of the Commonwealth Division, operating under the auspices of the United Nations. Over the next three years, until an armistice was signed on 27 July 1953, about 4700 New Zealanders served on the ground and 1300 in frigates. Forty-five New Zealand soldiers lost their lives. One welcome unforeseen impact of the war was a dramatic increase in demand (and rising prices) for New Zealand wool.[75]

For the Americans, the Korean conflict proved that the communists wanted to extend their influence into the Pacific and beyond. As the political scientist Richard Kennaway observed: 'Most Americans assumed . . . that both Russia and China were partners in North Korea's aggression in South Korea, and after the entry of Chinese "volunteers" into the war in November 1950, Communist China became America's chief military opponent and the image of China as the enemy, as an aggressor pursuing a policy of unlimited imperialism, became fixed'.[76] To combat this threat the United States were now prepared to commit to a strategic alliance in the area. The long-delayed peace treaty with Japan became an urgent priority.

Both New Zealand and Australia had wanted to preclude a resurgence of Japanese aggression in the Pacific after World War II by enforcing a peace treaty limiting her industrial capacity and potential to rearm. But to their dismay the Americans then favoured a lenient peace treaty with Japan, hoping to transform her into an ally against communist expansion in the area. Strenuously resisting what they considered to be a soft peace treaty, New Zealand and Australia were not prepared to accept Japanese rearmament without the guarantee of American support. Alister McIntosh, Secretary of External Affairs and Permanent Head of the Prime Minister's Department, expressed these sentiments in a letter to Carl Berendsen, New Zealand's ambassador in Washington:

It may be unrealistic to hope for the demilitarisation of Japan, but to let them rearm and range themselves alongside the anti-Communist forces means that they will only use their 'rearms' against us. After all, the essential point in New Zealand's long-term policy is safeguarding ourselves against the Asian countries — red, blue, black or yellow, or any blend thereof. More particularly, our aim is to obtain a guarantee against Japanese aggression and I still feel that if Japan is remilitarised to any extent it is merely an invitation to such aggression.[77]

America had been unwilling to make a commitment and the peace treaty remained unsigned. But the outbreak of the Korean conflict fuelled fears of Japan either collaborating with the communists or falling victim to their aggression. United States Secretary of State John Foster Dulles declared: 'Japan must have a full opportunity to become an equal partner within the community of free nations and thus be a bulwark against Communist aggression in the Far East.'[78]

The United States now saw a pact with the Pacific countries as an attractive proposition. By supporting America in Korea, New Zealand and Australia felt they had paid a 'fair price'[79] to gain US support, and used their involvement in that conflict to convince the Americans of their future value as allies.[80] Negotiations for the defence treaty were concurrent with those for the Japanese peace treaty. Although New Zealand and Australia originally envisaged a Pacific Pact that would include Britain, the United States was unwilling to find herself committed to British interests in South-East Asia. Finally, following several months of discussion, ANZUS, the 'richest prize of New Zealand diplomacy',[81] a tripartite agreement of mutual guarantee between Australia, New Zealand and the United States, was signed on 1 September 1951.

A landmark in New Zealand foreign relations, ANZUS was the first international treaty signed by New Zealand that did not include Great Britain. This provoked some disgruntlement. Winston Churchill grumbled: 'I do not like the ANZUS Pact at all . . . I am greatly in hopes that perhaps larger, wider arrangements may be made which will be more satisfactory than those which are at present in force.'[82] In the New Zealand Parliament, Walter Nash, leader of the opposition, reminded the House of 'the principle laid down by Mr Savage of where Britain goes we go. We should hold on to that principle. We have ties with Britain that cannot be cut, and the treaty would be more beneficial if the United Kingdom was a party to it.'[83] Prime Minister Holland, obliged to defend the decision, argued that closer solidarity with the United States did not mean any lessening of 'devotion to the mother country'.[84] On the contrary, because ANZUS guaranteed New Zealand's security in the Pacific, New Zealand could fulfil its obligations to Britain by sending troops to the Middle East in the event of war there:

It is our own feeling that the American guarantee . . . will strengthen, and in no way weaken, British Commonwealth interests. Indeed, we are strongly of the view that the Treaty reinforces the vital interests of the United Kingdom, Australia and New Zealand . . . and that the Southern Dominions will as a result be enabled to carry out in the Middle East those commitments to which the United Kingdom and we ourselves attach such great importance.[85]

ANZUS may have been a milestone on the way to New Zealand enunciating an independent foreign policy, but it did not lessen feelings of loyalty toward Britain and the Commonwealth. In 1962, Alister McIntosh was still expressing the view that 'the doctrine of "where Britain goes we go" . . . became firmly implanted in New Zealand hearts. I believe it still is, and that no New Zealand Government could ever ignore an attitude so firmly entrenched in our tradition.'[86]

Uncomfortable with Britain's exclusion from ANZUS, in 1952 New Zealand sought, unsuccessfully, to include her in the pact. Clashes between Britain and America over how to deal with the escalating problems in Indo-China further exacerbated the dutiful daughter's unease. Both Australia and New Zealand faced what historian F. L. W. Wood labelled 'The Anzac Dilemma': how to balance loyalty and traditional support for Britain, a declining power, with support for the United States, the new predominant power in the Pacific.[87] There was thus doubtless great relief all round when, in 1954, New Zealand signed the South-East Asia Treaty Organization (SEATO) Agreement. SEATO was created by the Manila Pact, signed in September 1954 by the United States, Great Britain, New Zealand, Australia, the Philippines, Pakistan and Thailand to create a bulwark against the extension of communist influence. It mollified Britain over its exclusion from ANZUS and satisfied a long-standing concern of the New Zealand government that both Britain and the United States should be allied in the Pacific.

Another milestone for New Zealand, this treaty was the first such document any New Zealand government had signed with an Asian country. Diplomatic links expanded: Foss Shanahan, appointed New Zealand's Commissioner to South-East Asia in 1955 and based in Singapore, also served as New Zealand's representative on the SEATO council. In 1956, New Zealand established an embassy in Bangkok; a High Commission in Malaya followed in 1958. Little by little, New Zealand developed political and diplomatic relationships with previously ignored Asian countries. One diplomat later commented that 'One practical effect of New Zealand's SEATO membership has been that since 1955

New Zealand has devoted much more detailed and continuous attention to South-East Asia than at any earlier period. Not only are there regular annual meetings of the SEATO Ministerial Council, but between sessions a body known as the Council Representatives meets in Bangkok normally once a month.[88]

The key factor behind increased diplomatic and cultural contacts in South-East Asia continued to be fear of communism spreading south. Alliances and deployments there were all made with an eye to containing communism and keeping the enemy as far from New Zealand shores as possible and to 'establish a claim upon our major allies for consultation, a voice in important decisions, and in the last resort, and most importantly, military assistance and protection in time of need. This requires New Zealand to demonstrate willingness and ability to assist our allies in matters affecting *their* national interests.'[89] This same logic and commitment to her alliances would lead New Zealand to participate in the longest, most controversial, politically divisive and bloodiest South-East Asian conflict — the Vietnam War.[90]

The Vietnam War presented a dilemma for the New Zealand government. There were real fears that a communist victory there might lead to further advances in the area. This was the heyday of the 'domino theory' (that is, the idea that if one nation fell to communism, so too would its neighbours). Moreover, the toppling dominoes appeared to be heading for Australia and New Zealand.[91] While acknowledging its commitment to the United States, New Zealand was nevertheless reluctant to become involved. On the one hand, policy-makers doubted that military intervention would be useful or effective; on the other, the defence forces still had commitments in Malaysia. In 1963, just as American calls for increased assistance in Vietnam intensified, New Zealand committed to increasing its troops to 1400 to assist in operations against Indonesian aggression in Malaysia. She had neither the resources nor the will for commitments in two theatres.

In the early 1960s, when the Vietnam conflict flared up with communist North Vietnamese incursions into the South, the United States decided to increase military and economic aid to the South Vietnamese government. It then made it clear to New Zealand and Australia that their participation in some way would be welcomed. Australia promptly offered assistance, sending a small team of military advisors in May 1962. The New Zealand government, more cautious, preferred a non-military option. Accordingly, in August 1962, it announced plans to provide a small civilian surgical team. But the United States wanted a military training team, a request publicly reinforced by the

South Vietnamese foreign minister on a visit to New Zealand in early 1963. In June that year, Prime Minister Holyoake announced that New Zealand would send a small team of military advisors to assist in a non-combatant role. In doing so, he carefully spelled out to the New Zealand public that the conflict in Vietnam remained 'essentially a struggle to be fought and won by the Vietnamese people themselves . . . In this struggle we are not to undertake combat duties; this has not been asked. And it would not be appropriate.'[92]

In reality, New Zealand was not so much sending aid to help the South Vietnamese as flying the flag alongside her American ally: 'The vital issue for Australia and New Zealand was not the need to restore stability in South Vietnam, but to preserve our position with the United States as our major ally.'[93] Holyoake's prevarication, combined with political instability in Saigon, delayed his acting for another year. An unequivocal request from President Lyndon Johnson for 'a strong show of flags in Vietnam' finally prompted the government into sending a 25-engineer detachment for road and bridge building.[94]

Holyoake doubtless hoped this show of support would staunch further requests from both the South Vietnamese and America. But as US involvement in Vietnam escalated (by 1968, there were over half a million American soldiers deployed there),[95] pressure for New Zealand to send troops intensified. Meanwhile, the government continued to hesitate, citing its meagre military resources and significant troop contribution in Malaysia, though officials were aware that not showing support could mean the loss of the American guarantee of security: 'The ultimate disaster for New Zealand would be for the Americans to wash their hands of us — to decide that we weren't worth the effort of cultivating or protecting — and if necessary we must be prepared to pay a high price to avoid this happening.'[96] On 20 April 1965, the president's special envoy, Henry Cabot Lodge, visited Wellington to persuade New Zealand to send troops and to point out the price of not doing so. On 27 May, Holyoake announced that New Zealand would send an artillery battery of 120 men to Vietnam.

As a political briefing paper at the end of April emphasised: 'if the contribution of an artillery battery by this country would help the United States administration to carry through its present policy of staying in and defending South Vietnam, and would at the same time reinforce the American guarantee which is the mainstay of our national security, then the contribution of such a unit would be in the best interests of this country and would be an acceptable price to pay.'[97] While this was the underlying rationale for New Zealand's involvement, Holyoake's explanation to the public emphasised the threat of communist aggression: 'If South Vietnam falls to the Communists, it will then be the turn of Thailand, and Malaysia and every other small country in the area. In this eventuality the threat to New Zealand would be that much closer to home . . . Communist terrorism must be halted . . . New Zealand's vital interests are at stake in this war . . . New Zealand's own security is involved. The people of South Vietnam must be supported in their struggle against Communist aggression . . .'[98]

The decision to become involved generated a certain amount of controversy and opposition, but hostility to communism and fear of China's growing power meant that by and large the New Zealand people initially supported New Zealand's entry into the war. As the *Dominion* of 14 May 1965 recorded: 'the Prime Minister spoke for the vast majority of New Zealanders when he said that South Vietnam must not be abandoned to the well-meaning demonstrators'.[99]

Although the evolution and social impacts of New Zealand's involvement in the war in Vietnam are explored more fully in Chapter 5 of this book, it is useful here to consider its significance as a watershed in foreign relations. This was the first war New Zealand fought without Britain and the last of its military involvements in Asia. It ended a historic bipartisan consensus on foreign policy, as Labour increasingly questioned the costs and benefits of unstintingly supporting the United States in security matters, and promoted a more independent, morality-based stance. Opposition to the war grew, leaving a legacy of distrust among sections of the New Zealand public of the perceived overbearing power of the United States, and scepticism toward its military interventions around the world. Participating in the war, in common with New Zealand's other involvements in Asia in the 1950s and 1960s, was strongly linked to defence considerations. New defence alliances and diplomatic links had not altered New Zealand's feelings towards Britain. They did, though, mark an end to the almost exclusive nature of the country's former relationship with the parent country and contributed to a growing sense of independence. Before World War II, New Zealand operated exclusively within an imperial framework that offered substantive economic and military benefits but also exacted an enormous toll in terms of military manpower and support. After the war, her role as an alliance partner was often more political in nature, and the material and military manpower element relatively negligible. The country not only shifted away from an alliance with one dominant partner, but the nature of its alliance support also shifted, enabling it to cultivate relations with a range of other international players. In contrast to its ignorance and fear of Asia prior to World War II, in 1966 New Zealand became a signatory and founder member of the Asian Pacific Council (ASPAC), an economic, cultural and social consultative body that included among others Japan, South Korea, South Vietnam, Thailand, New Zealand, Australia, Singapore and the Philippines. According to Ian McGibbon, 'New Zealand established a presence in the region that would persist long after security fears had been allayed.'[100] This was a happy but unanticipated by-product of a more pressing desire to draw the protective cloak of America tighter over the country. Defence considerations and diplomacy loosened old ties, but so too did changing economic relations, the growing influence and importance of global organisations, and developments closer to home.

Diversification and decolonisation

In the late 1950s, the first disturbing rumours reached New Zealand that Britain aimed to join the European Economic Community; in 1961, it openly announced its intentions. New Zealand, which regarded itself as having 'almost a divine right'[101] to export primary produce (namely cheese, butter and meat) to the British market unrestricted, did not accept lying down the prospect of losing its major agricultural export market. Instead, for the next ten years, between 1961 and 1971, Jack Marshall, Keith Holyoake's Deputy Prime Minister and Minister of Overseas Trade, skilfully spearheaded a political and diplomatic campaign to preserve privileged access for New Zealand's primary produce.

The campaign offers an insight into New Zealand and Britain's evolving, sometimes fraught, relationship. While New Zealand apparently accepted that it was appropriate and timely for Britain to join the EEC, this was with the intractable proviso that its access to the British market be allowed to continue. In arguing its case, it invoked sympathy and sentiment by highlighting cultural ties, the country's traditional dependent role as 'Britain's other farm',[102] and the loyal sacrifices offered up during two world wars. At the same time, many New Zealand officials and politicians held the view that the British, had they a free hand, 'would have sold New Zealand out as soon as possible'.[103] But they did not have a free hand. As one of Britain's leading EEC negotiators succinctly put it, Holyoake and Marshall effectively held the revered Mother Country 'over a political barrel'.[104] Opinion in Britain about joining the EEC was so divided that, if Holyoake rejected a settlement, an 'open and strenuous New Zealand campaign against membership' would preclude its ever obtaining parliamentary approval.[105] This is a testament to the emotional influence New Zealand still held in Britain. As late as 24 May 1971, British Foreign Secretary Sir Alec Douglas-Home admitted that 'it would be impossible to get anything but a fair deal for New Zealand through the House of Commons'.[106] New Zealand, aware of this trump card up its sleeve, was prepared to play it if necessary. In his discussions with Geoffrey Rippon, Britain's chief negotiator with the EEC, in September 1970, Holyoake said that while he trusted Britain to safeguard New Zealand's interests, he was also having difficulty dealing with the demands of Norman Kirk, the leader of the opposition, and other prominent New Zealanders who were prepared to campaign vociferously in the United Kingdom against Britain's entry into the EEC.[107] Underneath the sentimental rhetoric about family ties, hardball was being played, with mutual resentment, distrust and exasperation between mother and daughter evident throughout the campaign.

Britain made three separate attempts to enter the EEC; the first two, in 1961 and 1967, were vetoed by France's president, Charles de Gaulle. In 1973, when it finally succeeded in entering, New Zealand's years of skilful lobbying and negotiating paid off handsomely. Protocol 18 provided it with reduced but ongoing access to the EEC market until 1988, with residual access thereafter. Holyoake acknowledged in a television interview that this was 'the best deal they could possibly have got for us'.[108] The campaign had several spin-offs which together helped to loosen further the former reliance on Britain. New Zealand's diplomatic presence on the Continent expanded in the 1960s, as consuls and embassy officials were installed to proselytise the country's case. The longevity of the campaign allowed New Zealand time to make a concerted effort to diversify its export markets. When Britain finally did gain entry into the EEC, New Zealand's total exports to that country had dropped to 31 per cent of all her exports; by the next year (1974), that fell to 26 per cent.[109] By this time, talk of sentimental ties had ceased, a state of affairs the British High Commission in Wellington believed to be a healthy sign: 'Britain's entry into the EEC has served . . . as a catalyst to a recognition of the fact that New Zealand as "another six counties of Britain" is a notion that should have disappeared in the 1930s: that it has persisted is due as much to wishful thinking and very astute New Zealand propaganda.'[110]

The reality of the situation was that New Zealand was steadily moving away from reliance on Britain, and had in fact begun to do so before the EEC campaign commenced. The shift toward the United States in security matters coincided with a shift in trade and foreign investment partners. Throughout the 1950s and 1960s, the provenance of the bulk of foreign investment in New Zealand moved from Britain to the United States and Australia. So did the origin of imports:[111] by the late 1960s, the Australian share of New Zealand imports had reached 20 per cent while imports from the UK dropped from 60 per cent in 1950 to 19 per cent in 1970.[112] In 1961, New Zealand joined the International Monetary Fund (IMF) and the World Bank, thus reducing its former almost total dependence on Britain for overseas loans.[113] While New Zealand exports to Britain fell — from 65.5 per cent in 1955 to only 36 per cent by 1970[114] — her exports to a number of other markets expanded. Exports to the United States rose from 6 per cent of the total in 1955 to 16 per cent in 1970; to Australia, from 3 per cent in 1955 to 9 per cent in 1970; to Japan, from less than 1 per cent in 1955 to 10 per cent in 1970. As early as 1958, New Zealand and Japan signed a bilateral trade agreement which resulted in a 'massive increase in trade between the two countries'.[115] Britain's intended membership of the European Economic Community gave impetus to a search for new trade partners and 'world-wide trade diversification' that was already well under way.[116]

Britain's bid to join the European Common Market also prompted New Zealand and Australia to consider a closer trading relationship. An Australia–New Zealand Consultative Committee on Trade was set up and Australia's Trade Minister John McEwen and New Zealand's Deputy Prime Minister and Minister of Overseas Trade John Marshall started to work towards a free trade agreement. They succeeded, and on 31 August 1965 their respective countries signed the New Zealand–Australia Free Trade Agreement (NAFTA). Designed to progressively reduce tariffs and other trade restrictions between the two countries, it was described by McEwan as a 'historic landmark in trade relations' that would have 'far-reaching long-term effects on growth and development'.[117] Although NAFTA initially made only a slight difference to trade patterns, it set up a framework for trade consultation, so that when Britain finally did join the EEC, the mechanisms for closer economic ties were in place. It also prepared the ground for Closer Economic Relations (CER) negotiations and the eventual CER agreement of December 1982. Historian Philippa Mein Smith explains that 'Once NAFTA came into force in 1966, the trade ministers met at least once a year, and officials twice, supplemented by subcommittees and working parties, and reinforced by phone calls and day-to-day consultations between the high commissions and bureaucracy. The private sector also began to consult under the NAFTA umbrella.'[118] The proportion of New Zealand exports to Australia rose from 4 per cent in 1959, to about 9 per cent in 1970, to 12 per cent in 1980.[119] By the 1990s, Australia was New Zealand's biggest trading partner.

It is worth considering why trans-Tasman ties tightened so late in the day. Australia and New Zealand were linked by language, similar cultures, a British heritage and the ANZAC tradition. Citizens moved freely between the two countries, which benefited from a constant interchange of ideas and people.[120] But there was also surprisingly little trade, business or official political exchange and communication. Richard Kennaway wrote in 1972: 'perhaps the most striking feature of the first 60 years of this century has been rather the sparseness of direct bilateral contacts ... New Zealand ministers have until recently tended to regard Australia as a staging post, while Australian ministers have tended to ignore New Zealand.'[121] That the relationship between the two countries was 'fluctuating and largely ad hoc'[122] for a long time is borne out by the fact that between 1945 and 1970 only one Australian prime minister visited New Zealand, and vice versa.[123]

This lack of contact had roots in the Empire. Until 1943, when high commissions were established in Wellington and Canberra, communication on defence or foreign affairs was carried out through London: 'from spoke to hub, rather than directly to each other around the rim'.[124] The legacy of this situation, even once Britain no longer constituted the hub, proved tenacious. During World War II, the shift of superpower status in the Pacific from Great Britain to the United States compelled New Zealand and Australia to reconsider their mutual place in the region. But the regional zone of defence envisioned by the 1944 Canberra Pact was effectively 'stillborn'.[125] Ushering in closer trade and commercial relations also remained slow, with restrictive import licensing regimes hindering progress. Despite some efforts to coordinate economic development and discussions on trade issues, by 1959 only 4 per cent of New Zealand's exports were going to Australia. New Zealand received 17 per cent of its imports from Australia, however, making it the main market for Australian-manufactured goods.[126]

Closer relations were not helped by irritation, competition and lack of empathy between policy-makers on each side of the Tasman. Carl Berendsen, New Zealand's first High Commissioner in Australia (from 1943–44 and then New Zealand's Minister in Washington), grumbled in 1946: 'I am getting very fed up with Australia ... I don't remember any single instance where Australia has supported any action that I have taken here ... although whenever they have something to propose they very warmly canvass our support and certainly expect to get it ... I am getting a little tired of it.'[127] Alister McIntosh, Secretary of External Affairs, complained in 1950:

> it was never in our interests, and I doubt if it ever will be, to work in double harness with the Australians. We are much better to stick to our own line ...[128]

... you were right in saying that it doesn't pay to team up with them, because it is not possible to figure where they are going, nor will they play in a team, and it is a great pity that we are so much victims of geography that in a sense we must play in a team with them, but deal with them we certainly must.[129]

According to historian Ian McGibbon, with regard to involvement in the Korean War, communication remained unsatisfactory: 'Consultation between Australia and New Zealand had not been satisfactory either . . . In spite of the Australian–New Zealand Agreement of 1944 neither Australia nor New Zealand placed overriding importance on co-ordinating policy with the other.'[130]

Nonetheless, ad hoc cooperation between the two armed forces, cemented with the formation of the Australian and New Zealand Army Corps (ANZAC) troops during World War I, continued to evolve informally, with combined exercises, a naval exchange scheme, and the linking of troops in the Korean War, Malayan Emergency and Vietnam War. It was not until the 1970s, however, that the two countries took measures to provide closer defence cooperation and consultation at a political and ministerial level.

Decolonisation and the United Nations

In addition to altered military and economic relations after 1945, both Australia and New Zealand had to adjust to the rapidly changing nature of the Commonwealth, and to play a role in the newly created United Nations. After the war, the British Empire was reduced to fourteen British overseas territories. In 1949, the name 'British Commonwealth' was changed to 'Commonwealth' to reflect Britain's less dominant role in that increasingly diverse organisation. The number of Commonwealth members rose from twelve in 1960 to 31 by 1972, with the majority of new members from Africa, Asia and the Caribbean. Britain and the pre-1945 dominions came to be known informally as the 'Old Commonwealth' and the newer members as the 'New Commonwealth'. In 1960 alone, seventeen new African states achieved independence and joined the UN. By 1972, 70 per cent of the UN's 131 members came from the Third World.[131] Anti-colonialism and anti-racism became, not surprisingly, a preoccupation in both organisations.

In 1960, New Zealand voted for the United Nations Declaration for the Granting of Independence to Colonial Countries and Peoples, sponsored by the anti-colonial bloc in the United Nations. It then proceeded to 'decolonise' its own Pacific 'empire' of protectorates and trustee territories. Following a plebiscite, Western Samoa became fully independent in 1962; the Cook Islands in 1965; and Niue in 1972. Keith Holyoake's invitation in 1963 to a United Nations mission to monitor the process of decolonisation in the Cook Islands prompted protests from the British, Americans and Australians, all of whom felt worried that it might set a precedent for other colonial territories around the world. Nevertheless, Holyoake proceeded, resolute that the United Nations committee should verify the process, arguing that 'a small country like New Zealand cannot afford to antagonise the bulk of world opinion'.[132]

New Zealand strongly supported the United Nations from its inception, perceiving it as an important guarantor of peace and security, especially for smaller nations. Its tendency to take an independent stance in the United Nations did not go unnoticed in Britain, where concerns were expressed about New Zealand being 'much preoccupied with the figure she cuts in the United Nations' and showing 'undue susceptibility to the views of the African-Asian and anti-colonial sentiment as displayed in the United Nations'.[133] The way New Zealand handled the decolonisation of its Pacific 'empire', and its determined involvement of the United Nations in the process, certainly earned it plaudits from countries such as Tunisia and Algeria, among other UN members. Scholars influenced by post-colonial studies have recently offered a darker, less congratulatory view of the decolonisation process. Damon Salesa in particular has criticised New Zealand's earlier role as a coloniser in the Pacific. New Zealand's ulterior motives in the Pacific, he argues, are frequently either ignored or presented in a misleadingly roseate light by historians. In his view, formal decolonisation is better analysed as a change in tactics, which did not end New Zealand's primacy in the Pacific but rather altered its form.[134] New Zealand's eagerness to hasten decolonisation doubtless related to a perception that having friendly island nations rather than island dependencies and bastions was more in the national interest, and certainly the islands continued to be an important source of trade and of cheap labour.[135] Nevertheless, it proactively and rapidly decolonised.

New Zealand's determined use of the United Nations to direct and oversee the decolonisation process, sometimes in defiance of its major allies, was a significant development. The country's willingness to take an independent stance in the UN against the wishes of Britain and the US was also illustrated by its outspoken opposition towards nuclear testing in the Pacific. From the late 1950s onwards, New Zealand used the United Nations to express its disapprobation of its British and American allies for continuing the tests. In 1962, despite American disapproval and pressure from Britain, Prime Minister Holyoake spoke in the UN General Assembly supporting an immediate moratorium on testing as a first step toward a long-term test ban. In 1963, New Zealand became one of the first countries to ratify a UN Partial Test Ban Treaty in the atmosphere, outer space and underwater, and protested strongly against proposed French tests in the same year.

The United Nations became an important forum in which New Zealand could adopt an independent national stance on issues, often in opposition to its major allies — Britain and the United States. The formerly dutiful daughter's stance on decolonisation and anti-nuclear issues appeared to confirm Britain's unease at her tendency to succumb to 'the temptation of moral voting' and susceptibility to the views of the anti-colonial bloc of Africans in the UN.[136] So far the country would appear to clearly be on the side of the liberal angels, or at least the anti-colonial, anti-nuclear ones.

But its response to the 1965 Unilateral Declaration of Independence (UDI) by the government of Ian Smith in Southern Rhodesia showed another more conservative and ambivalent New Zealand response to colonialism. The Declaration effectively pre-empted British plans to move the white minority Smith government towards majority rule and eventual independence. Britain responded by seeking Commonwealth and UN sanctions against the Smith regime. In May 1966, the African states in the Security Council went one step further, calling on Britain to use all measures, including force, to bring about majority rule in Rhodesia. New Zealand was the only nation to vote against the proposal; the United States and Britain were amongst the eight nations who abstained. Zambia's Foreign Minister subsequently denounced New Zealand as 'the enemy of Africa'.[137]

Support for Smith within New Zealand was considerable. Sir Denis Blundell, New Zealand High Commissioner to London, believed that a majority (possibly as high as 80 per cent) condoned the regime. Some senior government ministers openly supported Smith, as did many of the country's newspapers. Barry Gustafson, Holyoake's biographer, has commented that 'on this issue, Holyoake clearly had to balance international opinion against offending those in his own parliamentary caucus and party and the electorate as a whole who sympathised with Smith's regime'.[138] Ongoing sporting links with South Africa also involved New Zealand transgressing international sanctions and precipitating international opprobrium. For some sections of the New Zealand populace, the shared cultural links between fellow members of the British Empire were more persuasive than arguments put forward by the anti-colonial anti-racist elements in the United Nations and Commonwealth. For older New Zealanders especially, because of a sense of shared identity, the white governing elite in Rhodesia deserved sympathy if not active support. They were fellow members of the British Empire who had fought for the same side in two world wars and like New Zealand had long been exporters of primary produce for the British market. Fissures over conflicting sets of values, one harking back to an older British Empire model and the other more internationalist and anti-colonial, would widen during the 1970s and 1980s.

During the two decades following World War II, New Zealand adhered to the Commonwealth framework and remained loyal to Great Britain. But her formerly exclusive dependence on the Mother Country steadily decreased. The new global economic and political situation resulted in her seeking and eventually entering into defence alliances not just with a declining Britain but with Australia and the new world superpower, the United States. The Cold War against communism prompted a shift in strategic efforts toward South-East Asia. In addition to involvement in a series of military conflicts in that region, by 1966 New Zealand had established embassies or other diplomatic offices in Singapore, Japan, Malaysia, Laos, Vietnam, Indonesia and the Philippines.

Britain's aim to join the EEC highlighted the need to adjust to changing global economic and international relations. In the process of campaigning for ongoing access of its primary produce to the EEC market, New Zealand created diplomatic posts and links on the European continent. It also successfully cultivated new markets and trading partners closer to home in Asia and Australia. Involvement in the United Nations helped foster New Zealand's growing sense of national autonomy and independence. Its critical stance on nuclear testing in the Pacific, at odds with Britain and the US, was particularly significant in this respect. While Britain gradually withdrew from the Pacific region, New Zealand's role in the decolonisation of its Pacific Island protectorates and trustee territories from the early 1960s onwards led to an increased awareness of its status and responsibilities as a south-west Pacific nation. In the post-war decades, foreign policy, like national identity, was shaped by a new globalisation and an accompanying set of evolving international relations. Emotional and sentimental ties with Britain might remain intact, but new links, both economic and diplomatic, were steadily forged as part of broader strategic considerations. In the words of historian Mary Boyd, 'it took a long time for New Zealand to make up its mind that it was a Pacific country, not a European outpost'.[139] That process, well under way by the mid-1960s, quickened and intensified over the next 20 years.

CHAPTER THREE

Creating New Zealand

CULTURE AND CHARACTER

The best contemporary painting (and literature, and music) is in fact creating New Zealand as a world of the imagination. This is a new development among us, which makes the present a particularly exciting and hopeful time to live in, because in these first stirrings of the native imagination an undiscovered world seems to be waking and opening before our eyes. In that world we may look for an expression of our spiritual identity as a people. — Charles Brasch, 1958[1]

The period between 1945 and the mid-1960s is often perceived as a golden age of suburban pastimes and aspirations: fathers mowing lawns; mothers filling baking tins and happily wielding newly purchased vacuum cleaners. These sorts of images conjure up a stereotype of bland conformity and cultural mediocrity. But while the suburban idyll did flourish in those years, so too did all manner of creative artistic endeavour.[2] A process of cultural self-assertion that began during the Great Depression gathered momentum, strengthened by the realities of post-war international relations. With Britain weakened and progressively shedding her empire, it seemed to many New Zealand artists and writers that forging a more self-reliant cultural identity outside the imperial framework was now both appropriate and overdue.

Writers, artists, musicians, critics, architects and social commentators all began producing work they proclaimed to be 'new': a 'discovery and invention' of New Zealand. They announced their emancipation from the immediate past, from what they believed to be the 'untruth of New Zealand' and the 'foreignness' of previous inspiration — that is, imported English or European styles that followed nineteenth-century romantic conventions and portrayed New Zealand through sophisticated, soft, sentimental eyes.[3] Painters and writers alike maintained that, although continuing to work in a European tradition, they needed to adapt it to 'individual vision and national consciousness'[4] and produce 'authentic' work.[5] The real New Zealand, they proclaimed, was one of barren isolated landscapes, waiting to be filled by the imagination; that is, by the works of writers and of artists. Art historian Francis Pound sums up their ideology as: 'Absence, blankness, solitude, silence. Such was the self-proclaimed origin of the quest of the 1930s, 1940s, 1950s and 1960s "to discover, or to invent, the true New Zealand".'[6] The task, according to the historian, poet and literary nationalist Keith Sinclair, was to create 'a New World', to make New Zealand less 'sheep and gold, more storied; through art and ideas more real and enhanced . . . We would find out what we were.'[7] New Zealand prose writers in particular focused on what they believed to be their country's repressive puritanism and conformity. It was, as Pound noted, a powerful ideology, constructed by intellectuals to distance themselves from what had gone before.[8]

The broader population did not necessarily share this desire for more cultural self-reliance and 'authenticity'. In his 2010 memoirs, the author and critic C. K. Stead recalls his dismay at the popular fervour surrounding the Queen's visit in 1953. So much frenzied devotion towards the ultimate symbol of the Empire and the British class system constituted a source of embarrassment that 'no self-respecting young New Zealand intellectual' could countenance: 'To see the huge New Zealand crowds in effect reaffirming those things was embarrassing. One felt ashamed, and looked to the writers, especially the poets, Fairburn, Mason, Curnow, Glover, Baxter, for an independent voice and an end to this ancillary status.'[9] These men were the self-avowed 'prophets to their people' who through their work would show the public the 'authentic' New Zealand.[10] For them, New Zealand was a land of harsh realities: a homogeneous, dull society of 'mean cities' and 'mortgaged farms' where 'settlers had to struggle to find their way in an often barren landscape'.[11] Denis Glover's celebrated poem 'The Magpies', which tells the life story of a farming couple, conveys this struggle with laconic, unblinking realism:

> The farm's still there,
> Mortgage corporations couldn't give it away

And Quardle oodle ardle wardle doodle
The magpies say.[12]

In conveying this version of authenticity, writers drew heavily on international literary movements and influences; notably modernism and neo-romanticism in poetry, and American realism in prose. Overseas influences also had an impact on art and architecture. Paradoxically, absorbing and adapting international ideas and trends went hand in hand with developing a more distinctive national culture. Finding inspiration overseas, although not a new phenomenon for New Zealand writers, artists and architects, was now augmented by a conscious desire to produce work that reflected their country's character — unique, unvarnished and true to life.

Pride in a distinctive national culture did not suddenly spring up, Athena-like, after World War II; it had steadily evolved within the imperial framework for over a century. But in the 1950s especially, as New Zealand increasingly opened up to influences other than that of Britain, its artists and intellectuals consciously pursued and attempted to foster a cultural identity separate from that of the parent country. This surge of cultural nationalism proved relatively short-lived however. By the latter 1960s, the country carried a sense of its independent identity more securely, and therefore proclaimed and celebrated it less compulsively. At the same time, issues of national identity also seemed less relevant, as New Zealand found itself drawn into an increasingly global culture.

Creative infrastructure

New Zealand's flourishing cultural scene after World War II was fostered by the creation of an artistic and cultural infrastructure. As in so many aspects of life, the state played a key role. The Labour government took the first and vital step by establishing the broadcasting system in 1936. In 1946, it also created a State Literary Fund to support and encourage local authors and publications. This enabled universities to set up fellowships for writers, and helped to sustain the fledgling publishing industry after the war. From 1961, the fund was incorporated into the Arts Advisory Council (the Queen Elizabeth II Arts Council from 1963) which supported a broader range of arts and established new awards, fellowships and scholarships.[13]

After a somewhat shaky start, the country's first national symphony orchestra — also founded by Labour immediately after the war — thrived and endured. In 1947, only two years after its creation, it performed Douglas Lilburn's *Song of the Antipodes*, the first orchestral music to be written by a

New Zealand composer and played by a New Zealand orchestra. Government set up the National Library Service at this time, and reconstructed adult education under university control. State support for the expanding university sector in ensuing decades indirectly fostered artistic productivity by providing secure paid work for many writers, critics, composers, artists and performers. In Auckland, a Community Arts Service brought drama, music and paintings to the remotest parts of the province. Its many fans hoped it might eventually form part of a national theatre, but that dream died after National's victory in 1949. Thereafter, state involvement in and support for the arts usually followed in the wake of private initiatives. In 1958, for example, a private endowment enabled Otago University to set up its Burns Fellowship for creative writers. In 1953 a Danish immigrant, Poul Gnatt, formed the New Zealand Ballet Company, and a year later Donald Munro, a New Zealand opera singer, founded the New Zealand Opera Company. Once established, these sorts of enterprises received state, local and corporate support.[14] A small number of war refugees, predominantly Jewish, also played a role in invigorating New Zealand's cultural scene — especially its music — often in alliance with the state. In 1945, for example, Fred Turnovsky founded the Wellington Chamber Music Society; by 1950, a national federation of chamber music groups worked in tandem with the New Zealand Broadcasting Service to cost-share when bringing overseas performers to the country or employing local performers.[15]

While the public might complain about the calibre and the frequency of local productions or performances, they soon took it for granted that New Zealand had its own artistic sector supported by a cultural infrastructure. The upsurge in creative activity, spurred by the desire for a more independent cultural nationalism, was something of a self-fulfilling prophecy, as works created by New Zealanders and aimed at a local market helped to forge a new sense of cultural identity and independence. Poets led the charge but, in doing so, started a battle within their own ranks.

Poetry wars

In 1945, the Caxton Press published *A Book of New Zealand Verse 1923–45*. The editor of the anthology, Allen Curnow, set out his views on New Zealand poetry in an extensive introduction. This established the terms of what became a protracted dispute about poetry and cultural nationalism. Curnow argued that the imagination of the New Zealand poet needed to 'seek forms as immediate in experience as the island soil under his feet'.[16] The best poetry, based on observed reality and experience, had a high mission: 'verse has begun to be recognised as purposive, a real expression of what the New Zealander is and a part of what he may become'. Rather than looking to the northern hemisphere, to that other 'Home' Great Britain, for inspiration and models, the best contemporary poets wrote from the immediate and the local before letting their 'imagination take flight' to explore universal and personal themes. For Curnow the problem was the 'fanciful aimlessness'[17] of conventional Victorian and Georgian poets, imbued with 'imitativeness and the facile exploitation of local colour'.[18] The solution lay with those who, in his words, 'accepted the disciplines of uncompromising fidelity to experience, of an unqualified responsibility to the truths of themselves, in this place, at that time'.[19]

While at university in Auckland and Christchurch during the 1930s, Curnow came under the influence of the modernist movement in literature, and upheld the kind of writing that 'broke with more formal, essentially British and middle-class conventions'.[20] He also contributed to the Auckland University student quarterly *The Phoenix* and was introduced to the poems of R. A. K. Mason and A. R. D. Fairburn, some of the best of which paid lyrical tribute to the New Zealand landscape. At this time, Curnow developed a lifelong friendship with the poet and publisher Denis Glover, who in 1934 founded the Caxton Press in Christchurch with the aim of publishing high-quality local literature. Glover's poems resound with images of mountains, lands, rivers and seas, and with nostalgia for a simpler time, when people were more directly linked to the land and to a life lived in harmony with nature.

Curnow, too, was searching for something in the 'unpeopled' New Zealand landscape, and forming ideas about its symbolic and metaphorical uses in poetry. During his time at university, he lost his strong Christian faith. His plan to follow in his father's footsteps and become an Anglican minister was consequently abandoned. Instead he became, in addition to a published poet, a journalist and an academic. From 1937 onwards, for over 50 years, he wrote satirical verses on topical New Zealand issues under the pseudonym 'Whim Wham'; first for the Christchurch *Sun* and later the *New Zealand Herald*. However, his lucid, authoritative introduction to the 1945 Caxton anthology first put his name at the forefront of national literary criticism.

Charles Brasch, the other prominent name in New Zealand literary circles from the late 1940s, was a contemporary of Curnow's. The title of his first poetry collection, *The Land and the People*, published by Caxton in 1939, signalled the direction his work would take. The second, *Disputed Ground: Poems 1939–40* (1948) confirmed it — a meditation on New Zealand landscape and his place within it. His elegiac poems, several of which appeared in Curnow's

1945 anthology, are infused with a strong sense of alienation and isolation, of seeking a place, a past and future, in the land of his birth. As Curnow observed, Brasch's poems are 'full of the failure of the New Zealander . . . to make the land his own'.[21]

Born in Dunedin to a wealthy Jewish family, Brasch was a reserved, somewhat solitary man of cosmopolitan tastes and sensibilities, who spent many years in England and Europe before returning to New Zealand in 1947. While living in England, he became more conscious and appreciative of his national heritage: 'It was New Zealand I discovered, not England, because New Zealand lived in me as no other country could live, part of myself as I was part of it, the world I breathed and wore from birth, my seeing and my language.'[22] Consequently, during these years he started writing poems that encapsulated what it meant to be a New Zealander, isolated and struggling to come to terms with a harsh, remote landscape: 'Always, in these islands, meeting and parting / Shake us, making tremulous the salt-rimmed air; / . . . The future and the past stand at our doors, / . . . distance looks our way'.[23] As with Curnow, his cultural nationalism was never of a patriotic or self-congratulatory kind; but rather imbued with a modernist sensibility, and a high sense of the importance of art and culture. His poems, which directly convey personal emotion while seeking communion and transcendence in the natural world, can also be placed within the romantic tradition. Like Curnow, he drew on the New Zealand land- and seascape to reflect on themes of identity, alienation and isolation.

In 1947, Brasch founded and edited the quarterly journal *Landfall*, New Zealand's foremost arts and literary journal. He aimed in doing so to promote New Zealand literature and the arts and to nourish a national literary and artistic consciousness. He later wrote: 'There was no such thing yet as a distinct New Zealand literature; but the small cloudy nucleus of one was already forming, and our journal would foster that, enabling it (I hoped) to define itself and so to define New Zealand.'[24]

Landfall's influence can hardly be overestimated. Brasch encouraged painters such as Colin McCahon and Toss Woollaston and reproduced their work in the journal long before they received any degree of public recognition. He regularly published new aspiring writers along with those already well established. As the young poet Ruth Dallas, a regular contributor to *Landfall*, later noted, 'now for the first time, I encountered the work of other young New Zealand writers; the platform existed on which we could speak; the rest was up to us'.[25] Reviews of books, exhibitions, operas, concerts and films, literary and social criticism, and articles on a wide range of political and social topics also regularly featured. New Zealand's foreign policy and relations with other Pacific countries, subjects such as education, broadcasting, civil liberties, the press and capital punishment, were all examined. Letters from Australia, Canada and later South Africa were an annual feature, and there were also reports from Samoa, Mexico, Western Europe, Russia, China, Japan and elsewhere.[26] The primary focus, however, was the development of a distinctive New Zealand consciousness and outlook. For the 20 years *Landfall* remained under his editorship, Brasch insisted that contributors had to be either New Zealanders, or living in New Zealand, or that their contribution be of special relevance to New Zealand. In this way, he created an almost wholly indigenous magazine that provided not only a forum for the country's artists, authors and academics, but a record of its intellectual and creative life during a formative period.

By the 1950s, a group of younger poets had begun to dispute what they perceived to be the narrowly nationalist prescriptions of Curnow and Brasch. Many of these dissidents were based in the capital, so the debate possibly incorporated an 'Auckland versus Wellington' element of competitive literary parochialism. The geographical boundaries of the ensuing schism were always rather fluid, however, as Brasch was Dunedin-based, while Curnow himself had been born and raised in Christchurch. The Auckland poets favouring a regional or national impulse included, among others, Keith Sinclair, Kendrick Smithyman, M. K. Joseph and C. K. Stead. The Wellington poets, most notably Louis Johnson, James K. Baxter, Alistair Te Ariki Campbell, W. H. Oliver and Peter Bland, were more inclined to write poetry that was not only more romantic but 'universal, international and political'.[27] For instance, Alistair Te Ariki Campbell's popular and romantic collection *Mine Eyes Dazzle* (1956) featured characters from ancient Greece and themes of love and death, loss and longing:

> At the great water's edge
> Golden Narcissus lies;
> Hand propped under his chin,
> Bees at his thighs;
> His eyes fixed upon nothing
> Where his image lies.
> O Echo, Echo.[28]

Campbell, born in the Cook Islands, was inspired more by the classical world than by New Zealand. This accorded with the Wellington group's desire to write international or universal poetry, not necessarily rooted in local soil, and more romantic in its direct expression of emotion.[29]

The central figure in the Wellington group, the poet and journalist Louis Johnson, in contrast to Curnow, refused to accept the principle of immediacy as a critical tool for writers.[30] His first two poetry collections, *The Sun Among the Ruins* and *Roughshod Among the Lilies*, both published in 1951, explored universal themes of personal anguish, sexual torment and domestic life. Rather than remote, people-less landscapes, his work focused on daily life in small towns and cities. A warm, gregarious man, Johnson played a crucial role as a literary mentor, fostering and encouraging new talent. In 1965, Charles Doyle wrote that 'Johnson has defined the working area for many of the poets of his generation. His is the poetry of suburbia, the domestic scene, the complexities of childhood. In content, Johnson's work teems with ideas. So many poets have been influenced by him, both as poet and editor.'[31] According to Keith Sinclair, Johnson founded the *New Zealand Poetry Yearbook*, an 'anti-Brasch, anti-Curnow annual', to 'prevent those two editors from determining, almost alone, what verse was published'.[32] Thanks to the *Yearbook*, which ran from 1951 until 1964, many young poets, unable to find a voice elsewhere, found readers and critical acclaim.

James K. Baxter was without doubt the most celebrated young New Zealand poet to emerge in the late 1940s and 1950s. From 1945, when his first collection of poems *Beyond the Palisade* appeared, until his death in 1972, he wrote poetry, literary criticism, social commentary and drama prolifically and energetically. A colourful, eccentric, romantic figure, his life trajectory attracted publicity as that of no other contemporary poet; playing out, as Elizabeth Caffin has written, as 'a myth enacted before the nation's eyes'.[33]

Many of Baxter's early poems explore the symbolic significance of very distinctly New Zealand scenery. His later work, however, moves on to universal concerns about the human condition, questions of spiritual and inner truth, with an increasing emphasis on social concerns. In 'Bucket of Blood for a Dollar', for example, he berates Holyoake for following the United States into the Vietnam War:

> 'You'll have to learn,' said Uncle Sam,
> 'The Yankee way of work
> Now that you've joined in our crusade
> Against the modern Turk;
>
> . . .

'Tell them straight,' said Uncle Sam,
'That it's a dirty war;
Mention the Freedom of the West
That we are fighting for;
But keep the money side of it
Well tucked behind the door.'[34]

Despite early admiration for Curnow, and affinities in their perceptions of how poetry should be written, Baxter eventually moved into the Wellington camp. Writing in 1951, he expressed the view that 'New Zealand poets have shied away from sociological themes . . . we have tended to write more readily of mountains than marriage'. He saw in the work of the younger generation of poets 'a new breakaway . . . the stereotypes established by older poets have been broken down and, broadly speaking, a new school has come into the open . . . a new and valuable stereotype is in process of being formed; the view of national history held by the poet who has grown up in entire acceptance of his environment, truly inhabiting the country'.[35]

Baxter's insight that New Zealand's poetic divides reflected differing generational preoccupations and perceptions was astute. Brasch was born in 1909 and Curnow in 1911; their somewhat austere modernism and emphasis on the necessary relationship between poetic vision and reality reacted against the kind of cloying sentimentality symbolised by J. M. Dent's *Kowhai Gold*, a 1930 anthology of New Zealand verse. Their reserved, erudite personalities and their age were possibly another source of resentment. Young poets disliked being told what was acceptable by older literary lions. Nevertheless, it is interesting to note that Curnow himself recognised that the next generation would be more comfortable with their New Zealandness: 'Not I, some child born in a marvellous year, / Will learn the trick of standing upright here.'[36]

For the poets of the 1950s, 'Curnow's was the inescapable voice of the father admonishing his sons'.[37] His prose, with its admonitions about a sloppy universalist romanticism and the need for intellectual rigour, has a magisterial, often censorious tone. But his nationalism, as the literary scholar Peter Simpson has pointed out, is often misread and misinterpreted. Curnow was fiercely averse to 'Little New Zealandism' and the sort of 'vulgar nationalism associated with patriotic ardours'. New Zealand was 'foregrounded' but not 'privileged'.[38] If one happened to be a New Zealander, New Zealand was 'the only possible place' because art needed to be related to 'reality, experience and truth'.[39]

The poetry debate turned into an open feud at the end of the 1950s when Curnow's second anthology, *The Penguin Book of New Zealand Verse* (1960), was about to be published. The Wellington group protested that too many young poets had been excluded because their work did not conform to Curnow's thematic preferences. Publication was delayed for two years. Commenting on the argument, Baxter believed that Curnow's limited definition of good New Zealand poetry prevented him from being able 'to recognise that much good writing, and new modes of writing, had come to light in our poetry since 1945'.[40] By contrast, the younger generation of poets, although showing evident regional roots, 'tend to lay far less stress on regional pieties than their predecessors did'.[41] Curnow, for his part, believed that regardless of regional pieties or their absence, there were simply very few new poets worth including: 'Nowhere in the last decade have there been any poetic departures worth mentioning, and New Zealand has not been privileged.'[42]

In addition to the contentious exclusion of younger poets from Wellington, Curnow's 1960 anthology was not rich with contributions by women. This partly reflected his personal aesthetic. For example, he dismissed the work of Eileen Duggan, who published copiously in the 1930s and early 1940s, as 'an emotional cliché' and excluded it from his 1945, 1951 and 1960 anthologies because it possessed the kind of 'decorative and precious' Georgian decorum he so abhorred.[43] Although full of local references and a patriotic concern for New Zealand history, it was anathema to his modernist sensibility. By contrast, in the 1960 anthology he included Ruth Dallas's work, which featured the natural landscapes of the South Island where she had worked as a land girl during the war. Dallas also frequently published in *Landfall*. Another successful poet, Ruth France, writing under the pseudonym Paul Henderson, practised the elegiac verse style favoured by Brasch. Her work appeared in *Landfall* and was published by Caxton.

Women poets operated in a literary milieu dominated by older male poets, many of whom dismissed domestic and interior subject matter as clichéd and emotional. Mary Stanley is a notable example of a poet whose ability to publish and earn critical recognition was adversely affected by this sort of bias. Her poems did not appear in *Landfall*, or in Curnow's anthologies, although they did feature in the *Yearbook of Arts in New Zealand* and *Here & Now*. The collection *Starveling Year* (1953, reprinted in 1994) has been described as 'landscape poetry of the house', written by an author whose voice was 'truly feminist' within the context of the times:

Being a woman, I am
not more than man nor less
but answer imperatives
of shape and growth. The bone
attests the girl with dolls,
grown up to know the moon
unwind her tides to chafe
the heart . . .[44]

The heated battles over the 1960 Curnow anthology marked a climax in the regional and generational disputes over nationalism versus universalism, modernism versus neo-romanticism in poetry. These sorts of conflicts gradually grew less relevant as both poetry and the poets themselves diversified, adapted, and modified their positions. The parameters of the debate had always been fluid, its misunderstandings rife and its complexities bewildering. The modernists Curnow and Brasch, for example, were sometimes accused of neo-romanticism of the 'solitary artist in the South Island landscape' kind. Most poets had a foot in both camps. As Curnow lamented with some exasperation: 'I am conscious . . . that this whole matter of New Zealand, and its arts and literature, is so bedevilled by intellectual shiftiness, pretentiousness and double-talk that it is unlikely that I can get my argument clean through the densely verbalised swamp where none of our critical pioneers have got off entirely uninfected.'[45]

What constituted local reality in an increasingly global culture was also becoming difficult to discern. With television and jet travel, New Zealanders were no longer at such a far remove from the cultural and social changes taking place in the rest of the world, and concerns such as the threat of nuclear war, civil rights in America, and the iconoclastic youth culture were part of their present observed reality. Young poets such as Fleur Adcock, Vincent O'Sullivan and Kevin Ireland either went beyond the local and national to respond to these international trends, concerns and events, or explored human existence by writing about family life and personal relationships. Whether their work reflected a New Zealand reality or something more universal was no longer a source of interest or dispute.

Traditional forms of poetry also changed as poets wrote in more colloquial tones, using a more 'informal personal speaking voice'.[46] Hone Tuwhare's 1964 collection *No Ordinary Sun* marked not only the welcome advent of a major Maori poet, but of a new popular voice. Poet Paula Green has suggested that

Tuwhare demonstrated that poetry was not the preserve of academics and intellectuals but could be 'of the people and for the people, not only in what was said but how it was said'.[47] 'That Morning Early' is typical of his accessible style:

> Started up that morning
> to stomach pinch and growls: listened
> to the sound of hail nick on glass
> and iron roof.[48]

Reprinted eleven times during the next 30 years, *No Ordinary Sun* became one of the most widely read individual collections of poems in New Zealand.[49] The older generation of poets such as Brasch and Curnow, both of whom produced some of their best work in old age, also evolved and changed; their poems became more personal and less preoccupied with questions of national identity or cultural self-reliance. Curnow perhaps best summed up the shift when writing of his own work in 1973: 'The geographic anxieties didn't disappear: but I began to find a personal and poetic use for them rather than let them use me up'.[50]

Prose writing: 'Things are stirring . . .'

Like poetry, prose fiction by New Zealand authors increased exponentially both in quantity and quality after the war. In 1946, J. C. Reid wrote a critical essay lamenting the lack of good prose writing in New Zealand to date, but added optimistically: 'Today, this country seems to stand at the entrance to a more virile period of writing than she has passed through before. Things are stirring'.[51] By 1960, M. H. (Monte) Holcroft, editor of the *New Zealand Listener* from 1947 to 1967, was able to note proudly: 'In the past four weeks thirty New Zealand books have been reviewed in *The Listener* . . . Novels, which for many years were low on the list, are now moving to the top.' No longer 'poor relations in a distant market, or rare and puzzling phenomena at home', they were now accepted as books amongst many worldwide, and judged 'on their literary merits alone'.[52]

In the years between these two statements, short-story writers and novelists produced distinctly realistic fiction, with identifiable themes. Unlike poets, New Zealand prose writers did not form opposing camps during the 1950s. They shared with poets, however, a desire to break away from what they labelled as imitative and facile conventions, and expressed the need to portray what they considered to be the 'real' New Zealand. Sometimes labelled 'provincial realism' or 'critical realism', these varied works share one overriding characteristic: an indictment of contemporary New Zealand.[53] Rather than an idyllic 'Better Britain', the country is portrayed as narrow-minded, materialistic, hypocritical and puritanical, with strong undercurrents of savage violence. A recurrent theme is the damage this repressive society inflicts on the isolated individual, families and entire communities.

An early critical realist novel, John Mulgan's *Man Alone*, was actually written in 1939, but only became familiar to New Zealand readers after being reprinted in 1949. Its laconic, Hemingway-esque protagonist Johnson is a newcomer from England who attempts to escape social and political responsibilities and to seek answers as a 'man alone' in the New Zealand bush. This proves a false, elusive dream. John Mulgan's father, Alan, a popular novelist and travel writer, had, in numerous popular works, presented New Zealand as cosily romantic and appealing. The country depicted in *Man Alone* is by contrast dark and unappealing. Yet the book has its own form of romanticism. C. K. Stead has observed that it is a 'piece of frontier mythologizing', with a hero who (patrimony notwithstanding) conforms to the popular stereotype of the frontier Kiwi (and/or the Aussie) male: pragmatic, resourceful, inarticulate and egalitarian.[54] Johnson in many ways resembles the Kiwi soldiers Mulgan observed abroad during the war and described so memorably in *Report on Experience* (1947).[55] His solitary quest is unsatisfying and misguided because, Mulgan seems to suggest, the real solution lies in collective action, in the company of other right-minded, left-leaning men.

A more typical if less well known example of critical realism is David Ballantyne's *The Cunninghams* (1948). Like Mulgan, Ballantyne was heavily influenced by American realist writers. Considered one of 'the finest works of New Zealand realism, unsurpassed as a picture of working-class family life',[56] the novel tells the story of a family struggling to survive at the end of the Great Depression. Crushed by the dullness, hypocritical religiosity, conformity and puritanism of provincial Gisborne life, the Cunninghams have little hope of escaping it or finding an alternative.

In an influential essay, academic and author Bill Pearson relentlessly excoriated what he, along with many of his contemporaries, considered New Zealand society to be — repressive and conformist. 'Fretful Sleepers', which appeared in the September 1952 edition of *Landfall*, was tellingly subtitled 'A Sketch of New Zealand Behaviour and its Implications for the Artist'. Written in the aftermath of the recent government crack-down on the Watersiders' Union, it was, despite its highly critical tone, apparently accepted without rancour by fellow New Zealanders as an important and astute piece of contemporary social analysis. The author, a left-wing intellectual and closet homosexual (coming out was not then an option, given its illegality), expressed a righteous anger toward his homeland, denouncing it as a conformist, judgemental society that 'runs by clockwork' and persecutes 'those who don't conform'. The average New Zealander, 'afraid of voicing any confident thought or unsanctioned emotion', denies 'real sensibilities and emotions for the sake of the almighty norm'.[57]

Literature, in Pearson's view, needed to 'expose ourselves to ourselves, explain ourselves to ourselves, see ourselves in a perspective of place and time' without 'the protective camouflage'.[58] His one novel, the celebrated *Coal Flat* (1963), achieved this aim by realistically evoking a West Coast mining town. Some thirteen years in the making, it initially featured a gay protagonist. But after either a failure of nerve or an altered authorial aim, Pearson jettisoned this character and positioned the working-class community centre stage instead.

James Courage, another author who experienced the frustrations of conformist provincial New Zealand, grew up among the pastoral gentry of North Canterbury and lived in England as an adult. Characters in his novels negotiate family conflict, sexual antagonisms and frustrations, boredom and isolation in a restricted, often destructive social milieu. In common with Pearson, Courage was homosexual and suffered from having to hide the fact. One of his later novels, *A Way of Love* (1959), set in England, openly focused on homosexual relationships. Banned in New Zealand on the grounds of indecency, it represented what Courage described as 'an attempt to write a serious novel about homosexuality . . . [which is] concerned with the heart and its deeper emotions'.[59]

Like Courage, Dan Davin lived and worked in England but usually wrote fiction about the New Zealand of his youth. An editor at Oxford University Press, he became friends with a wide range of writers, and acted as a genial host to numerous New Zealand authors visiting England. His fiction drew on his own experiences growing up in a large working-class Irish Catholic family in Southland. In common with other writers of the time, he explored what he saw as the often destructive impact of small-town attitudes and values. Many of his fictional characters, like Davin himself, escape the restraints of home only by becoming exiles from it.

Frank Sargeson, by contrast, remained at the heart of New Zealand's literary scene for many decades. In the late 1920s, he travelled abroad for two years to discover his European roots. Instead, as he wrote in his memoirs, 'In Europe I had discovered myself to be truly a New Zealander.'[60] He first began publishing in the 1930s, during the Great Depression, writing brief sketches that outlined character through a single event or encounter. The narrator was often a rootless, inarticulate drifter, and the sketches captured a distinctive Kiwi slang and cadence of speech.[61] 'New Zealandness' was conveyed not only by place but by language. Sargeson explained: 'I began to read all the New Zealand fiction I could lay my hands on; and it seemed to me that virtually always the formal language of the English novelists had been used . . . I asked myself the question whether there might not be an appropriate language to deal with the material of New Zealand life.'[62] Stories, character and details are developed through the narrator's dialogue — a recognisably New Zealand way of speaking that was laconic, understated, and often barely articulate. That Summer, published in three parts in Penguin New Writing over 1943 to 1944, prompted the English critic Walter Allen to describe Sargeson as 'the first New Zealand NATIONAL writer'.[63]

Sargeson's attack on a repressive and self-righteous moral code drew strength from the Depression ethos of egalitarianism and mateship, and from his own personal experience. In 1929, he was tried and convicted for a 'homosexual offence'. Janet Wilson has written that Sargeson 'subverts and reassesses puritan values, like goodness and love, through furtive buried scenarios which urge greater compassion towards the socially-stigmatised outsider. The assault on and redefinition of puritan repression is driven by the need to allude to the story that cannot be told openly.'[64]

Affectionately described by his friend C. K. Stead as 'gregarious, entertaining and lively; wicked, witty and waspish',[65] Sargeson was a mentor to many authors, who paid him the honour of imitating his style. His long, productive career also proved that being a full-time writer, although difficult in New Zealand, was not impossible. A letter signed by sixteen New Zealand writers to commemorate his fiftieth birthday highlighted his role as a literary pioneer: 'Your work, has had, in the past twenty years, a liberating influence on the literature of this country . . . it was your voice that said something true and original of life in New Zealand. You turned over new ground with great care and revealed that our manners and behaviour formed just as good a basis for enduring literature as those of any other country.'[66]

While the plight of the male non-conformist dominates Sargeson's work, and features prominently in other novels and short stories of the 1940s, 1950s and early 1960s, the interior voice of women is rarely explored. His fictional women are often vengeful, tempting figures who destabilise or threaten male mateship; and this has prompted charges of misogyny by later critics.[67] Sargeson also detested the work of author and journalist Robin Hyde, calling her *Passport to Hell* an 'obscene' work with 'bad prose'. He later referred to Hyde as a 'silly bitch'.[68] Male provincial fiction writers ascribed traditional roles to their women characters, who are generally portrayed as gaining satisfaction only from children and domesticity. The historian, political scientist and literary critic Robert Chapman noted that those female characters who attempt escaping this destiny often find it is too late, and suffer 'a nervous breakdown'.[69]

Literary magazines and literary criticism of the period, as well as more recent literary discussions about the 1940s and 1950s, focus almost exclusively on male writers. Female authors with successful careers have perhaps suffered neglect because their work was not in the dominant critical realist style. Romantic novelists such as Rosemary Rees, Dulce Carman, Mavis Winder and Nelle Scanlan, among others, while not considered 'literary', started writing in the 1930s and were still producing popular books decades later. Much of their work was set in New Zealand. Scanlan's Pencarrow tetralogy for example, which focused on the life and loves of ordinary New Zealanders, sold more than 80,000 copies in New Zealand by 1960. In 1934, Robin Hyde wrote that while '[s]everal have tried to catch the spirit of the New Zealand landscape — a subtle task . . . Nelle Scanlan has probably come nearer success than anyone else'.[70]

Another best-selling woman writer, Ngaio Marsh (1895–1982), one of four 'grande dames' of detective fiction, was probably New Zealand's best-known writer internationally. Her first crime novel appeared in 1934; of the 32 that followed, only four were set in New Zealand. Dividing her time between New Zealand and England, Marsh worked half of the year as a director at Christchurch's Court Theatre, struggling to establish a tradition of locally based professionalism.[71] Dorothy Eden, who started writing in the 1940s, also achieved an international reputation for her Gothic romances. Their setting moved from New Zealand to England after Eden moved there in 1954.

In the 1950s, established writers such as Davin, Courage and Sargeson were joined by several newcomers. Some, such as O. E. Middleton and Phillip Wilson, continued in the style favoured by Sargeson; with stories peopled by lone working-class male outcasts struggling in an indifferent society. Others found new themes or developed old ones in new ways. Ian Cross's critically acclaimed first novel, *The God Boy* (1957), for example, seemed to cover familiar ground (growing up in a provincial puritan society). But it achieved a new power and immediacy by using the thirteen-year-old Jimmy Sullivan as the unwitting first-person narrator. Ronald Hugh Morrieson's two lively novels *The Scarecrow* (1963) and *Came a Hot Friday* (1964) capture the seedy underside of New Zealand small-town provincial life. Racy and entertaining, with plenty of authentic colloquial dialogue, they were popular in Australia, but received a more ambivalent reception in New Zealand. *The Scarecrow* was criticised by some for its dark and thinly veiled portrait of Hawera (Morrieson's home town); while the copious violence and sex of *Came a Hot Friday* also generated mixed reviews. Although his work was praised in the daily newspapers, the literary establishment tended to view it with 'amused condescension'. Only in Australian literary journals were his books deemed to be of undoubted literary merit.[72] Morrieson's fame in the country of his birth was largely posthumous, skyrocketing in the early 1980s after his novels were made into successful films.[73]

Maurice Duggan's work, too, continued to critically examine the legacy of a constrictive society. C. K. Stead has described his stories about the Lenihans, an Auckland Irish Catholic family, published in the collection *Immanuel's Land* (1956), as 'some of the most perfect short fictions written by a New Zealander'.[74] These stories, and those that followed in *Summer in the Gravel Pit* (1965) and *O'Leary's Orchard* (1970), portray a rigid, loveless Catholic upbringing, not unlike Duggan's own. The ideal surface is peeled away to reveal the harsh reality underneath. Maurice Gee's first novel, *The Big Season* (1962), a portrait of 1950s small-town New Zealand, also pursued the familiar theme of the damage inflicted by a self-righteous conformist community on families and individuals. It was criticised, however, for its depiction of violence, both implicit and explicit, as a normal element of social life in New Zealand. Commenting on this dark strain, Gee later observed: 'I saw that human beings were lonely, that they lose what they most desire, that the passions that shake them produce cruelty more frequently than kindness.'[75]

Critical realist fiction was augmented at this time by a number of works exploring new themes and scenarios. Noel Hilliard's *Maori Girl* (1960), for example, examined Maori migration to the cities and the prejudice and discrimination that followed in its wake. The first in a tetralogy, it was a response to the racism Hilliard himself witnessed in Wellington:

Oh yes, there was a lot of racial discrimination around. You can go back and read old accommodation notices saying: 'Europeans Only'. Or there was a sign in a bar which appears in one of the novels: 'Native Women Will Not Be Served In This Hotel'. People think I invented that for the book, but it was for real.[76]

As he later noted, *Maori Girl* was 'really the first novel that portrayed Maori people as being members of contemporary society . . . all previous novels had depicted the Maori in their great heyday before the Pakeha arrived'.[77] Written at a time when New Zealand was proud of its racial harmony, the novel was criticised and rejected by many because of its 'passionate and unrelenting exposure of racial discrimination'.[78] These themes were further developed in the next three books in the series: *Power of Joy* (1965), *Maori Woman* (1974) and *The Glory and the Dream* (1978).

Marilyn Duckworth, like Hilliard, also explored a new theme. *A Gap in the Spectrum* (1959), her first novel, investigated the way women trapped in unsatisfactory relationships searched for ways to alleviate their pain.[79] Three more novels written in the 1960s pursued the theme of a vulnerable, dependent heroine, attached to an unsympathetic male, managing to find a way toward self-knowledge and independence.

Both Duckworth and Hilliard, while pursuing new subjects, were working within the established framework of exposing the hypocrisies, smug conventions and prejudices of puritan provincialism. A more substantive subversion of critical realism was undertaken by two innovative women writers. Sylvia Ashton Warner's *Spinster* (1958) might seem to occupy familiar territory (an unmarried woman teaching in provincial small-town New Zealand), but its loose structure, metaphorical language and emphasis on passion and emotion offered something decidedly different.[80] Her second novel, *Incense to Idols* (1960), diverged even more from the norm, consisting almost entirely of first-person stream of consciousness from another female protagonist. Although critically acclaimed abroad, Warner received a rather lukewarm reception in New Zealand, partly due to her divergence from the critical realist norm.[81] Her strong independent female heroines were determined to walk 'counter to the common' and rebelled against the 'suicidal cult of the average man'.[82]

Janet Frame, like Warner, also did not conform to the critical realist mould. Described as 'the most original talent to flower' in the 1950s,[83] her first volume of short stories, *The Lagoon* (1951), and her first novel, *Owls Do Cry* (1957), examined a theme that reoccurs throughout her writing — the disjunction between reality and a richly lyrical imaginative inner world. Frame's impressionistic style uses interior monologue and stream of consciousness to convey the intensity of interior experience rather than the external effects of society on the individual. Robin Hyde, an earlier New Zealand author, often employed this perspective, aiming 'to write from the inner centre of what people think, hope and feel', and convey, not the outside world looking in, but the inner person looking at the outside world.[84] Frame, by shifting viewpoints from symbolism to reality, from interior monologue to realistic description, poetry to prose, portrays characters for whom spoken language cannot communicate the essential. She explained in her autobiographical essay 'Beginnings' that she herself took refuge in the world of the imagination and its reality: 'As it was impossible for me to reconcile "this" and "that" world, I decided to choose "that" world, and one day when the Inspector was visiting my class at school I said, — Excuse me, and walked from the room and the school, from "this" world to "that" world where I have stayed, and where I live now.'[85]

Frame did not set out with the conscious intention of subverting realism; that she did so was the result of her sensibility. Maurice Shadbolt, by contrast, consciously aimed to depart from tried-and-true themes. Believing that New Zealand fiction was stuck in 'a rut running directly out of the 1930s', he wanted to move away from exposing 'New Zealand's puritan underside'.[86] Instead, he aimed to chronicle the fortunes of a wide spectrum of New Zealanders, 'fragments of a whole social and historical complex'.[87] His short-story collection *New Zealanders* (1959), greeted with high praise in England where it was first published, and where Shadbolt then lived, was less well received in New Zealand.[88] Nonetheless, it was the beginning of a long career that included best-sellers such as *Strangers and Journeys* (1972) and *The Lovelock Version* (1980), among others.

Interestingly, the most renowned and financially successful writers of the era, Mary Scott and Barry Crump, both wrote about rural life, tapping perhaps into a vein of suburban boredom or disaffection. Barry Crump sprang into prominence in 1960 with *A Good Keen Man*. This back-country, deer-culling, pig-hunting, 'man alone' yarn, written in amusingly colloquial 'New Zealand male vernacular speech',[89] sold nearly 50,000 copies within a year. By the 1970s, it had been reprinted fourteen times. Over the next 30 years Crump — or 'Crumpy' as he was affectionately known — published over 20 books, all in the same style and on a similar theme. By 1990, his total New Zealand sales exceeded one million copies, making him by far New Zealand's best-selling male author.

Mary Scott, who through the 1930s and 1940s wrote sketches for newspapers about backblocks life, published her first book, *Breakfast at Six*, in 1953. Twenty-five more romantic backblocks novels followed. Where Crump's books celebrated the resilient independent male in the bush, Scott's were about families and communities struggling to create lives in newly opened up rural communities. Country life was both character-building and a salutary contrast to suburbia: 'I know of a community a little out of the way of traffic and excite-ment where live a few people who have cut themselves off from the rat race, and are the happier for it.'[90]

With the notable exception of popular writers such as Scott and Crump, prose fiction during the 20 years after 1945 painted an unremittingly dark portrait of New Zealand. This bleakness is seemingly anomalous, given the protracted spell of 'golden weather' the country enjoyed in the 1950s, a decade of economic prosperity and increasing material comfort. Even bearing in mind the powerful influence of American realist writers, and a modernist sensibility that recoiled from sentimental romanticism, the almost unrelieved negativity of New Zealand prose fiction in the 1950s and early 1960s is remarkable. This was a high-water mark of New Zealand literary nationalism, yet its expression in fiction almost invariably took a bilious form.

This generally scathing authorial indictment of New Zealand dates back to the Great Depression. During this time, when several influential writers, most notably Sargeson, began their writing careers, the deterioration of social conditions 'broke up the crust of complacency, allowing artists to see what lay beneath'.[91] Having witnessed the injustices and hardships New Zealanders endured through no fault of their own, many prose writers embraced what they believed to be an unblinking social realism, and were determined to convey their version of New Zealand life, which they thought was often violent and harrowing. They rejected literature that portrayed their country in rosy terms, or refashioned it to accord with a lost English homeland, as inauthentic, imita-tive and inaccurate. During the more prosperous, materialistic and conformist 1950s and early 1960s, gritty social realism survived in a transmuted form — authors still unblinkingly examined the reality beneath 'the crust of compla-cency'. But in doing so they focused on the corrosive impacts of a conformist and constrictive puritanism, now happily married to thoughtless material-ism and flourishing in rural towns, cities and suburban enclaves around the country.

Several New Zealand writers, because they were homosexual, also experi-enced directly the loneliness and alienation that derived from being outside the norm at a time when idealisation of conventional heterosexual nuclear family life was in full flower. (Homosexual activity between consenting men aged sixteen or over was a criminal offence under the Crimes Act 1961 until the Homosexual Law Reform Act of 1986.) In 1987, Sargeson told Michael Beveridge: 'If you are alive to the fantastic loneliness and isolation of many people in this sort of society I think you find that deviation, or what people would call deviations, are much more widespread than the average person — if there is any such person as the average person — would suppose.'[92] According to Lawrence Jones, the conscious move away from English modes of novel writing towards a less formal American realist style was a way to express disaffection with the conventions of contemporary New Zealand society, because 'such [English] forms assumed an agreement with stable social norms and values'.[93] Like the less formal American realists, New Zealand prose writers often wrote works that had no conventional plot, and used an indigenous colloquial language. Ian Cross told a group of students in 1962 that this New Zealand idiom was more than just 'a kind of provincial variation . . . significant only as a colloquial phenomenon . . . it goes much deeper than that. I think it is concerned with our responses to what we have seen and heard since the day we were born.'[94]

Critical social realism in New Zealand fiction took root in the 1930s and flourished in the 1950s, and this critical anti-conventionalism had, by the 1960s, itself become a convention. The fact that New Zealand writers largely followed American realist rather than British literary models was in keeping with the socio-political realities of the post-war era; a time when both American military power and its cultural exports gained pre-eminence, while those of Britain retained associations with an older, more middle-class and waning colonial legacy. In the view of Sargeson and his many followers, genuine New Zealand fiction told the raw, observed truth, especially the pressure and pain endured by lonely, isolated, marginal or different individuals who failed to fit the conservative and conformist mould. In the immediate post-war period, prose fiction writers' bleak vision was also probably exacerbated by the ongoing struggle they faced making a living out of their art. Robert Chapman noted in 1952, New Zealand fiction 'is ignored by the public or resisted quite as much as if it had been thrown down from the highest of ivory towers.'[95]

One notable exception to all this gloom and critical indictment of New Zealand in fiction was a non-fiction book, albeit one with exceptional literary merit. Keith Sinclair's *A History of New Zealand*, published in 1959, enjoyed instant critical acclaim and enduring popularity. Written with great flair in seamless, accessible prose, it was an accurate, comprehensive, hugely influential book that placed New Zealand at the centre of its own story. A compelling opening prologue tells the story of 'The Fish of Maui', moving from myth and legend to recent ethnological and archaeological research. In doing so, it places the country firmly in context as an island in the Pacific. The British colonial heritage and race relations are examined, but always with the New Zealand experience to the fore; for example, the stress is less on what cultural baggage British settlers brought with them than on how they adapted to their new circumstances.[96] Generally, the country's history is portrayed as a commendable progression. John Stenhouse commented that Sinclair places an egalitarian New Zealand centre stage in a 'starring role' as a place where 'under Liberal and Labour governments, religious, and class, race and gender divisions' have been transcended 'better than anywhere else'.[97]

In addition to being the country's foremost historian, Sinclair was also, as noted, a poet. Although his poetry was never proselytising or jingoistic, he perceived literary cultural nationalism as both salutary and long overdue. As his memoirs unabashedly proclaim, he felt 'a burning desire to contribute to making a New Zealand literature — I was a literary nationalist'.[98] In his view, the 20-some years after World War II were when New Zealand art and literature came of age, and he was proud to be part of this unprecedented push for a more independent cultural identity.

This creative surge was boosted by a small but influential group of individuals determined to publish high-quality New Zealand literature. For a time, the Caxton Press was the sole publisher of high-production-quality New Zealand literature. Then in 1945 two Hamilton bookshop owners, Blackwood and Janet Paul, started a small publishing house called Paul's Book Arcade (renamed Blackwood and Janet Paul in 1964). As well as publishing literature and poetry, the Pauls commissioned New Zealand histories, including books on Maori history and culture, and children's books. In 1956, the Pauls persuaded popular novelist Mary Scott to publish with them. Producing a book every eighteen months which sold in excess of 7000 copies, Scott's work subsidised the smaller literary works of authors such as Sargeson, Pearson and various poets, thus allowing the Pauls to remain committed to quality literary publishing. By the early 1960s, they had succeeded Caxton as the leading publisher of New Zealand poetry and fiction; in many cases, this was undertaken jointly with overseas publishers.[99] The Pegasus Press, created in 1947, also published quality local literature, and like Caxton maintained high production standards.[100] Until its demise in 1980, it published numerous volumes of poetry, as well as fiction, with Janet Frame its most celebrated author. In 1947, the New Zealand University Press (NZUP) published its first book. Until 1961, when the University of New Zealand was abolished and the press with it, NZUP produced a small number of high-quality titles. In time, the newly autonomous universities created their own presses. During the 1950s, larger commercial local publishing firms such as Whitcombe & Tombs and

A. H. & A. W. Reed also started publishing more fiction by New Zealand writers, often in joint publication arrangements with overseas firms. By the mid-1960s, many overseas publishers had established branches in the country, providing an outlet for the burgeoning local publications across all genres. Between 1950 and 1960 alone, new titles published in New Zealand each year rose from 262 to 546.[101]

Journals and magazines also played a crucial role in advocating and publicising new works by New Zealand writers, artists, architects, actors and musicians. In addition to *Landfall's* seminal influence, the other important magazine was the *New Zealand Listener*. Established in 1939 under the auspices of the National Broadcasting Service, its original mandate was to focus on broadcasting matters. Its first editor, Oliver Duff, went beyond this brief, however, regularly publishing short stories, poems, and both fiction and non-fiction book reviews. From 1949, his successor, the author and critic Monte Holcroft, also believed that 'the official journal of the NZ Broadcasting Service had a duty to foster imaginative writing'.[102] By the time he retired in 1967, the *Listener* had become a leading literary magazine, with a broader readership and more popular appeal than *Landfall*.

In the 1940s, the Department of Education's *School Journal* was transformed from a dry moralistic magazine, primarily concerned with saving youngsters from 'the related evils of bad grammar and juvenile delinquency',[103] into a lively, entertaining publication that explored what it meant to be a New Zealander. Paying tribute to the *Journal* in 1951, J. C. Beaglehole commended its important role in introducing children to national art and literature, showing them that 'life in New Zealand can be a worthwhile and interesting experience, that New Zealand has a tradition and contemporary ways of living of its own; that New Zealanders are doing fascinating and important things here and now, that can best be written about and drawn by New Zealanders'.[104] New Zealand artists such as Louise Henderson, Colin McCahon, May Smith, Robin White, Rita Angus and Ralph Hotere all contributed work. Writers with established reputations such as Janet Frame, Frank Sargeson, Denis Glover, Ruth Dallas, Alistair Te Ariki Campbell, James K. Baxter, Roderick Finlayson, Louis Johnson, Helen Shaw, Maurice Duggan and Peter Bland wrote poems or stories specifically for the *Journal*. In 1961, the *Journal* launched the career of the celebrated children's writer Margaret Mahy by publishing her first poems and stories. Many artists and writers, such as Russell Clark, E. Mervyn Taylor, Juliet Peter, Roy Cowan, James K. Baxter, Peter Bland, Alistair Te Ariki Campbell and Louis Johnson, worked in the School Publications Branch where the *School Journal* and *School*

Bulletin were produced. Campbell, who edited the *School Journal* from 1955 to 1972, noted that their offices had a permanent buzz of creativity, imagination and the constant coming and going of established artists and writers, creating an environment where everybody flourished.[105] Over the years, established artists and writers have continued to contribute to the *Journal*, making it, in Dick Frizzell's opinion, an 'unauthorised history' of New Zealand art, or what Margaret Mahy once described as 'one of New Zealand's leading literary magazines'.[106]

In his essay 'Fiction and the Social Pattern' (1953), Robert Chapman accused New Zealanders of resisting or ignoring local writing.[107] By the mid-1960s, such a claim would have been clearly at odds with the flourishing New Zealand literary scene. Increasing numbers of young writers emerged every year, while older established ones continued to write and evolve. Influenced by social and attitudinal changes at home and abroad, they started moving away from the realist critique of a puritanical, homogenous, restrictive New Zealand society; their work and their authorial preoccupations reflecting altering social and cultural realities. Sargeson himself noted that gritty social realism could no longer express the complexities of society, with its diversity of experiences and multiplicity of relationships: 'the realism or the reality . . . in a few years, will have disappeared completely and all that will remain is the transmuted thing . . . I think there is a sophistication taking place which is becoming more complicated all the time. One has only to think of Janet Frame.'[108] By the late 1960s, writers adopted a wide variety of styles and chronicled an increasingly complex range of human experiences. Social changes — increasing urbanisation, the sexual and feminist revolutions, growing consumerism, an anti-authoritarian youth culture — gave a new generation of authors new themes and subjects to mine.

True colours: art, artists and the 'art scene'

As with literature, New Zealand art was transformed after 1945. International and local influences stimulated a range of innovative works that diverged from the unadventurous art of former times. Despite some resistance to the perceived excesses of modern art, by the 1970s the country boasted a vigorous 'art scene', several highly esteemed local artists and a small but growing number of dealer and public galleries with links to overseas artists and institutions.

This contrasts starkly with the situation before World War II, when there were no dealer galleries, few available art books, no contemporary national or international art magazines, limited access to good reproductions, and art schools that adhered to inflexibly old-fashioned teaching patterns. Local art societies run by predominantly middle-class Sunday painters exercised a blandly decorative aesthetic when deciding what was suitable for display. The one important exception was the Christchurch Group, a loose association of artists formed in Christchurch in 1927 by seven ex-students of the Canterbury College of Art. They aimed to provide an alternative exhibition opportunity for young, more adventurous artists whose work might not have been accepted for the more staid local Art Society hangings.[109] Although most of the artists who exhibited there were based in or around Christchurch, it also attracted artists from all over New Zealand. It has been claimed that 'Nearly every painter of note working in New Zealand during the nineteen-forties was either a member or had been asked to exhibit in the Group Shows as a "guest exhibitor",[110] and Dr G. M. Lester remarked when opening a Group exhibition in 1931: 'They represent a definite attitude towards art, one of revolt and experimentation.' In 1935, when he again opened a Group show, Lester pointed out that while Art Society exhibitions catered to 'a backward public taste', the Group's smaller exhibitions were important because 'they are for that part of the public that has art in view, and serve as a medium for the real expression of the age.'[111] Apart from this outpost of open-mindedness, however, local artists struggled, isolated and remote from the major centres of western art. To really explore modern artistic trends and themes, they had to leave the country. Frances Hodgkins, for example, was one who 'left New Zealand to develop a talent that could find no fulfilment in a colonial setting'. Based in Britain but travelling frequently in France and Spain, she achieved great success and was the first New Zealand-born artist to 'secure [a] place among the English avant-garde of the 1930s and 1940s'. In 1940, she was chosen to represent Britain in the twenty-second Venice Biennale, which did not go ahead because of the war.[112] Those artists who stayed needed to support themselves financially by painting popular landscapes and portraits.

Anything avant-garde met with derision from the general public. Government historian Dr A. H. McLintock declared approvingly in 1940 that the country remained largely insulated from, or hostile to, the artistic excess indulged in abroad: 'There was little experimenting with the more extreme schools of painting . . . In this respect New Zealand's remoteness and her inevitable delays in assimilating the artistic developments have proved definite assets, for at least she has been spared those excesses which stultify true progress in the arts.'[113] Artists tended to interpret the local environment in terms of 'the old and familiar features of the European scene'.[114] Landscape, for example, was portrayed as either 'a Pacific version of the English Home Counties' or the 'early colonial house o'ergrown by the native cliché'.[115]

After the war, however, a shift that had begun slowly in the 1930s began to accelerate, as a small body of artists moved away from the English-inspired academic style and aimed instead to convey New Zealand's 'rawness and hardness'.[116] This shift had in part been encouraged by the arrival of two young British artists at the end of the 1920s — Robert Field, a teacher at the Dunedin Technical College art school, and Christopher Perkins, who taught at the art department of Wellington Technical College. These two, along with other artists, had been brought to New Zealand under the La Trobe scheme instigated in 1920 by William Sanderson La Trobe, Superintendent of Technical Instruction for the Dominion, in an attempt to improve the quality of staff in technical schools which included art schools.[117] Promoting the use of local subject matter, they encouraged their students to paint everyday life in a realistic style with bold brushstrokes, defined edges and clear colours, to reflect the strong clear New Zealand light.

From the 1930s, works by William Sutton, Toss Woollaston, Eric Lee-Johnson, Doris Lusk and Rita Angus announced a new distinctive New Zealand style, by painters able to depict their country's true colours 'cleansed of the softer tones which came from English eyes when the earlier artists set up their easels beneath the cabbage trees'.[118] And from the 1940s, Colin McCahon, whose work reflected diverse international influences — cubist, American, primitive, the early Italian Renaissance paintings — also worked to convey a raw New Zealand landscape. From 1946, his series of religious paintings transposed religious figures into New Zealand's natural environment. For instance, *Crucifixion* (1949) or *The Marys at the Tomb* (1950) placed events of Christ's life in a New Zealand of light and dark contrasts.[119] *Takaka Night and Day* (1948), *Six Days in Nelson and Canterbury* (1950) and *Landscape series A* (1963) testify to the artist's 'spiritual relationship with the land'[120] and his perception of 'a land belonging not yet to its people, not yet understood or communicated, not even really yet invented'.[121]

Auckland Art Gallery director Peter Tomory believed Woollaston, Angus and McCahon to be not only the best contemporary artists practising, but 'the first consistently serious painters concerned essentially with the contemporary attitude'.[122] But, he pointed out, '[s]ubject painters like Eric Lee-Johnson and Russell Clark, with their realistic drawing, their romantic colour and their choice of significant subjects, were quickly admired . . . but the image makers like Rita Angus and M. T. Woollaston failed to generate the same enthusiasm'.[123] Woollaston, McCahon and Angus were also considered by some commentators to represent a nascent New Zealand nationalist art, in which landscape painting dominated almost to the exclusion of other modes.[124] Charles Brasch, for one, believed that 'If a national school of painting takes shape, it is likely to do so first in landscape, and by assimilating the findings of such independents as Rita Angus, M. T. Woollaston, and Colin McCahon. These painters have not been content to adopt the approaches commonest among us, which derive from the Impressionists, French or English and the English water-colour school . . . they are seeing a New Zealand of their own vision'.[125] Nonetheless, Woollaston owed much to post-impressionist artist Paul Cézanne, an influence he readily acknowledged: 'In all my years there [Mapua] I painted only a few landscapes over and over and over again . . . I seldom succeeded in doing what I wanted — which was to reach at one stroke the essence of the feeling I had for the landscape: and pay adequate homage to Cezanne, who mediated between it and myself . . .'[126]

That vision did not necessarily make them especially popular with either the public or critics.[127] McCahon's paintings in particular, with their cryptic words and numbers and religious subjects, elicited incomprehension and derision. In 1948, for example, the poet A. R. D. Fairburn, after acknowledging McCahon's talent and originality, went on to describe his paintings as 'pretentious hocus' that 'might pass as graffiti on the walls of some celestial lavatory'.[128]

In the course of the 1950s and early 1960s, decades after modernism had been established in Europe, New Zealand began haltingly and belatedly to accept and respond to modern art. Howard Wadman, editor of *The Yearbook of the Arts in New Zealand*, wrote in 1947: 'heroes of the Resistance, Matisse and Picasso, Epstein and Henry Moore, Klee, Kandinsky and many others are no longer young men. The revolution is fifty years old, although New Zealand is only just beginning to experience it.'[129]

One of the pioneers of modernist ideas and techniques in New Zealand, John Weeks, studied in the atelier of cubist painter André Lhote in Paris in the 1920s, before returning to Auckland in 1929 to teach at Elam School of Fine Arts. He introduced his students to European modernism, and encouraged them to experiment with form, abstraction and colour at a time when draughtsmanship, drawing and attention to accurate scale and detail were emphasised. But it would be another two decades before this type of painting was widely shown.[130] Louise Henderson, attracted by Weeks's cubist-inspired work, studied under him in 1950 before going to study in Paris for a year. Upon returning to Auckland, an exhibition of her cubist-type paintings in 1953 attracted wide attention and critical acclaim.[131]

Purely non-representational art, however, met with intense hostility. The art historian Gordon Brown has pointed out that when such paintings did manage to be shown publicly, they 'usually provoked abuse along with the accusation that they were simply a bad joke intended to affront the gullibility of an unsuspecting public'.[132] In 1947, for example, Gordon Walters, inspired by viewing Maori rock drawings in South Canterbury, exhibited a series of simple abstract figures, drawn in one tone on white paper. Public response was so hostile that Walters did not exhibit again until 1966, for, as he later wrote, he found the climate to be unsympathetic: 'The atmosphere in New Zealand was so hostile to abstraction, there would have been little point in showing any more than this.'[133]

Another pioneer of non-representational abstraction, Milan Mrkusich, a New Zealander of Dalmatian origin, trained and worked as an architect in Auckland. He decided not to study at Elam because its curriculum held little appeal. Uninterested in nature, landscape — 'You want a landscape? Take a drive in the country'[134] — or figurative art,[135] he looked to European abstract painters, whose art and theoretical writings he was able to find in the increasing number of art books and magazines coming into the country. Labouring 'singularly, solitarily, and with minimal celebration',[136] he produced purely non-representational modernist art from the 1950s onwards. This was 'an almost untrodden path as far as New Zealand painting was concerned'.[137] But it was not until the 1970s that these abstract artists started receiving positive critical endorsement and were able to sell their paintings to an increasingly receptive public. Mrkusich and Walters were no longer on their own. Influenced by Mrkusich's methods, 'pictorial structures' and 'concern with surface and texture', they were joined by younger artists such as Roy Good, Geoff Thornley, Ian Scott and Stephen Bambury. Pure abstraction had, journalist Michael Brett wrote in the *Auckland Star*, 'finally come in from the cold'.[138]

By the late 1950s, other artists such as Don Peebles and Jean Horsley, among others, were producing innovative works that reflected their observation and experience of New Zealand combined with an assimilation of overseas trends and ideas about abstract art. Despite some critical support, resistance from the general public and more conservative art galleries remained. When the exhibition *British Abstract Painting* was brought to New Zealand by the Auckland City Art Gallery in 1958, neither the staid National Art Gallery in Wellington nor the Dunedin Public Art Gallery would exhibit it. G. G. Watson, the chairman of the Management Committee of the National Art Gallery, declared it not worth showing because it was 'a collection of works of a particularly extreme section of ultra-modernism in art'.[139] Nonetheless, in 1959 the Auckland City Art Gallery dauntlessly mounted an exhibition of Louise Henderson, Kase Jackson and Colin McCahon under the title *Three Abstract Painters*.

Gordon Brown has described the 1950s as the 'decisive decade in New Zealand painting', when artists discovered and felt their way towards new forms. For a time, especially in the late 1940s and early 1950s, the notion of a national artistic style had been discussed and prophesised. The Auckland City Art Gallery director Eric Westbrook, for example, promoted the idea of a distinctive New Zealand art: 'Today we are seeing the birth of a real New Zealand. In future years the '50s will be looked upon as the era when New Zealand found its soul, not bits of someone else's soul. Now we are developing a national consciousness in which national art must play an important part.'[140] He later declared that 'the day of a typical New Zealand form of art may be dawning. Already there is evidence that some local artists are moving away from the traditional styles and colourings established in Britain and Europe'.[141]

By the 1960s, this search for a 'typical New Zealand art' seemed both elusive and less relevant, as artists confidently assumed 'artistic authority', and the country in which they lived and worked grew increasingly outward-looking and attuned to international trends and developments.[142] Contemporary art flourished, and its practitioners pursued widely different styles and influences. Art writers Hamish Keith and Gordon Brown have noted: 'the directions that emerged from 1960 were not marked by any common intention among painters. If anything, developments during the decade were remarkable for their variety.'[143] The notion of a recognisable national style receded as artists responded in myriad ways to the physical or spiritual environment in which they lived and worked. What John Summers had written in a review of a Christchurch Group show in 1949 could be applied to this new generation of artists: 'They have begun to live in New Zealand as painters, neither self-consciously stressing the fact by putting in the obvious and typical detail, nor on the other hand, painting in some no-man's-land of the spirit as if New Zealand was totally irrelevant to their purposes. It does exist for them, quietly and naturally.'[144] Artists such as Don Binney, Michael Smither, Pat Hanly, Garth Tapper, Don Peebles, Robin White, Ralph Hotere, Robert Ellis, Michael Illingworth, Gretchen Albrecht and Rudi Gopas produced works that covered the spectrum of artistic styles, and dealt with all aspects of New Zealand life — urban, rural, historic and contemporary. The range of work being created precluded any one defining label or school.

Most artists lived and worked abroad for a time, and some on their return were able to continue as professional artists. In this they were supported by the gradual development of an artistic infrastructure, and the expansion of venues that were willing to show modern art. The monopoly of the conservative art societies had been challenged from the late 1940s when some public libraries and coffee houses began to hold exhibitions of contemporary art. The Wellington Architectural Centre, opened by young architects in 1946, became another popular place to exhibit modern works. Two years later, also in the capital, Helen Hitchings opened the first New Zealand commercial dealer gallery. (Unfortunately, this lasted only three years, as Hitchings moved to Europe.)

In terms of curators and arts administrators, Auckland led the way. In 1952, Eric Westbrook was appointed director of the Auckland City Art Gallery, the first full-time professional director of a public gallery in the country. He set out to transform the gallery from 'a Victorian mausoleum into a modern art museum',[145] organising a number of cutting-edge exhibitions of contemporary works. *New Zealand Paintings by Nine Artists* (1952) was followed a year later by *Young Contemporaries*. In 1955, *Art and Image* presented abstract paintings by artists such as Milan Mrkusich and John Weeks among others. After Westbrook left the gallery in 1956, his replacement, Peter Tomory, continued to promote New Zealand artists. For example, in 1959, at a time when sculpture was rarely exhibited, he organised an exhibition of three women sculptors, Anne Severs, Alison Duff and Molly Macalister. Macalister, whose work had been influenced by the gallery's 1956 Henry Moore exhibition, was subsequently given several large public commissions, including *Maori Warrior* (1964–66), which was placed at the bottom of Queen Street in Auckland, and *Little Bull* (1967), in Hamilton Gardens. While at the gallery, Tomory bought contemporary New Zealand work, devoted exhibition space to it and organised travelling exhibitions. This allowed people to view art from other centres and began to 'whittle down parochial attitudes and preference for local painters'.[146] Moreover, artists who had often been isolated from each other were able to observe their peers' work at first hand. Consequently, New Zealand art started to move from being local to national. 'Localism, which dominated so much of this country's artistic life from its earliest days, was being challenged seriously. Exhibitions selected nationally by the Auckland Gallery and toured throughout the country, were to become part of the New Zealand scene.'[147]

Tomory also increased the number of overseas exhibitions by contemporary artists. One of the first, a Henry Moore exhibition of 1956, was vilified by the press and sparked enormous controversy. As a result, attendance at the gallery reached a record of more than 36,700 visitors. Auckland City Art Gallery also started its own magazine, the *Quarterly* (1956–78), and began to produce art books. Informative, well-researched catalogues accompanied shows, and reviews and articles were written for the national press, the *Listener* and *Landfall*. The Auckland City Art Gallery became the most important publisher of literature on the arts in New Zealand, responsible for the lion's share of art publications between 1952 and 1962.[148] Under Westbrook and Tomory, it was transformed into the most active visual arts institution in the country. As a consequence, Auckland became a centre of contemporary art, with a growing number of dealer galleries,[149] replacing Christchurch as the hub of artistic activity.

The way was now open to a new generation of artists able to benefit from the changes and advances made since 1945. Their isolation had diminished; they could keep abreast of international movements by travelling overseas or by reading the growing number of art magazines available in the country. Art schools became more contemporary in approach, and increasingly dealer galleries showed and sold contemporary New Zealand art. Public art galleries were also becoming receptive and started building up collections of contemporary work. Touring exhibitions exposed the broader public to contemporary artists, and the government-funded Arts Council helped galleries to fund tours and buy new works, and also offered grants to individual artists.[150] In 1963, New Zealand participated in the Paris Biennale for the first time; in 1964, a collection of contemporary New Zealand painting and ceramics toured Japan; in 1965, a major exhibition of New Zealand art was shown in London and contemporary New Zealand paintings exhibited in the Australian state galleries.

Maori art

Although modern New Zealand art acquired infrastructural support and some popular acceptance in the 1950s and early 1960s, appreciation for Maori art remained limited. Gordon Walters, an early advocate of non-representational abstraction and tribal art, later recalled: 'It's difficult to explain just how opposed to these areas Pakehas were at the time.'[151] Maori art was considered to be strictly decorative, useful only for the tourist industry. Motifs such as the kowhaiwhai accordingly adorned brochures, postage stamps and magazine covers. In 1966, *The Encyclopedia of New Zealand* consigned traditional Maori art to the past and to the status of craft: 'their meaning and purpose is of the past and they linger on in practice only as traditional crafts . . . No Maori artist of stature has yet arrived. The process of integration has isolated the Maori of today from the living meaning of the arts of his forefathers, and his culture must, from now on, be one with that of his European neighbours.'[152]

The two main art schools taught a European academic style, using examples of classical antiquity as models. Sculptor Arnold Manaaki Wilson recalled: 'Maori art was relegated to the far corners. The nearest I got to it was when I made a sculpture of Tangaroa, god of the sea. I did it in realistic form — a man holding up a taiaha, the cherubs beside him. The subject was Maori, not the style.' When Wilson suggested going to the museum to study Maori art he was told: 'You want to be a Maori, go back and wear a grass skirt.'[153]

Despite lack of encouragement from the art establishment, young Maori artists did begin to combine traditional art with western modernist influences. After leaving art school in 1954, Wilson and five other trained Maori art teachers and advisors — Selwyn Wilson, Selwyn Muru, Ralph Hotere, Katerina Mataira and Muru Walters — were sent by Gordon Tovey, Supervisor of Arts and Crafts in the Department of Education, to Northland to teach art. There they developed works that reconciled western art traditions with Maori cultural inheritance. Wilson has written of that time: 'The 1950s was that period where things were really beginning to bubble through . . . It all started from there, from Kawakawa . . .'[154] Works by these six artists were shown at the Auckland Education Centre in 1958, in what was the country's first exhibition of contemporary Maori art.[155] This was not, however, the first of many. While this group of artists became influential teachers, inspiring future generations of young Maori, their own art continued to be neglected. Although Hotere and Wilson had works included in exhibitions at Auckland City Art Gallery, and Hotere's *Black Painting* (1964) was purchased by the gallery, this was the era in which Stewart Maclennan, director of the National Art Gallery, declared: 'No Maori artist of stature has yet arrived.'[156] In 1969, Hotere was the first Maori 'written into the history of mainstream New Zealand art' as one of the few painters of advanced abstract art then being made in New Zealand.[157] By the 1970s, recognised and acclaimed for his ability to express 'empathy with people and nature',[158] Hotere had become, and remained, one of New Zealand's pre-eminent modernist artists, and one of the earliest to sustain a full-time career as a painter.

The archaeologist Roger Duff of Canterbury Museum also discounted Maori rock drawings in South Canterbury as art. In his view, 'relatively few of the drawings would be beyond the artistic powers of a pre-school child'.[159] Fortunately, the artist Theo Schoon, a war refugee from the Dutch East Indies, convinced the authorities that these drawings were indeed art: 'I was immediately struck by the high artistic quality of these drawings, and secondly by the obvious departure from naturalistic subjects.'[160] For about three years from 1946, he copied, photographed and catalogued the works, and discovered more in the process. He invited Gordon Walters to visit the sites, and the drawings inspired Walters' ground-breaking works in 1947 (not, as noted, well received at the time). In 1949, the poet A. R. D. Fairburn also recognised the drawings' merit: 'Their aesthetic quality for the student of art is astonishing . . . There is hardly a drawing, of the many I have seen, that does not have some high aesthetic quality — sometimes reminiscent of modern painters such as Paul Klee and Miro.'[161] This remained a minority view. Until the late 1960s, most Maori art was consigned to museums as an ethnographic artefact, rather than exhibited in galleries.[162] With the Maori Renaissance, however, Maori artists began to make a real impact on New Zealand. During that time, Ralph Hotere, Rei Hamon, Arnold Manaaki Wilson, Selwyn Muru, Para Matchitt and Muru Walters, who had been practising since the late 1950s and had initiated a form of Maori modernism which combined Maori spiritual thought and concepts with European art-making traditions, were finally recognised for their innovation and influence.[163]

By the mid-1970s, New Zealand art both Maori and non-Maori was flourishing, stimulated by a range of national and international influences. A growing number of dealer galleries provided artists with space to show their works and exposed the public to contemporary art from New Zealand and around the globe. What had formerly been a hobby or part-time recreational occupation now became for many a viable profession. The work of artists throughout the country reflected a plurality of expression, but did so without 'chasing the chimera of a singular national identity in art'.[164]

Absorbing influences: architecture

The quest for a distinctive national style of architecture went hand in hand with the absorption of overseas influences. After World War II, young architects who had formerly lived and worked overseas returned to New Zealand determined to introduce European modernist concepts of functionalism (light-filled, free-flowing open buildings, large windows and easy movement

from interior to exterior spaces) and adapt them to the local climate, materials
and lifestyle. Christchurch architects Paul Pascoe and Humphrey Hall assured
readers in 1947:

> There is a group of professional architects in this country who apply modern
> principles to house design . . . The conditions in this young country are wholly
> suitable to modern design. Our indigenous materials are suitable. Our earthquake
> risk demands studied structural systems which confirm the cantilever principle, the
> simple forms and other features of modern design.[165]

The number of these enlightened advocates of modern architectural principles swelled from the late 1930s with the arrival of talented émigré European
architects such as Ernst Plischke, Heinrich Kulka, Imric Porsolt, Friedrich
Neumann and Helmut Einhorn. These men were Jewish refugees from Nazism
(the exception being Plischke, who was married to a Jew). All were educated
in the internationalist modernist traditions of Le Corbusier, Walter Gropius
and Ludwig Mies van der Rohe. Understandably, they continued to design
continental-style modernist houses in the antipodes.

Modernism was compatible with the search for an indigenous architecture
— the stress that the French architect Le Corbusier placed on local traditions,
environment and materials, for example, encouraged the quest for a national
style.[166] Paul Pascoe noted in 1940 that 'although modern architecture shows a
tendency to become international, it may also be expressive of national character'.[167] Three New Zealand architects — Pascoe and Hall in Christchurch,
and Vernon Brown in Auckland — played a critical role in developing a New
Zealand architectural style in the post-war period.[168]

Vernon Brown, an English-born architect, arrived in Auckland in the mid-
1920s and by the early 1940s had built several distinctive, affordable creosoted
houses. Dismissing European modernism's characteristic flat roofs and white
plaster walls as 'enriched white bread',[169] he promoted simple wooden houses
that were rather like 'big baches' or sheds, which he believed more appropriate
for New Zealand. He explained his structures in strictly functional terms: 'All
cant and humbug were avoided. The roof was low pitched, because there is no
snow in Arney Road'.[170] As a teacher at the Auckland School of Architecture
from 1942 until his death in 1965, he exerted an enormous influence on the
development of an indigenous style of architecture. At the same time, Pascoe
and Hall in Christchurch were designing not dissimilar houses — with painted,
timber-clad exteriors, sloping mono-pitched roofs and long low windows. Both

became prolific architectural commentators whose ideas and designs featured in a growing number of arts and/or architectural publications that reached a national audience.[171]

In 1946, some of Brown's Auckland students formed a group variously called the Architectural Group, Group Architects or Group Construction. Being socialists, they aimed to create a distinctive New Zealand architecture based on economic affordable houses for ordinary people: 'overseas solutions will not do. New Zealand must have its own architecture, its own sense of what is beautiful and appropriate to our climate and conditions.'[172] Residences designed by the Group were to reflect the owners' lifestyle; form would follow function. The founder, Bill Wilson, explained: 'This pattern of movement becomes the plan of the house — it is the plan of the lives of the people. The architect does not invent plans — he discovers them.'[173] Efficient design went hand in hand with efficient use of materials and, in the interests of economy, local materials were used whenever practicable. The *New Zealand Herald* described the Group's famous First House, constructed in 1950 on a Takapuna back section, as 'revolutionary'. Open plan and simple, with exposed beams and rafters and walls lined with sheets of ply, it also contained specially fabricated plywood furniture. Although seemingly influenced by modernist principles, the Group insisted it was a purely vernacular design based on Maori whare and early Pakeha houses: 'The Maoris lived here for hundreds of years so they ought to know what goes on . . . They evolved a style of house suited to the climate, and that is exactly what we are doing . . . The basic design is peculiar to New Zealand.'[174]

Twenty-five years later, Christchurch architect Miles Warren paid tribute to the first and second Group houses of Bill Wilson, Ivan Juriss, Brett Penman, Campbell Craig, Jim Hackshaw, Bruce Rotherham and Allan Wild as 'the best of architecture 25 years ago. They demonstrate its principles, hopes and ideals. The Group houses were the first expression of modern architecture in the country. Early so-called modern buildings provided the trappings and style but not the essence.'[175] As individual architects, the Group went on to build a diverse body of work, drawing on a wide range of influences and criteria.[176]

Whether the Group admitted it or not, the new vernacular styles of architecture were linked to international influences and trends, most notably modernism. Émigré architects who designed sleek white modernist European-style houses adapted them to local conditions, and learned in the process how to use local materials such as weatherboard. In Auckland, for example, Imric Porsolt and Heinrich Kulka created modernist homes substituting timber for the concrete and brick they would have used in Europe. In doing so, they created aesthetically pleasing homes adapted to harmonise with the local environment.[177] Ernst Plischke, who arrived in 1936, chose New Zealand as his destination because he believed it would be ideally suited to his 'International Style'.[178] In his view, architecture was 'a response to needs and environment, both of which had a certain international commonality, rather than to any individual national culture'.[179] New Zealand, though, seemed to think otherwise. Although Plischke arrived with an established international reputation, he was not admitted as a member of the New Zealand Institute of Architects as he refused to sit the necessary examinations, believing his experience and qualifications should be sufficient. His application for the chair of design in the School of Architecture in 1947 was turned down because his work was considered too European. (It was not surprising then that when he was offered a position as Professor of Architecture in Vienna, he accepted with alacrity.)[180] On arrival in New Zealand, he was employed by the Department of Housing Construction in Wellington until 1948, when he went into partnership with Cedric Firth and started designing private houses, the occasional public building, and several churches. Initially, his clients consisted primarily of fellow émigrés, but his reputation grew steadily. By the mid-1940s until his departure in 1963, he was the architect of choice for many of Wellington's academic, business and cultural elite.[181] His striking houses featured white interiors and exteriors and frequently wall-to-ceiling glass to achieve transparency and lightness.

By the late 1950s and early 1960s, growing prosperity enabled more people to afford architect-designed houses. The School of Architecture in Auckland turned out an increasing number of architects; a wider range of construction materials was available; and architectural styles for residences diversified. Japanese, American and Scandinavian influences were now assimilated and adapted. Some architects favoured high-style international modernist houses, others moved toward a 'Pacific style' of modernism featuring relaxed informal open wooden structures.[182] Guy Natusch in Hawke's Bay for example built tent-like open houses that were a 'natural extension of the terrain'.[183] These open houses with large expanses of glass suited the warmer north. In the mid- to late 1960s in Wellington, Ian Athfield and Roger Walker burst on to the architectural scene with buildings 'like no other in New Zealand'.[184] Using a wide range of materials, and rejecting modernism, they both designed in a neo-colonial style, with pitched roofs, dormer windows, gables, visible chimneys and weatherboards, or later on, Mediterranean-style white plasterwork, combined with the neo-colonial forms. Popular with the public and architects alike, Athfield and Walker made neo-colonial houses fashionable and soon architects throughout New Zealand were designing them. By the mid-1970s, 'the Colonial house, new or old, became the most popular on the market'.[185]

In the south, architects also searched for a more casual style of living but had to build more solidly against the elements. Interiors were often cutting edge, but exteriors remained solid, with pitched roofs. Miles Warren, influenced by his work with the London City Council, and realising that the Group's style of timber housing was not suitable for the colder Christchurch climate, began using concrete block.[186] In 1959, his Dorset Street Flats, which were in fact more like modern townhouses, featured exposed concrete beams and concrete-block walls. Among the most celebrated domestic buildings of the decade, the Dorset Street Flats captured the imagination of architects and their clients.[187] By the 1960s, a distinctive Christchurch style had evolved, which drew on the city's colonial heritage by incorporating traditional cottage-style traditions, but also integrated new principles of light and flow and modern technology.

The modernist impulse was not restricted to domestic architecture. Once post-war building restrictions were eased, public and commercial buildings entered a boom period. Churches, office buildings, airports and war memorial halls all exhibited modernist influences in their innovative design and light open spaces. In large commercial buildings, the influence of international architects was evident in rectilinear forms and the extensive use of glass. One architect of the era commented: 'Every architect working on office buildings at that time was in love with glass boxes.'[188] One of the very first in Wellington was Plischke's Massey House (1951–53). Commissioned by the New Zealand Meat and Dairy Board, it was eight storeys of glass and aluminium, with a light open interior, natural wood veneers and built-in furniture, and strikingly modern compared with its neighbours.[189] In Auckland in 1950, government architect Gordon Wilson, who had travelled in 1949 to New York to study public buildings, designed the new Auckland government offices, named the Bledisloe Building. Its rectilinear shape, columns, pilotis and extensive use of glass closely resembled Le Corbusier's United Nations Headquarters building in New York.[190] One of the most successful modernist office buildings in Auckland was the AMP Building (1958–62) in Queen Street, designed by Jack Manning. With its glass curtain wall framed by stainless steel and ebony black granite-clad ground-floor columns, it was, in the words of architect David Mitchell, 'a scaled-down version of the glass skyscraper of America'.[191]

During the 1960s in Christchurch, large heavy concrete buildings were constructed alongside the glass boxes. This was soon followed by 'a spate of unlovable concrete buildings in Wellington and elsewhere'.[192] By the end of the 1960s, commercial architecture, like domestic, had become more varied, incorporating different styles, materials and technologies. In the 20 years after World War II, architecture grew and diversified within the framework of the modernist movement, with New Zealand architects absorbing the influences of modern international architecture and successfully adapting them to the country's specific needs and self-perceptions.[193]

'Different but not very'

This productive interplay between national and international influences was a crucial component of the artistic upsurge after World War II. Assisted by the development of an artistic and cultural infrastructure, the sense of a separate national cultural identity intensified. Nationalism and national pride was not new; having quickly taken root in the nineteenth century, it flourished and evolved for over a century within the framework of the British Empire. New Zealand politicians and diplomats regularly and astutely manipulated imperial ties to national advantage. After the war, however, Britain's weakened status encouraged a broadened outlook; the international situation was conducive to adopting a more independent cultural stance.

In consciously shifting away from the formality and conventions of the colonial past, artists and writers, architects and musicians drew heavily on international influences — most notably the modernist movement, without which a more distinctive and independent national culture would arguably not have flourished with such rapidity and success. What has been described as a 'salutary, sanitary, necessary'[194] phase of cultural nationalism reached a peak in the late 1950s and early 1960s; thereafter it did not disappear but simply became less relevant. The need to emphasise a separate identity diminished as that identity grew increasingly secure. There was also a growing sense of the country's increasing participation in a global culture. In *Distance Looks Our Way*, a 1962 book of essays on the cultural impact of New Zealand's geographical remoteness, Robert Chapman observed: 'Our most sensitive intelligences have devoted themselves to articulating authentically New Zealand attitudes, a national pattern which all have shared in creating and feeling. But we live in an age when national differences constitute no more than regional variations on international modes of living. We are different: but not very.'[195]

CHAPTER FOUR

Leisure and Popular Pastimes

UNSETTLING INFLUENCES

Our main pursuits were only cultural in the broadest sense. They were horse-racing, playing Rugby football and beer drinking — especially playing football.
— John Mulgan, 1945[1]

New Zealanders' traditional passion for playing and watching rugby remained undiminished after World War II. Many workingmen also enjoyed attending and betting on horse or dog races and drinking beer with mates. As in other aspects of life, the state played a part in determining when and how the time-honoured trio of 'rugby, racing and beer' could be indulged. Pubs shut at 6 p.m. This early closing, introduced in 1917 as a temporary wartime measure, apparently enjoyed widespread approval, because in a 1949 referendum voters opted overwhelmingly to maintain it.[2] The spectacle of the 'six o'clock swill', with men crowding into drinking holes after work, quaffing pints in quick succession and rolling home for dinner, continued to be part of daily life until 1967. In addition, strict licensing laws made it difficult to sell alcohol in shops and restaurants. From 1951, government extended its embrace to racing: all bets on the horses or dogs were laid at Totalisator Agency Board (TAB) outlets. The TAB, the first government-run betting agency in the world, proved a successful revenue earner and cultural export, soon copied in Australia and elsewhere around the globe.

The state also shaped and directed various other leisure pastimes. It controlled broadcasting, for example, carefully vetting what programmes and music people listened to; and a government-appointed film censor cut or banned anything deemed unsuitable for the movies. In 1945, along with setting a 40-hour working week, Labour passed legislation to ensure that (apart from dairies) shops did not open on weekends. Saturday trading, which prior to 1945 had been countenanced for at least part of the day, did not resume until 1980. Sunday trading was made legal only in 1990.

As the 1950s progressed, state control steadily waned. Society grew both more complex and less quiescent. Teenagers (a confounding new phenomenon), and a youth culture heavily influenced by American rock 'n' roll, began to challenge the more conservative and complacent aspects of social life and recreation. Even among 'square' mums and dads, leisure patterns evolved. Prosperity, full employment, affordable labour-saving domestic appliances and reduced working hours meant increased time for recreation. More people joined clubs, went to films, watched or played sport, listened to radio, read comics, shopped, danced, played music, attended concerts and even occasionally dined out. Speedier DC-6 airplanes from 1954 and jet travel from 1959 made journeying abroad progressively faster and more affordable. Cars, consumerism, suburban and urban growth, and the advent of television in 1960 drew New Zealand into an increasingly global culture. In endeavours such as sport and pop music, success on the international stage augmented national pride. Overseas influences also played an increasing role in determining what people listened to, ate, watched and wore.

American versus British

Despite New Zealand's proud cultural links to Great Britain, a great many of those overseas cultural influences were American. The twentieth century is sometimes described as 'the American century', but the key year is 1945, when the United States emerged as the pre-eminent superpower.[3] American popular culture exerted a profound influence on New Zealand well before this, however, largely due to Hollywood's domination of the film industry. In order to foster Commonwealth films and 'give our people a clearer idea of British history, of British countries, and British customs and ideals', the Coates government in 1928 legislated that at least 20 per cent of films imported into New Zealand had to be British.[4] Although in place until 1976, this quota neither diminished the flow of American films into the country nor their popularity. New Zealand's belated acquisition of television meant that, right through the 1950s, Hollywood continued to cast its spell without any competition from the new medium. As Geoff Lealand has observed: 'The consequences of so many New Zealanders spending so many hours in the darkened cinema, watching American actors and actresses go through their paces, listening to American voices and absorbing the powerful perennial mythologies of Hollywood cannot be easily measured.'[5]

American influence extended beyond films. New Zealand employed a range of inventions, new technologies and industrial and agricultural methods pioneered in the United States; the dairy industry, for example, benefited greatly from American innovations and technology. Michael Joseph Savage's Labour government watched Roosevelt's 'New Deal' unfold with interest and admiration, even borrowing the name for its seminal 1938 Social Security Act from the American version passed three years earlier.[6] During World War II, between 1942 and 1944, Auckland, Wellington, Pukekohe and Warkworth hosted thousands of US marines, army and navy men. This friendly invasion of well-paid young American soldiers caused some unease whilst 'our boys' were overseas (and romance did frequently blossom: 1400 New Zealand women married American servicemen and went to the US as war brides).[7] At the same time, the Americans brought energy, excitement, glamour and good times to a country battened down by wartime restrictions. Places like Auckland's Peter Pan Cabaret and Wellington's Majestic Cabaret became lively hot-spots, where 'sedate cheek-to-cheek foxtrots' gave way to 'razzle-dazzle-gee-whiz jitterbugging'. Restaurants and coffee bars with exotic names like 'Hot Dog' and 'Florida' sprang up, catering to the visitors' tastes for hamburgers, coffee, sodas, milkshakes and steak. Wellington's Green Parrot restaurant in Taranaki Street opened all night during the war years for the 'after-movie Marine crowds', whose favourite order was steak, raw tomatoes and milk. Throughout the country, florists, taxis, cafés, restaurants, nightclubs, confectioners and jewellers did a roaring trade. American popular music, from swing bands to jazz, to Bing Crosby and the Andrews Sisters, became hugely popular.[8]

After the war, the influence of American popular culture, to the discomfort of some, showed little sign of abating. American mass consumerism, American fads and an American way of life continued their seemingly inexorable advance. This 'cultural imperialism', part of a worldwide trend, evoked criticism in the late 1940s and 1950s. Several New Zealand literary figures expressed disdain for American popular culture, warning of its pernicious influence. *Landfall* in the late 1940s, for example, contained little American content, but in its pages, various writers heartily condemned that country's popular culture. Movies came in for special opprobrium: P. J. Downey memorably denounced Hollywood for having 'vomited forth the festering mass of selfish materialism that has given it one of the most frightening collective psychoses that have ever been developed.'[9] In early issues of the *New Zealand Listener*, too, correspondents warned about the grave dangers posed by American slang, while the country's pre-eminent film critic, Gordon Mirams, extolled the superiority of British over American films.[10] Despite the influence of American realist writers on New Zealand literature at this time, New Zealand journalists, writers and critics often dismissed American culture as synonymous with the lowbrow and popular; many believed its encroaching tentacles threatened both local culture and a proud British heritage. A 1952 magazine article entitled 'Preserving Culture from the Vulture' by the novelist Noel Hilliard expressed distaste for the perceived Americanisation spreading around the globe:

This is the epoch of the Truman Doctrine, dollar diplomacy, Coca-colonisation. Local cultures have no chance to compete. They are subverted, squeezed out; the American article is forced in. England, France and Italy have been experiencing this for years. And it is not the best that America has to offer (even if it be a poor best) that is forced on these peoples; it is the worst, and the worst is filthy.

Hilliard went on to commend Australia, where a 'Citizens Movement in Defence of Art and Culture' aimed to protect that country's cultural heritage from 'a flood of crude and vulgar presentations of sex, horror and violence'.[11] Similarly, an earlier (1951) Canadian report expressed concern about the perceived danger to Canadian culture of America's dominance.[12]

Although no such groups or reports featured in New Zealand, the correspondence columns of the *Listener* in the 1950s continued to reflect dismay about American 'cultural rubbish':

What I, in common with many other thinking citizens, am deeply concerned with is the deplorable results which have followed the vast export from America to our own country of cultural rubbish, of which films are only a small part. By far the worst is commercial radio, with its ceaseless 'earbashing', its accent on crime and violence and its gross materialism. It has suborned so many of our young people with its 'education by propaganda'.

Another correspondent in the same issue expressed the view: 'The USA may well be the second most powerful nation in the world, but from the point of morality and culture it lies near the bottom of the barrel.'[13] Nevertheless, these views were not universal; most New Zealanders could simultaneously loyally support the Queen and Commonwealth, and value their country's British cultural heritage, while at the same time enjoying and appreciating American films, books, comics, music and magazines. New Zealand's growing number of young people in particular enthusiastically absorbed whatever American musicians and film-makers had to offer — by 1957, 97 per cent of records in the New Zealand top 20 came from the United States.[14]

Peter J. Read's study of imported popular culture in 1950s New Zealand tells the at once amusing and horrifying story of 'Davy Crockett' mania. In 1956, the film *Davy Crockett, King of the Wild Frontier* proved incredibly popular with children around the globe. Stores in New Zealand, as elsewhere, sold a range of associated merchandise, including Crockett outfits, with hats made of rabbit rather than the authentic but inaccessible American raccoon. Gripped by a passionate desire to obtain a hat like that of their hero, Kiwi boys began to kill cats (usually by hanging them) to obtain their tails. Some schools banned the wearing of the hats, and one parliamentarian expressed the hope that a Rabbits Amendment Bill would make rabbit skins so hard to come by that the coveted Crockett hats could no longer be found in shops. Several children attempted to scalp their playmates during the Crockett mania and two unsuccessful hanging attempts (of children by children) took place in Wellington and Dunedin.[15]

Various other items — predominantly from the United States, such as pogo sticks and hula hoops — became leisure fads, 'must-purchase' playthings until the next one came along. Interestingly, with the exception of softball, neither children nor adults took much to American sport: baseball and gridiron never threatened to oust rugby and cricket in New Zealand. Once television took hold in the 1960s, however, the number of American programmes almost rivalled those from Britain. Moreover, as a survey conducted in 1987 by historian Jock Phillips indicates, the ratio of American to British programmes steadily increased over time. In 1967, shows of US origin were 28.8 per cent and British 34.4 per cent; by 1987, the US figure was 42.7 per cent and the British 24.3 per cent. Phillips also surveyed the origins of films shown in Wellington in the first two weeks in May every decade between 1947 and 1987. The results conclusively indicated Hollywood's continuing dominance, with US films at 71.4 per cent in 1947, 87.9 per cent in 1957, 90.1 per cent in 1967, 85.5 per cent in 1977 and 83.3 per cent in 1987.[16]

If elements within the older generation continued to disdain American popular culture during the 1960s, discussions about its threat to New Zealand's British cultural heritage gradually diminished. This partly reflected the country's opening up to a broader range of global cultural influences, and was partly generational. The British versus American dichotomy simply seemed less relevant to a younger generation that grew up with American popular culture, and to a considerable degree looked to America for ideas about contemporary issues such as racism, gender and imperialism. Increasingly, events occupying America had 'a worldwide ripple effect'.[17] New Zealand's expanding educated elite became more interested in and knowledgeable about America, as New Zealand universities began to offer courses in American history. Canterbury University even introduced an American Studies Department.[18]

In the immediate post-World War II period, however, although American military might was clearly ascendant, the politicians and the people of New Zealand still looked loyally to Britain and perceived their own cultural identity within the Commonwealth framework. American films and American music had eager fans in New Zealand but also numerous detractors, especially among the educated middle classes. Government took active steps to shape the leisure and popular pastimes of New Zealanders to accord with the kind of wholesome, family-oriented, productive lifestyle they aimed to foster. Radio, which had from its inception in the 1920s been both a vital news source and an immensely popular font of entertainment, was the obvious place to start.

One voice: radio

In 1945, 84 per cent of New Zealand households owned a radio; this figure rose to over 90 per cent by 1960.[19] In 1936, recognising the power of radio to sway and control public opinion, the newly elected Labour government nationalised broadcasting:

> Well, the government took over radio with the avowed purpose of making it a means of communicating government policy to the people, because they reckoned they weren't getting a fair go from the newspapers. So they were going to make broadcasting their own, and for a while they did. They used it without any compunction for direct political purposes.[20]

The government either bought or shut down all but two of the smaller privately owned commercial radio stations. It then created two new government departments: the National Broadcasting Service (NBS) ran the non-commercial and the New Zealand Broadcasting Corporation (NZBC) the commercial stations. Although the latter answered to the Minister of Broadcasting, it was quasi-independent, with separate administrative and engineering staff, and the ability, within certain limits, to choose its own programmes.

In 1943, however, government amalgamated the departments to form the New Zealand Broadcasting Service (NZBS).[21] Now advertisers could only choose programmes purchased by the NZBS, the model of operation, technology and administration of which essentially followed the BBC.[22] James Shelley, who presided over the newly amalgamated service, believed that radio should 'inform, educate and entertain',[23] while upholding moral standards: 'If the New Zealand public really wants vaudeville, it is not the slightest use appointing me Director of Broadcasting . . . Are we going to use such a tremendous instrument merely to fill in the gaps, or as a back-ground for noises we make when we eat our soup?'[24]

New Zealand radio became heavily censored. From 1943 and for the next two decades, 'broadcasting lived quietly within accepted limits — no crisis, no conflict, no confrontation'.[25] A discussion panel entitled 'ZB Citizens Forum', for example, set up in 1948 to 'stimulate public thought and discussion', only considered safe government-approved topics such as 'Do New Zealand men lack a clothes sense?'[26] Politically sensitive topics such as 'That equal work should be rewarded with equal pay, regardless of sex' were banned.[27] Audience participation, although initially encouraged, was soon forbidden. Even comedy was censored. In a 1957 lecture to Auckland University College students, J. C. Reid noted: 'The fact that all radio programmes are under the control of the New Zealand Broadcasting Service makes sure that comedy programmes on radio do not offend against good taste, and are not crude in their allusions . . .'[28]

The Information Section of the Prime Minister's Office supplied news bulletins — radio news was effectively the propaganda arm of the government.[29] The NZBS read the news but did not write it. Despite NZBS directors begging successive governments throughout the 1950s for the right to start a news service, government had no desire to relinquish control. Its readiness to use the broadcasting service for its own ends was apparent in 1951 when it denied any airtime or publicity to the Watersiders or their supporters. Then, as one opposition MP declared: 'By the emergency Regulations the press was practically blacked out except in relation to Government statements. The radio was used only by those who were in support of the Government.'[30] Again in 1960, pressure from Prime Minister Nash and the Ministry of External Affairs ensured there was virtually no discussion concerning the controversial All Black rugby tour of South Africa.[31]

Government applied censorship even to school broadcasts: the programme *How Things Began* ended in 1947, for example, after groups and individuals protested at the teaching of evolution.[32] In 1949, Sir Thomas Hunter, Principal of Victoria University College, criticised New Zealand broadcasting as undemocratic, censored and controlled. His warning that 'until all shades of opinion may be heard on the air the totalitarian character of our broadcasting system will remain'[33] was as relevant in 1960 as it had been in 1949. The NZBS remained a strictly controlled government department 'under the rigid aegis of a Minister of the Crown'.[34] A breakthrough finally occurred in the early 1960s, when the NZBS was allowed its own news service with a dedicated team of reporters. By the mid-1960s, with the threat of television luring away its customers, the NZBS began to change, allowing more freedom and exerting less control over content. Talkback radio was introduced in 1965 to immediate and widespread success. All the local commercial stations renamed their women's programmes *Person to Person*, and extended their duration from one to two and half hours, including a talkback segment.[35] *Checkpoint*, a current affairs programme introduced in 1967, provided a forum for public controversies to be aired and for politicians to be questioned about their policies and actions.[36] Local stations were granted more freedom over content. But government still controlled the airwaves and would continue to do so until the early 1970s.

Strict government vetting notwithstanding, listeners avidly tuned in to what was on offer. The commercial ZB network attracted over 80 per cent of the radio audience[37] and remained 'unashamedly designed to attract the masses'.[38] Mornings and early afternoons were geared towards women. The 3ZB Christchurch programming schedule for Monday 2 May 1955 is typical of the daily fare: 9.00 Morning session with Aunt Daisy; 9.30 Music while you work; 10.00 Dr Paul; 10.30 The Layton Story; 10.45 Portia Faces Life; 11.00 Music Stand; 11.30 Shopping Reporter; 12.00 Lunch Session; 2.00 This is My Story; 2.30 Women's Hour.[39] ('Dr Paul, a story of adult love' was an enduring favourite, broadcasting every morning nationwide from 1950 to 1972.)[40] Fans of both sexes followed the evening serials with fervent devotion. As one listener remembers, 'we would have walked over broken glass rather than miss an episode'.[41]

Despite their popularity, radio producers were concerned about serials' malevolent influence, particularly on the young. Radio executive Alex O'Donoghue's view was not untypical: 'What frightful things the majority of the recorded plays are! Portraying as they do all the fundamental details of every desperate crime imaginable . . . And sometimes as many as three or four of these ghastly serials are broadcast in one evening from a single station.'[42] Broadcasting executives purchased no American serials between 1946 and 1956, believing them to have the most corrupting content. It was difficult to obtain British serials, so most of those featured on New Zealand airwaves were Australian.[43] British comic serials such as *Hancock's Half Hour* and (from the early 1950s) *The Goon Show* were, however, hugely popular.

Amidst all the imported programmes, a few local radio personalities became household names. For example, the whole country seemed to know and love rugby commentator Winston McCarthy's catchphrase 'Listen . . . Listen . . . it's a goal!'[44] Maude Ruby Basham, better known as Aunt Daisy, was the unrivalled queen of morning radio. She introduced her programme at 9 a.m. sharp every weekday, in her characteristically cheerful, brisk 'Good morning, good morning, good morning everybody'. From 1936 until her death in 1963, she offered pragmatic household management tips and recipes, uplifting thoughts, and commentary on contemporary events in a lively, entertaining manner. In addition to her popular 'Ask Aunt Daisy' column in the *New Zealand Listener*, her books on household management were instant best-sellers.[45]

The avuncular Selwyn Toogood enjoyed a reputation and presence 'almost as formidable as that of Aunt Daisy'. The biggest male star on New Zealand radio,[46] his career commenced in 1949 with *Posers, Penalties and Profits*, a quiz show staged in the four main centres and played over the ZB stations. As he later recalled, this 'took the country by storm. Literally everything stopped while it was on . . .'[47] From 1954, Toogood's *It's in the Bag* gripped audiences nationwide as contestants either took the money after three easy questions or struggled on with increasingly difficult questions, choosing either more money or risking 'The Bag'. The latter could contain large expensive prizes such as refrigerators, washing machines and radiograms or a booby prize such as a clothes peg. Recorded all over New Zealand in community halls with locally selected contestants, people queued by the hundreds (sometimes thousands) to be allowed to compete; then queued again to be part of the audience. The show was so universally popular that 'on the night Selwyn was doing *It's in the Bag* cinemas virtually closed their doors because it wasn't worth opening'.[48]

Music then, as now, was a radio staple; in 1947, it comprised nearly 76 per cent of everything broadcast.[49] But radio executives decided what to play, and they chose only what they deemed acceptable to the whole family. One baby boomer recalls: 'Our pet hates were the interminably mush orchestras

— Mantovani was only worst because he was most prominent. There were Frank Chacksfield, Andre Kostelanetz, Victor Sylvester, Glenn Miller, David Rose . . .'[50] For half an hour each week at 8 p.m. the *Lifebuoy Hit Parade* (*Lever* from 1955) broadcast records from the UK or USA hit charts, providing they were family friendly.

Rock 'n' roll, considered decadent and unsuitable for family listening, took some time to reach the New Zealand airwaves. Johnny Douglas, who began working as a programming cadet at NZBS in 1956, remembered: 'I was very conscious that overseas, Elvis had arrived, and rock 'n' roll and pop. There were very good pop artists around — Connie Francis, Ricky Nelson, Cliff Richard — who were not terribly noisy. But in New Zealand we were very much sheltered from all those things.'[51] For the conservative middle-aged executives who controlled the airwaves, rock 'n' roll evoked incredulity and disgust. James Hartstonge, a broadcasting manager in the Wellington district during the mid-1950s, declared that 'the orgiastic writhings of pop singers' made him turn away with a sickened stomach.[52] Peter Downes, an NZBS programmer in the 1950s, later recalled:

> [A]ll the Elvis songs and those thing arrived here suddenly, more or less in a block. Nobody knew what to do with them, there was no alternative youth station. Whereas we had been going along safely with Perry Como and Andy Williams and all the rest, suddenly we were confronted with this music, which was not on the ZB Hit Parades, at the start. The radio people dealing with it were not teenagers and certainly not rebellious. They had been brought up on the Bing Crosbys and Dinah Shores. What were we going to do with this new music? Nobody had the foggiest idea, and there weren't really young people on any of the radio stations to say, 'This is our music and this is the popular music of the future.'[53]

Much of the public shared the view that rock 'n' roll was linked to 'moral turpitude' and the first step toward juvenile delinquency.[54] The press warned against its pernicious influence: 'The rhythm and blues numbers which have been in epidemic form in the United States have given way to a new fever — the "Rock 'n' Roll" craze. Be prepared for it is bound to strike us sooner or later . . . it has been banned in some parts of the States and has caused controversies in newspapers and aggravated negro-white segregation difficulties in some parts.'[55]

Towards the end of the 1950s, radio executives grudgingly realised they had to modernise and things slowly loosened up. After all, if young people

A peaceful suburban scene with state houses, a car, and a mother with young children. Below, the teenagers' looming presence suggests potential trouble in paradise. *Neg A 1658, AALF 6122, 15-1-20, 187 tif, Archives New Zealand; Ans Westra*

Aerial top dressing at Bethells Beach on Auckland's west coast in the 1950s. This agricultural innovation dramatically increased farm productivity. *O. Peterson, Auckland War Memorial Museum*

An idyllic rural scene in the Gisborne region in 1952. The handsome farmhouse in the middle distance was burned down by Ruatoria Rastafarians in the late 1980s. *Peter Bush*

Interior of the Naenae Co-op, 1950s. Consumer co-ops were formed in the 1940s and 1950s on state housing estates throughout the country. These sorts of general stores were superseded by the advent of supermarkets. Below, a crowd in Otahuhu in 1958 eagerly awaits the opening of a Foodtown, one of the first supermarkets in New Zealand. *PWD neg. G3077, AALF 6112, 22-2-13, 795tif, Archives New Zealand; courtesy of Countdown Supermarkets*

Contrasting scenes: city work and country life in 1950s New Zealand. *Ans Westra*

Sir Edmund Hillary (left) and radio personality Selwyn Toogood (right) give away samples of 'Rinso' during the opening of the Lambton Quay Self Help store, Wellington, 1956. Below, Aunt Daisy (Maude Ruby Basham), the queen of New Zealand radio, speaks to shoppers at the new store. *EP/1956/2503, Evening Post Collection and EP/1956/2504B-F, Alexander Turnbull Library*

Drinkers at the Porirua Tavern in 1967 enjoy the last days of the 'six o'clock swill'. *Peter Bush*

Rugby legends Don ('The Boot') Clarke and Bob Scott engage in a kicking contest at Athletic Park in 1966. Scott (right) is kicking barefoot. *Peter Bush*

Dedicated rugby fans wait outside the gates of Athletic Park, Wellington, the night before the first test between South Africa and New Zealand on Saturday, 31 July 1965. The All Blacks won 6–3. *Peter Bush*

New Zealand Olympic champion Yvette Williams jumping at the Carisbrook sports meeting on 26 January 1954. *F-42423-1/2, Archives New Zealand National Publicity Studios Collection, Alexander Turnbull Library*

Impressively uniformed marching girls participate in a northern regional championship at Titirangi in 1974. *Max Oettli, PADL-000098, Alexander Turnbull Library*

couldn't hear rock 'n' roll on the radio, they would find it in a dance hall or on a jukebox. Popularised by the Americans during World War II, and a standard fixture in milk bars throughout the country by the 1950s, jukeboxes played music banned by the NZBS, such as Little Richard's 'Tutti Frutti'.[56] Musician Sonny Day recalled that those who wanted to hear banned records would 'get out of school and go and put our jeans on and blue suede shoes and bright socks and go straight down to the milk bar and buy a Coke and sit there playing the jukebox. Little Richard and those guys: Fats Domino, Elvis, Bill Haley. Most of them were American.'[57]

Appreciating that radio needed to move with the times, new fast-talking deejays such as Neville Chamberlain ('Cham the Man'), Des Britten and Peter Sinclair, among others, dared to 'deviate from the set format written down in front of us'.[58] This new breed disregarded established rules, spoke in 'rapid-fire Austral-American accents', and revolutionised both the style of presenting and the type of music played.[59] Young listeners loved them: 'Des, Cham the Man, Pete Sinclair — they knew our language. They started off saying [things] like "Hi there, you there, Pete here" and "See ya round — like a record". My favourite was "another groove from the grave", which I thought was real witty.'[60] The NZBS, reluctantly conceding that rock 'n' roll was indeed here to stay, began from the late 1950s to give pop music and local artists more airtime, established more regional commercial radio stations, and modernised existing ones. Regional hit parades emerged to rival the *Lever Hit Parade*.

But until this loosening up process commenced in the latter part of the 1950s, government control of the airwaves was remarkable. Politicians and broadcasting executives worked together to reinforce and maintain what was deemed a desirable 'norm' — a homogenous society full of hard-working, family-oriented husbands and wives. Rebellious or discordant notes were not allowed to sound. Pakeha culture prevailed. Historian Patrick Day has noted that 'Broadcasting may have been a major influence in the establishment of a New Zealand nationality, but it defined that nationality by declining to focus on the differences among New Zealanders.'[61]

Popular Maori songs and bands played on the radio, but Maori broadcasting was extremely limited — from 1942, there was a weekly quarter-hour general news bulletin, and in 1954 a weekly quarter-hour talk in Maori. In December 1963, these were amalgamated into one weekly half-hour programme called *Te Reo o Te Maori*. Challenges to cultural homogeneity and harmony increased by the mid to late 1950s and intensified as the 1960s progressed. The new music and fashions embraced by the young during the 1950s were all copied from overseas, but that did not make them any less alarming. The NZBS, despite the valiant efforts of some radio executives, had not been able to hold back young New Zealanders' taste for rock 'n' roll. Instead of comprising one big homogenous happy family, the country, like other developed nations around the world, was confronted in the 1950s by that unfathomable phenomenon: youth culture.

'Menace in our midst'

In mid-1954, two events shattered New Zealand's complacency. On 22 June, Honora Parker was battered to death by her teenage daughter Pauline and her friend Juliet Hulme in Christchurch. Murders were so rare at that time — only two or three a year, and rarely committed by women — that those convicted became household names. Teenage murderesses and matricide were simply unheard of. After psychiatric evidence revealed that the relationship between the two girls was considered to be 'grossly homosexual', moral panic, disbelief and horror spread throughout the country.[62] A month later came the revelation that Hutt Valley teenagers were involved in a 'shocking degree of immoral conduct which spread into sexual orgies perpetuated in private homes during the absence of parents, and in several second rate Hutt Valley theatres where familiarity between youths and girls was commonplace'.[63] Forty-one boys and sixteen girls aged from thirteen years were, according to Petone senior police sergeant Frank Le Fort, meeting at Elbe's milk bar in Lower Hutt with the express purpose of arranging sexual liaisons to indulge in 'carnal knowledge and indecent assault'.[64]

To many New Zealanders, these two disturbing events reflected a decline of juvenile moral standards that threatened society's equilibrium. Hilda Ross, Minister for the Welfare of Women and Children, declared that: 'The problem of juvenile delinquency is a grave menace in our midst today which threatens to destroy the basis of our civilisation.'[65] She attributed blame for this 'national emergency' to an abundant and easily accessible supply of filthy literature. 'The cure is strictness, not laxity — this terrible laxity which has produced the spectacle of unhappy children and broken-hearted parents . . .'[66] Press editorials cautioned the public against the dangers of complacency. This would 'condone a lowering of public standards generally, a trend which many fear has already gone too far'.[67]

Faced with a public outcry, on 23 July the government appointed an official investigation into this 'grave social problem'.[68] It charged a committee headed by Dr Oswald Mazengarb with inquiring into the 'conditions and influences that tend to undermine standards of sexual morality of children and adolescents in New Zealand . . . and to make recommendations to the Government for positive action by both public and private agencies, or otherwise'.[69] Two months later, on 21 September, having considered oral evidence from 145 people and received 203 written submissions, the Special Committee on Moral Delinquency in Children and Adolescents presented its report.

The reasons for juvenile immorality in New Zealand, the report maintained, were many and varied. They included the ready availability of indecent literature; inappropriate films; suggestive music; radio serials; advertising 'based on sex attraction, horror and crime'; having too much money; the availability of contraceptives; a lack of spiritual values; the absence of community spirit; and coeducational schools. At the root of it all, however, was lack of parental responsibility. This 'stood out as a matter of grave concern. Many of the parents of children affected by recent happenings throughout the Dominion showed a deplorable lack of concern for their responsibilities . . .'.[70] The report singled out working mothers: 'Some mothers may need to work: but many of them work in order to provide a higher standard of living than can be enjoyed on the wages earned by their husbands, or because they prefer the company at an office, shop, or factory to the routine of domestic duties'.[71] This posed a threat to family life: 'It is the view of the Committee that during the past few decades there have been changes in certain aspects of family life throughout the English-speaking world leading to a decline in morality . . .' It urged that a remedy be found 'before this decline leads to the decay of the family itself as the centre and core of our national life and culture'.[72]

The government hastily passed into law three amendment acts in 1954 to curb the flood of immorality. The Indecent Publications Amendment Act aimed to cut off the flow of indecent literature. The Child Welfare Amendment Act (No. 2) enabled courts to hold parents responsible for their children's delinquent behaviour and extended the definition of delinquency to include any female less than sixteen 'who incites a male to carnally know her or to commit any indecent act upon her'.[73] Finally, the Police Offences Amendment Act prevented the sale of contraceptives to children under sixteen. To make sure the public realised the enormity of the problem, 300,000 copies of the Mazengarb Report were printed and delivered to households throughout the country.

Was the view that juvenile delinquency threatened the moral fibre of society justified, and how unique was this perceived problem? Bronwyn Dalley has shown that young New Zealanders' behaviour in the 1950s was 'not necessarily any "worse" or any "better" than that of earlier generations': in fact, the number of court appearances by juveniles in the mid-1950s was less than the pre-war rate.[74] During the Mazengarb inquiry, social and welfare workers directly involved with youth argued there was no evidence of widespread immorality, and few real changes in juvenile behaviour; a certain number of adolescents had always been and always would be 'abnormally interested' in sex.[75] They also made the salient point that the Hutt Valley 'problem' resulted from a large adolescent population in a new suburb with few amenities. The inquiry and the press ignored this sensible assessment and read delinquency, immorality and the imminent decline of society into what was little more than youthful behaviour instead.[76] The 'moral panic' about juvenile delinquency (or what was perceived as such) and teenage culture generally (the two were often seen as synonymous) was not unique to New Zealand. Throughout the developed world, various groups expressed opposition to the conventional values and lifestyles of their parents in similar ways and met the same alarmed reactions. In England in the 1950s, there were teddy boys, working-class males who dressed like Edwardian dandies. In Australia by the late 1950s, concerns about the antics and attire of bodgies and widgies (see below) reached a crescendo.[77] In the early 1960s, British mods and rockers, influenced by American biker gangs, engaged in highly publicised clashes in Brighton and elsewhere.

Some young people in New Zealand emulated the fashions, along with some of the less problematic behaviour, of these groups. David Ausubel, an academic visiting and working in New Zealand in the late 1950s, observed that the 'causes and symptoms' of the country's juvenile delinquency 'disease' appeared to be 'much the same as in New York, Paris, Sydney, London and Moscow'.[78] The disease followed the cure, and was in a sense its direct result. The desire for a return to 'normality' after the trials of war resulted in a conformist era. In New Zealand, as elsewhere throughout the developed world during the 1950s, strict notions of convention and uniformity reigned.[79] While suburbs and nuclear families flourished according to plan, by the mid-1950s, some young people began to behave in a manner that clearly challenged the accepted norm. The baby boom and a buoyant economy created a youthful section of the populace with increased leisure and more disposable income. These young people could drive cars or take public transport to socialise together in dance halls and milk bars away from parental control.

'Teenagers' (a word coined in mid-twentieth century America) now formed their own culture and sought to express their individuality and identity through music, clothing, language and entertainment. Glen Fearnley, a Wellingtonian who grew up in the early 1950s, recalls: 'Teenager was a new thing, a postwar thing . . . Teenager meant fun . . . My parents didn't have a teenage experience . . . they went straight from school to work. Kids were at school as children then out to work as adults. There was no in-between.'[80] An important consumer market, teens listened to music that shocked their parents and wore clothes that deliberately defied convention. This perplexing, pleasure-seeking new adolescent society frightened many adults, who labelled it delinquent.[81]

During the 1950s, young people throughout New Zealand met on main streets in towns and cities on Friday and Saturday nights to shop, frequent the ever-increasing number of milk bars serving American-style hamburgers and shakes, or just wander along in their best clothes and watch the world go by. The Christchurch *Press*, commenting on this street activity in 1955, noted its apparent aimlessness with some asperity: 'In twos and threes the boys and girls wandered from place to place, from street to milk bar, from milk bar to street.'[82]

At the more visible cutting edge of youth culture were bodgies and widgies, milk-bar cowboys, and teddy boys. Milk-bar cowboys frequented milk bars, indulged in loud behaviour and dressed to be noticed. In Auckland, 'Curries Cowboys' (many of them working-class apprentices) wearing army greatcoats or leather jackets and train-driver's peaked caps, milled around the jukeboxes of Curries milk bar on Queen Street, or roared up and down the street at high speed on motorbikes. Girls who rode at the back were known as 'pillion pussies'. Despite their formidable attire, the cowboys generally caused little more trouble than blocking the traffic.[83] Christchurch's milk-bar cowboys 'stood and talked either astride their machines or near them, and were seen more often with their own sex'.[84]

Bodgies were males who 'wore unusual and exaggerated haircuts' and suits with trousers shorter and tighter in the legs than was then the style, exposing 'garishly coloured socks'. Brightly coloured shirts, pullovers or windbreakers, and neckerchiefs completed the look.[85] They admired all things American and some even assumed Bronx accents. Their female counterparts, widgies, wore bright lipstick, abundant costume jewellery and favoured tight black clothing with contrasting white socks.[86] Their long hair was 'drawn tightly back and tied in a tail' or worn in a 'bushy windswept style fringing carelessly over the forehead'.[87] In Australia, where they originated, bodgies were urban working-class youths, some of whom engaged in shoplifting, minor vandalism and, occasionally, racist attacks.[88] Although the latter behaviour does not appear to have been evident among the New Zealand bodgie population, two shocking, highly publicised crimes featured prominently in the press. In 1955, a nineteen-year-old bodgie called Paddy Black was tried and convicted for knifing a rival by the jukebox in a Queen Street café. Known as 'the jukebox killing', this took place only nineteen days after another bodgie, Frederick Foster, shot and killed a teenage girl in a Queen Street milk bar. Redmer Yska has described these two events as 'inner-city crimes of youthful passion, set in a movie, pulp novel and rock'n'roll saturated world'. Their perpetrators were both hung.[89]

In the public mind, fuelled by hyped media reports, bodgies and widgies were knife-carrying, sexually promiscuous rock 'n' roll addicts, hooligans and vandals who engaged in a wide range of loutishness and unlawful activity.[90] Auckland psychologist A. E. Manning, in his 1958 book *The Bodgie: A Study in Abnormal Psychology*, examined a sample of youths and girls in Australia and New Zealand and concluded that they needed psychiatric treatment. He attributed their unsavoury behaviour to unhappy childhoods, with divorced or inattentive parents.[91] Bodgies themselves did not agree with this diagnosis. During an interview on the radio series *Youth Without Purpose*, one bodgie noted: 'We are just ordinary sensible jokers, or try to be . . . I mean we think as other human beings think, the jokers who wear square clothes as they call them . . . We think like them, we work like them, do everything like them only we wear different clothes to them, so we get called a bodgie.'[92] Another contemporary recalled the species as 'just normal teenagers . . . a bit brash, a bit show-off-y, a little bit bolder . . . They'd do all those things that would be thumbing the nose of authority slightly, very slightly. I suppose . . . I would have been slightly envious of them because they had a lot of fun.'[93]

Bodgies and widgies were apparently addicted to rock 'n' roll,[94] but they were by no means alone in this habit. Most conventionally attired and well-behaved young people growing up in late 1950s New Zealand (that is, the vast majority) also considered rock 'n' roll to be *their* music. Some teenagers believed rock 'n' roll evened things up: 'Now we had our music, they had their music'; others felt that just listening to the new music was rebellion by proxy: 'we could all listen to rock'n'roll and feel like bodgies'.[95]

Following the Mazengarb Report, and the sensational bodgie murders, juvenile immorality and delinquency continued to concern officials and educationalists, but did not dominate headlines again until 1960. In that year, 'hooliganism' and 'mob violence' by teenagers at the Hastings Blossom Festival caused another outcry from concerned politicians, the press and irate citizens. The behaviour of 'jeering, booing youths and teenage girls', 'the sounds of drunken singing, the crash of breaking glass and the roaring of car engines' prompted many alarmed articles and letters. A newspaper editorial asked plaintively: 'Must The Hooligan Take Control?' Politicians advocated stronger measures against juvenile crime and delinquency, which was decried as 'a festering problem . . . the canker in our midst . . . blotting the fair name of our nation'.[96] Demands for increased discipline in schools, calls for work camps, detention centres and borstals, and suggestions to increase church youth activities, youth clubs and youth welfare organisations, ensued. However, this furore died down quickly. The press and the older generation tended to panic and/or despair over the antics of youths in the wake of particular events, and this often led to exaggerated claims about young rebellious 'enemies of society'.[97] Yet by the late 1950s and early 1960s, there was some real cause for concern, as the number of problem children (as opposed to occasional youthful outbursts of riotous or what was perceived as immoral or alarming behaviour) steadily grew. A booming population, with an increasing percentage of young people, rising ex-nuptial births, and rapid social changes in the wake of urbanisation and suburbanisation led to increases in children and teens in trouble with the law or with behavioural problems. While the number of children appearing before the courts rose steadily after 1948, from the mid-1960s onwards the rate accelerated markedly. As demands on child welfare services increased, government established more residential institutions for problem children and expanded the Child Welfare Division of the Education Department. The number of 'experts' — from therapists and psychologists to counsellors — also rapidly grew. The state, keen to expand its population after the war and more sensitive to the care and nurture of children, put in place all appropriate measures to encourage children and teens to grow into good and useful citizens.[98] Serious criminal or anti-social behaviour among the young, however, was often conflated with occasionally riotous group 'misbehaviour', which waxed and waned. Enhanced public awareness of juvenile behaviour, and waves of popular panic about more rebellious or unconventionally attired young people, also doubtless affected the rate of notification and detection of children's offences.[99]

Megan Ritchie's study of 1950s youth culture in Auckland reveals how concern about what was deemed unsuitable or morally questionable youth culture drove adults to increased efforts to organise recreation for young people, and recruit them into groups such as scouts and guides. An Empire Youth Day Parade in May 1955 saw 3500 smartly uniformed young Aucklanders posing a welcome contrast to the dreaded bodgies. The *New Zealand Herald* noted approvingly:

As they strode past six abreast, with heads high and shoulders squared, these youths and the thousands who followed them — scouts, guides, boys' brigade and the rest — made a brave showing. Said an old man in the crowd with some emotion: 'You can't tell me there's anything wrong with the youth of New Zealand.'[100]

Churches and schools provided space for young people to meet and dance with proper adult supervision. In 1957, the Jaycees (Junior Chamber of Commerce) organised a 'Community and Youth Week' that incorporated numerous worthy causes such as a drive for blood donors, firefighting and street-cleaning demonstrations, and water sports with accompanying instruction about water safety. In 1957, the Auckland Youth Council focused on promoting groups that encouraged youngsters to play sports and engage in other worthwhile hobbies, and many communities started a teenagers' or youth club, which offered organised adult supervision and/or parentally accepted pastimes such as darts, draughts and table tennis, in addition to rock 'n' roll dancing and jiving.[101] It was thus possible for well-behaved and hard-working conventional teens to engage with youth culture to some degree without alienating their parents or becoming bodgies or widgies.

After radio executives grudgingly accepted the rock 'n' roll phenomenon in the latter 1950s, local record companies also jumped somewhat belatedly on the bandwagon. HMV, after initially refusing to import Bill Haley's 'Rock Around the Clock', soon realised its mistake. Popular musician Johnny Cooper, 'the Maori Cowboy', a country and western singer under contract to HMV, was asked to record it.[102] A poor imitation of the original, it was not a great success; nor was Cooper's next effort. But he adapted his style and in 1957 recorded 'Pie Cart Rock 'n' Roll'. New Zealand's first rock 'n' roll composition had light-hearted lyrics explaining how the song was written in exchange for a pie from a Wanganui pie cart.[103] Cooper, who topped the bill at the rock 'n' roll jazz concerts in Palmerston North and Wanganui in March 1957, was dubbed New Zealand's King of Rock 'n' Roll. (As he was New Zealand's only recorded rock 'n' roll artist at the time, there were few pretenders.)

In the meantime, another distribution company, TANZA, picked up the rights to Bill Haley's 'Rock Around the Clock' and released it in September 1956, to coincide with the movie being screened in New Zealand. The record sold 50,000 to 75,000 copies and the movie became the biggest box-office hit of the 1950s. From this time onward, according to music historian John Dix, 'New Zealand went rock'n'roll crazy'.[104] New dance venues catering exclusively for young people opened and flourished, with hundreds of rock 'n' rolling teens packed in on weekends; the rock 'n' roll phenomenon, rather than fading away, as many parents hoped, seemed if anything to steadily gather momentum. The Jive Centre in Auckland became the country's number one venue, attracting some 600 dancers every Friday and Saturday night.[105] Ben Tawhiti, a teenager in Auckland during the late 1950s, remembered: 'There were so many dances on at the time. You just poked your head in and if you didn't like the music, you went to another one. The Manchester, Trades Hall, Catholic Social Centre, the Metropol, the Playhouse, the Oriental, St Seps — many, many places that you could relate to. Yes, that was the entertainment scene of that time.'[106] In Wellington, regular dances had long been held at the Empress, the Trades Hall and the Majestic, 'but when Elvis came in and rock'n'roll started up Ngati Poneke was the place to go. The band at Ngati Poneke played rock'n'roll and people went there in their hordes.'[107]

Ngati Poneke's counterpart in Auckland, the Maori Community Centre in Freemans Bay, was 'the jazziest, jumpingest place in the city. Its talent quests were legendary, and on a long weekend the festivity and feasting hardly stopped, day and night. Taxis banked up outside.'[108] Every weekend, the Centre pulsed with young aspiring Maori amateur musicians, hoping to become one of the regular bands at Auckland's numerous dance halls. Established artists and groups such as the Hi Fives, the Maori Volcanics, Toko Pompei and Dusky Nepia, among others, would also 'come for miles just to get on that stage. It was the "in thing" . . . if you didn't get into the Maori Community Centre, you weren't a name at all.'[109] Kiri Te Kanawa and Hannah Tatana sang light opera there, and overseas acts visiting Auckland would frequently receive a Maori welcome at the Centre.

The 1950s and early 1960s were a golden era not just for the Maori Community Centre but also for Maori musicians generally. Their prominence in New Zealand entertainment was out of all proportion to their numbers. From the 'poshest night clubs'[110] to the wildest dance halls, from country halls to local marae, Maori dance bands played and Maori vocal groups sang as young people rock 'n' rolled, jived and twisted to their music.[111] In 1949, Ruru Karaitiana recorded 'Blue Smoke', the first 'complete New Zealand pop song'.[112] After this milestone, Maori musicians remained at the forefront of the popular music scene, forming trios, quartets, jazz bands and show bands. The latter, a unique hybrid of New Zealand and American influences, were phenomenally popular with people of all ages. Show bands, such as the Maori Volcanics and the Hi Fives, sang and played popular music of all kinds, from rock 'n' roll to country to romantic ballads, but were also accomplished comics, dancers and entertainers. According to Rimini Paul, a member of the Hi Fives: 'We were professional "show people" as well as well as "professional musicians" . . . the main focus was on the presentation and the visual aspects of live performance.'[113]

Maori show bands were soon a profitable export commodity, especially to Australia: 'When the Hi Fives arrived on the Gold Coast around 1960, they were an unbelievable hit. In fact from that time on, Maori show bands controlled the entertainment scene on the Gold Coast for a number of years because of their popularity. These groups were complete cabaret and dance music combinations . . .'[114] From Australia, the Hi Fives successfully toured the world, and in June 1964 acted as the Beatles' support group during their Hong Kong concert.

By the mid-1960s, Maori show bands seemed ubiquitous in Australia, Asia and the Pacific.[115] Including a Maori segment in their shows was 'a necessary tool for Maori show bands to implement because that's what made us unique and different from others and that was an attraction. Whether it was in Australia, Vietnam, England, Europe or the States, it was different to see us performing our own culture, and yes, it had to be in there and we felt almost naked if we didn't do the traditional Maori show.'[116] Interestingly, most Maori show bands achieved more success and fame abroad than they did at home.

One Maori group hugely popular both at home and abroad, the Howard Morrison Quartet, was originally Rotorua based. Music promoter Benny Levin spotted the band there and brought them to Auckland in 1957 to perform and record. Their first hit, 'Hoki Mai' (the signature song of the 28th (Maori) Battalion), had customers queuing outside record stores. More original hits followed; one of the best known, 'My Old Man's an All Black', was a satire and protest at the exclusion of Maori from the 1960 All Black tour of South Africa. In January 1960, as part of music impresario Harry Miller's 'Summertime Spectacular' New Zealand-wide tour, the Quartet drew such large crowds in Wellington that the rush to buy tickets caused an inner-city traffic jam. Despite being 'the most popular family entertainers in New Zealand history', they broke up in 1964 after five years of incessant touring in Australia and New Zealand and numerous hit records. Morrison pursued a solo career, and was for decades one of New Zealand's leading television and concert entertainers. He died in 2009.[117]

New Zealand musicians quickly adapted to the craze for rock 'n' roll. Many dance and concert bands previously specialising in jazz or swing introduced rock 'n' roll numbers into their repertoires, despite not being fans themselves:

'We couldn't believe it was so popular yet so *dumb*', recalled drummer Harry Voice.[118] Rock 'n' roll dance marathons attracted large numbers of young participants keen to literally 'rock around the clock'.[119] Every small town soon had its own band or bands. In Invercargill, where 'ballroom dancing was being blown off the stage by electric rock'n'roll and beat music',[120] several rock 'n' roll bands formed. The Echophonics, one of the first in Southland, played Sunday-afternoon dances in the Orange, Buffalo and St Mary's halls to crowds of teenagers. They joined rising international superstars the Rolling Stones, Ray Columbus and the Invaders, the Newbeats, and Roy Orbison for impresario Harry M. Miller's 'Big Beat Show' then touring the country. This was a rock 'n' roll production on a scale never seen in Southland before or since. Two sold-out shows in the Civic Theatre on 2 February 1965 played to 2000 screaming teens.[121]

Despite sensationalist newspaper accounts linking rock 'n' roll to delinquency, some establishment figures expressed surprising acceptance early on. Four years after his famous report, for example, Oswald Mazengarb postulated in 1958 that rock 'n' roll might well offer a healthy outlet for excess youthful energy, while Walter Nash announced serenely: 'I've seen nothing that I would not have done at your age had I been so agile.'[122]

Not everyone was so non-judgemental. Concerts featuring rock 'n' roll, invariably lively events, frequently elicited irate letters of protest to the newspapers. One jazz lover wrote that the concerts provided an opportunity for hundreds to 'throw off civilisation for two or three hours and take on animalish and wild manners — screaming, catcalling, etc, instead of listening to the music'.[123] Another correspondent described rock 'n' roll as 'the nadir of depravity. Any doubts on that point must be quickly dispelled by observing the deportment, dress and general behaviour of those who indulge in the practice. Its devotees stand in need of a stiff dose of psychiatric medicine.'[124] In the late 1950s, Bill Roper Smith, seventeen-year-old lead singer of Invercargill band the Skiffling Five, emulated Elvis's pelvis gyrations and hip wiggling while the band played at the opening of a large new restaurant in Dee Street. Teenagers in the audience went mad and pandemonium ensued, leading to the arrival of the police and the shutting down of the venue. Bill was hauled before a committee of three clergymen, a police chief and the full city council, who cautioned him never to do it again. The mayor concluded by telling him: 'Let's stamp this out right now.'[125]

In October 1956, prompted by an Australian report that denounced such venues, and rock 'n' roll, for promoting 'lust at first sight', a combined South Island church group surveyed local dance halls. What they saw (low lights, gyrating bodies, scantily dressed girls and hanky-panky in the corners) sparked indignation: 'It is bad enough to have such animalistic music with nothing more than a primitive sexual basis. But we find dance promoters emphasising sex with subdued lighting and lustful types of dances.' They called, unsuccessfully, for brighter lighting, and declared rock 'n' roll dancing to be 'a shameless showing of crudity which completely degrades the dancers'.[126]

This sort of moral concern about licentiousness and depravity exerted no apparent impact on the youth music scene. In January 1958, Johnny Devlin, an eighteen-year-old Wanganui bank clerk, debuted at Auckland's Jive Centre to hysterical rapture. He later recalled with some incredulity:

> I came out on stage and started shaking around, doing the Elvis thing. All these
> girls started screaming and I thought I had left my fly undone or something.
> I quickly turned round and checked that, and found that no, we were right there.
> I had heard that it happened overseas but I hadn't witnessed anything like it myself.
> I didn't know why the audience was screaming. I thought they must like the music.
> I shook my leg and they screamed, then I shook it again and they screamed again.
> It was the actions, the movements. I don't think it's a sexual thing, I never believed
> that. I think they're just excited with the music and the whole deal, wrapped up in
> the song and the singer.[127]

Night after night, Devlin played to a packed floor, with disappointed fans turned away. In June 1958, his first recording, a cover version of 'Lawdy Miss Clawdy', launched him as a national star. Towards the end of the year, he began a six-month tour of the country, during which frenzied followers regularly ripped off his shirt. Devlin's concerts, and the hysteria surrounding them, featured in the press nearly every day throughout the tour. The *Otago Daily Times*, for example, reported both the positive and negative repercussions of Devlin mania: 'Conservative Oamaru "let its hair down" last night . . . Johnny Devlin . . . had teenagers stamping, clapping, yelling and rocking in the Opera House in what must have been the most uninhibited demonstration in the town's history. It was certainly one of the liveliest shows to come to Oamaru in recent years.'[128] However, the next day the paper reported that teenagers had damaged the Opera House: 'some let themselves be carried away and caused damage totalling more than £100 . . . Several seats had their backs kicked out . . . several were torn from their mountings, and one was found outside the theatre after the performance . . . Rotten tomatoes were squashed into the floor and were lying over all parts of the theatre . . . During the show riotous performances were given by teenagers wielding chairs in the stalls.'[129] Devlin's first hit record appeared in June 1958; by May 1959, when he left New Zealand permanently for Australia, his recording sales had reached 'astronomical proportions'.[130]

Christchurch was the home of New Zealand's next big musical sensation, Ray Columbus and the Invaders. 'She's a Mod' was released in June 1964, at the same time the Beatles were touring New Zealand. By the end of the year, it topped the Australian and New Zealand charts. The band became megastars; during an Australasian tour in 1965 with the Rolling Stones, Newbeats and Roy Orbison, they generated as much hysteria as the Stones.[131] 'Til We Kissed', released in 1965, sold over 50,000 copies in New Zealand alone and won the first Loxene Golden Disc Award in 1965.[132] Later described as 'one of the most influential New Zealand has produced',[133] the band broke up in 1965, but its members all went on to have successful individual musical careers.

During the Beatles' 1964 tour of New Zealand, as elsewhere around the world, crowds of frenzied female teenagers screamed and wept uncontrollably upon glimpsing their idols. The tour also exerted an immense influence on the New Zealand music scene. After the Beatles' departure, more bands formed than during any six-month period in the history of Kiwi rock, and every high school started at least one beat band. Music styles changed as 'established groups immediately dropped their Shadows covers and quickly adapted to the pulse of British R&B'.[134] The youth music market was now influenced by British as much as American music.

Teenagers constituted a force to be reckoned with in the music industry. Sales of 45 rpm singles rocketed from 200 in 1955, when they were first introduced, to 576,000 in 1957: most were bought by teenagers.[135] Because, as Peter Downes later pointed out, teenagers spent big money, 'the recording industry changed gear and concentrated on that age group. It didn't happen overnight but it happened fairly quickly.'[136] Rock 'n' roll created such an unprecedented demand for records that distributors and retailers struggled to keep up. Fred Noad, a record distributor, later noted that 'rock and roll [was] the biggest money spinner the industry has ever known'.[137] To meet demand and encourage local artists, big record companies and the growing number of small independents increasingly recorded local artists. The late 1950s and early 1960s were thus boom years for local music: many of the early rock 'n' roll groups recorded and small independent labels proliferated.[138] Musical entrepreneurs emerged to organise tours, promote local and international musicians, and organise concerts and dances. The hit parades, formerly selected by NZBC executives, were now driven by teens.

The teen market extended beyond music. Magazines and retailers quickly exploited youth fashion, another lucrative consumer market.[139] The *New Zealand Woman's Weekly* and *Australian Women's Weekly* (widely available in New Zealand since the 1950s) devoted increasing page space to teenage fashion and beauty. Teenagers also emulated the make-up and fashion trends depicted in American publications such as *Seventeen*, or British ones such as *Honey*. Retail stores catered to teen tastes. It became more and more acceptable for young women not to dress exactly like their mothers. One woman reminisces: 'We bought material and patterns to sew our frocks: ming blue, shocking pink and burnt orange. We also bought wide black belts with large clasps and full net ½ petticoats. One girlfriend had three layers of net with rope sewn through the bottom.'[140] Some girls, emulating widgies, wore black dresses with slits up the sides; others sported woollen dresses that 'fit like a glove', with 'wide spikey belts made of plastic in bright colours, spikey shoes and spikey bras'.[141] But many young women were slower to change. Author and journalist Rosemary McLeod, who finished school in the 1960s, later remarked: 'You left school, you dressed like an image of your mother, you had your first pair of high heels, you went off and had your hair permed. Teenage fashion? You went straight from high school to lipstick, powder, perm, high heels and stockings. One minute you were at school and then you were debbed and looking for a husband.'[142]

Young men too now had choice. It was no longer compulsory to dress like their fathers in grey trousers, dull ties and sports jackets. Many chose to do so, but others struck out boldly: 'My first pay packet went on clothes. A green glitter jacket, yellow shirt with glitter thread, green trou, yellow socks to match the shirt, brown slip-ons. For some reason my parents regarded the slip-ons as the most controversial. And it was so good to get out of the grey uniforms.'[143] A great many young New Zealanders in the 1950s and early 1960s still retained the grey uniforms however. They did not rebel, but rather remained happily accepting of the status quo. Journalist Gordon Campbell, reminiscing about the 1950s, wrote in 1982: 'For every gone cat there were a hundred squares look-ing on in fear, loathing and some curiosity.'[144] Sam Elworthy, in his history of University of Otago students, has written that, after World War II, the student body became both more cohesive and more attuned to traditional student cus-toms and rituals such as capping. In keeping with a new conservatism, univer-sity students felt a strong call to be like the rest of society.[145] Both sexes sported long university scarves of Cambridge blue and gold; women favoured fawn raincoats and men wore flannels or corduroy and a university blazer. By the late 1950s and early 1960s, some long-haired arty beatniks and politicos disdained the world of 'racing, football and booze' created by the 'materialistic boneheads in power', and objected to sport's unrivalled status as 'the national religion'.[146] They remained a small minority, however, until the mid-1960s, when a more rebellious youth culture began to challenge the post-war consensus. Before that time, despite all the media attention and parental concern, the sartorial bravado of various rock 'n' roll enthusiasts or rebellious bodgies and widgies did not signal any real disaffection with the status quo, nor was it linked to political disaffection. But it did reflect the growing power of international cultural influences on the burgeoning youth demographic. With the rise of Beatle mania, pop music shifted away for a time from its former dominance by America to Britain. By the early 1960s, too, the fashion epicentre had moved to 'Swinging London', where Mary Quant sold the first miniskirt from her shop in Carnaby Road in 1964. Despite the desire after the war to bolster and encourage a conventional, homogenous, family-oriented society, parents and government were powerless to suppress these new trends. Youth culture mimicked overseas precedents, emulating not only American and English music and fashion trends, but also what was portrayed on the silver screen.

Movie mad

A new brand of film aimed directly at young people began to appear from the 1950s, as Hollywood started to churn out movies portraying juvenile delinquency, adolescent rebellion, violence, and sex and rock 'n' roll. These films, coinciding with widespread alarm about juvenile delinquency in New Zealand, sparked fears that teens would emulate what they saw on screen. Along with comics and crime novels (Mickey Spillane's in particular), the 1954 Mazengarb Report cited movies as a malign moral influence. The censor was very cautious. *The Wild One* (1953), one of the earliest teen films, starred Marlon Brando as the leader of a motorcycle gang that terrorises a small town. The Auto Cycle Union for one exerted pressure to secure its suppression, arguing: 'this film can do damage to the motorcycling movement and boost the egos of our comparatively tame cowboys. It is up to the Transport Department, the union, the trade, every club and every rider to condemn this film and press for a ban against it.'[147] They were successful. The film was banned in New Zealand until 1977.

Many other teenage films did make it onto New Zealand screens but were cut to remove bad language, sex or violence. *Rebel Without a Cause* (1955), for example, initially banned by chief film censor Gordon Mirams for depicting objectionable behaviour such as 'necking at high school, drinking, slashing of car tyres, and general vandalism, insolence towards adults . . .',[148] was passed by the appeal board with only very minor cuts. When *Rock Around the Clock* screened in 1956, there was understandable trepidation, because screenings in New York, London and Sydney had been followed by riots and vandalism. In New Zealand, Auckland and Christchurch audiences behaved. But in Wellington fans smashed the doors of the Regent cinema and assaulted the manager. In Dunedin, 'movie patrons danced out of a cinema and down Moray Place where they broke a fire alarm'.[149] Fears about negative screen role models were apparently justified.

In June 1956, the censor expunged 'all exaggerated hip movements and references to 'Elvis, the Double Pelvis' from a Cinesound newsreel entitled *Rock'n'roll comes to Sydney*.[150] Nonetheless, films such as *Blackboard Jungle*, *The Tommy Steele Story* and *Jailhouse Rock*, among others, screened to keen audiences: 'The best ever double feature was *Rebel Without a Cause* and *East of Eden*. The Roxy kept bringing it back every few months. I don't know how many times I saw it because it was a continuous theatre and you could stay in all day'.[151]

Teenagers also frequented dark movie theatres for reasons other than just watching the latest film. Writing about the small township of Waitara in 1953 and 1954, Glenda Leader reminisced how every Friday night her crowd of friends attended the local cinema. Upon arrival, girls sat with girls and boys with boys. But once the lights dimmed:

> Seats flap up as their occupants vacate them and the whole theatre seems on the move . . . There is more happening in the theatre than on the silver screen . . . Eyes adjusting to the dark see male arms go around the girls next to them, hands find hands, many pairs of heads merge into single shadows, and contented sighs are heard.[152]

Enthusiasm for movies was not restricted to rebellious or amorous teens. With more than 500 cinemas around the country and average annual attendances of nearly 21 per head of population, the 1940s and 1950s were the golden age of the movies in New Zealand.[153] By 1945, New Zealanders were second only to Americans in the frequency of their cinema-going, and had the highest number of cinema seats per head of population — one for every six people as compared to America's one for every twelve. The smallest communities boasted at least one cinema; many had two.[154]

The great majority of films came from the United States. In 1954, for example, 65 British films were competing for the audience attendance against 279 from the United States.[155] Gordon Mirams wrote in 1946 that New Zealand culture was Hollywood culture:

> We New Zealanders are a nation of film fans . . . It follows that our picture-going habit exerts an enormous influence upon our manners, customs, and fashions, our speech, our standards of taste, and our attitudes of mind . . . If there is any such thing as a 'New Zealand culture', it is a large extent the creation of Hollywood.[156]

Hollywood movies even dictated New Zealand fashion. After seeing Jean Harlow in *Hell's Angels*, women besieged beauty parlours demanding to be made to resemble 'that girl with the lovely shimmering hair'. Women were not alone in emulating American stars: in Ruatoria, Maori wore big hats in honour of the 'Singing Cowboy', Gene Autry.[157]

Mirams was not the only commentator to feel uncomfortable with Hollywood's perceived negative influence on New Zealand culture. In 1953, in response to a film review by Brian Bell, the author and academic Bill Pearson declared: 'American films are far more of a danger than he recognises. They are sometimes the most effective propaganda for the American way of life, for the crusade against communism, for the decivilisation of the "free world" . . . morality never enters the question, ends justify the means . . . Hollywood is a Voice of America indoctrinating millions of foreigners by means of sensation.'[158] There was little in the way of local alternatives however: only four New Zealand films were made between *Rewi's Last Stand* in 1939 and Roger Donaldson's *Sleeping Dogs* in 1977.

Every Saturday night, a large proportion of New Zealanders chose to be happily (if unwittingly) indoctrinated by the 'voice of America', with Westerns, comedies, war films and Disney movies the most popular types of feature films.[159] Going to the movies, the social high point of the week, was an occasion to get dressed up: 'On Saturday night the paper was consulted, the best film chosen, the best clothes donned and off we went.'[160] In provincial centres and city suburbs, many people held permanent reservations for a Friday or Saturday evening. Cinema historian David Lascelles has described how: 'People booked the same seats every week, dressed up and came along in time for the womenfolk to chat in the foyer and their husbands to put their feet up in the auditorium and read the paper. Evening-suited managers greeted patrons by name and would telephone those who failed to turn up and enquire as to the trouble.'[161] Socialising during the intermission was almost as important as the movie itself. In Remuera, one of Auckland's more prestigious suburbs, the community newspaper ran a regular column from the late 1940s called 'As Seen at the Tudor', which simply listed who had been seen at the local movie theatre.[162]

Children eagerly awaited Saturday-afternoon matinees, and cinemas across the country established children's clubs to assure their viewing loyalty. The Kerridge Odeon group, for example, set up the Young New Zealanders' Club, which by 1947 boasted some 75,000 badge-wearing members. On Saturday morning before afternoon matinees, sing-alongs, cartoons, competitions, prizes, magic tricks, lolly scrambles and birthday cakes entertained the young members. The high-spirited audiences, not always easy to control, rolled jaffas down the aisles, shouted encouragement to their heroes, and booed, stamped, and threw jaffas at the screen when disappointed. Sometimes a typewritten message interrupted the screening: 'Be quiet or the film stops'.[163]

In 1960, annual movie admissions peaked at over 40 million. But only a short time later, after national television arrived in New Zealand, the golden age of cinema began to draw to an end. The number of movies attended per annum per person plummeted from 17 in 1961 to 7.3 in 1966, to 4 in 1973.[164] In the ten years between 1962 and 1972, the number of cinemas fell from 545 to 210, which meant that most small towns, and many city suburbs, lost their local cinema.[165] Despite a small revival in numbers in the late 1970s, the arrival of home videos in the early 1980s brought another slump, and by the end of that decade annual cinema admissions fell to a mere six million.[166]

Television takes over
The dramatic decline in movie attendance and in the number of cinemas attests to television's enormous popularity in New Zealand. The new medium, having been long deferred, was embraced all the more fervently. In England, television commenced in 1936, but closed for the war; in the United States, commercial television programming began in 1941.[167] In Australia, it was introduced in 1956. But despite pressure by various individuals and commercial organisa-tions, government purposely delayed the advent of television in New Zealand until 1960. Ronald Algie, Minister of Broadcasting in the National government (1951–57), admitted later: 'As minister of Broadcasting some years ago . . . I took care to do as little as I could towards the introduction of television.'[168]

The reasons for this 'slowing up' were partly financial (it was a much more costly medium than radio) and partly reflected a determination to retain con-trol. Private consortiums and companies such as Pye and the Kerridge organ-isation offered to set up a nationwide television network provided they could have guaranteed access for ten years. But government, realising television was 'a much more potent weapon than [radio] broadcasting',[169] demurred. When transmission finally started on 1 June 1960 it was very limited — two hours a night twice-weekly in Auckland. By January of the next year, Aucklanders could watch television for two and a half hours seven nights per week. By the end of 1961, Wellington and Christchurch had television; Dunedin had to wait until July 1962. Hours of transmission increased slowly, reaching 50 hours per week by 1964.

Once New Zealanders first glimpsed the new medium, enthusiasm was boundless. Crowds blocked pavements outside television retailers, gazing transfixed through the windows at the flickering black-and-white screen.[170] In Symonds Street, Auckland, furniture shops selling sets 'actually put forms on the footpath so people could sit on the footpath and watch TV displays all night. People took to it like ducks to water and just watched it and watched it and watched it.'[171] The number of licence holders jumped from 4809 in 1961 to 80,000 with an estimated 300,000 viewers at the beginning of 1963, to over 500,000 in 1966.[172]

Television irrevocably altered leisure patterns and usurped radio as the primary family home entertainment. An article in the *Mirror* magazine in August 1961 entitled 'Lose a Lounge and Gain a Family' argued that television exerted a beneficial impact on family life: 'The teenagers stay at home at night now . . . Families find fresh contact with each other in sharing and enjoying TV programmes.'[173] Advertisements for televisions often reinforced this view, featuring pictures of cosy domesticity, with a family settled together viewing programmes. Visiting neighbours to watch television (it was not uncommon for those who had a set to invite over those who didn't) also served to strengthen community bonds.

For the first decade, sports telecasts, quiz and music shows, and some local news programmes were the only New Zealand-produced content. Two current affairs shows started in 1964: *Column Comment*, a critical weekly discussion of newspapers, and *Compass*, the first programme to consider domestic and international issues from a New Zealand viewpoint.[174] The latter's scope was somewhat limited, however, and often subject to politicians' interference. Ian Johnstone, an early television interviewer, remembers the ritual involved whenever the Prime Minister was on *Compass*: 'The DG, the director of television, the head of public affairs and the station manager would stand in a row . . . The prime minister would be welcomed and . . . all four gentlemen would bring him up the stairs and I would be there . . . You would then negotiate in as firm a way as you could as the minion there what the questions would be.'[175] As interviews were not live, the Prime Minister could, if dissatisfied, request a re-recording.

Lack of equipment and poor studios, combined with high production costs, meant that New Zealand-produced dramas were practically non-existent. One reviewer lamented in 1961: 'The New Zealand made programme, the home-product that helped establish television in other countries, plays a Cinderella role . . . it is necessary to proceed along a road sign posted in our language and not in one New Zealanders do not speak.'[176] Indeed, New Zealand television relied more heavily than any other country on imported programmes from the United States and Britain.[177] Until 1967, only about one piece of local drama was produced every other year.[178] In 1963, New Zealand was the BBC's biggest customer and also bought heavily from British independent television companies. British programmes were still the dominant fare, but American came a close second.[179]

As with radio, programming was conservative. At first, the NZBC's director Gilbert Stringer viewed nearly all the programmes offered before buying. When he could no longer find time to do so, his wary paternalism continued to directly influence content. In his view, television programming should reflect rather than lead public taste. As he apparently judged public taste to be his own, programme selection was extremely cautious. Nothing experimental was allowed. The country was to be 'led gradually into television fare'.[180]

Like radio, television news bulletins were predominantly information supplied by government departments, combined with a small selection of local items of interest. International content was mainly taken from (and selected by) the BBC. Journalist David Edmunds remembers:

> We really had no chance to select what we wanted. We got what they thought we wanted which tended to be as they would see the Commonwealth through British eyes. They sent us a lot of the Queen doing fairly minor things. We would get a lot from other Commonwealth countries . . . We didn't get stories like Commonmarket [sic] stories, we didn't get many stories from Eastern Europe, from the Soviet Union. We tended to get nice comfortable picture stories.[181]

Until 1969, national networking was not possible, so programmes were flown to the four stations (Auckland, Wellington, Christchurch and Dunedin) and broadcast on separate nights. Consequently, a regional emphasis developed as each station had its own announcing staff and locally produced programmes, gardening, sport, interview, game and music shows. Local television personalities such as AKTV2's Alma Johnson, WNTV1's Relda Familton, CHTV3's Judy Cunningham and DNTV2's Cathy Dowling came under intense public scrutiny. Cunningham later commented: 'People wanted to know all about you . . . [and] felt very much that you belonged to them. They didn't feel at all reticent about coming up to you as if you were an old friend.'[182] Less positively, broadcasters' private lives became the subject of gossip and rumour.

With the exception of regional programmes, most shows were imported, and watching them drew viewers into the common culture of the increasingly global village. Shows like *I Love Lucy* and the *Dick Van Dyke Show* portrayed a sanitised, humorous view of American family life, while English and American hospital dramas such as *Emergency — Ward 10* and *Dr Kildare* unfolded night after night in New Zealand living rooms. Along with other countries around the world, New Zealand enjoyed popular American Westerns such as *Bonanza* and *Rawhide*, and police dramas such as *87th Precinct*. From 1964, *Coronation Street*, a programme that remains popular to this day, began offering an insight (of a kind) into working-class life in the north-east of England.

New Zealand's geographical remoteness seemed to diminish with this closer daily contact with the rest of the world. News was also now more immediate, graphic and powerful. Pictures of the assassination of US president J. F. Kennedy on 22 November 1963 beamed into sitting rooms around the country; in 1964, New Zealanders watched and celebrated the success of their athletes at the Tokyo Olympics. These sorts of achievements on the international stage helped to define New Zealand's distinctiveness and foster a sense of national identity. One important component of the country's character was exceptional sporting prowess.

Sport: pride and prowess

According to Barry Gustafson, sport was 'probably the major catalyst and the most visible expression of New Zealand's emerging sense of national identity during the fifties and sixties.'[183] New Zealanders have always valued physical prowess; it is sportspeople more than intellectuals or artists who are admired and emulated. Given the country's small population, the number of individuals who have achieved international sporting success per capita is remarkable. Although rugby has always been the unrivalled national sport, New Zealand has produced outstanding athletes in a wide range of endeavours, from cricket and athletics to yachting, golf and motor racing. In 1950, when the country proudly hosted the British Empire Games in Auckland, it won 54 medals and placed second overall: per head of population it was the most successful team.[184]

In the two decades after World War II, greater leisure time, more prosperity and increased mobility saw participation levels in sport increase dramatically. New sports clubs formed, and old ones burst at the seams. Never before had so many people joined so many clubs.[185] Almost entirely run by volunteers, who spent long hours raising money, holding working bees, coaching teams and doing the administration, sports clubs were often the centre of social and community life for their members.

At every level, sport was for amateurs. Teams like the All Blacks were made up of working men, who took time off from paid employment to tour. Olympic athletes such as Peter Snell, Murray Halberg and Yvette Williams all held regular jobs and trained at weekends or evenings. This did not prevent them from achieving phenomenal success. Yvette Williams won a gold medal at the Empire Games in Auckland in 1950, and three for the long jump, discus and shot at the Vancouver Empire Games in 1954. She was the first New Zealand woman to win an Olympic gold medal when she competed in the long jump at Helsinki in 1952. Peter Snell won gold at the 1960 Rome Olympics for the 800 metres, and at Tokyo in 1964 for both the 800 and 1500 metres. Murray Halberg won the 5000 metres at the 1960 Rome Olympics.

But funding always remained a problem. In line with the amateur ideology, government kept its distance, but did bestow some indirect help through lottery grants, and from 1962 the Rothmans Sports Foundation became a significant source of funding for all major sports.[186] However, maintaining amateur status gradually became more and more difficult. Bit by bit, commercial sponsorship became a major source of funding, and sportspeople began to turn professional. In 1995, the last bastion of amateurism fell — rugby became professional.[187]

Rugby was of course the most major sport of all. It was, and is, an unwavering national obsession. New Zealanders' passion for the game has deep historical roots: by the mid-1890s, over 300 teams were affiliated to the Rugby Union.[188] After a triumphant tour of Britain in 1905, in which New Zealand won 34 games and lost (contentiously) one, the All Blacks became symbols of the nation, greeted as heroes on their return to Wellington. By 1924, there were 670 rugby teams and an estimated 40,000 players throughout the country.[189] The novelist John Mulgan, writing in the 1940s, described rugby (along with lonely beaches and family at Christmas) as the embodiment of what it meant to be a New Zealander: 'it was best of all our pleasures, it was religion and desire and fulfilment all in one'.[190] After the war, the 'rugby, racing and beer' culture entered a halcyon period. Amendments to the Factories Act in 1945 and 1946 guaranteed a 40-hour working week: men now had more time to play rugby for a local club and to attend games.

The author Piet de Jong has described the huge crowds attending Eltham post-war rugby games, and underlined the importance of such games to the finances of many small businesses in small-town New Zealand.[191] After-match camaraderie was almost as important as the match: spectator and players alike indulged in excessive drinking at the clubs, RSA halls, or pubs (at least until 6 p.m.). In 1958, consumption of alcohol, particularly beer, had almost doubled from its pre-war figure of 48.3 to 94.5. litres a head.[192] Post-match revelry doubtless accounted for a significant part of that rise.

Rugby was compulsory for male primary and secondary school students. When boys were not playing matches, they practised; when doing neither of those two things, they watched and supported: 'Most effort went into rugby. It was warfare. No time for its build-up was begrudged. The juniors were there with the war chants to egg the First XV on to do or die.'[193] Every schoolboy had his hero: 'I went to several rugby games at Athletic Park when I was 11 with my cousin, who was 20. I divided my burgeoning emotions between him and wing-three-quarters Ron Jarden, a real hero of mine. I even named my dog, a Cairn Terrier, Sandy McJarden.'[194]

Not only schoolboys worshipped rugby heroes. Colin Meads, a physically imposing, laconic farmer, became an All Black in 1957. He seemed the embodiment of how New Zealanders wanted to see themselves: decent, pragmatic, modest, and making a living from the land while playing glorious rugby.[195] Before long, he attained the status of a national icon. His biographer Alex Veysey wrote: 'It is not easy to convey what Meads has meant to New Zealanders. They have ridden on his back to glory in the field which means most to them.'[196] Meads's All Black career commenced one year after the famous Springbok tour of 1956.

Rugby inspires the same reverence in South Africa as it does in New Zealand, and the rivalry between the two countries has always been intense and emotionally charged. Donald Woods, a former South African newspaperman, remembers: 'Springbok–All Black rugby was full of tradition and lore. For us it was the greatest of international rivalries, and during World War II whenever South African and New Zealand troops encountered each other, whether in a Cairo street or a London pub, they would scrum down on the spot.'[197] National honour was at stake with each game. In 1949, the Springboks trounced the All Blacks. In 1956, there came a chance for revenge. (Ironically, given its name, the 1949 All Blacks touring team had been, by stipulation of the South Africans, all white.)

The 1956 tour completely dominated New Zealand life for three months. Businesses paused as workers listened to radio commentaries; debates in Parliament were delayed, and schooling was disrupted. The press wrote of almost nothing else. Over 600,000 people from a population of just over two million attended matches in stadiums around the country.[198] In Poverty Bay, for example, an attendance of 16,000 represented about 70 per cent of the total population of the Gisborne area.[199] For many, the games left an indelible memory:

> The 1956 Springbok tour is my first enduring memory of New Zealand sport. I was nine years old at the time, and my father was an enthusiastic follower of the game. We followed the fortunes of the All Blacks, along with the rest of the country. For me, it was like the Farmers' Christmas parade going on for three months. For my father, it was probably more like war without the bullets.[200]

New Zealand won the series in a decisive final test before a crowd of 60,000 in Auckland.

The next clash between the two rivals was in 1960, when New Zealand toured South Africa. In contrast to 1956, however, when the press and public ignored the political situation in South Africa, by this time New Zealanders had awoken to the injustice of excluding Maori from the rugby team. The issue had long been a source of debate, especially since 1928, when the popular George Nepia was excluded from an All Black tour of South Africa. The Citizens All Black Tour Association (CABTA) launched an anti-tour campaign with the slogan 'No Maoris, No Tour'. Despite presenting a petition of over 162,000 signatures to government, it did not succeed in stopping the tour.[201] But it did stir public awareness, which continued to grow until 1981, when it exploded into countrywide public protests and demonstrations against 'the Tour'.

Rugby is frequently described as 'a man's game' because it is tough, physically demanding, and was historically a male preserve. The historian Jock Phillips claims that, in the past, men dominated rugby even at the spectator level: 'While the men were off at Carisbrook and the pub, the women were at home bottling jam, knitting jerseys, looking after the kids or, if they were single, they may well have been at the movies.'[202] Recent research by Jennifer Curtin, however, emphasises that women have long played an important role supporting club rugby in innumerable ways, and have also long been part of the spectator crowd.[203] It is not possible to ascertain with any accuracy how many women went to rugby matches. From the late 1800s, Auckland women had been allowed into matches free of charge, but how many took advantage of this opportunity is not known. In 1949, the Otago Rugby Football Union built ladies' toilets in the ground for the first time. This suggests either increasing numbers of female spectators, or that they were finally becoming more assertive (if the latter, it was somewhat belated, given that women were charged admission to the ground from 1928).[204]

The question of New Zealand women's involvement in sport is beleaguered by lack of data. One of the first studies of recreational patterns, which focused on Auckland in 1971, showed men's participation rate in all sports to be double that of women.[205] On the other hand, women vastly outnumbered men when it came to home-based leisure pursuits such as gardening, sewing, knitting and baking. These findings were reinforced by a survey of 4000 New Zealanders over the age of ten in 1977 which showed that although 18.9 per cent of women respondents cited sport as their preferred leisure category, those who did so were largely in the under nineteen years old group. The percentage fell steeply after women reached their twenties, and had turned to more domestic pursuits.[206] Once married, they usually stopped playing competitive sports such as netball, hockey and tennis. This pattern was doubtless even more marked in the 1950s and early 1960s, before the advent of second-wave feminism. Former national netball coach Lois Muir, who married in 1954 at the age of nineteen, recalls the general expectation that women would relinquish sport after marriage: 'People tended to get married a lot younger then, but very few managed to keep up their sport afterwards. I did and found it very difficult . . . Surprised officials and players would ask what I was doing back there. As soon as you were married they expected you to stay at home, have children, and rock the cradle.'[207]

When women did engage in competitive sports, hockey, tennis, bowls and golf were popular choices, but none more so than netball. As early as 1929, this sport (which until the 1970s was called basketball) was described as the 'national game . . . for women'.[208] Introduced in the first decade of the twentieth century, it was less aggressive than hockey and therefore deemed ideal for women: 'Basketball provides splendid exercise for those engaged in it, but it has the added charm of not being too rough. Science counts in it more than strength, and it is a fact which makes it so good a game for girls.'[209] By 1924, the year the New Zealand Basketball Association formed in Wellington, there were 124 affiliated teams. The first national competition took place in 1926. By 1940, netball had become a compulsory part of the education curriculum. By this time, too (with the exception of the Auckland Catholic Basketball Association), women controlled all aspects of the game — coaching, refereeing and administration. Many moved into these roles after marriage, when they ceased playing.

The number of players increased after the war. By 1948, with the exception of rugby, netball could boast the largest number of players in any sport in New Zealand.[210] Courts were in such short supply that in Greymouth, for example, Saturday mornings in winter saw the main street closed off for several hours to allow play.[211] Saturday-morning games in cities needed to start earlier and earlier, just to get through the growing number of matches. By 1951, 35 provincial associations and 2180 teams were affiliated to the New Zealand Basketball Association.[212] But without the financial and government administrative backing or enormous spectator support that rugby enjoyed, netball struggled. International tours were rare, due to financial constraints, and even when organised, often had to be cancelled. The game received none of the wide media coverage bestowed on male-dominated sports such as rugby or cricket. Journalists did not attend matches, and until the 1970s, match results were only reported when supplied to the press by netball officials keen to give the game at least a mention. Despite all these difficulties, the game continued to expand. By 1988, there were an estimated 155,600 women and schoolgirls playing — nearly 10 per cent of all New Zealand females. Matches are now covered in the press and on television, and financial sponsorship has been forthcoming, as the New Zealand Silver Ferns have established themselves as one of the top teams in the world.[213]

Marching, another sport that, like netball, was considered ideal for women, originated in New Zealand in the 1920s and 1930s, when young women in shop, factory, business, YWCA or church teams marched at local sports and show days. The Physical Welfare Branch of the Department of Internal Affairs, keen to encourage women's participation in sport, promoted it as a summer sport for young women. It had many virtues. It required little finance, no expensive equipment, and no specialist space or facilities. Moreover, it provided discipline and promoted pride in appearance, good posture, friendship and team loyalty. The sport really came into its own in the 1940s, its popularity boosted after the Women's War Service Auxiliary included it as part of their ground drill routine. When the New Zealand Marching Association formed in 1945, the sport was formalised with an organisational structure, rules, grade hierarchy, judging panels and criteria, a national championship and a common set of conditions for competition.[214] Many former male drill sergeants and army officers participated as coaches, administrators and judges: 'adapting their methods of army drill to competition marching'.[215] In contrast to netball, which was completely run by women, marching was a uniquely female sport administered and coached by men.

Marching soon became, along with tennis, the leading summer sport for girls and young women in New Zealand. It had its detractors: in 1952, the poet A. R. D. Fairburn described it as a sign of 'cultural decadence . . . attractive only to factory slaves and office-functionaries already adapted to mechanical regime'.[216] In 1958, the *New York Times* expressed the view that marchers were unfeminine and ungraceful: 'resembling the strutters of dictatorship'.[217] Nevertheless, young women and girls flocked to participate. In 1951, New Zealand boasted over 80 district marching associations. In 1952, a Dunedin marching team toured England and Scotland. By the mid-1950s, 360 teams throughout New Zealand competed in local, regional, inter-island and national competitions. Marching teams also featured in displays of national culture — for example, the civic welcome to the Queen Mother in 1958. No local street parade was complete without teams of girls in regimental uniforms with pleated skirts swinging, keeping perfect time marching in strict, highly disciplined formation. By the mid-1970s, however, the sport's popularity was starting to wane, and by the 1990s only a handful of teams still existed.

Sport continues to loom large in New Zealand life, with ongoing achievements in rugby and sailing being particularly notable. In 2011 — to the great relief of rugby fans throughout the nation — the All Blacks won the Rugby World Cup. (Despite being the only team to play in all the World Cup finals between 1987 and 2003, their last win, prior to 2011, was in 1987.) In sailing, the late Sir Peter Blake achieved two successive America's Cup victories, in 1995 and 2000, and Sir Russell Coutts has notched up four America's Cup victories.[218] The country has earned more than 60 world yachting titles along with more Olympic medals for yachting than for any other sport.[219] New Zealanders also excel at a range of other water sports, regularly winning medals and trophies in rowing, canoeing and boardsailing/windsurfing. Sporting success on the water has been matched on land. In athletics, Yvette Williams, Peter Snell, Murray Halberg and John Walker have joined the national pantheon of sporting legends, while many others compete successfully at international level. Equestrians Mark Todd and Blyth Tait have both enjoyed long and distinguished careers, while Richard Hadlee — the first bowler to take more than 400 test wickets — is widely regarded as one of the greatest fast bowlers and all-rounders in the history of cricket. Bruce McLaren and Denny Hulme became internationally celebrated Formula One racers, and Robert (Bob) Charles, Michael Campbell, and most recently, Lydia Ko have excelled in golf.

A mobile and material lifestyle

During the 1950s, many long-established leisure patterns remained unchanged; New Zealanders continued to enjoy and excel in a range of sports, avidly attended movies, joined and supported a wide range of voluntary organisations, service and church groups, and relaxed at the beach over summer. In the country, and in towns and cities, annual Agricultural and Pastoral Association (A & P) shows provided an opportunity to show livestock and celebrate a range of rural skills and produce. But despite the enduring popularity of A & P shows, from the 1950s rural life was receding, as more people lived in suburbs on the outskirts of cities. Cars and consumer goods fuelled an increasingly mobile and materially oriented lifestyle. Late-night shopping on Friday nights was a keenly anticipated ritual for many, and American-style shopping malls began to spring up around the country. Visiting a basic bach (or for South Islanders, a crib) in a remote spot far away from both suburbia and the demands of city life became a popular summer ritual for many from the late 1940s onward.

City entertainments and amusements were becoming more sophisticated and diverse. By the late 1950s, most New Zealand cities boasted a few European-style cafés such as Harry Seresin's café above Parsons bookshop on Wellington's Lambton Quay; Leon Langley's Attic House in Christchurch; the Kiwi Café on Auckland's Ponsonby Road; and from 1961, Nelson's legendary Chez Eelco, which attracted a bohemian, artistic clientele. Milk bars offering American-style fare abounded, as did takeaway places furnishing Chinese, fish and chips, or pies. A few fine dining establishments, such as Orsini's in Wellington, and Otto Groen's 'Gourmet' in Auckland's Shortland Street, flourished. Eating out gradually became more of a popular pastime; the number of restaurants in Auckland City rose from 59 in 1946 to 184 by 1965.[220] That city, in addition to numerous rock 'n' roll dance venues and jazz clubs, had strip joints, nightclubs, brothels, and even a criminal demi-monde. Cities grew simultaneously more vibrant and more problematic — the latter reflected in the rise of crime and disturbing developments such as motorcycle gangs. Rock 'n' roll and youth fashion mimicked American and British cultural trends, as young people began to signal their distance from the older generation. Paternalistic radio executives found their family-friendly music selections rejected in favour of Elvis. Television underscored and augmented such unsettling international influences — it also mitigated the remoteness that historically played such a crucial role in New Zealand's sense of identity and interactions with the rest of the world.

At the same time, aspects of New Zealand popular culture remained buttoned down. Six o'clock closing endured; shops stayed closed on weekends; licensing laws made it extremely difficult for most restaurants to sell alcohol. The majority of the population quietly accepted the status quo. For every widgie and bodgie, legions of young women in twinsets and pearls and young men in ties and sports coats married young and settled into suburbia to raise a family. Like so much of the country's history after 1945, this pattern mirrored what was occurring abroad. Indeed, New Zealand's post-war popular culture was so directly influenced by overseas precedents that it is often difficult to distinguish its distinctive elements. The historian Miles Fairburn has argued that what was exceptional about New Zealand was its domination by three other cultures — American, British and Australian. A culture comprised of a 'pastiche dominated by imported elements',[221] however, was not that exceptional. Popular culture in the second half of the twentieth century was increasingly transnational; what is interesting and telling is how New Zealanders selected and adapted those elements. By the early 1960s, despite some alarming new trends and fashions among the young, the homogeneity and consensus fostered after the war remained fundamentally intact. Although government could no longer exercise the same degree of control over how people chose to spend their leisure time, or what they listened to on the radio, an underlying consensus about societal norms and aspirations remained. That soon disappeared, however, in the more tumultuous late 1960s and early 1970s, when all kinds of previously shared (or decreed) values became subject to loud and passionate debate.

CHAPTER FIVE

In Ferment

CONTESTED AND PROTESTED VALUES

*Something is happening to New Zealanders. They are behaving in ways
quite uncharacteristic of the species as recognised by their ancestors.*
— New Zealand Monthly Review, May 1965[1]

*We live in a turbulent, nervous, worried world. There is ferment and turmoil
and violence everywhere . . . The building up of colossal armaments by the
superpowers . . . internal strife and fratricidal wars . . . nationalism and racialism
. . . the revolt of youth . . . the sit ins-the sit downs-the love ins-the hippies-the go
slows-the strikes . . . these are the most difficult times in which to govern.*
— Prime Minister Keith Holyoake, 1971[2]

On 1 December 1966, 'Radio Hauraki' began transmitting pop music from
Tiri, a 35-year-old wooden scow painted a defiant bright yellow. Strategically
moored just outside the 3-mile limit of territorial waters in the Hauraki Gulf,
the pirate radio station effectively broke the New Zealand Broadcasting
Corporation's monopoly of the airwaves. The young men responsible — journalists David Gapes and Bruce Baskett, Denis 'Doc' O'Callahan, a radio ham
and yachtie, and radio producer Derek Lowe and announcer Chris Parkinson,
both ex-NZBC employees — joined forces in 1965. In their view, the radio
currently on offer in New Zealand was dull and stifling. A formula that was

already a proven success overseas was needed: a private commercial station dedicated to non-stop pop, interspersed with brief news spots.[3]

Initially, fortune favoured their endeavour. Jim Frankham, an older man who headed a small coastal shipping company, was sympathetic to their cause, and offered the *Tiri* at a low cost along with some financial support. They spotted and promptly purchased an old American wartime radio transmitter for only $300. O'Callahan, described as 'the sort of bloke who makes radio sets go better just by standing near them', used his formidable technical and administrative talents aboard ship while Gapes and Lowe attracted the advertising contracts necessary to make the station commercially viable.[4] But a series of dramatic battles with authorities — some legal and some physical — captured headlines and resulted in frustrating delays. The pirates, their determination hardened by adversity, finally managed to steal out to sea in late November 1966. In 1968, having survived several storms and misadventures, *Tiri* was wrecked on the rocks at the entrance to Whangaparapara Harbour on Great Barrier Island following an engine failure. Frankham provided a new ship, however, and *Tiri II*, also painted yellow, was soon up and running.

Under-resourced but indomitable and enterprising, the young pirates caught the public imagination. They attracted a solid teenage fan-base, but many older New Zealanders also supported the cause. In May 1966, when the proposed venture first hit the headlines, a *Dominion Sunday Times* article entitled 'Break this Monopoly' observed: 'Everyone is exhilarated by a pirate story.' It went on to express the view that the state should release its 'suffocating grip' on the NZBC.[5] 'Radio Hauraki' enjoyed four tumultuous but rewarding years on the water before the Holyoake government finally bowed to pressure and passed legislation opening up broadcasting to private commercial radio. The station got a licence and moved to dry land in 1970.[6]

This story, with its rebellious young protagonists, illustrates the spirited anti-authoritarianism that, in New Zealand as elsewhere, characterised the late 1960s. The fact that the piracy had an overseas precedent (the pirate ship *Radio Caroline* began transmitting off England's Essex coast in 1964) also reflects a key aspect of the time. More than ever before, both literally and figuratively, New Zealand began to open its airwaves, rapidly absorbing and emulating global influences. In the process, government control over the media and various aspects of popular culture steadily decreased. At the same time, a new breed of politician learned to use the media to political advantage.

Like other developed countries around the globe, New Zealand felt the impact of an iconoclastic youth culture. Everything from hair and hem length to drinking habits and drug use, gender roles, sexuality and race relations was suddenly in ferment and contention. In the press, on radio and television, in homes and on the streets, young people raised in a period of peace and prosperity engaged in a conflict of values with an older generation who had experienced the austerity of the Great Depression and the tragic losses of World War II. High-profile contemporary causes such as environmentalism, opposing the Vietnam War, and objecting to nuclear testing in the Pacific attracted many passionately committed young activists. Such movements, while linked to and influenced by international ideas and events, were also underscored by a strain of domestic nationalism. Many of those who advocated these causes wanted to see New Zealand operating as an independent nation, with its own distinctive policies, ethics and priorities. Through activism and protests — some moderate and peaceful but others disruptive and violent — people of all ages expressed varied views about individual and collective values, and about New Zealand's identity and place in the world.

In 1967, the long spell of economic golden weather ended abruptly, with a fall in wool prices. Apart from a brief rally in the early 1970s, this darker economic climate proved tenacious. A worldwide phenomenon, its impacts were keenly felt in New Zealand's export-driven economy. Politicians strove to protect ordinary New Zealanders from rising prices and unemployment, while steering a careful course through the generational and ideological upheavals.

Opening up and acting out

On 29 January 1966 at 12.30 p.m., following a proud speech by Prime Minister Keith Holyoake, Governor-General Brigadier Sir Bernard Fergusson officially opened New Zealand's first international airport at Mangere, Auckland. The culmination of sixteen years of planning, five years of physical work and a £10 million budget, the new airport represented an aviation milestone. Located in the country's most populous and rapidly expanding city, it offered a gateway to the world. One journalist enthused that the facility symbolised 'a new era of progress in a century's steady advancement from primitive days of bullock wagon and pack-track, to the introduction of the jet age, and the thunder of supersonic boom in the high blue sky'.[7] A spectacular three-day air pageant to mark the airport's opening featured over 300 types of planes: modern and vintage, commercial and military, many of which had never before been seen in New Zealand. Thrilled crowds watched aerobatic displays, and parachutists who 'dropped in free falls, trailing streams of vapour strapped to their bodies'.[8] Over 100,000 people, more than 17,000 cars and 100 buses attended the pageant, marvelling not only at the planes but at the new terminal. Operated by the Auckland Regional Authority, this served both domestic and international passengers, and boasted the first air-bridges in the country as well as escalators.[9]

There was reason to marvel and to celebrate. Improvements in jet-plane travel, notably Air New Zealand's purchase of DC8s in 1965, dramatically increased air travel and brought New Zealanders into closer contact with the rest of the world. A trip from Auckland to Sydney now took just four hours. Instead of the long expensive journey to London by ship, jet travel offered an economical alternative of some 24 hours. By 1973, there were no longer any passenger liners coming regularly to New Zealand.[10]

Air travel increased exponentially. In 1963, the New Zealand international carrier Tasman Empire Airways Ltd (TEAL) carried 102,341 passengers; its successor Air New Zealand, created in 1965, had nearly tripled this figure by 1970.[11] By 1967, the South Pacific was the fastest-growing tourist destination in the world. In 1972, total traffic for overseas airlines entering and leaving New Zealand was 519,887; by 1976, it was 884,310.[12] Government investment in tourism, notably through hotel construction under its Tourist Accommodation Development Scheme, proved a sound and timely investment. From 1965 to December 1975, New Zealand's average visitor intake increased by 17.4 per cent a year compared with an international average of 6.9 per cent.[13]

The new improved jet age transformed numerous aspects of economic and cultural life. With its spectacular scenery and vibrant Maori culture, New Zealand had much to offer tourists. On the other hand, overseas visitors did not expect to find shops closed on weekends and a dearth of restaurants or bars. The abolition of the infamous 'six o'clock swill' in 1967 enabled customers to drink in pubs in the evening until 10 p.m. Liquor licensing laws for restaurants gradually relaxed, and by the late 1960s and early 1970s a growing number of ethnic restaurants began to cater not just to tourists but to the increasing number of New Zealanders who had travelled abroad and developed a taste for exotic cuisines.

In 1965, the *New Zealand Listener* noted: 'All New Zealand cities are at least moribund on Sundays, but Wellington is openly and unashamedly dead. It is a shell from which nearly all the weekday people have withdrawn to their homes in the suburbs.'[14] That situation was improving in most places by the late 1960s and had disappeared altogether in others. In Ponsonby in Auckland, for example, a mix of artists, hippies, Pacific Islanders and Maori, university students and transients enjoyed urban pastimes and an inner-city lifestyle seven days a week.

In addition to becoming less like small towns writ large, New Zealand cities grew more ethnically mixed. Although the overwhelming majority of the population remained European/British in origin, by 1971, 9.5 per cent of the 2,862,631 overall population was Polynesian (i.e. 227,414 or 7.9 per cent Maori and 45,413 or 1.6 per cent Pacific Islanders). There were also 12,818 (0.4 per cent) Chinese and 7807 (0.3 per cent) Indians, 2021 (0.1 per cent) Fijians and 4702 (0.2 per cent) other ethnic groups.[15] In the course of the 1970s, urged on by the United Nations and its allies, New Zealand also accepted more than 10,000 South-East Asian refugees from Cambodia, Vietnam and Laos.[16] These immigrants spent their first six months at the Mangere Immigration Hostel, learning English and basic living skills. Many prospered, working in factories, holding several jobs at once, and eventually setting up businesses of their own. While urban race relations posed serious challenges, an increasing diversity of ethnic cultures made for a less monochromatic society.

By 1972, 82 per cent of the population was classified as urban. Agricultural employment, following a trend that started in the 1950s, contracted further as large farms replaced small ones and land prices rose steeply. By 1976, 47 per cent of the nation's male workforce was blue-collar, working predominantly in the building, transport and manufacturing industries. Seventy per cent of Maori males worked in blue-collar jobs and almost all Pacific Island migrants did so.[17] At this stage, most of the 200 business computers in the country were unwieldy mainframes requiring large air-conditioned rooms in which to function. Operators fed them punch cards; the computers then disgorged data out on huge plan printers.[18] Although advantageous for some business functions, few would have predicted their future technological sophistication and far-reaching economic and social ramifications. IBM developed the first 'PC' home computers in 1981, but it was not until the late 1980s, in New Zealand as elsewhere, that the growing use of computers created jobs across many industries.[19]

In the late 1960s and early 1970s, although the 'computer revolution' was some way off, 'revolution' was a word much used by the younger generation. A transnational 'counter-culture', with popular music its deity and long hair, free love and marijuana its attendant priests, rejected parental conventions and values. Local music festivals, inspired by overseas precedents, celebrated an 'alternative' way of life. In 1973, four years after Woodstock, New Zealand had its own Ngaruawahia festival. Later festivals such as Nambassa and Sweetwaters followed in 1976 and 1980 respectively. The atmosphere at these events was charged, excessive, hedonistic, and according to rock historian

John Dix, at times downright dangerous, with people '[d]rowning, stabbing each other, raiding tents and generally making a terminal mess of their lives'.[20] One colourful high-profile counter-cultural phenomenon, Bruno Lawrence's Electric Revelation and Travelling Apparition (BLERTA), a group of actors and musicians led by the charismatic Lawrence, when not performing at festivals, travelled the country in a bus putting on plays, playing music, smoking dope and incurring the ire of local authorities.[21]

Such bohemian antics posed a contrast to the docility decried in Bill Pearson's 1952 essay 'Fretful Sleepers': 'The New Zealander delegates authority, then forgets it . . . generally he does what he is told, partly because everyone else is doing it . . .'[22] Diffidence in the face of authority receded from the late 1960s, as the baby boomers made their voices heard. Some opted to 'drop out', forgo contemporary consumerism, go 'back to the land' and adopt an apolitical stance. Others chose impassioned engagement with causes such as opposition to the Vietnam War, feminism, Maori activism, anti-racism, environmentalism and anti-nuclearism. Both internationally and nationally, the younger genera-tion played a leading role in these movements. A surge in New Zealand births (some 1.5 million) between 1945 and 1970 represented a virtual doubling of the numbers born from 1920 to 1945. University campuses became vital centres of debate and protest: between 1960 and 1975, the number of students enrolled in universities and polytechnics rose from under 20,000 to over 50,000.[23] In the course of the 1960s, New Zealand gained two new universities: Waikato in Hamilton and Massey in Palmerston North; while Auckland, Wellington Christchurch and Dunedin universities became separate entities after the dis-solution of the University of New Zealand in 1961. Not all New Zealanders welcomed this new trend toward higher education. One correspondent to the *Listener* in 1975, for example, after denouncing the various trendy 'isms' espoused by pretentious intellectuals, concluded with a biblical paraphrase drawn from the farm: 'Consider the buttercups in the paddock, they toil not neither do they spin, they're just useless weeds.'[24]

University students, and the academics who taught them, were exposed to international ideas and trends in learning. They had the time to protest and were attuned to a global youth culture angrily averse to capitalist consumerism and convention-bound suburbanism. Tony Judt, describing Europe's youth culture of the 1960s, has noted that:

The gap separating a large, prosperous, pampered, self-confident and culturally autonomous generation from the unusually small, insecure, Depression-scarred and war-ravaged generation of its parents was greater than the conventional distance between age groups. At the very least, it seemed to many young people as though they had been born into a society reluctantly transforming itself — its values, its styles, its rules — before their very eyes and at their behest.[25]

According to Andrew Marr, the legacy of the 1960s in Britain was 'racing consumerism and pop democracy'.[26] In New Zealand, as in America and elsewhere, youth culture similarly became commercialised and conformist in its non-conformity. But many young people also passionately and actively opposed the war in Vietnam. While the older generation might dismiss some of the 'do your own thing', 'back to the land', 'flower power' elements of the late 1960s and early 1970s as 'pretentious and impractical romanticism',[27] opposition to the war gave the younger generation a credence and moral authority it might otherwise have lacked.

Television both played a key role in bringing the Vietnam conflict into powerful view and continued to draw New Zealand into the 'global village'. By 1971, 84.6 per cent of the country's households possessed a television.[28] Daily, in their living rooms, residents could view the suffering in Vietnam, the angry anti-war student protests in the United States, the 1969 Woodstock festival, the fashions and fads sweeping through the developed world. Events at home were also shared. The NZBC footage of the tragic *Wahine* shipwreck on 10 April 1968, in which 53 people lost their lives, screened on televisions around the world.[29]

Although British and American programmes dominated New Zealand television, in 1966 a New Zealand Television Quota Committee formed with the aim of ensuring the preservation of national identity by the planned development of locally made productions. *Country Calendar*, a documentary series about farming and rural life, first screened that year and remains phenomenally popular to this day. Despite the fact that the majority of New Zealanders lived in cities by 1966, there was (and still remains) a strong sense that rural life is intrinsic to national identity. This rural bias extended into politics — for most of the 1970s, farmers, who constituted some 7 per cent of the adult population, comprised about half of the Cabinet.[30] Comedian John Clark's black-singleted farmer Fred Dagg, a popular figure on early 1970s television, satirised aspects of the traditional rural Kiwi male during a time of changing social mores. Murray Ball's popular *Footrot Flats* cartoon strip mined the same rich vein.

From 1967, *C'mon*, a cross between Dick Clark's *American Bandstand* and Britain's *Ready Steady Go!*, occupied the prime-time Saturday-night television spot.[31] The show drew on overseas chart hits while showcasing local talents, as did its popular successor *Happen Inn*, which ran until 1972.[32] From the mid-1970s, programmes such as the soap opera *Close to Home* added New Zealand characters and locales to imported genres, bolstering a sense of national identity and providing a training ground for local actors, writers and producers. Hosting and participating in televised international sporting events also fostered a sense of national identity and pride. The opening ceremonies of the successful 1974 Commonwealth Games in Christchurch, for example, included some 2500 New Zealand schoolchildren in red, white and blue rain slicks (colour television commenced in 1973) running onto the field and forming an NZ74 symbol. The royal family attended and participated in these formal opening ceremonies, which included a Maori concert and haka. Television both connected New Zealand to global popular culture and helped to define its identity within that culture.

The media, especially television, now played a crucial role in presenting and interpreting contentious causes and issues. Activists and politicians on the left and right used it to woo the hearts and minds of the inactive but crucial silent majority. For example, from 1968 the influential New Zealand television current affairs programme *Gallery*, produced by Des Monaghan, offered an assertive approach to current affairs and a new appreciation of the journalists' mandate as a public watchdog. Dr Brian Edwards, the articulate expatriate Irishman fronting the show, adeptly engaged with politicians, drawing out their views. Elections focused increasingly on images and personalities. During his last seven years in office, Keith Holyoake's aversion to the new medium considerably weakened his leadership. He did not shine on the small screen, and resented its new-found influence in politics. In 1971, a year before the Prime Minister's long-anticipated retirement, Brian Edwards observed:

> Holyoake's reputation as a television performer could not have been worse . . . he
> expected as of right to be told the questions in advance and had been known to
> refuse to answer certain questions at all . . . The studio Holyoake was everything
> that an interviewee should not be — evasive, pompous, patronising, overbearing,
> long-winded, repetitious, pretentious, boring.[33]

By contrast, Robert Muldoon, a rising young National politician who in 1967, aged 45, became the country's youngest ever Minister of Finance, ably exploited television. In *The Rise and Fall of a Young Turk* (1974), the first of several popular autobiographies, he wrote: 'In the early days I used to watch playbacks to see if they came over as me. When I was satisfied with that I simply used the same style, relaxed and concentrated on what I wanted to say.'[34] This 'style' — speaking straight down the barrel of the camera and expounding one or two easy-to-comprehend points — served him well.

Norman Kirk, who emerged in 1969 as leader of the Labour Party, also used television adroitly. A formidable debater with a facility for bold language, his views about New Zealand's place in the world began to attract attention. He advocated a new style of government, more in tune with the times and responsive to change. Conservative elements in New Zealand society, however, did not endorse this positive response to change. Rather, they felt uneasy about the permissive paths that opened up in the late 1960s, resented protesters who engaged in violent tactics or overstepped the law, and lamented the decline of former unquestioned standards of propriety.

Secular and permissive: moral battle lines

From the latter 1960s, a marked shift occurred, both internationally and nationally, toward a set of cultural values not only more liberal and sexually permissive but more secular. The percentage of those who identified as having no religion or who objected to stating their religion in the national census rose from 9.1 per cent in 1966 to 10.6 per cent in 1971, to 17.2 per cent in 1976.[35] Professed (as opposed to actual) attendance at all the major churches in New Zealand declined markedly from the 1960s: Anglicanism from 33.7 per cent to 18.4 per cent between 1966 and 1996; Presbyterianism from 21.8 per cent to 13.4 per cent; Methodism from 7 per cent to 3.5 per cent, Catholicism from 15.9 per cent to 13.8 per cent. The only increase occurred in the Pentecostal churches which increased fivefold between 1966 and 1981, with the last five years of that period witnessing the greatest rise.[36]

Even some professional clerics appeared to be following the liberal secular trend. In 1967, Lloyd Geering, Principal of Knox Presbyterian Theological College, was tried for heresy by the General Assembly of his church for challenging the orthodox version of the resurrection. He was acquitted but eventually left his former position and took up the post of foundation professor of religious studies at Victoria University in 1971, where he was soon 'proclaiming the end of all traditional religions'.[37]

Broader social patterns influenced the trend towards an increasingly secular society. Women's increasing participation in the workforce, for example, adversely affected church-related activities. With the demands of running households and paid employment, many women now had little time left over for church and other voluntary associations. The historian John Stenhouse has noted that: 'As the suburbs expanded, more people spent more time each day commuting between home and work, leaving less time and energy for much else. Civil society began to creak.'[38]

To the dismay of some more traditional Christians, sex (and sexuality) was by the late 1960s and early 1970s openly discussed as never before, and statistics underscored the more carefree and careless attitudes that the birth-control pill helped to engender. In 1967, for example, 27 per cent of babies born to mothers in the 16 to 25 age group were illegitimate; some 40 per cent of first babies born to married women arrived less than eight months after marriage.[39] In the 1950s, news that teenagers engaged in premarital sex was deemed scandalous and a sign of imminent moral collapse. By the late 1960s, youthful premarital sex no longer constituted 'news'. Increasingly, too, with the rise of the feminist and gay rights movements, the nuclear heterosexual suburban family came under critical scrutiny. This was an age of experimentation in personal relationships, with many young people finding 'liberation' through unconventional arrangements such as communes and 'open' marriages. Tim Shadbolt, a university dropout turned concreter and the poster boy for youthful rebellion in New Zealand, writing later in life about the commune he lived in at Huia in the Waitakeres from 1972, emphasised the idealism of those times:

> The commune was not just a rejection of orthodox society. We genuinely believed we could create a whole new world. We would reverse the history of evolution, the agricultural revolution, the Industrial Revolution, and all the wars and famines of the world simply by staying at home and growing organic vegetables.[40]

Communes came in all shapes and sizes. By 1975 New Zealand had about 200. Some opposed consumerism and private property; others rejected the traditional gender roles of the nuclear family in favour of more 'open' relationships; others advocated environmentalism and self-sufficiency.[41] All, however, shared the desire for a lifestyle that diverged from the conventional parental mainstream.

Only a minority of young people in the late 1960s and early 1970s embraced communal living, but New Zealanders of all ages experienced the various impacts of an increasingly permissive age. Monte Holcroft, the veteran journalist and *Listener* editor, in a somewhat prematurely elegiac editorial about the 'age of permissiveness' written in 1973, described the 'loosening up' that New Zealand experienced from the latter 1960s onwards:

'Permissive' became a vogue word, but it described better than any other, the temper of the age; an impatience with control or discipline, a conviction that nothing should be hidden. The cinema entered a new phase of candour, and nudity reached the theatre. Four-letter words came so much into use that printers aged prematurely if they had to produce students' papers.[42]

Contemporary debates over film censorship offer an insight into the battle lines arising from the new permissiveness (as well as which side was prevailing). Cinemas, in response to television's capture of the family market, moved toward more sexually explicit and violent films, a trend illustrated by film classification statistics. In 1965, the censor found 39 films suitable for general exhibition. By 1976, this number had decreased to ten. Meanwhile, those deemed suitable for 'adults only' (people over sixteen) rose from 22 in 1965 to 36 in 1972; and films 'restricted' to those above a certain age (usually 18, but from 1972 onwards, 20 was sometimes specified) rose from 16 in 1965 to 39 in 1976.[43]

What was considered acceptable for public viewing also changed rapidly. In 1967, the explicitly sexual language in *Ulysses* caused the New Zealand film censor to insist that audiences watching it be segregated by gender. But by 1971, female nudity in *Blow Up* caused no problem whatsoever; a year later, *A Clockwork Orange* (rated R20) included scenes of rape and murder. Whereas obscene language had previously been censored, by 1975 the film *Lenny* (about American comedian and master of profanity Lenny Bruce) passed uncut with an R20 restriction. One notable exception to the generally more free and open censorship decisions prevailing in the late 1960s and early 1970s was *Last Tango in Paris*. This film was not shown in New Zealand until 1976, following the advent of a less restrictive Cinematograph Films Act.[44]

This 1976 legislation represented the (undesired) culmination of a protracted morality campaign commenced in 1970 by Patricia Bartlett, a teacher and former Catholic nun. Disgusted by what she saw as society's increasingly lax morals, 'Miss Bartlett', as she was known, organised a petition of 49,802 signatures seeking a tightening of film censorship laws to include scenes of sexual intercourse, displays of nudity, and same-sex love scenes as indecent. Although unsuccessful, she remained undeterred and quickly founded the Society for the Protection of Community Standards (SPCS). By 1975, its numbers had reached 21,000.[45]

The SPCS battled sexual permissiveness on several fronts apart from film. In 1972, for example, when theatrical impresario Harry Miller was acquitted of indecency charges for staging *Hair* in New Zealand (some four years after its triumphant premiere overseas), Miss Bartlett and the Society denounced the decision as opening 'the floodgates of decadence'.[46] She also had several skirmishes with shopkeepers over the years for selling pornographic magazines or books. The Society achieved some success with regard to the latter in 1972 when certain amendments in line with its submissions were made in regard to the Indecent Publications Act 1963. However, this success galvanised Miss Bartlett's main opponents, notably the various liberal-minded film societies in New Zealand, who began to lobby intensively and concertedly for no censorship to adult films. The 1976 Cinematograph Films Act, viewed as a victory for their cause, gave applicants discretion as to whether or not to accept the censor's cuts. Moreover, the censor's decisions were now no longer based on what was 'decent' but what would be injurious to the public good.[47]

Although frequently mocked and ridiculed in the media, Patricia Bartlett had, as the Society's large membership indicates, a core of committed supporters. In 1977, she was made an OBE for service to the community. Interestingly, the various churches, which were moving towards a more liberal position on many issues, including censorship, offered little support for her or the Society. For example, the New Zealand Inter-Church Council on Public Affairs (which included the Anglican, Presbyterian, Roman Catholic, Methodist and Baptist churches) expressed approval of the proposed Cinematograph Films Bill in 1976; only the Associated Pentecostal Churches of New Zealand and the Church of Jesus Christ of Latter-day Saints opposed it.[48]

The latter churches figured prominently among those involved in another high-profile protest against society's perceived moral decay and permissiveness. In 1972, some 70,000 New Zealanders participated in 'Jesus marches' throughout the country. Auckland's effort in May attracted some 10,000 participants; Christchurch's in September boasted around 15,000, many of them university students. The last and largest march, to Parliament in Wellington on 8 October 1972, involved between 15,000 and 25,000 people (estimates vary). Described as a 'grass-roots conservative Christian response to changes in society',[49] the marches were both a protest against moral decline and a positive celebration of Jesus.

Unlike the 'Jesus people' in America, most of whom were counter-cultural hippies, Jesus marchers in New Zealand came from all ages and income brackets. The marches were loosely modelled on Britain's Festival of Light of 1971 (although, again, marchers here were generally less 'alternative' than in Britain). Participants derived from every religious denomination, but Pentecostal and charismatic churches played a prominent role. One leading figure was the Maori evangelist Muri Thompson; another was the Auckland civic leader and one-time mayor Keith Hay. The marches acted as 'a catalyst for increasing conservative Christian mobilisation over the next 15 years',[50] and for an upsurge in support for charismatic and Pentecostal churches. Whether protesting declining morals or pushing for legislative or attitudinal change, committed minorities — conservative and liberal — held strong views about what sort of society New Zealand should become.

Protest and identity: Vietnam

One reason some conservative Christians may have been drawn to the Pentecostal and charismatic churches is disapproval of other denominations' opposition to the Vietnam War. From the outset, despite the danger of being lumped with leftist radicals and alienating their own flock, many clerics from the established churches energetically protested against the war. Opinions diverged within and between denominations, but as the historian Laurie Guy has noted, 'the public voice of the churches was on the whole against the war'.[51] By contrast, most New Zealanders supported it. The only national opinion poll conducted about New Zealand involvement in the Vietnam War, in July 1965, showed 70 per cent of the population believed the level of military aid offered by the government was appropriate or should be increased; 23 per cent thought it too much.[52]

But although the majority endorsed the country's involvement, the opposed minority were passionate and proactive. When a visit to Wellington by Henry Cabot Lodge, the US ambassador to South Vietnam, coincided with the Campaign for Nuclear Disarmament's (CND) annual peace march,[53] the idea arose among marchers to hold all-night vigils outside Cabot's hotel. Within a week, a Committee on Vietnam (COV) formed in Wellington. More COVs in other cities soon followed. The early activists included CND members, church members and Christian pacifists, left-wing groups such as the Progressive Youth Movement (originally the Youth Action Committee on Vietnam and the Socialist Action League), trade unionists, some communists, left-leaning academics, politically radical students, and Quakers.[54] Protester Cath Kelly later recalled her family's time-consuming dedication to the cause: 'It was the subject of discussion at breakfast, dinner and tea — what was the next move to try and get New Zealand troops taken out and the war ended.'[55]

New Zealand's anti-war movement was characterised by a lack of over-arching structure, diversity, and a persistent localism.[56] In addition to the local COVs, different groups and committees on Vietnam burgeoned, engaging in heated disagreement over ends and means. Protests ranged from burning flags and hurling smoke bombs to silent vigils, rallies, marches and sit-ins, to more conventional but equally effective tactics such as newsletters, letters to the editor, articles, leaflets, posters and pamphlets. 'Teach-ins', an idea copied from America, involved seminars led by academics, church people, journalists, activists and politicians. They became an important means of extending debate about Vietnam to wider numbers of people outside of left-wing and pacifist fringe groups. The first teach-in, held at Victoria University in July 1965, lasted over fourteen hours and attracted an audience of over a thousand.[57]

Visits by VIPs provided an ideal focus for protests. When President Lyndon Johnson visited in 1966, he received a warm welcome, with up to 200,000 New Zealanders lining the streets to catch a glimpse of him. At the same time, a 300-strong anti-war demonstration took place in Auckland, along with smaller ones in Christchurch and Dunedin, and a 1500-strong demonstration in Wellington. In 1966, during Vice President Hubert Humphrey's visit, four young people chained themselves to the steps of Parliament in protest. A year later during a visit by Air Marshall Ky, Prime Minister of South Vietnam, 'Ky protest committees' sprang up around the country. Later, in August 1967, when the US president's advisors Clark Clifford and General Maxwell Taylor visited Wellington, 2000 people protested outside Parliament, and Victoria University students bore a coffin 'in memory of New Zealand democracy'.[58]

In 1968, a 'Peace, Power and Politics' conference, held at the same time that the SEATO Council of Ministers met in the capital, attracted several international speakers, including Irish MP and intellectual Conor Cruise O'Brien and V. K. Krishna Menon, former Indian Defence Minister and architect of that country's non-alignment policy. O'Brien led a march on Parliament, and nailed a petition on the door. One crucial appeal, for a non-aligned foreign policy, underlined the degree to which the domestic debate about Vietnam had become focused on the relative 'independence' of New Zealand foreign policy.[59] In addition to the many international ideas and events influencing the anti-war movement, there was an element of nationalism.

The anti-war activist and publisher Alister Taylor later recalled that the conference received 'total media penetration'.[60] While opinions about the war in the press and correspondence columns remained mixed, all newspapers unanimously expressed the view that unruly or violent protests would antagonise ordinary law-abiding New Zealanders. During the 1969 election campaign, for example, jeering anti-war protesters disrupted several election meetings around the country, throwing firecrackers before being seized by police. The press united in denouncing the behaviour, predicting that 'a massive backlash against the demonstrators may outweigh all other factors in returning the government to office'.[61]

During that campaign, the opposition Labour leader Norman Kirk announced that, if elected, his government intended to withdraw New Zealand's troops from the conflict. National, however, won the election, and New Zealand maintained its presence in Vietnam. Public opposition to the anti-war protesters' antics may, as Kirk believed, have played a part in Labour's loss.[62] However, over the course of the next three years, whatever their views on the more radical, unruly elements among the anti-war movement, opposition to the war by mainstream New Zealanders rose to new levels.[63]

The more radical elements of the anti-war movement also stepped up their efforts. On 16 January 1970, during a visit to Auckland by American Vice President Spiro Agnew, police forcefully dispersed a core group of about 300 people (many of them members of the Progressive Youth Movement) still protesting outside Agnew's hotel in Princes Street at 11.45 p.m. The *New Zealand Herald* reported: 'Before the crowd had time to move off dozens of policemen waded in. Many of the young demonstrators were pushed to the ground. Some were kicked.'[64] A bitter controversy erupted over the degree of force the police used. Eventually an investigation by Ombudsman Sir Guy Powles found fault on both sides. After the Agnew fracas, a series of attacks and bombings took place around the city. Angry at *Truth* newspaper's support for the police's behaviour, on 27 January 1970 a 'direct action' fringe of the anti-war movement, the ALF (Auckland Liberation Front), attacked the paper's office in Symonds Street with ball-bearing missiles fired from a customised rifle. A note at the scene read: 'The damage done to this building tonight is because this building houses the most bigoted right wing press in the country. This is only a warning. Print the real Truth.' Over the next few months the group bombed more targets, including the Fox Street military base in Parnell, the Auckland Supreme Court and the Wellington headquarters of the SIS. Eventually, in late 1970, three men were tried for the bombings. John Bower and Bob van Ruyssevelt were sentenced to four years' jail and Kevin Bower received four years' borstal.[65]

In April 1970, the American and South Vietnamese incursion into Cambodia sparked angry protests in the United States and around the world, including New Zealand. Then, on 4 May, the Ohio National Guard fatally shot four anti-war student protesters at Kent State University. New Zealand's *Monthly Review* commented sombrely on the new militancy among university students and staff following this event:

Effigies have never been burned in our streets before. Students at our universities have never boycotted classes before in protest at an incident occurring on the other side of the world. Graduation ceremonies have never before seen, added to the colourful array of academic gowns and hoods, anything like white armbands labelled 'CAMBODIA, KENT' . . .[66]

One of the most dramatic protests occurred in Auckland where students in capping processions carried four bloodstained coffins bearing the names of those killed in Ohio. Nixon's unexpected re-escalation of the war drew criticism even among those formerly supportive of the American administration. At this time, mass mobilisations — mirroring the 'moratoriums' in America and Australia — marked a high point of popular support for the anti-war movement.

The first Mobilisation Day, on 17 July 1970, saw marches and teach-ins in Wellington and Auckland. Well-coordinated and non-violent (the Progressive Youth Movement disassociated itself from this 'overcautious' event), it attracted some 4000 people nationwide.[67] As the National government gradually reduced New Zealand's presence in Vietnam (there were only about 264 service personnel there by May 1971), a committee formed in Wellington at a National Anti-War Conference to plan the next 'mob'. Their work preparing newsletters and badges and newspaper adverts paid off dramatically. The mobilisation on 30 April 1971 — the largest anti-war demonstration to date — drew between 29,000 and 35,000 nationwide.[68] Despite increasing factionalism among the various groups comprising the Wellington and Auckland COVs, another mobilisation, organised for 30 July 1971, attracted some 32,000 marchers nationwide. On 14 July 1972, a final 'mob' took place, with the largest crowd (over 10,000) in Christchurch; Wellington's 3000 turn-out represented only half of the figure for July 1971 however.[69]

One notable aspect of the final 'mob' was the appearance of the 'politics of identity'. Gays, Maori, women and even high school students marched both as members of a particular group and as opponents of the war.[70] By this stage, anti-Vietnam War feeling, formerly not a serious hindrance to National's popularity, added to Labour's pre-election momentum, with Norman Kirk eloquently espousing justice, humanity and an independent foreign policy from the hustings. Historian Roberto Rabel has pointed out that 'Growing public acceptance of the anti-war movement's critique challenged the presiding Cold War consensus and led to more widespread questioning of the costs of unstinting support for the United States. It also meant foreign policy could no longer be the exclusive domain of politicians, diplomats and bureaucrats.'[71]

The anti-war movement, in disagreeing with the policies and actions of the United States, fed a growing sense that New Zealand needed to find a more independent identity on the international stage. People's right to voice concerns and take action to effect change, a suspicion of imperialism and of superpower (especially American) motives: these were part of the movement's legacy. At the same time, in the course of opposing the war, some young people 'developed a disrespect for the entrenched political parties, the Labour Party as much as the National Party, and the whole system'.[72] Tim Shadbolt's 'counter-culture' memoir *Bullshit & Jellybeans*, published in 1971, offers a taste of how the younger generation's opposition to the Vietnam War fed its disdain for politicians: 'Anyone who has seriously studied this war must realise our country is an absolute shithouse to support it. Anyone who supports the war is either an ignorant fascist peasant, or worse still — a politician'.[73] The book's title derives from an incident on 23 March 1970 when Shadbolt's use of indecent language in a public place (in this case, standing on a truck outside Mt Albert Grammar School) resulted in his arrest. He had referred to New Zealand's involvement in Vietnam as 'based on a firm foundation of solid bullshit'.[74] Reviewing Shadbolt's book in the *New Zealand Listener*, Alexander MacLeod noted that its author, 'far from being the desperate renegade his detractors paint him', was in many ways 'a typical New Zealander — by turns impatient, sentimental and ingratiating, light on analysis and strong on attitudinising'.[75] Shadbolt also wrote the original prose poem that the radical activist Auckland Progressive Youth Movement modified and then used as its 1970 manifesto. A hard-hitting indictment of the older generation, this began: 'Damn your war. / Damn your petty morality. / Damn your closed eyes when a peasant's guts spills into Vietnam's bomb-soaked soil — and open wide when someone says damn . . .'[76]

New Zealand Vietnam War veterans received only one official 'welcome home'. In May 1971, 161 Battery and members of the SAS who had served in Vietnam marched up Queen Street in Auckland. Although cheering supporters lined the street, a small group of protesters tossed eggs and red paint and shouted insults. Several threw themselves under the feet of the band, causing an altercation that ended up with one protester taking the battery commander to court for offensive behaviour. (The judge dismissed the case as 'misconceived'.) Not uncommonly, anti-war activists assailed returned Vietnam veterans, who frequently found themselves embroiled in arguments or fights, and denounced as mercenaries or 'child killers'.[77] Veteran Dave Douglas later commented: 'You were sort of expecting to be, I suppose, welcomed with open arms, so to speak. But we weren't, you know. We were shunned'.[78]

The majority of New Zealanders continued, if not to actively endorse official policy on the war, to accept it philosophically. The Christchurch *Star* wrote in August 1971: 'there has been an abundance of sound and fury but with this country's military contribution never rising above 550 men — more a moral than an effective commitment — Vietnam did not personally affect the majority of people'.[79] According to Holyoake's deputy and successor Jack Marshall, 'the great New Zealand public never really got worked up about the Vietnam war'.[80] Nevertheless, the anti-war movement had a significant impact on New Zealand society. Labour's opposition to it from 1969 ended a long-standing bipartisan consensus on foreign policy. Several of the movement's ideas about peace and support for an independent foreign policy extended into other protest movements and causes, most notably the anti-nuclear campaign. One anti-war activist later declared: 'I don't know that we'll ever be able to fully appreciate the significance of the Vietnam war in shaping people's opinions for a generation, to generalise them on to contacts in sport with South Africa, race relations in New Zealand — a whole broad range of issues.'[81]

Saving Manapouri

In 1969, as anti-Vietnam War demonstrations gathered momentum, another protest movement began to attract media attention. The 'Save Manapouri Campaign' united a variety of New Zealanders — young and old, radical and conservative, urban and rural — from public servants, academics, and eminent scientists to farmers, housewives and 'back to the land' enthusiasts.

By the late 1960s, both the media and a substantial body of international literature warned of resource depletion and looming environmental catastrophe. Protecting the environment was a topical contemporary cause, but the roots of the Manapouri dispute reached back to 1959, when the Labour government secured an agreement with an Australian company to develop Lake Manapouri's hydro-electric potential to fuel an aluminium smelter. After the company reneged on the costly task of building the smelter, the government assumed responsibility for both the smelter and the hydro-electric project. The latter drew water from the West Arm of Lake Manapouri, drove it through underground turbines and out a tailrace into Doubtful Sound. The Comalco aluminium smelter built at Tiwai Point on Bluff Harbour reaped the benefits of this cheap electricity.[82]

In 1969, when the West Arm turbines became operational, it was revealed that empowering legislation from 1960 allowed the lake to be raised up to 11 metres, to permit generation of an extra 200 megawatts of electricity. Because of a connecting waterway, Lake Te Anau would also be raised in the process. Environmental impact reports outlined the dire repercussions of this scheme: some 160 miles of shoreline would be inundated and 800 hectares of shoreline forest drowned, along with all of Manapouri's beaches and 26 of its 35 islands; landslides might occur on steep slopes surrounding the lake; tree trunks and branches could become hazards for people seeking recreation; and silting would destroy the lake's ecology. Such threats to two of the South Island's scenic treasures seemed a high price to pay for a small increase in electricity output. Moreover, farms in the Waiau Valley would be destroyed as would tourist revenues generating an estimated $10 million annually.[83]

In October 1969, National Party MP Norman Jones launched the Save Manapouri Campaign at his home in Invercargill. Its driving force, Ron McLean, a Southland farmer and community leader, was a far cry from the popular stereotype of a long-haired protester. Nineteen regional Save Manapouri branch committees quickly sprang up around the country. Newspapers unanimously rallied behind the campaign, as did several prominent New Zealanders. The national committee, with McLean as president, included VIPs Sir Jack Harris, Sir Ronald Algie, zoology professor John Salmon and Dr (later Sir) Charles Fleming, scientist and pioneering conservation advocate.[84] In Auckland, Sir Edmund Hillary joined that city's Save Manapouri Committee, created in 1970.

Innovative techniques helped to raise both funds and public environmental awareness. Some 30,000 share certificates were issued to promote the cause and any surplus income to the issue was promised to Fiordland National Park for improving public amenities. On 26 May 1970, Royal Forest and Bird Protection Society officers wheeled a trolley with a 264,907-signature petition into Parliament objecting to raising the lake — by far the largest ever submitted. In 1970, Wellington's *Dominion* newspaper named Ron McLean New Zealand's 'Man of the Year'. There were national conferences on Manapouri, and numerous protests with placards, banners and chants.[85]

The government, taken aback by the public response, appointed a Commission of Inquiry which, after considering some 2000 pieces of evidence, concluded that the Crown was contractually bound to raise the lake. The campaigners vowed to fight on. In November 1971, when Prime Minister Holyoake and a few cabinet members flew to Invercargill to open the aluminium smelter at Tiwai Point, they encountered some 1000 protesters. One of the placards read: 'Who Owns This Country: The New Zealand People or Comalco?' After

Holyoake, speaking through a loud-speaker, assured the crowd that it belonged to the people, he was jeered.[86]

As the stalemate continued, in March 1972, 'with Manapouri as its midwife',[87] the first Conference on Environment and Conservation was held. Four months later, National created the Commission for the Environment, a concessionary measure that did not repair the dent to its popularity Manapouri had made. The Save Manapouri Campaign had raised questions concerning national values, and in doing so highlighted a critical, still ongoing debate about the environmental and cultural cost of 'progress' and economic development. Its success 'kick-started the politicisation of the environment',[88] signalling to politicians that managing and maintaining the nation's natural resources could no longer be left to politicians making decisions behind closed doors.

Preserving time: environmental awakening
Environmental issues now exerted an increasing impact on party politics, with the Labour Party in particular taking a strong pro-environment stand during the 1972 election campaign. One Labour poster depicted a large preserving jar labelled 'Environment, 25/11/72'. Inside the jar, a line drawing depicted various native flora and fauna while a text caption announced: 'It's preserving time. It's time to preserve what we have, while we still have it.'[89]

A few months prior to the election, in May 1972, the Values Party formed in Wellington. Sometimes billed as the first 'Green' party in the world, its primary aims of zero population and zero economic growth reflected a desire to 'meet the needs of the people rather than the needs of the system'.[90] A number of its policies — such as encouraging waste recycling, sustainable resource management, de-emphasising cars and investing in rapid-rail transit systems, preserving and maintaining heritage buildings, and advocating MMP — proved prescient. Several founding members of the future Green Party of Aotearoa New Zealand, formed in 1990 (notably Jeanette Fitzsimons, Rod Donald and Mike Ward), were active in the Values Party, which earned 2 per cent of the vote in 1972 and an impressive 5.2 per cent in 1974.[91] Values supporters, most of whom worked in the public service, the health sector and teaching, wanted to lift the country out of a perceived 'depression of values'.[92] They associated this depression with materialistic capitalism.

Controversies surrounding the environmental cost of economic development were fed by television and press reports of similar issues overseas, and by leading environmentalists, many of whom had trained abroad. In addition to having been influenced by overseas ideas and movements, several of these individuals also played a role in international environmental lobby groups and organisations. The geologist, ornithologist and conservationist Charles Fleming (1916–1987), for example, was elected to the Royal Society of London and to life membership of several other prestigious overseas scientific bodies and organisations. Bing Lucas (1925–2000), the first Director of Parks and Reserves in the Department of Lands and Survey in the 1970s and later Director General of Lands and Survey, was associated with the International Commission on National Parks for three decades, actively involved with the International Union for the Conservation of Nature in Switzerland, and vice-chair of World Heritage in 1995.[93]

These eminent environmentalists would seem at first glance to have little in common with more radical 'back to the land' types. In terms of preferred tactics and lifestyles, differences were indeed often vast. Yet the apparently disparate environmentalist elements shared an intense emotional commitment to the cause. A shared perception of the natural world as a source of salvation from the evils of modern man-made society gave environmentalism cohesion, force and crusading zeal. The value ascribed to the pristine landscape and natural resources of New Zealand fostered a form of eco-nationalism. At the same time, this linked into and was fostered by broader international ideological currents and environmental lobby groups and organisations. If these national and international strands represented the combined forces of good, they were engaged in a series of skirmishes with both the imperatives of global capitalism and national economic 'progress' and development.

The campaign to save native forests, which commenced in the early 1970s, offers an insight into the interplay between national and international environmental interests, the tension between a desire to preserve New Zealand's natural heritage and the requirements of (often international) business interests, and regional socio-economic considerations (notably work in native timber sawmills). In 1971, the Forest Service signalled its intention to log some 340,000 hectares of indigenous forest — mainly beech but some rimu — in Westland, Nelson and Southland, to be chipped for the Japanese pulp industry. This plan evoked a chorus of irate responses from conservation groups, public servants, scientists, concerned private citizens, counter-culture radicals and tangata whenua. Forest and Bird secured 80,000 signatures on a petition for a stay of execution on the logging. Opponents effectively wanted a say in decisions regarding national resource management.[94]

Logging continued, but in 1974 the Nature Conservation Council and a newly formed Beech Council pursued the issue of protecting native forests.

Rush to Destruction (1975), a book by Graham Searle, a young science graduate and co-founder of the British arm of Friends of the Earth, 'marked a new
kind of public style in environmental campaigning'.[95] It presented a number of
economic arguments, sceptically assessed company tax incentives and other
subsidies supplied by taxpayers, and reminded readers that while New Zealand
native forests rapidly diminished, Japan's remained intact.[96] Within one month
of publication, government launched an investigation into beech felling and
a subsequent report concluded that beech utilisation in both Westland and
Southland made 'unacceptable demands on the environment'.[97]

Despite this success, felling of native forest continued. Guy Salmon and
his partner Gwenny David formed the Native Forests Action Council (NFAC)
in 1975. One of its early initiatives, the 1975 Maruia Declaration (signed by 40
conservationists on the scenic banks of the Maruia River near Lewis Pass),
wanted native forests recognised and protected in law. It advocated that logging
of state-owned virgin forests be phased out by 1978, and that remaining publicly owned native forests be placed 'in the hands of an organisation that has
a clear and undivided responsibility to protect them'.[98] Bitter debates ensued
within the conservation movement between groups such as the NFAC, which
accepted some 'sustainable yield' development (its plans in 1977 recommended
maintaining West Coast sawmills by sacrificing lesser-valued native forests),
and those who believed it imperative to cease all native forest logging.

Guy Salmon's involvement at the centre of the native forest campaign was not
surprising. His father John, a biologist at Victoria University College from 1948,
published a book called *Heritage Destroyed: The Crisis in Scenery Preservation
in New Zealand* in 1960, warning against the adverse environmental impact of
the various development works then being undertaken on a vast scale. He raised
public concern and awareness about conservation at a time when few were
attuned to the issue, convincing government to form a Nature Conservation
Council, on which he served as a foundation member from 1963–83. Active in
the Save Manapouri Campaign and in the Forest and Bird protection society,
in 1972 he became the first chairman of the National Alliance of Environment
and Conservation Organisations (CoEnCo, known as ECO from 1976) and was
chairman of Conservation New Zealand from 1975–81.[99]

Overseas movements and organisations exerted a major impact on both
John and Guy Salmon's environmental activism. In the course of mid-career
study tours abroad, both in England on a Nuffield Fellowship in Natural Science
in 1950–51 and in the United States as a Carnegie Travelling Fellow in 1958,
John came into contact with scientists who were committed to conservation

and working actively to raise public awareness about it. Upon returning to New Zealand, he devoted time and energy to teaching, writing and broadcasting about natural history for the general public. His popular books on native trees and plants especially helped to foster public interest in planting and conserving native vegetation. As a boy, Guy accompanied his father to Oregon, where he observed at first hand grass-roots activists campaigning to save Douglas firs. Later, as a student, he attended the Stockholm United Nations Conference on the Human Environment, which considered environmentalism in an international context.[100]

Despite the ongoing conflicts over native forest policy, conservationists won numerous notable victories in the 1970s and early 1980s. New Zealand came to enjoy international renown for its successful campaigns to save endangered birds — from takahe, kiwi, native ducks and saddlebacks to the Chatham Island black robin.[101] Plans to log rimu and miro in South Okarito halted after a rare brown kiwi was found in the area (which became part of Westland National Park in 1981). In the late 1970s, intentions to mill Pureora (a remnant of podocarp forest in the central North Island) threatened the continued existence of endangered kokako, which relied on it for its habitat. In 1978, after fourteen protesters hoisted themselves onto platforms among the trees at Pureora and remained there for two days, milling came to a standstill. By 1982, an NFAC letter-writing protest had brought all logging at Pureora and Waihaha forever to an end, and the remaining virgin forest became ecological reserves. In 1984, the forests at Whirinaki, and in 1987, the region south of the Cook River, all came under protection.[102] Many private landowners also embraced conservation of native forest and natural resources. In 1977, the creation of the Queen Elizabeth II National Trust, brainchild of a farmer called Gordon Stephenson, enabled private owners to sign covenants protecting all manner of landscapes, from forests to wetlands, to archaeological sites and geological formations. Five years later 1400 covenants covered some 50,000 hectares of land.[103]

Preservation and conservation protests extended beyond forests. In the early 1970s, Les Molloy, a DSIR soil scientist and ecologist, led a successful campaign to prevent the mining of the Red Hills in South Westland. Numerous protesters also vociferously opposed mining in the Coromandel Peninsula in the 1970s and early 1980s. In both cases, environmentalists argued that these special scenic places possessed natural wilderness and heritage values worth preserving.[104]

From the late 1960s onwards, environmentalism attracted a wide range of New Zealanders of all ages and occupations and lifestyles, who perceived their country's unique flora and fauna to be a valued part of national identity. The combination of passionate, almost quasi-religious commitment, nationalism and international influences also characterised the anti-nuclear movement, another high-profile cause inextricably linked to environmentalism, and like the anti-war protests, to peace.

The anti-nuke movement: 'A nation on our own'
The environmentally damaging impacts of nuclear tests in the Pacific region and the threat to the global environment posed by the possibility of nuclear warfare became a focus of growing protest from the 1960s onwards. The movement originated overseas but before long enjoyed a level of support in New Zealand unparalleled elsewhere. By the mid-1970s, New Zealand was renowned for its anti-nuclear stance, and the anti-nuclear cause had become closely tied up with national identity.

New Zealand's status as the world's leading anti-nuclear crusader seemed unlikely in 1960. In the preceding decade, it cooperated with Britain and America in the development of nuclear weapons, and its warships participated in British nuclear tests in the Pacific and Australia.[105] The country's first anti-nuclear group, the Campaign for Nuclear Disarmament formed in 1959 and based on a British model, was left-leaning, earnest and tiny. In the early 1960s, however, the anti-nuclear movement rapidly expanded in response to France's proclaimed intention to test nuclear weapons at Mururoa Atoll in French Polynesia (2650 miles from the East Cape). The New Zealand government swiftly voiced its objections to French president Charles de Gaulle. In September 1963, the New Zealand Parliament received an 80,000-signature petition seeking a nuclear-free southern hemisphere. Angry university students formed the Committee for Resolute Action Against the French Tests (CRAFT). France remained impervious, however, commencing tests in 1966. The National government issued diplomatic protests, but not wanting to alienate the French on trade issues, avoided any confrontational action.[106]

In the late 1960s, the Vietnam War overshadowed the anti-nuclear movement, as did proposals, which did not eventuate, to establish an Omega navigation 'spy' system in New Zealand. The French temporarily suspended testing in 1969, the same year New Zealand ratified the UN Non-Proliferation of Nuclear Weapons Treaty. In 1971, in response to pressure from environmentalists and concerns by other allies, the government made it clear to the US that it would not agree to visits by its nuclear-powered vessels unless liability in the event of an accident was accepted.[107]

In 1972, a watershed year for the anti-nuclear movement, French testing resumed at Mururoa. The National government continued to object quietly and diplomatically, but since some of the negotiations over the Common Market had been settled, now adopted a more assertive stance. At the 1972 United Nations Conference on the Human Environment in Stockholm, for example, Minister for the Environment Duncan MacIntyre criticised France's decision to resume tests and attracted support for opposing nuclear testing in the Pacific from 100 nations (but not, predictably, from the nuclear superpowers).[108]

Meanwhile, the New Zealand Labour Party angrily and unequivocally opposed the nuclear tests. For a wide range of non-governmental groups that formed its support base, the time for diplomacy was over. The Federation of Labour imposed a ban on carrying goods to the French Pacific territories; a move that the National government criticised as inimical to national interests. The public mood grew increasingly impatient and there were growing calls to break off diplomatic relations with France.

On 26 June 1972, a group called Peace Media, which included several prominent Labour Party members, sent out a 'peace flotilla' of boats from New Zealand into the French testing zone to shame the government into more direct confrontation.[109] Public figures such as author Maurice Shadbolt, poet and former Polynesian studies lecturer Barry Mitcalfe and MP Matiu Rata were present on three different boats, which helped to fuel public and media interest. One of the vessels, the *Boy Roel*, went missing in early July, after its engine died and radio transmitter malfunctioned. Despite widespread anxiety among the boat's supporters and families of the crew, the government refused to launch an immediate search-and-rescue mission. This was partly because it was widely believed that the radio silence was deliberate (in order to fool the French), and because Prime Minister Jack Marshall did not want to give any help that could be seen as support. The media coverage became politically embarrassing and eventually the government ordered two Orion aircraft to search for the missing vessel. This coincided with the *Boy Roel* crew reporting themselves safe in American Samoa, where they arrived under sail on 7 August.[110]

During the 1972 election campaign, the Labour Party plugged into an increasingly nationalistic mood among New Zealanders angry at the tests. Norman Kirk's stirring rhetoric directly linked anti-nuclearism with the need to assert a more independent foreign policy:

We are no longer hanging on the shirts of the major powers. We are a nation on our own and we are prepared to stand up and face the world and our own responsibilities . . . instead of having others fight our battles for us while we quietly support them in international forums. Let us have some dignity and honour and face the world as an independent nation.[111]

Slimmed down, with fashionably longer hair and sideburns, Kirk appeared distinguished and authoritative. Campaigning with the slogan 'It's Time for a Real Change', he led the party to a 23-seat majority on 25 November 1972. This triumph owed much to his personal leadership. Wellington's *Dominion* newspaper pronounced him 'Man of the Year'.[112] The country now had a Prime Minister who supported several causes that had galvanised protesters for several years, from the war in Vietnam to Manapouri and France's nuclear tests.

'Time for a real change': the Kirk years
While several of Kirk's policies aligned with the aspirations of radicals and youthful activists, he was wary of what he saw as polarising protests by long-haired middle-class university students and intellectuals, and deeply conservative on some social issues, notably abortion and gay rights. Born in Waimate in 1923 to working-class parents who were devout Salvation Army members, he finished school to find work at thirteen, taught himself manual skills in several jobs, and eventually became an engine driver. After settling in Kaiapoi, he successfully ran for mayor, and then won the Lyttelton seat for Labour in 1957. Five years later he was president of the Labour Party and leader of the parliamentary party. He shared many of the older generation's key values and beliefs, and understood ordinary working-class New Zealanders. At the same time, he supported several causes dear to youthful radicals. This enabled him to act as a unifying figure between two groups frequently at loggerheads — one young, internationalist and liberal and the other older, more focused on the national and parochial, and socially conservative. A pragmatic, principled, complex man, he rarely spoke of socialism but endorsed a state-managed economy and society that fostered equality of opportunity and helped those in need.

First and foremost strongly nationalistic, Kirk was concerned with New Zealand's independence and place among nations in the post-war world. At the 1968 Labour Party Conference he proclaimed: 'We aim to accelerate New Zealand's journey towards nationhood . . . The New Zealand Labour Party is the NEW ZEALAND party. The words New Zealand are as important as the word Labour.'[113] When a series of extracts from his speeches appeared a year later, the book's self-chosen title was *Towards Nationhood*.[114]

As Minister of Foreign Affairs, he announced soon after the 1972 election that New Zealand would withdraw its few troops from Vietnam and recognise communist China. In his view:

> The Vietnam conflict caused a revolution in public attitudes to the kind of wars in which the civil population is inevitably the chief sufferer. It marked the end of an era. By its close it had become plain that military intervention by great powers in the affairs and on the territory of smaller nations is no longer acceptable to world opinion.[115]

In the annual report of the Department of Foreign Affairs that year he declared:

> From now on, when we have to deal with a new situation, we shall not say, what do the British think about it, or what would the Americans want us to do . . . Our starting point will be, what do we think about it? What course of action best accords with the fundamental principles of our foreign policy?[116]

Believing that New Zealand had a specific role to play in the Pacific, he envisaged a new regionalism based on cooperation between independent neighbours: 'Now we do not consider ourselves the Britain of the South. Instead we recognise that New Zealand is the southernmost country of the Asia and Pacific region. Indeed New Zealand is connected to Asia by more than the stepping stones of a submerged continent.'[117] Overseas development assistance increased under the Kirk government, especially the proportion channelled to the South Pacific.[118]

Kirk wanted New Zealand's foreign policy to express 'national ideals as well as reflect our national interests'.[119] Doing this meant taking a principled stand on issues and actively participating in international bodies such as the United Nations and the Organisation for Economic Co-operation and Development, which New Zealand joined in 1973. It also meant drawing international attention to injustices against the small but principled country of New Zealand. Losing no time in initiating a more resolute stance on French testing in the Pacific, he wrote to the French ambassador outlining New Zealand's opposition, but added a significant new threat. His government was prepared to use all available means to end it. In 1973, he sent Deputy Prime Minister Hugh Watt to Paris to try to dissuade the French from testing. When this proved unsuccessful, he began considering sending a frigate to the test sites in active protest.[120]

Meanwhile, Kirk launched a case against France at the International Court of Justice in The Hague. The government submission garnered an impressive amount of legal, scientific and political evidence, and the Court upheld New Zealand's request, voting eight to six that 'the French Government should avoid nuclear tests causing the deposit of radioactive fallout on the territory of New Zealand, the Cook Islands, Niue or the Tokelau Islands'.[121] This landmark decision legitimised New Zealand's anti-nuclear stance in international law. Although France had already given notice that it would not accept the Court's jurisdiction in matters of defence, the case focused attention on the issue and spurred opposition to the tests around the world.

Within New Zealand, support for the government's anti-nuclear stance steadily rose. France's non-recognition of the ruling prompted Kirk to go ahead and dispatch a frigate to the testing zone. HMNZS *Otago*, crewed by volunteers and farewelled by thousands, left Wellington Harbour for the test sites on 28 June 1973.[122] Kirk's speech on the occasion painted New Zealand as a little nation taking a big moral stand:

> We are a small nation but in the interests of justice we claim the world's attention . . . This is a voyage of peaceful but serious purpose. Today the *Otago* leaves on an important mission. She leaves not in anger but as a silent accusing witness with the power to bring alive the conscience of the world.[123]

As fully intended, the frigate's actions attracted global media interest. The *Otago*'s departure, and the rhetoric that endorsed it, stirred national pride. The former dependent colony was now a player on the international stage, taking on more powerful countries and endeavouring to end war and save the planet.

Dispatching the *Otago* marked a high point of anti-nuclear sentiment and publicity during the Kirk years. After this gesture, the government directed energy towards working for a comprehensive test ban treaty at the United Nations, supporting bilateral negotiations in SALT1 (the first round of the Strategic Arms Limitation Talks involving the US and the Soviet Union), and continuing to oppose nuclear proliferation. In 1974, France announced its intention to undertake all future tests at Mururoa underground. In October 1975, New Zealand co-sponsored, with Fiji and Papua New Guinea, a proposal for a South Pacific nuclear weapons-free zone. Labour and anti-nuclear activists could feel justifiably pleased about the success of their cause.

In 1973, Kirk also compelled the New Zealand Rugby Football Union to call off a proposed tour by South Africa, refusing to grant visas to the non-racially integrated Springboks. This move respected prevailing UN sanctions against sporting contacts with South Africa but angered more conservative elements of the populace who believed sport should be kept separate from politics. With considerable political astuteness, the Prime Minister defended cancelling the 1973 rugby tour not just on moral grounds but because anti-apartheid protesters might disrupt or jeopardise the impending Commonwealth Games in Christchurch.[124]

Kirk opposed racial discrimination nationally and used the media with panache to convey his message of a partnership between Maori and Pakeha based on mutual respect. At Waitangi in February 1973, he took the hand of a small Maori boy and walked with him to the rostrum before making his speech. The now famous photograph of this apparently spontaneous gesture became a powerful symbol of biculturalism.[125] He also quickly fulfilled his election promise to prevent the raising of Lake Manapouri, passing innovative legislation that appointed six leaders of the Save Manapouri protest movement as Guardians of Lakes Manapouri and Te Anau. The 'cream of the rebels' now managed the lakes.[126] This move endeared the new Labour government to environmentalists, who included among them those keen to embrace a self-sufficient existence by moving 'back to the land'. Remarkably, the Kirk years witnessed a government 'Ohu' programme to provide public land for people wanting to form 'back to the land' communes. Few other nations could boast a state-sponsored counter-culture.

The Ohu name derives from a Maori word meaning to achieve something by means of friendly help and work. Evidence suggests that the scheme (the brainchild of either Kirk or MP Matiu Rata) appealed to Kirk's nationalism. In a 1972 interview with the *Australian Financial Review*, he referred to Israeli kibbutzim as a possible model, and seemed to perceive these sorts of communities as a temporary stage in the lives of young New Zealand nation builders: 'He says he intends to start off with three kibbutzim into which younger New Zealanders could go for a period as a means of contributing with their own hands and sweat to the building of a nation.'[127]

Although this notion of Ohu as a temporary mecca for young nationalists appears to have got lost over time, it was perhaps more viable than the dream of permanent communities. The scheme has been described as 'a classic case of an idea coming from the top levels of government and being almost immediately undermined by the bureaucracy'.[128] In early March 1974, Margaret Hayward, Kirk's secretary, wrote:

... press officer Peter Kelsey, who has transferred from our office to work on the [Ohu] scheme, of which he is an enthusiastic advocate, tells me that the Lands and Survey Department has decided that applicants should have only land designated as suitable for nothing else, 'and that's pretty bad land to go on to'.[129]

In addition to the poor-quality land, obtaining permission to proceed frequently involved frustrating obstructions and delays at district office level, and overly severe applications of local by-laws and regulations. Some groups persisted and survived, however, the most enduring being the Ahu Ahu Ohu on the Ahu Ahu River, a tributary of the Whanganui River, which lasted for over 20 years.[130]

Less contentiously, Labour introduced a scheme of national walkways to encourage New Zealanders to venture into the countryside. Another popular policy, consistent with party traditions, was a 'Christmas bonus' for all means-tested beneficiaries. As Minister of Finance Wallace (Bill) Rowling observed, the new government regarded economic growth as 'the servant of our social needs and not as the master of our environment'.[131] In keeping with election promises, Labour implemented innovative social welfare programmes. A Domestic Purposes Benefit (1973) gave benefits to solo parents, enabling them to stay at home and look after their children. Following the recommendations of a 1967 Royal Commission report, Labour passed the 1972 Accident Compensation Act, which set up a no-fault accident compensation scheme, funded by levies and government contributions, for all accidental injuries.[132] Labour also abandoned wage controls instituted by the previous government; introduced tax breaks for wage and salary earners; controlled post office, rail and bulk power charges; and offered bigger subsidies to hold down the domestic prices of sheep meats, milk, woollen goods and sugar.

The newly created New Zealand Export-Import Corporation, a government body dedicated to increasing trade, along with a Rural Banking and Finance Corporation, fostered rural growth. After Britain's entry into the EEC in 1973, the government cultivated new markets and attempted to encourage more diverse exports and economic versatility. It also made efforts to promote tourism through the government's Tourist Hotel Corporation, and created a government Shipping Corporation in July 1973 to revitalise coastal shipping. From August 1974, a New Zealand Superannuation Corporation implemented the contributory superannuation scheme promised during the election. Education, housing and health spending increased as a slightly more relaxed immigration policy between 1973 and 1975 pushed up demand for services in those areas.

Between a third and a half of new houses were in some way state-funded, and education spending at this time (as a percentage of total government expenditure) was higher than for the rest of the century.[133]

These policies and initiatives signalled an energetic government that initially seemed on track for success. Kirk became Prime Minister in 1972 when the country experienced a short-lived export-led boom (which saw the trade price index increase by nearly 35 per cent between 1972 and 1974).[134] This newly buoyant economy augured well, bolstering government plans to create a more egalitarian, caring, moral nation. But the economy, and with it Labour's plans, soon foundered. Rising wages, unstinting government spending and burgeoning import costs pushed inflation up rapidly. By August 1973, wage pressures were so high that government announced a wage stabilisation order, which meant that no wages could rise above the level set by government. Unions began to flex their muscle at this attempt to curb wage-price inflation, and strikes and industrial unrest ensued.[135]

The first oil crisis following the Yom Kippur War in October 1973 adversely affected the entire western world, but for New Zealand, so dependent on its export trade, the impact was doubly traumatic, with a massive collapse in wool prices. The government tried to insulate New Zealand from external pressures by borrowing overseas. However, the huge contraction in the terms of trade — some 43 per cent in little more than a year — was too great to cushion against.[136] Meanwhile, government spending proceeded unabated. In July 1974, Labour introduced a contentious 'maximum retail price' system, creating considerable confusion and even some ridicule.[137] A month later, Norman Kirk, after a short illness, died of heart disease, aged 51.

The nation responded to this premature loss with shock and grief. Over a thousand mourners attended the state funeral, held at St Paul's Cathedral in Wellington, and a massive crowd listened to the proceedings outside. The *Evening Post* wrote: 'Wellington showed the face of New Zealand's grief, in a crowd of more than 10,000 that waited in uncanny silence for the funeral service of the Prime Minister, Mr. Kirk.'[138] Kirk had inspired confidence, respect and a broad fan-base. In January 1974, a Wellington band called Ebony achieved a top ten hit with a tribute song called 'Big Norm'. Although the government's popularity waned in early 1974 as the economic crisis deepened, respect for Kirk himself had not diminished.

The capable but uncharismatic Bill Rowling, who became Prime Minister upon Kirk's death, was a tertiary educated teacher and sometime university lecturer. These origins accurately reflected the evolving character of the Labour

Party, which now attracted more white-collar members; most notably, education, public service, welfare and other professional services providers. In 1957, professionals such as lawyers and teachers comprised one quarter of Labour MPs; by 1984, the figure had risen to three quarters.[139] As the 1975 election loomed, Rowling faced a dire situation. The buoyant economy of 1972–73 had vanished. A $1 billion inherited balance of payments surplus was replaced by a deficit of more than $1 billion. Unemployment rose above 5000, and inflation trebled to 15 per cent.[140] External public debt stood at $863 million by 1975. An estimated 18 per cent of the population (about 550,000) were in poverty.[141] The government appeared increasingly beleaguered as the economic crisis deepened, and it was not clear that Rowling had the qualities required to sort out the mess.

To add to the government's troubles, in 1974, Dr William Sutch, a leading economic and cultural nationalist and former permanent secretary of the Department of Industries and Commerce, was arrested and tried for espionage. (He had several le Carré-esque rendezvous with a Russian diplomat in unlikely locations.) The scandal attracted frenzied media attention. Although Sutch was acquitted in February 1975, suspicions lingered. In July 1975, *Truth* ran a sensational series of articles exposing what it dubbed 'the Plot' — a 'sinister scheme to socialise New Zealand'.[142] The paper breathlessly revealed (courtesy of leaked SIS documents) that Kirk had authorised Labour MP and vice-president of the party Gerald O'Brien to seek monetary and economic advice from a team of experts (including, among others, Sutch and Trade and Industry Secretary Jack Lewin) about possible tactics to deal with the increasingly problematic economy. Some discussion of nationalisation of the finance sector ensued. As Redmer Yska has noted, the sensational manner in which *Truth* conveyed this information was 'bound to unsettle Labour at the next election'.[143] Sutch, decried as an arch-villain by *Truth* (in the 29 July edition he figures as a grinning octopus wrapping tentacles around banks and insurance companies), died of cancer in September 1975.[144]

Troubled paradise

Austin Mitchell, an English academic who lived and worked in New Zealand from 1959 to 1967, later wrote a droll, occasionally acerbic critique of Kiwi life and culture entitled *The Half-Gallon Quarter-Acre Pavlova Paradise*. Published in 1972, the book portrayed New Zealand as a parochial, pragmatic, puritanical, 'DIY' and rugby obsessed, egalitarian, anti-intellectual society, hungry for external validation: 'The only thing wrong with New Zealand was the number of people asking how I liked New Zealand.'[145] Some elements of the society Mitchell had observed, such as its passion for rugby and DIY, endured into the 1970s and beyond. Yet the 'pavlova paradise' changed rapidly from the late 1960s. The cultural consensus and economic prosperity of the post-war years ended. Television and improved jet travel further opened the country to global influences. The population grew more culturally diverse and the younger generation especially became better educated and less conformist and quiescent than many of their elders.

Protests, an important means of trying to effect change, attracted not just long-haired university students but eminent clerics, public servants, doctors, trade unionists, academics, teachers and journalists. Over time, activists initially decried as extremists or caricatured as trouble-makers in the popular press often came to be viewed in a different light, as policies, ideas and tactics initially perceived as extreme or outlandish by middle New Zealand gradually became absorbed into the mainstream. Not all protesters and activists aimed to overturn the status-quo. Some worked to preserve and protect the natural environment, others to defend beliefs increasingly under siege in an age of permissive non-conformity and 'doing your own thing'. Generational divides formed only part of a broader uncertainty and flux, as the country felt the push and pull of those aiming to radically transform society and those determined to protect and preserve it; those wanting to dive headlong into the waters of change and those happier to submerge themselves incrementally, if at all.

CHAPTER SIX

Schisms

A SOCIETY DIVIDED

*He saw the studio, press conference or platform as battlefields, and walked on
to them with two aims — dominate the occasion, intimidate the participants . . .
We have not had a politician to match him for gall, balls and gunfire.*
— journalist Ian Johnstone on Robert Muldoon, 1998[1]

*I found myself sitting next to a middle-aged lady, who offered me a sandwich.
She said her husband, a farmer, had made them for her while he was making his
own to eat at the match. They came from the Wairarapa together, amicably. He to
see the match, she to join the protest.* — a protester against the Springbok tour,
Wellington, 1981[2]

The National Party's new leader, Robert Muldoon, conducted the 1975 election campaign with a characteristic mixture of pugnacity and populist flair.
From the hustings, he inveighed against the country's economic woes, derided
Labour's general incompetence, particularly its handling of the Sutch affair,
and dismissed his opponent Bill Rowling as 'a shiver looking for a spine to run
up'.[3] National, he contended, was both more committed to individual freedom
and choice than the Labour Party, and more sensitive to the interests of the
'ordinary bloke'. His campaign slogan, 'New Zealand the way you want it', could
cleverly mean different things to different people.[4]

For those disaffected with recent trends in New Zealand society, such as the increasingly problematic economy, 'New Zealand the way you want it' was New Zealand the way it used to be. Muldoon's sanguine assertion that he would fix the ailing economy particularly appealed to older people on fixed incomes struggling during inflationary times. The same demographic also responded enthusiastically to the promise of a very generous national super-annuation scheme. Described by Keith Sinclair as 'the biggest election bribe in the country's history', this policy offered a retired married couple 80 per cent of the average ordinary wage at the age of 60.[5] At a series of public meetings throughout the country — replete with balloons, bands, boaters and badges — Muldoon attracted thousands of excited supporters.

One event on the evening of 25 August unsettled but did not derail the campaign momentum. During a television debate hosted by British journalist David Frost about the state of unions in New Zealand, passions ran high, and even Muldoon's supporters felt he did not come off well. Later that evening, invited by businessman Bob Jones to address the Landlords' Association, and stimulated by the preceding fierce debate (and probably by alcohol), Muldoon 'thumped' a demonstrator outside the Peter Pan Cabaret in Auckland's Queen Street, then pursued others down the street, shouting. While this street brawling alarmed some National supporters, others expressed admiration for Muldoon's display of vigour. Jones later commented: 'That night provided the foundations for the evolvement of "Rob's Mob"; for the transfer in allegiance of the mainly male, normally Labour-voting ordinary Joe, not from Labour to National but Labour to Muldoon. This was the sort of street-fighting leader they usually only dreamt about.'[6]

For many Labour supporters, such unbridled aggression was the stuff of nightmares. A group called 'Citizens for Rowling', which included eminent figures such as Sir Edmond Hillary and Bishop Paul Reeves, formed to oppose what they saw as Muldoon's bigotry and divisiveness. But in the end, despite some determined opposition, the election results proved resounding. Neatly reversing Labour's 55 to 32 majority, National now had a 55 to 32 majority itself.[7]

While highly intelligent, capable and energetic, the new Prime Minister was also truculent, outspoken and domineering. His personality and leadership style stimulated admiration, dislike and, not infrequently, fear. As Muldoon was born in 1921, a significant proportion of his youth took place against the backdrop of the Great Depression. He absorbed from his socialist grandmother the values of frugality, hard work, self-reliance and a keen appreciation for the welfare state. While serving in Italy during World War II, he completed

Poets Allen Curnow and Denis Glover, the printer and publisher Bob Lowry
and an unidentified friend in front of a movie hoarding in Christchurch, c. 1948.
PA Coll-2146-008, Bridget Williams Collection, Alexander Turnbull Library

Author Frank Sargeson (right), with friend and partner Harry Doyle, at Sargeson's
Takapuna bach, c. 1950. *F-27776-1/4, John Reece Cole Collection, Alexander Turnbull Library*

Writer and teacher Sylvia Ashton-Warner helping children in a classroom, c. 1951. *PA Coll-2522-2-001, Sylvia Ashton-Warner Collection, Alexander Turnbull Library*

Artist Louise Henderson, March 1963, in front of a tapestry she designed for the New Zealand Room in the Hong Kong Hilton. *PA Coll-7796-93, Evening Post Collection, Alexander Turnbull Library*

A pioneering modernist: the painter Milan Mrkusich, photographed in 1969 in the Remuera home he designed and built himself. *Max Oettli, PADL-000101-Milan Mrkusich.1969tif, Alexander Turnbull Library*

Photographers Ans Westra
(left, in her Wellington studio,
c. 1959–60) and Marti
Friedlander (shown below, at
work, c. 1970) both immigrated
to New Zealand from Europe
in the late 1950s. *Ans Westra;
Gerrard Friedlander*

Artist Colin McCahon, in his Partridge Street studio, Auckland, 1967. *Gil Hanly*

Icons of high and popular culture: poet James K. Baxter and best-selling author and 'Good Keen Man' Barry Crump. *Ans Westra; Peter Bush*

Maori youths outside a typical rural 1950s cinema in Te Kaha. *Ans Westra*

Women at the beach model the latest fashions in bathing suits, c. late 1940s. *F-37093-1/2, Gordon Burt Collection, Alexander Turnbull Library*

Shearers and models pose together as part of New Zealand Wool Board promotions in the early 1960s. *Peter Bush*

Maori youths practising rock 'n' roll in the Maori Community Centre, Freemans Bay, Auckland, 1962. *Ans Westra*

Rock 'n' roll dancing at Wellington Town Hall, 1957. *EP/1957/0643, Evening Post Collection, Alexander Turnbull Library*

Mabel Howard, New Zealand's first female cabinet minister, jives with rock 'n' roll star Johnny Devlin in Christchurch, 1959. *PA Coll-5679-01, Lou Clauson Collection, Alexander Turnbull Library*

'The Chicks', sisters Judy and Sue Donaldson, released their first single in 1965. *PA 1-f-192-35-14, Lou Clauson Collection, Alexander Turnbull Library*

A royal welcome: The Beatles on the balcony of the Hotel St George, Wellington, June 1964. *F-071852-1/4, Morrie Hill Collection, Alexander Turnbull Library*

exams to become a cost accountant. In 1960, he won the suburban Auckland Tamaki seat and in 1967 assumed the powerful role of Minister of Finance. Short, rotund, and porcine in appearance (hence the nickname 'Piggy'), even before assuming the party leadership in 1974, his caustic wit and media-savvy confidence made him a ubiquitous political presence. One journalist noted that through television, Muldoon, more than any previous leader, was 'incessantly in everybody's living rooms, stirring hate and devotion'.[8]

This propensity to polarise rather than conciliate set the tone for his tenure as Prime Minister, which extended from December 1975 to July 1984. Muldoon's uncompromising stance on several contentious issues, combined with his combative leadership style, exacerbated socio-cultural and generational divides, pitting liberal, often urban and tertiary educated elements against older, more conservative New Zealanders. His disdain for the liberal left accompanied a keen eye for its hypocrisies, which he mocked with hard-hitting barbs and one-liners. This truculence intensified societal tensions at a time when the country's ongoing economic problems resulted in rapidly rising unemployment and financial hardship. At the same time, Muldoon sincerely aimed to assist and protect ordinary people from the negative impacts of economic forces outside of their control. Like Kirk, he placed a high value on the welfare state and aimed to conserve this time-honoured element of New Zealand political culture.

In attempting to combat the country's worsening economic plight, however, Muldoon embarked upon several development schemes that angered environmentalists, while his scornful opposition to the anti-nuclear movement galvanised activists to pursue the cause with determination and energy. Despite the schisms and debates that preoccupied New Zealand during Muldoon's tenure, this turbulent time stimulated an upsurge in creativity and cultural dynamism. But by the early 1980s, as the violent eruptions surrounding the 1981 Springbok rugby tour unfolded, it became apparent that strains in the social fabric could rapidly and frighteningly tear apart.

Determined economic interventionism

Muldoon promised during the 1975 election to fix the economy. Upon forming a government, he assumed the dual roles of Prime Minister and Minister of Finance to facilitate this recovery. Yet these efforts notwithstanding, the economy continued to deteriorate. By mid-1976, inflation reached 18 per cent and the country had slipped from fourth position on the OECD list of wealthy nations to around seventeenth.[9] Real income per capita fell by over 11 per cent between 1973 and 1977. At the same time, unemployment rose. The number of registered unemployed climbed from 10,617 in January 1976 to 17,155 in October 1977. In 1978, unemployment soared, the total out of work reaching 46,894 in July.[10] Maori and Pacific Islanders employed as unskilled factory hands and labourers were particularly vulnerable to job losses. A range of social ills was associated with increasing unemployment, including gang warfare, crime and a widespread sense of disillusionment. In 1978, the overall population of New Zealand actually fell for the first time since World War II, as people sought jobs abroad — some 45,000 in 1977–78 alone. This was a costly and unsettling 'brain drain' of the young and skilled.[11] Between 1976 and 1983, 150,000 more people left New Zealand permanently than arrived.[12]

Faced with this ongoing economic and social malaise, Muldoon remained a determined economic interventionist. Unwilling to ignore the impact of any major restructuring reform on individuals, families and communities, he was, as his biographer Barry Gustafson has written, 'temperamentally and philosophically' opposed to the kind of 'New Right' economic and social theories ascendant in Britain, the United States and Australia from the late 1970s and early 1980s.[13] He was not only concerned at the human pain such policies would cause, but convinced that they would lead to election defeat by angry voters, and unprecedented industrial relations upheavals. Muldoon regarded a regulated economy as most desirable. The state would be responsible for providing infrastructure and would attempt to balance the needs of various sectoral interests. Despite his reputation for ruthless decisiveness, both his willingness to tinker with established arrangements and his vision of a regulated economy never wavered.

The National government did, however, initiate some retrenchment and reform. It built fewer state homes and encouraged renters to purchase. In contrast to Labour, education did not receive extra funding, as Muldoon commenced a 'back to basics' debate, as well as urging a shift towards applied, vocational learning at tertiary level. He initiated some liberalisation of the financial sector, removing most interest rate controls in 1976, but when various efforts to retrench public spending between 1975 and 1977 resulted in voter grumbling, economic contraction and rising unemployment, he pulled back.[14] Ad hoc interventionism, an unpredictable 'pick and mix' approach to the day-to-day running of the economy, remained his preferred modus operandi.

Concerted efforts to cultivate new markets for New Zealand agricultural exports, notably in the Middle East, Japan, Australia and the USSR, and to diversify exports such as manufactured goods, met with some success.

Manufactured exports grew from 5 per cent of exports in 1965–66 to 19 per cent in 1980–81, with both the range of products and range of markets expanding.[15] In 1977, National attempted to diversify the economy and expand trade contacts by introducing an 'Entrepreneur' category for prospective immigrants. The government successfully targeted wealthy Chinese business people and professionals who needed to bring in $200,000 in the hand plus sufficient capital to underwrite their business enterprise. This scheme attracted 553 applicants in the first two years.[16] Government subsidies and government-fostered joint ventures also boosted fish exports, while new pastoral products such as deer and goats found markets, along with racehorse bloodstock exports. Some horticultural products, notably kiwifruit, boomed, as did the tourism industry.

The Muldoon government provided struggling farmers with a range of subsidies, including tax and production incentives, loan schemes, reductions in estate duty, and additional finance through the Rural Bank. From 1978, it established Supplementary Minimum Prices (SMPs) for meat, wool and dairy products, offered export incentives to manufacturers and maintained key import controls. As a result of strained relations with the unions (1976 was the worst year for industrial disputes since 1951), Muldoon imposed a freeze on wages, salaries, professional charges and directors' fees, as well as rents, for 1976–77. An independent Wage Hearing Tribunal established by the government awarded a generous 6 per cent rise from March 1977. In 1978, farmers and several of Muldoon's political colleagues, dismayed by his soft stance on militant unionism after he conceded to freezing workers' wage demands, began to view his interventionism as erratic at best.[17]

In addition to the costly new superannuation scheme promised during the election, National gave young single-income families tax rebates, motivated not just by compassion but by a desire to bolster the nuclear family. A Cabinet Committee on Family Affairs set up after the 1975 election concluded that this bedrock institution was foundering. In 1965, one in twelve marriages broke down; by 1976, it was one in three. Concerned that the increasing number of people on the Domestic Purposes Benefit facilitated this decline (6000 people received it in 1972 at a cost of $6.5 million; by 1977, 28,400 were receiving it at a cost of just over $100 million),[18] National introduced checks to ensure that beneficiaries were not in de facto relationships, and reduced benefits for the first six months. This action earned opprobrium from feminists, as did the conservative 1977 Contraception, Sterilisation and Abortion Act (see Chapter 7). The government's often insensitive, confrontational stance on immigration and race relations also angered sections of the public. In addition to these controversies, National's policies on various environmental issues, especially its dismissal of the growing anti-nuclear movement, resulted in a groundswell of spirited opposition.

Pro- and anti-nuke

Upon winning the 1975 election, Muldoon, who dismissed Kirk's independent anti-nuclear stance as 'sanctimonious humbug about a moral foreign policy',[19] promptly announced that New Zealand would no longer lobby the UN for a South Pacific nuclear weapons-free zone. Instead it would invite nuclear-powered (and possibly nuclear-armed) United States naval vessels to visit New Zealand. While embracing traditional defence alliances, notably ANZUS and SEATO, Muldoon attended every South Pacific Forum meeting, using the opportunity to urge qualified support for the South Pacific nuclear weapons-free zone that would enable the free passage of American ships in the Pacific.[20]

From being able to rely on government support during Kirk's time in power, anti-nuclear activists now had to react against policies opposed to their aims. Auckland's Peace Squadron, founded by the Reverend Dr George Armstrong of St John's Theological College, swung into action in 1975, launching a squadron of small boats to picket New Zealand harbours against American nuclear warships. This form of protest had considerable popular appeal. Armstrong described it, with characteristic flair, as 'a symbolic gesture of resistance to the destruction of humanity by fire . . . [and something that] could make New Zealand an island of sanity in an ocean of peace'.[21]

When the USS *Truxton* visited in 1976, the New Zealand Defence Department, anticipating problems with Auckland's Peace Squadron, organised for the vessel to arrive in Wellington. However, a union ban on the waterfront prevented it from berthing. (A succinct piece of graffiti: 'Truck off Fuxton' appeared in the capital around this time.) Later in the year, the USS *Long Beach* sailed into Auckland, to be met by a protest 'squadron' of small yachts, dinghies and other pleasure craft. Former Labour Education Minister Phil Amos, in his boat *Dolphyn*, was among those arrested for obstructing the visiting ship en route to the wharf.[22] During subsequent visits by the nuclear-powered submarine *Pintado* in December 1977 and the USS *Haddo* in 1979, Peace Squadron protests became more dangerous and high-profile, as all involved (on both sides) took more direct action to protect their interests. During the *Haddo*'s visit, for example, several kayaks and small craft were sunk and one daring individual (Stephen Sherie, a 27-year-old Waiuku labourer) even managed to actually board the nose of the submarine, where he 'began a dance, half of defiance, half of joy'.[23]

The Peace Squadron protests generated immense publicity and attracted a great deal of support internationally from various peace groups. Within New Zealand, by the late 1970s, a growing assortment of anti-nuclear groups frequently worked together, employing tactics other than direct action. Prior to the *Haddo*'s arrival, for example, the Peace Squadron, Friends of the Earth, the New Zealand Foundation for Peace Studies, Greenpeace, CND and the Auckland Branch of the United Nations Association sought a Supreme Court injunction, hoping to prevent that vessel from entering Auckland.[24]

In addition to its invitations to nuclear ships, the National government began inquiring into the viability of nuclear-generated electricity in 1976. Immediately, the Campaign for Non-Nuclear Futures (CNNF), a loose coalition of anti-nuclear and environmental groups, mounted a massive public education exercise. A 'Campaign Half Million', aiming for half a million signatures on an anti-nuclear energy (and anti-nuclear ship visits) petition, also commenced. This resulted in the largest petition in the country's history to date, with 337,087 signatures by October 1976.[25] In September 1976, National set up a Royal Commission on Nuclear Power Generation. The ensuing report, tabled in Parliament in May 1978, in general rejected the need for nuclear power generation in New Zealand. When the Muldoon government, unable to ignore the depth of public feeling against nuclear power, declared the decision on nuclear-generated power would be deferred, it was widely recognised as a face-saving backdown. The CNNF disbanded shortly thereafter, having achieved a major victory.[26]

Nevertheless, although unpopular with anti-nuclear campaigners, the Prime Minister still struck an appreciative chord with the majority of New Zealanders. Prior to the 1978 election, he remained preferred leader by an impressive 60 per cent. Just before the election, this fell rapidly to 48 per cent, largely due to Rowling's more positive, confident image and Muldoon's counter-productive, aggressive tactics during the campaign.[27] The Social Credit leader Bruce Beetham, who won the former National stronghold seat of Rangitikei in a February 1978 by-election, also attracted favourable media attention as a personable contrast to Muldoon. Journalist, author and political commentator Colin James has described Social Credit as standing for 'the small operator, beleaguered in a world of big business, big unions and big government'.[28] With its credit reform policy now de-emphasised, it attracted a 'protest' vote away from both major parties. In the 1978 election, National, at 39.8 per cent, actually polled fewer votes than Labour on 40.4 per cent. National's majority decreased to ten seats, and Rangitikei remained Social Credit. An electoral boundaries redistribution in 1977, plus a diversion of possible Labour protest votes to Social Credit, helped stave off defeat.[29]

Meanwhile, the anti-nuclear forces continued to energetically work for the cause. In 1978, a regional group of non-governmental peace and religious groups in Suva, Fiji, formed the People's Charter for a Nuclear Free and Independent Pacific. Endorsed at conferences in 1980 and 1983, this called for a nuclear-free zone in the Pacific, including all nuclear power generation and uranium mining. In 1981, 'Peace Movement Aotearoa', a loose national network aiming to coordinate New Zealand's various peace activists and groups, emerged and began publishing a national journal, *Peacelink*. In the same year, the Canadian-born activist Larry Ross formed the Christchurch-based Nuclear Free Zone Committee. In addition to organising tours for overseas activists and publishing a newsletter, Ross tirelessly traversed the country, speaking about the dangers of nuclear war. The United States' recent switch from nuclear deterrent strategies to 'first-strike counterforce' doctrines, and the Reagan administration's statements about the possibility of 'winning' a nuclear war, aided his cause. Ross encouraged his audiences to form local anti-nuclear groups and to lobby.[30]

Women's groups and church groups around New Zealand soon began declaring their homes and buildings 'nuclear-free'. Not waiting for government, people took action themselves. The Nuclear Free Zone Committee saw this happening and decided to encourage groups throughout the country to urge local governments to declare themselves nuclear-free. A visit by the Australian-born paediatrician and anti-nuclear campaigner Dr Helen Caldicott in 1983 further aroused public feeling against the arms race. In 1984, a group called International Physicians for the Prevention of Nuclear War helped raise awareness about the medical consequences of nuclear warfare. Anti-nuclear campaigners could no longer be stereotyped as long-haired lefties. Kevin Clements has noted: 'It stretched credulity to assert that doctors, lawyers, engineers and scientists were communist stooges or subversives seeking to undermine New Zealand's defence and security.'[31] By 1984, 65 per cent of New Zealanders lived in 'nuclear weapons-free zones', proclaimed by city, county and borough councils, and a clear majority of the population — 57.4 per cent — opposed the entry of ships equipped with nuclear weapons into New Zealand waters.[32]

Conservation versus development

Environmentalists' calls for greater openness, accountability and safeguarding of natural resources made progress in the latter 1970s but also experienced opposition and frustrating failure. In 1976, for example, the National government proposed to raise the Clutha River in Central Otago to generate hydro-electricity. This prompted controversy from the outset, as it entailed flooding the Cromwell Gorge and obliterating scenic historic sites as well as picturesque productive orchard land. Public opposition increased once it became apparent that the end goal was to generate cheap electric power for a proposed aluminium smelter at Aramoana. The smelter site, located directly across Otago Harbour from Taiaroa Head and the world's only royal albatross colony, was highly contentious.

The heated disputes surrounding the proposed dam and smelter moved to the courts. Eventually, the smelter proposal lapsed due to the withdrawal of likely corporate investors, but a High Court appeal against the dam proceeded. The objectors claimed that the end use of the power to be generated by the Clutha dam had not been taken into account, and that this was contrary to law. The Court upheld this claim.[33] Determined not to have the project stymied, Muldoon responded with empowering legislation. The Clutha Development (Clyde Dam Empowering Act) of 1982 conferred the rights to dam the river on the Minister of Energy, thereby reversing the Court's decision to the advantage of the government, and giving the Act what Nicola Wheen has described as 'a constitutional notoriety unmatched in New Zealand's legal history'; one which revealed an intention to see the dam built regardless, and 'a derisory attitude towards the objectors and the courts'.[34] The Prime Minister got this legislation passed by calling on the support of Parliament's two Social Credit members. The Clyde Dam construction costs ran dramatically over budget, helping to escalate the national debt, which jumped from $1 billion in 1976 to $9 billion by 1984.[35]

In 1979, the world experienced a second oil shock in the wake of the Iranian Revolution, and the ensuing scarcity and steep rise in fuel prices compounded other inflationary pressures such as rising wage rates and increased government spending.[36] In response, the National government, like administrations elsewhere around the globe, adopted some innovative measures. 'Carless days' aimed to reduce petrol consumption. Every car owner nominated one day per week when they would not drive. Colour-coded windscreen stickers indicated the selected day; infringements resulted in a fine. Exemption stickers proved something of a fatal mistake, however, as a black market soon flourished.[37] The policy only lasted until May 1980, having made little impact on fuel consumption. Similarly, banning petrol sales on weekends also proved ineffective and lasted only eighteen months.

A more far-reaching and costly initiative, the 'Think Big' energy projects embarked upon at this time, aimed to decrease dependence on costly overseas oil by developing New Zealand's own abundant energy resources. As an added bonus, the government assured the public, an estimated 450,000 new jobs would be created in the process. Muldoon, an enthusiastic exponent of the various Think Big schemes, gave Minister of Energy and National Development Bill Birch the task of overseeing their implementation. Maui gas, which came on stream in 1979, was to be used for methanol and ammonia-urea plants at Waitara, a synthetic petrol plant at Motunui, and for CNG and LPG. The Marsden Point oil refinery was to expand, along with New Zealand Steel. New Zealand electricity and gas would power the electrification of the North Island main trunk line, as well as aluminium smelters at Tiwai Point and Aramoana.[38]

From the outset, however, the Think Big projects were both controversial and staggeringly expensive. Imported oil, expected to reach US$60 a barrel by the 1980s, in fact levelled out at a mere $15, undermining the financial viability of these large-scale projects. Massive construction cost overruns, industrial disputes, bad management and a spiralling overseas debt compounded problems. Government borrowing rose from $1 billion in 1976 to $3.1 billion in 1984; servicing the debt rose from 6.5 per cent of the government budget in 1975 to 17 per cent by 1985.[39] Jobs did not eventuate in anything like the numbers anticipated.

In 1979, Muldoon pushed through a National Development Act to 'fast track' the major Think Big projects, some of which were attracting vocal criticism from environmentalists. This legislation was opposed as undemocratic from without the National Party. A 'Coalition for Open Government' headed by Sir Guy Powles formed to lead the attack. Perhaps more disturbingly, within the party, three MPS (Marilyn Waring, Ian Shearer and Mike Minogue) crossed the floor on the issue. This negative response reflected growing concern at what was perceived as Muldoon's arrogant exercise of executive power. The Coalition for Open Government, made up of environmentalists as well as those concerned about perceived threats to labour rights and participatory democracy,[40] worked for five years from 1979 to increase public accountability and pushed for more open government. The passing of the Official Information Act in 1984, which set out processes for accessing official information and created ombudsmen to help the community in its dealings with government, answered the Coalition's desire for more accountable government. Opposition to the National Development Act also reflected growing public scepticism about the Think Big strategy and concern over the ever-worsening economy. Writing in the *New Zealand Listener* in December 1979, the economist Brian Easton pronounced the 1970s to be 'by almost every economic measure . . . a disastrous decade'.[41]

Government did, however, take some steps to halt the destruction or alienation of New Zealand's coastal and marine resources in the course of the 1970s. In 1972, the Labour government, just prior to the United Nations Conference on the Human Environment at Stockholm, had set up a Reserve Acquisition Trust Fund, with $1 million committed annually to purchase coastal land. Between 1974 and 1978, this acquired some 20,000 hectares. A Marine Reserves Act, passed in 1971, created the country's first marine reserve, near Leigh north of Auckland. In 1978, the National government passed a Marine Mammals Protection Act, and in the same year Muldoon announced, in opening a New Zealand Oceans Conference, his party's long-term objective to create 'a series of protected environments in key areas around our coasts — certainly not the creation of reserves in a haphazard fashion'.[42]

The degree of destructive overfishing then being pursued underlined the importance of marine reserves. In 1968 alone 6,300,000 kilograms of Chatham Island crayfish were landed.[43] Pair-trawling rapidly depleted the formerly abundant snapper fishery in the Hauraki Gulf, and the use of monofilament nets saw stocks of shark, moki and yellow-eyed and grey mullet plummet. Two international initiatives adopted and applied nationally helped to address this pressing issue. In 1982, the United Nations Convention on the Law of the Sea enabled states such as New Zealand to define the 'exclusive economic zones' over which they controlled rights to fishing and the seabed. In 1978, New Zealand formally took jurisdiction out to the 12-mile nautical limit. In 1983, this extended to 200 nautical miles.[44]

New Zealand's anti-whaling activists, part of a worldwide movement with global impact, also achieved a major victory in the late 1970s. Greenpeace New Zealand, formed in 1972, challenged the nation's poor voting record at International Whaling Commission (IWC) meetings, which it perceived as a cause for shame. In Wellington in 1979, Greenpeace New Zealand set up a 'whale embassy' to represent the 'whale nation' during IWC meetings. In a mock funeral procession, its members carried a giant model sperm whale through Wellington streets, drawing attention to the country's pro-whaling voting record.[45] In 1979, Greenpeace New Zealand sent environmental activist Michael Taylor to the IWC conference in London, where, dressed in an orca suit, he attended a Friends of the Earth 'Save the Whales' rally in Trafalgar Square. In response to public pressure, the New Zealand delegation at the 1979 conference reversed its traditional pro-whaling vote. In May, the Minister of Foreign Affairs Brian Talboys publicly announced the change of policy. A breakthrough occurred in 1982, when the IWC voted 25 to 7 in favour of halting commercial whaling, which was to be phased out over three years.[46]

Social unease and cultural dynamism

During the Muldoon era, differences of opinion on several causes and issues, from anti-nuclearism and environmentalism through to feminism and the push for Maori land rights, resulted in some powerful creative responses. Art served both as a refuge and a means of exploring conflicting values, whether new and iconoclastic or traditional and threatened.[47] Painting, art, literature, poetry and music flourished, with many works reflecting a prevailing sense of social unease and disaffection. Writers, artists, sculptors, composers, musicians and craftspeople living and working in New Zealand absorbed and adapted influences and ideas from abroad, fusing them in their creative work with distinctively local elements.

Arts and crafts was one area in which New Zealand achieved distinction and world-class standing, with potters such as Len Castle, Campbell Kegan, Beverley Luxton and Chester Nealie, glass artists like Gary Nash and Ann Robinson, and weavers such as Judy Wilson earning international renown.[48] The painters Gretchen Albrecht, Robin White and Don Binney, among others, began to attract critical acclaim at home and abroad. Several artists responded to contemporary conflicts by conveying a political or environmental message in their art. Ralph Hotere, for example, produced several works opposing construction of the proposed Aramoana aluminium smelter, while Pat Hanly, Bill Hammond and Colin McCahon produced a range of works expressing opposition to the use of nuclear weapons. In literature, a more assured, less apologetic tone replaced earlier self-conscious debates about national identity. Maurice Gee's novel *Plumb* (1978), for example, considers universal themes amidst an unselfconsciously New Zealand setting.[49] Poets such as Sam Hunt, Vincent O'Sullivan, Bill Manhire and Ian Wedde, novelists and short-story writers such as Owen Marshall, Fiona Kidman and Elizabeth Smither, embarked upon long and productive literary careers. In the burgeoning theatre scene, hard-hitting works like Greg McGee's *Foreskin's Lament* (1981), described by Peter Simpson as 'a trenchant analysis of society through the metaphor of rugby',[50] drew appreciative audiences, as did lighter fare such as Roger Hall's popular comedies of middle-class manners.

In music, local artists and musicians often imitated overseas cultural trends or movements, then tweaked them to fit New Zealand's unique mix of Pacific Island, Maori and Pakeha influences. Jamaican reggae, for example, was enthusiastically received and adapted by Pasifika and Maori musicians. In 1975, 'Back Yard', a Ponsonby-based trio of Pacific New Zealanders, added reggae covers to their repertoire. By 1980, having changed their name to 'Herbs', they had evolved into an influential band, with a Polynesian sound within a reggae/rock framework. A break-dancing craze originating in urban America swept across New Zealand in the early 1980s, proving particularly popular with Maori and Pacific Island adolescents.[51]

Internationally renowned artists such as Kiri Te Kanawa raised New Zealand's profile and helped to sell its global 'brand', while an avant-garde group such as Split Enz, which achieved numerous chart successes abroad, countered preconceptions about New Zealand's staid and conservative culture. In 1977, National's Minister of Arts Alan Highet, appreciating the relationship between the arts and strengthening national identity and the country's global profile, advocated legislation to set up a state-supported film production industry on the grounds that

> [f]ilm makers will interpret the country's lifestyles in lively and entertaining ways which will contrast with the previously largely unrelieved diet of films from other cultures. New films will help New Zealanders to come to a better understanding of their responsibility as a significant South Pacific nation. There will be new incentives for skilled performers, writers, directors, cameramen and designers, technicians and others to stay in New Zealand to pursue their craft. The new era of New Zealand film will enable the world to see New Zealand and its people as they see themselves.[52]

In 1977, Roger Donaldson and Ian Mune's feature film *Sleeping Dogs* constituted a breakthrough in New Zealand film-making. A loose adaptation of C. K. Stead's 1971 novel *Smith's Dream*, set in a New Zealand run by a totalitarian state, its commercial and critical success helped spur the creation of the New Zealand Film Commission (NZFC). Prolonged lobbying combined with the enviable example of a vibrant Australian state-supported film industry also played a part. The first films sponsored by the NZFC (*Angel Mine*, 1978; *Skin*

Deep, 1978; *Middle Age Spread*, 1979; and *Sons for the Return Home*, 1979) criticised the values and institutions of New Zealand society. These were followed in the early 1980s by a 'significant flowering of New Zealand cinema', with offerings such as *Beyond Reasonable Doubt* (1980), *Goodbye Pork Pie* (1980), *Smash Palace* (1981), *The Scarecrow* (1982) and *Utu* (1983).[53]

In 1983, *Patu*, a film by Merata Mita, became what *Listener* reviewer Peter Wells described as 'the hottest documentary ever made in New Zealand'. Its subject was the 1981 rugby tour of New Zealand by the South African Springboks. This event brought to a head long-building tensions and divisions surrounding societal values and beliefs. The debates and conflicts that characterised the Muldoon era spurred creativity and artistic diversity. Less positively, social strains and angrily competing points of view could, as the tour vividly demonstrated, fuel divisions that rapidly spiralled out of control.

The tour: rugby, New Zealand, South Africa

The 1981 Springbok tour prompted 'the worst scenes of disorder and violence since the Anglo-Maori wars of the eighteen-sixties'.[54] For a period of eight weeks, New Zealand was embroiled in a state of angry conflict. Viewers in New Zealand and around the world watched incredulously as television news showed footage of police in riot gear facing off against protesters wearing protective helmets and padded vests. In the country and the city, among young and old, passions ran high. 'The tour' evoked bitter battles not just between protesters and police but within families, workplaces, sporting groups, churches and schools.

Although no one had anticipated just how spectacular the disputes surrounding the 1981 tour would be, tensions about playing rugby with South Africa had been mounting since early in the century. From 1928, the first year the All Blacks toured South Africa, Maori were excluded from the team. When South Africa played Maori in New Zealand, the games were marked by ill feeling, with allegations of rough play by Maori and racial insults by Springboks.[55] In 1960, the announcement that Maori All Blacks would be excluded from a tour of South Africa sparked some high-profile protests, and as many as 150,000 people signed a petition stating 'No Maoris, No Tour' spearheaded by the National Council of Churches.[56] The tour proceeded, but another in 1967 was cancelled, with Prime Minister Holyoake arguing in 'a clear non-directive directive'[57] that 'in this country we are one people; as such we cannot as a nation be truly represented in any sphere by a group chosen on racial lines'.[58] There was widespread opposition by New Zealanders to excluding Maori from

All Black teams, but much less opposition to playing racially selected (that is, all white) sports teams from South Africa.[59]

For the next tour of South Africa in 1970, the South Africans were forced to allow Maori players, who were accorded the status of 'honorary whites'. In anticipation of this proposed tour, a new anti-tour protest group arose in 1969. Halt All Racist Tours (HART), led by Trevor Richards, was created to oppose all sporting contacts with South Africa. Its members, predominantly university students and professionals concerned about international race relations, organised demonstrations, started petitions, wrote letters, issued press statements and delivered speeches. This young, earnest membership helped to fuel a caricature of HART as a group of long-haired lefties opposed to or uninterested in sport. In fact, many were passionate rugby supporters.

They were also (and this was a key aspect of the organised anti-tour movement in New Zealand) internationalists. HART developed close relationships with a number of African governments, with the Organization of African Unity and with the United Nations. The latter provided an internationally backed moral legitimacy that HART persistently invoked. In 1968, the General Assembly of the UN called for all states to suspend cultural, sporting and educational exchanges with South Africa. In 1969, HART organised activities all around the country in support of the UN resolutions and against the proposed 1970 tour.

They also sought support from prominent New Zealanders who would help in the crucial battle to swing public opinion. The group Citizens' Association for Racial Equality (CARE), headed by Tom Newnham, was, like HART, committed to opposing rugby links with South Africa. In 1970, it published a book entitled *I'm Against the Tour* which featured celebrities such as Sir Guy Powles, James K. Baxter, Lady Louise Hillary and Auckland mayor Dove-Myer Robinson among others. HART and CARE were from the outset media savvy, recognising the critical importance of keeping sporting links with South Africa under discussion.[60] Although unsuccessful in halting the 1970 tour, they continued working energetically to ensure that the issue of playing rugby with South Africa remained in the public eye.

In the course of the 1960s and early 1970s, international criticism of apartheid steadily intensified. South Africa was expelled from FIFA in 1961, and excluded from the 1964 Olympics. In 1970, a proposed South African cricket tour to England had to be suspended due to protests. Many countries, even before the 1968 UN resolution, had ceased to engage in sport with South Africa.[61]

The majority of New Zealanders, however, remained impervious to these trends. Opinion polls in 1972 showed 80 per cent keen to allow the 1973 Springbok tour.[62] Rugby, and particularly the zealously contested rivalry with South Africa, was a key component of national pride and identity. When Prime Minister Norman Kirk banned the 1973 tour he was careful to emphasise that protests could prove disruptive and that playing the Springboks might result in a boycott of the imminent Christchurch Commonwealth Games. During those successful games, he welcomed the opportunity to meet visiting Commonwealth leaders and made strong speeches opposing racism. Having stopped the tour, he could take this stance at the games without hypocrisy.[63]

The Soweto riots occurred almost on the eve of the All Blacks' ill-fated 1976 tour of South Africa. The massacre helped to further harden international censure and sanctions against South Africa and led to widespread criticism both of the New Zealand Rugby Football Union's decision to proceed with the tour and the National government's failure to stop the tour going ahead. The 1976 tour not only ended in sporting defeat, but has also been described as 'a diplomatic disaster unprecedented in the country's history'.[64] Twenty-nine African countries resolved to boycott the Montreal Olympics because of it. Overnight, New Zealand became 'an international pariah'. At Montreal: 'Not even John Walker's victory in the 1500 metres could save New Zealand from embarrassment.'[65]

The arguments put forward by the pro-tour lobby had considerable resonance among large sections of the New Zealand public, however, and continued to be reiterated as passions flared in 1981. They were captured in the slogan 'Keep Politics Out of Sport'. As National's 1975 election manifesto stated, 'each individual should be free to follow his own conscience, without having someone else's morality forced on him'.[66] Although Labour sympathised with the anti-apartheid movement, it would not have intervened to stop the 1976 tour. Its leader Bill Rowling explained, however, 'we would have made sure our opposition was well understood by the Rugby Union and the world'.[67]

The price of separating politics from sport was dear. Minister of State Keith Holyoake observed with some alarm in 1976 that there were some perceptions abroad that the National government was 'racist in its outlook and action'. This had caused serious differences of opinion with traditional friends such as Canada, Australia and Britain: 'Most New Zealanders believe that politics should be kept out of sport. This government is strongly opposed to political interference in sporting affairs and we are doing all we can to stop it. But we have to be realistic.'[68]

At the 1977 Commonwealth Heads of Government meeting, under the 'Gleneagles Agreement', member countries agreed 'vigorously to combat the evil of apartheid by withholding any support for, and by taking every practical step to discourage contact or competition by their nationals with sporting organisations, teams or sportsmen from South Africa'. Another section stated that it was for 'each Government to determine in accordance with its laws the methods by which it might best discharge these commitments'.[69]

For the Muldoon government, vigorously combating apartheid did not extend to prohibiting a proposed South African rugby tour in 1981. In May 1981, 41 per cent of the electorate approved of the tour and 43 per cent were opposed.[70] Support for the tour was stronger outside of the major cities. With an election to be held two months after the tour, electoral considerations might well have played a part in ensuring that it proceeded: six crucial marginal seats with a strong pro-tour contingent might have defected from National to Social Credit if the rugby was stopped.

For the baby-boomer, tertiary educated, predominantly urban and Labour voting generation that had come of age in the late 1960s and 1970s, this was an issue worth fighting for however. The same country that had gained international praise and recognition for leading the moral vanguard against the nuclear threat now faced international opprobrium for failing to take a stance against a notoriously racist regime. At the same time, for the many New Zealanders who supported the tour, there was the quasi-religiously charged passion for rugby and the perception that any attempt to prevent the long-standing rivalry between the 'Boks' and the All Blacks was almost unpatriotic: an unwelcome challenge to a much enjoyed cornerstone of Kiwi culture.

Despite the acknowledged ideological and emotional divides within the country on this issue, the violence and divisiveness that characterised the 56 days of the 1981 rugby tour came as a massive shock. Over 150,000 people demonstrated in over 200 protests; almost 2000 arrests were made; and the cost to the government of defending the tour reached $7,200,000.[71] While the leaders of organised protest movements such as HART were young and left-leaning, the vast majority of those who demonstrated against the tour were not. Only 6 per cent of a large Wellington sample were frequent protesters; over 50 per cent had university degrees. Nor were they particularly young. Surveys indicate that a minority were under 25 and that the largest age group was in their thirties. The majority were liberal and middle class, with a preponderance of teachers and educators, researchers, scientists, media workers, public administrators and social workers.[72]

By the early 1980s, New Zealand had one of the most active, well-organised anti-apartheid movements in the world. In August 1980, its two main components, HART and the National Anti-Apartheid Council (NAAC) which included numerous affiliated groups such as CARE and the National Council of Churches, merged under the name HART. In addition to this major national organisation, 1981 witnessed the sudden growth of 'coalitions' such as MOST (Mobilisation to Stop the Tour) in Auckland and the organised and effective COST (Campaign to Oppose the Springbok Tour) in Wellington. These spontaneous groups sprang up in all the major centres. Within them, HART was one of many voices, which included Maori groups, trade unions, churches, student organisations and women's groups.

Outside of this organised opposition, many prominent individuals made a stand against the tour. One of the most high-profile, the All Black captain Graham Mourie, publicly announced he would not be available to play. Several local councils also moved resolutions to oppose the tour, and these had varying success. In some instances, for example, it was resolved to deny facilities to the team.[73] A 'mobilisation' spearheaded by HART and the coalitions on 1 May saw some 7500 people out on marches around the country. On 3 July, there was an equally impressive turnout. When the Springboks touched down in New Zealand, 2000 protesters greeted them at Auckland Airport.[74] Among the protesters were at least two bishops and some 60 students and staff from St John's Theological College, who held a 'Service of Repentance and Solidarity with the Black People of South Africa'. They sang hymns and took communion but were banned from entering the terminal building on the grounds that the Cross they carried might be used as an offensive weapon.[75]

In Gisborne, at the first match, some 300 protesters rammed through a fence surrounding the rugby ground and a vicious fight ensued, with police and irate rugby fans battling protesters in the mud. The violence and ferocity of the conflict was dramatic, but the game went on unimpeded. At the second match in Hamilton, on 25 July, events took a different turn. This time, protest marchers numbered some 5000, and a plan dubbed 'Operation Everest', whereby some 400 protesters peacefully occupied the rugby ground, succeeded. The police were told that a pilot had stolen a light plane and was flying toward Hamilton, intent on doing whatever was necessary to stop the match. The game was called off.[76] This was a moment of triumph for the protesters but the pent-up anger of the disappointed rugby fans soon boiled over. Despite the appearance of the newly created 'Red Squad' (a special unit, replete with batons and helmets, to police the tour), chaos and violence ensued.

The impact of stopping the Hamilton game was a key determinant of subsequent events. It marked a turning point for the New Zealand police, many of whom perceived it as a day of shame and professional humiliation. Ross Meurant, second in command of the Red Squad, later recalled his emotional distress: 'I remember opening my mouth but the words would just not come. The tears welled in my eyes . . .'[77] From this point onward, Meurant believed the police 'no longer saw the tour as a moral issue but a matter of law and order and believed it was imperative that the tour proceed so the police could reassert the rule of law'.[78] Another police officer, watching the events at Hamilton on television, felt that it was 'the most humiliating experience of my police career'.[79] A 1982 survey showed that these feelings were widespread throughout the force. The idea prevailed that the issues surrounding the tour now involved not just opposition to apartheid but a threat to the rule of law.

The question of law and order, as opposed to anti-apartheid ideals, was also invoked after Hamilton by National, who perhaps sensed its potential as an election plank. It was not uncommon to couple this stance with reference to the left-leaning leaders of the protest organisations. Speaking in Parliament, for example, National MP Jim McLay warned:

[p]rotesters themselves have now changed the issue from one of apartheid which is opposed by most New Zealanders, to a threat to the institutions of any democratic society . . . There can be only one answer to such threats — the rule of law must prevail.[80]

Minister of Immigration Aussie Malcolm also criticised the fact that 'figureheads of several of our Christian Churches have been associated with leading people into lawlessness'.[81]

Four days after Hamilton, in what came to be known as the 'Battle of Molesworth Street', peaceful protesters marching towards the house of the South African consul were batoned by police determined to prevent their proceeding. For those watching the events in front of their televisions, the sight of the protesters' distressed expressions, including those of elderly women whose faces dripped with blood, was both frightening and hard to credit. As one marcher recalled: 'We stopped walking and I saw the first young people being helped from the front, blood on their heads and faces. We stood, frozen in disbelief.'[82] Afterwards, police congratulated themselves on having handled matters well. For some protesters, however, the events of Molesworth Street galvanised their commitment. As one 24-year-old scientist wrote: 'After Molesworth Street the right of New Zealanders to protest peacefully without fear of police intimidation and violence also became a reason to protest for me.'[83]

The increasingly embattled situation afflicting the country did not diminish over the ensuing few weeks, as games took place at stadiums throughout both the North and South Islands. Barbed wire, first used to surround the stadium before the Palmerston North match, soon became standard. Police wielding long batons and brandishing riot shields also quickly became a familiar sight. Most protesters now wore helmets and protective vests. Tense standoffs between police and protesters became almost ritual, but no further tests were cancelled due to protest action. Frustration and anger mounted on both sides as the tour ground inexorably on. To protest against the tour now, despite the peaceful tactics endorsed by the anti-tour organisers, meant the very real possibility of encountering violence.

Protests also occurred on a smaller scale in country towns and suburbs, where protesters were frequently jeered, pushed and booed. A woman protesting in Eltham, for example, was challenged: 'Why don't you fuck off back to Russia, you red, fascist, commie, hippie bitch?'[84] Abuse directed against the anti-tour movement often played on its perceived link with left-wing subversives. The attempt to portray protesters as unwitting puppets of 'reds under the bed' was fuelled when, prior to the second test in Wellington, Muldoon published an SIS report identifying the political affiliation of some leaders of the protest movement. As he told the *Evening Post*, he released the document in the hope of influencing 'thousands of idealistic people . . . associated with the protest movement . . . [to] think twice about the people with whom they are associating'.[85] For some, this tactic had the opposite impact. One secondary school teacher and mother of five later observed: 'What encouraged me to be involved [in protests] was the publication of the list of names of subversives. The whole thing struck me as totally ludicrous. I thought it had to be shown that quite ordinary people, and masses of them, are opposed to the tour.'[86]

Conflict was not restricted to organised protests. Throughout the country, the tour issue elicited passionate, polarising responses amongst people of all ages. Intense arguments flared and tensions strained within workplaces, and between friends and among families. For one 27-year-old public servant, the repercussions of deciding to protest were uncomfortable and prolonged:

> Family's still pretty strained. Do I just keep myself apart, do I make an effort to go back there, not pretending that things haven't happened? The family's reaction is to laugh about it, to patch it up, but I haven't allowed that to happen.[87]

Conflicts within workplaces and organisations mirrored those dividing families. The various Christian churches found that adopting an anti-tour stance and participating in protests often generated considerable strife and opposition from within their congregations, and sometimes between senior clerics with opposing views. A number of clerics who played leading roles in the anti-tour protests suffered physical violence. Father Terry Dibble, for example, who was secretary of CARE and acted as 'on the field' negotiator when the Hamilton match was cancelled, had his nose broken in the violent mayhem following that announcement.[88]

Apprehension and tension mounted prior to the final games in Auckland and Whangarei. John Minto and Dick Cuthbert led the MOST coalition in Auckland, with the Anglican priest Andrew Beyer, from the inner-city church St Matthew's, as its chair. By the time of the first Auckland game on 5 September, the biggest police operation in New Zealand's history had turned Eden Park into 'a veritable fortress'. On the morning of the match, the protesters, organised into three squads — Biko, Tutu and Patu — were kitted out in helmets and face masks, while 'padding of every kind was taped to limbs and torsos'.[89] Some confrontations ensued, but for the most part, the violence did not extend beyond intermittent clashes.

However, 12 September, the bizarre, frightening day of the final test in Auckland, saw the worst violence of the tour.[90] The test fell on the anniversary of the death of Steve Biko, and a commemoration march was planned. The mood of the estimated 7000 protesters was keyed up and militant. During the test, to the astonishment of players and spectators, a Cessna repeatedly dive-bombed the pitch. The pilot, Marx Jones, assisted by Grant Cole, kept up a relentless attack, dropping some 60 flour bombs in a barrage that lasted for the entire game. One flour bomb hit All Black Gary Knight on the head, knocking him to the ground; another landed on top of a television camera. When Marx Jones returned to the airfield, he announced: 'I did it to fight apartheid.' Before being taken away by police, he handed a reporter an envelope containing money for the charter of the aircraft.[91]

Meanwhile, violence unprecedented in intensity erupted outside Eden Park. Street battles on Marlborough Street in particular resulted in the worst injuries of the tour, with many people hospitalised and several requiring surgery. An amusing account by Bruce Ashby, a high school teacher, offers some insight into the battle and the fear it provoked:

Up till then, the air was relatively free of hardware, except for some smoke cans, crackers and a few stones, but the charge out and the inability of the officer in charge to control his men, precipitated a full street riot. Protesters dismantled fence pickets, took scoria boulders from fence lines, bottles from residents' rubbish piles and hurled them at the Red Squad. It was then I joined 'Cowards Against the Tour' and ran . . .'[92]

The end of the tour prompted a national collective sigh of relief. The sudden cessation of hostilities left some protesters with the welcome luxury of weekend leisure time. Protests had taken place regularly throughout the tour, and not just at match or test venues. The extraordinary tumult of the last 56 days evoked considerable incredulity and not a little lingering anger and indignation on both sides. Opinion polls in September showed that opposition to the tour rose eleven points from May to 54 per cent;[93] how much this was due to the perception that the tour was not worth the turmoil is open to conjecture.

Muldoon's stance on the tour paid off politically. Eleven weeks after the Springboks' departure, the election resulted in a narrow National victory. The winning party's pro-tour stand paid dividends in rural areas and provincial towns such as New Plymouth, Gisborne and Taupo. Some 17.4 per cent of those voters who switched to National did so because of the tour.[94] As in 1978, Labour won more votes but fewer seats (43 to National's 47); Social Credit held on to its two, leaving National (after excluding the Speaker of the House) with a majority of just one.

Internationally, the extent of the protests counteracted much of the damage that the government's 'interpretation' of Gleneagles had done to New Zealand's reputation. Black South Africans responded with overwhelmed gratitude that 'people thousands of miles away cared so much'.[95] International news coverage had made it clear that nowhere outside of South Africa had protests on the issue reached such a height as in these two small islands on the other side of the world.

The question of why this issue so spectacularly divided New Zealand in 1981 occupied New Zealanders both during the tour and in its immediate aftermath. The journalist Tom Scott remarked that 'The tour has not created divisions so much as exposed differences which were already there.'[96] This sentiment featured strongly among respondents asked to comment about the tour in the *Listener*. According to the writer Bruce Jesson, for example:

The significance of the tour was its symbolism. It provided a focus for a deeply felt conflict between competing sets of attitudes — broadly speaking liberal versus traditional — that animates much of our political life. Ordinarily these differences in attitude tend to be intangible. The function of the tour has been to highlight these differences in the most dramatic way possible.[97]

These differences reflected varying ideas about New Zealand and its place in the world. To many members of the baby-boomer generation — especially those who had attended university and been exposed to contemporary ideas about capitalism, colonialism and racism — opposition to the war in Vietnam, anti-nuclearism, environmentalism and anti-racism were causes that reflected their values. In ignoring international sanctions against a racist regime, they felt that their country had abrogated those values. For many of their parents and for the more conservative among their contemporaries, however, the long-standing, passionately contested rugby rivalry with South Africa, a tradition critical to their identity as New Zealanders, was not something they were prepared to jettison because of international sanctions.

Despite the fact that the bulk of the protesters in 1981 were middle class and eminently respectable, old discourses based on resentments and stereotypes about protesters dating back to the late 1960s were revived and brought into play. The tendency to perceive the anti-tour protesters in these pejorative terms was possibly exacerbated by the perception that two of the forces spearheading the previous decades' 'politics of identity' — feminists and Maori activists — firmly opposed the tour. Yet opposition to apartheid remained the crucial factor cementing the protest movement. Internationalism and nationalism amongst the anti-tour forces intertwined, as many expressed shame that their nation was now regarded as racist by the international community. Chants of 'Shame, Shame' and 'The Whole World is Watching' reflected this perceived blot on the national character.

Several of those who wrote about the impact of the 1981 tour straight afterward expressed a dark view about the future of the game; and there was (misplaced) scepticism that it would ever 'regain the place it once held for us'. The 'cynical manipulation' of the tour by politicians, the transformation of the issue at hand into one of 'law and order', and the abrogation of civil liberties all came in for criticism.[98] A *Listener* editorial described the tour as a 'jarring time' that had 'aggravated further the distance between city and country attitudes', erected barriers between communities and between friends, and

jarred so many accepted notions about ourselves — about our tolerance, our social concern. Above all, it jarred our sense of security. Most New Zealanders tend to regard their country much as a child understands his family. The underlying quality is security. The Springbok tour upset the comfort that is part of that security.

Many aspects of our society can no longer be taken for granted; many questions have been raised, the answers to which might be unacceptable. The recent events have been a vivid reminder of how artificial our political order is. To make this order work requires constant effort.[99]

For the playwright Roger Hall, the long-term significance of the tour was not the tour itself but how it was handled, and the tendency on the part of government to 'grind down all forms of opposition'.[100] Bruce Jesson noted, more positively, that New Zealanders could no longer be considered 'passionless'; and Johnnie Frisbie-Hebenstreit, a Dunedin housewife and supporter of the tour, expressed the view that lack of unanimity was not necessarily new or inimical to democratic health.[101] Whether, as one historian has suggested, Muldoon's decision to allow the tour was 'one of the most cynical in modern times, a blatant attempt to win votes especially in the provinces', is a moot point.[102] During the period and in its aftermath some citizens felt a need to support and champion national unity. In March 1981, for example, a formerly unknown sales rep called Tania Harris, in response to a period of strikes and industrial closures, organised a lunchtime 'Kiwis Care' march in Auckland. The march aimed to show that Kiwis still felt pride in their country. Harris's message that 'pride and unity' were important, and that 'we must pull together and not apart', together with the almost 50,000 turnout, attests to the perceived sense of imperilment.[103]

A period of personal rule

The early 1980s have been described as Muldoon's period of 'personal rule',[104] and while this is obviously an exaggeration, he was increasingly a man alone. His drinking, an issue since the early 1970s, became worse and his temper more domineering. He remained determinedly interventionist. Many people, both within the party and among its traditional voters (notably farmers and business interests), wanted to see a move towards more 'market economics', not costly state investment in energy infrastructure facilitated by massive borrowing. In 1980, during the Prime Minister's absence overseas, several disgruntled MPs, led by Derek Quigley, Jim McLay and Jim Bolger, attempted what came to be known as 'the Colonels' coup', challenging Muldoon's leadership. It was doomed, however, because Brian Talboys, the charming and eminently capable Deputy Prime Minister, was reluctant to firmly assume control. Not unreasonably, he feared that a vengeful Muldoon might well destroy the party. Talboys retired from politics soon after, succeeded by Duncan MacIntyre, a loyal Muldoon supporter. Those MPs who stood by Muldoon during the failed coup found themselves rewarded and promoted.[105]

Faced with high wage demands, the costly Think Big projects and inflation at 15 per cent, in June 1982 the Prime Minister imposed a wage and price freeze, a move embarked upon in the face of unanimous opposition from Treasury, Trade and Industry, and the Governor of the Reserve Bank. Income tax legislation designed to prevent tax evasion in the kiwifruit industry proved unpopular with business and horticultural interests. In 1983, a Finance Bill to bring down interest rates passed only with the assistance of Social Credit and dissident Labour MPs, against opposition from leading free-market National Party members such as Derek Quigley, Ruth Richardson and Dail Jones. In early November, Muldoon announced regulations to bring down mortgage interest rates to 11 per cent for first mortgages and 14 per cent for subsequent mortgages; this covered all property transactions, including commercial ones.[106]

One significant exception to all this proactive interventionism was the signing in 1983 of a Closer Economic Relations (CER) free trade agreement with Australia. Although the main architects of this agreement were Brian Talboys and Hugh Templeton, Muldoon was eventually converted to the concept. Later, he liked to take full credit for it, despite the fact that, as his biographer has pointed out, 'it was concluded despite him rather than because of him'.[107] Britain's EEC membership notwithstanding, Muldoon remained staunchly loyal. If economic imperatives required a search for new markets, in foreign policy matters he did not hesitate: when the 1982 Falklands War broke out, he immediately severed relations with Argentina and (unasked) sent a frigate to support Britain. He then wrote an article in *The Times* of London entitled 'Why We Stand With Our Mother Country'.[108]

By the early 1980s, Muldoon faced opposition from a proliferation of diverse sources: liberal conservatives and free marketers in his own party, financiers, farmers, feminists, trade unionists, the media, radical Maori activists, environmentalists and anti-nuclear campaigners, and of course his long-standing enemies the liberal middle classes. In 1981, a Royal Commission of Inquiry report by Justice Peter Mahon into the tragic loss of 257 lives in the 1979 Air New Zealand plane crash on Mt Erebus in Antarctica added another high-profile controversy to the mix. Muldoon and Air New Zealand objected to Mahon's findings concerning 'an orchestrated litany of lies' by Air New Zealand's witnesses to the inquiry. The matter proceeded to the Court of Appeal and eventually, in 1983, to the Privy Council, which found the evidence did not substantiate Mahon's charges regarding a 'litany of lies' and a 'conspiracy to deceive'. The protracted controversy aroused conflicting views — some members of the public felt Air New Zealand had been too quick to blame pilot error and downplay other contributing factors to the crash; others perceived Muldoon as too partisan in defending the airline's board and senior management.[109]

The Prime Minister's outspoken belligerence seemed increasingly to define his leadership, and there was a lonely, besieged aspect to his final years in power. His relations with everyone from colleagues to the press deteriorated. In 1983, he banned Tom Scott of the *Listener* from his press conferences, and refused to be interviewed on television by journalists Ian Fraser and Simon Walker. In September, he denied Wellington's *Dominion* newspaper any interviews or official government material in retaliation for publishing a leaked document concerning long-term tripartite wage-fixing negotiations. The ban was lifted after 48 days, following a decision by the Press Council which, while not supporting the offending article, condemned the government's response to it as a clear attack on freedom of the press.[110] The death of his mentor Keith Holyoake in December 1983 left Muldoon grief-stricken and even more isolated.

In 1983, Muldoon's former friend and ally Bob Jones, a libertarian property magnate who wanted more freedom in the economy and in personal life, formed the New Zealand Party. Although Muldoon amusingly dismissed the new party as 'the greedies',[111] it was soon running at 10 per cent in the polls, and drawing supporters from National's traditional constituency, especially younger people working in farming, business or the finance sector. Jones also espoused an anti-nuclear non-alignment position on defence matters.[112]

Muldoon's failure to fully appreciate the growing anti-nuclear sentiment in the country was soon brought home to him. In early June 1984, MPs Marilyn Waring and Mike Minogue crossed the floor to support Richard Prebble's Nuclear Free New Zealand Bill, which was narrowly defeated 40 to 39. The anti-nuclear stance was a key issue for Waring, whereas for Muldoon, preoccupied with various financial matters, it was just a nuisance that could imperil relations with a close ally and trading partner. During debates on the Bill, Waring was thwarted from expressing her views freely in the House. Annoyed by this muzzling, she wrote to the Chief Whip on the morning of 14 June stating she would not attend any select committee or government caucus meetings for the remainder of the parliamentary term. Discussions as to what this letter meant ensued, with Muldoon at one stage launching an abusive verbal attack on Waring. Later that evening, despite her promise not to bring down the government, he called a snap election. Anger and alcohol mixed with diabetes medication prompted this fateful decision.[113]

The ensuing election campaign was disastrous for National. While Muldoon seemed lacklustre, Labour now had a confident and witty new leader. David Lange, a civil rights lawyer from a Methodist background, was an eloquent advocate of the anti-nuclear cause and clearly won an important television debate against a curiously deflated Muldoon, who came across as tired and mean-spirited. On 14 July 1984, National received the lowest percentage of the popular vote since its inception, with 36 per cent compared to Labour's 45 per cent, the New Zealand Party's 12 per cent and Social Credit's 8 per cent.[114] Disaffected voters found a viable alternative in the New Zealand Party.

It is telling that during a period of economic depression and cultural turbulence, when irate protesters and the jostling politics of identity replaced the consensus of the post-war years, Robert Muldoon was the nation's leader of choice for three consecutive terms. His emphatic disdain for the many 'isms' transported to the country from abroad and adopted by a younger, more idealistic generation, and his identification with traditional 'Kiwi' values, appealed to many members of the older generation especially, who felt former certainties increasingly under threat.

In one television interview, Muldoon expressed the view that he wanted to leave the country 'at least as good as when I took it over'.[115] This now famous observation is often interpreted as denoting a lack of vision, but in fact reflected a fundamental conservatism and appreciation for those aspects of New Zealand culture that he (and many others) valued and had come to expect. Like Kirk and Savage before him, he was not prepared to see the welfare state, a central component of New Zealand's historical development over time, replaced by faith in blind market forces. However, he only really began to perceive of New Right philosophy as an evil enemy during his last beleaguered years as Prime Minister, and did engage with some forms of retrenchment and reform during his time in office.[116]

As he pointed out at the outset of the disastrous 1984 election campaign, during his period in office, in addition to CER, transport had been de-licensed and voluntary unionism introduced. Shops now opened on Saturdays and Air New Zealand had been reformed. Modernisation of the railways was under way, and a start had been made on rationalising industry, removing farm subsidies and lowering import controls. Some freeing up of the financial sector had been effected, a new system of setting wages adopted, and the tax system was being overhauled. In addition, he argued that his recent wage and price freeze, a temporary necessity to hold inflation, wages and interest rates, was a resounding success. No less an influential source than the British *Financial Times* endorsed the latter claim, noting in June 1984 that New Zealand's inflation had declined from 16 per cent in 1982 to an expected 5 per cent in 1984.[117]

Muldoon's rejection of New Right solutions is sometimes portrayed as a Canute-like attempt to hold back an inexorable wave.[118] While Thatcher in Britain and Reagan in America embraced New Right free-market ideas and policies, it is perhaps not surprising that those solutions were initially resisted in a country famous for its ground-breaking social welfare legislation. Nor, as the above figures relating to inflation indicate, was state intervention in the economy a byword for reaction and failure. It was not solely a commitment to state economic management that sealed Muldoon's fate in 1984. Rather, there was a widespread appreciation that he had ruled too long. His assumption that he alone knew what was good for society increasingly appeared to reflect a disturbing autocratic bent. On the issue of anti-nuclearism in particular, he failed to discern the shifting sensibilities and expectations of mainstream New Zealand. His nine years in office during one of the most turbulent periods in New Zealand's recent history ensured his legacy as one of the more colourful and controversial leaders of the late twentieth century. But he had lost touch with the 'ordinary bloke', and with the changing temper of the times.

CHAPTER SEVEN

Feminism and Gay Rights

LIBERATION AND ITS LEGACY

A revolution doesn't have to be bloody, there don't have to be guns and grenades.
A revolution can take place inside people's heads . . . — Dunedin Collective for
Woman, 1972[1]

In the early 1970s, the women's and gay rights movements gathered momentum in New Zealand, raising the hopes of some and the hackles of others. Supporters embraced these causes with varying degrees of exhilaration and relief, finding in them a means of 'liberation'. Opponents perceived them as an unwelcome reflection of permissive times and a threat to society's lynchpin, the nuclear family.

Like other contemporary 'isms', New Zealand's second wave of feminism originated overseas. Once introduced here, it quickly adapted to local conditions and flourished. Sue Kedgley, a prominent feminist in the 1970s, recalled that while 'in the very early days, feminism was an intellectual event', it 'rapidly became intensely personal, fire in the belly, a clutching at the throat, a rage that would not go away'.[2] For Kedgley and many others of her generation, the feminist moment had arrived.

The women's movement had two dominant strands. One was radical, holistic, liberating and collective. It raised public consciousness about sexism and drew attention to the oppressive legacy of traditional notions of femininity. At the same time, it placed a high value on motherhood and domesticity and celebrated women's collective decision-making processes as an alternative to the perceived aggressive, competitive hierarchy of a patriarchal male culture. The other strand opposed discrimination against women, and sought parity with men by operating within established systems. Advocates of this more pragmatic, equal rights-based approach became more zealous and high-profile in the 1970s, aiming to eradicate gender inequities and expand women's opportunities. Divisions between these two strands were often neither neat nor clear-cut, and many women operated within groups that contained elements of both.[3]

Most feminists agreed about key issues: the need for better childcare facilities, equal pay and anti-discrimination legislation, the right to legal abortions, the importance of contraception and sex education and of raising public awareness about sexism and male violence. From the outset, however, some feminists expressed dissenting views on specific issues (notably abortion), and about how best to achieve desired ends. Rifts grew wider as radical collective, moderate liberal, Maori, lesbian and socialist elements pushed increasingly different agendas. By the early 1980s, feminism had transformed the social landscape and improved the rights and protections of New Zealand women under the law. Yet factionalism increasingly soured the movement. It also remained unclear what degree of 'liberation' if any had accrued to women at the bottom of the socio-economic scale.

In the course of the 1970s, gay rights activists lobbied and campaigned to diminish the former secrecy and stigma surrounding same-sex relationships. But New Zealand did not decriminalise male homosexuality until 1986, following an acrimonious battle. In the early 1980s, its legislation on abortion and sex education also remained more conservative than that of other developed nations such as Britain, Australia and Canada. The more liberal attitudes towards love, sex and sexuality that swept over the country during the late 1960s and early 1970s had effective and influential opponents.

Feminism: origins, ideals, disputes

The first organised women's liberation groups in New Zealand emerged out of frustration at women's subordinate role in various left-leaning movements. During a Radical Activists Conference in Wellington in 1969, the male majority silenced an attempt to discuss women's issues. A Wellington Women's

Liberation Front originated a year later. The group's first president, Therese O'Connell, described its impetus as 'a combination of personal grievances against women's set role in society, reinforced by literature on overseas women's liberation, and discussion in a committee of the Victoria [University] Socialist Club'. At the first meeting, twelve women and six men determined to fight for: 'a.) promotion of women's rights, ie. equal pay for equal work and b.) re-evaluation of women's role in society . . .'[4] Setting up daycare centres, liberalising abortion laws, ensuring access to contraception, and re-education of women were other key aims. An Auckland Women's Liberation Front, which formed shortly after this, was linked to the socialist Progressive Youth Movement. Members believed women's liberation would only succeed within a socialist society, and criticised the profit-oriented beauty industry for distracting women from their true interests of collective mobilisation against patriarchal gender expectations and capitalist exploitation.[5]

Within a short time, other women's liberation groups, varied in organisation and aim, began to multiply. By 1972, at least 20 had sprung up across the country.[6] These groups were not restricted to left-wing university students but included a range of predominantly middle-class mothers and wives from the suburbs. The intensity with which women embraced the movement, and the different kinds of feminist organisations that mushroomed, attests to the level of receptivity among all manner of women.

In 1966, women made up 41 per cent of the country's paid workforce. Most occupied low-status, low-paying jobs; the median income was 51 per cent that of men. Only 1.9 per cent of women as opposed to 20.9 per cent of men earned over $3,000 per annum.[7] Working women faced the prospect of unsatisfactory or non-existent childcare facilities, coupled with the expectation that they maintain a happy home while earning a salary. Suburban housewives, trying to conform to an idealised role as wife and mother, frequently suffered boredom, anxiety and loneliness. American feminists had begun consciousness-raising groups and campaigns for women's liberation early in the 1960s. Books such as Betty Friedan's *The Feminist Mystique* (1963) offered a beacon of hope for many New Zealand women, long before the advent of organised 'women's liberation' groups. In 1965, for example, the poet Lauris Edmond came under Friedan's spell while working as an adult education tutor for Playcentre mothers in the Wairarapa:

> We had a visit from another tutor who asked me if I'd read *The Feminine Mystique* by Betty Friedan, and lent me her copy. At once I was in the middle of a whole series

of mental somersaults, a carnival of sudden new views and changed ideas — a revolution. I could hardly believe it. Thousands of women all over America were saying in interviews again and again that their families were well, happy, busy fulfilling their ambitions, their husbands likewise, and yet beneath this apparently perfect façade they themselves suffered a profound and inexplicable malaise.[8]

The word 'liberation', borrowed from the United States civil rights movement, was eminently suited to a time of sexual revolution and youthful anti-authoritarianism. Its appearance signified a new wave of feminism.

Working for women's rights was of course not a new phenomenon, and in the course of the 1960s, significant milestones (notably the 1960 Government Service Equal Pay Act)[9] had been achieved. In 1964, the New Zealand Federation of University Women and the Wellington Business and Professional Women's Club held a successful conference on 'Women's Contribution in a Changing Society' in Wellington. One important outcome of this event was the formation of a Joint Committee on Women and Employment (JCWE) to lobby for a government advisory committee on women in employment. Another was the formation of a Society for Research on Women in 1966. This voluntary organisation rapidly flourished: by 1973, it had branches in Auckland, Wellington, Christchurch, Dunedin and the Waikato. The Society's first major project, *Urban Women*, which commenced in 1967, surveyed over 5000 women in the four major centres. Published in 1972, this study covered employment patterns, retraining needs, education, community involvement and leisure interests. One of its more explosive findings was that 60 per cent of all New Zealand women left school without qualifications and ended up in low-paid, low-status jobs.[10] During the 1970s, a period when the overall percentage of women in the workforce increased from 29.8 to 39.1 per cent, the Society for Research on Women played a key role in revealing women's inequality and disadvantage.[11]

In 1967, in response to prompting by women's organisations (notably JCWE), the Holyoake government set up a National Advisory Council on the Employment of Women (NACEW), a body that later encouraged the passing of key employment legislation in the 1970s. Independently chaired, but serviced by the Labour Department, this brought women from various women's organisations together.[12] It also provided a conduit into the Department of Labour and negotiations with government for equal pay in the private sector, a cause persistently lobbied for, especially by the clerical unions, many of whose members were women.[13] While this goal was pursued, some important new legislation strengthened women's rights under the law. From 1968, for example, a Domestic Proceedings Act required fathers of ex-nuptial children to pay maintenance not just towards their children but the mothers of their children. In 1969, the Status of Children Act accorded equal status to all children, regardless of the marital status of their parents. In the same year, an Independent Women's Party formed in Auckland and fielded four (unsuccessful) candidates in the general election. The platform focused on reform of the marriage laws. As candidate Esther James complained: 'A woman spends, on an average, 25 years of her married life in her home — without praise or pay . . . Then her husband can take her matrimonial home away from her.'[14]

In the late 1960s, New Zealand women began scrutinising the role of wife and mother as never before. *Thursday*, a magazine for the 'new woman' founded in 1968 and edited by Marcia Russell, aimed to attract a younger audience, to whom *Woman's Weekly* articles about 'royalty, recipes and romance' no longer appealed.[15] Yet as the magazine's letters columns soon revealed, many older women enjoyed reading the new publication. The letters also exposed widespread concern about the value of full-time wife- and motherhood versus a career, and conveyed ideas about employment being fulfilling in itself, not just a means of supplementing the family income.[16] The organised liberation groups that flourished after 1970 grew from fertile, well-prepared ground.

Unlike the circumscribed demands of those who had effectively campaigned for equal pay in the public service in the 1960s, 'women's libbers' queried traditional roles and aimed to raise public consciousness about women's subordination by using attention-grabbing tactics. By 1970, some women (and a few men) had begun energetically crusading to draw public attention to the cause. The writer and historian Christine Dann, who belonged to a socialist women's liberation group at the University of Canterbury in the early 1970s, recalls:

On Suffrage Day we dressed up as suffragettes and chained ourselves to the cathedral railings under the banner 'Yesterday's Suffragettes: Today's Marionettes'. There were equal pay and abortion pickets and stalls, and a float in the capping parade in which my flatmate Malcolm made a wonderful outsize baby driving his housebound mum to distraction while we handed out leaflets alongside. We demonstrated outside the Miss New Zealand show at the Theatre Royal and got called ugly. I think I wrote the leaflet for that, and I was also getting better at hand-lettering placards.

It wasn't all outrageous militancy . . . We spoke at school, on radio and television — wherever we could get an audience . . .'[17]

In addition to left-wing groups linked to university campuses or existing socialist organisations, another important strain of feminism, determinedly structureless and collectivist, began to attract committed adherents. Radical collectivist feminists espoused a 'sisterhood' that would consciously avoid the competitive hierarchy of male-dominated organisations and institutions. A key word was *oppressed*; the enemy was the male *patriarchy*.[18] Formed in 1971, the Dunedin Collective for Woman, a successful example of this more radical branch of women's liberation, rejected hierarchy and 'platforms':

> Starting with what we don't have: we don't have leaders, we don't have a platform, we don't have dues, we don't have any organisation.
>
> We don't have <u>leaders</u> because we hate the whole idea of the superwoman, the woman who is special, the woman who can make it alone way out ahead of other women in a man's world.
>
> We have <u>no platform, no party line</u>; there is nothing to which anyone has to sign their name.[19]

Yet an emphasis on egalitarian sisterhood and consciousness-raising did not preclude effective practical engagement with various issues. By 1972, the Dunedin Collective was publishing *Woman*, a fortnightly newsletter, and had seven different focus groups actively working on abortion, contraception, childcare, equal pay, women in trade unions, research and publicity. Many of its members were well-educated mothers who had garnered personal experience of the women's movement overseas. By 1975, the collective boasted 80 active committed members, all dedicated to a non-hierarchical structure and shared decision-making. It undertook several notable initiatives, including the publication in 1973 of *First Sex, Second Sex*, an influential booklet about sex-role stereotyping in infant readers. The Dunedin Collective also acted as an umbrella organisation for special-interest groups and projects, and conducted significant research surveys. It confidently and ambitiously aimed at 'nothing less than the total transformation of the whole world'.[20]

The idea of 'consciousness raising', a term borrowed from the Chinese Revolution, involved both heightening women's awareness of their own oppression (hence the relevance of the American catch-cry 'The Personal is Political') and engendering a feeling of solidarity with other women. In small groups, women discussed questions relating to topics such as male chauvinism, sexism in the workplace and media, and the iniquitous domestic division of labour.

Such groups encouraged open discussions about sex and sexuality. For many women, this was both a departure and a revelation. According to author and feminist Mary Varnham, when Sue Kedgley told the BBC's Alan Whicker in 1973 that the New Zealand male's idea of sex was 'a thrusting penis — he wouldn't know a clitoris if he came across one' on national television, it sent 'shock waves through suburban living rooms'. As Varnham observed: 'Once women started comparing notes, feminism became the biggest kick in the balls imaginable for male sexuality. The fact emerged that there were a lot of hopeless lovers out there.'[21]

Often those involved in radical feminist activism began to experiment with new kinds of domestic relationships and living arrangements. Fern Mercier, a member of Auckland's Women for Equality liberation group, moved into a commune in Freemans Bay that both embraced a collective lifestyle and rejected traditional sex roles:

> The feminist revolution opened the doors to change on personal and sexual, racial and cultural, social and political levels. 'Free Love!' and 'Death to the Nuclear Family!' were our battle cries. But for us the ends could never justify the means, and our revolution became the means, the process of the daily and local input of our most intimate and personal lives. This stuff became the eye of a revolutionary storm that carried us all along. Battles were fought within and without, and there was never any turning back.[22]

From 1972, those women keen to work for women's rights but not inclined to be part of a liberated sisterhood or embrace communal living could join the National Organisation for Women (NOW). Modelled on similar groups in the United States, NOW councils set up around the country. They aimed to achieve full equality for women within the law, the workplace, education and family life. Unlike radical liberation groups, they were structured and could include men (though few took up the option). Within a month of forming in 1972, the Auckland NOW group boasted 250 members; by the end of the year, it had 400. Primarily educated career women in their late twenties and thirties, well placed to influence the media, politicians and professional groups, they provided speakers on the status of women to various groups and helped raise public awareness about women's rights. Views on some key issues such as abortion, however, remained divided. The historian Raewyn Dalziel has noted that 'NOW sat rather nervously in the centre of the women's movement, viewing feminists to the right and left warily'.[23]

The most influential women's organisation to the right of NOW, the National Council of Women (NCW), founded in 1896, worked to achieve justice and freedom for women without making opponents of men, and prioritised family issues. An umbrella organisation to which many women's groups with conflicting aims and ideas belonged, the Council respected and attempted to accommodate members' views. Although to many women's liberationists, it represented a conservative body all too given to compromise, it played a role as a 'consciousness raiser' both during the high tide of feminism in the early 1970s and in the ground-setting decade of the 1960s. It brought information about women's issues to its disparate members, politicians and the general public, participated in the campaign leading to the 1960 Government Service Equal Pay Act, and throughout the 1970s supported initiatives for pay equity and equal employment opportunity by lobbying and submissions. It also maintained strong international links with the United Nations, and played a role in supporting key UN declarations that had an impact on New Zealand's social legislation.[24]

The Broadsheet Collective, on the left of NOW, and therefore substantially to the left of the National Council for Women, commenced in 1972. For the next 26 years, the *Broadsheet* periodical was the irate, irreverent, crusading voice of New Zealand feminism.[25] Founded by Sandra Coney, Anne Else, Rosemary Ronald and Kitty Wishart, it critiqued and commented on women's issues with rigour and humour. Its existence was crucial because, as Sharon Cederman stated in a 1971 edition of Auckland's student newspaper *Craccum*:

> Newspapers, TV, radio and magazines seem determined to exploit Women's Lib as a sensational, controversial subject. Most people seem to have a very limited idea of what we are trying to do and this idea is entirely supplied by the media. Consequently people are very hostile. Once people find out what we are really trying to achieve the reaction is usually agreement because what we are trying to achieve is a better, more equal life for men, women, and children.[26]

The Dunedin Collective for Woman also lambasted the media's portrayal of women's libbers as joyless earnest zealots:

> The attacks on us take familiar forms now! What did you burn your bras for? You are all man-haters, child neglecters, house-slovens, power-lovers, freaks, foreigners, and communists. In answer to all these, education, repetition, reasonableness, wit and clear evidence are our weapons. People are very willing to listen.[27]

Allison Webber, who was a young reporter on the *New Zealand Herald* when the women's movement came into full force in the early 1970s, remembers that the media 'didn't and still haven't come to terms with feminism as a movement which was equally as far-reaching as free market economics. Instead they tended to marginalise and label leaders of the movement, and treat feminists as a vociferous and temporary minority group.'[28] To expose sexism in the media, *Broadsheet* ran a popular 'Hogwash' feature highlighting examples of sexist advertising, for which there was never a shortage of copy.

Feminists criticised the media for ignoring important issues such as equal pay and perpetuating negative stereotypes, yet at the same time courted media attention, recognising its value in publicising their cause. For example, 'pub liberations' (as fully intended) made great news stories and attracted headlines. Women's libbers marched into public bars, at that time restricted to men only, and demanded service. In addition to the fact that drinks in the lounge bars (where women *were* allowed) cost more, pub liberations signalled that some women resented the unspoken expectation that they should be home preparing evening meals. Nor did they feel that their sensibilities required protection from the atmosphere of the public bar.

The first two pub liberations, at the Britomart in Auckland in August 1970 and Wellington's New City Hotel in September 1970, were smooth and successful. Later liberations proved more fractious. Fisticuffs broke out when feminists liberated the Great Northern Hotel in Auckland in June 1971, with disappointed TV cameramen rushing in a few seconds too late to film the action. Victory was short-lived, however, as under the Sale of Liquor Act publicans could refuse to serve whoever they wanted if the bar was private. Accordingly, the Great Northern bar was rechristened 'private' in August. In Christchurch, the publican of the United Service bar acquiesced peacefully to a 1972 liberation, but in the same year, feminists took the less accommodating proprietor of the Masonic Hotel to court. After pleading guilty, he was discharged without conviction, although the magistrate did admit that gender was not a 'reasonable cause' to refuse service.[29] Excluding women from public bars eventually disappeared, although one Auckland public bar did so as late as 1981.

While pub liberations attracted media attention, the visit in early March 1972 of Dr Germaine Greer was a veritable public relations bonanza. Barbara Brookes has described how 'a coven of liberationist witches' from the Auckland Women's Liberation Front, led by Ngahuia Volkerling (attired in a witch's hat and gown), met the 'tall, outspoken and glamorous' Greer at

Auckland Airport.[30] This was the first of many media opportunities. Greer, then at the height of her fame as the author of *The Female Eunuch* (1970), spoke with characteristic candour over the next few days about the constrictions of the nuclear family and women's sexual needs, evoking a storm of controversy. Open-line telephone broadcasts were even temporarily prohibited from discussing 'the subject of politics and Dr Germaine Greer'.[31] While Greer attracted new adherents, especially among young women, some feminists remained ambivalent. Connie Purdue, chairperson of the National Organisation for Women, for example, was offended by Greer's disdain for the union movement. The president of the National Council of Women also pointedly observed that many women 'don't want to be liberated because they are very happy'.[32]

Controversy deepened when, at an Auckland luncheon to celebrate International Women's Day, Greer received a summons bearing two charges for indecent language ('bullshit') and one for obscene language ('fuck'); offending words employed when answering questions at a public talk. The next day, she addressed a crowd of over 2000 at Victoria University and some 250 people who supported her use of the naughty words later demonstrated in front of the police station. This protest, which resulted in 20 arrests, made front-page news. In Greer's ensuing trial, a judge found her guilty on the obscene language charge. When this became known, a fracas erupted in front of the court. Protesters threw eggs, tomatoes and jellybeans, and police arrested 29 people.[33] For a considerable time afterwards, New Zealanders — young and old, male and female — debated feminism, and sales of *The Female Eunuch* soared throughout the country.[34] Marilyn Duckworth recalled:

> Feminism was rampant. It was called 'women's lib'. At a meeting on the university campus Germaine Greer informed us she wore no knickers. Karn and Beth and I devoured her book *The Female Eunuch* and relished her public use of the word 'bullshit'. It seemed truth was raising its head above the sticky waves of conservatism that had threatened to silence us.[35]

Another significant event in 1972, the first National Women's Liberation Conference, took place one April weekend in Wellington, attracting 500 women and 30 men. In an atmosphere of enthusiastic unanimity, attendees resolved to pursue equal pay and equity in the workplace; push for childcare centres; raise awareness of the housewife's plight; implement women's studies programmes at tertiary level; support gay rights and gay pride; campaign to repeal all abortion laws; and support contraception advice and sex education in schools.

By this time, the high profile of the women's movement's commanded attention, especially from aspiring politicians in an election year. As Sue Kedgley declared in a talk to the Workers' Educational Association (WEA) in September 1972:

> The party to whom women will give their political allegiance will be the party that, first, takes a genuine stand on women's issues, and second, gives more than lip-service adherence to female equality. We are not going to deliver our votes, energies, and efforts for nothing. We are demanding something in return.[36]

In 1972, the newly formed Values Party — the first party in the country to have a woman leader (Margaret Crozier) as well as a deputy leader (Cathy Wilson) — ran feminist candidates and policies. The Labour Party, too, promised to look seriously at the status of women with the aim of eventually introducing anti-discrimination legislation. After its election win, the new Labour government followed through on its promise, setting up a Select Committee on Women's Rights in 1974. A year later, it created a Council on Women, which aimed to open up communication between various women's groups and government.

In 1973, the first United Women's Convention, held in Auckland to commemorate the eightieth anniversary of women's suffrage in New Zealand, attracted some 1500 women. In a positive and mutually supportive atmosphere, a wide range of women's organisations — from conservative groups such as the League of Mothers and the Catholic Women's League to radical women's libbers and Sisters for Homosexual Equality — mixed together. Viv Walker, a working-class mother, recalled the feelings engendered by the occasion:

> It was a really huge event for us, and we thought we were pretty smart going off to this convention. Our husbands didn't mind; they were pretty good about it. But there was still a lot of effort before we went — we had to get all the teas ready and put them in the freezer. Then off we went on a plane to Auckland. I don't remember anything about it really. I don't think I heard a word the whole time, except that song at the end — the Helen Reddy song. It was like being at a Billy Graham revival; it was just amazing. I don't think I'd ever been to a meeting like that. I didn't even know what a conference was! It was neat. I felt really stroppy and came back and laid down the law.[37]

Despite the numbers and inspiring ambience, press coverage of the conference, in the *Auckland Star*, featured a photo of a mother holding a baby with a caption explaining that the reason baby (Oliver) was there was because 'he couldn't stand on his own feet and tell his mother . . . that he would sooner be at the Rugby Test with all the boys. So Oliver figures he'll form a new organisation — the BBLM. And that stands for Baby Boys' Liberation Movement.'[38] The delegates unanimously voted to send a note of censure to the Press Council. Toni Church also wrote to the *Star* editor Ross Sayers, who apologised (with the qualification that the response was an overreaction that 'does less than credit to your cause'). Sayers published more coverage of the conference on Monday, as well as several letters of protest from women. In the *Listener*, the journalist Tom Scott wrote that while the photo was a 'pathetic, stupid, harmless enough gesture', the anger it evoked stunned him: 'I began to perceive the enormity of the despair and rage. It was yet another petty humiliation heaped upon a mountain of insults. A road toll statistic, part of a whole too huge for comprehension.'[39]

Despite the unity of the 1973 convention, the movement, already comprising several strands (socialist, radical collectivist, liberal), began to acquire more subgroups — notably, increasingly vocal lesbian and Maori activists. Means and ends, and how best to achieve real liberation, became a source of increasing friction and debate over the next few years. For example, liberal feminists hailed the Equal Pay Act of 1972, which extended equal pay into the private sector, as a major achievement. By contrast, radical feminists decried it as legislation with 'tiny little teeth and hardly any guts'.[40] In response to pressure from NACEW, National had established a Royal Commission of Inquiry into Equal Pay in 1971. Both political parties agreed that equal pay was desirable, so the Commission's mandate was to consider how best to introduce it. The ensuing 1972 Act dismayed radical feminists because its provisions were to be implemented gradually over a five-year period. They also objected to the fact that while the Act stipulated that rates paid to women were to be based on those paid to males with the same or substantially similar skills, responsibilities or service, issues of comparability remained murky.[41] After the end of the implementation period, women's earnings relative to men rose from 65 to 75 per cent, but the gap did not then close any further, and most women remained clustered in occupations at the bottom of the labour hierarchy.[42] The much discussed issue of a wage for stay-at-home mothers also divided New Zealand feminists and politicians. As Melanie Nolan has commented, this was 'simply an issue on which neither women nor the state could agree in the 1970s'.[43]

The Labour government's Domestic Purposes Benefit (DPB) of 1973 was a milestone, however, for solo mothers with no other source of income. At the time, New Zealand's support for single mothers lagged far behind that of Europe, and 28 submissions to the 1972 Royal Commission on Social Security recommended its introduction.[44] The 1973 Act provided for a benefit based solely on being a single parent, rather than demonstrable need. Numbers receiving the benefit rose steeply from 3092 in 1970 to 17,231 by 1975. By 1976, 43 per cent of never-married women supporting children received the benefit introduced under the 1973 Social Security Amendment Act.[45] A network of organisations to support single mothers sprang up around the country. In 1973, the Auckland feminist and solo mother Joss Shawyer became involved in forming the Council for the Single Mother and her Child, to advocate for solo mothers' rights. The Council's 1976 publication *Everything a Single Parent Needs to Know* was timely. In that year, Bert Walker, Minister of Social Welfare, accused single mothers in de facto relationships of 'ripping off the system'.[46] This marked the start of a campaign in which welfare officers were instructed to cancel benefits in cases where a DPB recipient was in an alleged sexual relationship with a man. Social workers busily searched for men's clothing in cupboards and inspected sleeping arrangements. Feminists protested loudly against such measures, which they perceived as unfair harassment. In 1976, a government committee reviewed the DPB and concluded that it should be continued, but introduced a number of cuts.[47]

Free and legal abortion, without doubt the most passionately contested issue on the women's liberation agenda, provoked disputes among feminists themselves. The Chairperson of the National Organisation for Women, Connie Purdue, for example, a long-time trade unionist and feminist but also a Catholic, staunchly opposed abortion. NOW resolved not to have an abortion policy. There was considerable unanimity within the movement overall, however, on the need to make abortion safe and legal: in 1972, the first National Women's Liberation Conference had agreed to adopt the stance of 'a woman's right to choose'.

From the outset, anti-abortion activists in New Zealand comprised a passionate, organised and effective united front. The Society for the Protection of the Unborn Child (SPUC), formed in 1971, proved a formidable lobby group. A majority of its members opposed abortion on religious grounds.[48] The Abortion Law Reform Association of New Zealand (ALRANZ), a moderate, low-key group advocating law reform, commenced in 1971 in response to SPUC. The feminist Women's National Abortion Action Committee

(WONAAC), formed in 1973, uncompromisingly advocated repeal of all abortion laws.

The saga of the Auckland Medical Aid Centre (AMAC), New Zealand's first legal abortion clinic, offers an insight into the antagonistic polarisation surrounding this issue. Run by ALRANZ and set up in Remuera in May 1974, this heavily utilised facility, staffed by several prominent feminists, experienced a police raid in mid-September. To the outrage of doctors throughout the country, the police took away patient files, to search for incriminating evidence. As a result of the raid, the clinic doctor James Woolnough soon faced twelve counts of procuring illegal abortions. Following three trials, he was eventually acquitted. In 1976, a Bill passed requiring that abortions be conducted in licensed hospitals. Accordingly, the AMAC shifted into one. For some four months, anti-abortion campaigners protested outside, chanting around a cross and thumping on a miniature wooden coffin. In 1976, the hospital suffered some $100,000 worth of damage after an arson attack.[49] Feminists continued meanwhile to busily prepare submissions for the Royal Commission on Contraception, Sterilisation and Abortion, which the National government had appointed in 1975.

While abortion was a major preoccupation for the women's movement, so too were health issues. The hugely influential American book *Our Bodies, Ourselves* (1973) argued that women needed to wrest control over their own bodies from a patronising male medical establishment and, armed with relevant information, engage in proactive self-help.[50] Different kinds of feminists adopted a varied range of methods to facilitate this goal; some lobbied for change within the existing system; others turned their back on it altogether. Radical feminists, in defiance of the law, handed out contraception leaflets to high school students, and Women's Health Clinics run by women for women set up files on local doctors, who they rated 'hot' or 'cold' on a scale of sexist attitudes. What was perceived as a patronising and unforthcoming approach towards women patients by many male doctors drew increasing feminist criticism from the early 1970s onwards, but it was not until 1987, as examined more fully in Chapter 10 of this book, that issues surrounding the treatment of a group of cervical cancer patients at National Women's Hospital in Auckland precipitated a major public outcry. The ensuing Cartwright Inquiry, which resulted in regulatory and legal changes to a number of fields of medicine, represented the culmination of a long-standing feminist challenge to the medical establishment. In addition to casting a critical eye upon the medical profession, some feminists in the course of the 1970s began to ask questions about the safety of the birth-control pill, as well as the perilous side-effects of other contraception options such as the Dalkon Shield and Depo-Provera.

Male violence and its impact on women's health also came under feminist scrutiny. In 1974, the first women's refuge opened in Christchurch. This initiative, one of the enduring success stories of second-wave feminism, saw no fewer than 34 refuges operating throughout the country by 1985, with more in the process of being opened.[51] The refuges, run as much as possible along collectivist, non-hierarchical lines, from the outset encouraged the principle of self-help. In 1973, too, the first rape crisis centre, a part-time service conducted by phone and run by volunteers, opened in Wellington. Feminists put rape, an issue not previously discussed openly, squarely in the public domain. In addition to establishing a network of support services for victims, they commenced a consciousness-raising campaign to publicise the nature and extent of this underreported crime. They also made a concerted attempt to raise awareness of the invidious impacts of pornography, a cause shared by moral right crusaders such as Patricia Bartlett, who were, in all other respects, vehemently opposed to women's liberation and everything it stood for. Issues surrounding male violence towards women continued to be a focus within the feminist movement in later years: the first 'Women Reclaim the Night' march against male violence took place in 1979; by 1981, a National Collective of Independent Women's Refuges was established and three years later received government funding. In 1982, a Domestic Protection Act helped protect women from domestic violence through use of non-molestation orders and emergency occupation and tenancy orders.

Another United Women's Convention in Wellington in 1975 attracted a record 2000 attendance, with hundreds having to be turned away. Radical collectivists and liberal feminists engaged in a few more disputes this time. The former held a separate Radical Feminist Caucus later in the year and in 1976 formed a Radical Feminist Network. Radical feminists, in contrast to liberal feminists, took a somewhat jaundiced view of the fact that 1975 was United Nations International Women's Year. While approving of the attention to their cause, they resented government's perceived hierarchical, top-down control. Writing in the *Listener* at the end of the year, Pauline Ray noted: 'In a way, the women's year dilemma mirrored the dilemma of the feminist movement — whether to keep plugging away through established channels or to set up alternative channels and institutions.'[52]

A national conference entitled 'Education and the Equality of the Sexes', the government's first formal contribution to International Women's Year, proposed measures to lessen sexism and inequality in the school system and spurred the creation of groups dedicated to improving women teachers' rights and opportunities. The PPTA, for example, set up a Sex Equality Advisory Committee. In 1975, the report of the Labour government's Select Committee on Women's Rights concluded that the main source of inequality between the sexes was the preconception that only traditional domestic roles were suitable for women. Consequently, it recommended measures to advance women's opportunities in education, work and public life. Later, joint initiatives between government and women's groups included the Women in Social and Economic Development Conference (1976) and a Women and Health Conference (1977).

Eradicating inequality and achieving parity with men — one of the key goals of liberal feminism — gained an effective new voice in 1975. The Women's Electoral Lobby (WEL) aimed to increase women's election and appointment to public office, and to advance gender equality. Modelled on an Australian precedent, it rapidly proliferated: within eight months, there were around 2000 members in eighteen branches.[53] Many, such as Marilyn Waring, Margaret Shields, and Ruth Richardson, went on to enjoy prominent political careers. The group, formed in an election year, attracted a great deal of media attention, especially because it rated political candidates according to their stance on women's issues. The long-term impact of the push to attract more New Zealand women into public and political roles was dramatic and successful. Dawn Ibbotson later remarked that:

> My daughter and I attended the United Women's Convention in 1975. If anyone had told us at that time that within 25 years we could have had two women Governors General, two women Prime Ministers, a woman bishop and a woman Attorney General — we would have laughed. It would have seemed quite impossible.[54]

By 1975, rifts between variants of feminism showed no signs of closing. Moreover, the broader community's perceptions of the movement grew even more ambivalent. In a 1975 *Listener* editorial, Michael Dean took stock of what feminists had achieved, noting the movement's loss of support due to 'the emotional Calvinism of some of the leadership'. In his view: 'The optimism in which International Women's Year began has turned sour. The acceleration of social change has produced anxieties in the ranks of the movement itself.' There were no easy answers when liberation was often only feasible for a privileged few. For working-class women, leaving the prison of their homes was not so attractive when the alternative was 'the prison of the factory bench'. Warning that it 'is self-interest in the disguise of enlightenment which argues that women who abandon their babies to day-care centres are doing the best by their children', Dean went on to contend:

> Philosophically the movement is in a mess. Much of its jargon has been borrowed from the New Left, which itself lies in ruins, but its protagonists range from blinkered Marxists to the self-styled moderates of the political centre . . . This kind of pluralism, of course, is both the movement's disabling weakness and its truly democratic strength.[55]

This rather bleak assessment neglected the substantive achievements feminism had effected in a short period of time. Nor did it celebrate the fact that the pluralistic melange produced a remarkable creative outpouring.

Creative liberation

Women's art burgeoned in the 1970s. Rita Angus, Lois White, Evelyn Page and Olivia Spencer Bower were among the many New Zealand artists whose work feminists rescued from obscurity and celebrated. In 1974, the women's professional association Zonta organised a show of 20 contemporary New Zealand women artists in Auckland; and in 1975 a women's art show featured at the Robert McDougall Art Gallery in Christchurch. In 1976, *Broadsheet* toured a women's photography exhibition, 'Womanvision', throughout the country, with works by Marti Friedlander, Gil Hanly and Fiona Clark among others. In 1979, Christchurch hosted a women's art festival and the National Art Gallery set up a women's Art Archive. In the same year, a Women's Gallery opened in Wellington. In 1980, a national Association of Women Artists formed, supported by Outreach, Auckland's cultural centre for the visual and performing arts. Feminist Art Networkers, an offshoot of the Association of Women Artists, created in Auckland in 1982, encouraged links between New Zealand women artists and the thriving international women's art movement.[56]

Women writers also flourished, with authors such as Fiona Kidman, Patricia Grace, Marilyn Duckworth, Lauris Edmond, Sue McCauley, Margaret Mahy and Tessa Duder attracting a wide readership and critical acclaim. In 1975, no less than nine poetry collections by New Zealand women poets were published. *Private Gardens*, an anthology of New Zealand women's poetry, appeared in 1977.[57] *Spiral*, a women's art and literary journal, commenced in Wellington in 1976 and soon became a floating imprint, used by a variety of feminist groups. It also published books by New Zealand women writers unable to find another publisher (most famously, Keri Hulme's *the bone people*, which went on to win the 1984 Booker Prize).

Feminists made a concerted attempt to highlight outstanding women in history such as Kate Sheppard, Katherine Mansfield and Robin Hyde, and to find out more about the past lives of ordinary New Zealand women. Suffrage Day on 19 September, instigated by the Auckland Women's Liberation Front in 1971 to help raise the profile of women's history, became a popular yearly event. Feminist bookshops also opened in Dunedin, Christchurch and Auckland. After demand grew among university students for more courses about women's history and women-related subjects, in 1974, Rosemary Seymour at Waikato University offered the first credited women's studies courses, followed a year later by Phillida Bunkle at Victoria University. An informal Women's Studies Association formed at Waikato in 1974 came formally into being in 1977. By this time, women's studies courses and departments proliferated nation-wide. In 1984, a Women's Studies Association journal commenced, the first issue pursuing the theme of 'rowdy women'.[58] In addition, several publishing companies, such as Bridget Williams Books, specialised in feminist books and/or women's history.

In the performing arts, feminist drama and comedy conveyed social and political ideas, and opened up hitherto unexplored or taboo subjects. The Dunedin-based *Cure All Ills All Star Travelling Medicine Show* toured the country in 1975 with a satirical review that dealt frankly with subjects such as menstruation. Numerous other reviews followed, some directed at topical issues like abortion, others about lesbianism. The Hen's Teeth comedy collective toured to great acclaim in the 1980s. In 1981 alone, five feminist plays or dramatic shows premiered in Auckland, including Renée's *Setting the Table* (about feminists who tackle a rapist) and *Secrets*, about incest. *Broadsheet* mounted its first touring theatrical review in 1982 with Renée's *What Did You Do in the War, Mummy?*[59]

Television documentaries and features examined the reality of contemporary women's lives. In 1975, the Committee on Women asked government to make a film about New Zealand women for International Women's Year. Deirdre McCartin produced and directed *Some of My Best Friends are Women* assisted by a predominantly female crew. This film focused on three women, aged 18, 34 and 61, at work, home, and with family. As McCartin explained, a major theme was 'about choice . . . We wanted to explore the choices available to women and the extent they take them up, or don't.'[60] In 1977, a subsequent series produced six documentaries on women-related issues, including domestic violence, media stereotyping, marriage, Maori women, sexuality and childcare. Series such as *Pioneer Women* and Merata Mita's films on the 1981 rugby tour and Bastion Point followed in the early 1980s.

In 1981, upon returning to New Zealand after a stint in the International Women's Secretariat of the United Nations in New York, Sue Kedgley saw little evidence of corporate culture having been transformed by feminism's humanising influence. The world of mirror glass and tailored suits and profit margins remained generally impervious to the sort of transformative ideals of sisterhood and non-hierarchical equality espoused by groups such as the Dunedin Collective for Woman. Yet in Kedgley's view, 'the women who didn't join the stampede into the corporate world, the artists, writers and women who work from home or have set up their own businesses have been extraordinarily successful in forging a new female culture and a new female voice'.[61] Whether these non-corporate women artists and writers identified as 'feminist' or not, they worked in an era when women's creativity was recognised, celebrated and supported as never before, in no small part due to the efforts of the feminist movement.

Trouble, strife, backlash

The artistic creativity that feminism inspired in the late 1970s and early 1980s did not extend to other aspects of the movement. To borrow a phrase from Queen Elizabeth II, 1977 in particular was something of an 'annus horribilis', during which feminism faced challenges both from within its ranks and without. The first blow, the Contraception, Sterilisation and Abortion Act of April 1977, in contrast to more liberal abortion laws being passed internationally,[62] made abortion law in New Zealand more restrictive. Leading figures in the National Party supported this conservative legislation. In September 1974, while still in opposition, Muldoon came out against abortion, having received 1057 letters against it and only 179 in favour.[63] In the 1978 election, the only political party to argue for women's right to decide whether to have an abortion was the Values Party, which failed to come third in any seat.[64] Following the 1977 Act, women seeking a termination would now have to present their case before a medical panel, and abortions were only legal if the danger to a woman's health could not be averted by any other means. The abortion clinic in Auckland closed with just one day's notice.

Feminists responded by organising the Sisters Overseas Service (SOS), which assisted women to fly to Australia for abortions. By September 1978 some 1000 women had used this service, spearheaded by activist Joss Shawyer.

Broadsheet aided the cause by including an SOS leaflet in its January 1978 issue along with a sticker on the cover announcing 'Where to get an abortion — see inside'. By February 1978, a feminist-launched petition calling for the repeal of the 1977 Act quickly garnered 318,820 signatures.[65] The Petitions Committee gave it a low rating for consideration, however, and thus prevented its presentation to Parliament. In 1979, an arson attack seriously damaged the SOS office in New Street, Ponsonby.

Nevertheless, the situation regarding access to abortion gradually improved, partly because Parliament's advisory body on abortion, the Abortion Supervisory Committee, in response to criticism, requested changes to make the 1977 law workable. The interpretation of the law also gradually liberalised, until there were sufficient certifying consultants and facilities to provide a service in New Zealand. The Auckland Medical Aid Centre received a licence and reopened in 1979, and public abortion facilities opened in Auckland and Wellington. By 1981, flights across the Tasman for terminations virtually ceased. According to Laurie Guy: 'Conservatives won the battle over parliamentary legislation, but lost the war over abortion practice.'[66]

In addition to its tightening up of abortion, the 1977 Contraception, Sterilisation and Abortion Act also included clauses that further restricted teaching about contraception and sex education in schools. These stipulations represented a victory for conservative groups on the 'moral right' who had been lobbying against any attempts to loosen those restrictions since the early 1970s. Sex education in New Zealand was prohibited in primary schools and only inconsistently provided at secondary school. In 1973, the Ross Report sought to revise sex education in order to take into account recent 'vast changes in public attitudes'.[67] Commissioned under the then Labour government, the report recommended offering introductory programmes in human development and relationships at primary school, and compulsory sex education courses at secondary school.

A group of parents who fiercely opposed these proposals formed the Concerned Parents' Association to lobby against it. Another group, the Family Rights Association, created in 1973, aimed to protect the traditional nuclear family from the perceived threat of 'permissive elements' such as feminists and gay rights advocates. Other groups such as the Society for the Protection of Community Standards and SPUC endorsed this stance. These conservative groups objected to liberal sex education guides the *Little Red School Book* (1972) and *Down Under the Plum Trees* (1976) as obscene, and submitted them to the Indecent Publications Tribunal. That body subsequently found the former to be 'decent' but stipulated that only those over eighteen could read the latter, unless instructed by parents or professional advisors. In 1978, London Bookshops was fined for publicly displaying *Down Under the Plum Trees* and Alex Comfort's sex guide *The Joy of Sex*.[68]

A Save Our Homes (SOH) group, formed in 1977, organised an anti-feminist convention to coincide with the feminist United Women's Convention in Christchurch that year. SOH laid the break-down of family life at feminism's door, arguing that 'when it comes to the governmental arrangement of the family there is no equality, the husband is the head of the home. The husband is the provider and the protector.'[69] Traditional moralists like SOH feared that state involvement in sex education would interfere in what they saw as the rightful province of family control and impose the new permissive morality on children. Feminism challenged the traditional gender roles (not just in advo-cating sex education but in promoting non-sexist readers) that such groups aimed to maintain.

In 1977, the Johnson Report (a follow-up to the Ross Report, also initiated by Labour) endorsed integrated sex education and relationship programmes within schools. The public had until 1979 to respond to its recommendations. Conservative moral right groups again mounted a concerted campaign of opposition, uniting to form the Council of Moral Education (COME) in 1978. This aimed to protect the sanctity of the traditional nuclear family and reject (acronym notwithstanding) any curriculum involving sex education and contraception.

Despite the fact that the majority of the 2700 submissions on the Johnson Report supported its proposals, Merv Wellington, the conservative Minister of Education from 1978, ignored its recommendations.[70] It was not until 1985 that the Education Amendment Act set the parameters for sex education in primary and secondary schools. For the first time, sex education formed part of the syllabus for primary schools, with sexual health education from form one (ten years). This moderate legislation contained the proviso that parents be consulted on the health syllabus every eighteen months, and gave them the right to withdraw their children from classes on sexual education if desired.[71]

As battles with moral right groups gained momentum in the late 1970s, the women's movement itself became more bitterly divided internally. At the 1977 United Women's Convention, intense battles raged between women's lib-erationists and liberal reformist feminists, lesbians and heterosexuals, Maori and Pakeha. At one stage, radical feminists evicted male reporters from the premises on the grounds that men could never be objective. Several women journalists, feeling conflicted about this ejection, later created 'Media Women', a group aiming to both improve women's depiction in the media and raise their status and influence within it.[72]

In 1978, increasing conflict between lesbians and non-lesbians resulted in what came to be known as 'the great split' at the *Broadsheet* collective, when half of the members left the magazine. Angry disputes between lesbians and hetero-sexuals, Maori and Pakeha, also marred the Radical Feminist Caucus at Piha in 1978. A year later, the United Women's Convention at Waikato University made a mockery of the conference name, as different kinds of feminists engaged in vitriolic disputes. Some women graffitied university buildings with crude slogans, justifying this on the grounds that these premises were male property. Eventually, the conference organisers, after receiving death threats, called in the police. Although this convention attracted record numbers, it was a painful occasion, never to be repeated.

Writing in 1993, Sandra Coney traced the point when women's liberation 'inexorably set on the path of self-destruction' to the 1978 Radical Feminist Caucus at Piha, and described the 1979 convention in Hamilton as 'the death knell of the women's liberation movement':

> Women were meant to be better, kinder, more nurturing people than harsh, aggres-
> sive, power-hungry men. And yet women indulged in purges, coups, ostracisation,
> and brutal confrontations, which often included a special manipulativeness that
> they had learned to get their way in a man's world.[73]

Coney observed that many women left the movement disillusioned in the late 1970s and moved into causes such as campaigning for ecological issues, peace, or anti-racism. She contrasted the early 1970s period, in which the key word was liberation, with all its positive joyful connotations, to a later preoccupation with women's subservience and victimhood.[74]

Factionalism and intolerance undeniably existed among some sections of the women's movement from the late 1970s. Perhaps the most notorious exam-ple of unauthorised physical aggression towards men occurred on 1 February 1984 when six feminist vigilantes kidnapped University of Auckland lecturer and playwright Mervyn Thompson and chained him to a tree in a local park.[75] They then sprayed the word 'rapist' on his car. A press release subsequently explained that the action had been necessary because the status of some men exempted them from accountability through the court system.[76] This incident did not improve feminism's public profile, and indeed the perception of some activists as zealous, man-hating extremists threatened to overshadow many of the movement's positive achievements.

In the course of the 1970s, feminists dramatically raised public awareness about sexism in the workplace, media, schools, Parliament and families. Breakthrough legislation such as the Equal Pay Act of 1972 helped to alleviate women's iniquitous position under the law. More legal protections followed: in 1977, for example, the Human Rights Commission Act legislated against, and provided remedies for, discrimination against women.[77] Older women's independence was increased by the introduction of national superannuation, which replaced earlier pension provisions based on the marital unit, while the Citizenship Act of 1977 ensured that women enjoyed the same nationality rights as men (that is, they too could now pass on their citizenship to their husband and children). In 1980, the Maternity Leave and Employment Protection Act allowed women to take pregnancy leave for up to 26 weeks and prohibited dismissal on the grounds of pregnancy or maternity leave. In 1983, a Minimum Wage Act entitled women over 20 to the same minimum wage as men, and an Equal Employment Opportunities (EEO) programme was introduced in the public service. In 1983, New Zealand ratified the International Labour Organization Equal Pay Convention, which covered equal pay for work of equal value.[78]

Women were taking advantage of opportunities in tertiary education to train for professions such as the law. A study of Victoria University graduands doing Bachelor's and Master's degrees in the period 1963–66 showed that only 0.4 per cent of female students studied law, with arts attracting 77.5 per cent.[79] By 1992, almost half of new lawyers were women, compared to only 2 per cent in 1975.[80]

In 1982, Sue Wood was elected president of the National Party; two years later, Margaret Wilson became Labour's president. By 1984, New Zealand had ten Labour women MPs. When, in 1983, the Society for Research on Women and the Women's Advisory Committee of the Vocational Training Council embarked upon a 'Girls Can Do Anything' campaign, it seemed to many to be already patently the case. This initiative did lead, however, to a further significant leap in the number of women in non-traditional careers such as horse racing and firefighting.[81]

Even those who played little or no part in the women's movement were affected by it. Many women's lives took new directions, altered by the sudden surge of feminine energy and aspiration. This did not necessarily involve the adoption of an unconventional or alternative lifestyle. Penny Jamieson, who in

1989 became the seventh Anglican Bishop of Dunedin (and the first woman in the world to be elected a diocesan bishop), remembers, for example, the liberating impact of reading a book by Mary Daly called *The Church and the Second Sex* in a local theological discussion group:

> Sharing that together was enormously revealing. It just blew our minds. Some of us went on to become continually active and really quite strong in church leadership because we could see the feminist issues, and others dropped right out, but life would never be the same afterwards. It was quite formative for me personally.[82]

Mary O'Regan, the first secretary of the newly created Ministry of Women's Affairs from 1985 (and the first New Zealand woman to head a government department), initially acquired feminism at a practical, community level:

> I started with issues of employment and training, and then began to make connections with other aspects of women's lives . . . you can't actually deny the systems that are there, so to that extent I'm a reformist. A lot of the systems are not worth keeping, but because they are fairly entrenched I've tended to say, 'Let's see what we can do with them or around them or in them.' I have experienced varying degrees of elation and despair working that way. I don't think there has been radical change or development in the time that I've been involved, but I do think there has been a general shift in people's consciousness — in the heads, if not the hearts, of men and in women's expectations.[83]

Raising consciousness about women's roles and rights helped to broaden education and career options. Dramatically improved educational achievement was one of the great legacies of second-wave feminism. At the start of the 1970s, more boys than girls were likely to stay to form six at secondary school, but from the mid-1970s, that pattern reversed and proportionately more girls than boys continued to sixth form. The number of girls remaining until form six increased from 40 per cent in 1970 to 72 per cent in 1989. In 1979, 30 per cent of girls left school with no qualifications; a decade later this had dropped to 18 per cent. In 1966, women accounted for 28 per cent of university enrolments; by 1988, they comprised 51 per cent.[84] By the 1980s, New Zealand women were confidently striking out on more diverse career paths, adopting routes that would have seemed highly unlikely in 1970.

Despite such advances, the majority of New Zealand women were neither active supporters nor vehement opponents of feminism. Rosemary Barrington and Alison Gray's *The Smith Women*, a set of 1981 interviews of 100 diverse women with this common surname, illustrated views about feminism ranging from the cautiously supportive to the distinctly negative. A commonly held perception was that feminism went too far, was anti-male, and difficult to combine with a workable family life. Many interviewees felt that the women's movement agitated for more self-centredness, and saw this as having a detrimental impact on home life and society in general. 'Cheryl', a young mother (and the only working-class woman to comment on feminist issues), perceived women's lib to be a threat to the natural order:

> A lot of women's libbers think today there should be half and half — the husband should do the washing one day and all that. But I think that's the woman's place. The jobs for the wife are laid down; she cooks, cleans, and all that. Not half and half, with her husband doing the cooking one night. Colin will help me to a certain extent, but not to the point where I'll say, 'Well, you cook the tea tonight. I'm going to sit and watch TV'; or something like that.[85]

Several interviewees expressed the view that the movement was too extreme and surplus to requirements. Sarah, for example, stated: 'I agree to a certain point with the feminist movement. I think the danger is, as with all groups, that a few people get carried away with their cause. Women in New Zealand on the whole can do what they want to do, if they want to.' Others, such as Melissa, perceived it to threaten femininity itself: 'I don't like women's lib to the extent that some of them carry it. I still love being female. Mostly it's the old-fashioned idea that the men look after you. I think if you had to go without that there wouldn't be much use in being married.' Alma, another interviewee, believed that 'women's lib has broken up a lot of homes and families because each one is out to do their own thing, no matter what. They're not going to stick at home because of the family and neither of them is going to give in, so they each go their way and who are the losers? The family. I'm just not a women's libber at all.'[86]

The nuclear family did suffer some serious blows in the course of the 1970s. Between the early 1970s and the mid-1980s, the marriage rate fell by a third and the introduction of no-fault divorce doubtless helped the divorce rate to rise from under five per thousand marriages in 1970 to well over fifteen in the early 1980s. Households were smaller, marriages occurred later, and, more remarkably, only just over a third of New Zealand homes now consisted of a traditional nuclear family — that is, mum, dad, and at least one child. Now, a great many New Zealand households were a mix of solo parents, childless couples, same-sex unions and multi-family groups.[87]

One feminist initiative that attracted considerable criticism from more conservative groups was the New Zealand Working Women's Charter, promulgated by labour activist Sonja Davies. This bill of rights for working women advocated equal pay, equal opportunity, paid family leave, and the elimination of all discrimination on the basis of sex, sexuality, age, race, and marital or parental status. More controversially, it also supported freely available sex education and birth-control advice and the removal of all impediments to safe abortion, contraception and sterilisation.[88] In 1980, it was adopted as policy by the Federation of Labour, and the Labour Party formally endorsed it in 1981.

Conservatives particularly objected to those clauses of the Working Women's Charter that advocated 'wide availability of quality childcare with government, employer and community support for all those who need it, including industrial crèches, after-school care and holiday care'.[89] The National Council of Women refused to support the Charter because it interpreted this clause as an unreasonable demand for 24-hour childcare. It also refused to endorse the clause relating to freely available birth control because of its reference to abortion. In Parliament, the Labour MP and anti-abortion campaigner Dr Gerard Wall referred to childcare centres as 'dumping grounds for parents who offload their children'.[90] Fundamentalist Christian groups also commenced a well-orchestrated campaign, denouncing the Working Women's Charter as promoting:

> . . . the Marxist vision of the family . . . it's fine political and economic theory to rear infants in day-care centres but it flies in the face of Mother Nature and common sense . . . The Working Women's Charter calls for the state to become the principal custodian of children. It denigrates the role of the housewife in society.[91]

Meanwhile, any progress in getting government commitment to improve childcare facilities and training proved elusive. Writing in 1978, the National MP Marilyn Waring reviewed the actions undertaken since the recommendations of the Report of the Select Committee on Women's Rights, concluding: 'The prize for total non-implementation goes to . . . childcare . . . there is no progress.' She noted the Minister of Social Welfare's view that: 'Present government policy does not accept that central government has a responsibility to initiate and promote the establishment of childcare centres . . . the family has and should retain the primary responsibility of childcare.'[92]

As the number of mothers working with children under five rose (in 1976, they numbered 45,030, 26,250 of whom were part-time and this figure continued to rise), childcare arrangements remained largely 'makeshift'. One 1981 study of mothers in Newtown in Wellington, for example, showed that 68 per cent had taken on work of some kind with a pre-schooler but only 10 per cent had used childcare services. Using friends, family or private minders was the more common option. The number of employers providing childcare services rose from eleven in 1971 to 41 in 1980, but generally they did not as a group accept this responsibility and like many others were waiting for the government to act.[93]

Conservative Christian groups concerned about the perceived weakening of the traditional nuclear family campaigned in 1983 against the proposed ratification by the government of the United Nations Convention on the Elimination of All Forms of Discrimination against Women (CEDAW). They viewed this agreement as yet another threat to women's roles as wives and mothers. A mass campaign against ratification was waged by various conservative and religious groups such as the Country Women's Institute, the Women's Division of Federated Farmers, Women for Life, the Catholic Women's League, the Salvation Army, the Baptist churches and a number of Pentecostal churches. In response to this mounting pressure (which included a 46,000-signature petition), National decided against ratification.[94] Similarly, National never endorsed the New Zealand Working Women's Charter.

After Labour's election win in 1984, the new government held forums around the country to discuss women's issues, and to formulate the agenda for the newly created Ministry of Women's Affairs. Conservative Christian women, fearful that the new government would ratify CEDAW, seized their chance and hired buses and car-pooled to organise mass turnouts and express their anti-ratification views. A representative from the Australian anti-feminist group called 'Women Who Want to be Women' visited at this time to lend support.[95] The campaign by conservative women not only resulted in some stormy exchanges with feminists, but highlighted the issue in the media.[96] Just prior to Christmas 1984, Labour ratified CEDAW. Although its opponents had been unsuccessful, their organisation and volubility attests to the widespread feeling among conservatives that family values were under siege.

Facing such vocal opposition helped to renew a sense of purpose and unity among feminists, but only for a brief time. As the 1980s drew to a close, the women's movement began to feel enervated and conflicted. The radical feminist collectivist model based on consensus and cooperation in particular increasingly seemed a pipe dream. While some elements did live on in various service providers, most notably in the health sector, non-hierarchical women's collectives generally wound down or disbanded. To many women, it appeared that full-time motherhood was being devalued. At the same time, armies of besuited 'superwomen' attempted to prosper in a hierarchically ordered male world only to bang their heads against a 'glass ceiling'. Despite equal pay legislation, significant gaps still existed between men's and women's earnings. Moreover, domestic duties still lay primarily with women. A 1976 survey by the Federation of University Women revealed that only 42 per cent of women had any help with housework from men, and a National Council of Women study in 1985 showed little change in men's contribution in this area.[97]

When in 1983 Jenny Phillips's *Mothers Matter Too* had appeared in bookshops, mothers at home responded instantly to its message, hoping for recognition of their neglected status and needs.[98] In addition, while middle-class women steadily acquired tertiary qualifications and rewarding careers, in recessionary times, working-class women, who included many Maori and Pacific Islanders, found themselves out of work and impoverished. Between 1976 and 1986, the female unemployment rate was almost twice that of New Zealand men.[99] In 1982, 'Women Against the Cuts' groups formed in Wellington and Auckland to protest the impact that government cuts to health, education and welfare had on women.

Like other countries throughout the western world, New Zealand's second wave of feminism in the 1970s played a part in a broader cultural transformation that resulted in a more socially diverse, less conventional and constrictive society. While the women's movement owed much to international ideas and trends (particularly American feminism), it had several distinctive elements. In contrast to the United States, where radical libbers split away from established moderate liberal-feminist groups, in New Zealand the radical collectivist strain of women's lib from the outset comprised a distinct, influential force. Yet, long before 'women's lib' became a phenomenon, moderate liberal feminists had looked for, and had considerable success in obtaining, legislative and other assistance from the state to improve women's status and opportunities relative to men.

Liberal feminists continued to comprise an important part of second-wave feminism in the 1970s and 1980s, successfully lobbying for legislative change and social policies to improve women's opportunities. The radical, non-hierarchical, collective approach to women's issues, although less enduring, helped to transform old stereotypes and offered a communitarian alternative to the liberal model of women gaining equity in a hierarchical, competitive, individualist workplace. The critiques of radical Maori feminists, for whom many of feminism's preoccupations appeared beside the point in what they perceived to be a racist society, also added another layer of complexity to second-wave New Zealand feminism. Finally, feminists keen to change long-standing notions about women's roles had to contend with that tenacious breed, the 'Kiwi bloke'.

Blokedom under fire

Whatever their views on the women's movement, few New Zealand men in the 1970s remained oblivious to its indictment of chauvinism and sexist stereotyping. Feminists criticised the 'rugby, racing and beer' culture, but by the late 1970s, so too did Kiwi men. In *The Passionless People* (1976), a humorous indictment of contemporary New Zealand, Gordon McLauchlan pilloried the national cult of the laconic, lawn-mowing, rugby-playing bloke:

> If a man has a steady job, grows main crop potatoes in his vegetable patch, keeps his lawns down, can fix a tap and paint a roof and maintain his car, played Rugby as a young man and now watches the main game at The Park every Saturday and doesn't actually fall over and vomit on someone else's carpet when he's drunk, then he can screw paupers for money and beat his kids mercilessly and treat his wife like a pet cat, and still be admired.[100]

In December 1978, Auckland University was the venue for the first New Zealand Men's Conference, organised by the Men's Alliance for Liberation and Equality, which attracted some 150 men and 30 women. A *Listener* article called 'Unmoulding Men' captured the conference's fraught ambience and doomed attempts at male expiation:

> The best thing to be at New Zealand's first men's conference . . . was female. Gay was good, too. Black was great. The worst thing to be was male, white and heterosexual; those who automatically qualified as Oppressor, bent on keeping women, blacks and gays in subjugation every working minute . . .'[101]

What it meant to be a New Zealand male was a subject pursued with growing interest in academic circles. In 1980, Jock Phillips began exploring the enduring impact of Kiwi male stereotypes and myths, a subject he later made the focus of a full-length historical study, *A Man's Country*, in 1987.[102] Alison Gray's *The Jones Men* (a 1983 companion volume to the aforementioned *Smith Women* of

1981) also illustrated that blokedom, rugby and a matey drinking culture were still central to many men's lives. All of the 100 interviewees worked hard and felt responsible for supporting their wives and children, but many still perceived housework and child-minding to be women's work. As one man remarked: 'We split the chores right down one side. She does it all.'[103] Another observed:

> Let's face it, the wife brings up most children. She does the hardest stage. I can honestly say I didn't have a lot to do with bringing the children up. But that is probably the case in 99.5 per cent of all families. Most of the stress comes on when you're trying to pacify your wife, who thinks it's because she's depressed. You're always trying to keep the balance.[104]

Yet some men, especially younger middle-class ones, made an effort to share household chores, and a number openly and eagerly expressed their love and gratitude towards their partners.[105] The mere existence of the book reflected a heightened appreciation of men's changing roles. Women were not the only ones oppressed by the hard-drinking, mate-ish culture of the Kiwi male. Men themselves suffered, especially those who did not conform to the heterosexual norm.

Prejudice and pride: lesbian and gay liberation

During the 1970s, a watershed decade for lesbians and gay men in New Zealand, openness and pride replaced secrecy and shame. Lesbianism, although legal (its possibility not apparently countenanced in the nineteenth century), was a word most young New Zealanders in the 1950s and 1960s rarely heard. Schools offered little or no sex education, and young women were generally expected to marry and raise children. When lesbianism did receive publicity, it was through two highly publicised murder cases — that of Thelma Mareo by her husband Eric in 1935, and the sensational Parker-Hulme murder of 1953. Being a lesbian was thus linked in the public mind with 'being mad, bad and violent'.[106]

For homosexual men, the law compounded the situation. Being discovered to be engaged in homosexual acts could result in a criminal conviction, loss of career, or even blackmail, all compelling reasons to remain within the closet. The example of writer and academic Bill Pearson offers an insight into the stress and strain facing homosexual men in 1950s New Zealand. Faced with the daunting prospect of leaving London and returning to his homophobic homeland, Pearson consulted a psychiatrist about his homosexuality, touchingly hoping for a 'cure'. When the doctor advised him to accept his 'condition' and get on with his life, Pearson's telling response was: 'I am going back to a very puritan country.'[107]

Homosexuality was considered an unnatural affliction or pathology, linked to mental illness. This belief was widely held around the world and by no means unique to New Zealand. In 1966, for example, the Australian edition of *Time* magazine described homosexuality as a 'pernicious sickness'.[108] The religious also frequently denounced homosexuality as sinful. In Maurice Gee's novel *Plumb*, the Reverend George Plumb's response upon discovering his son in homosexual activity is shocking in its ferocity: 'I cried that they were unclean, that they were filth. And I called down death upon them, I called down brimstone, fire; I smote them so they died.'[109]

In 1964, six young men beat Charles Aberhart to death in Christchurch's Hagley Park, but were acquitted on a charge of manslaughter because he had made homosexual approaches. The successful use of 'homosexual panic' as a defence sent a message that gay men and lesbian women could be killed almost with impunity and that 'discretion and caution were essential'.[110]

Nevertheless, during the 1950s and 1960s, New Zealand cities included lesbian and gay meeting places. Auckland had the Vic, the Oxy, the Shakespeare, Gleeson's and the Queen's Ferry; in Wellington, 'packed, noisy, smoky' venues such as the Royal Oak Hotel, the Sorrento (later the Sunset Strip), and coffee bars such as Chez Paree, Carmen's, the Tete a Tete, Man Friday and Let's Be In, had a 'volatile, bizarre, and risky, though always exciting' ambience.[111] The first lesbian club, KG (for Karangahape Road Girls' Club), opened in Auckland in 1971. Its clientele, largely working class, with a strong Maori presence, viewed middle-class 'libbers' with some wariness.

As with feminism, overseas events and cultural influences profoundly influenced gay liberation in New Zealand. The 1969 Stonewall Riots in New York City, for example, which triggered the American gay liberation movement, evoked a stir of sympathy, excitement and solidarity. It was only a matter of time before New Zealand followed suit and a gay rights movement was officially founded. The catalyst occurred in 1972, when the New Zealand University Students' Association nominated the lesbian feminist activist Ngahuia Volkerling (Te Awekotuku) to undertake a tour of campuses in the United States. After being denied a US visa on the grounds of 'sexual deviance', she proceeded to the University of Auckland campus and delivered an impassioned speech calling for more openness about sexuality. As a result, an inaugural meeting of a gay liberation group met on the Auckland campus on 21 March 1972. More groups rapidly sprang up around the country. National Gay

Liberation conferences were held between 1972 and 1976, and a National Gay Rights Coalition (NGRC), formally established in June 1977, included some 30 affiliated groups by 1978.[112]

Again, like feminism, the gay rights movement incorporated different strands, with varied views about how best to achieve desired goals. One strand focused on incremental law reform. The first formally organised New Zealand homosexual group, the Wellington Dorian Society, founded in 1962, formed a legal subcommittee to promote law reform in 1963. This was the precursor of the New Zealand Homosexual Law Reform Society, founded in 1967. Made up of straight and gay individuals, it aimed for gradual legislative change. Its members were willing to accept legislation that included different ages of consent for gays and heterosexuals, including the unsuccessful [Venn] Young Bill of 1974 and an equally dormant successor, promoted by Warren Freer, in 1979.

But for more radical and militant elements, any legislative age differential meant an inadmissible acceptance of less than equality with heterosexuals. These reformers wanted a radical transformation of society: a revolution that would liberate gays and lesbians from oppression, denounce homophobes, and initiate a tolerant and liberal acceptance of different sexual preferences. Aims were often both ambitious and undefined. Gay rights activist Lindsay Taylor observed of the formative early 1970s period:

> [We had a] very grandiose scheme of overthrowing the nuclear family, polymorphous sexuality, breakdown of the difference between homosexuality and heterosexuality, which were ideas which had been picked up from the women's movement. On the one hand we had a very limited law reform, and on the other hand this complete overthrow of society. There was nothing in between really. Our political ideas on a strategic basis were virtually non-existent, but we all seemed to have quite similar concepts at that stage. All the people who joined the movement or wanted to form it at that time had backgrounds in the women's movement or the anti-war movement or Maoist politics or whatever, so they shared a fairly common view.[113]

Nevertheless, despite these shared left leanings, methods and cultures often clashed. For example, the divergence between some lesbian feminists and the insouciant theatricality of homosexual drag artists could hardly have been more pronounced. Lesbians frequently criticised the fact that homosexual men did not sufficiently support women's issues. Laurie Guy has written that 'the overall impression of gay liberation co-ordination is one of fragile unity coupled with a great deal of factionalism and fragmentation.'[114]

The first autonomous lesbian political organisation, Sisters for Homophile Equality (SHE), formed in Christchurch in 1973. It aimed to improve lesbians' low self-esteem, and to pursue various lesbian and feminist aims, such as ending discrimination. Another SHE group formed in Wellington later in the same year. This group founded a lesbian magazine, *Circle*, which facilitated the creation of lesbian networks of communication throughout the country. In March 1974, SHE organised the first national lesbian conference in Wellington. In 1979, the Auckland Women's Centre in Ponsonby became home to Auckland's first lesbian support group. Lesbian summer camps, softball teams, and in 1984, a lesbian radio programme, followed. Poets such as Heather McPherson published 'full-bodied, direct and sexy' lesbian love poems.[115]

In 1980, beginning with a hui on Waiheke, a Black Dykes organisation, heavily influenced by black American and Marxist sources, formed. Its membership included Maori and Pacific Island women, and fighting racism was a priority issue along with Maori nationalism. Later in the decade, this group became a more tribally focused entity, and proclaimed itself 'Wahine mo nga Wahine' ('Women for Women').[116] In the early 1980s, two Pakeha comedians and musicians, Jools and Lynda Topp, began to attract a growing fan-base. Identical twins and the daughters of Huntly dairy farmers, they were funny, quintessentially Kiwi, and openly and proudly lesbian.

Gay men and lesbian women could, from the 1970s onward, read a range of newsletters, as well as newspapers such as *Gay News*. Chris Brickell maintains that in the course of the 1970s, gay men in particular came to be recognised as a particular consumer group:

> . . . to be gay implied a particular personality, style and attitude. The gay man knew what he wanted because he knew who he was: somebody with a clearly demarcated sexual identity and a place to stand in the world. After a hundred and forty years of European settlement, the gay New Zealander had finally arrived.[117]

The gay community and its heterosexual supporters raised public awareness of what it meant to be gay or lesbian. A *Listener* feature in 1973 posed the question: 'Is Being Gay Reason to be Glum?' The answer was an emphatic 'No'. In the 1970s, according to John Croskey, Wellingtonians' tolerance of drag surpassed even that of Londoners: 'Wellingtonians didn't bat an eyelid when they saw a drag queen sailing up Cuba Street in full regalia.'[118]

Some events, however, highlighted the limitations of apparently more tolerant and accepting public attitudes. In 1976, for example, Prime Minister Robert

Muldoon (temporarily) destroyed the career of Labour MP Colin Moyle, who had been picked up by the police for alleged homosexual activities a few months earlier, by pointing out discrepancies in Moyle's explanations regarding the incident. Following an inquiry, Moyle resigned. The 'Moyle affair' as it came to be known, attracted much press coverage. Quite a few editorials, and many letter writers, decried Muldoon's campaign of 'personal vilification',[119] but the 'affair' reminded the gay community that an accusation of homosexuality could still damage or even destroy a career.

Muldoon's stance on homosexuality was that while distasteful to most people (even 'sinful'), it was less than a crime and should not be punishable by law.[120] He defended the outspoken young National MP Marilyn Waring when she was attacked about her lesbianism. Waring's involuntary 'outing' occurred in the same year as the Moyle affair, but resulted in a very different outcome. *Truth*'s dramatic front-page announcement of 24 August 1976 that Waring shared a 'Wellington love nest' with a former housewife and mother of three prompted an upsurge of public sympathy for the MP and a backlash against the paper.[121] Hundreds of protesting letters flowed in, while the other dailies maintained a discreet silence. Even allowing for the fact that lesbianism was not illegal, the sympathetic public response to Waring seems to indicate a watershed in public opinion. Yet tolerance on this issue was not universal and opposition was considerable. In 1980, four years after the Moyle affair, for example, the Wellington City Council refused to place a Lesbian Centre advert on city buses on the grounds that 'a small boy might see it and ask his mother what a lesbian was'.[122]

Despite New Zealand's impressive record of legislation for women's rights, in the early 1980s, its laws regarding homosexuality remained notably unreformed. In Britain, decriminalisation occurred in 1967; in Canada, in 1969; in Australia, states began passing decriminalisation legislation from 1975, commencing with South Australia. For many gay rights activists in New Zealand, however, the emphasis during the 1970s was less on legislation and law change, and more on a transformative awakening; an attempt to encourage all of New Zealand, not just its lesbian and gay inhabitants, to come out of the closet — 'that metaphorical space of darkness, silence, repression and self-denial'.[123]

It was not until March 1985 that the Labour MP Fran Wilde introduced a Homosexual Law Reform Bill into Parliament. Despite the more tolerant and permissive beliefs that had swept over the country over the past fifteen years, opposition was heated and protracted. For fourteen months, fundamentalist Christian groups (specifically the Salvation Army, the Associated Pentecostal

Churches of New Zealand, the Reformed Churches of New Zealand, the Church of Jesus Christ of Latter-day Saints, as well as moral right Christian groups such as the Concerned Parents Association), expressed horror at the Bill, which they deemed to be inherently evil; a threat to the family and to morality:

> It is a watershed in the struggle between the forces of good and evil, traditional morality and humanistic liberalism in New Zealand. The outcome will in large measure determine the moral, spiritual and social direction New Zealand takes in the immediate future. Quite apart from the appalling public health consequences of legalising sodomy, the implications of giving rights to homosexual teachers constitute a moral and educational dilemma for nearly every parent of schoolchildren in the country.[124]

The Coalition of Concerned Citizens formed a united front to fight the Homosexual Law Reform Bill by spearheading a variety of activities on moral issues. According to the Coalition's press officer, 'homosexuals came along at the very wrong psychological moment', when the new Labour government was perceived by moralists to be in bed with the enemy — namely, groups such as women's rights and gay rights activists.[125] At this time, Jack Swann, a veteran of the anti-gay campaign in New York, and Jackie Butler, president of Australia's anti-feminist 'Women Who Want to be Women', visited New Zealand to lend support to the anti-homosexual law reform campaign.[126] Selwyn Dawson, a retired Methodist minister, wrote an article in *Metro* magazine called 'God's Bullies', which criticised anti-gay rights campaigners, and depicted them as the counterpart of the American Moral Majority and New Right.[127]

Opponents of the Bill expressed alarmist predictions about the threat posed by HIV/AIDS once homosexuality was legal, describing the illness as a plague brought down by God to punish the sexually perverse.[128] However, the Bill's supporters also invoked AIDS, arguing that legalisation would result in less promiscuous behaviour among homosexuals and enable the disease to be effectively and openly reported and combated. The Bill's opponents presented a massive petition bearing an ostensible 800,000 signatures (there were false signatures as well as some from children) to Parliament under the slogan 'For God — For Family — For Country', a process accompanied by the singing of hymns and choruses.[129] Nevertheless, the Bill eventually passed by a vote of 49 to 44.

The Homosexual Law Reform Act was a milestone for homosexual rights campaigners. Like feminists, in the course of the 1970s, gay rights activists raised the general public's consciousness about and understanding of their cause. The younger generation embraced liberation through self-discovery and freedom of expression, and rejected many former prescriptions about gender roles, sex and sexuality. Calls to ensure equal rights under the law, both for women and for homosexuals, were accompanied by a desire to foster a more open, equitable and tolerant acceptance of diversity with regard to how people lived their lives. Not all New Zealanders shared this desire however. The high-profile, impassioned opposition to homosexual law reform in the mid-1980s highlighted the fact that for some New Zealanders the more permissive attitudes toward sex and sexuality in recent decades presented an unwelcome threat to the traditional heterosexual nuclear family. Although these opponents swam against the tide, they were by no means a spent force. Secularising currents generated 'counter-secular reactions'[130] in the final years of the twentieth century, both in New Zealand and elsewhere around the world.

From the late 1960s onwards, the post-war social consensus came under sustained attack from younger women in particular. While married women had begun challenging notions about stay-at-home mothers by returning to work long before this period, it was not until the rise of second-wave feminism that a number of New Zealand women fervently and often angrily rejected traditional notions about their domestic role in the nuclear family. At the same time, some radical collectivist feminists celebrated domesticity, and aimed for the ascendance of a uniquely female way of operating that would provide an alternative to a hierarchical and competitive 'male world'. Both of these strands contributed to a push for change in the 1970s, as feminists of all persuasions worked for greater equality for women at home, at work, in Parliament, under the law, and in society generally. Gay rights activists also worked to effect a change in social attitudes and prejudices and strove for equality under the law. While both movements achieved considerable success, they also faced significant opposition. In the case of homosexual law reform, a substantive change in civil rights did not occur until 1986. In the long term, however, these movements transformed innumerable aspects of economic and cultural life, altering not only rights under the law but individual and collective sensibilities.

On 17 April 2013, New Zealand became the first country in the Asia Pacific region and the thirteenth country in the world to legalise same-sex marriage. Gay Labour MP Louisa Wall's private member's bill passed with a resounding 77 to 44 vote. Upon hearing the result, Wall commented: 'I think the cross party working group has been incredibly effective, but it also shows we are building on our human rights tradition as a country.'[131]

CHAPTER EIGHT

Race Relations

RENAISSANCE AND REASSESSMENT

We were told we had the best race relations in the world, and believed it because there was nothing at the time to contradict it. It might even have been true, but, if so, we would slowly have to learn, and learn to accept, that that was only in the sense that everyone else's race relations were worse. — C. K. Stead, 2010[1]

In the early 1960s, a consensus prevailed that New Zealand, in addition to its benign climate and spectacular scenery, enjoyed two distinctive social blessings: an egalitarian ethos and harmonious race relations. As K. C. McDonald's 1963 school textbook *Our Country's Story* proudly claimed: 'there is no country in the world where two races of different colour live together with more good will towards each other'.[2] Politicians regularly invoked Lieutenant Governor Hobson's famous pronouncement at the signing of the Treaty of Waitangi: 'He iwi kotahi tatou' ('We are now one people'); Prime Minister Holyoake, for example, frequently sprinkled it into his speeches. By the early 1970s, however, cracks had begun to spread across the veneer of racial harmony. Radical activists took to the streets, and race-related issues featured prominently in the media. Anger, frustration and mounting resentment among both Maori and Pakeha soon displaced the apparent equanimity of the recent past. In 1982, the office of the Race Relations Conciliator published a report that warned: 'The myth of New Zealand as a multi-racial Utopia is foundering on reality.'[3]

Before the high-profile activism of the 1970s and despite evidence to the contrary, New Zealanders' pride in their country's harmonious and equitable race relations remained unruffled. However, Ernest and Pearl Beaglehole's *Some Modern Maoris* (1946), an anthropological study of Maori life in a rural service town, revealed that most Maori worked as unskilled labourers, and lived in crowded, substandard homes. Maori and Pakeha in the community rarely socialised together and both races expressed ambivalence, and frequently open opposition, towards mixed marriage. This latter view was obviously not exceptional. In 1952, the poster text for John O'Shea's film *Broken Barrier* tellingly exclaimed: 'A White boy, a Maori girl, Facing the Challenge of Prejudice!'[4] In 1959, news that the Papakura Hotel had banned Dr H. R. Bennett, a senior medical officer at Kingseat psychiatric hospital, from its lounge bar because he was Maori inspired Allen Curnow, as 'Whim Wham', to write a poem satirising New Zealand's idealised perception of its race relations: 'IF it happened as stated, we'd rather it hadn't occurred — / An unflattering Fact after many a flattering Word.'[5] In 1960, Noel Hilliard's novel *Maori Girl* exposed contemporary racism in Wellington. In the same year, David Ausubel's non-fictional *The Fern and the Tiki* angered some readers with its account of the racial prejudice and discrimination the author witnessed in New Zealand as a Fulbright scholar during the late 1950s.[6]

The myth of racial harmony and equality was easier to maintain when Maori and Pakeha did not live in close proximity. As a boy growing up in 1930s Auckland, the writer C. K. Stead rarely saw a Maori.[7] That situation rapidly changed after the war: in 1961, 38.4 per cent of Maori lived in cities; by 1981, 78.2 per cent did.[8] Many Maori successfully negotiated the difficult transition from rural to urban, but others became lost and alienated. In the late 1960s and early 1970s, a second generation of young, angry, urban Maori activists (along with some radical young Pakeha) added racism and Maori socio-economic disadvantage to the list of contemporary society's failures.

What has come to be known as the Maori Renaissance, an affirmation of Maori cultural and political identity, commenced in the 1970s. It was closely linked to and augmented by international opposition to racism and support for the rights of indigenous people. The American civil rights and Black Power movements, the Australian Aboriginal rights movement, and Amerindian pan-tribal activism featured regularly in the media in the 1960s and early 1970s. At the same time, academics and students on university campuses around the world endorsed anti-racist and anti-colonialist views, as did international organisations such as the United Nations and the Commonwealth.[9]

While United States President Lyndon Johnson received a warm welcome from the majority of New Zealanders during his 1966 visit, opponents of the Vietnam War used the occasion to protest. *Peter Bush*

Young women protest against the war in Vietnam outside the American consulate in Auckland, 1972. *John Miller*

Battling permissiveness: Christian marchers in Auckland in 1972
advocate a return to religion and traditional values. *Marti Friedlander*

Youth activist and hippie Tim Shadbolt (wearing overalls and headband, centre) rehearses with the Norfolk Street Theatre in Ponsonby, Auckland, 1972. *John Miller*

Bruno Lawrence and band perform at the Ngaruawahia music festival in 1973. *John Miller*

Germaine Greer (left) during her 1972 visit to New Zealand; with New Zealand feminists Sue Kedgley and Ngahuia Volkerling (Te Awekotuku), dressed in witch's hat and gown. *John Miller*

Delegates at the United Women's Convention at Waikato University, Hamilton, in 1979. *Marti Friedlander*

Billboards on Auckland's Karangahape Road advertise the kind of male entertainments that angered second-wave feminists. Below, a women's art project of the early 1980s critiques female domestic drudgery. *Gil Hanly*

Separated by a rope, male and female students at Victoria University of Wellington in 1967 watch the film *Ulysses*. The New Zealand film censor had ruled that it be shown only to segregated audiences. *EP/1972/3506/15, Dominion Post Collection, Alexander Turnbull Library*

Allen Maddox and Philip Clairmont at fellow artist Tony Fomison's home in Grey Lynn, Auckland, c. 1977. *Marti Friedlander*

Artist Robin White in front of her painting of poet Sam Hunt, c. 1977. *Marti Friedlander*

Gretchen Albrecht, a major contemporary New Zealand artist, in her Titirangi studio, 1980. *Rod Wills*

Comedians, singers and lesbian feminists Lynda and Jools Topp perform at a
women's concert at Outreach Gallery in Auckland, c. 1982. *Gil Hanly*

Rock musicians playing on the steps of Parliament in the 1960s.
Robin Morrison, N5.4 11, Auckland War Memorial Museum

The United Nations proclaimed 1971 to be the International Year for Action to Combat Racism and Racial Discrimination. Younger, often tertiary educated New Zealanders, who were especially receptive to these international ideas and influences, soon focused their attention on race relations at home.

Although the Maori Renaissance owed much to contemporary ideas opposing racism and advocating indigenous rights, its roots lay in government policies adopted in the formative years after World War II. The Hunn Report of 1961 is a requisite starting point for understanding the various responses of both Maori and Pakeha to race relations in the latter part of the twentieth century.

What the shark said to the kahawai

The Labour government had commissioned the Report on the Department of Maori Affairs (now commonly known as the Hunn Report) in January 1960. Walter Nash, then Prime Minister and Minister of Maori Affairs, concerned about the high Maori crime rate, wanted a better knowledge base for addressing problems associated with the growing numbers of urban Maori. The man chosen to undertake this task, Jack Kent Hunn, was deputy-chairman of the Public Service Commission and Acting Secretary for Maori Affairs. The newly elected National government launched his influential report in January 1961.

The Hunn Report provided dramatic proof that Maori in New Zealand lagged far behind Pakeha in all statistical social welfare indicators. Maori infant mortality was 57.7 per 1000 in the 1954–58 period, as compared to 19.8 per 1000 for Pakeha; there was 3.34 per cent unemployment among Maori in 1956 compared to 0.85 per cent for Pakeha. Maori crime figures were three and a half times that of Europeans; 58 per cent of Maori homes had a bath compared to 93 per cent of Pakeha; in 1958, only 0.5 per cent of Maori students reached the sixth form, as compared to 3.8 per cent of Pakeha. At tertiary level, Maori enrolment was only one eighth of what it should have been given their population.[10] One of the report's positive impacts was to raise public awareness of Maori social and economic disadvantage. Another was the development of policies to reduce these inequities. Its proposals, all of which came to fruition in the following twelve years, included a plan to facilitate and hasten Maori land development; the establishment of a Maori Education Foundation to assist Maori higher education; increased state housing assistance and trade training; a continuous Maori health campaign; changes in land tenure to prevent ongoing fragmentation of Maori titles; and the elimination of discrimination in New Zealand legislation.[11]

Hunn depicted his end goal, racial integration, as an evolutionary imperative: 'Evolution is clearly integrating Maori and Pakeha. Consequently "integration" is said to be the official policy whenever the question is asked.' Unlike assimilationism, integration

> implies some continuation of Maori culture. Much of it, though, has already departed and only the fittest elements (worthiest of preservation) have survived the onset of civilisation. Language, arts and crafts, and the institutions of the marae are the chief relics. Only the Maoris themselves can decide whether these features of their ancient life are, in fact, to be kept alive.[12]

Government racial policy could hasten or lengthen this process, but not dispel it. In a letter to a colleague, Hunn expressed the view that eventually there would be no need for any statutory recognition of Maori. The Maori seats, Maori Land Court, the Department of Maori Affairs — all would inexorably disappear, as integration, and especially education, put Maori on the same footing as Pakeha. It might take decades, but eventually 'a need for these sorts of protections will diminish'.[13] Special measures necessary now would ultimately vanish and the 'one nation' model prevail.

Some Maori welcomed the policies Hunn recommended as progressive and overdue; others worried that integration was a cover for assimilation. A pamphlet by the Maori Synod of the Presbyterian Church compared integration to 'what the shark said to the kahawai'.[14] Matiu Rata, MP for Northern Maori, speaking in Parliament in 1963, lamented the government's lack of consultation with Maori about integration, and the complete neglect of the Maori language.[15] Many Maori resented the report's assumptions of Pakeha racial superiority. The Maori Synod declared: 'A race cannot be forced into taking steps towards its own elimination . . . let it be understood that, while we are willing to join with the Pakeha in becoming New Zealanders, we have no desire whatsoever to become Pakehas.'[16]

The colour of the game
Like the Hunn Report, playing rugby with South Africa brought racial issues under closer scrutiny.[17] In 1961, the Commonwealth expelled apartheid South Africa, and in 1962 the United Nations advised member states to boycott that country's exports and break off diplomatic relations. New Zealand, like the UK, US, Australia and Canada, was slow to endorse this stand and either voted against or abstained on most United Nations resolutions on South Africa.[18] In 1965, thousands of well-wishers greeted the touring Springboks, who played

an All Black team that, in contrast to the all-white 1960 All Blacks, included Maori. A group called Citizens' Association for Racial Equality (CARE) led the small (but vocal) minority of protesters. Formed in 1964, CARE aimed 'to assist in promoting harmonious race relations based on equality of status and opportunity'.[19]

The New Zealand Maori Council's decision to welcome the Springboks in 1965 divided Maori. MP for Northern Maori Matiu Rata spoke out against a Maori welcome on the grounds that it would be seen as approval for apartheid. MP for Southern Maori Eruera Tirikatene stated: 'The very composition of the [Springbok] team is a visible manifestation of apartheid. It therefore seems entirely inappropriate and unnecessary to me that the President of the Maori Council should hold the view that the Maori people are in any way bound to treat the Springboks as honoured guests.'[20]

In 1967, Holyoake effectively cancelled a proposed All Black tour of South Africa by making his 'No Maoris, No tour' backing clear.[21] But the controversy did not end there. Further tours eventuated and continued to generate protest as the issue moved away from Maori exclusion from the All Blacks (which most New Zealanders opposed) to whether it was acceptable to play rugby with apartheid South Africa. This provoked much less opposition (according to opinion polls, only 16 per cent).[22] The persistent controversy about playing rugby with South Africa kept issues surrounding racism repeatedly in the public eye. Among a section of the population, concern about racism abroad led to an increased awareness of it at home.

Groups such as CARE, and from 1969, Halt All Racist Tours (HART), became proactive about race relations in New Zealand. They worked in tandem with Maori and Pacific Island radical activist groups to help migrants adjust to their new country.[23] By 1969 in Auckland, for example, CARE, in conjunction with the Workers' Educational Association, had set up English classes for new citizens; a homework centre for high school pupils; and Maori and Samoan language classes for beginners in the basement of the Unitarian Church in Auckland's Ponsonby Road. In 1970, HART, CARE, the Wellington Association for Racial Equality and several unions and churches involved in the anti-apartheid campaign formed a New Zealand Race Relations Council 'to promote and extend understanding, co-operation and harmony between the races'.[24] Its patron was Sir Edmund Hillary and vice-presidents included the Ombudsman Sir Guy Powles, the Maori Queen Te Arikinui Dame Te Atairangikaahu, Cardinal Peter McKeefry, the four Maori MPs, and the Anglican bishops of Auckland and Dunedin.

In 1971, New Zealand (in keeping with the UN Convention on the Elimination of All Forms of Racial Discrimination signed in 1965) passed a Race Relations Act to 'affirm and promote racial equality in New Zealand'.[25] This outlawed racial discrimination and created a Race Relations Conciliator to investigate practices apparently in breach of the law. Although sporting links with South Africa remained a bone of contention, by the early 1970s, policy-makers were legislating against racism and the general public was discussing race-related issues as never before. The 'anti-tour' movement, and the 1971 Race Relations Act, reflected a growing international influence on New Zealand attitudes and legislation about racial equity and justice.

The 'Last Land Grab' Act of 1967

Arguably the most decisive factor stimulating Maori activism in the late 1960s was government policy relating to Maori land. The Hunn Report recommended moving away from communal ownership of Maori land on the grounds that it precluded efficient utilisation. In 1966, the Prichard-Waetford Report,[26] following a Committee of Inquiry into the laws affecting Maori land and the operations of the Maori Land Court, advised that government compulsorily acquire uneconomic interests in Maori collectively owned land. Under the Maori Affairs Act of 1953, the Maori Land Court could compulsorily vest uneconomic interests in Maori land (worth less than £25) in the Maori Trustee for administration (that is, it would usually be sold to other Maori, who had greater shares in the same land).[27] The Maori Affairs Amendment Act of 1967 gave the Maori Trustee further powers to compulsorily acquire 'uneconomic' interests in Maori land valued at less than $50. A 'conversion fund' was established for the Maori Trustee to use. The Act also stipulated that land owned by four or fewer owners lost its designation as Maori land and became general land. Such 'compulsory conversions', which had to be registered in the Land Transfer Office, were undertaken without any reference to the Maori owners, in the interests of economic efficiency.[28] The 1967 Amendment, which one member of the Maori Council dubbed the 'last land grab',[29] spurred the Maori Renaissance, galvanising both conservative and radical Maori alike.

In the *Rotorua Post* of 8 November 1967, retired Maori Land Court Judge Bartholomew Sheehan condemned the legislation as:

The worst exercise in race relations since Culloden 220 years ago . . . The Pacific today requires the highest diplomacy and the greatest tact in race relations and to me the haste with which the Bill is being pushed through is a flagrant act of tactlessness . . . [It is like] putting a pistol to a man's head.[30]

On 7 November, the MP for Western Maori Iriaka Ratana warned her fellow parliamentarians: 'This Bill is so revolutionary in destroying Maori interests and Maori ideals that no Maori who has the welfare of his race at heart could possibly be in favour of it.'[31] Maori, young and old, rural and urban, left and right wing, voiced their opposition to the legislation at hui throughout the country, discussing the complicated ramifications of the reforms and resolving to make submissions opposing the Bill to Parliament. Even the conservative Maori Council began, as Richard Hill has observed, to 'place the government under greater scrutiny'. The Crown could no longer 'automatically rely on the support of its own creature'.[32]

In 1969, the National government, alarmed at the common cause being shown between the Maori Council, Maori MPs and liberal Pakeha, declared that the Act would be 'cautiously' implemented. But it was too late. Momentum built: land became a rallying point and discussions about rangatiratanga (chieftanship) and Maori autonomy revived. Another government policy enacted in 1969, the elimination of separate Maori schools, also met considerable opposition from Maori because these schools (whatever their assimilationist origins) had long been part of a distinctive Maori identity.[33] Their sudden closure appeared like yet another step on the government's road towards seamless integration, or even assimilation.

Ratana leaders began reviving the long-standing idea of a separate Maori Parliament, and there were some calls for the government to honour the Treaty of Waitangi.[34] Disaffection coalesced with a sense of injustice to shape the sensibility of many young urban Maori. Contemporary ideas of black liberation helped to motivate the new generation to fight for indigenous rights in New Zealand. But the fact that some of the aims and objectives of these young radicals in the late 1960s began to be shared by conservative organisations such as the Maori Council owed much to government policy.

The new activism

In 1968, a group of Maori activists in Wellington started an underground newspaper called *Te Hokioi*, and another activist group, Maori Organisation on Human Rights (MOOHR), soon emerged from it. Both vehemently opposed the 1967 Maori Affairs Amendment Act, had trade union links, and perceived indigenous rights to be inextricable from the class struggle.[35] They criticised government's repeated failure to uphold the Treaty of Waitangi, and complained that Maori language (te reo) was not on the school syllabus. The teaching and revitalisation of te reo was a concern shared by Nga Tamatoa (young warriors). This high-profile activist group grew out of a Young Maori Leaders' Conference on urbanisation at Auckland University in 1970. Academics, students, kaumatua,[36] and members of gangs such as the Stormtroopers and Black Power, came together and resolved to strengthen Maori language and culture, raise public consciousness about race issues, and take stronger political action to achieve those aims. Nga Tamatoa's protests and high-profile activism raised critical ire both within Maoridom and from Pakeha. At the same time, the group achieved several key goals.

Initially, the more uncompromising radicals such as John Ohia, Paul Kotara and Ted Nia — who spoke the language of American Black Power leaders such as Stokely Carmichael and H. Rap Brown — advocated Maori liberation and 'Brown Power'. Another faction, comprised for the most part of university educated students such as Syd and Hana Jackson, Peter Rikys and Donna Awatere, hoped to initiate self-help programmes and were not averse to pursuing conventional channels in order to improve conditions for Maori. This latter group gained ascendancy in the early 1970s.[37]

Hana Jackson organised a petition to have Maori language taught in primary and secondary schools. (By the early 1970s, 50 per cent of Maori were under fifteen, but only some 15 per cent of that age group could speak Maori.)[38] Activists circulated this petition at protest marches and door to door, until it had enough signatures to present to Parliament. When sceptics pointed out that there were not enough qualified teachers, Nga Tamatoa called for the establishment of a one-year training scheme for adult native language speakers. After the 1972 election, in 1974 Labour's new Minister of Education Phil Amos introduced a 'link' system of teaching Maori at primary and secondary school, and also set up a one-year training scheme for native speakers. Nga Tamatoa's idea of a Maori Language Day on 14 September 1972, to call attention to the crisis in Maori language, was also adopted by the education system and later evolved into Maori Language Week. By 1976, there were 123 secondary schools teaching Maori, compared to only eleven previously. At the primary school level, 100 schools offered Maori Studies programmes. By the mid-1970s, lecturers in Maori Studies were appointed in all teacher training institutions.[39] Maori Studies flourished in the early 1970s, when it became a distinct programme of study at university and steadily expanded.[40]

The number of Maori and Pacific Island students at university also rose.

At the University of Auckland, Maori and Pacific student enrolment increased from 3 per cent to about 15 per cent between the early 1970s and 1997. Steven Webster has noted: 'The university appointments of the early 1970s reflected a gathering awareness of neglect and sense of guilt invoked among liberal intellectuals.'[41] On campuses throughout the country, the combined impact of protests against the 1967 Act, the gang problem, and the high-profile activism of groups such as Nga Tamatoa increased concern about New Zealand race relations and socio-economic inequality between the races. During the 1970s, 'Polynesian Preference' schemes at universities made provisions for Maori and Pacific Island students where, in the absence of open entry into courses such as Medicine, Engineering and Law, competition might have excluded them.[42]

For those not able to take advantage of the opportunity to study at university, Nga Tamatoa offices in Auckland and Wellington interviewed migrants from the country and helped them find work. The group also extended assistance to Maori offenders who needed advice or legal aid, and spent considerable time and energy making submissions to the Select Committee on the Race Relations Bill. Members travelled the country, speaking about race issues and trying to raise public awareness of Maori goals. Nga Tamatoa's most contentious protests took place at Waitangi Day celebrations, and were widely reported on national television and in the press. In 1971, members wearing wreaths and black clothing, in mourning for lost Maori land, dramatically advanced through the crowd at the Treaty Grounds. During a speech by Robert Muldoon (who was deputising for Prime Minister Holyoake), a young Nga Tamatoa woman ran from the crowd and stood waving behind the speaker's rostrum, where, as the press reported: 'Above the general hubbub she could be heard shouting out the words "honour" and "freedom".'[43] When another protester attempted to set fire to the New Zealand flag, sailors snatched it off him before much damage was done. A *Herald* editorial commented on the day's events: 'The spirit of the treaty will best be nourished by creating and seizing opportunities to forge one people. On any balanced view, it is difficult to see how any measure of militant activity emphasising distinctions between the races can be helpful.'[44]

Derision and adulation

The rising tide of Maori activism and the general prominence of race issues met with derision in some quarters. Letters to the editor often queried bilingualism and dismissed te reo as an impediment to national growth. One correspondent to the *New Zealand Herald* wrote in 1971, for example: 'It is difficult to understand . . . headmasters who allow the teaching of the Maori language

. . . [it] is a primitive language with a very limited vocabulary and is entirely unsuited to our civilized way of life'.[45] In June 1973, a *Sunday Times* editorial expressed dismay at the 'mushrooming groups, mostly well intentioned but in some cases frankly malevolent, who emphasise racial differences, language barriers, cultural gaps and illusory ancestral rights'. It went on to categorise any form of discrimination, whether favourable or otherwise, as racism. Thus, Nga Tamatoa, the Maori rugby team, the Maori Education Foundation and the four Maori seats were all racist impediments to 'the peaceful integration of all racial types into New Zealanders'. Speaking Maori was deemed a racist act:

> Every time Maoris use their attractive but quite useless language in the presence
> of non-Maori, every time they employ the insulting term 'pakeha', they aggravate
> the differences between the races. They create resentment where none previously
> existed and risk turning a tolerant Kiwi joker into a racist.[46]

Maori as well as Pakeha disagreed with the aims and tactics of radical activists such as Nga Tamatoa. Maori leaders frequently criticised the 'young warriors' of the day for failing to practise true Maoritanga. Some kaumatua regarded the young activists as a disgrace to Maori values, and roundly criticised their methods of protest and resistance.[47] At the same time, many members of the younger, anti-establishment generation not only perceived Maori activism as commendable; they romanticised Maori culture, lifting it to the 'uncritical elevation of an imaginary social ideal'.[48] The poet James K. Baxter was a particularly high-profile example of a Pakeha who embraced Maori culture as a romantic alternative to a materialist, individualist, consumerist society. In 1969, he set up a Maori-influenced commune at Jerusalem on the Whanganui River. In one of his *Listener* columns that year, he succinctly summarised his preference for Maori culture over Pakeha: 'The difference between the Maori and Pakeha cultures is the difference between a community of neighbours and a society of strangers.'[49]

It was not coincidental that the 'back to the land' communes known as 'Ohu' introduced under Norman Kirk's third Labour government (see Chapter 5) had a Maori name. Miranda Johnson has commented that 'Maori values were associated with rusticity and with an aboriginal connection to the land. Urbanised Pakeha lacked these values because of their obsession with rapid technological change in the name of "progress"'.[50] Many young people, disaffected with contemporary Pakeha culture, perceived Maori culture as an appealing antidote to competitive capitalism. Not all Maori were sympathetic to this socio-cultural critique, however, or willing to engage in protest marches. Yet even among more conservative groups, a groundswell of energy began moving towards improving Maori socio-economic conditions and facilitating Maori self-reliance.

Administrative and legislative change

The advent of the third Labour government in 1972 raised Maori hopes. Just before the election, Nga Tamatoa set up a Maori embassy, Te Whare o te Iwi, on the steps of Parliament House.[51] Traditionally, Labour was the party most sympathetic to Maori interests, as well as to international anti-racism policies and biculturalism. Prime Minister Kirk was outspoken about making the Treaty the foundation stone of the nation.[52] While noting that the Treaty 'stressed equality', Kirk still believed there was a case for allowing affirmative action in fields such as Maori education.[53] He also opposed Hunn's views on 'integration', proclaiming in Parliament that 'integration is what cats do to mice. They integrate them.'[54]

The third Labour government decided to jettison a long-standing de facto 'white New Zealand' policy, and as a result, assisted immigration from Britain effectively ceased in 1975. National or ethnic background was no longer a criterion for immigration selection. Kirk also made Matiu Rata the first Maori Minister of Maori Affairs in 28 years. Aware that Maori wanted more involvement in managing their own affairs, during his time in office Rata worked to restore funding levels to the Maori Affairs Department and increased its number of state houses.[55] A new section added to the 1953 Maori Affairs Act, which outlined the Department's aims (the preservation of Maori language and culture, and the promotion of the health, education and wellbeing of all Maori), potentially allowed the Department to oversee other government agencies' work.[56]

Rata set up a new Maori Land Board with an increased Maori representation of five members to ensure a clear Maori majority. Maori Land Advisory Committees, again with Maori appointees, were also created in departmental districts to consider proposals for improvements to Maori land titles and any change in the use of Maori land. Rata also repealed the much-hated 1967 Maori Affairs Amendment Act and expanded the powers of the Maori Land Court.

As a result of these combined efforts, sales of Maori land dropped dramatically.[57] Rata set up a Royal Commission on Reserved Lands, which in its 1974 report recommended owners be allowed to choose whether they wanted their land to remain under the legal and administrative control of the Maori

Trustee. He also increased subsidies to marae and community centres and reformed electoral legislation. Under the 1956 Electoral Act, only those Maori who had half 'Maori blood' were allowed to register on the Maori electoral roll. But the Electoral Amendment Act 1975 defined Maori much more generously as 'a person of the Maori race of New Zealand; and includes any descendant of such a person who elects to be considered as a Maori'.[58] Maori could now decide whether they registered on the Maori or the general roll. This signified an important new conception of Maori status, premised on self-identification. At the same time, Maori and Pakeha intermarriage steadily increased: as early as 1960 in Auckland, for example, 42 per cent of all Maori marriages were to Pakeha.[59]

The push for more Maori agency and self-determination became increasingly evident even in conservative groups such as the New Zealand Maori Council, which appeared to be moving inexorably in the same direction as the more radical activists. Under Graham Latimer, who assumed the presidency in 1973, the Council began to become more assertive and proactive. In 1974, for example, the government, embarrassed by the annual Nga Tamatoa protests at Waitangi, sought the Council's advice about Treaty breaches. It responded with a submission citing some fourteen statutes that contravened Article 2. The Maori Council also successfully pressed for an amendment to the Town and Country Planning Act that took into account the relationship of Maori people with their ancestral land. In 1975, it also sought and obtained an amendment to the 1953 Maori Affairs Act, stipulating that Maori land acquired under the Public Works Act be returned to its original owners if it was no longer being used for the purpose it was taken.[60]

Labour introduced all these initiatives and legislative reforms within a fairly short time. Rata was thus perhaps understandably distressed to hear of plans for a massive protest march, highlighting Maori grievances. He felt, erroneously, that this reflected badly on his performance as Minister. In fact, it resulted both from Maori frustration and the tenor of the times. The march aimed to unite Maori and to focus Pakeha attention on Maori land loss. It succeeded in uniting Maori for a short time only, but its impact in raising public awareness about Maori land loss was significant and enduring.

The Land March of 1975

The great hikoi, or Land March, of 1975 pushed Maori land grievances to the forefront of the national consciousness. Led by the redoubtable 80-year-old Whina Cooper,[61] it commenced at Te Hapua in the north on 14 September

1975 and concluded on the steps of Parliament in Wellington on 13 October. By that time, there were 5000 people in its ranks. Numbers swelled as the group proceeded 700 miles down the North Island, stopping at 25 marae en route. Some people joined the march temporarily as it passed through their towns. Others, Maori and Pakeha alike, expressed support by beeping their car horns and waving.

The slogan which became a catch-cry in the course of the march: 'Not one more acre of Maori land', encapsulated the sense of urgency surrounding the marchers' cause. Out of some 66 million acres of land in New Zealand, Maori retained only 2.5 million. Ten years earlier, the figure had been 4 million.[62] The prospect of future landlessness loomed. Radical activism and rhetoric focused increasing attention on land and this was augmented by a groundswell of resentment against unpopular legislation.[63]

The idea for the march originated at a hui at Te Tira Hou marae in Panmure in April 1975, when several groups united with the aim of combating further land loss. They called themselves Te Roopu o te Matakite: the last word means 'seers' or 'prophetic visionaries'. The name was suggested by Whina Cooper, whose idea to hold a 'sacred' march to galvanise support was also endorsed with alacrity. (This idea had a high-profile precedent: in 1972, American Indians marched on Washington in a highly publicised 'Trail of Broken Treaties'.)[64] For the next four months, an organising committee, chaired by Whina, fundraised, planned the route, and rallied supporters. Committee members included Graham Latimer, chairman of the New Zealand Maori Council, Mira Szászy, president of the Maori Women's Welfare League, Ranginui Walker of the Auckland District Maori Council, and Syd Jackson and Titewhai Harawira of Nga Tamatoa.

In addition to planning logistics, Whina gave special attention to the symbolic aspect of the march. Her son-in-law carved a pouwhenua, an upright stake denoting tribal land ownership, to be carried at the head of the march and never touch the ground. A Memorial of Rights, written in archaic language in order to link present and past petitions by Maori to the Crown, was to be signed only by recognised rangatira (chiefs) at each marae visited. The general public would sign a more general Petition of Support that included among its aims the recognition of communal tribal land ownership as equal to individual title. Whina also wrote a song, 'Na Te Kore I Mohio', to keep up spirits, the last verse of which exhorted: 'Let us unite / people of the four winds / consolidate all our aspirations / bind them with love / with the power of God's blessing / to benefit all mankind / to benefit all mankind.'[65]

Whina exerted firm control during the march. She allowed no alcohol, insisted on frequent prayers, and expected marchers to behave in an exemplary fashion. Participants experienced fatigue, trepidation, sore feet and ennui but also exhilaration and a sense of shared commitment. The spectacle of the hikoi reaching the steps of Parliament, in the pouring rain, on 13 October was captured on television camera and recounted by the national press. When Whina presented the Memorial of Rights, signed by 200 elders, and the petition, with 60,000 signatures, to Prime Minister Bill Rowling he assured the marchers: 'You will find that your march is not in vain', to loud cheers and applause.[66]

After the march, the movement fractured, as some of the more radical marchers (against Whina's wishes) stayed on in a tent embassy in Parliament Grounds.[67] Nevertheless, in a decade full of protest marches, this one etched itself on the nation's collective consciousness. Its scale and symbolic aspect, restrained demeanour and dignity, made it a memorable event that inspired an upsurge of goodwill from Maori and Pakeha alike.

Land issues featured prominently in the media again in 1976, when Te Matakite lent its support to the Tainui Awhiro people at Raglan, who, under the leadership of Eva Rickard, were pressing for the return of the Te Kopua block. This land had been taken for military purposes, but then vested after the war in the Raglan County Council and leased to a local golf club. In April, Maori demonstrated on a sacred burial site that had been converted into a bunker. A letter was also sent to the Minister of Maori Affairs, requesting that the land be returned. This campaign succeeded, and the disputed land was vested in Tainui Awhiro under the 1953 Maori Affairs Act.[68]

The impact of high-profile groups such as Te Matakite helped to facilitate important policy initiatives. The most significant of these, the creation of the Waitangi Tribunal, was effected by Matiu Rata just before Labour lost power in 1975. The three-member Tribunal, under the chairmanship of the chief judge of the Maori Land Court, could initially only hear complaints about post-1975 Treaty breaches. At this stage, it was somewhat toothless, with no ability to determine distributions of legal rights and duties, and no powers of legal enforcement: it could only hear (post-1975) cases and report and recommend on them to the executive arm of government.[69] Nevertheless, it was a major step to give the Treaty this recognition. A document that in the early years of the decade attracted precious little attention was on its way toward a remarkable shift in status.

By the late 1960s and early 1970s, Maori radical activists were acutely aware of the contrast between the Treaty of Waitangi and the treaties affecting North

American Indians. The latter, being part of constitutional arrangements, had led to concessions in favour of indigenous people. By contrast, New Zealand's Treaty had no legal basis. Indeed, a series of cases in the 1960s rejected it as a basis for granting rights.[70] At the same time, despite denunciations of it as a fraud by some radicals, most Maori never gave up on the Treaty. The document itself was not perceived to be at fault; rather, Pakeha failure to honour it.[71]

Pakeha New Zealanders' knowledge and understanding of the Treaty increased considerably during the 1970s. Academics such as the historian Ruth Ross played a considerable role in enhancing public awareness of its historical context, as well as highlighting the difference between the Maori and English texts.[72] Writing in 1976, the anthropologist Joan Metge paid tribute to the Treaty's ideal of 'two races united in friendship and equality', and referred to the Treaty itself as a 'standard of value against which particular actions and situations are to be judged'.[73] Increased awareness of the Treaty and respect for its ideals, while notable among some sectors of the populace, did not, however, signify a victory over the 'one New Zealand' model of racial harmony. That remained robust, strengthened by the laudable ideal of a tolerant multiculturalism. Waves of Pacific Island migrants to New Zealand in the 1960s and early 1970s added 'a fresh complication to the country's racial dynamic'.[74] From 2159 in 1945, New Zealand's Pacific Island population reached 61,354 in 1976. Other ethnicities, such as Chinese and Indian-born migrants, remained small minorities. Despite what James Belich has described as a 'persistent mean-minded attitude to refugees', politicians regularly invoked rhetoric praising multiculturalism, and generally sang their country's praises as a tolerant melting pot.[75] But many Maori perceived multiculturalism as a means of sidestepping their special status as tangata whenua under the banner of unified racial diversity.

Successive governments sought to position Waitangi Day as a symbol of national multiculturalism, rather than a celebration of the special relationship between Crown and Maori. During the 1960s and 1970s, when the Education Department directed schools to commemorate the national holiday, an official message was usually read which included notions of the Treaty's primacy as a founding document of multiculturalism. In a speech to the Founders' Society on Waitangi Day 1970, for example, Minister of Maori Affairs Duncan MacIntyre hoped that

[a]s a Nation we will progress into the '70s and into the future as a united country of one people . . . New Zealanders . . . where the different lives and ways of life — English, Dutch, Scottish, Maori, Chinese and many others, interweave and

interlock, to form a truer New Zealand identity and an identifiable New Zealand way of life.[76]

Like Maori, Pacific Islanders in New Zealand comprised a visible element in the multicultural mix: a 'brown proletariat' employed in low-paid labouring and factory jobs.[77] The majority were Samoan, and entered on a negotiated quota system; but there were also temporary work visas for both Samoans and Tongans. Cook Islanders, Tokelauans and Niueans had free right of entry as New Zealand citizens. Each group had its own distinctive culture, so it was often frustrating, as it was for Maori, to be identified under the umbrella label 'Polynesian'.[78]

Young urban radical activist elements among the Maori and Pacific communities had much in common, but Pacific Island migrants also faced formidable language and cultural hurdles. Some fondly remembered aspects of growing up in their adopted land. Samoan-born Ta'afuli Andrew Fiu, who grew up in Ponsonby in the 1970s, for example, recalled:

> . . . brown grinning faces running in and out of houses, the aroma of newly baked banana cakes and pineapple pies that wafted in the breeze and — the dead giveaway — the corned beef cans used for wheels on neighbourhood trolleys.
>
> I still remember the absolute unity of this multicultural street of ours . . .[79]

Other experiences were less rosy. Another Pacific Islander who grew up in Ponsonby found that, by secondary school, fellow students hurled racist taunts:

> It was not until I attended secondary school that I began to notice racist jibes — 'Black bastards', 'nig nogs', and so on — that all Islanders and Maori are familiar with. The disappointing thing about these racist jibes was that they came from the minds and mouths of pakeha boys who had adopted these views from their parents' generation.[80]

The most testing times for race relations between Pakeha and Pacific Island migrants resident in New Zealand occurred halfway through the 1970s, when the economic downturn began to affect views about the desirability of migrant workers. The government's sensitivity towards 'overstayers' — that is, those migrants from the Pacific Islands who remained in the country illegally following the expiration of their temporary work permits — suddenly increased when the economy began to falter.

Panthers and dawn raids

The Polynesian Panthers participated in Whina Cooper's 1975 Land March, and supported the aims and aspirations of Nga Tamatoa. Formed in 1970, the Panthers were deeply influenced by America's Black Panthers, notably Huey Newton. They primarily comprised young Pacific Islanders from the Ponsonby, Grey Lynn and Newton areas of Auckland who wanted to assist and support Pacific migrants in New Zealand. Like Nga Tamatoa, they used the highly charged leftist language of the day; seeking liberation from racist, imperialist and capitalist oppression. The Panthers' most prominent leader, Will 'Ilolahia, had links to overseas indigenous rights groups. In 1972, Bobby Sykes invited him to attend a Black Moratorium in Sydney; two years later, he and Billy Bates were interviewed in the *Black Panther* (USA) magazine.[81]

Dedicated to non-violent protest, the Polynesian Panthers also engaged in a range of social welfare initiatives, from after-school care to food co-ops, to prisoner transport and rehabilitation, to assisting those vulnerable to rack-renting or any form of racial discrimination. They worked alongside CARE, the Auckland Committee on Racism and Discrimination (ACORD) and Nga Tamatoa, as well as left-wing groups such as the People's Union for Freedom and Survival. In 1973, they helped Nga Tamatoa to organise Maori Language Day.

The first 'dawn raids' took place in March 1974. Pacific Islanders suspected of overstaying their work visas were woken in the early hours of the morning by police and immigration officers. Having answered the door, they were asked to produce proof that they were in the country legally. Raids were also conducted during church services. One participant recalled how, during a church service at 64 Crummer Road in Auckland,

> all of a sudden the place was swarming with police, officials and dogs. They asked for passports. There were 18 that didn't have them, including the priest. They were taken to Mount Eden. There was great shame in seeing the people taken away, and it was seen in the court the next day.[82]

The Kirk government initiated these first raids, which focused on Tongans, at a time when the oil crisis and the accompanying economic downturn prompted fears about unemployment. Few newspapers voiced objections, although the Catholic weekly *Zealandia* did report that the Bishop of Tonga (Patelesio Finau) had condemned them as 'shameful'.[83] However, Polynesian leaders and members of various groups, including Nga Tamatoa, ACORD, the New Zealand Race Relations Council, the Free Church of Tonga, the Samoan Branch of the New

Zealand Labour Party, the Auckland trade unions, the Polynesian Panthers and the People's Union for Freedom and Survival debated and protested about the raids. In response, on 21 March, the Minister of Immigration Fraser Coleman announced they would cease immediately. On 1 April, Prime Minister Kirk intervened, suspending entry permits for Polynesians until tighter controls could be implemented on applications. He introduced a two-month amnesty period, in which illegal Tongan immigrants could register with the Department of Labour and be granted a two-month extension on their visa, along with immunity from immediate prosecution. After this amnesty, 1500 Tongan overstayers returned home and a further 2000 registered to have their visas extended.[84]

During the 1975 election campaign, immigration from the Pacific Islands again became a prominent issue. National's now notorious television adverts, produced by the American cartoon studio Hanna-Barbera — which featured dancing cartoon Cossacks and brown-faced overstayers — prompted accusations of racism from Labour. But even within the National caucus, there was division over the professed aim of putting limits on immigration from the Pacific Islands. Venn Young argued that National 'didn't want to be painted as a racist party', while Keith Holyoake and Jim Bolger attempted to have a section about restricting immigration deleted from the party manifesto.[85] National eventually endorsed the section after Muldoon expressed the view that it would have a positive impact in marginal seats such as Eden, Birkenhead and Auckland Central.

Why opposition to immigration from the Pacific Islands suddenly intensified in the mid-1970s is, according to James Belich, unclear, because the economy was worsening but not yet dire. He suggests that the concern reflected a 'scapegoat hunt' caused by 'the Pakeha identity crisis'.[86] Another less abstract factor was rising crime, some of which was associated in the public mind with Polynesian gangs such as the Nigs. In his column in *Truth* newspaper in September 1975, Muldoon expressed the view that most New Zealanders shared his desire for 'criminal Islanders' to be sent home.[87] But economic factors appear to have been critical, as concern increased about the pressure ongoing immigration would place on housing, health, education and employment options. In 1975, immigration policy was reviewed in the wake of a record annual gain of 30,000; a figure that evoked alarm.[88] The *Auckland Star* in January 1975 ran an article headlined: 'New Zealand can't stop influx from some islands', which noted that while newly implemented regulations would 'quickly eliminate' itinerant Tongan workers, others such as Cook Islanders,

Niueans and Tokelauans retained free entry because of their New Zealand citizenship. Concern about unemployment was paramount. President of the Federation of Labour Tom Skinner called for a complete halt to all immigration during 'the current work crisis'.[89]

The frightening, alienating experience of the dawn raids, which resumed under Muldoon's government, caused not a little scepticism among Pacific Island migrants about claims that New Zealand police were friendly and helpful. By this time, it was common practice for the raids to include the use of police dogs, which not surprisingly created fear.[90] In his evocative memoir of growing up in 1970s Auckland, Ta'afuli Andrew Fiu recalled the experience of a dawn raid from a child's perspective:

> The negative perceptions of policemen stick in the mind of an Island kid, especially when you're dawn raided while watching *Spot On*. Especially when you have a European presenter on TV talking about how you can ask a policeman for help any time and then they show a picture of the same bastards standing in your (our) house. I can tell you they weren't smiling like the two cops on *Spot On*. 'Need help? Ask a policeman', I think the presenter said.
>
> I looked from the TV to the police in the house to the TV again and thought, we'll take our chances thanks. Replacing doors can be expensive . . .'[91]

A new group, Amnesty Aroha, made up of Pacific Island organisations, trade unions, feminists, social workers, churches, and university and anti-apartheid organisations unhappy with government policy on overstayers, commenced in Wellington in 1975 and soon spread to Auckland and Christchurch. Its aim was to raise public awareness of racism and lobby against what it believed to be unfair and discriminatory immigration policies.[92] When on 10 April 1976 the Minister of Immigration announced a temporary amnesty for overstayers, 4674 people, all but 77 of whom were Pacific Islanders, took advantage of the opportunity. On 12 April, Minister of Immigration Frank Gill reported that there were some ten to twelve thousand overstayers in New Zealand, two thirds of whom were Pacific Islanders.[93] According to police historian Susan Butterworth, there were some 4000 overstayers in Auckland and 6000 in the rest of the country. These figures would indicate that the response to the government's amnesty was relatively low, perhaps because police heavy-handedness during dawn raids had induced considerable fear and distrust.[94]

Another policy that came under scrutiny by anti-racism groups for its perceived persecution of Polynesians, a police 'Task Force', targeted drinkers in pubs in an attempt to stem street and tavern disorder. Police travelled in convoys to various inner-city pubs frequented primarily by Pacific Islanders and cracked down on any drunkenness and disorder. In 1974, a report prepared by ACORD labelled the Task Force 'An Exercise in Oppression'.[95] But many Aucklanders welcomed it as a positive step: in July 1975, about 100 parents, most of them Pacific Islanders, clapped and cheered when the Task Force members received a certificate for services to the community, during a ceremony at Newton Central School.[96]

A steep rise in complaints to the Race Relations Office, from 92 in 1973–74 to 150 in 1974–75, reflected the public's increasing sensitivity and awareness of racism. Complaints alleging incitement of racial disharmony jumped from 25 to 55. Of the 150 complaints, 139 were lodged against Pakeha compared with seven against Maori, two against Chinese, and one against Dutch and English individuals respectively. Of the 150 total complaints, 125 derived from Auckland.[97]

Operation Immigration

In 1976, 'Operation Immigration' took place over some ten days from 21 October. Police, having been asked by the Immigration Division of the Labour Department to address the overstayers issue, responded by stopping hundreds of Pacific Islanders on Auckland streets,[98] in pubs, at taxi ranks and bus stops, requiring proof of their right to be in the country. They questioned nearly 600 people, arrested some 40 who could not produce residence documents, and also stopped Maori, whose skin colour caused suspicions about their right to be in the country.[99]

The day after the operation commenced, the *Auckland Star* bore the headline: 'Police: If you don't look like a Kiwi, carry a passport'.[100] Beneath this article, which described the random checks and arrests, another headline ('Sobbing Man Wrongly Held') told how a young Samoan who worked as a Post Office linesman was arrested while walking down a Grey Lynn street, spent a night crying in jail, and then was released fourteen hours later, with no apology, after he was found to be working in the country legally. David Lange, then a lawyer and chairman of the Council for Civil Liberties, denounced Operation Immigration as both 'reprehensible' and 'incredible'.[101]

Letter columns in the newspapers soon filled with irate correspondence, comparing the operation's tactics to South Africa and even Nazi Germany, although there were also many letter writers supporting the police.[102] The *Auckland Star*, which endorsed Chief Ombudsman Sir Guy Powles' suggestion of a total amnesty for overstayers, noted that if the Minister of Police did not understand why others were so outraged by the 'operation', he was badly out of touch with 'the Auckland attitude'.[103] The *Star* then engaged in a battle of proof with Muldoon, who claimed the affair had been blown out of all proportion by liberal journalists. On 28 October, its reporters obtained (and flew down to Wellington) six sworn statements in response to the Prime Minister's challenge to produce proof of complaints about the random checks.[104]

It became increasingly clear that (despite engendering a small amount of support) the whole exercise had proved a public relations disaster for the government. Eventually, an inquiry, an apology and a hasty retreat by police followed. The overstayers' amnesty register reopened again until 31 January 1977.[105] Immigration from the Pacific decreased in the latter part of the decade, as annual quotas reflected the deteriorating economic situation and fewer employment options: about 24,000 Pacific Islanders immigrated in 1971–76, but only 7000 in 1976–81.[106]

In January 1978, Race Relations Conciliator Harry Dansey[107] spoke to a journalist about the state of New Zealand race relations. Despite the fact that complaints to his office had reached a record high of 177 (a rise of 71 over the previous year), he remained unalarmed. Perhaps most astonishing to him were the number of complaints the office received from Pakeha about perceived threats to their culture. When local authorities began to provide information pamphlets in Polynesian languages, for example, numerous complaints ensued, and when Auckland University offered a scholarship for Pacific Island students, Dansey's office received six written complaints and 20 critical phone calls.[108] This reaction reflected the persistence of the 'one New Zealand' model of race relations, and the view amongst some Pakeha that any policy based on racial differentiation was both racist and unfair.

Creative renaissance

Maori culture's rising profile perhaps exacerbated the perception that Pakeha culture was under threat. In the 1960s, and increasingly through the 1970s, Maori art and creativity blossomed — supported and encouraged by tribal elders, voluntary associations such as the Maori Women's Welfare League, as well as a range of government-sponsored initiatives. Notable among the latter was the Arts and Crafts Branch of the Department of Education, which offered courses and publications for teachers and students, and university extension programmes in Auckland and Wellington. The Maori Purposes Fund also diverted a not inconsiderable portion of its funds to subsidise arts and crafts activities associated with community projects.

From the mid-1960s, government made efforts to make Rotorua a 'show-piece of Maoridom'.[109] By 1966, a new two-storey Maori Arts and Crafts Institute opened, funded and supported with the burgeoning jet-propelled tourism industry in mind. Carving was a major focus, with master carver John Taipa employed to teach a select group of young Maori trainee carvers in view of novelty-seeking tourists. The Institute proved, despite some tensions among the staff, a great success; a new block was added in 1975 to provide more space for displays.[110]

In addition to this subsidised Maori art and culture, the advent of a youthful counter-culture, the rise of Maori activism, and a loosening of previously constrictive societal conventions all helped to create a favourable climate for a spontaneous creative upsurge. Maori culture was suddenly vibrant and visible as never before. The koru was adopted as the national airline's symbol. It also became the name of a literary magazine produced by the New Zealand Maori Artists and Writers Association, formed in 1973. That group's inaugural hui, convened by the poet Hone Tuwhare at Te Kaha marae, fulfilled the aim of discussing ideas and creative projects against a background of cultural traditions and taonga (treasures).[111]

The rapid pace of the Maori artistic renaissance is best illustrated in literature. As late as 1968, the author and academic Bill Pearson expressed the hope that someday a Maori novelist of outstanding talent might emerge.[112] Some fifteen years later, writers such as Witi Ihimaera, Keri Hulme and Patricia Grace, among others, were well established. Ihimaera's *Tangi*, the first novel by a Maori author, was published in 1973. A 1974 review of his second book, *Whanau*, testifies to literature's positive influence in eroding racial stereotypes:

> Too often we have heard of the Maori who is fat, lazy, rather untidy, who drinks and goes to parties that never end, and who plays a guitar because he has rhythm and the Pakeha has none. And, so it is in this book. It all fitted — at first.
> But slowly the book develops, or maybe one's own outlook begins to change. Gradually the people stop being 'typical' and become individuals and real. .

This reviewer concluded that *Whanau* 'commands respect not because, like *Tangi*, it is written by a Maori, but because it is fiction of merit'.[113]

In the art world, Rei Hamon, Selwyn Muru, Para Matchitt and Muru Walters continued to effectively adapt traditional Maori conventions and patterns into innovative original works, as did master carvers such as Paki Harrison, Cliff Whiting and Arnold Manaaki Wilson.[114] In fashion, clothes using Maori motifs and patterns by designers such as Sandy Ansett, Kura Ensor and Janice Hopper became increasingly popular. The Labour MP for Southern Maori Whetu Tirikatene-Sullivan regularly made public appearances wearing cutting-edge Maori fashion. By 1970, the *New Zealand Woman's Weekly* featured an all-Maori fashion show.[115] A few Maori artistic endeavours were linked to radical activism, focussing squarely on past and present perceived racial injustices. In Harry Dansey's 1972 play *Te Raukura*, for example, Syd Jackson played the role of Tamatane, who accused Pakeha 'who took the land' of the 'greed of conqueror and thief'.[116] But much Maori art was neither radical nor overtly political.

Michael King, one of the more influential Pakeha writers to celebrate the Maori cultural renaissance, came into contact with a range of Tainui elders (in particular members of the Turangawaewae marae in Ngaruawahia) while working as a reporter for the *Waikato Times*. Drawing on these contacts, he produced biographies of Maori leaders Whina Cooper and Te Puea, and histories of Maori life and culture.[117] In 1974, he wrote and acted as an advisor for *Tangata Whenua*, a popular ground-breaking series of television documentaries that interviewed various Maori personalities and explored tribal culture. The historian Jock Phillips, reviewing the series in the *Listener*, lauded it as 'the finest achievement of New Zealand television'.[118] King believed that Pakeha needed to participate in the revival of Maoritanga and his writings and media work helped to raise the general public's knowledge and understanding of Maoridom. Alan Ward's *A Show of Justice*, published in 1974, also greatly raised Pakeha awareness of historical race relations. Dick Scott's book about the persecution and survival of Parihaka pa in the nineteenth century, originally published in 1954, was revised, expanded and reprinted as *Ask That Mountain* in 1975 to critical acclaim.[119]

From 1973, the *New Zealand Listener* featured 'Korero', a column on Maori issues by academic and community leader Ranginui Walker.[120] This generated considerable criticism, especially at the outset, from readers who perceived its perspective as biased, racially divisive, or simply surplus to requirements. One irate Pakeha correspondent complained:

Maori culture has no place in my life and although I would not want to stop anyone practising it, I do not want it forced down my throat.

Despite the writer's desperate attempt to make me do so, I do not feel guilty that my ancestors defeated or otherwise conned the Maoris into giving up land. That was their fight, and there is nothing I or any modern-day Maori can do about it.[121]

For those who advocated a more proactive biculturalism, television (with the notable exception of the 1974 *Tangata Whenua* series) was a Pakeha preserve. The *Listener*, in July 1978, included an article on this subject entitled 'Maori TV: A Presence for a People'. Rawiri Rangitauira, chairman of the Te Reo Maori Petition Committee, who had organised a 25,000-signature petition calling for more Maori content on New Zealand television, was quoted: 'There are more blacks on New Zealand television than Maoris . . . If we say we live in a multi-cultural society, then we are only paying lip-service to it in broadcasting.'[122]

In 1980, *Koha*, a weekly half-hour Maori magazine programme, began screening on Sunday afternoons. Critically acclaimed and popular, it was moved a year later to Monday, prior to the 6.30 evening news on TV One. In 1983, a five-minute Maori news segment, *Te Karere*, produced by Derek Fox, began screening daily on TV2 just before that station's news at 6 p.m. The Maori comic Billy T. James, whose eponymous, enormously popular television series commenced in 1981, soon featured 'Te News', a comic take-off with Billy (the newsreader) attired in a black singlet with yellow towel slung around his neck. This skit, along with several others, prompted intermittent accusations that the show perpetuated racial stereotypes. James countered that he was in fact raising public awareness about racial issues. In the early 1970s, he experienced racism first hand, when a landlady who agreed to rent a flat to his Pakeha fiancée withdrew the offer upon discovering Billy was Maori. The incident later featured in several of his jokes and skits.[123] His amusing versions of Captain Cook discovering New Zealand, or the signing of the Treaty of Waitangi, caused many New Zealanders to both think about race relations and to laugh at themselves. The first Maori performer to have his own television series, James was loved by Maori and Pakeha alike and regularly voted Entertainer of the Year. In 1986, he was made an MBE for his services to entertainment.

While Maori were playing an increasing role on television, whether in prime-time comedy or indigenous news slots, radio too began to pay increased attention to providing Maori and Pacific Island content. In 1973, the Adam Committee on Broadcasting called for a separate Radio Polynesia in Auckland, 'for the expression, enjoyment and understanding of New Zealand's Polynesian cultures by New Zealanders of all cultures'.[124] Although plans for its establishment were shelved by the National government in 1976, a year later a small Maori and Pacific Island radio unit was set up, with five staff in Auckland and two in Wellington. In addition, by 1978 the National Programme had daily news bulletins in Samoan, Cook Islands Maori, Tongan, Niuean and Tokelauan, as well as four vernacular Pacific-language magazine programmes and a weekly English-language Pacific magazine show.[125]

Pacific Island art and culture, like that of Maori, flourished in New Zealand during the 1960s and 1970s. One outstanding author, Albert Wendt, was born in Western Samoa and grew up in Auckland's Freemans Bay. His novel *Sons for the Return Home* (1973) tells the story of a relationship between Sione, a Samoan man, and Sarah, a Palagi woman.[126] Talented visual artists included Fatu Feu'u, John Pule and Ani O'Neill among others. Several Pakeha artists were also deeply influenced by Pacific culture. Tony Fomison, for example, began being tattooed in the traditional Samoan way in 1979, a two-year process that almost claimed his life when the tattoos went septic. He completed his celebrated painting *The Ponsonby Madonna*, which recasts the Virgin Mary and Christ Child as Pacific people, in 1983.

Pacific arts and crafts, music and dancing contributed to a more vibrant culture. In 1970, the Maori Purposes Fund made a grant of $5,000 to organise the first annual Polynesian Festival. Held in Rotorua, this enormously popular competition was by the mid-1970s biennial. Festival chairman Kingi Ihaka expressed the hope in 1975 that the event would evolve into something less competitive and more celebrative.[127] The Mana Arts Festival, on the Kapiti Coast, commenced in 1970 and drew on performers from Porirua's large Maori/Pacific Island communities as well as others from throughout the country. In 1976, the festival was launched with a Pacific Spectacular, featuring 138 performers visiting New Zealand for the South Pacific Arts Festival being held in Rotorua.[128]

Festivals celebrating Maori and Pacific cultures helped to foster a growing sense of New Zealand's identity as a South Pacific nation. Such events — popular with all ethnicities — contributed to an era when, within a relatively brief period of time, public understanding and appreciation of Polynesian culture rapidly increased. In 1977, the New Zealand public's consciousness of racial diversity and racial sensitivities heightened further still, when a Maori protest placed race relations at the epicentre of current affairs for seventeen months.

Takaparawha, Bastion Point, 1977–78

Whina Cooper chose Joseph Parata Hohepa Hawke of Ngati Whatua, a young Auckland builder, to bear the pouwhenua across the Auckland Harbour Bridge during the 1975 Land March. In 1977, he was once again at the centre of the Maori land rights movement, leading those opposed to the newly elected National government's development plans for 60 acres of Crown land at Bastion Point.[129]

For Hawke, these 60 acres were all that remained of wrongly dispossessed ancestral land, and he wanted it returned to Ngati Whatua. The Crown, despite 1868 legislation proscribing its alienation from Maori, steadily acquired the 700-acre Orakei block by sale, long-term lease, and compulsory acquisition under the Public Works Act. As a child in 1951, Hawke witnessed the forcible eviction of the few remaining residents of the papakainga (village settlement) at Okahu Bay and the subsequent demolition and burning of their homes and the tribal meeting house. The evictees were then moved into state rental housing nearby. By that stage, Ngati Whatua's landholdings in the Auckland isthmus were reduced to a quarter-acre urupa (cemetery).

Upon hearing of the Crown's plans for Bastion Point, the Orakei Maori Committee set up an action group to occupy the site, under the leadership of Joe Hawke and Roger Rameke.[130] Some 150 protesters duly settled into the camp on 5 January 1977. It quickly grew from 'Tent Town' (a few tents and caravans) into a proper community. Whina Cooper, who was among the first visitors, managed to acquire a shed for the protesters' use. The occupiers eventually built a large meeting house called 'Arohanui', replete with cooking facilities and sleeping and office accommodation, and dug 3 acres of garden, planted with kumara, corn, beetroot and broccoli.

Throughout the 506 days of occupation, alcohol and drugs were banned and daily classes in Maori language, culture and history were offered for children and adults. A visiting Catholic priest, Father Terry Dibble, remarked after a visit there:

> I saw the development of a sense of pride, discipline and aroha. I saw young Maoris absorbing their language, their culture, their history and their customs. Many admitted to never having had real contact with anything specifically Maori before. Together, on Takaparawha, the meeting house, which was itself a masterpiece of ingenuity, Maori people discovered a sense of purpose and identity.[131]

The support the protesters received from Maori and Pakeha alike surprised and encouraged them:

> On at least two Sundays, thousands of people visited Tent Town. Food, tools, lamps, tents and money were donated to us by both Maori and Pakeha supporters. On January 16 we organised a peaceful demonstration of 1,500 people which processed along the waterfront to the papakainga in Okahu Bay and then up to Bastion Point.[132]

From the outset, local residents were opposed to the development. Environmentalists, Nga Tamatoa, the Socialist Unity Party, Te Matakite o Aotearoa, CARE, the Auckland District Maori Council, the Values Party, the regional council of the Labour Party, the New Zealand University Students' Association, and the Auckland University Students' Association endorsed the protest. In addition, the Auckland Trades Council declared a 'green ban' on the area, effectively precluding any building work. Prime Minister Muldoon received over a thousand letters and petitions, the overwhelming majority of which opposed the sale of Bastion Point and wanted the remaining unused land returned to Ngati Whatua.[133] Letters to the newspapers also expressed solidarity and hope that the government would respond positively.[134]

At the same time, many Maori and Pakeha believed it wrong to engage in illegal actions, however just the cause. Others, as the occupation persisted, despaired of the issue ever being resolved. An injunction was filed in the Supreme Court to order the protesters' leaders from the land. The elders of Ngati Whatua tried to find a peaceful resolution and began in February 1978 negotiating a deal with the government.[135] The Action Committee members rejected this course, however, and remained staunchly in situ. The impasse, when it broke, did so dramatically.

On 25 May 1978, 600 police, assisted by the army, forcibly removed the occupiers:

> More than 50 vehicles, including 30 army three-tonners, were in the convoy from Hobsonville, where about 400 policemen from other parts of New Zealand were billeted for the night.
>
> As the protesters, numbering between 175 and 200, broke into songs and hymns, police jumped from the troop carriers and moved to encircle the protest camp.[136]

There were 222 people evacuated, arrested and charged with wilful trespass: 108 Maori, 104 Pakeha and 10 Pacific Islanders.[137] The sheer scale of this process, as one television news report observed, was like something from a World War II movie. The *Herald* wrote: 'The grim procession of army trucks trundling through Auckland streets was like a flashback to unhappier lands and times. We would never want to see them again.'[138] Whetu Tirikatene-Sullivan denounced the government's 'rodeo-type round-up' and the 'dishonourable conclusion' it had orchestrated.[139] Matiu Rata, in the course of an extremely fiery parliamentary debate about the Bastion Point arrests, observed: 'Very few actions have been taken [in New Zealand] about which I can truthfully say the country should be ashamed. Parihaka was one, and I believe today's events represent another.'[140] A *Herald* editorial written a day after the arrests warned:

> Let those at the heart of the protest, who resisted the Government's plans, be given credit for the sincerity of their stand. And let no one underestimate an underlying legacy of concern from colonial days that still attaches to Maori land questions.[141]

Despite divergent views on the rectitude of the occupants' stance, Maori land grievances were, throughout the seventeen-month protest, firmly in the public eye. The protest increased appreciation among Pakeha of the injustices experienced by Maori, not only in the present but in the past, and enhanced their understanding of the land's emotional and spiritual significance for tangata whenua.[142]

From the outset, the occupation was a media event. This interest persisted long after the climax of 25 May 1978, with later films such as Merata Mita's documentary *Bastion Point: Day 507* drawing on television footage of the evacuation. Lines of helmeted police converging on the makeshift camp, and a bulldozer later razing the village, were powerful images. In addition to raising public awareness about Maori land grievances, Bastion Point left another, more tangible, legacy. The magnificent landscape in dispute remained unsubdivided. In May 1981, Maori protesters, supported by the Auckland Trades Council and others, briefly reoccupied Takaparawha, objecting to the proposed construction of Housing Corporation units on the site. After a discussion in caucus on 18 May, the National government decided to demolish all buildings and remove the protesters. Six years later, following the 1987 Waitangi Tribunal report on Orakei, the Crown returned the Bastion Point lands in their entirety to Ngati Whatua along with compensation of $3 million and an apology.[143]

The haka party

After Bastion Point, many of the protesters joined or continued to engage with a variety of activist groups such as Waitangi Action Committee (WAC), the Maori People's Liberation Movement of Aotearoa, and Black Women, which often went on protest marches and challenged politicians in public places. But on 30 April 1979, fourteen WAC members' involvement in a unique and contentious event prompted frenzied media attention and renewed concern about New Zealand race relations. For over a decade, Maori had been writing to complain about a long-standing feature of the Auckland University engineering students' capping week festivities — a 'mock haka' performed by students wearing grass skirts; their bodies decorated with imitation moko and obscene images. During a practice, the WAC members (now calling themselves Te Haua) assaulted the students, tearing off their grass skirts and inflicting bruises and cuts in the process.

Initial wildly exaggerated press coverage (under the headline 'Gang rampage at varsity') reported that six carloads of gang members had conducted a violent attack wielding clubs, softball bats, iron bars and metal rods.[144] A more realistic account gradually emerged. Although a statement released by Race Relations Conciliator Harry Dansey and his assistant Pita Sharples disavowed the use of violence, it soon became apparent that most of conservative Maoridom, including the Auckland District Council, supported the attackers' actions. This was because they objected so strongly to the cultural insult of the mock haka. Pakeha public opinion about the incident diverged. Some saw it as evidence of a lack of humour on the part of Maori, others as an overreaction. A few commentators, such as *Listener* editor Tony Reid, condemned it as a sad reflection of cultural arrogance: 'It is a sad fact that Pakeha attitudes are still so overwhelmingly arrogant that we need a sharp course of contemporary Maori education. As we enter the 1980s it is time to listen carefully to rather than sneer at Maori "overreaction".'[145]

Charges of rioting, rather than assault (the former carried a more severe penalty), were laid against Te Haua. In the ensuing court case in July, Maori elders clarified the nature of the insult. Erihapeti (Elizabeth) Rehu-Murchie, president of the Maori Women's Welfare League, referred to the haka as a 'cultural gem', while Graham Latimer, president of the Maori Council, revealed the support for Te Haua in marae across the country. Although the judge ruled out the defence of provocation and cultural insult, conscious of the complex cultural issues involved, he imposed a sentence of periodic detention rather than imprisonment.[146] The haka party incident raised a great deal of heated controversy about race relations, and ends and means.[147] Less controversially, important changes through more conventional channels started to accelerate from the late 1970s onwards.

Tu Tangata, Whaka-Whaiti

The appointment of Kara Puketapu, of Te Atiawa descent, as Secretary of Maori Affairs in June 1977 gave impetus to the Maori push for self-reliance. He determined to revitalise the Department of Maori Affairs using two guiding precepts: Tu Tangata, to recognise the stance of the people; and Whaka-Whaiti, to harness the resources and strengths of all the people.

The Department held a series of wananga (discussions) throughout the country for women, youth and kaumatua, to gather ideas for programmes to benefit Maori. Community development and youth (in 1979, two thirds of Maori were under 24) were priorities. The first initiative to emerge from these meetings, a marae enterprise scheme, encouraged rural Maori communities to expand their economic base by stimulating awareness of business opportunities in spheres such as arts and crafts, tourism, and development of natural resources. Seminars were offered, along with direct financial assistance and loans.[148] Interestingly, despite the National government's recent engagement in 'high-wire' politics at Bastion Point, it facilitated administrative reform and policy initiatives within Maori Affairs designed to augment rangatiratanga.

Kokiri (advance) Centres were another initiative designed to enable communities to make their own decisions. Community advisory groups were initially set up in every departmental district, to give advice to the Department and to make decisions about financial allocations for programmes. In Wellington in 1980, an experiment overseen by the State Services Commission saw the district Maori Affairs office replaced by three Kokiri administration units. These had departmental officers working under a community management group who set priorities and field tasks. The experiment proved so successful that a network of Kokiri Centres was created throughout the country. In many cases, the Department's involvement was limited to seeding funding.[149]

Kohanga reo (language nests) aimed to provide a pre-school environment that enabled Maori children to become fluent in te reo and knowledgeable about traditional Maori culture. The first nest, begun as an experiment in Wainuiomata in 1982, proved so successful it received strong departmental backing a year later. Within a decade, some 600 kohanga reo flourished throughout the country, attended by over 30 per cent of Maori pre-schoolers. One of the great success stories of the Maori cultural renaissance, and the most successful under the Tu Tangata umbrella, kohanga reo are often used as a model by overseas groups attempting to revive indigenous/ethnic languages. In time, many language nests came to be associated with or located at marae, and the term 'whanau' (family) used to describe the team of teachers, parents and kaumatua who ran them. Kohanga reo rely heavily on volunteers. 'Determinedly independent' and 'as much a political movement as . . . a language recovery programme', the kohanga reo movement has been described as 'an element in its own right of the Maori Renaissance'.[150] In January 1984, over a thousand people attended the first national kohanga reo hui at Turangawaewae marae in Ngaruawahia. The final Maori Affairs programme, Matua Whangai, run in conjunction with the Justice and Social Welfare departments, aimed to assist young Maori in trouble with the law, and to develop whanau structure so that they could be removed from institutional care and placed in the care of Maori people.[151]

Maori Affairs now employed more Maori personnel at all levels than ever before. With the 1980 appointment of Edward Taihakurei Durie as chief judge of the Maori Land Court and ex-officio chairman of the Waitangi Tribunal, for the first time in history, the Minister, secretary and chief judge were all Maori. The call by Maori for more involvement in their own community affairs led the government to take the unprecedented step of asking the Maori Council for input into the new Maori Affairs Bill, introduced into the House in 1978. Eventually, the Maori Council Legislative Review Committee produced a 'brown paper' setting out a desire for recognition of biculturalism in legislation, and stressing the importance of land ownership to Maori identity. In 1982, a further paper, 'Kaupapa', reinforced this message but added a preamble emphasising both government's right to rule and its fiduciary responsibilities to Maori under the Treaty. The new Bill was drawn up in serial form but the snap 1984 election halted its process.[152]

Te Whare Tapa Wha: Maori health
The growing desire by Maori to have more direction of their own affairs also spurred a grass-roots health movement. By the early 1980s, health rivalled land loss as a central focus of Maori concern. The Hunn Report had highlighted the poor state of Maori health relative to Pakeha, an inequity still evident in the 1970s. In 1977, the Maori Women's Welfare League launched the Rapuora project, an extensive study surveying 1177 North Island Maori women. This research project, conducted by Maori according to tikanga Maori (Maori traditional rules, culture), was a milestone, and the women researchers involved gained confidence to return to their communities and play a role in regional and national health organisations. Whare rapuora (health centres) were recommended and several set up on marae over the next five years. Project director Erihapeti (Elizabeth) Rehu-Murchie, appointed in 1981, believed that Maori health was so poor due to inadequate tribal leadership and the need for more Maori input in the health system.[153]

In December 1979, Dr Peter Tapsell, an orthopaedic surgeon and member of the Maori Advisory Committee on Health, wrote a feature article in the *Listener* entitled 'Maori health — the push for parity' which contained disturbing statistics about the poor state of Maori health relative to Pakeha. Infant mortality and life expectancy were particularly problematic, despite a marked improvement since the dismal state of affairs in the 1950s. Between 1954 and 1958, the Maori death rate per 1000 live births was 57 compared with 20 among non-Maori. By mid-1975, this had dropped to 21 for Maori compared to 16 for the total population. In terms of life expectancy, Tapsell noted: 'A Maori child born today can expect to live for 61 years if a male, and 65 years if a female. A male European child can expect to live eight years longer, and a female European child 10 years longer. Only one Maori in a hundred lives to more than 70 years of age, compared with six in every hundred for non-Maoris.'[154]

A year later, Dr Eru Pomare, a Wellington gastroenterologist and the grand-son of New Zealand's first Maori doctor, published a report on Maori health covering the 1955 to 1975 period. Commissioned by the Medical Research Council of New Zealand, this contained a wealth of comparative data, all of which reinforced the preface's warning — there was 'no cause for compla-cency'.[155] Socio-cultural factors such as cigarette smoking, obesity and alcohol consumption adversely affected Maori health, while infant mortality by acci-dent was three times greater among Maori than non-Maori. From the age of six onwards, deaths associated with homicide were six times greater among Maori than non-Maori. First admissions for mental disorders in 1974 showed that schizophrenia and paranoid states in the age group 25–44 years at 5.5 per 10,000 was the highest rate for any mental disorder in any age group, Maori or non-Maori.[156]

In 1982, a health hui at Palmerston North Hospital provided an opportu-nity to discuss the state of Maori health, and further discussions ensued at the tenth Young People's Hui at Raukawa in May 1983. At this latter event, Mason Durie, a prominent Maori medical doctor, spoke about a 'whare tapa wha' model for Maori health, which would balance spiritual, mental, physical and whanau (extended family).[157] Maori mental health was now a pressing concern. Whereas before 1970, Maori were underrepresented in psychiatric hospitals, by 1982, their figures were two or three times higher than for non-Maori, with alcohol-related admissions the greatest area of increase.[158] In 1982, the National government passed a revamped Health Amendment Act and even-tually appointed a Standing Committee on Maori Health, led by Puti O'Brien. A number of health professionals and Maori community leaders held meetings on marae about how to achieve a more bicultural health service. In March 1984, the Hui Whakaoranga on Hoani Waititi marae in Auckland resolved to push for more health clinics on marae, recommending that 'health and educational institutions recognise culture as a positive resource' and that 'the feasibility of including Maori spirituality in health education programmes in schools and in tertiary educational institutions be investigated'.[159]

Hard times

The disturbing figures relating to Maori mental health were linked to the financial downturn. This had a particularly dramatic impact on Maori and Pacific Islanders, because they tended to work as semi and/or unskilled labour and were vulnerable to lay-offs and cutbacks. By 1981, 14.1 per cent of Maori workers were unemployed compared with only 3.7 per cent of the non-Maori labour force.[160] House ownership among Maori had declined: in 1961, one in four Maori households owned their own house; by 1981, the figure had decreased to one in eight. From 1979, Maori (under 9 per cent of the overall population) comprised more than 50 per cent of the prison population,[161] and with Maori unemployment rising, fears mounted that more Maori youths would opt for a life of crime.

Escalating gang-related crimes received much press attention. In 1976, police shot dead a seventeen-year-old Mongrel Mob member called Daniel Houpapa in Taumarunui during a confrontation outside the local police station. Speaking at the tangi for his son, Sonny Houpapa urged gang members to 'throw down your uniforms, your chains and weapons, and return to Maoritanga'. In the newspapers following Daniel's death, front-page headlines quoted the Police Minister Alan McReady supporting Houpapa's plea as 'right on the ball'. At the same time, news reports highlighted the Minister's rather sanguine assertion that he intended to 'put an end' to gang violence.[162]

The Muldoon government funded several work trusts and cultural and craft programmes for gang members in the late 1970s and early 1980s.[163] The Prime Minister believed, having been counselled by his friends Whina Cooper and Graham Latimer, that reacquainting gang members with their traditional culture was the key to their reintegration into society. At the same time, reintegrative policies were balanced by 'tough rhetoric and support for the police against the gangs' violence and criminal activities'.[164] In 1979, following a pitched battle between rival gangs at Moerewa in Northland, police adopted a PR-24 long baton to help curb violent behaviour.[165]

The negative impact of a worsening economic situation on Maori continued, and in November 1979, Matiu Rata, disenchanted with the situation and with two-party politics generally, resigned from Labour. In April 1980, he launched a new party, Mana Motuhake,[166] dedicated to Maori self-reliance, and contested a by-election. Rata gained 38 per cent of the vote to Labour's 53; a respectable showing. By June 1981, Mana Motuhake had 100 branches through-out the country and some 15,000 members. Although its four candidates for the Maori seats were defeated in the 1981 election, they all polled higher than the National or Social Credit parties.[167] The emergence of a possible new rival in those seats doubtless concerned Labour. Many of Mana Motuhake's key platforms, especially its emphasis on active biculturalism and honouring the Treaty, were adopted by Labour later in the decade.

After the violent confrontations of the 1981 South African rugby tour (see Chapter 6), race relations at home seemed to acquire new resonance. Some young radical Maori and Polynesian activists became more radicalised, and more at odds with their Pakeha counterparts within various anti-racist, feminist and left-wing groups. In 1982, for example, Donna Awatere (still embroiled in legal proceedings due to her protest at the Hamilton rugby match) wrote a series of articles entitled 'Maori Sovereignty' in *Broadsheet*. When these were pub-lished as a book in 1984, their message reached a wider audience. In Awatere's view, feminism's grievances paled into insignificance compared to Pakeha racism. Past injustices against Maori could only be answered by Maori sover-eignty, which sought 'nothing less than the acknowledgement that New Zealand is Maori land, and further seeks the return of that land'.[168] Awatere's angry, force-ful prose and vehement arguments attracted attention in the press, adding to a darkening public perception about the state of New Zealand race relations.[169]

In the early 1980s, newspapers featured a diverse range of items about racial issues, many of which related to cultural misunderstandings and the parame-ters of biculturalism. In 1983, for example, several articles dealt with the offence caused to Maori by post-mortem examinations conducted without familial con-sent, or by bodies being retained by the medical establishment, which delayed tangi.[170] In June 1983, Ponsonby's Outreach Gallery exhibited souvenirs and other items for sale in city shops that portrayed Maori as 'objects of fun and car-icature'.[171] Maori dolls with key rings protruding from their heads, and images of rangatira on tea towels and ashtrays, were offensive to many Maori and Pakeha alike. The Auckland *Star* commented that 'It seems obvious . . . that the time has come to set limits on the exploitation of Maori artefacts and images'.[172]

While sensibilities became more attuned to respecting Maori culture and tikanga, public opinion of Maori was often critical. Maori unemployment and prominence in crime statistics frequently featured as subjects on talkback radio, and in the correspondence columns of newspapers and magazines. Ben Couch, Minister of Maori Affairs, himself a Maori, blamed 'a certain type of Maori' for wallowing in a grievance culture.[173] In 1982, the public's response to the 1981 unemployment statistics, as revealed in the correspondence columns of the *Sunday News*, was sceptical and unsympathetic: 'All these reports in the paper make out as if Maoris are useless and can't get a job but I think half of them aren't even looking . . .' These sorts of reader comments were placed under the headline: 'Fair go, mate, they're not up to it!'[174]

Resentment about affirmative action also simmered. In 1983, the Auckland Nurses' Association suggested a form of positive discrimination to ensure the recruitment of more Maori and Pacific Island nurses who could respond to that city's large Polynesian population. While this met with approval in some quarters, others expressed alarm. One member of the Auckland Hospital Board, for example, likened the proposal to apartheid.[175] In the same year, the Auckland Regional Authority decided to drop its non-elected Maori representative as a cost-cutting measure, evoking criticism from the Auckland District Maori Council.

High-profile annual Waitangi Day protests, led by the Waitangi Action Committee, heightened a sense of worsening race relations. The yearly turmoil on 6 February precluded complacency about racial harmony. Governor-General Sir David Beattie, a liberal thinker sympathetic to Maori aims, in his 1981 Waitangi Day speech acknowledged: 'We are not one people, despite Hobson's oft-quoted words, nor should we try to be.'[176] The protests featured prominently on television and in the press, and the number of protesters arrested increased yearly.[177] The increase was linked to the protesters' actions (in 1982 an egg hit the Governor-General and smoke bombs were thrown) but also to an escalating response: police wielded batons against protesters for the first time in 1982. The annual strife at Waitangi was soon all too predictable. In 1983, concern in the established churches about being involved in the ceremonies led to a proposal by the National Council of Churches that a moratorium be held on the 1984 celebrations.

This did not eventuate. The 1984 Waitangi Day protests were larger and more spectacular than ever, but there were no arrests. Once again, a peaceful hikoi brought together a diverse range of participants. These ranged from members of two of the oldest Maori protest groups, Kotahitanga and the Kingitanga, to Pakeha groups such as CARE, ACORD and HART, students, feminists, members of Mana Motuhake, the Labour and National parties, and Maori clerics, among others.

The hikoi aimed to stop the celebrations by force of numbers, and to present Maori grievances directly to the Governor-General. At a hui at Waahi marae, the home of Dame Te Atairangikaahu, Eva Rickard was elected president of the hikoi and Titewhai Harawira its secretary. The marchers, who eventually numbered in the thousands, walked over 300 kilometres, stopping one night at Bastion Point, where they were hosted by Ngati Whatua.[178] On the evening before the celebrations, they received news that Governor-General Beattie agreed to meet a delegation and to receive their petition. They decided, however, not to break the unity of the hikoi. Either all or none of the protesters would meet the Governor-General. Before crossing the bridge to Waitangi, the Archbishop of New Zealand, the Rt Reverend Paul Reeves, and the Bishop of Aotearoa, the Rt Reverend Whakahuihui Vercoe, joined the marchers. The police did not let the hikoi into the Treaty Grounds, ushering them instead into Bledisloe Park, and negotiations ensued. The Governor-General waited for several hours and then departed.[179]

Some Maori deemed the protesters' behaviour to be discourteous.[180] However, in an open letter to Sir David Beattie published a few days later, Eva Rickard praised his decision to meet a delegation as 'the most significant historical initiative in Maori–Pakeha relations since the signing of the Treaty'. She noted that because he had graciously retired when his offer of a meeting was not taken up, the spirit of the offer remained intact.[181] The press also printed protesters' submissions, including requests to 'examine sympathetically the issues troubling Maoridom' and also to make the Waitangi Tribunal 'a more effective institution to rectify past injustices'.[182] This latter hope was realised after the election of the fourth Labour government in 1984.

A seismic shift

Writing in the *Listener* in 1979, Michael King observed that contemporary historians no longer used the term 'Maori Wars' on the grounds that '[i]t is pejorative of Maori, implying that they alone were responsible for the outbreak of the wars in the 1840s and 1860s, which they were not'. He went on to discuss the reasons behind the name change of Murderers Bay to Golden Bay, concluding that while individually such linguistic changes were unimportant, 'the important thing is the direction rather than the destination: the fact that in New Zealand efforts are being made to incorporate Maori views of the nation's shared experience rather than the partial view of early European observers'.[183]

This sensitivity towards language and terminology reflected how far New Zealanders' racial sensibilities had developed over the preceding decades. Less than 20 years after its publication, the Hunn Report, with its references to Maori cultural 'relics', seemed itself like a relic from another century.[184] Pakeha awareness of the need to understand a Maori perspective increased, along with an awareness of the legacy of colonialism. The myth of New Zealand's exemplary racial harmony no longer prevailed. When an establishment newspaper such as the *Herald* commented after Bastion Point that it was time for past injustices inflicted on Maori to be addressed, a seismic shift in appreciation of race issues had clearly taken place.[185]

International movements opposed to racist regimes, as well as those advocating the rights of indigenous people and ethnic minorities, were highly influential in inspiring and spurring radical Maori activism from 1970. A new generation attuned to the language of liberation and protest began to demand recognition of Maori land rights and culture. Individuals and groups of all kinds — anti-racist, religious, tribal, government-subsidised and charitable — worked to improve living and working conditions for Maori and Pacific Island people in New Zealand cities. The Maori desire for self-reliance made steady progress, enabling district Maori councils and iwi to better organise their own affairs. Initiatives such as Tu Tangata saw more devolution and consultation, and government departments, voluntary agencies and iwi-owned and -operated commercial bodies worked to improve all aspects of Maori life — from health to education, to housing, to economic prosperity. The hugely successful kohanga reo movement fostered Maori language and pride in tikanga Maori. The creation of the Waitangi Tribunal in 1975 was a milestone, raising both the status and public recognition of the Treaty of Waitangi.

Yet while a great deal had changed, a great deal remained the same. Despite many well-intended policy initiatives, as the economy worsened, so did the relative deprivation of Maori and Pacific Islanders in low-paid unskilled jobs, many of whom were made redundant and struggled to make ends meet. Attempts to overcome this situation by affirmative action were welcomed by some but decried by others. A tenacious 'one New Zealand' ethos was often tethered to an egalitarianism that rejected as discriminatory any differentiation or special status under the law. More extreme adherents of this view perceived Maori 'privileges' such as the Maori Land Court and the Maori seats as a form of 'apartheid' and anathema to 'the Kiwi way'.[186] Liberals, by contrast, argued that special privileges and affirmative action measures countered rather than abetted racism, and helped to ameliorate inequity. Some Maori viewed the ideal of a tolerant multiculturalism as a means for Pakeha to avoid committing to biculturalism.[187] After the election of the fourth Labour government in 1984, the increased powers given to the Waitangi Tribunal, combined with the ongoing impact of economic restructuring and retrenchment, ensured that race relations remained topical, contentious and pressing.

CHAPTER NINE

Transformations

DOING THE IMPOSSIBLE

The fourth Labour Government threw open our doors to the world and the winds of change nearly blew us away. — Margaret Wilson, 2005[1]

On 14 July 1984, Labour triumphed at the polls. The victory date, Bastille Day, was symbolically appropriate. The election of the fourth Labour government marked the start of a 'free market' revolution that deregulated the hitherto heavily protected economy and 'downsized' the responsibilities the state had steadily assumed since the period of post-war reconstruction. It ousted the old guard — the generation of politicians who grew up in the Depression, fought in the war, and believed that the role of government was to intervene in the economy and the lives of citizens to bolster the commonwealth. In their place emerged a younger generation of politicians convinced they could 'restructure New Zealand from top to toe'.[2] Their reforms gathered a seemingly unstoppable momentum, altering and transforming aspects of life and culture from employment options to schools, social organisations and consumer preferences. After Labour's defeat in 1990, the momentum continued, as National trod a similar policy path, introducing a 'user pays' corporatist model into areas of social policy and industrial relations where its predecessor had feared to tread.

New Zealand's adoption of a free-market ethos after 1984 followed a strong current of international policy thinking, advocated by agencies such as the World Bank and the International Monetary Fund.[3] In Britain, Margaret

Thatcher, after becoming Prime Minister in 1979, began restructuring and deregulating to reignite the ailing British economy, privatising state-owned companies, lowering direct taxation, increasing indirect taxation, and attacking the power and influence of trade unions. 'Thatcherism', Tony Judt contends, 'stood for various things: reduced taxes, the free market, free enterprise, privatization of industries and services, "Victorian values", patriotism, and "the individual".[4] In the United States between 1981 and 1989, President Ronald Reagan espoused family values while following a monetarist policy similar to Thatcher's. 'Reaganomics' reduced government spending, deregulated the economy and cut taxes, and also took a hard line against trade unions. From 1983, Australia's newly elected Labor government under Prime Minister Bob Hawke and Treasurer Paul Keating also introduced a programme of financial deregulation and reform.

Speed and comprehensiveness distinguished the 'New Right' reforms applied by New Zealand's Labour government after 1984.[5] A feature of New Zealand economic deregulation in comparison with other countries was that government made radical changes rapidly and simultaneously across a wide range of fronts. A unicameral political system, and a strong tradition of cabinet rule, helped to facilitate the fast and far-reaching process of change. According to Keith Sinclair, Finance Minister Roger Douglas and like-minded Treasury officials, who quickly swept away the economic controls established by the first Labour government, possessed 'the evangelical fervour of born-again capitalists'.[6] Douglas spoke of a revolution when pushing the case for swift, uncompromising reform: 'We can lead the world again, both in standard of living and in social justice. To do that we need to have a revolution . . . It means doing things our way, doing the impossible.'[7] It also meant 'rolling back' the paternalistic, pervasive, authoritarian, bureaucratic state, and encouraging citizens to become responsible for their own individual wellbeing rather than relying on government.[8] The new post-1984 breed of Labour politician perceived Muldoon's interventionism as old-school and ineffective. They blamed it for holding back economic recovery and rationalisation for too long. The way of the future was market forces. The economist Brian Easton has argued that the Labour government's crusading zeal took hold because

The Muldoon generation reflected the old structure: pastoral farming, importing based on licensing, protected manufacturing and staid banking. Many of Muldoon's activities were aimed at protecting that old political economy . . . as the old structure was undermined, despite the subsidies and patronage being used to support it,

Muldoon grew increasingly out of touch with the pro-market proponents and the evolving new political economy.'[9]

The new guard

Labour's 1984 Cabinet, the youngest since the 1850s,[10] was also the best educated in the country's history. Seventeen of its 20 members came from professional/semi-professional occupations, including eight former teachers and six with law degrees.[11] Labour party politicians, and many of their supporters, were now white-collar, tertiary educated liberals rather than, as had been the case with the first Labour government, predominantly working-class trade unionists and socialists.

David Lange, a genial, quick-witted South Auckland lawyer, became, at 41, New Zealand's youngest Prime Minister of the twentieth century. The son of a doctor, he grew up in Otahuhu, worked as a lawyer for some of the country's most vulnerable and disadvantaged groups, and then entered Parliament as Labour MP for Mangere in 1977. Both the general public and his fellow parliamentarians quickly recognised Lange's wit and powers of oratory. Jim Bolger described him as 'a master of parliamentary debate and an outstanding orator; few could match him in my years in Parliament. His mastery of the English language and his gift of almost instant rebuttal with penetrating one-liners on all subjects made him a formidable parliamentarian.'[12]

In 1979, Lange became Labour's deputy leader. In 1983, when he replaced Bill Rowling as party leader, he had high expectations: 'I knew when I was elected leader that I had been given the greatest chance of my life. There would be an election in less than two years and I believed that this time Labour would not lose. It was a chance to make a different kind of country in New Zealand. I knew that this could be a country which had the assurance to stand up for itself and make its way confidently in the world.'[13]

The other key member of the 1984 government, Minister of Finance Roger Douglas, also wanted to make a different kind of country. In 1983, Lange, who admired his drive and focus, made him Labour's finance spokesperson. Unlike the personable Lange, Douglas was a poor public speaker and not particularly prepossessing. He came from a political family with strong links to the union movement and to Labour, and had served as a cabinet minister under Norman Kirk. Douglas fervently believed in the need for major economic reform. Shortly before the official 1980 Budget, Douglas published, to Rowling's chagrin, an 'Alternative Budget', spelling out the need for a complete overhaul of the economy, tax system and state sector. Later in the year, he followed this with his book *There's Got to be a Better Way! A Practical ABC to Solving New Zealand's Major Problems*, which summarised his thoughts on how New Zealand could 'break out of our present economic and social morass'.[14] He lamented the fact that New Zealand had one of the highest levels of gross official indebtedness in relation to GDP of all OECD countries, as well as relentlessly rising unemployment and spiralling inflation. He also expressed concern that its standard of living had fallen from third in the world in the 1950s to twenty-first in the early 1980s:[15]

> Thirty years ago New Zealand led the world. We were the richest country in the world, and we had the most developed system of social security, free education and health care. Today, relative to other countries, we are falling faster than any other developed country.[16]

This publication advocated policies that later became central to the Lange government's 'free market' reforms (soon dubbed 'Rogernomics'). It attacked trade unions as short-sighted and conservative, state departments as wasteful and inefficient, and advocated abolishing subsidies that propped up inefficient industries, along with introducing a user-pays system for government services. Income tax stifled enterprise, and needed to be replaced with a sales tax (GST). State-owned companies needed to be streamlined for efficiency and profit, and tourism and agriculture developed more effectively.

New Zealand's economic decline galvanised the new breed of monetarists like Douglas, who perceived it to be linked to Muldoon's autocratic economic interventionism. Writing in 1986 about the twilight years of Muldoon's leadership, the journalist Bruce Jesson observed:

> A climate of right-wing anti-Muldoonism developed during his last years in government. With his removal, free-market individualism automatically filled the vacant space. Now our political affairs are dominated as thoroughly by free-market individualism as they were by Muldoonism.[17]

Ironically, Muldoon himself created the ideal circumstances for the advocates of a free market to seize the initiative and begin dismantling 'fortress New Zealand'.[18]

A crisis and a gift

On 14 July 1984, the Labour Party routed the National government by nineteen seats. The newcomers, confident and keen to take the helm, were unaware that New Zealand was on the brink of insolvency. When the election was announced, both a change of government and currency devaluation were widely anticipated, prompting a massive run on the New Zealand dollar. Muldoon borrowed heavily from overseas to keep it propped up, ignoring pleas from the Reserve Bank to devalue. A *New Zealand Listener* article later in the year recounted the former Prime Minister's intransigence and secrecy with some incredulity:

> From the moment the election was called, and our foreign exchange reserves were stampeded, the Reserve Bank chants its cries of doom like a Greek chorus. Memo by memo, it implores the implacable Sir Robert to devalue the dollar and save the day . . . Yet . . . Sir Robert publicly stated that he believed reports of foreign exchange trading on the Friday were exaggerated . . . In the final week, $120 million a day was leaving the country, and borrowing was stretched to the limit . . . Sir Robert was even refusing to meet his advisers.[19]

After the election, Muldoon refused to heed the advice of the incoming Labour government to deal with the crisis, announcing in a television interview that there would be no devaluation. Lange hit back in a subsequent television interview:

> This nation is at risk. That is how basic it is. This Prime Minister, outgoing, beaten, has in the course of one television interview, tried to do more damage to the New Zealand economy than any statement ever made. He has actually alerted the world to a crisis. And like King Canute he stands there and says everyone is wrong but me.[20]

Years later, looking back on this time, Lange described it as 'an extraordinary gift to the new government . . . putting the reality of the currency crisis squarely in front of the public and forever identifying the old regime with recklessness and irresponsibility'.[21] It also enabled the new government to act rapidly and with impunity. Labour immediately devalued the dollar by 20 per cent, removed interest rate controls, and imposed a three-month freeze on wages and prices. In Lange's view, the post-election exchange rate crisis

> determined the entire course of the government . . . By the Wednesday we had . . . got the devaluation. And that sealed it, because once we had devalued there were

certain inexorable outcomes . . . It was then absolutely illogical to carry on with an eastern European-style regulatory structure with what had become a more market-orientated economy . . . the circumstances of those first few days in government gave Roger the opportunity to do what he had always wanted to do anyway.[22]

For Douglas, the crisis was 'a great window of opportunity. It got the ball rolling and in a sense I made every endeavour to make sure the ball didn't stop rolling. I had the principle that it was much harder to shoot me down if I kept one pace ahead.'[23] Like all revolutionaries, he had a ruthless disregard for the adverse effects of his revolution on the general populace. Interestingly, however, industrial relations for the time being remained immune from the reforming mania; upon assuming power, Labour promptly repealed legislation introduced by the Muldoon government that introduced voluntary unionism.

Out of control
A raft of deregulatory measures implemented in the immediate aftermath of the crisis moved New Zealand from being one of the most highly regulated of all OECD countries to one of the least regulated economies in the western world. The rapidity of this transformation was remarkable. Controls on foreign exchange, including overseas investment and borrowing, were progressively removed, culminating in the floating of the dollar on 5 March 1985. After being progressively deregulated, banks and other financial institutions increased in number from four in 1984 to nearly 20 only five years later. As Douglas later observed with some gratification: 'We actually introduced all the changes in the financial market between July 1984 and 1 March 1985. We went from being the most regulated [economy] in the developed world to being the least regulated.'[24] In 1989, the Reserve Bank Act put in place a nil to 2 per cent inflationary target, imposed transparency, and made the Reserve Bank independent of government. This freed it up to implement monetary policy unhindered by political interference.

The government abolished supplementary minimum prices (SMPs), which guaranteed prices to farmers and insulated them from the vagaries of the open market. It lifted agriculture subsidies, such as those for fertiliser, and brought interest rates charged by the government-owned Rural Bank into line with open-market rates. It also progressively phased out industrial tariffs, import licensing and export incentives. In November, the fourth Labour government lifted wage and price controls introduced by the first Labour government in 1947, when they enacted the Control of Prices Act which had given the government power to fix the price of any good or service. A large number of items had been affected by price controls, thus killing competition and keeping prices either artificially high or low.

A major overhaul of the tax system simplified and reformed taxes and closed loopholes. In October 1986, all wholesales taxes were abolished and replaced with a general goods and services tax (GST) of 10 per cent (increased to 12.5 per cent in 1989) on goods and services with the exception of financial services and charities. Income tax rates were incrementally lowered, with the top personal tax rate reduced from 66 to 48 per cent in 1986 and then to 33 per cent in 1988. Company tax was also reduced from 45 to 33 per cent. In 1987, notwithstanding indignant denials that 'anyone who suggested Labour would cut superannuation was spreading rumour with malice', government imposed a surcharge on other income earned by people receiving national superannuation; specifically, a 25 cents in the dollar tax for private income over $5,200.[25] Superannuitants were outraged. One irate correspondent to *North & South* magazine denounced the new tax as: 'One of the shabbiest acts of political duplicity in our history . . . The solemn promises of his [Roger Douglas's] colleagues that national superannuation would not be interfered with were simply part of the grand deception'.[26]

A lobby/protest group called the Auckland Superannuitants Association soon formed, and other comparable groups quickly sprang up around the country. Dubbed 'Grey Power', this proved a force to be reckoned with, keeping the superannuation issue in the media eye.[27] In 1993, Grey Power had over 55,000 members nationwide. By 1997, its focus having expanded to include other social and political issues affecting retired people, it numbered 84,000.[28]

Easing the path: ANZUS and the Rainbow Warrior

The Lange government began implementing neo-liberal economic policies at a time when its resolute anti-nuclear stance was earning high praise from the liberal middle classes. In 1982, the Labour Party conference had called for active promotion of a nuclear weapons-free zone in the South Pacific and withdrawal from ANZUS. The virtually identical aspirations of the party and the peace movement became a significant source of electoral strength to Labour in the build-up to the 1984 election.

Once in power, the Lange government's uncompromising anti-nuclear stance quickly brought matters to a head with the United States. What came to be known as the 'ANZUS crisis' was the inevitable result of the government's determination to ban all ships carrying nuclear weapons from entering into New Zealand ports. In January 1985, it accordingly declined to receive a visit from the USS *Buchanan*, which in keeping with US policy, would 'neither confirm nor deny' that it carried nuclear weapons. The United States responded swiftly, severing all military and intelligence ties with New Zealand. Suggestions in the US press that this staunch anti-nuclearism reflected a left-wing government were far from accurate. The reactive surge of nationalism in 1985, and David Lange's personal identification with the anti-nuclear cause (his widely televised Oxford Union debate with the right-wing evangelist Jerry Falwell had made him 'a poster boy for nuclear disarmament'),[29] in fact helped to ease his government's monetarist path. For many people, Lange's government could be cut some slack, despite its abrupt turn to the right in economic policy, because it remained so solidly and unequivocally 'anti-nuke'.

Gerald Hensley, a former head of the Prime Minister's Department under Muldoon and then Lange, notes: '[I]n 1984, the activists on Labour's Left abandoned economics to the free-market reformers and concentrated instead on the country's international relationships through the ANZUS quarrel.'[30] Lange pursued a 'two-handed diplomacy'; while reassuring the Americans, British and Australians that he was willing to negotiate, he was at the same time reassuring the New Zealand public that the government's position banning nuclear-powered ships in New Zealand waters was non-negotiable. Once they understood this, 'the Americans lost confidence, deciding that the Prime Minister was simply playing them on a line until they got tired'.[31]

Both sides in the ANZUS crisis held to their determined course because they could do so with impunity. There were no trade sanctions as a result of the rift with the US, and New Zealand could rely on its Australian ally for defence. For the US, there was 'no strategic or economic incentive to take special care with New Zealand'.[32] The ANZUS crisis and the accompanying rhetoric surrounding a nuclear-free and independent foreign policy was well under way when a surprise occurrence prompted another reactive upsurge of nationalism related to the anti-nuclear cause.

On 10 July 1985, the Greenpeace ship *Rainbow Warrior*, in Auckland prior to embarking for Mururoa to protest at more French tests, was bombed and subsequently sunk. This astonishing event, which resulted in the death of the Portugal-born Greenpeace photographer Fernando Pereira, evoked shock, anger, sorrow and incredulity. As the *Auckland Star* wrote on the day: '. . . even as terrorist acts go, this must be one of the most pointless. To blow up a boat dedicated to putting the peace back into the Pacific is not going to win any friends for the perpetrators. Just the opposite.'[33]

The perpetrators, French secret agents Alain Mafart and Dominique Prieur (two leading figures in a larger team of saboteurs), left 'a trail so Gallic', one French agent later admitted, 'that the only missing clues were a baguette bread loaf, a black beret and a bottle of Beaujolais'.[34] Among New Zealand's allies, only Australia sternly condemned the attack; the reactions of Britain and the United States were lukewarm at best. Richard Northey, then Labour MP for Eden, stated that this had important repercussions:

> It gave rise to a reappraisal of our national identity and of our place in the Anzus alliance. After a supposed Western ally bombed us, we had to rethink our role as a Western ally. And with the failure of the US and British Governments to condemn the bombing, people felt betrayed. There was already a strong anti-nuclear consensus, but since the bombing, and after the US and French treatment of New Zealand and the people of the Pacific, New Zealanders have become more willing to support independence in the Pacific.[35]

On 8 August 1985, the unrepentant Lange government, having garnered considerable popularity through its anti-nuclear stance, signed the Treaty of Rarotonga, which created the South Pacific Nuclear Free Zone.[36] In July 1987, US Secretary of State George Shultz announced: 'We part company as friends, but we part company as far as the [ANZUS] alliance is concerned.'[37]

The anti-nuclear cause, which had its origins in a left-leaning minority protest movement with environmental and pacifist elements, became central to the country's identity, and linked to surges of populist nationalism. The latter, largely reactive, arose in response to events such as the United States' unequivocal severing of ties over ANZUS and the *Rainbow Warrior* bombing. Tellingly, the public's desire both to remain within the ANZUS alliance but also to ban nuclear-powered ships was quite tenacious. Polls in 1986 consistently showed that a narrow but clear majority of New Zealanders would accept ship visits if that were the price of remaining within ANZUS.[38] Only in 1989 did polls indicate that a clear majority of New Zealanders were willing to jettison traditional alliances in favour of the anti-nuclear policy.[39] New Zealand's anti-nuclear stance was nevertheless, from 1984 onwards, the strongest in the world. The stirring and dramatic crises of 1984–85 helped to boost the Labour government's popularity, at a time when its economic policies were causing considerable hardship for various sectors of the populace, including the public service.

Gliding out: reforming the public sector

After 1984, state-owned companies and state services, many of which were notorious for complacent inefficiency and overstaffing, were shaken up, downsized, restructured, streamlined, corporatised and expected to operate as commercial businesses with the same levels of accountability, profitability and efficiency as the private sector. The State-Owned Enterprises Act 1986 corporatised the large public utilities into nine state-owned enterprises (SOEs), along with several other companies owned by the government. They were now to be run commercially and profitably.[40]

In April 1986, Dr Roderick Deane became chairman of the State Services Commission, with a mandate to transform the public service before the next election.[41] Government services offered 'a job for life for one-fifteenth of the total workforce'.[42] Cumbersome and often unresponsive, they were frequently overmanned, usually due to 'poor management, union pressure, mixed objectives, or political pressures to take on staff'.[43] *Gliding On*, a popular television sitcom written by Roger Hall, caricatured the all-too-familiar situation — a typical Wellington government department with too many employees filling in time gossiping or doing the crossword but objecting indignantly when asked to actually do anything. The State Sector Act 1988 aimed to change all this. Positions formerly filled from within the public service were now to be advertised. Department heads, renamed chief executive officers (CEOs), were hired on five-year contracts and given freedom to run their departments as they saw fit — hiring and firing, determining pay and conditions, setting targets, and implementing systems to maximise outcomes. Large unwieldy departments underwent drastic downsizing and restructuring, with trading activities shorn off and turned into SOEs. The Post Office, for example, which encompassed banking, postal delivery and telecommunications (the latter two protected monopolies), was split into three SOEs — Post Office Bank (now owned by ANZ), Telecom (now a public company) and New Zealand Post (an SOE).[44]

Financial accountability, transparency and efficiency, and moving to accrual accounting became mandatory under the Public Finance Act 1989. Justice Minister and Deputy Prime Minister Geoffrey Palmer, who took charge of the process, later noted of these reforms: 'what you got were three statutes that completely changed the face of New Zealand public administration. The SOE Act, the State Sector Act and the Public Finance Act. You take those three statutes together and the entire public sector of New Zealand has been turned on its head and I would suggest, notwithstanding a few teething problems, that

that has been for the better.'[45] By April 1987, fourteen SOEs had been established, and about 36 core public service departments remained. Employees in the public service decreased by 15.3 per cent. Actual numbers fell from 85,738 in March 1985 to 60,940 in March 1988.[46] This restructuring, with its accompanying corporate-speak and inevitable lay-offs, provoked protests from the Public Service Association. In February 1988, for example, 13,000 state servants from throughout the lower North and upper South Islands assembled to oppose the State Sector Bill, chanting 'Stop the Bill'.[47]

Richard Prebble became Minister of State-Owned Enterprises in 1987 and announced the next major reform, privatisation of SOEs, at the end of that year. Sales proceeded quickly: government sold $8.3 billion worth of assets by July 1990.[48] By the mid-1990s, in addition to SOEs, government sold various state-owned companies such as the Rural Bank and New Zealand Steel. The ensuing rationalisation of these enterprises resulted in massive staff redundancies. Trades people, young apprentices, unskilled workers, civil servants and state forest workers lost jobs in the thousands — the Electricity Corporation shed 3000 staff; Coal Corporation, 4000; Forestry, 5000; and New Zealand Post, 8000.[49] This did not necessarily affect productivity; for example, the railways workforce alone was slashed from 23,000 to 5000 but the organisation still increased its freight tonnage handled.[50] Railways, Coalcorp and Forestry Corp each laid off up to 65 per cent of staff, with little reduction in output. Cuts in staff numbers of 10 to 25 per cent were common in SOEs.[51] According to Alan Gibbs, chairperson of the new Forestry SOE: 'We had two and a half times the people we needed and that was right through the state sector. Every single SOE within two or three years of corporatisation reduced its staff by at least a half, so that was fundamental efficiency.'[52]

The reformers justified their slashing of jobs and application of private-sector principles of reducing costs and increasing returns by reporting what they insisted were the resultant dramatic turnarounds. Gibbs, with Chief Executive Officer Andy Kirkman, for example, maintained that they presided over a rapid and phenomenal change in Forest Corp's productivity. Staff numbers were reduced from 7070 to 2770, including full-time contractors, and increased prices were sought for wood. An operating deficit in 1986/87 of $71 million was transformed into a $61 million surplus in 1987/88.[53] In a later television interview, commenting on the question of the impact of job losses, Gibbs observed: 'Those people [who lost their jobs] rightly felt aggrieved . . . Half the people working for the state at that time were effectively digging holes and filling them in. Of course, I thought about the people; nobody likes dislocating lives . . . It was best for them to get the [redundancy] cash, and to have a chance to redirect their lives . . .'[54]

Moreover, the business people who took over state-owned enterprises maintained that they encountered numerous examples of waste and inefficiency. They frequently found no inventory of what the business owned, while at the same time huge supplies of goods never used by staff languished in warehouses. In a 1996 book recalling his experiences as Minister of State-Owned Enterprises from 1987, Richard Prebble wrote that in the Post Office 'clipboard consultants' from the Ministry of State-Owned Enterprises discovered a warehouse containing more desks than the Post Office would need for a decade. The purchasing clerk unapologetically explained that he had not spent his allocated budget and, as unspent money could not be carried forward, had purchased desks. Realising that they were not actually needed, he had them designed to be collapsible and rented a warehouse in which to store them.[55] Prebble recounted numerous examples of what he deemed to be ill-conceived decisions by government departments, some relating to unnecessarily complex work or pay systems, others to botched attempts at computerisation in the latter 1980s. One of the most astonishing stories was about the Post Office, which, after experiencing problems tracking and recording telephone lines (the records were then all kept manually), bought a Swedish computer program for $2 million to solve the problem. However, the program was written in Swedish, 'a language few New Zealand linesmen were confident in', so managers budgeted another $2 million to translate the program into English. Eventually, after paying some $37 million, they ended up cancelling the program altogether as unworkable.[56]

New Zealand's rapid transformation from 'the Poland of the South Pacific' to 'a paradise for free marketeers' hit the manufacturing sector particularly hard.[57] Previous governments had buoyed up manufacturing and exporting companies with subsidies, export incentives and protective tariffs. Many such businesses were poorly run, producing expensive goods consumers did not particularly want. In the hope of making manufacturing more efficient and responsive to consumer demand, the fourth Labour government withdrew tariffs, protections and subsidies. After struggling to keep producing, many companies eventually went bankrupt. Insolvencies reached record levels.[58] Long-established firms such as Crown Lynn Potteries closed, unable to compete with cheaper produce from the Philippines. The formerly heavily subsidised motor assembly industry dramatically decreased in size. Those enterprises that remained came under the ownership of overseas parent companies, streamlined production and became more efficient, resulting in a 20 per cent drop in car prices. Footwear manufacturers faced intense pressure from imports, which soared from 10.5 per cent to 53 per cent of the total domestic market between 1983 and 1993. The labour-intensive, low-technology textile industry, which made a narrow range of expensive, largely undifferentiated clothes for a small market, either closed down or moved into creating specialised upmarket garments offshore, where labour was cheaper.[59] Bendon, for example, closed factories in Auckland and Cambridge and opened them in Fiji.

Counting the cost

Economic rationalisation and deregulation resulted in massive job losses. A net 68,700 manufacturing jobs disappeared between 1986 and 1989; between February 1984 and February 1990, jobs in that sector decreased by 18 per cent.[60] Maori and Pacific Islanders, many of whom worked in the freezing works, timber mills and factories that were closing down, were hit particularly hard. By 1990, Maori unemployment was at 18.1 per cent and Pacific Island unemployment at 18.3 per cent compared with 5.6 per cent for Pakeha and 7.1 per cent for the population as a whole.[61] Unemployment started to rise in 1972 following an economic downturn. But after 1984, and more particularly after the 1987 share market collapse, it rose ever more rapidly, peaking at 11.2 per cent in 1992.[62] The number of beneficiaries on the Domestic Purposes Benefit, sickness and invalids benefits, and the unemployment benefit increased dramatically.

Small towns suffered numerous negative social and economic repercussions from the new free-market economy, particularly ones that depended on a single major industry such as coal mining, forestry, freezing works or railway engineering. Without work, many people were forced to move elsewhere, and community social institutions, clubs and organisations shut down. In 1986, the Whakatu freezing works in Hawke's Bay closed with the loss of 2000 full- and part-time jobs. Unemployment in the area shot up to 12.75 per cent, nearly 1.5 per cent above the national average. In 1987 the *New Zealand Outlook* wrote that many laid-off workers felt deeply reluctant to leave the area: 'At Hastings the closure of Whakatu has shell-shocked the community. Many families with three generations suddenly out of work do not want to follow the government's signposts pointing to Auckland and Wellington. Many hang onto the fragile hope that they will get one of the 250 jobs likely to be reinstated under new management.'[63]

Crime increased — two dozen burglaries took place in Hastings on one July weekend alone in 1990 — and violent crime also rose.[64] Throughout the country, individuals, families and communities experienced similar loss and dislocation. The Huntly coal mines shut down, and railway workshops closed, ending thousands of jobs. Milling towns were particularly hard hit. In forestry towns where the company owned the houses, losing a job also meant losing accommodation. Tom Gallot, for example, who worked in the Golden Downs Forest for 31 years, lost his job and never managed to find another. He died ten years later. His widow Ann remembers:

And once Tom was rejected two or three times it started to sink in pretty quickly that this was it . . . No home if we don't have a job. What happens then about our home? . . . That was when we made the decision to put our redundancy money into a home and at least stay in Tapawera which we loved . . .

But where before Tapawera had been a tight community, now all the values that held that community together were destroyed:

Community groups fell to bits; people didn't go out any more, people didn't do voluntary work any more, people didn't become involved any more because you had to look after yourself.[65]

In the Rotorua district, over 700 people were laid off. Residents of villages such as Kaingaroa, Rotoehu and Minginui, where forestry was the only employer and owned all the houses, became reliant on welfare, with more than 90 per cent of the workforce unemployed. Rotorua's unemployment rate reached 22.5 per cent in 1992, the highest in the country. Every day another shop or business closed its doors, and the Housing Corporation repossessed another house. Crime, vandalism and drunkenness spiralled. As one resident remarked despairingly: 'Rotorua's a depressing old town now. Hopeless. Dirty. The Mall's full of crap, there's rubbish strewn along the streets. No one could care less any more.'[66]

When railway workshops were closed in Wanganui East, residents simply abandoned the whole area. Ian Turner, who had worked there, bitterly recalls the impact of losing both job and community:

The broken promises! They promised in their manifesto and in their policy statements they put around the railways that they would retain the workshops . . . They closed us down . . . Many of those people have never worked again and for many of them their lives ended prematurely because they couldn't cope. This wasn't just a workplace, it was a microcosm of society with the same clubs and sporting activities . . . All those traditions, cultural and sporting things, all disappeared with the place.[67]

The planned closure of six hundred post offices in 1988 added to the already severe difficulties rural towns faced. As post offices were the cornerstone of the community and the only bank, many believed that if they went, the whole community would die. Opposition was particularly strong on the West Coast, where a large number of closures were planned. Protest meetings were held in various rural townships, and local MPs lobbied against the closures. A West Coast United Council took the issue to the High Court in Wellington but to no avail: 432 post offices closed as planned on 5 February 1988.

In Karamea, however, nine people staged a post office sit-in, refusing to leave for twelve days. A correspondent to the Christchurch *Press* expressed support for this stand: 'Congratulations to the residents of Karamea. Their post office is more than just an office for distributing mail. It is the very heart of the community. Nobody has a right to take that from them, not even a Minister of State-Owned Enterprises'.[68] Within two days a picket line stopped officials from moving furniture and private mailboxes off the premises. Meanwhile, inside the post office, the *Press* reported that

> things were warm and cosy and townsfolk were busy supplying meals. 'We are certainly not going short of grub,' said Mr Malins. 'In fact we are putting on weight.' Mr Malins is a store keeper in Karamea. He said the townsfolk believed that without the post office and PostBank in the township, local people would have to travel the 100km to Westport to obtain cash and do their shopping.[69]

After several days, more than 400 people turned out to show their support, including some protesters aged over 80, who stood outside the post office 'waving placards for three hours'.[70] However, after 12 days the sit-in was abandoned, and the post office closed.

The problems confronting small country towns in the late 1980s were compounded by the plight of farmers. For some 20 years before 1984, government grants and subsidies for the agricultural sector steadily increased. In the 1960s, agricultural support comprised just 3 per cent of farm income; by 1983, it was nearly 40 per cent in the sheep sector alone.[71] Farmers received all manner of assistance, from concessionary livestock valuation schemes and fertiliser subsidies to cheap loans, to lucrative incentives for land development and ample tax rebates. In addition to these different forms of assistance, supplementary minimum prices, or SMPs, effectively encouraged farmers to produce more sheep and beef than the market wanted.[72] Guaranteed a stable income despite the fact that prices were sliding, they had little incentive to change. Increased output from the agricultural sector by 1984–85 was generally less than the actual costs of production and processing.[73] The neo-liberal Labour government saw the farming sector as ripe for reform, and moved quickly in 1984, abolishing minimum price schemes for beef, sheep meat, wool and dairy products. It withdrew tax concessions for farmers and eliminated free government services. Producer boards found their access to concessionary Reserve Bank funding withdrawn, and land development loans, fertiliser and irrigation subsidies and subsidised credit were all reduced and eventually phased out from 1987.

The rapid speed and scale of these measures resulted in hardship and considerable pain for farmers. Encouraged by the previous government's incentive schemes and tax concessions, many had bought and developed more land (often not suitable for development) and increased stock numbers. Now, having lost all those subsidies and concessions, they struggled with high interest rates. Many could no longer buy fertiliser, use rural service industries, purchase equipment, or even new clothes. Companies supplying these needs lost money and often went bankrupt, leaving the main streets of some small country towns lined with empty, boarded-up shops. Land prices, formerly artificially inflated by subsidies, fell sharply, in some cases by as much as 50 per cent.[74] Farmers unable to pay high mortgages lost their farms.

Angry protests about the farmers' plight attracted large numbers: 10,000 turned out in Wellington, for example, and when Lange visited Invermay, near Dunedin, he encountered a group of irate placard-waving farmers.[75] As he later recalled: 'There was rebellion sometimes. I was attacked by a group of farmers in Otago. I was burnt in effigy by farmers all round the place.'[76] But all the marches, placards, and burnt effigies changed nothing.

In some cases, farmers remained solvent only because their wives went off to work in the nearby town. Alice Hood, a farmer and coordinator for the Rural Trust in the Manawatu/Wanganui district, remembered:

> Well of course when the crunch came, all these women went back looking for their old jobs and basically they got them . . . They were working full-time and also trying to hold a family together. The stresses on them were incredible in terms of the time they worked, and the lengths they had to go to to satisfy the creditors because a lot of their wages were taken wholesale by the banks as well.[77]

Tom and Mary McNaught of Hunterville lived on a hill-country farm that had been in Tom's family since 1914. In 1978, they borrowed heavily to buy the neighbouring farm. In 1984, when interest rates increased from 5 per cent to 14 per cent, they were forced to sell at a mortgagee sale. Mary remembers the sale as being like a death. Her husband was devastated.

> Yes it chased me back to work quite quickly. A lot of rural women were doing the same. I'd never thought that I would return to work, a semi-breadwinner. But at the end of 1985 we sat down and looked at it and it wasn't looking very good at all and I had to get a job quite quickly . . . [I] got a permanent job in teaching. And that was the start of an enormous change, personal change.[78]

Tom eventually found work as a shearer.

The (government-owned) Rural Banking and Finance Corporation estimated that in 1984 out of a farming population of some 60,000, some 15,000 were at severe risk and 5000 were in a critical debt situation facing foreclosure.[79] In 1986, an article in *New Zealand Outlook* magazine aptly entitled 'Out in the Cold World: Farming Reaches a Crucial Turning Point' noted that 'Hardship is a near certainty for at least the next two years, and the farming community has reached within itself to cope.' It described how Waikato Federated Farmers had set up an advisory group of 40 different farmers from various backgrounds, and that similar groups had formed in the Wairarapa and South Canterbury. The leader of the Waikato advisory group, Sam Lewis, expressed the view that the costs of returning farming to greater self-reliance would have proven worthwhile by the time the pain had ceased: 'We're trying to tell farmers to stay there. If you're in such a bad situation you've got nowhere to go it's better to fight it out to the bitter end.'[80]

Ideas about the benefits of self-reliance were not new to the sector; Federated Farmers had in fact been advocating many of Labour's market-oriented reforms for 20-odd years. Federated Farmers president Peter Elworthy, interviewed by *North & South* in 1986, while not opposed to many of the reforms, pointed out that their negative impact was compounded when combined with other government policies such as the floating exchange rate and the sudden increase in borrowing costs. He saw the present as a transitional period between 'the agriculture of the past and the agriculture of the future', requiring leadership which 'as far as possible gets agriculture through without having rural sectors die.'[81]

The sheep sector experienced the most dramatic change in the wake of the reforms. Termination of SMPs and other government support at the end of the 1984/85 season resulted in significant falls in the prices paid to producers. One estimate reported was of a 50 per cent fall in works door return per lamb. The national sheep flock reduced in number from 70 million in 1983–84 to 40 million in 2004–5.[82] After 1984, many sheep farmers had to think about ways to diversify and innovate to boost returns. In 1987, Angus Gordon, who farmed the Clifton station near Cape Kidnappers in Hawke's Bay, decided to try augmenting income by growing early squash for the Japanese market. For the first few years this proved fraught and not profitable enough to continue, but in 1989, J. M. Bostock, a large organic orchardist firm, persuaded him to try again:

> By now, on the pastoral side of farming, things were at an all time low. Clifton was getting between $4 and $10 for the old ewes, sometimes below $3 for a kilo of wool, about $17 for our best lambs, and $350 for our best weaners. I was game for anything! This seemed like at least an opportunity to try and control our own destiny . . . The 1990 squash crop was such a success that I was able to buy a new Ford station wagon, which we nicknamed the Squashmobile.[83]

While many sheep farms did not survive the difficult period following the 1984 reforms, those that did shifted their focus from quantity to quality. Reduced numbers of sheep resulted in many processing companies closing in the mid-1980s; the firms that remained became more modern and sophisticated. Prior to the reforms, carcasses accounted for 82 per cent of New Zealand's lamb exports. In the more market-oriented era after 1984, producers, necessarily more responsive to international consumer demand, began to consult with overseas supermarkets about cutting and pre-packing meat, for example, and some companies located processing facilities in overseas markets to better supply supermarket chains with specific cuts on request. Over time, spectacular gains were also made by improved sheep breeding. In 2002, for example, revenues from a sharply reduced stock exceeded those generated from the 70 million-strong flock of the early 1980s; lambing levels had also increased by 25 per cent compared with 1984/85 levels.[84]

The dairy industry, too, experienced dramatic changes in the wake of the 1984 reforms. The national herd increased from 2.3 to 5.3 million between 1983/84 and 2004/5; average herd size also increased from 150 to 270; and the volume of dairy production rose by 75 per cent.[85] The dairy sector's rapid expansion — in part the result of the reforms and in part improving access to international markets — resulted in New Zealand firms such as the Livestock Improvement Corporation (LIC) becoming world-leading innovators in pastoral stock genetics, an expertise which helped the country's dairy exports retain a competitive edge globally. New Zealand is currently the world's largest exporter of butter, skim milk powder and casein, and the second-largest exporter of cheese and whole milk powder. In 2007, it accounted for up to 33 per cent of internationally traded dairy production. General agricultural productivity growth is three times greater than in the economy as a whole.[86]

New Zealand farmers' need to survive in the post-1984 economic climate led in many cases to a 'flowering of entrepreneurial activity'. The dramatic and rapid economic restructuring 'shocked the existing system into a heightened understanding of the need for change'.[87] Two sectors that particularly flourished in the brave new world were horticulture and viticulture, which prior to the reforms had been small subsectors, largely domestically focused. In the deregulated economic environment they became successful 'growth industries', serving both the national and the more significant international market; wine exports worth less than US$10 million in 1984–85 had increased to $125 million by 2004–5; similarly, horticultural exports rose from $140 million in 1983–84 to $827 million in 2004–5.[88] In addition to innovation in these sectors, farmers survived the economic reforms through diversifying, often by finding innovative ways to supplement their incomes. Tourism was one notable option: in 1984–85, for example, four agriculturalists created 'Agritour', a company offering farm tours for tourists as well as more 'technical tours' that encompass sheep and deer production, animal breeding, processing plants, waste control and disposal facilities. The firm also designed various 'add-ons' in the form of hunting and fishing trips through to white-water rafting and jet boating.[89]

With considerable resourcefulness and resilience, the country's agricultural sector successfully met the challenges it confronted in 1984. However, this was a protracted process, involving trial and error and experimentation. As Angus Gordon wrote:

> What it [the post-1984 reforms] achieved for the farmers who survived was an
> entrepreneurial spirit that helped them adapt quickly to a diverse range of other
> possibilities . . . There were many mistakes, such as the goat boom, which spawned
> a host of overnight goat companies. These crashed with spectacular rapidity, leaving
> a lot of bankrupt and red-faced farmers. Many farmers close to the main centres
> survived by selling off small blocks of land for what has become the ubiquitous life-
> style block. What also emerged out of this time was the growth of the larger-scale
> farmers and farming businesses, such as J.M. Bostock or Brownrigg Agriculture in
> Hawke's Bay, both of which now lease and own vast acreages of land.[90]

James Williams, another Hawke's Bay sheep farmer, expressed the view that:

> Pre 1984 farming was often a comfortable, subsidised, traditional family business
> ... But with the removal of government support schemes, farmers had to adapt to
> survive ... There was a change in land use to forestry, dairying, arable and lifestyle.
> More precise management and grazing systems based on objective measurement
> were introduced along with improved genetics ... This change in efficiency has
> resulted in the same tonnage of lamb produced today, as in 1970, but from half the
> number of breeding ewes.[91]

While many within the agricultural sector adapted and adjusted and in
the long term benefited from the withdrawal of subsidies, for some farming
families the painful reality of the situation on the land in the late 1980s left
bitter memories. Alice Hood, who worked with the Rural Trust, witnessed at
first hand successive farmers pushed to the wall, forced to yield up all income
directly to the creditors:

> I still feel a sense of shock. It was a very emotional time. All the power had been
> given to the banks and the stock firms with deregulation but no power was given to
> the borrower on the other end of the line. And it was the way they used that power.
> They used every means they could to intimidate people and back them against the
> wall.[92]

Peter Elworthy, commenting on the numbers of farmers forced to leave their
land in the late 1980s, noted that there were not as many as initially feared:
'Some people thought ten thousand but in the end we probably lost, forcibly,
upwards of a thousand out of say thirty thousand. So it wasn't as dramatic
for all sorts of reasons including, most importantly, the pressure we put upon
bankers to keep good farmers on the land.'[93]

In 1996, Roger Douglas claimed that farmers' discontent and anger after
the removal of government support in the late 1980s helped the process of
extending the free-market revolution:

> In a way, farmers were quite helpful in ensuring other change came about. Once
> they realised the government was not going to go back to subsidies and tax breaks
> and the like, they became in some ways our best supporters. They were out there
> saying we want fairness, we want the ports reformed, we want railways reformed,
> we want government reformed.[94]

David Lange, who shared Douglas's conviction that the reforms to the rural sector were necessary, later admitted that the cooperation of Federated Farmers had assisted the government's aims. He also noted that it was not long before the farmers' pain 'came to be shared in huge measure by many thousands of New Zealanders . . . The pain was pretty widely diffused by the time 1990 came.'[95]

The gilt off the gingerbread

The hardships and tribulations experienced by many in the rural sector in the latter 1980s contrasted with a boom in the cities. Inflation shrank to about 5 per cent for the first time in twelve years, the 1987 Budget was in surplus for the first time in a generation, and the trade deficit fell.[96] The deregulated economy combined with rising interest rates encouraged overseas investors into the market. Wages rose sharply to keep up, consumers spent up large on goods newly released from import controls, and credit became readily available. Indeed, banks fell over themselves to lend to new entrepreneurs and property companies. Olly Newland, one of Auckland's more successful high-profile property developers, later recalled: 'the banks were pushing money down people's throats because they had it. The money was flowing into the banks. The farmers and the manufacturing sector weren't borrowing it so they had to lend it to someone.'[97] Takeovers and mergers proliferated, as a raft of newly created investment companies sold and bought other companies trading in goods and services. They made substantial profits with each transaction, as spending was diverted from productive to speculative investment.[98] One of the largest enterprises, Brierley Investments, owned hundreds of New Zealand firms as well as companies in Australia, Britain and the US. The darlings of the stock market were the newly formed merchant banks, financial companies, property developers and speculators. Richard Carter, head of Carter Holt Harvey, one of New Zealand's largest companies in the 1980s, later commented ruefully about this period: 'During all the hype throughout 1985 to 1987 we hardly got a mention. We were not a property developer or a merchant banker. They were in all the greatest newspaper articles. We were simply the backbone of New Zealand industry.'[99]

Fuelled by the incessant takeovers and mergers, and by the creation and listing of new companies, the share market surged, tripling in value between 1984 and 1987. In October 1987, the New Zealand Stock Exchange had 309 listed companies, far more than at any previous time in its history.[100] Speculative investment became the rage:

With the freeze regulations all but melted, and the economy released from decades of financial stranglehold, investment in general and into the stock market in particular began to take off in earnest. Public companies, and especially those in property or speculative investment, became all the rage. The riskier the better. There seemed no end for the public's appetite to throw money at the market or entrepreneurs who might be the flavour of the month.[101]

Everybody wanted a part of the action. Close to 900,000 New Zealanders — about 40 per cent of the adult public — eagerly invested in the boom. All over the country, as the stock market kept on rising, share clubs sprang up, and groups of amateur investors happily got together to trade tips on this seemingly infallible way to make money quickly. According to historian David Grant: 'Joining a share club or attending an investment seminar had become as common as buying a lottery ticket or going to the races. Most brokers were offering one simple message: Buy!'[102] Many new investors mortgaged their houses, sold their cars and cashed in superannuation to finance stock market speculations.[103] Brian Gaynor, a financial analyst, recalls the investment culture of that time as 'kind of evangelical . . . everybody wanted to hear the business gurus and everyone wanted to buy their shares'.[104]

The boom altered the urban skyline. Construction of new office blocks rose 32 per cent in 1984, 24 per cent in 1986 and 39 per cent in 1987, as property developers erected huge new office buildings.[105] Newly rich investors, lawyers, accountants and brokers rushed to fill them at exalted prices. Opulence was the hallmark of the new corporate work spaces: Zealcorp, a specialist arm of the Development Finance Corporation, for example, luxuriated in a first-floor suite of offices that opened onto a wide indoor avenue of silver trees. Fay Richwhite's foyer was lined in black marble, at a 'staggering expense'. Employees, in addition to working amidst such splendour, enjoyed vast salaries.[106] Champagne flowed and consumption was conspicuous as newly wealthy investors indulged in European cars, opulent houses, designer clothes, shopping trips and exotic holidays abroad, large boats and expansive holiday homes. They paid record prices for real estate and investment art, and entertained lavishly. Olly Newland's description of a soirée thrown by the property development firm Chase Corporation captures some of the ostentatious excess of the times:

The Chase boys threw a Christmas party on 15 December at Highwic House Epsom. It was a fairytale evening of snow-white tents, black-liveried servants, fairy lights winking on and off in the darkness and important people, wonderful food, music, dancing, costumes and elegance. BMWs, Mercedes and Rolls-Royces slid to and fro all night long carrying inebriated VIPs and slightly tipsy women.[107]

One of the more glamorous newcomers to the share market, Ray Smith, a devotee of fast cars and beautiful women, appeared on the cover of *Personal Investment New Zealand* magazine in October 1986 dressed in athletic gear and 'looking more like a tennis pro or an international playboy than the governing director of the Auckland Coin and Bullion Exchange'.[108] In the accompanying article, he offered advice to would-be gold investors.

Although a large section of the public had initially disliked Labour's free-market reforms, by mid-1987, as the election approached, much of the population began to see some benefit. The rural recession seemed to be lessening, unemployment was falling slightly, and the share market boom looked like it would never end. Labour started to rise in the opinion polls, and in the August election, increased its vote from 44 per cent in 1984 to 48 per cent. It took three seats from National and almost won the two safe blue-ribbon National seats of Remuera and Fendalton.

Untrammelled entrepreneurialism seemed on an unstoppable upward trajectory. Then, on 'Black Monday', 19 October 1987, a global stock market crash commenced, moving inexorably from Asia to Europe to the United States and elsewhere. In New Zealand, because of the time difference, the crash occurred on 'Black Tuesday', 20 October, wiping $5.7 billion from share values in just under four hours.[109] Over the next three weeks, the value of shares fell by 37.4 per cent. The crash was international, but New Zealand's stock market suffered one of the highest losses in the western world: within two months, nearly 50 per cent of the market was wiped away.[110] Valued at $50 billion in 1987 before the crash, it dropped to a low of $14.5 billion in January 1991.[111] Other stock markets around the globe recovered faster than New Zealand's, which had risen higher and fallen further. (Its trading volumes had increased by 100 per cent in one year, while the equivalent markets in Australia, New York and London only increased 20, 30 and 30 per cent respectively.)[112] In the year following the crash, the performance of the New Zealand stock market was the worst in the world.[113] Recovery remained elusive until 1991, when the market was stimulated by 'New Zealand's biggest-ever share sale', the $420 million Telecom share float.[114]

The fallout of the 1987 crash was dramatic and widespread — as firms went into liquidation, company bankruptcies climbed from 305 a year at the beginning of the 1980s to over 2000 in 1988.[115] Share brokers, big and small, either laid off huge numbers of staff and closed down whole departments or, like Renouf Partners, one of Wellington's oldest and largest firms, closed down completely. Gwen Parker, who ran a thriving one-woman share-broking business in Oamaru, was also forced to close. Her clients were small investors — country people, housewives, share clubs, students and the like — all of whom simply stopped investing after the crash.[116] A great many small investors lost money, and some, such as retired businessman and former president of Grey Power Harold Roberts, lost their retirement funds:

> I went on advice from a very reputable firm of share brokers and invested my money, as they advised, in Chase, in Equiticorp, in Goldcorp; in all these gilt-edged securities which crashed something dreadful in 1987 . . . So I lost very severely, which completely curtailed my way of life . . . I had to move from the type of residence that I had . . . I effectively lost my life savings. It was a feeling of terrible loss, a feeling of inadequacy, of being unable to do anything about it, nothing. All gone.[117]

Others lost redundancy payouts. In 1987, for example, Lloyd Evans, having been laid off from a forestry job, invested his redundancy money in the share market:

> At the time the Labour Government was telling us we should be investing in this country, so I put it into Equiticorp, Brierleys and Chase. And I put some off-shore because I wasn't convinced that things here were as safe as they should have been. Then the share market crashed, and I lost most of it. It was shocking, a very traumatic time for me, trying to live on $129 a week.[118]

Property values collapsed, cars and houses were repossessed, the retail sector became static, restaurants emptied, car yards stopped selling fancy cars; even supermarkets were affected. Mark Wills, marketing manager of Progressive Enterprises at the time, commented that: 'The crash has made people more price-sensitive . . .'[119]

The economy had been weakening since 1984, but was buoyed by the speculative boom. Now it rapidly spiralled into a five-year recession.[120] Growth dropped to zero, retail spending dropped 4.3 per cent, GDP contracted by an average of 0.6 per cent, and companies either downsized or closed their doors. This meant more job losses but there was little investment to create new jobs. Unemployment soared from 100,000 in 1988 to 216,000 in 1992.[121] Public debt rose, and as imports increased, so did foreign debt, and with it huge interest bills that consumed about one fifth of the country's export earnings. This situation so concerned the American credit rating agency Standard & Poor's that it considered dropping New Zealand's rating, a situation that the new National government had to contend with in 1990.[122]

The bubble had burst spectacularly, and with it the massive overnight profits and the confident culture of speculation and expense account lunches. Many high-flyers fell to the ground with a thump, and were facing charges for illegal business practices. Former entrepreneurial princes such as Ray Smith found themselves suddenly devoid of assets, and facing not only legal charges but also 'public ridicule and contempt'.[123] Smith chaired Goldcorp Holdings, a company floated in early 1987.[124] Upon going into receivership in 1988, it did not hold enough gold bullion to pay out all the investors. A group of about 1600 investors, who had collectively lost millions following the company's collapse, took Smith to court on fraud charges centring on misleading advertising statements. Although acquitted of those charges in 1991, in 1993 Smith was convicted on fifteen of 29 charges of concealing assets from creditors and doing business while a bankrupt. Jailed for six months in the light-security Rangipo Prison, he served only half the sentence. In 1994, Smith's book *Where's the Gold?* described his lavish and glamorous pre-crash lifestyle, and ingenious tax avoidance schemes. It also revealed his lack of remorse for his role in Goldcorp's downfall.[125]

Allan Hawkins, another high-profile 1980s business hero who fell dramatically from grace, founded the profitable merchant bank Equiticorp in 1984. In August 1987, Hawkins, whose estimated worth was US$361 million, ranked second on the *National Business Review* 'Rich List'. In keeping with the times, he enjoyed a sumptuous lifestyle, living in an imposing cliff-top Auckland home that boasted a swimming pool cantilevered over the harbour. Bad timing played a role in Equiticorp's demise. Just hours before the Wall Street slump, the firm purchased the government's 89 per cent stake in New Zealand Steel for US$327 million. Hawkins paid for this with 92.9 million Equiticorp shares that he agreed to buy back at a fixed price. Equiticorp shares, trading at $3.50 on 19 October, decreased to $2.90 the next day. By February 1988, they had slumped to one dollar.[126] On 22 January 1989, Equiticorp collapsed, bringing down with it the 153 companies in its stable.[127] Its statutory manager sued the Crown to recoup shareholders' losses deriving from the New Zealand Steel purchase, and was awarded $328 million by the High Court in 1996. This comprised the most expensive legal suit in New Zealand history to that date.[128] In the course of the trial, the Labour government's role in the New Zealand Steel purchase came under critical scrutiny, for benefiting at the expense of Equiticorp investors and for 'turning a blind eye' to the murky nature of the transaction.[129] In 1998, rather than appealing, the Crown agreed to pay an out-of-court settlement of $267.5 million.[130] Meanwhile, in 1992, Hawkins was sentenced to six years in prison (he served less than three) on fraud charges relating to the running of Equiticorp and the financing of the New Zealand Steel purchase. The Serious Fraud Office Director Charles Sturt compared this case, with its complex web of share market manipulation, fraudulent foreign exchange dealings and money laundering, to 'completing a 1000 piece jigsaw from a million pieces . . . The dilemma was to work out which 900,000 pieces did not form part of the final picture.'[131] Property magnate Sir Bob Jones, quoted in the *New Zealand Herald* in 2007, expressed the view that Hawkins was unfairly singled out: 'After crashes the public, fuelled by the media, look for culprits.'[132] According to business historian Graeme Hunt, Hawkins was 'too big a fish to be allowed to resurface in the way several failed 1980s property developers had'.[133]

The fall of various former high-flying businessmen in the aftermath of the October 1987 crash had all the elements of a medieval morality play. The culture of speculation and high spending had come at a cost, and in the sobering post-crash economy, several entrepreneurs, previously esteemed, admired and envied for their glamorous lifestyles, were exposed for engaging in unethical and/or illegal business practices. In 1987, the television 'glitter-soap' *Gloss* cast a satirical glance at the 'If you've got it, flaunt it, if you haven't, get it' aspect of contemporary urban life in late 1980s New Zealand.[134] Its protagonists, the wealthy Redfern family, presided over a lucrative high-fashion magazine business in Auckland. Full of glamour, yuppies, shoulder pads, and melodrama, the series was an entertaining commentary on the times:

> Kiwi viewers had seen American super-soaps *Dallas* and *Dynasty*. They got that this local media-and-money show reflecting Rogernomics and the long-lunch years of excess was both of the genre and a send-up. The series largely screened after the bubble had burst in 1987 and the often cynical and un-politically correct tone caught the mood.[135]

In particular, the theme song, with its caustic take on aspirational materialism, took on a new resonance after the crash:

> It's the gilt off the gingerbread
> The icing on the cake

It's monuments and mirror-glass
The city's on the make
Devil take the hindmost
So no one counts the cost
Such a sweet seduction
Glossssss![136]

Tomorrow's shake-up

The dramatic reform of the financial and state sectors was only part of New Zealand's extreme makeover during the early years of Rogernomics. With resolution and fervour, the Labour government proceeded to review, reorganise, rationalise and shake up every aspect of public life. Task forces were accordingly commissioned to assess education, health, local government, social welfare and housing.

Businessman Brian Picot headed up an education task force that, in its April 1988 report, argued for 'decentralisation of educational decision-making' and 'management of schools by local parent representatives'.[137] Despite evoking a storm of protest from teachers, teachers' unions, university staff and students' associations,[138] the government accepted most of Picot's recommendations, incorporating them as the basis of a reform package called 'Tomorrow's Schools'. The Department of Education became the Ministry of Education; boards of trustees, comprised of parents, the head teacher and some teachers, replaced regional educational boards. Trustee boards now effectively governed schools: setting policies in place, managing the annual budget and overseeing staffing. An Education Review Office and a New Zealand Qualifications Authority were created to monitor schools and set national standards. David Lange, then Minister of Education as well as Prime Minister, rationalised the changes by promising that they 'would result in more immediate delivery of resources to schools, more parental and community involvement, and greater teacher responsibility [and] would lead to improved learning opportunities for the children of this country'.[139]

Opinion on the results of this policy path has been divided. A survey in 1991, for example, found that teachers (who were asked their views on both the impact of the educational reforms to date on their school, and on the wider educational system) did not believe change had been for the better. Of the 70 per cent who responded, only 4 per cent made a positive comment on the effects of the reforms on New Zealand education as a whole.[140] A later review in 2000, however, found the great majority of trustee boards believed they were successful and functioned well, and that involving parents resulted in better education.[141] Hoe-o-Tainui, a country school near Hamilton, for example, was pleased and grateful for the advances Tomorrow's Schools had facilitated:

> The extra work that these changes brought and greater responsibility was, and still is, taxing on Board members, but it has also allowed for greater control in the direction that parents, Boards and teaching staff have deemed important for our own children . . . Whilst the responsibility carried by the Board is greater, so too is the freedom we have to determine just what are the greatest needs of our own children and also to specifically apply our time, effort and funds to answer these needs.[142]

Labour's desire to streamline and economise also extended to the health sector, where expensive new technologies and an ageing population had seen rapidly escalating costs. Consequently, two task forces were commissioned — the 'Health Benefits Review Taskforce', which reported in 1986, and 'Unshackling the Hospitals' headed by businessman Alan Gibbs in 1988. Commonly known as the 'Gibbs Report', the latter recommended sweeping changes to hospital management and administration, which Labour rejected as too radical. Instead it continued what the previous National government started: decentralisation of the Department of Health's operational and public health responsibilities and restructuring 27 hospital boards into 14 regional locally elected area health boards (AHBs). Each AHB was to integrate various service providers — primary, secondary and tertiary — develop local services, and promote good health and preventative medicine.[143]

Upon becoming Minister of Health in 1989, Helen Clark restructured and streamlined the Health Department and introduced a Health Charter requiring each AHB to set 'health goals' and to sign an accountability agreement with the Minister.[144] She appointed general managers to run hospitals, clearly defined public health goals and targets, and focused on preventative strategies such as reducing tobacco and alcohol consumption, heart disease and cervical and skin cancers, and improving nutrition.[145] Despite some complaints from workers, the health system became significantly more efficient as a result. Health spending fell from 15.76 per cent of total government expenditure in 1980 to 12.75 per cent in 1990, by which time the sector overall seemed to be working well.[146]

The scythe of cost-cutting efficiency also descended on local government. A Local Government Commission, known as the 'Elwood Commission' after its chairman Brian Elwood, a lawyer and the mayor of Palmerston North, was appointed in 1985 to consider possible options. Michael Bassett, the Minister of Local Government, believed that a reorganisation was imperative, warning: 'local government must bear its share of the pain entailed in economic restructuring.'[147] Although the Commission produced a discussion document, 'Reform of Local and Regional Government', the government was in a hurry, and did not pause to discuss strategies. Bassett promptly introduced the Local Government Amendment (No. 3) Act 1988 even before submissions to the Commission had closed. He then proceeded with 'the first comprehensive reform of local government in New Zealand since the abolition of the provinces in 1876'.[148]

The reforms were implemented at great speed. Graham Bush has remarked: 'The breadth was astonishing: to be covered were the functions, structure, funding, and organisation of both the territorial and ad hoc sectors. The reforms would have to be completed within two years if the inaugural elections of the reformed authorities were to proceed normally in October 1989.'[149] Approximately 700 different regional, council, special purpose boards (for example, harbour boards, drainage boards etc.) and local bodies were reduced to 14 regional councils, 14 city councils and 59 district councils. Bassett later described many of the bodies restructured out of existence at this time as 'semi-moribund ad hoc authorities'.[150]

Labour then turned its attention to welfare expenditure, which in its view had recently spiralled out of control. Until the 1970s, providing generous benefits to meet citizens' needs worked well. But in the late 1970s, as recession hit and unemployment soared, spending on social services, including health education and social security, rose from 13 per cent of GDP in the 1950s to 23.5 per cent.[151] It continued to escalate along with unemployment in the 1980s. By 1989, net expenditure on social welfare reached $8,177 million annually. Unemployment benefits soared from $2.1 million in 1968 to $987 million in 1989, with 8.4 per cent of the labour force out of work. Domestic Purposes Benefit payments almost quadrupled from $252 million in 1982 to $962 million in 1989.[152] In addition, there were income supplementary benefits for low-income families, a large number of cash emergency benefits and special needs grants, accommodation subsidies, along with a growing range of supplementary services.[153] Superannuation absorbed the largest portion of social security spending however. In December 1975, Muldoon introduced universal superannuation at 80 per cent of the average wage to all men and women aged 60 or over. As a result, the cost spiralled from $114 million in 1977 to $4,314 million in 1989, equalling over half of all social security spending.[154] Labour's surcharge on superannuitants' other income temporarily, but only slightly, reduced the

Norman Kirk speaking at the 1972 Labour Party Conference. The campaign slogan,
'Time for a real Change', proved prophetic. After being in opposition since 1960,
Labour won the November 1972 election decisively. *Peter Bush*

Prime Minister Robert Muldoon shakes hands with a gang member employed on a work scheme
in Otara, 1979. From the 1970s, gang membership in New Zealand rose dramatically.
Box 7/16, Footprints 00222, Courier Collection, Manukau Research Library

The great hikoi, or Land March, of 1975 drew public attention to the loss of Maori land.
This photograph shows the marchers, by this time numbering some 5000,
walking along the motorway from Porirua to Wellington. *Peter Bush*

Maori leaders and activists (left to right) Dame Whina Cooper, Eva Rickard and Titewhai Harawira singing waiata at a Waitangi hui, mid-1980s. *Gil Hanly*

Members of the Nomads gang enjoy a peaceful moment, relaxing outside Wellington Railway Station, 1988. *EP/1988/1687, Evening Post Collection, Alexander Turnbull Library*

Young supporters of the Polynesian Panthers and of the Progressive Youth Movement march in Auckland in the early 1970s. *John Miller*

The writer Albert Wendt (left) and Polynesian Panthers co-founder Will 'Ilolahia (centre) with Longman Paul editor Rosemary Stagg on Ponsonby Road, Auckland, in the early 1970s. Ponsonby was then home to many Pacific Island people, as well as hippies and artists. *John Miller*

On 25 May 1978 some 600 police, assisted by the army, forcibly removed the Maori land rights activists who had occupied a site at Bastion Point, Auckland, for 506 days in opposition to the National government's land development plans. *Gil Hanly; Robin Morrison, NEG 446, Auckland War Memorial Museum*

Tangi (1973) by Witi Ihimaera (centre) was the first novel published by a Maori author. Ihimaera is shown here with Ngahuia Volkerling (Te Awekotuku) at an artists' and writers' hui at Te Kaha, Bay of Plenty, in June 1973. Poet Hone Tuwhare (bottom left) is having a snooze. *John Miller*

At the Dowse Art Gallery, Lower Hutt, a 1979 exhibition by Selwyn Muru commemorates the historic events at Parihaka in 1881. Sitting underneath his paintings are Netta Wharehoka, Ngahina Okeroa and Matarena Rau-Jupa with a photo of Te Whiti. *Ans Westra*

Sir William Lily, founder of the Society for the Protection of the Unborn Child, Dr Diana Mason, Mrs Ruth Kirk and the Roman Catholic Archbishop of Wellington at an anti-abortion rally in August 1974. *EP/1974/6130/33, Dominion Post Collection, Alexander Turnbull Library*

Pro-abortion graffiti scrawled across the driveway of Minister of Social Welfare Bert Walker in December 1977. Walker supported the conservative Contraception, Sterilisation, and Abortion Act of 1977. *Box 7/3 Abortion 5085, 508516/12/1877, Alexander Turnbull Library*

The 1981 Springbok tour divided New Zealand. Above, Reverend Dr George Armstrong of St John's Theological College, Auckland, addresses police squads on the playing field at Rugby Park, Hamilton, on 25 July 1981. The game was eventually cancelled for security reasons after police received reports that a light plane stolen from Taupo was heading for the stadium. Below, rugby supporters and anti-tour demonstrators clash violently on their way to the third and final test at Eden Park, Auckland, on 12 September 1981. *Gil Hanly; EP/1981/3106/17a, Dominion Post Collection, Alexander Turnbull Library, Wellington, New Zealand*

cost. In 1986, when the net rate increased by 5 per cent to compensate for GST, costs immediately rose again.

Beneficiaries and officials expressed considerable discontent with the social welfare system in the early 1980s. Lange accordingly promised during the 1984 election campaign to review and overhaul the system to meet the changing needs of the New Zealand public. After three difficult years of restructuring, he believed people should benefit, and that government 'should now make the economy fit for people to live in'.[155] In October 1986, a Royal Commission on Social Policy, with extremely wide terms of reference, was set up to review what people wanted or expected from social welfare. Its mandate was

> to inquire into the extent to which existing instruments of policy meet the needs of New Zealanders, and report on what fundamental or significant reformation or changes are necessary or desirable in existing policies, administration, institutions, or systems to secure a more fair, humanitarian, consistent, efficient, and economical social policy which will meet the changed and changing needs of New Zealand and achieve a more just society.[156]

However, the findings produced in April 1988 ran completely counter to the government's austere 'downsizing' path. The Commission opposed neo-liberal economic reform, advocating instead new forms of expensive state support. Historian Margaret McClure has written: 'The report documented the hopes of ordinary people, but lacked a coherent, concise, moral rationale for its ideals of community, or an economically convincing argument on how a more generous society could be achieved . . .'[157] In a 1987 *Listener* article, journalist and Labour party advisor Simon Walker dismissed the Commission and its report as: 'a sop to party internal critics. In practice, Roger Douglas's idea of "delivery" is likely to be quite different from a traditional socialist approach . . . It was an open secret . . . that no one had any faith in the ability of the Royal Commission to sort out priorities.'[158]

This view proved prescient. The Commission's massive report — thousands of pages long and comprising four unindexed volumes — was largely ignored by politicians and public servants, but apparently served as a doorstop at the Commission's concluding celebration party.[159] Nonetheless, the social policy aims and ideals endorsed in the report traditionally drew support from Labour. They were also important to one prominent member of the government. Prime Minister David Lange felt genuinely reluctant to cut welfare and take the knife to social policy.

'Time for a cup of tea'

By April 1987, the cohesiveness that allowed the fourth Labour Government to achieve so much so quickly was disintegrating. According to Michael Bassett:

> The government tiptoed into April [1987] determined to keep on keeping on. Speed was enormously important to managing change . . . Yet below the surface . . . the tensions were building that would ultimately destroy the Fourth Labour government . . . On the one hand Douglas kept up the momentum, believing it to be the secret to our success so far.[160]

On the other hand, Lange wanted to slow down, believing that more radical reforms would only increase hardship for the unemployed, the poor, and the farmers. Having countenanced a great deal of radical monetarist reform, he now believed that 'we ought to start to remember that people could not endlessly change, could not endlessly be restructured, could not endlessly be ground down. That we had to start thinking about them rather than theory.'[161] In August 1988, when addressing the National Press Club in Canberra, he expressed the view that it was time 'to stop and assess our situation and let those who had fallen behind catch up with us. It was time for a cup of tea.'[162]

Roger Douglas (and many of the Cabinet) did not want tea: instead they aimed to forge ahead and restructure social policy. In Douglas's view, 'Lange wasn't really prepared to face up to the waste in the social policy areas in the way that he was prepared to do it in the more economic-type areas like railways, telecommunications and so on'.[163] The April 1987 Budget sparked the first in a succession of major differences of opinion between the two. Douglas proposed radical measures — a flat tax rate, extreme expenditure cuts, and the sale of almost all government assets. The proposals shocked Lange: 'I could hardly believe what I was reading. It was an unaccustomed addition to the burdens of office to have the finance minister take leave of his senses.'[164]

After convincingly winning the election in August 1987, Lange proceeded to reshuffle his Cabinet, appointing ministers who would support his less reformist stance: 'I no longer trusted Douglas and wanted to use the allocation [of portfolios] to put some restraints on him . . . My greatest concern was to put ministers in place who would protect the social services from the onslaught I knew would be made on them . . .'[165] But despite this attempt to bolster his position, matters did not improve. Lange, by this time unwell and increasingly disenchanted, continued to battle Douglas and his allies, growing to dislike and distrust them all in the process:[166]

Dear God! What a terrible lot of people they were. It is hard to believe I used to think so much of them . . . I thought that if we stopped to pick up the casualties of our first term in office we would get the politics right . . . His [Douglas's] politics lacked understanding and humanity, and I will always believe I was right to take issue with them.[167]

According to Bassett, Lange had lost his earlier willingness to pursue economic reform, and was becoming more reclusive. A key reason for Lange's change of heart, Bassett believed, was the influence of Margaret Pope, his speechwriter and the woman who would become his second wife. Describing her as intelligent, manipulative, and an 'old time' socialist, Bassett perceived her influence to be 'the biggest single factor in the collapse of the Lange government'.[168] Others on the left wing of the party were also increasingly uneasy with the free-market path, and unwilling to follow it any longer. Jim Anderton, for example, resigned after refusing to accept the sale of the Bank of New Zealand. He formed the New Labour Party, taking many of the faithful with him. Cabinet, as Lange later recalled, became a battleground:

Cohesion was gone for good, and any kind of philosophical unity. It was a place of contest. We could turn our collective mind only to inconsequential issues; anything of moment was subject to dispute and settled by shifting alignments of support.

Douglas as leader of the opposition had the constant encouragement of Bassett and Prebble.[169]

In January 1988, the irreconcilable differences between Lange and his Minister of Finance aired before the public. Without consulting Cabinet or caucus, Lange unilaterally declared that the flat income tax rate of 24 cents in the dollar, announced in December, would not be implemented. As he later admitted: 'I killed it without proper process. I killed it by going direct to the press conference. I didn't even wallow around in it in caucus. The caucus came out, including members of the Cabinet in caucus, and discovered that I had gone public and killed this flat-tax package because it had to be killed.'[170]

The year ground on, beleaguered by public squabbles between the Lange and Douglas factions over economic and social policies. By this stage, Margaret Pope later commented, 'All sense of common purpose had vanished from the government and with it David's power to speak for it. He could only hedge or equivocate and sounded as if he was never entirely sure of himself . . . Confidence in the government — already eroded by recession — plummeted, and polls soon had National comfortably ahead.'[171] Finally, on 14 December 1988, Douglas resigned, writing to Lange:

> Mistrust has infected our offices, and destroyed the internal coordination of both policy and communication. Public confidence in the Government, its directions and its ability to manage the economy in a consistent way, have all suffered fundamental damage, with results now reflected in the opinion polls. These are matters of the most profound seriousness, not just for the Government but for the country as a whole. They have impacted repeatedly on the level of interest rates, the attitudes of investors, our ability to maintain and create jobs, and on the length of the unemployment queues at the dole office. The nation has paid a high price for it — an avoidable price . . . As Prime Minister, you should not be aggravating such risks for the nation. You should be playing your part in the collective process . . .'[172]

However, after pressure from caucus and Cabinet, Douglas was re-elected to Cabinet on 3 August 1989. This provoked Lange into resigning. His deputy, Geoffrey Palmer, replaced him, but as the election loomed and Labour spiralled even further downward in the polls, Palmer was in turn supplanted by Mike Moore. The government limped into the election on 27 October 1990 and was thoroughly trounced by National, which won 67 seats to Labour's 29.

Commenting on the fourth Labour government and its legacy in 2004, some 20 years after it first swept into power, Michael Cullen, who served as Senior Whip during Labour's first term and Associate Minister of Finance and Minister of Social Welfare during its second, wrote that 'there was a tendency for the government to become so convinced of its own intelligence, courage, and competence in the pursuit of change that change became the end not the means. In so doing, the government lost sight of the innate conservatism of most New Zealanders, particularly faced with simultaneous change on almost every front.'[173] Labour's defeat in 1990 did not, however, mark the end of 'the most ambitious and comprehensive structural reforms undertaken by any OECD country'. The 'New Zealand Experiment' was about to enter its second and most controversial phase, as reformist attention shifted towards both industrial relations and the welfare state.[174]

CHAPTER TEN

'Focused by Events'

A SECOND WAVE OF REFORM

We knew the time had come for the second wave of reform . . . And just as we had seen a Labour Government courageously, as you would expect, show leadership . . . so also were we ready to show that leadership. — Ruth Richardson, 1996[1]

If voters hoped that by electing a new government in 1990 they would slow down the pace of reform, or even initiate a shift away from a market driven, laissez-faire approach and return to a more collectively responsible system, they were mistaken. The revolution that commenced in 1984 was about to enter a second stage. National forged ahead with more reforms that would have adverse social and economic impacts on individuals and families, particularly those at the lower end of the socio-economic scale. Promises were broken, welfare slashed, unions destroyed, and a 'user pays' philosophy introduced into education and health. The new National government headed by Jim Bolger, with Ruth Richardson as Finance Minister, assumed power with a vague commitment to 'redesign the welfare state'. This did not mean undoing the funding cuts of the previous two years, but rather completing what Roger Douglas had been unable to finish — namely, slashing welfare benefits and 'taking Rogernomics into social policy'.[2]

Public hopes for a better future and an end to radical reform evaporated. In 1993, weary of change and sick of politicians who did not listen to the will of the majority and who acted without any apparent concern for the impact of their reforms on the lives of ordinary people, the electorate voted to adopt a new system of political representation. In doing so, they aimed to regain a voice and to add some checks and balances to governments that acted arbitrarily.

Stiff medicine

Prime Minister Jim Bolger, who left school at fifteen to work on the family farm, became National MP for the King Country in 1972. A farmer, and a devout Catholic with a large family, he was a pragmatic politician who preferred to govern by consultation and consensus. Ruth Richardson, on the other hand, was an uncompromising libertarian, driven, as she herself acknowledged, 'by a vision of what the country could do when we let freedom drive our agenda. I believed that the state was stifling us as New Zealanders and was knocking the stuffing out of our economy.'[3] She particularly wanted to reform social policy and the labour market: 'we needed to move into the no-go areas for Labour — the labour market, social policy, the size and the role of the state.'[4] Richardson drove through the next lot of reforms, aware that 'Jim was going along with these measures through gritted teeth as he felt the fiscal imperatives gave him no option'.[5]

Just as National came to power, New Zealand slid into recession, with an unemployment rate at levels unprecedented since the 1930s Depression.[6] Two major shocks, developments the outgoing government had not disclosed, compounded the economic situation. Firstly, the new government learned of a completely unexpected budget deficit of $3.7 billion, which was expected to rise to $5.2 billion by 1993 if steps were not taken to control it. Secondly, the Bank of New Zealand was in trouble, requiring a government bail-out to the tune of $620 million.[7] This dire state of affairs provoked threats from credit rating agency Standard & Poor's to drop New Zealand's credit rating.

As in 1984, an economic crisis gave Ruth Richardson the mandate to imme-diately start implementing cuts across the board:

> My advice from Graham Scott [Secretary of Treasury] was if you leave policy
> running just as it is now you are looking at a deficit of 5.2 billion dollars. So we
> were galvanised into action . . . within six weeks of taking office we had effectively
> announced a framework for action that would sustain this National government
> for over six years. So it gave us a running start to a relationship. We were focused by
> events.[8]

That framework, the Economic and Social Initiative (ESI) package, announced in December 1990, was a 'stiff medicine, designed to bring the economy back to full health as rapidly as possible'. It emphasised that the cost of the unemployment, sickness, invalid and domestic purposes benefits alone rose from $850 million in 1984 to $3 billion in 1990, noting: 'It is a generous provision by international standards, and unsustainable for one of the worst performing economies in the developed world.'[9]

The ESI package forecast removing $1,275 billion from the social welfare budget.[10] On 1 April 1991, welfare benefits were to be cut by 10 per cent across the board: the single unemployment benefit would fall by $14; the sickness benefit by $27; and couples with children as well as solo parents would lose between $25 and $27 a week. Rules for eligibility were tightened: youth rates extended from age 20 to 25, and a longer stand-down period (before applying for the unemployment benefit) was imposed. As Richardson later commented: 'the potential source of both short- and long-term savings was undoubtedly social welfare spending.'[11]

Richardson and Social Welfare Minister Jenny Shipley wanted not only to save money but to change the philosophy and rationale of the welfare system. Tougher criteria, targeting and less generous benefits were to encourage people back to work. National aimed to renew the work ethic, lift people's dependence on the state, return them to self-reliance and independence, and 'arrest New Zealand's drift from work to welfare'.[12] Benefits were to be reduced to below the level of the minimum working wage, as both Richardson and Shipley believed non-workers were not entitled to the same benefits as those in work: 'Redesigning the welfare state is at the heart of any serious attempt to rescue New Zealand from economic decline. Work must be rewarded more highly than continuing dependence on benefits intended to provide temporary assistance.'[13] Shifting away from a commitment to income support at a level that enabled recipients to 'belong and participate' in society (in the words of the 1972 Royal Commission), the underlying ideology changed. Self-sufficiency was now to be encouraged by the setting of a benefit level which would ensure only the necessities of life – food, clothing, power and housing.[14] At the same time, National announced its intention to reform other areas: appointing a task force on health along with a review of social services, and foreshadowing changes to industrial relations.

All this caused considerable public outrage. Newspaper headlines dramatically announced 'Welfare State in tatters' and 'Outrage over impact on poor as spending cuts bite deep' and even 'Social warfare predicted'. The latter article, in Wellington's *Dominion*, forecast that benefit cuts would force people into abject poverty, and cause increases in crime and suicide rates. Beneficiaries were 'being reduced to unsurvivable poverty'.[15] An editorial in the same edition, under the heading 'The Welfare State No More' warned:

> Let there be no misunderstanding, the Welfare State was put down in Parliament
> yesterday. Finance Minister Ruth Richardson not only administered the death of
> a thousand cuts, but also removed the raison d'etre which has sustained it to the
> present. The little people of New Zealand have been dealt a cruel blow while the free
> marketeers have had a glorious victory . . . The Welfare State has been sacrificed to
> the free market gods.[16]

Anti-government protesters marched all over the country, and burned Bolger's effigy alongside those of Richardson and Shipley.[17] Around this time, information about the proposed Employment Contracts Bill that would adversely affect unions began to feature in the press, and prompted equally fierce opposition: 'Unions ready to act on lunatic bill', warned one headline.[18] Another newspaper article suggested that 'the Government's new industrial relations legislation would destroy national education standards', while health services feared that 'the bill in its present form would allow the law of the jungle to operate in the health service'.[19] The Council of Trade Unions called for a week of rolling work stoppages and protests throughout the country and a $150,000 publicity campaign to get changes in the Bill.[20]

Then, in July 1991, Richardson produced what she aptly termed 'the Mother of All Budgets'. This not only made more cuts across the board, but announced a fundamental shift in the role of the state in people's lives. Social security support would henceforth be targeted and minimal, and a user-pays philosophy introduced in housing, education and health services. Minister of Social Welfare Shipley explained:

> The major shift in perspective of social welfare in New Zealand is simple. The state
> will continue to provide a safety net — a modest standard below which people
> will not be allowed to fall provided they demonstrate they are prepared to help
> themselves . . . The Government affirms its commitment to protect those who
> are unable to protect themselves. It will provide sufficient assistance to maintain
> individuals and families in the daily essentials of food clothing, power and housing
> at a decent level. Assistance will be closely targeted on genuine need and people will
> be expected to support themselves when they have the ability to do so.[21]

The uncompromising Budget caused more outrage. Catherine Goodyear, direc-
tor of the Anglican–Methodist Family Care Centre in Dunedin, later recalled:
'It was controversial, there was a lot of publicity. There was marching, fighting,
heckling of Government — people were angry. They felt absolutely second class
. . . They were made to feel a class apart.'[22] The National Party Conference in
August required heightened security amidst the growing backlash against the
Budget. As MPs arrived under tight security, about 250 rowdy demonstrators
shouted, heckled and harassed them, waving placards protesting against the
Budget decisions, hammering on windows and shouting insults.[23] Letters of
protest against the Budget also began to proliferate, providing an outlet for
public anger:

> Sir, The Annual budget presented the National Government with a unique oppor-
> tunity to break out of the past two decades of economic dogma. Regrettably, it now
> seems that this Government is as much a prisoner of the Treasury and the nouveau
> riche policies of the New Right as was its predecessor . . . this budget delivers more
> hurt than relief and perhaps more important, strips those without employment of
> hope in the future.[24]

One of the most contentious cuts announced in Richardson's 1991 Budget
was to superannuation. Contrary to its election promise to abolish the
surtax and restore superannuation to former levels, National introduced a
much harsher income test. This meant that recipients with even very small
incomes from other sources would have their superannuation significantly cut.
Moreover, there would be no adjustments to the rate paid until 1993, and the
eligibility age was to rise to 61 immediately and to 65 by 2001.

The outcry was immediate and loud. Pressure groups such as Age Concern
and Grey Power held public meetings around the country, appeared on television, and initiated letter-writing campaigns to MPs and to newspapers.
In the Auckland Town Hall, for example, when George Drain, president of the
Superannuitants Federation, denounced Bolger as dishonest and untrustwor-
thy before an audience of 2700: 'Suddenly there were all these oldies stamping
their feet and shouting "Out! Out!" . . . it built to a crescendo.' Drain toured the
country speaking at public meetings and encouraging new members. Cited in a
New Zealand Listener article entitled 'Greys are Great', he warned: 'Grey Power
revolution is just beginning. Superannuitants can be extremely influential . . .
This organisation could be so powerful it would be frightening in the wrong
hands.'[25]

Faced with the formidable force of elderly activism, the government backed off the harsher income testing and reinstituted the surcharge at an increased rate. But the rise in the age of entitlement as well as the freeze remained. In 1993, Labour, National and newly constituted left-wing party the Alliance signed a multi-party accord. This retained the surcharge and the raised eligibility age and pegged the level of superannuation to between 65 and 72 per cent of the average wage — down from the previous 80 per cent.[26] The raised eligibility age decreased superannuitant numbers from 510,000 in 1992 to 470,000 in 1995.[27] Despite the 1993 multi-party accord, the issue remained a bargaining chip for political parties running up to the 1996 election. National succumbed to pressure, and announced that from April 1997 only the very wealthiest would have the surtax imposed.

On 1 July 1993, government introduced means testing for those in long-stay care in public hospitals and rest homes. Once again, Grey Power mobilised, holding meetings all over the country in protest. In Wellington, for example, 2000 marchers descended on Parliament: 'They came in a thick grey line up the hill, brandishing placards like battle-shields, medals glinting in the sun . . . Many had actually seen battle — the Returned Servicemen's Association Grey Power battalion of about 550, from as far away as Invercargill.' Once at Parliament, they booed and jeered the Social Welfare and Senior Citizens Minister Peter Gresham, while 'any mention of Health Minister Shipley brought forth ugly noises from the crowd.'[28] Bowing again to pressure, the government partially amended its means testing. This was not enough, however, and protests continued. Nonetheless, despite promises from succeeding governments, it was not until 1 July 2005 that the asset-testing threshold was considerably raised, resulting in a spike in the numbers of elderly eligible for the residential care subsidy.[29]

In addition to tackling superannuation, National proceeded, through the Employment Contracts Bill, to radically restructure the labour market. New Zealand workers, the new government believed, had been under the sway of powerful unions far too long. This led to job protection, mistrust and antagonism between workers and employers, and an inflexible labour market. Consequently, change and growth had been severely inhibited.[30] The economist Brian Gaynor, writing in 1987, when the fourth Labour government still held power, argued that by holding on to outdated practices, 'the trade union movement is protecting the few at the expense of the majority'. He cited the managing director of the country's largest meat company (Waitaki NZR) who at the 1984 Economic Summit regretted that it was much more economic to establish meat processing operations offshore than to process in New Zealand. The unions 'needed to accept that New Zealand is operating in an internationally competitive environment'.[31]

When arguing for the Employment Contracts Bill in Parliament in 1991, the Minister of Labour Bill Birch, like Gaynor, also emphasised that 'a more flexible labour relations system is crucial to our economic development'. He advocated the proposed legislation as a means of increasing not only competitiveness and profitability, but personal freedom: 'In the past our system has arbitrarily restricted employers and employees from making arrangements that suit themselves. Astonishing as it may seem, the parties that work in our factories and our work-places throughout New Zealand have been unable because of the law to negotiate terms and conditions of employment that suited them.'[32]

Compulsory unionism, in Prime Minister Bolger's view, had to go, because it 'simply gave power to the union leaders to dictate to their members how they work, when they went on strike and what sort of wage negotiations should be conducted' and produced 'endless strikes and stoppages'. As Minister of Labour under the Muldoon government, Bolger managed to get voluntary unionism introduced, but it had been instantly repealed by Labour. Now he was determined to 'drag industrial relations in New Zealand into the 20th century' and push through legislation that would get rid of the strikes and stoppages which he believed hindered growth and productivity. The Employment Contracts Act 'was developed on the important premise that workers and their employers have a common interest in improving the productivity and profitability of an enterprise. One has their job on the line and the other their business.' Aware that they faced 'an impressive wall of opposition' to the proposed legislation, from the unions, the Labour Party, social activists and church leaders, and even some employers, Bolger and National remained convinced that 'if we provided New Zealanders with a sensible framework to operate within, then much of the bloody nonsense of the past would stop'. As he later remarked, however, at the time: 'Our conviction wasn't shared by many.'[33]

Despite demonstrations, marches and strikes in which more than 50,000 working days were lost over just a few days, and in the face of opposition from some 250,000 workers around the country, the Employment Contracts Act (ECA) passed on 15 May 1991, ending compulsory unionism. Employees would now have the right to bargain individually, either directly with the employer or via whomever they chose to represent them, thus cutting out the unions' automatic right to negotiate. At the same time, the Act limited the right to strike to contract and wage negotiations. An Employment Tribunal and an Employment Court were established to hear workplace grievances. Critics saw the Act as a way to drive down wages. Union leader Ken Douglas, for example, maintained that it was designed 'to achieve a dramatic lowering of wages, very quickly, by allowing high levels of unemployment to pull the cost of labour down; that the market would determine and an oversupplied market would reduce the price',[34] while its defenders believed it created a stronger, more flexible workplace, with much improved labour–management relations.[35] One commentator described it as 'a devastating defeat for the union movement. Not only did union membership subsequently fall by over 50 per cent, strike activity declined to the lowest level seen since the 1930s'.[36] Another deemed it 'a blatant attack on trade unions and human rights' that would 'inevitably lead to exploitation and injustices being committed against New Zealand workers'.[37] Union membership fell from 603,118 or 42.3 per cent of the total labour force in May 1991 to 329,919 people or 17.7 per cent of the total labour force in 2001. The number of days lost through industrial action fell from 331,000 working days in 1990 to 114,000 in 1992. By 1997, this figure had fallen to just 24,000 days lost.[38]

Official reviews of the Act's impact were generally positive. The 1993 Report of the Labour Committee on the Employment Contracts Act, for example, concluded that 'The weight of evidence received by the committee pointed to a distinct improvement in employer/employee relations under the Act, mainly because of the removal of third party involvement at the workplace where employees and management did not want it'.[39] The Committee visited several companies in the course of their inquiry and reported: 'Witnesses said that altered work practices and productivity gain-share schemes for staff, have led to increased productivity, and are the result of conditions of employment negotiated under the Employment Contracts Act 1991'.[40] The Committee also noted that since the Act, measured rates of productivity growth (expressed as international competitiveness) had increased substantially.[41] Less positively, there were concerns about delays in dealing with cases before the Employment Tribunal, and considerable evidence that some employers were 'either in breach of certain provisions in the Act or certainly in breach of the spirit of the Act allowing for freedom of association'. The Committee recommended that government keep this under 'active review'.[42] It noted widespread public concern about the exploitation of young workers, and while evidence presented about this was largely anecdotal, it recommended that legislating for minimum youth rates could solve the problem.[43]

The New Zealand Employers' Federation and the New Zealand Business Roundtable,[44] in a 1992 publication, unreservedly praised the new Act as benefiting employers, workers, and the economy as a whole:

> The Employment Contracts Act has . . . [allowed] employers and employees much greater freedom to decide on the terms of their contracts. In general, the results have been a pronounced shift to enterprise-based collective and individual contracts, greater trust, cooperation and information sharing between firms and their staff, and better incentives for performance including the removal of restrictive and uneconomic conditions. The Act is making an outstanding contribution to productivity growth . . .[45]

In a 1993 interview, Anne Knowles of the Employers' Federation pointed out that the Federation had been pushing for the ideas in the legislation for many years, and that well before the ECA's passing there had been a groundswell among employers saying: 'this is not working, we cannot continue to have centralised wage fixing when we're working very much in a competitive international market . . .'[46] Employers' Federation briefing sessions prior to the Act regularly attracted over 2000 attendees, as opposed to the usual figure of between three to four hundred.[47]

The unions' response to the ECA was by contrast unreservedly negative, citing poorer wages and deteriorated working conditions. Ashley Rush of the Building Trades Union, for example, interviewed in 1993, recounted that:

> Our wages eventually were reduced by up to 30%. Good employers maintained the 1990 conditions for a considerable period beyond May of 1991 but the crook employers taking advantage of the Employment Contracts Act and the depth of the depression that had hit the industry by that time entered upon a wholesale destruction of the award, abolished overtime, abolished special pay, in some cases unilaterally abolished payment for statutory holidays and things like that. Sick pay went down the drain, travelling time which formed a fifth of workers [sic] wages went out the door, conditions like tool money gone . . . The whole effect of the act was to restructure wages and conditions to such a degree that restructuring is entirely in the hands of the employers right now.[48]

Steph Breen of the New Zealand Nurses Organisation, also interviewed in 1993, agreed that the National government had 'effectively given more power to the employers and that's the way we see it really'. When asked how the Act had affected the Nurses Organisation, she replied: 'It's nearly killed us in the past three years. We have to adapt and be flexible and adjust to what's ahead . . . be clear about what our core services are, stick to our mission and live through it . . .' In her view, the Act's major disadvantage was that: 'it goes against collective bargaining and the whole contract system has been broken down and fragmented into enterprise bargaining . . . the fundamental principle of the Employment Contracts Act is to be divisive, to pit worker against worker and it does that but that has caused problems as well.'[49]

While employers supported the Act and unions opposed it, the New Zealand public's view of it was more ambivalent. A 1995 *National Business Review*–Consultus poll showed that 37 per cent of respondents acknowledged the Act had been good for the economy; 34 per cent said it had been bad; 13 per cent thought it made no difference; and 16 per cent didn't know. But 49 per cent disapproved of the ECA, 30 per cent liked it and 21 per cent did not have an opinion. This disapproval rate existed despite the fact that only 18 per cent claimed the Act had been personally detrimental, while 68 per cent claimed it had made no difference to them.[50] In 1996, five years after the Act was passed, a *North & South* feature article entitled 'What's so Awful about the Employment Contracts Act?' asked why, despite a drop in unemployment and a reviving economy, there was still a persistent clamour to have the ECA changed: 'The ECA is working as planned. Why then do so many people want to fix something that ain't broke? Why do they hate the ECA so much they're prepared to risk our new affluence?'[51]

Roger Kerr, executive director of the Business Roundtable, believed that one reason why a considerable proportion of the public disliked the Act may have been that 'ideological attachments to the former view of labour relations are deep-rooted and can only be expected to change slowly'; another was that many of those who gained work as a result of the freer labour market 'may not recognise the link between the freer labour market and the fact that they now have a job'. For Victoria University industrial relations lecturer Rose Ryan, the public's disapproval of the ECA reflected the fact that: 'The act is predicated on the basis that the employee and employer are on an equal footing, but it takes no stretch of the imagination to appreciate that that assumption is false . . . While the vast majority of employers are responsible and don't abuse their predominance, New Zealanders don't like a law which can be used unfairly.'[52]

Stuart Robb, a linesman in the Hutt Valley for eighteen years, when interviewed about the Act's impact, said: 'We're earning more but working more too.' The fact that he and his colleagues worked on average 30 hours per week overtime took a toll in terms of stress: 'Marriages are breaking up and families suffering.'[53] At the same time, he acknowledged a real improvement in relations between workers and management:

> We've learned to live with the ECA . . . It's just part of other changes in the industry — deregulation, restructuring, amalgamations. We get on well with top management now, whereas once before it was us versus them. Some of middle management are a bit slow to adapt though — old habits die hard and they're still a bit rattled having been restructured themselves.[54]

The *North & South* article concluded that the ECA was 'neither the draconian law its critics claim it to be, nor as effective as its supporters pretend'. But it pointed out the difficulty in ascertaining how much of the country's recently improved economic performance was linked to the ECA.[55] A 1996 study by the economist Andrew Morrison also emphasised that the ECA was only one of many factors that had influenced the economy since 1991 and advised: 'Care is required when interpreting data.' One problem, for example, was that many surveys did not include small employers, where conditions for workers might well have deteriorated.[56] Morrison concluded that evidence indicated the ECA had exerted a positive effect on economic growth, though its exact impact was hard to measure. Econometric analysis showed that the Act accounted for at least one sixth of the total growth of employment between 1991 and 1995. It had little apparent effect on the aggregate level of wages, and although 'conditions of employment appear to have worsened . . . it is difficult to quantify the extent'. New Zealand labour relations had clearly transformed, with unionisation halved. While women's hourly wages and salaries actually improved relative to men's in the wake of the Act, as did those of unskilled and part-time workers, the hourly earnings of Maori worsened relative to Pakeha.[57] Morrison cited a 1995 survey that showed that while 54 per cent of respondents believed the ECA 'means NZ business can be more responsive to the needs of the international marketplace', and 46 per cent believed it had improved workplace productivity, 41 per cent saw it as unfair to youth workers, 29 per cent agreed that it was unfair to part-time workers and 20 per cent that it was unfair to women.[58]

Views about the Act, as revealed in books and correspondence columns, varied predictably according to occupation and political persuasion. The prominent businessman Alan Gibbs, interviewed in 1996, saw the ECA as marking the end of an era when 'pig-headed' unions, through disruptive work practices, effectively put many companies out of business.[59] Lion Breweries

CEO Douglas Myers saw it as simply quickening a process that would have happened anyway, as management and labour needed to seek solutions that would serve the consumer: 'in an open economy, Employment Contracts Act or not . . . if the brewery worker and the brewery manager don't get together to make products that the consumers want for a price they're prepared to pay, they're both out of a job . . .'[60] For long-time trade union leader Ken Douglas, the Act constituted an assault on notions of what was fair and equitable in New Zealand society. Noting that the government was in trouble with the International Labour Organization (ILO) because the ECA did not enhance or protect collective bargaining, he observed: 'I think we will go through a period of debate about why institutions, and why a collectivist society, is the only sort of society that can build a progressive equity and fairness into the system.'[61] To trade union organiser Quentin Noble-Conway, the post-ECA shift in industrial culture was 'towards "shonkiness", towards chaos and towards a loss of dignity for people in work'.[62]

When the health service came under more reforming scrutiny in the early 1990s, like the ECA, the ensuing proposals met considerable resistance from sections of the New Zealand public. Although health costs had been brought under control by the previous government, and despite Treasury advice that area health boards (AHBs) were performing well, National resolved to pursue the policies outlined in the Gibbs Report.[63] In July 1991, Minister of Health Simon Upton released *Your Health & the Public Health: A Statement of Government Health Policy*, which proposed a complete restructuring of the sector. Funding and service provision were to be separated, and a Public Health Commission established to purchase public health services and provide advice to the government. AHBs were to be replaced by four regional authorities, which, as funding agencies, would contract for services from private, public or voluntary health providers. Hospitals were to become Crown Health Enterprises with appointed boards of directors. Expected to run on commercial lines, like businesses, they would compete for contracts from the Regional Health Authorities.[64] Part charges for hospital services were introduced, prescription charges tripled from $5 to $15, and subsidies for doctors' visits cut by $4. Shipley rationalised these changes on the grounds that services provided free of charge 'led to excessive use of those services . . . Part charges for hospital services will halt the trend of users viewing hospitals as a cheap alternative to a visit to the doctor . . . it will encourage New Zealanders to focus on healthy living rather than medical treatment.'[65]

But widespread opposition in the form of protests from the public and medical profession alike, and the refusal of many people to pay, combined with the difficulty of administering part charges, saw inpatient charges abandoned within a year.[66] (Outpatient charges remained, but following heavy boycotting were finally withdrawn on 1 July 1997.) Again, Grey Power was a driving force behind the protests. At a Grey Power meeting of 2000 members at the Auckland Town Hall on 14 February 1992, Neville McLindon, vice-president of the Superannuitants Federation, called for 'a fight until we've won' against hospital charges, arguing: 'If we don't, all we've fought for in war and peace, what we've built with our hands, and what we've paid taxes for, will mean nothing.'[67] Writer and activist Omar Hamed has shown that at least 50,000 members of the public, including a Member of Parliament, refused to pay the charges and were consequently pursued by debt collectors. He describes the mobilisation against hospital charges as a 'mass revolt, the largest civil disobedience campaign in New Zealand since at least the 1981 Springbok Tour protest in terms of participants'.[68]

Closing or downsizing a number of small, mainly rural hospitals was another unpopular component of National's health cost cuts. Labour closed 26 hospitals between 1986 and 1990; National intended to close many more. Some shut down with little or no protest, but others remained open as a result of determined community campaigns. In 1991, for example, plans to close Greytown Hospital and cut services at Masterton Hospital were shelved after a demonstration of 16,000 people at the latter and 6000 at the former. A 5000-strong march on Parliament to present a petition followed.[69] When Southern Regional Health Authority (SRHA) proposed removing surgical services from Ashburton Hospital in 1994, the local community reacted very strongly, organising protest rallies, and meetings with the Minister to argue their case. In September, it presented a petition of 11,700 signatures to Jenny Shipley. In October, 25,800 people marched in Ashburton against health cuts as part of a Grey Power coordinated 'day of action' that saw 23 protests across the country.[70] In December, the *Dominion* reported: 'Ashburton residents came out in force yesterday for the town's third show of strength against health charges. More than 3000 people turned out for the Hands around Our Hospital rally and formed a human chain around the hospital they are fighting to retain.'[71] Finally, the SRHA announced in mid-1995 that Ashburton Hospital would retain its full range of services.

Kaitaia Hospital in the Far North, a facility threatened with cuts since the early 1980s, remained open due to continual community mobilisation. Action culminated in a day of protest on 9 February 1995, when nearly all the town's businesses closed and a 7000-strong march proceeded down the main street behind a 'Save Our Hospital' banner. The hospital was finally saved with all its services intact.[72] Reefton managed to keep its hospital open by a campaign of badgering officials, protests at the SRHA's headquarters, and a sit-in at the hospital. A *Listener* report captured the scene: 'a thousand people (in a town of 1200) linked hands around the hospital while the TV crews risked the thunder and lightning to helicopter in. For every argument the hospital board put up, they had one of their own. They won. The hospital stayed.'[73]

Endings were not always so happy: many small towns either lost their hospitals or had them downgraded. Taumarunui's hospital, for example, despite several well-attended protest meetings, was downgraded, and as a result residents now had to make the four-hour round trip to Hamilton for surgery — even for operations as minor as a fifteen-minute D and C or the insertion of grommets.[74] A letter to the editor pointed out:

> a 90-minute drive, when in discomfort and pain and emotional stress, is a very long time indeed. Something I don't see city people facing — the whole issue is rural … Close the rural hospital, what's next? Close the rural school perhaps … I am not prepared to pay taxes at the same level as a city person if I can't have the same standard of health and education as them.[75]

Many small rural hospitals were transferred from government ownership into community health trusts, funded in part by the government and in part by the community.[76] Over the next two decades, health was re-reformed several times as the objectives of more efficient and effective expenditure and better health outcomes proved difficult to achieve and public and doctor criticism of each new system became more and more strident. 'In just over a decade (1989–2000), New Zealand had four different public health system structures, giving it the title of the "most restructured" in the developed world.'[77]

While issues of efficiency and economy dominated health reforms in the 1990s, earlier ideas and events precipitated reforms and attitudinal changes that altered the patient/doctor relationship and medical culture generally. Although difficult to verify, it is likely that these attitudinal changes influenced the proactive response to National's subsequent reforms to the health system. People had become more conscious of their role as consumers (and not always happy ones) of health services. In the 1970s, many New Zealand women, influenced by second-wave feminism, began to question what they perceived to be an authoritarian and paternalistic culture among the medical profession.[78] The idea that relationships between patients and doctors should be more open and collaborative gained momentum, as many patients of both sexes wanted to be informed about, and to participate in, decisions about their treatment. Progress on this front was relatively slow, however, as the medical profession guarded its autonomy and right to treat patients as it saw fit. Then, in June 1987, *Metro* magazine published an article by two well-known feminists, Sandra Coney, a journalist, and Phillida Bunkle, an academic. Entitled 'An "Unfortunate Experiment" at National Women's Hospital', it catapulted these issues into the public arena and acted as a catalyst for change.

The article reported that Dr Herbert Green, an associate professor in the Postgraduate School of Obstetrics and Gynaecology at the University of Auckland's Medical School had, since 1966, been withholding conventional treatment from women at National Women's Hospital, Greenlane, with carcinoma in situ of the cervix (CIS). Instead, he had been monitoring them with regular smears and biopsies, believing that, contrary to common opinion, CIS did not necessarily lead to invasive cancer. Hospital colposcopist Dr Bill McIndoe and pathologist Dr Malcolm (Jock) McLean had, since the 1970s, been alarmed by the number of women under Green's care who developed cancer. They tried to get the hospital to review the study but did not succeed. In 1984, along with several other doctors, they published a paper in *Obstetrics & Gynecology*, the prestigious journal of the American College of Obstetricians and Gynecologists, highly critical of Green's management of his patients. This showed that in contrast to what Green maintained, women with abnormal smears had a significantly heightened chance of developing full-blown invasive cancer.[79] Although this paper produced no result from National Women's, it was the impetus for Coney and Bunkle's article.

'An "Unfortunate Experiment"' had an immediate impact, provoking a widespread public outcry. Within two weeks of its publication, the Minister of Health Michael Bassett appointed District Court judge (later Dame) Silvia Cartwright to head a committee of inquiry into the treatment of cervical cancer, along with various other matters, at National Women's Hospital. After sitting for six months and calling a great number of witnesses, she submitted the report, along with recommendations, to the Minister in July 1988. Many of the recommendations related to wider issues concerning medical training and practice and accountability, research approval, patient information and consent, and medical ethics.

These set the agenda for numerous regulatory and legal changes to all fields of medicine that followed the inquiry.[80] A new national system was put in place for granting ethical approval for research and audit systems were implemented in hospitals to limit individual doctor autonomy and protect patients. Doctors henceforth needed to obtain informed consent from all patients, and patients' rights were updated and made readily available to all. A nationwide cervical screening programme commenced. A patients' advocate position established at National Women's Hospital in 1989 was an initiative other hospitals throughout the country soon adopted. A Health and Disability Commissioner was appointed to 'promote and protect the rights of health consumers and disability services consumers' and facilitate 'the fair, simple, speedy and efficient resolution of complaints'.[81] A legally enforceable Code of Rights came into operation in 1996. Widely acknowledged to be very successful, this 'has earned widespread support from the public, patients and practitioners and has required only one amendment since 1994 . . . For the most part it is simple and easily understood . . . making it accessible to consumers as a tool for empowerment.'[82]

Attitudinal change, both on the part of health professionals and consumers, accompanied these legal and regulatory changes. According to Sandra Coney: 'The major positive change to occur as a result of the Cartwright Inquiry has been attitudinal . . . Health care consumers have become more assertive and aware of their rights, and health professionals' awareness of issues such as informed consent has been heightened.'[83]

In addition to its health reforms, National in the 1990s also applied user-pays principles to tertiary education by increasing fees, which had been introduced under the fourth Labour government (and which National in the run-up to the election had promised to remove). In 1995, the government raised the level of student contribution to 25 per cent of tuition cost, which for many meant a significant fee increase.[84] Student allowances became means tested on the basis of parental income and a government-funded student loan scheme was established to assist tertiary students to pay fees and support themselves.

The 1990s proved a frugal and challenging decade for beneficiaries. The amount government spent on social welfare by 1993–94 was down to 12.9 per cent of GDP; by 1997–98, that had reduced further to an estimated 11.7 per cent. Beneficiary numbers rose from 304,000 in 1990 to 354,000 in 1997.[85] Beneficiaries on average lost about 20 per cent of their disposable income, which fell from the equivalent of 72 per cent of that for all households to 58 per cent.[86] Those living in what could be considered poverty (that is, less than 60 per cent of the median equivalent disposable household income)[87] more than doubled between 1984 and 1993, rising from 4.3 per cent (159,000 people) to 10.8 per cent of households (393,000 people).[88] Unemployment continued its upward trend, peaking at 10.6 per cent in September 1992. It most affected the young, with an unemployment rate of 24 per cent for those aged between fifteen and nineteen, and rates of 26.9 and 30.9 per cent for Maori and Pacific Islanders respectively.[89]

For many people, benefit levels became insufficient to cover basic living costs such as food, housing and other essentials.[90] This translated into a rise in those applying for supplementary benefits, special needs grants and disability benefits. More and more turned to charities to help meet daily needs.[91] Newspapers regularly reported the plight of beneficiaries who could no longer afford to see a doctor, had to resort to food parcels from charitable organisations, and could no longer pay their rent. Some even withdrew their children from exams because they could not pay the fees.[92] Voluntary agencies reported a huge increase in demand for food and clothing. Food banks increased dramatically — from very few in the 1980s to 365 by 1994. They provided 40,000 parcels a month to a value of $25 million annually.[93] In Auckland, for example, there were sixteen food banks in 1989 and over 130 in 1994.[94] The Salvation Army, which ran a large number of food banks, reported the number of people receiving food assistance jumped from 1226 in 1991 to 14,906 in 1994, with a major surge in 1992, when numbers increased from 2124 to 10,261.[95] The director of Dunedin's Anglican–Methodist Family Care Centre, Catherine Goodyear, observed: 'During the 1970s and '80s most of the people seeking emergency food parcels had been transient individuals and families with unexpected crises. Now the foodbank has two full-time staff and caters for between 10,000 and 12,000 a year.'[96]

Restructuring public housing exacerbated the hardship and poverty many New Zealanders experienced in the 1990s. The Housing Corporation, now renamed Housing New Zealand, became a state-owned enterprise expected to operate along commercial lines. Rents increased gradually to meet the market. Low-interest mortgages provided and managed by the Housing Corporation were sold and were now to be paid at market rates. State housing stock was sold, as more people were encouraged into private rentals. (Between 1994 and 1997, Housing New Zealand sold 3622 properties and acquired only 259 new ones.)[97] By 1999, when National lost the election, housing stock numbers had decreased by about 10,000.[98]

National both decreased the number of state houses and replaced all existing housing benefits with a new, simplified 'accommodation supplement' to assist low-income households with housing costs. An indirect subsidy available to all low-income households would supposedly increase affordability and provide greater choice and equality to all renters. In reality, it meant that tenants paid an increased percentage of their incomes in rent. Whereas before 1991, state housing policy set rents at 25 per cent of income, by 1996 a quarter of all households and more than half of those renting paid more than 30 per cent of their disposable income on housing,[99] while 9 per cent paid more than half their net income on housing costs.[100] One family, the Nysses, tenants in a state house in Miramar for about 40 years, were shocked by a 20 per cent rent rise, which devoured more than half their total income: 'This leaves me with just enough to pay for my power and my gas. No doctors or anything like that. They're squeezing us against the wall . . . I think the Government shouldn't make it unfeasible for me to follow my very modest lifestyle.'[101]

These rent rises placed huge pressure on household budgets. People could not meet their basic needs, and many shifted from place to place in search of cheaper housing. Some families doubled up to share accommodation, which resulted in chronic overcrowding. (A 1999 survey showed 40 per cent of low-income households were overcrowded.)[102] In some areas, the number of empty state houses increased, as tenants vacated them, unable to afford the rent. In Cannons Creek, Porirua, for example, the primary school roll plummeted as so many families had left, unable to afford the increases.[103] Demands for emergency housing escalated. Charles Waldegrave, a housing researcher, estimated:

> prior to the reforms, at least those in state houses on a benefit, paid an affordable rent and kept 75% of their residual after tax income, while those in the private sector rentals struggled with market rents. It appears as though the reformed housing policy simply equalised everybody downwards to the insecure level of those in private sector rentals.[104]

Despite protests from church, community and welfare groups that the housing changes were causing undue hardship, the government persisted with its market rents. Only after the 1996 election, when National and New Zealand First formed a coalition government, did attitudes soften. The accommodation supplement slightly increased, rents temporarily froze, and new instructions: 'replacing the profit focus of Housing New Zealand with a new brief to meet the Crown's social objectives in a businesslike manner', were issued.[105]

National's unaccommodating cost-cutting throughout the 1990s, combined with a failing economy, endeared it to few. By the 1993 election, voters had had enough of broken promises, tough measures, high unemployment and a seemingly never-ending recession. Confidence in politicians and Parliament plunged to an all-time low, with polls showing politicians ranked alongside used-car salespeople as the least-respected occupations in New Zealand.[106] Only 11 per cent of electors were prepared to say that Labour was trustworthy in 1990, while only 19 per cent expressed trust in National.[107] Both Labour and National's support plummeted — their combined share of the vote the lowest in 65 years.[108] National, within one year of coming to power, reached an all-time low for any government: its ratings nosedived from a high of 50 per cent support just after the 1990 election to 22 per cent by late 1991.[109]

After scraping back into power by one seat in the next election, Bolger, in an effort to win back the confidence of the electorate, replaced Ruth Richardson with Bill Birch: 'We knew from market research that we were often seen as arrogant and uncaring and I was determined to correct that.'[110] Announcing the Cabinet changes to the public, Bolger declared: 'We, the New Zealand people, accept that our nation had to change. The process was painful but the benefits are now apparent and must be retained. However, we believe the time has come to recognise the big moves are behind us and a different form of management is needed.'[111] This was the beginning of the end of nine years of unprecedented reform, and of a free-market revolution that changed so much so quickly. It was also the end of Richardson, who refused to accept any other post in Cabinet. In her memoirs, she wrote that: 'Jim had grown tired: tired of my reforming zeal . . . tired of reforming the economy . . . He also knew I would not be prepared, if reappointed Minister of Finance, to live with a diminution of the programme.'[112] She returned to the back benches, staying long enough to drive through the Fiscal Responsibility Act,[113] before resigning in July 1994.

For the remainder of the 1990s, Bolger and Birch followed a much more moderate path, with slight increases in social spending and promises of tax reductions in the future. They were helped by an improving fiscal situation. After near-zero growth from 1987 to 1991, the economy started growing again in 1992. In 1993, it grew by 1.2 per cent, peaking at 6.2 per cent in 1994 and levelling out to 2.8 per cent in 1996.[114] Inflation fell from 5 per cent in late 1990 to 1 per cent in 1992, when there was a surplus for the first time since 1978 and unemployment started declining. After peaking at 10.4 per cent in 1992, it fell to 8.1 per cent in 1994. For the next decade, it continued its downward momentum, reaching 3.7 per cent in 2005,[115] making it the fourth-lowest unemployment rate in the OECD countries, and well below the OECD average of 6.9 per cent.[116]

MMP: the end of 'elective dictatorship'
The 1993 election signalled the end of 'first past the post'. Disaffection with a

system that allowed one party to govern by 'elective dictatorship' grew steadily from the mid-1970s onwards.[117] Distaste for Muldoon's authoritarian style, widespread anger and dismay at Labour's neo-liberal reforms, followed by National's broken promises and tough social measures, encouraged increasing numbers of people to push for change. They wanted to move away from a system in which a single party could be elected without obtaining the majority of votes, but by obtaining the majority of seats in Parliament. Instead, they desired a system that would reflect the majority will of voters, and provide checks and balances to prevent arbitrary and unilateral government decisions. In 1985, a Royal Commission had investigated the electoral system and, somewhat surprisingly, recommended adopting a completely new system: mixed member proportional representation (MMP), closely modelled on the German system.[118] Although neither major party particularly wanted change, recognising that it would disadvantage them, public pressure forced Bolger to hold a non-binding referendum in 1992. An overwhelming 85 per cent of voters opted for change. A second, binding, referendum was held at the same time as the 1993 election. Voters now 'took revenge' on the politicians they had so come to distrust.[119] When MMP was voted in, the dominance of the 'big two' decreased. Any party that obtained more than 5 per cent of the votes would now get representation in Parliament. Over the next three years, several new parties emerged: a disparate mix of disillusioned Labour and National party members and/or MPs along with many complete newcomers. By the 1996 general election, 27 parties had registered with the Electoral Commission.[120]

Amongst those formed was New Zealand First, created in 1993 by Winston Peters, who had been Minister of Maori Affairs in the 1990 National government but was sacked from Cabinet in October 1991 after disagreements with Bolger. He resigned, forcing a by-election in Tauranga, which as an independent, he won easily. A populist, he garnered support by criticising National's free-market policies, alleging that the rich were defrauding New Zealand and foreign business interests were taking over the country. But the 'race card' — particularly opposition to the Waitangi Tribunal and an anti-Asian stance in the early 1990s — gained him the most support. After adopting an anti-immigration policy, his party's popularity soared. It won seventeen seats in Parliament in 1996, including all the Maori electorates. Peters was now 'king maker'.

In 1996, the first election under the new system was indecisive. After nearly two months of wrangling, National and New Zealand First formed a coalition government with Peters negotiating himself into the powerful positions of Deputy Prime Minister and Treasurer. (This was a surprise, as throughout the campaign Peters had consistently insisted he would go with Labour.) The coalition was shaky, however, unpopular both with voters and National MPs. The former had hoped for a new government, not just a rejigged version of the old one, and the latter resented the policy concessions made to New Zealand First, and the difficulties of working with inexperienced New Zealand First ministers. The operating culture of the National–New Zealand First coalition has been described as 'scarred from the outset by feelings of resentment and suspicion at all levels of both parties'.[121] Disappointment with the government manifested in a vertiginous plunge in the polls for National. At the same time, polls indicated soaring support for Labour under Helen Clark. After calls from within National for a more aggressive leader, Jenny Shipley toppled Jim Bolger on 8 December 1997, becoming New Zealand's first female Prime Minister in the process.

Initially, National climbed in the polls, as Shipley returned to the reforming politics of the early 1990s, cutting pensions, introducing state house market rents, and deregulating accident compensation. But the 'honeymoon' was short-lived. The government started unravelling in August 1998 when the proposed sale of Wellington Airport split the increasingly fragile alliance with New Zealand First. After Shipley sacked Peters from Cabinet, he immediately withdrew his support for the government. New Zealand First splintered, with some members becoming independent and staying with the government. Shipley cobbled together enough support from 'a ragtag collection of miniature parties and independents'[122] to stay in power. Her unpopularity grew, however, as she mismanaged various crises and pursued hard-line policies at a time when the electorate wanted nothing more than to move back to more centrist politics. According to Colin James, she sowed the seeds of her downfall by 'veering right in 1998 when the electorate was chorusing its wish for a new centre, in pinching pennies off pensioners and calling it "progress", in time after time mismanaging micro-scandals into crises . . .'[123]

A new centre

On 26 November 1999, fifteen years of zealous monetarist reform came to an end when National suffered its greatest-ever electoral defeat. Helen Clark, New Zealand's first elected female Prime Minister, headed a new Labour–Alliance coalition government. A former academic noted for her pragmatism, analytical ability, discipline and tough-mindedness, Clark first entered Parliament in 1981 as MP for Mt Albert. Although uncomfortable with the Lange government's radical economic restructuring after 1984, she sat on the back benches and kept her thoughts to herself.[124] In 1987, she was given the Conservation and Housing portfolios and in February 1989 became Minister of Health. In August 1989, following Lange's resignation, she was appointed Deputy Prime Minister. After Labour's 1990 election defeat, she replaced Mike Moore as party leader.

Recognising that New Zealanders were sick of radical restructuring, and the hardship it entailed, the new Labour government 'softened the neoliberal policy regime in small but significant ways while retaining and embedding all of its most important features'.[125] During its first month in power, it increased the minimum wage and raised the youth wage to 80 per cent of that of adults; restored the unions' right to be the only agent for collective employment contracts under the Employment Relations Act 2000; increased the top tax rate from 33 to 39 per cent; and restored income-related rents to 25 per cent of household income for tenants in state houses (this did not affect those renting in the private sector, who had to continue to pay market rents). It placed a moratorium on state house sales and announced a house acquisition and upgrading programme.[126] It also introduced parental and holiday leave, inflation-adjusted benefits, stopped the state asset sales programme, and renationalised accident compensation. Health-care funding and service were once again integrated under the Ministry of Health, which began to reconsider health priorities and policy, moving away from a commercial model to a more social-service system. Twenty-one district health boards, each with a combination of elected members and appointees, replaced the Health Funding Authority. Health policy turned full circle, with a consultative, community-building style once again ascendant.[127]

Clark promised that her government would strive to achieve a better balance between a market economy and a fair society. Like Tony Blair in England, and Bill Clinton in America, she looked to a 'third way' which sought a balance between domestic economic and social policy and justice, the needs of the community, and the expectations and demands of global finance and trade.[128]

> Labour takes the view that neither the excesses of hands-on nor of hands-off have served New Zealand well. That's why we have articulated a third way for the state in the economy. That third way sees government as a leader, a facilitator, a co-ordinator, a broker and a partner. It is a strategic role which also sees us apply funding where there is public interest and/or market failure.[129]

While many of the fundamental changes introduced over the preceding fifteen years remained, others were modified. Social policy moved away from a safety-net approach toward a more proactive role for the state in achieving and maintaining social justice and equality of opportunity. Launching its policies in June 2001, government spelled out the ideological changes: rather than redistributing income, the new policies would help people develop skills needed to participate in a rapidly changing working world. Signalling this change of direction, the various social ministries were amalgamated into a Ministry of Social Development and Employment.[130]

This change in name reflected the government's philosophy that 'work in paid employment offers the best opportunity for people to achieve social and economic well-being'.[131] Creating training for work schemes and helping individuals get back into work replaced the National coalition's work-for-the-dole scheme (known as the 'community wage'). Policy now focused on 'active forms of assistance that lift skills and abilities and overcoming obstacles that impede movement into paid employment'.[132] In 2001, Minister of Social Development and Employment Steve Maharey announced: 'the DWI [Department of Work and Income] is introducing personalised Job Seeker Agreements which detail how DWI will assist each unemployment beneficiary back into the workforce. The Agreements will include training opportunities, work experience and other support which the Department agrees to provide and the obligations on the job seeker to take up those opportunities.'[133]

The 2004 'Working for Families' policy, to support working families on low incomes, underscored the importance the Clark government placed on work. Designed to be fully implemented by April 2007, it included housing assistance, childcare subsidies, and an 'in work' tax credit for those working 30 hours in a two-adult household or 20 hours in a single-adult household.[134] Those 'substantially dependent on the state' — in other words, beneficiaries — were not eligible. A 2007 evaluation of the policy found it had successfully benefited a large number of working families, and that the in-work tax credit encouraged people to transit from welfare to work.[135] Working for Families attempted to redress the neglect of family assistance over the previous two decades.[136] At the same time, the supplementary benefit system was tightened; discretion for granting temporary benefits was eliminated, replaced by a rules-based system; and the length of time beneficiaries were eligible was reduced. Economist Susan St John argued that

> there was significant redistribution to low- and middle-income working families who received the IWTC [in-work tax credit] and who gained entitlement at much higher levels of income . . . they have not reduced the hardship or child poverty

among families not classed as 'working' . . . Rather, a much bigger gap has been opened up between families 'in work' and those not 'in work' . . .[137]

The 2006 Social Security Amendment Bill proposed further changes, requiring all those claiming any benefits to undertake work- or training-related activities and to look for and accept any offer of work. Their benefit would be halved if they refused. Social commentators and workers' groups attacked this policy as 'the biggest benefit cut since 1991',[138] perceiving it as a return to the work-for-the-dole scheme.[139] The government was accused of wiping 'away any notion that our social security system is about ensuring everyone can participate as citizens. Instead, it makes getting people into a job, any job, the fundamental duty of citizenship. The principle is baldly stated "Work in paid employment offers the best opportunity for people to achieve social and economic well-being."'[140] Despite such criticism, the Bill passed into law in June 2007. A final confirmation of the government's focus on getting people into work, it stated: 'work in paid employment offers the best opportunity for people to achieve social and economic wellbeing, the priority for people of working age should be to find and retain work, and if work is not appropriate people should be either assisted to plan for work in the future or supported'.[141]

In November 2012, a *New Zealand Herald* feature article entitled 'Counting the True Costs of Poverty Trap' by Charles Waldegrave and Bob Stephens, writing on behalf of the New Zealand Poverty Measurement Project, endorsed the 'massive achievement' of the Working for Families policy in reducing child poverty:

> In 1995 the authors published the first data showing that a third of New Zealand children lived in relative poverty. That figure stayed close to 30 per cent until the Working for Families package reduced it to between a fifth and a quarter depending which measure is used. That is a massive achievement for one policy intervention, but it still leaves far too many children in poverty.[142]

To families with children, including beneficiaries who could not meet their daily essentials in the future, the authors recommended giving tax credits, or some form of 'direct income', to lift them above 'agreed poverty thresholds'. Only then, the authors argued, could work incentive payments be applied. They concluded by noting that if New Zealand seriously wanted to end child poverty this would require transparent goal setting along with careful measuring and monitoring: 'we need measurement and reporting in the social sphere as well'.[143]

Weighing the balance

The legacy of New Zealand's 'free-market revolution', both economic and cultural, has been subject to considerable debate. On one hand, many social commentators, academics and economists, while acknowledging that some change was needed, believe the reforms were carried through in 'a single-handed and non-consultative way', with no transitional assistance given to help businesses and individuals adjust.[144] This group believes that the reforms were ideologically and theory driven, and completely disregarded the adverse social and economic impact on ordinary New Zealanders. The result, they maintain, was an unacceptably high human cost. Poverty and inequality increased, while many in the business community became wealthier and more powerful. Paul Dalziel was expressing the opinion of many when he wrote in 2002 that instead of achieving its core aims of alleviating poverty and increasing productivity, the Labour government achieved the reverse. Productivity declined and poverty increased:

> the New Zealand economic experiment did not succeed, despite achieving greater
> microeconomic efficiency in some industries and obtaining its intermediate
> objectives of price stability and fiscal balance . . . Seventeen years later, with higher
> unemployment and lower real incomes at the bottom end of New Zealand's income
> distribution, it is clear that the comprehensive reforms of the late 1980s and early
> 1990s did not achieve that core objective.[145]

Individualism, selfishness, competition and materialism, many believe, have replaced universality, shared community values and working in the interests of the majority.

Others, however, including many business people, economists and social commentators, applauded the reforms, believing that they markedly improved New Zealand's economic prospects and international competitiveness, made industry more efficient, and the New Zealand people more accountable and self-reliant. A review of the reforms by Lewis Evans, Arthur Grimes, Bryce Wilkinson and David Teece in 1996 concluded: 'After decades of policy errors and investment blunders . . . [New Zealand] is on a trajectory to maintain its economy as a consistent high performer among the OECD. New Zealand once again appears to be emerging as a laboratory from which results will animate economic debate and policy throughout the world.'[146] Roderick Deane, an economist who was Deputy Governor of the Reserve Bank, Chief Executive of the State Services Commission (1986) and later served as CEO of both the Electricity Corporation of New Zealand and Telecom New Zealand, believes that 'the reforms . . . set New Zealand up in a much stronger position than would otherwise have been the case to cope with the onslaught of the global financial crisis in 2007–08 (the GFC) . . .' and allowed New Zealand to weather the storm with 'a resilience that it had not previously enjoyed'.[147]

Whether the New Zealand economy would have fared better or worse had 'market fundamentalism and managerial efficiency'[148] been less fulsomely embraced after 1984 is obviously debatable. What is not is that New Zealand had, in 1984, an ailing economy on a downward spiral, with rising unemployment, inefficient state-run companies, a highly subsidised farming sector and inefficient protected manufacturing industries. It was no longer a prosperous country. Successive governments had increasingly, but with little success, imposed controls to try and halt the decline. Things had to change.

Free-market ideas rapidly took hold and were incorporated into a range of government reforms from that time. The economy began to improve in the 1990s, as manufacturing continued to rally, business regrouped and diversified, and niche markets were developed.[149] Unemployment reduced from 10.4 per cent in 1992 to 3.8 per cent in 2005, giving New Zealand one of the lowest unemployment rates in the OECD. After the GFC, the unemployment rate increased to 6.2 per cent, which still compares very favourably with most other OECD countries.[150] Towns adversely affected by the dramatic policies of the 1980s proved remarkably resilient and adaptive. The agricultural sector successfully responded to the withdrawal of government support and subsidies by diversifying, improving efficiency, and generally becoming more responsive to what the market, both at home and overseas, demanded.

The reforms have made the New Zealand of 2013 a more diverse, dynamic, varied society with choices and opportunities that did not exist in 1984. Thanks to the reforms, New Zealand has become more competitive in an increasingly global marketplace and able to react more quickly to fluctuations and changes in trading conditions. Overseas investors have gained confidence in the country's accountable and transparent banking and financial arrangements (although many New Zealanders would argue that there is too much overseas investment), and are more willing to invest here than they were before 1984.

Yet aspects of New Zealand's former cultural identity have altered irrevocably. Within just a few years, two of its most proudly proclaimed characteristics

— the welfare state and an egalitarian ethos — suffered a sustained attack. Statistics showed the income gap between rich and poor widening by the late 1990s; while the long-standing Kiwi goal of home ownership became less viable for many.[151] At the same time, a 1998 survey of national political values found that most New Zealanders still overwhelmingly endorsed a substantial degree of central government intervention, and believed that helping those in need was part of government's responsibility; that providing a decent standard of living for the old was central government's role, as was providing decent housing for those who could not afford it. Despite the recent free-market revolution, the responses to their questions hardly indicated 'a population keen to minimise government involvement in their lives'.[152]

The New Zealand public did not drive the post-1984 free-market revolution. Rather, it was imposed from above — by government policy. New Zealand's unitary political constitution, particularly the strong role played by Cabinet, made it possible for Douglas to effect change quickly, with little or no regard for the general will of the electorate or the effects on the social and economic lives of numerous New Zealanders. Many suffered vicissitudes and hardships as a result of the reforms, responding at first with some incredulity, and frequently with protest and anger. For those who are struggling with life's everyday necessities in the early years of the twenty-first century, the anger remains. New Zealand has become a more socially divided country with greater extremes of poverty and wealth. As individualism has grown, so too has conflict, division, and social and economic inequality.

The consensus about the basic values that underpinned New Zealand society and politics for the many decades since 1936 — collective responsibility, and a balance between individual and community needs and interest — has eroded. But the values and ideals of the free-market ethos are here to stay. 'Fortress New Zealand' is well and truly dismantled — now the country operates as part of a global market, seeking out and cultivating new trading partners. Even after the Labour/Alliance victory in 1999, neo-liberal ideas and policies were softened but by no means disposed of: attitudes about self-reliance and personal responsibility continue to influence government social policy, and few have advocated a return to economic protectionism.

CHAPTER ELEVEN

Shifting Tides

MAORI, PAKEHA AND THE TREATY AFTER 1984

You know, when we stand at the foreshore, we do not always see the movement of the tide. We see no more than the regular breaking of the waves, as if no painful inch is gained. But look back to the creeks and inlets. There, silently, it is plain to see the tide running at full flow. — Judge Edward Taihakurei Durie, Waitangi Day, 1989

During the 1984 election campaign, the Labour Party announced its intention to 'honour' the Treaty of Waitangi — a promise popular both with liberal Pakeha and Maori voters. Once elected, the new government began fulfilling its vow. It incorporated the Treaty into legislation and policy, promoted its history, and introduced bicultural practices into workplaces. Dismissed as a 'simple nullity' in the nineteenth century and frequently denounced as a 'fraud' in the militant 1970s, the Treaty moved to centre stage in the latter 1980s.[1]

Labour's promise to honour the Treaty had unforeseen consequences that shaped and augmented the ongoing Maori economic and cultural renaissance. In 1985, the Waitangi Tribunal Amendment Act extended the Tribunal's jurisdiction back to 1840. This legislation simultaneously gave the Tribunal teeth, profoundly influenced New Zealand race relations, and spurred tribal revitalisation, as iwi around the country began to research, organise and plan tribunal claims. While the Lange government's 'New Right' policies resulted in economic hardship for many Maori, they also brought welcome opportunities for increased tribal self-reliance/tino rangatiratanga. Two convergent streams: tribal revitalisation and a free-market ethos, strengthened the flow of race relations reforms after 1984.

Nationalism also played a part. Labour's support for Maori land rights and for a more proactive biculturalism commenced at a time when its David versus Goliath 'anti-nuke' stance was grabbing headlines around the world. This resolutely independent anti-nuclear policy prompted an upsurge of nationalism, which swelled further in the wake of the 1985 *Rainbow Warrior* bombing. The various pro-Maori government policies introduced at this time were often couched in terms of safeguarding and fostering a unique element of New Zealand's national identity. The post-1984 push for a more proactive biculturalism gained impetus from a mutually reinforcing mixture of nationalist and internationalist elements: Labour's advocacy of Maori rights was indebted to overseas anti-racism and pro-civil rights movements — ironically, many of them American in origin — which in turn influenced Maori ideas about tino rangatiratanga and self-reliance.

Commitment to the Treaty, and to a more substantive bicultural partnership between Maori and Pakeha, experienced a 'high tide' after 1984. By the late 1980s, this began to ebb, however, as a significant backlash gathered momentum among sections of the New Zealand public, which called into question both Treaty rights and the claims process. Although this development altered the course of electoral politics, it did not erase the various Treaty-related policies and initiatives implemented in the action-packed years following the 1984 election.

The Hui Taumata and a 'Decade of Maori Development'

Since 'Tu Tangata' in the 1970s, Maori Affairs policy reflected a strong Maori desire for self-determination and community empowerment. Following Labour's 1984 election win, many Maori hoped that the tino rangatiratanga[2] promised under Article 2 of the Treaty might finally be more fully realised. This desire dovetailed with Labour's plans to shrink the state. Devolving power to iwi offered Maori the chance to control their own affairs, and assisted the government's downsizing ambitions. Labour perceived iwi as the most practical and manageable 'devolution' partner. Long-standing predictions that Pakeha culture would subsume traditional Maori culture had not eventuated; iwi remained a vital focus of Maori cultural identity. Although significant pan-tribal, non-tribal and hapu (clan or descent group) associations existed, Maori desire for more self-reliance married well with the government's laissez-faire ethos, and iwi played a key role in facilitating the union.[3]

In the course of an economic summit in 1984, Maori leaders voiced concern that Labour's free-market policies would have a disproportionately detrimental impact on their people. At the same time, they recognised the need to respond to the government's proposals, and saw the potential opportunities for exercising more tino rangatiratanga. A push for a separate summit to plan for the future resulted in a Maori Economic Development Conference, the Hui Taumata, which took place in the Legislative Council Chamber at Parliament, Wellington, in October 1984.

A wide range of Maori tribal and community representatives attended the hui. The chairperson, Professor Ngatata Love, later described it as a 'turning point', when Maori moved from 'being told what to do to establishing a determination to take control of our destiny'.[4] Six themes emerged to guide an impending 'Decade of Maori Development': the Treaty of Waitangi, tino rangatiratanga, iwi development, economic self-reliance, social equity, and cultural advancement.[5] The best recipe for the future combined self-help, self-reliance, and Maori solutions to Maori problems: 'let us seize the opportunity to exercise our right to self-determination. However, in exercising this right we must first embrace and adhere to a philosophy that recognizes the rights and freedoms of all New Zealanders.'[6]

To act on the hui's recommendations and encourage iwi self-reliance and autonomy, the government set up a Maori Economic Development Commission in December 1984. Its 'progeny' included the Maori Enterprise Development Scheme (1986), Mana Enterprises (1986) and the Maori Resource Development Corporation (1987). The latter aimed to trade at the 'top end' of the commercial sector and included members of Fletcher Challenge and Brierley Investments on its board.[7]

Between 1985 and 1987, the Maori Affairs Department experimented with various initiatives to facilitate the transfer of responsibility for social and economic programmes away from government and towards tribal groups. In 1987, it created an iwi-based Maori ACCESS scheme to offer training and vocational skills. To successfully benefit from devolution policies and processes, tribes and subtribes developed mechanisms with which to engage. Tainui, for example, created a Development Unit to deal with MANA and MACCESS programmes.[8] The resources Maori Affairs received to ensure its various schemes operated to best effect increased dramatically — the departmental vote rose from $67 million in 1983–84 to $234 million in 1987–88.[9]

The Treaty centre stage

The Waitangi Tribunal Amendment Act of 1985 helped to defuse the often angry activism that had characterised the 1970s. In the latter 1980s, although activists continued to work for Maori rights, archives and briefcases now took precedence over protests and placards. Treaty claims absorbed much iwi time and energy. Tribunal hearings, often a cathartic process for the claimants, provided an opportunity to address long-standing historical grievances and seek reparation for past land and resource loss. They frequently took place on marae, where oral testimony from claimants augmented expert evidence. A sizeable 'Treaty industry' quickly sprang up, providing employment for lawyers and historians. Some of the early claims lodged — notably by Ngai Tahu, Tainui and Te Atiawa — involved vast amounts of land; others of all types and sizes quickly followed. By 1987, 140 were lodged with the Tribunal. Two years later, the Tribunal faced a backlog of 180 claims; by 1999, the figure had reached 700.[10]

Evidence presented to the Tribunal focused both on historic injustices incurred during colonial times and on more contemporary sources of complaint. Exposing and criticising monoculturalism and the negative legacy of colonialism was part of the 'zeitgeist' in the 1980s, and featured in numerous popular non-fiction books. In 1985, for example, Michael King in his book *Being Pakeha* observed:

> . . . every possible legislative and social condition should be created to ensure the flourishing of Maori language, institutions and wider culture. There is a moral obligation on the part of the majority Pakeha culture to rectify the destructive policies of the past. The British have not been noted for their tolerance of the ways of other peoples; themes of racial and cultural superiority have been far too strong in their history.
>
> . . . Maori and Pakeha will have to approach the task of nation and culture-building in a spirit of reconciliation . . . Pakeha people *must* acknowledge and attempt to rectify mistakes made by their representatives or their ancestors or the agents of their culture.[11]

Histories such as James Belich's *The New Zealand Wars* (1986) shifted attention towards Maori agency and military prowess, critically assessing Victorian racial preconceptions in the process. Claudia Orange's best-selling *The Treaty of Waitangi* (1987) traced the Treaty's story over time; from long-standing neglect to its recent status as a blueprint for a more equitable bicultural partnership.[12]

When Paul Reeves, a liberal Anglican archbishop, became New Zealand's first Maori Governor-General in November 1985, the appointment seemed to symbolise the advent of a new, more active commitment to biculturalism. In 1986, Reeves launched Project Waitangi, a government-funded educational organisation that soon offered courses on the Treaty in schools and workplaces, as well as resource kits for teachers and employers. In addition, Russell Marshall, Labour's Minister of Education, provided more support and resources for the Taha Maori (literally, the Maori side) cultural programmes, which had been introduced in schools in the early 1980s. The 1984 Education Department publication 'Taha Maori in Schools — Suggestions for Getting Started' highlighted the centrality of Maori language and culture to national identity:

> Maori culture is unique to New Zealand. It gives New Zealand a distinct characteristic and it will maintain its vitality only if fostered in this country. The language of a people enshrines its living spirit and whoever would seek to understand that people must start to understand their language and their culture. An awareness of taha Maori contributes to the New Zealand identity . . .[13]

In 1986, the Waitangi Tribunal 'Te Reo Maori' Report recommended that government take steps to protect Maori language as a Maori 'taonga', or treasure, but also as a form of property right guaranteed under the Treaty. The government subsequently created a Maori Language Commission, and in 1989 the Maori Language Act recognised te reo as an official language of New Zealand.[14]

On 23 June 1986, Cabinet instructed that, in future, all government departments needed to consult with Maori about the Treaty, and consider Treaty principles when framing legislation. In 1986, the Environment Act duly stipulated that the newly created Ministry for the Environment needed to take a full and balanced account of the Treaty and its principles. A year later, the Conservation Act both established a Department of Conservation and required it to give effect to the Treaty.[15]

Impeding the juggernaut

In May 1987, a Treaty clause presented an unforeseen impediment to the 'Rogernomics' reforms. Government planned to divest itself of landholdings and hand them over to state-owned enterprises (SOEs). Once sold on to a third party, however, those lands could no longer form part of a Tribunal claim. The Maori Council, aware that section 9 of the State-Owned Enterprises Act 1986 stipulated that nothing in the Act should permit the Crown to act in a manner inconsistent with the Treaty, filed an injunction in the Court of Appeal. On 29 June 1987, five judges unanimously granted the injunction.

Now commonly referred to as the 'Lands case', this was the first judicial ruling on the principles of the Treaty.[16] Others soon followed. When Coalcorp tried to sell its Waikato mining interests, the Tainui Trust Board sought an injunction in the Court of Appeal to protect its claim on a million acres of confiscated land in the Waikato. Once again, the Court granted the injunction.[17] Then the Muriwhenua tribes of the Far North brought a claim before the Tribunal in 1987, arguing that fishing quotas created a property right in the sea from which they were excluded. The Tribunal upheld this claim as a clear breach of Article 2. The Muriwhenua tribes and the Maori Council then filed for another injunction that the Court granted. Later that year, the Maori Council, Tainui Trust Board, Ngai Tahu Trust Board and other tribes lodged an injunction against the fishing quota regime in all tribal waters around New Zealand. Yet again, the Court of Appeal ruled that the quota system cease until issues surrounding Maori fishing rights were resolved.[18] In 1989, after protracted dispute and discussion, government created a Maori Fisheries Commission to receive and distribute 10 per cent of the quota. This was an interim measure only, as negotiators for both sides continued to search for a permanent solution.[19]

In each of these cases, the New Zealand judiciary consistently upheld Treaty principles. The government's liberal Treaty policies now threatened to stymie the Rogernomics 'juggernaut'.[20] At the same time, the Court of Appeal's pronouncements confirming the Crown's duty to abide by Treaty principles proved highly influential. The 'Lands case' judgment in particular, with its eloquent call for a partnership in which each party needed to 'act towards the other reasonably and with the utmost good faith', signalled that the judiciary perceived the Treaty as a 'living instrument', the spirit/wairua of which could guide future race relations.[21]

Institutional racism and Pakehatanga

Commitment to the Treaty did not grant Labour immunity from criticism about racism in its own back yard. In 1984, the nine-member Women Against Racism Action Group (WARAG) wrote a report exposing 'institutional racism' in the Department of Social Welfare's Auckland office, where only 2 per cent of staff spoke Maori and 3 per cent Samoan.[22] In response, the Department appointed a Ministerial Advisory Committee on a Maori Perspective.

Chaired by John Rangihau, a public servant and Tuhoe kaumatua, its 1986 report, *Puao-Te-Ata-Tu (Day Break)*, claimed that 'New Zealand institutions manifest a monocultural bias and the culture which shapes and directs that bias is Pakehatanga . . . Institutional racism is the basic weapon that has driven the Maori into the role of outsiders and strangers in their own land.'[23] Monoculturalism and racism were said to be both endemic and frequently unconscious:

> If a person works within an institution that practises institutional racism, that person need not necessarily be racist. However, if those in positions of influence within institutions do not work to reduce and eliminate the monocultural bias that disadvantages Maori and minorities, they can be accused of collaborating with the system, and therefore of being racist themselves.[24]

Institutions needed to become more culturally inclusive, and implement affirmative action to redress the socio-economic disadvantage that monocultural hegemony inflicted on Maori. This report has been described as 'a charter in the development of government policies for the delivery of equity to Maori people'.[25] In 1988, the State Sector Act officially recognised biculturalism, requiring chief executives in the public service to incorporate Treaty principles into operations and policies.[26] As a result, all departments soon had a Maori name, and official functions included traditional Maori ceremonies.

Encouraging a more proactive biculturalism extended beyond government departments into a wide range of institutions and organisations. These efforts met with varying degrees of success, often because the parameters of biculturalism were unclear and the process underresourced. In 1987, for example, the School of Social Work in the Auckland College of Education persuaded the college council to allocate 20 of the 40 available trainee places to Maori, 10 to Pakeha and 10 to Pasifika people. The college lacked the resources to appoint extra Maori staff, so strains and 'dissonance' among staff and students resulted.[27]

Some efforts to increase biculturalism drew success from defeat however. A bid by the Aotearoa Broadcasting Trust (ABT) for a Maori television channel in 1985, for example, floundered over funding. But a by-product, a Maori Programmes Department, helped raise the profile of Maori culture on national television, with shows such as *Take Maori*, a bilingual current affairs programme, and a daily ten-minute kohanga reo programme for mothers and little children.[28] The ABT submission to the 1985 Royal Commission on

Broadcasting made a case for Maori television on the grounds that government had a Treaty obligation to preserve and protect Maori culture.

Various official reports and documents in the late 1980s depicted honouring Treaty obligations as central both to national harmony and national identity. The 'Culture and Heritage' section of the 1987 National Curriculum statement, for example, noted:

> Studies of our heritage recognise the importance of both Maori and Pakeha traditions to all New Zealanders. They affirm the special place of Maori as tangata whenua; they recognise the importance of all New Zealand cultures; and they acknowledge the Treaty of Waitangi as a central feature of our country's identity.[29]

Following the Tomorrow's Schools reforms, school charters incorporated a Treaty of Waitangi goal, the first objective of which was to 'ensure the curriculum reflects Maori perspectives'. A Project Waitangi resource kit entitled 'School Charters and the Treaty: A Guide for Trustees from a Pakeha Perspective' warned: 'It is not enough for teachers to just become more skilled at delivering education to Maori students and maintain the current Pakeha structures and Pakeha control. The Treaty requires equal participation of both Maori and Pakeha in decision-making and control.'[30] A 'Treaty check-list' offering a guide to more effective biculturalism recommended Treaty training workshops; school signs in Maori and English; Maori language and protocol used as well as Pakeha at assemblies and other school occasions; staff selection panels with at least two Maori representatives; special budget allocation for teaching te reo; recognition of and consultation with local tangata whenua; and the desirability of occasionally holding staff meetings on local marae.[31]

Tomorrow's Schools also recommended fostering 'kura kaupapa'. The first two such schools, set up in West Auckland in 1985, enabled Maori language immersion teaching beyond kohanga reo. In 1987, a working party of Maori academics and community leaders considered the development of the kura kaupapa school model, with the goal of promoting further schools nationwide. Full government funding of six kura kaupapa schools as a pilot scheme commenced in 1990.[32] A year later, another five were funded, and 23 other groups expressed an interest in joining the scheme. By the early 1990s, six privately funded kura kaupapa were established.[33] Such schools helped to realise the long-standing Maori aim for more self-reliance and also fostered te reo and tikanga Maori. These aims were also central to the wananga — tertiary institutions offering diploma and degree courses in tribal development, health, social services, lore and philosophy, education, art and design — that developed from the early 1980s onwards. The first, Te Wananga Te Raukawa, grew from humble beginnings out of a tribal development programme in 1981.[34]

Social welfare and health policy increasingly recognised and incorporated Maori values and cultural practices. In 1985, a Matua Whangai community-based Maori fostering scheme provided whanau- and hapu-based care for 'youth at risk'. The Children, Young Persons, and their Families Act of 1989 required social workers to recognise tribal and family relationships and to be aware and supportive of traditional cultural preferences and customs.[35] Supporting Maori solutions to Maori problems resulted in some notable initiatives. West Auckland's Te Whanau o Waipareira Trust, for example, developed a portfolio of health and education, disability support, work training and small business services. This group, while not aligned to an iwi, adhered to a philosophy built on Maori values.[36]

A dramatic rise in Maori mental illness in the 1970s gave rise to two cultural therapy units: Whaiora, at Tokanui Hospital, and Te Whare Pai, at Carrington Hospital, Auckland. Established in 1983, both aimed to incorporate Maori values and beliefs into treatment. Whaiora was highly successful, but Te Whare Pai attracted unwelcome notoriety in 1988 when its director Titewhai Harawira and four staff members were charged and eventually convicted for beating a patient.[37] The unit, which operated in 'self-imposed isolation', and often denied access to hospital staff, eventually closed down.[38] Media attention surrounding these events helped fuel public unease about the potentially divisive aspects of biculturalism. A *New Zealand Herald* article, for example decried Harawira's 'vicious, violent' assault, while the judge, addressing her supporters in court, admonished: 'We have known from day one that this has not been a legal case but a political one.'[39]

A degree of autonomy

Government supported Maori self-reliance and autonomy, but only within certain prescribed limits. In 1986, an advisory committee on legal services suggested that the Maori Land Court be restructured to return decision-making to tribal groups. Maori Land Court judges made the same suggestion to the 1988 Royal Commission on Social Policy. In 1988, the Maori activist Syd Jackson wrote a report advocating a parallel justice system for Maori. These proposals, and others in a similar vein, never received serious credence or support.[40]

Government adherence to the Treaty was also sometimes more evident on paper and in bureaucratic committees than in practice. For example, several groups, including a Maori Local Reform Consultative Group (MCG), were set up in 1988 to consider the Treaty implications of proposed local government reforms aiming to make councils '[f]ewer, leaner and meaner'.[41] When the reforms eventuated, however, they neither mentioned the Treaty nor referred to Maori identity and values. In response to criticism (primarily from Maori) about this omission, government requested a report from the MCG. This recommended that 'there should be a fifty per cent manawhenua (the authority of local Maori communities) membership on regional and territorial authorities'.[42] It also recommended Maori wards; Maori standing committees to vet authorities' policies and actions; a Treaty of Waitangi audit office with powers similar to those of the Commissioner for the Environment to consider Treaty matters; and a Maori Local Government Commission with the same powers as the Local Government Commission.[43]

The Minister of Local Government Michael Bassett rejected these proposals, and denounced the MCG as a body 'highjacked' by 'unrepresentative activists'.[44] Further criticisms from Maori resulted in calls for a discussion paper that would recognise the Treaty and provide a mechanism to ensure Maori input into decision-making at local government level.[45] A draft bill ensued, proposing mandatory Maori Advisory Committees (MACs) to facilitate communication between regional councils and territorial authorities and tangata whenua. This attracted 170 submissions from Maori and Pakeha, both for and against, but Labour was voted out of office in 1990 before it passed.[46]

From the moment Labour announced its intention to reform local government, debates about the Treaty implications of this process had been lively. Some Maori rejected a relationship with local authorities on Treaty matters because they saw the Treaty as an agreement between Maori and the Crown (which later became central government) only. Many local authorities also protested at the notion that they should be involved in Treaty matters, because they viewed them as issues for central government to address and resolve. Several of the submissions from local governments about the MAC proposal, for example, argued that because the Local Government Act of 1974 contained no specific reference to the Treaty, local authorities were not bound by it.[47] In the end, the fourth Labour government extensively reformed local government in New Zealand without reference to the Treaty. As Janine Hayward has pointed out: 'Despite the often-repeated warning that "the Crown cannot divest itself of its Treaty obligations", the reform of local government had done precisely that.'[48]

Generally, however, as more claims were lodged, and workplaces and associations tried to become more bicultural, the Treaty's status and impact on New Zealand society had never been higher. Judge Edward Taihakurei Durie, presiding chair of the Waitangi Tribunal, remarked in 1989: 'The Treaty is moving in as surely as the tide. In the statutes of our Parliament, in bureaucratic operations, in the legal administration of the Courts, and in local authority planning, the Treaty is well known.'[49] For some, however, the tide was advancing at an uncomfortable pace, and threatening to carry away too much with it.

A backlash begins

In 1987, after the Waitangi Tribunal's *Orakei Report* unequivocally upheld Ngati Whatua's claims, the *New Zealand Herald* commented that 'many people will wonder just where Maori claims are going to stop'.[50] National Party leader Jim Bolger noted that claims were 'starting to gnaw away at New Zealanders'.[51] Winston Peters, National's new spokesperson on Maori Affairs and Race Relations, warned of future claims amounting to hundreds of millions.

The handsome, always immaculately attired Peters came to prominence in 1986–87 by exposing the 'Maori loans affair'. This much-publicised scandal involved a negotiation between Tamati Reedy, Secretary of Maori Affairs, and a Hawaiian financier, to raise a loan of some $600 million. Although Peters did not force Minister of Maori Affairs Koro Wetere to resign, his criticisms arguably hastened the demise of the Maori Affairs Department. He emerged from the 'loans affair' as National's rising star. Critical of the 'Treaty industry', and scathing about radical Maori activists, he believed individual initiative was needed today, not 'sickly white liberals' who focused on past wrongs.[52] Speaking at the Party's 1988 National Conference, he denounced the Treaty as 'a talisman of the past'.[53] The son of a Maori father and Pakeha mother, he was essentially a populist who homed in on popular grievances — in this case, Treaty claims.

In 1988, the Treaty of Waitangi (State Enterprises) Act extended the Waitangi Tribunal's powers with regard to Crown land transferred to SOEs. If the Tribunal found that the land had been acquired in breach of the Treaty, it could order rather than recommend its return to Maori claimants. The Tribunal expanded to include some eighteen members, and its research capacity increased.[54]

A chorus of complaints — in Parliament, letters to the editor and radio talkback programmes — began to mount, criticising the Tribunal as biased and unfair. Early in the year, Ralph Maxwell, Parliamentary Under-Secretary for Agriculture, wrote an opinion piece for the *New Zealand Herald* entitled: 'That

Treaty? Scrap it and Substitute Another Pact'. A *Herald* headline a few weeks later erroneously warned: 'Treaty Bill Could Force out Farmer'.[55] Sir Robert Muldoon referred to the Tribunal as a 'recipe for racial disharmony' and suggested its abolition.[56] The One New Zealand Foundation, a newly created group headed by Peter Clark and located in Tauranga, also called for the Tribunal's abolition. It argued that 'one law, one people, one New Zealand' was the desired aim, not 'racist privilege'.[57] However, in June 1988, a *North & South* article called 'Learning to Live with the Waitangi Tribunal: the facts without fear' assured Pakeha readers that their property would not be arbitrarily confiscated to settle claims:

> Fearful Pakehas listen for the scrape of motorbike boots up the suburban front path and ask: Will it really happen?
>
> The answer is no. The Waitangi Tribunal doesn't have the power to hand your home to Maori claimants. It can't do it — and it doesn't want to.[58]

While the Tribunal claims process obviously evoked some alarm and resentment, so too did the actions of a small number of radical Maori. Between 1985 and 1990, a series of arsons ravaged the small rural town of Ruatoria, on the East Coast of the North Island. The perpetrators were a group of Maori Rastafarians, who had links to the Black Power gang and who 'grew, sold, and smoked a lot of cannabis'. According to journalist and author Angus Gillies, one of their aims in setting fire to farm buildings, schools, homes, churches, and even the local police station-cum-courthouse, was 'to drive off the white settler families and return all the land around Ruatoria to the original Maori owners'. Before long they were burning down 'anything that represented authority and the establishment', including the property of Maori they believed had slighted them.[59] Drugs and gang culture, often perceived as urban problems, adversely affected many rural communities, especially those that experienced severe unemployment in the wake of the fourth Labour government's post-1984 reforms. Ruatoria's unemployment rate in the early 1990s, for example, was 80 per cent, as compared to around 10 per cent in the Gisborne and Bay of Plenty regions.[60]

The Ruatoria arsons attracted much media attention. In 1988, in addition to the adverse publicity surrounding the aforementioned charges against Titewhai Harawira and staff at Te Whare Pai, there was more controversy after the Maori rights activist Hana Jackson told a group of Auckland University law students to 'kill a white person before you die and be a hero'.[61] Complaints were laid with the Race Relations Conciliator, who decided that the remarks were not actionable, having been made in a private place (in this case, a marae). Jackson claimed her comments were taken out of context:

> I was predicting that this is what people would have to do out of desperation for their situation. I would have clarified it if all those people had not walked out. And I never said to kill a white. To me a white is an American or someone, but a Pakeha is a New Zealander. I wouldn't call a Pakeha a white.[62]

The perceived prominence of both Maori culture and liberal guilt also provoked ongoing criticism in the media. A 1986 *Metro* article entitled 'Te Pakeha: The Search for White Identity' mockingly referred to 'guilty liberals who hang bone carvings around their necks, adopt Maori spellings of their names, call New Zealand Aotearoa and flock to the Te Maori exhibition as if it will assuage their guilt'. In the same article, the playwright Greg McGee was quoted: 'The cultural cringe has turned into a Pakeha cringe for those with the curse of no Maori in them. Most Pakeha are so consumed with guilt that it turns into a paralysis.'[63] A *North & South* article in November 1988 entitled 'Bleeding White: Middle Class and Carrying the Can' complained that '[t]o be white and middle class, we are led to believe, is a kind of moral crime. We are told we are responsible for bigotry, social injustice, even the past.'[64]

In 1989, the eminent author and academic C. K. Stead wrote an opinion piece called 'The New Victorians' in *Metro*, lamenting what he perceived to be a constrictive climate of 'moral fervour' surrounding feminism and anti-racism in New Zealand; a fervour which 'destroys both the sense of history and all thought of future consequences'. Referring to recent correspondence and reviews in the *London Review of Books* about anti-anti-racism, he observed:

> . . . it's a sign of the health of the British intellectual community (which New Zealanders often affect to despise) that such a debate can be carried on at a high level in a liberal paper; and that no such thing is imaginable in this country.[65]

He also expressed the view that

> Pakeha New Zealanders . . . were not a party to the treaty and I think for that reason do not feel responsible for it or in sympathy with its present-day consequences. One may feel, as many liberal-minded Pakehas do, that that is wrong; but if I'm right that it is a fact, and if that fact is not recognised, then it's hard to see how we can even begin to understand one another.[66]

In his opinion, 'worse trouble — confusion, misunderstanding — springs from the Pakeha disinclination to speak out frankly'.[67]

But Pakeha reluctance to speak out frankly was apparently lessening. A survey of New Zealand values conducted by Hyam Gold and Alan Webster of Massey University in 1989 showed that only about four in ten New Zealanders sympathised with the Maori rights movement, and two thirds disapproved of special land and fishing rights for Maori. Three out of four wanted to limit claims under the Tribunal or abolish the Tribunal altogether.[68] In overview, Gold and Webster stated that while 'government and political elites have moved far in recent years towards greater sympathy for the notion of Maori rights under the Treaty, it is clear that they have not succeeded, at least as yet, in carrying the bulk of the population with them'.[69]

The irate response to the acquittal of Tom Te Weehi in 1986 and Jack Hakirau Love in 1988 on charges of illegal shellfishing under section 88(2) of the Fisheries Act (which stated that 'nothing in this Act shall affect any Maori fishing rights') illustrated the public's resentment against perceived special privilege. According to Andrew Sharp, these cases evoked 'the greatest outcry of the 1980s against Maori legal privilege'.[70] The media frequently fanned public indignation, denouncing the acquittals as 'racist law' and 'separatism' without attempting to explain the nature of indigenous rights under the Treaty or the common law of aboriginal rights.[71]

Reasserting control

In 1987, the United Nations Indigenous Peoples Preparatory Meeting in Geneva endorsed indigenes' right to 'whatever degree of autonomy or self-government they choose'.[72] Aware that this sort of resolution could fuel a spreading fire, and already burned by Court of Appeal rulings that hindered its economic reforms, government began to assert more political control over the Treaty arena. It created a Crown Task Force, consisting of a Cabinet Committee on Treaty issues, core officials from various government departments, and a new Treaty of Waitangi Policy Unit (TOWPU) to help clarify Treaty policy and research and negotiate claims. By commencing 'direct negotiations' with iwi, government would effectively bypass the underresourced Waitangi Tribunal, cut costs and litigation times, and sit firmly in the driver's seat.[73]

In 1989, TOWPU produced 'Principles for Crown Action on the Treaty of Waitangi', a policy statement aiming to increase transparency in government relations with Maori. The five principles — kawanatanga, or government; rangatiratanga, or self-management; equality; co-operation; and redress

— proved durable and were frequently utilised by Maori and supporters of Maori causes in subsequent years. At the same time, Maori adamantly upheld the primacy of the Treaty itself. In 1985, when Attorney-General and Minister of Justice Geoffrey Palmer proposed a Bill of Rights, and later in 1994, when Prime Minister Jim Bolger argued in favour of becoming a republic, both suggestions met largely negative responses from Maori, many of whom saw them as threats to the Treaty's pre-eminence and mana.[74] The *Principles for Crown Action* were nevertheless generally welcomed as realistic, workable guidelines for race relations between Crown and Maori that comprised 'a major statement of intent to honour the Treaty'.[75]

The sesquicentennial and the 'national symbol of unity'

In 1987, the government set up a '1990 Commission' to plan and coordinate sesquicentennial celebrations. After debating whether it was viable to 'celebrate' a treaty so consistently ignored or breached in the past, the Commission's mission statement, released in June 1988, emphasised 'commemorating' the Treaty and celebrating New Zealand's natural advantages. Its 1989 booklet 'The Treaty of Waitangi: The Symbol of our Life Together as a Nation' described the Treaty as 'a national symbol of unity and understanding between cultures'.[76] This was a dominant refrain in the various sesquicentennial events.

A 'Waitangi Working Group' within the Department of Internal Affairs coordinated the proposed Waitangi Day celebrations. These included a costumed re-enactment of the historic 1840 signing at Waitangi; an official ceremony at the Treaty Grounds; cultural events in eight different locations (ranging from Maori contemporary dance to a performance by the New Zealand Symphony Orchestra); and an Aotearoa Maori Arts Festival at Waitangi as well as a ceremony honouring Maori elders. Queen Elizabeth II was to speak at the official ceremony, and waka from iwi around the country would gather on the water.[77]

In contrast to these enthusiastic official plans and pronouncements, a *Listener* editorial on the eve of Waitangi Day 1990 expressed ambivalence about the Treaty:

> Sacred covenant or fraud? Founding document or Victorian relic? Pact of partnership or symbol of disunity? In the confused and divided New Zealand of 1990 . . . these conflicting views could all be regarded as valid interpretations of the current status of the Treaty of Waitangi. The debate is intense and often angry. The treaty is certainly a major thread in the fabric of the nation but at times it almost seems the fabric cannot hold.[78]

Despite such concerns, media coverage of the commemoration emphasised unity and celebration. National pride in the day and its associated events was heightened by the fact that New Zealand had just hosted the 1990 Commonwealth Games in Auckland, and farewelled the Whitbread Round the World Race yacht fleet.[79] The public mood was buoyantly nationalistic and positive.

Queen Elizabeth's speech sounded a subtly less congratulatory note, acknowledging: 'Today we are strong enough and honest enough to learn the lessons of the last 150 years and to admit that the Treaty has been imperfectly observed.'[80] The Maori Anglican Bishop Whakahuihui Vercoe pursued the theme of failing to honour the Treaty more damningly:

> . . . since the beginning of that Treaty 150 years ago you have marginalised us. You have not honoured the Treaty. We have not honoured each other in the promises we made on this sacred ground.[81]

This speech elicited a mixed response. Some media reports described it as moving; others selectively edited it to accord with the idea that the Treaty was a symbol of unity and 'one nation'.[82]

As in the past, protesters at the Waitangi marae ceremony received considerable media attention. But the overall message conveyed in newspapers and on radio and television was that, ultimately, national unity had been enhanced by the commemorative events. As one television news report concluded:

> . . . recapping on Waitangi Day 1990. It brought together one of the biggest tribal gatherings in 150 years. It also brought determined protest, which refuses to be silenced, even in the presence of royalty. But at the end of the day it brought a hope of moving two people, Maori and Pakeha, together.[83]

The repeated emphasis on the Treaty as New Zealand's founding document during the sesquicentenary weakened its chances of being relegated to the dustbin of history by those unhappy about its recent rise to prominence.

Devolution, division, unity

While the sesquicentennial celebrations were being planned, the Department of Maori Affairs was gradually shedding many of its operational programmes. From 1989, it ceased to exist. A new Ministry of Maori Affairs (Manatu Maori) now offered a Maori perspective on policy creation, while an Iwi Transition

Agency (Te Tira Ahu Mahi) helped tribes develop a sound base for service provision by 1994.[84]

For many Maori, the Department's demise evoked concern and unease: they feared that tribes would become increasingly self-interested and divided, competing against each other in vying for government mandating and funding. If Labour had not consciously implemented a 'divide and rule' policy, some believed that would be the long-term impact of free-market devolution and a claims process that fuelled inter-iwi competition and rivalry.

In 1987, Koro Wetere and Hepi Hoani Te Heuheu Tukino VII, paramount chief of Ngati Tuwharetoa, set up a Federation of Maori Authorities to be a forum for Maori resource-based trusts, incorporations and other businesses. This became an important national voice, but Hepi Hoani Te Heuheu believed that a further body was now needed, a pan-tribal organisation totally independent of government, to present a united Maori front on key issues. He accordingly convened a hui on 23 June 1989 at Lake Taupo to discuss its formation. On 14 July 1990, a National Maori Congress (later, Maori Congress), which included all of the major tribes, formed. As with the Kotahitanga movement, self-funded meetings rotated throughout the country.[85]

In December 1989, Labour introduced its Runanga Iwi Bill. Iwi runanga (governing councils) would provide devolved government services to their members. To gain official recognition, they were expected to meet specific criteria such as authenticated boundaries and appropriate financial structures. They also needed to adopt a corporate management model similar to that established by the government in the public sector. The National Maori Congress opposed the Bill on the grounds that it was too prescriptive, defining iwi strictly within boundaries that reflected Crown aims and goals. Pantribal organisations and urban-based tribal authorities also felt neglected and objected to the emphasis on iwi runanga.[86]

In response to Maori feedback, when the Bill passed in August 1990 it included some references to the principles of the Treaty of Waitangi, attempted to be less prescriptive, and acknowledged that an authorised Maori collectivity could include a body other than a tribal runanga, such as a marae committee or a trust board.[87] In the event, the Act did not last long enough to make an impact. It was repealed by the new National government in May 1991; the notion that Maori were in some sort of officially franchised partnership position thus deflated.[88] Under National, as part of the 'mainstreaming' process, groups offering services for Maori would be just one among many competing providers.

At the same time, National's new Minister of Maori Affairs, Winston Peters, wanted to address the economic and social gulf between Maori and Pakeha. He had gained political traction by exposing incompetency within the Department of Maori Affairs and by opposing the Treaty. In May 1990, prior to the election, he created a furore by telling the media that he had caucus support for wiping the Treaty from all existing legislation. This fell on receptive ears; in July 1990, a *North & South* cover story entitled 'Winston Peters, The Man YOU Want as Prime Minister' observed:

> While liberals and Maori Activists see him as a menace, conservative and middle New Zealand hails Peters as a messiah . . . He's the man they can trust, the man to fix their problems and allay their fears, the man they want as Prime Minister.[89]

As Minister of Maori Affairs, Peters focused on Maori socio-economic disadvantage, arguing that if such inequities continued, New Zealand would suffer. To lift Maori up, he advocated better education along with a stronger, larger Maori Affairs Department.

Creating a centralised 'super-ministry' to facilitate Maori development was a key component of *Ka Awatea*, a report produced by a ministerial planning group in 1991. Its recommendations, which included a training unit and health promotion unit, were neglected, however, because Treasury was not prepared to allocate the requisite resources. Funding a larger department for Maori Affairs went against the 'downsizing' trend. Peters' less sympathetic political colleagues also saw it as a 'grab' for power and resources.[90]

In 1992, a Ministry of Maori Development, Te Puni Kokiri, replaced the Iwi Transition Agency and Manatu Maori. Policy rather than service delivery was now a focus, along with improving the performance of mainstream departments to meet Maori needs. Under National, partnerships with Maori stemmed from the neo-liberal belief that culturally appropriate services were a response to market demand.[91] The National Party's 1990 election manifesto paid homage to the Treaty as the 'founding document of the nation', then confidently promised to end all settlements by 2000 — an aim which apparently proved popular with voters.[92]

At the same time, devolution and benefit cuts continued to exact a toll. Socio-economic disparities between Maori and Pakeha were widening alarmingly rather than closing. If the Treaty process was helping some iwi, large numbers of deracinated urban Maori remained unaffected by it; their poverty and malaise a source of pressing social concern. In 1991, the Maori teen childbearing rate was three times higher than that of non-Maori; and 46 per cent of the prison population identified as Maori. Maori comprised 30 per cent of all solo parents, even though those aged 15 to 59 comprised just 10 per cent of the population in that age group. Sixty-six per cent of Maori solo parents had no educational qualifications, compared with 40 per cent of Pakeha. In 1992, four out of ten Maori left school with no qualifications, compared with one in ten non-Maori.[93]

A *North & South* feature article in 1993 responded to 'One New Zealand' adherents who bemoaned the 'hundreds of millions of dollars' poured into special Maori programmes and schemes as a 'separatist Maori burden on Pakeha taxpayers' by stating:

> There is indeed a Maori burden but the facts show it is borne by the Maori community, which is this country's poorest, unhealthiest, worst housed, least educated group . . . The state of Maoridom is the shame of New Zealand. It's a nonsense to claim we are one nation when tens of thousands of people from one distinct group live on a poverty-ridden fringe of society.[94]

The article cited numerous statistics chronicling Maori socio-economic disadvantage, and noted in doing so that the problem was largely a socio-economic rather than a 'Maori'/racial one. In ensuing years, Maori socio-economic disadvantage did not show any signs of improvement. By 1995, 19.6 per cent of the Maori labour force was unemployed, compared to 5.8 per cent for Pakeha.[95]

'The tyranny of political correctness': anti-Treatyism and cultural safety

Despite such statistics, the backlash gathered momentum, and books opposed to the Treaty began to proliferate. In 1990, for example, Robin Mitchell's book *Treaty and the Act: 1840 and the Treaty of Waitangi Act 1975* declared:

> . . . the partly Government funded sickly-white-liberal group Project Waitangi [had] made me aware that if people such as I did not study the Treaty and make an unbiased interpretation of it, misinterpretations were liable to be the order of the day, with a risk that the whole place would be handed over to the Maoris — as indeed almost seems to be in the process of happening.[96]

Another author, Stuart C. Scott, depicted the Treaty as a 'kind of legal blank cheque . . . currently being filled in and cashed by Maori opportunists'.[97] His first book, *The Treaty of Waitangi*, self-published in 1995, went into its sixth printing eleven months later, having sold 18,000 copies. A profile about the book by television current affairs programme *60 Minutes* invited viewers to express their views. At the end of the week, 10,000 calls had been received, 91 per cent in support. A successor volume, *Travesty after Travesty*, published in 1996, exposed 'the advances of Maori influence, property ownership and political and financial power' since 1993.[98]

One chapter of Scott's second book was devoted to the 'cultural safety debate'. In 1992, the Nursing Council had made 'cultural safety' a requirement for nursing and midwifery courses. A culturally safe nurse would know 'not to blame victims of historical and social processes for their current plight', and would be 'open-minded and flexible in their attitudes towards people from differing cultures to whom they offer and deliver service'.[99] A *Metro* article entitled 'Cultural Shock' responded to this initiative with alarm:

> From November, student nurses may fail their State Final registration exams if they don't follow the party line on Treaty objectives. From this year, 20 per cent of the State Final examination will be something called 'cultural safety', a concept involving sensitivity to Maori (but not Pacific Island, Indian, Chinese or any other minority) cultural differences, anti-racism and a liberal interpretation of the Treaty of Waitangi.[100]

The article went on to ask whether being medically safe was less important than holding 'politically correct attitudes' and described the programme as 'social engineering'.[101] The issue attracted further negative attention when Anna Penn, an ex-Christchurch Polytechnic student, wrote a six-page letter to the Christchurch *Press* on 7 July 1993 attacking cultural safety. She claimed she had not met the course requirements because of 'failing a hui'.[102]

All media, including television and radio, then took up the debate. A *Press* editorial on 14 July attacked political correctness as 'an instrument of tyranny, characterised by bullying, moral blackmail, and the stifling of argument'. On 27 July, the *Dominion* attacked the 'thought police' behind cultural safety, and on 6 August another article denounced 'the self-righteous aura of the politically correct'.[103] A few publications supported cultural safety as an important element of nurse training. The *Listener*'s Bruce Ansley noted that '[t]he cry of cultural safety certainly brought rednecks tumbling out of the closet' and concluded: 'Hell hath no fury like a failed student. Perhaps it is as simple as that.'[104] An article by *North & South* writer Cate Brett in October 1993 debunked several myths surrounding both Penn's case and the broader cultural safety debate.

No one had 'failed a hui'; the state exam did contain 20 per cent cultural safety, but cultural safety comprised a much smaller component (in Christchurch, 3.5 per cent) of the diploma/degree courses nurses had to pass beforehand; there had demonstrably been no falling off of academic training or standards.[105] After acknowledging growing public resentment about emphasis on the Treaty, Brett concluded that the Penn debate 'has vividly demonstrated the growing gap between where the legislators and the public are coming from on treaty issues'.[106]

In 1995, an *Evening Post* article by a polytechnic tutor again attacked cultural safety, suggesting that devoting so much time to it compromised nursing standards.[107] Another round of criticism ensued in newspapers and on talkback radio. A further student complaint in June 1995 prompted an investigation by Parliament's Education and Science Select Committee. In 1996, the Nursing Council produced a report and subsequent draft guidelines for the teaching of cultural safety which refined the concept to include nurses' awareness and sensitivity towards patients of differing age, gender, religion, sexuality, ethnicity and disability.[108] As a result, the furore over cultural safety receded. But the idea that teachers were to blame for subverting the will of the majority continued to feature prominently in 'anti-Treaty' writings in the 1990s. Walter Christie, for example, who published four anti-Treaty books between 1997 and 2000, claimed that 'masses of propaganda for treatyism is flushing through education of every kind everywhere'.[109]

'Confrontational and unsettling': Once Were Warriors

Alan Duff, the most famous anti-Treaty writer of the 1990s, had a Pakeha father and a Maori mother. His first novel, *Once Were Warriors*, burst onto the New Zealand literary scene in 1990. The story concerns Beth and Jake Heke and their six children, residents of a government housing estate who lead dissolute lives marred by alcoholism, unemployment, sexual abuse and domestic violence.[110] For many New Zealanders, the 'raw reality' of the novel was a 'confrontational and unsettling experience'.[111] This surprised Duff: 'I presumed my book would hardly be a revelation to them, the middle-class whites. I presumed they already knew of the quite different social state of the Maori compared to themselves. I presumed wrong . . .'[112]

Although a national and international best-seller, the novel generated controversy, with opponents claiming it blamed the victim, perpetuated negative stereotypes, and fostered the notion that violence and abuse were problems specific to Maori.[113] Its essentially libertarian message rejected debasing welfare, and presented Maori self-help as the way forward.[114] Duff's views were widely disseminated through his fiction and in weekly (later, fortnightly) columns for the *Evening Post*, syndicated to another eight newspapers throughout the country. In 1993, his non-fiction *Maori: The Crisis and the Challenge* castigated Maori for their crisis of 'underperformance' as students, parents and providers. Only individualism and 'get up and go' would staunch further failure: an archaic collectivist tribal culture represented the past, not the future. Duff objected to Treaty claims as just another handout: 'I think Maori have made a bad error of collective judgement in waiting around for the bus of grievances to come and collect them.'[115]

In 1994, *Once Were Warriors* was made into a feature film. Directed by Lee Tamahori, this became a cultural phenomenon, breaking all previous box-office records for a New Zealand film. Internationally, in addition to doing well at the box office, it won an array of coveted film prizes.[116] Like the novel, it attracted criticism for its harrowing portrait of contemporary urban Maori life, but was positively received overall.[117]

Over time, the phrase *Once Were Warriors* became a kind of verbal short-hand for a range of problems prevalent within an impoverished urban Maori 'underclass'.[118] For Duff, like Winston Peters, education was the only answer to Maori problems — a crucial exception to the 'no handouts' from government rule.[119] Both men also believed in a unified Maoridom, rather than teams of competing iwi. This, combined with their mutual antipathy to Treaty claims, made them unwilling to accept that settlements were opening up new opportunities for Maori.

Settlement progress

In 1991, following Peters' ejection from the National cabinet, the Minister of Justice, Douglas Graham, assumed responsibility for Treaty settlements.[120] He faced a monumental challenge. Over 400 claims awaited hearings and the repeal of the Iwi Runanga Act meant that questions about who to negotiate and settle with were often complex and contentious.

There is some irony in the fact that settlements forged ahead under National, given its de-emphasis of the Treaty in social policy. In his 1997 book *Trick or Treaty*, for example, Graham noted that early in National's first term it was resolved that: 'Henceforth Maori would qualify for government assistance on the basis of need like everyone else and not because they were Maori.'[121] National proceeded down the settlement path for several reasons: the journey had already started, Maori expectations were high, and it was in the interests of social harmony to do so. Moreover, the process accorded with a neo-liberal agenda. As Graham noted:

> Maori self-respect would be re-established, they would be able to move away from dependence on the state for so much, they could preserve their cultural taonga or treasures as they saw fit, and they could if they wished, but of course were not obliged to, provide health and educational facilities for their people in the manner of their choosing. Over time this seemed likely to be a far better investment by the taxpayer than simply paying out millions with apparently insignificant return. And, of course, settling the claims was the right and honourable thing to do.[122]

The first major settlement completed under National was a unique pan-tribal one. The Treaty of Waitangi (Fisheries Claims) Settlement Act of 1992, now commonly known as the 'Sealords deal', involved the Crown putting up some $150 million to buy a 50 per cent share in Sealord Products Ltd, a large seafood company.[123] In addition, the Maori Fisheries Commission would receive 20 per cent of the quota on new species entering the Quota Management System. This offer, which comprised some $170 million, was enabled by the timely sale of Sealords: a window of opportunity not to be missed. Proceeds were to go to the newly reconstituted Treaty of Waitangi Fisheries Commission/Te Ohu Kai Moana, which would administer and distribute them.[124]

Controversy over the deal was deep and bitter. For some Maori, the cost was too high, because the quid pro quo stipulated by government was relinquishing customary aboriginal rights over fisheries. The government now knew exactly how much it was in for with regard to Maori fishing rights. Maori, for their part, could never ever again litigate or make further claims in the area of commercial fishing. For some, this was a diminution of tribal rangatiratanga, a question of conceding too much principle for too little profit.[125] There were also valid criticisms from urban iwi that their rights had been neglected under the deal,[126] and ongoing wrangling over quota allocation to iwi. Nevertheless, as Richard Hill observes: 'Despite all such problems, and however inadequate the final fisheries settlement may have been considered by many Maori, a pioneering transfer of major resources had been conceded. And a compensation precedent of considerable magnitude had been set.'[127] By 1996, Te Ohu Kai Moana was the major stakeholder in New Zealand's fishing industry, with assets of $507.4 million.[128]

The other major direct settlement negotiation under way at this time, the Waikato-Tainui Raupatu, commenced in 1989–90 and resumed in 1992 under Graham and his officials. The final settlement, signed in May 1995, involved some $170 million; a significant sum, especially as not five years earlier, government negotiators offered $150 million less.[129] Importantly, in addition to money and land, the Crown expressed 'profound regret and apologised unreservedly for the loss of lives . . . arising from its [1863] invasion' and now sought 'on behalf of all New Zealanders to atone for these acknowledged injustices'.[130] This fulsome apology, crucial to the settlement and an important step in mending New Zealand race relations, set national and international precedents.

The National government in the early 1990s, despite the anti-Treaty rhetoric of some of its key members, also passed a number of important pieces of legislation that incorporated Maori values and perspectives. For example, the Resource Management Act of 1991 specified that Maori environmental values must be taken into account, along with the recognition of cultural values pertaining to any building, land or water or other resource utilisation.[131] In 1993, the Te Ture Whenua Maori Act promoted the 'retention, use, development, and control of Maori land as taonga tuku iho by Maori owners, their whanau, their hapu, and their descendants'.[132] In contrast to many previous laws, Te Ture Whenua made alienating Maori land more difficult. Multiple ownership, formerly discouraged as an impediment to economic progress, was now encouraged through the Act's provisions for a variety of trusts and incorporations. It also provided for improved management structures to increase financial returns on tribal land.[133]

A year of angry protest

Despite this positive momentum, Maori opinion unanimously hardened against the National government in December 1994, after it announced a new overarching claims settlement policy. This policy answered two of National's fervent wishes: to know how much future settlements would cost, and to set a deadline for ending the claims process. The 'fiscal envelope' set a billion-dollar cap on settlements within a ten-year timeframe. Settlements would be voluntary, full and final — the more one tribe got, the less would be available for those that remained. The conservation estate was not up for negotiation except in extreme circumstances, nor were natural resources.[134]

Maori throughout the country expressed indignation that government set the fiscal cap unilaterally, without consultation. A hui convened by Sir Hepi Hoani Te Heuheu at Hirangi marae in January 1995 sent a unanimous message: Maori rejected the fiscal envelope, and wanted a major constitutional review. A series of regional hui organised by the Crown in February to March proved a public relations disaster, with Maori expressing frustration at their continued inability to exercise tino rangatiratanga as promised under Article 2 of the Treaty.[135]

Racial tensions heightened. Protests at the 1995 Waitangi Day ceremonies were more heated than usual due to Maori anger over the fiscal envelope. In the early evening, before the flag-lowering ceremony, officials discovered Tino Rangatiratanga and Kotahitanga flags hung on the official flagpole, and that some of the pins holding up the scaffolding for the seats had been removed. Deputy Prime Minister Don McKinnon cancelled the evening ceremonies due to fears for public security.[136] For the next four years, official Waitangi Day celebrations were held at Government House in Wellington, with only a small retinue of government officials at the Waitangi site.

On 28 February 1995, Maori activists occupied Moutoa Gardens (Pakaitore) in Whanganui, an ancient pa site and reserve that, as conservation land, would be excluded under the fiscal envelope from any future Treaty settlements. Commenting on the occupation, the *Listener* asked: 'So it's to do with the fiscal envelope?' and answered:

> Directly, no. Indirectly, yes, yes and yes again. Whatever Doug Graham's hope
> for the fiscal cap proposal, the manner of its delivery represents a grade A policy
> disaster. National misread the mood of Maoridom by presenting what looked like a
> signed and sealed policy at the very time when Maori wanted a hand in creating the
> policies under which they would have to live.[137]

Although a Waitangi Tribunal report on the Whanganui River and its environs was to appear later in the year, the occupiers claimed not to recognise the Tribunal, the High Court, or any other legal body. They set up tents in the gardens, decapitated a statue of John Ballance, New Zealand's first Liberal premier, and displayed a banner proclaiming: 'Pakaitore is Maori Land — Return Now!' Throughout the occupation, local authorities tried to deal with the protesters without provocation or intimidation.[138]

For 79 days, the occupation elicited polarised responses from the public. Methodist, Anglican and Catholic clergy wrote to the occupiers seeking forgiveness 'for our years of silence and ignorance concerning your hurts'.[139] By contrast, the One New Zealand Foundation organised an Anzac Day procession in which some 500 people marched past Moutoa against the occupation.[140] Talkback shows and letters to the editor were largely opposed. In April 1995, the columnist Tom Scott noted: 'Any suggestion that a Maori minority would be ruling over a Pakeha majority is mana from heaven for talkback radio, and one popular school of thought on the airwaves was that Moutoa Gardens should be nuked.'[141] The tone adopted by some Pakeha about Maori at this time was often openly negative. In the same article, Scott referred to a remarkable incident earlier in the month, when the Chief Whip John Carter rang up fellow National MP John Banks' talkback show pretending to be a Maori dole bludger called 'Hone'. This ruse caused widespread offence and Carter was removed from his role (but reinstated a year later). On the same day Carter pretended to be 'Hone', another caller defended his Maori workmates as good blokes. Banks' riposte was: 'Oh yeah, can you name one?'[142]

By the end of March, Moutoa activists numbered over 400, and included veterans such as Titewhai Harawira, Mike Smith and Ken Mair. The latter described the occupation as an assertion of wider Maori sovereignty rights. This issue was so topical in 1995 that two books were published about it; one canvassing Maori views and the other Pakeha. Maori interviewees generally supported increased sovereignty, although ideas about what that entailed differed widely. For John Tamihere, chief executive officer for Auckland's Te Whanau o Waipareira Trust: 'Sovereignty to me simply means marking out quite clearly our share of the action and going for it.' Waireti Walters, a Maori health worker in Glen Innes, observed: 'Sovereignty to me is being in the kitchen and at least sitting at the table.'[143]

Pakeha perspectives ranged from unequivocal opposition to warm support. Glyn Clayton, editor of the *Christchurch Mail*, warned: 'it's . . . the end of New Zealand, if we have Maori sovereignty, because we have tribalism and tribal-ism is what's buggered the world since it began'. By contrast, John Paterson, Anglican Bishop of Auckland, believed: 'the rights and privileges of Maori under the Treaty, is . . . an issue that's really critical to our continued well-being as a society'. Douglas Graham, Minister in Charge of Treaty Negotiations, observed: 'I'm happy to talk about self-management and tino rangatiratanga and what it means, and kawanatanga, all that sort of thing, until the cows come home. But we are not going to waste time on something which isn't going to happen in a country like New Zealand.'[144]

Prime Minister Bolger agreed with Graham. In a letter to Sir Hepi Hoani Te Heuheu in September 1995, a week before a second Hirangi hui was held, he made it clear that 'the sovereignty of Parliament is not divisible'. After a third hui in April endorsed 'decolonisation' and called for indigenous sover-eignty and constitutional change, the Prime Minister remained adamant that any increase in tino rangatiratanga would have to occur within the existing political and constitutional framework.[145]

The activists left Moutoa peacefully on 18 May, faced with the prospect of an impending eviction order. Several other protest actions, however, occurred around the country. The final act in a year of racial protest took place in September 1995, when Maori protesters torched the Takahue school and community hall in the Far North.[146]

Despite moves by the Maori Congress to promote a national Maori political organisation, there was no agreement among Maori that this was desirable. Some tribes felt it could undermine tribal authority and compromise the right of iwi to organise their own affairs. Others saw tribal economic development as a first priority. The 30 per cent of Maori not affiliated to iwi felt understandably concerned that a national Maori organisation would favour tribes. By 1996, the Maori Congress itself had been reduced to about 30 iwi.[147] The united front and independent voice that Te Heuheu hoped to foster for Maoridom proved elusive; in its place, inter-iwi competition and rivalry intensified as tribes organised to participate in the settlements process and post-devolution service delivery. The Maori Congress withered away in the course of the late 1990s, weakened by 'differences within and between Maori components'.[148]

The events of 1995 made it clear that government would not countenance any dilution of parliamentary sovereignty. Yet many leading Maori appreciated that the Treaty settlement process comprised a means of augmenting tribal prosperity and rangatiratanga. In 1995, the existing Treaty of Waitangi Settlement Unit within the Justice Department, renamed the Office of Treaty Settlements, received more funding, staff and autonomy. It was now a special unit to facilitate Treaty settlements through direct negotiation with the Crown.

On 29 September 1998, the legislation for the settlement of the Ngai Tahu claim passed its third and final reading in Parliament. The culmination of eight years of negotiations, it reached a value of $170 million.[149] Along with Waikato-Tainui and the Sealords deal, it was seen as an important step towards interracial harmony, offering prospects for future iwi self-reliance and prosperity. As a 1992 *North & South* article pointed out, Ngai Tahu was already a significant corporate player:

> He [chief negotiator Tipene O'Regan] represents a tribe that counts among
> its closest strategic advisers the celebrated Rogernomics exponents C. S. First
> Boston and hires some of the best legal brains in the country . . . A tribe that is
> already heading some of the South Island's brightest hopes in the fast-growing
> nature tourism market, including a monopoly hold on Kaikoura's whale-watching
> venture.[150]

Although that article assumed an imminent settlement, negotiations continued for several more years. Unease among Ngai Tahu negotiators concerning the unknown situation that might prevail after the first MMP election hastened the settlement.[151]

Influence, agency and MMP

Mixed member proportional representation (MMP) enabled Maori to achieve more influence and agency within the political system. Initial plans to jettison the four Maori seats altered after a deputation of tribal elders met with the Prime Minister and argued for their retention. As a result, the seats were not only retained, but their number linked to the size of the Maori electoral roll. They consequently rose to five in 1996, six in 1999 and seven in 2002.[152]

The 1996 election has been described as the 'dawn' of Maori political might because it dramatically demonstrated the ability of the Maori seats to determine the balance of power.[153] After New Zealand First won all five Maori seats, Winston Peters, supported by voters disillusioned and adversely affected by economic liberalisation and recession, assumed the powerful role of 'kingmaker'.[154] When New Zealand First formed a coalition with the minority National government, Maori political influence enjoyed unprecedented prominence. In addition to the Maori seats' 'balance of power' role, there were now four Maori cabinet members, and fifteen Maori MPs in a House of 120.[155]

Before long, disagreements arose between Peters and the Maori members of New Zealand First, known as the 'Tight Five', who wanted a greater say in the party's governing council. By the end of the three-year term, four of the five Maori members had left the party. Tau Henare, the MP for Northern Maori, deputy leader of New Zealand First and Minister of Maori Affairs, was banished from the party following disagreements over funding for Maori programmes. After 1998, when the coalition collapsed, Henare and several other New Zealand First MPs supported National, enabling it to retain a small majority.

In the 1999 election, New Zealand First did not contest the Maori seats, as Peters now advocated their abolition. Labour, however, wooed them all back, a draw card being its avowal to restore the Treaty to social policy.[156] Maori featured prominently in the new Labour/Alliance coalition government, which included two members from the Mana Motuhake Party (list MPs Sandra Lee and Willie Jackson), and three Maori cabinet ministers: Dover Samuels, Sandra Lee and Parekura Horomia. Maori political influence was evident when

Maori MPs brokered a deal whereby government awarded a quarter of radio frequency spectrums to Maori — not as a property right, but as a means of helping to reduce socio-economic disparities. In the 2002 election, Maori again supported Labour, helping it to another conclusive win. A record total of 20 Maori took their seats in Parliament after the election.[157]

The change to MMP facilitated increased levels of representation among minority groups and provided added 'strategic incentives' for the major parties to take account of Maori concerns.[158] At the same time, although Maori under MMP played a more influential political role, Maori and Pasifika people at the lower end of the socio-economic scale continued to bear the brunt of neo-liberal reforms. In 1996, over 40 per cent of Maori children had no parent in the workforce. One in every two Maori women aged fifteen and over received a government benefit, compared with one in five non-Maori women, and 45 per cent of Maori women lived in households where annual before-tax income was $30,000 or less. In 1998, Maori unemployment was 18 per cent, compared to 7 per cent for non-Maori.[159]

'Enough is enough': from the 'Hikoi of Hope' to 'Closing the Gaps'

In 1998, the Anglican Church organised a 'Hikoi of Hope' to focus public attention on the growing gulf between rich and poor. Its key aspirations were affordable housing, a higher minimum wage, and restoring welfare benefits to the pre-1991 level.[160] The Roman Catholic, Methodist, Presbyterian and Salvation Army churches also supported the march, which commenced in September 1998 from both ends of the country, and concluded with some 8000 people converging on Parliament on 1 October. Some 40,000 New Zealanders, both Pakeha and Maori, marched at various times.[161] Media attention was extensive and generally positive, although some critics noted that identifying problems was easier than finding solutions. The columnist Jane Clifton, for example, while acknowledging the hikoi's symbolic significance, described it as 'a Care-bear convention of beaming vicars'.[162] With an election looming, however, the hikoi catch-cry 'Enough is enough' became 'the most potent political slogan of '98'.[163]

Goodwill towards the hikoi diminished considerably following a meeting between the Prime Minister, Cabinet and the hikoi leaders in December 1998. On that occasion, Professor Whatarangi Winiata advocated a three-tikanga governmental structure modelled on that adopted by the Anglican Church in 1992. He also warned that ignoring Maori demands for some form of sovereignty would result in revolution. These arguments both deflected attention away from government's social policy failures, and exposed a lack of unity among the hikoi organisers.[164]

The hikoi's call for social justice and a more equitable, humane society did have some enduring influence. From 1999, Prime Minister Clark initiated annual meetings with church leaders, during which the hikoi hopes were discussed. Whereas National had supported Maori capacity to deliver services in health, education and welfare without any mention of the Treaty, the new Labour/Alliance government intended to bring the Treaty back into the social policy arena by 'Closing the Gaps'.

This was not a new term or concept, having been the title of a 1998 Te Puni Kokiri report highlighting Maori socio-economic deprivation relative to Pakeha,[165] and calling for more Maori control over their own resources. National's response was that separate measures to address relative deprivation were divisive and unnecessary. In the *Dominion* in July 1998, Education Minister Wyatt Creech warned that 'lies, lies and damned statistics' could distort the picture. Maori living standards were in fact getting better, but because they were also improving for non-Maori, an immovable gap remained.[166]

In the lead-up to the 1999 election, however, Labour enthusiastically took up the phrase 'Closing the Gaps'. Its election manifesto on Maori Affairs declared an intention not only to close gaps but to return the rhetoric of Treaty partnership to social policy: 'Labour is committed to fulfilling its obligations as a Treaty partner to support self-determination for whanau, hapu and iwi.'[167] These promises helped the Labour/Alliance to victory, as Maori returned to their traditional political ally. Clark hailed 'Closing the Gaps' as the government's 'flagship' social policy. Her Speech from the Throne in December 1999 repeatedly invoked the Treaty, and described 'Closing the Gaps' as an obligation under Article 3 (which guaranteed equality in the rights of citizenship). She herself chaired the newly formed 'Closing the Gaps' Cabinet Committee, thereby underlining its importance. Yet 'Closing the Gaps' was destined for a short, rather ignominious life.

A scandal involving alleged inappropriate behaviour by Minister of Maori Affairs Dover Samuels in early 2000 deferred criticism for a time, but in November, opposition leader Jenny Shipley launched the first attack. She denounced the 'Gaps' policy on the grounds that Maori were not the only New Zealanders in need, and that need, not race, should determine entitlement. National continued to disparage the policy on the grounds that it was divisive, unfair, and did not accord with the country's egalitarianism. Towards the end of 2000, a paper often referred to as the Chapple Report (after its author) added to the critical momentum by pointing out serious deficiencies in the statistical analysis undertaken by the Ministry of Maori Development in 1998 to determine the gaps.[168]

Labour, perceiving increasing public disquiet about its flagship policy, began to change tack. Former rhetoric to the contrary, 'Closing the Gaps' had not apparently focused on reducing Maori socio-economic deprivation. Rather, it was to assist all disadvantaged New Zealanders. Before long the 'Gaps' policy was what the *Sunday Star-Times* described as 'the cause that dare not speak its name'.[169] The 'Closing the Gaps' Cabinet Committee disbanded, replaced by a Reducing Inequalities Cabinet Committee. Use of the phrase 'Closing the Gaps' by ministers and officials ceased.

Although the New Zealand Maori Council accused Labour of 'pandering to rednecks',[170] the government was more concerned about changing attitudes among middle New Zealand. Michael King, in the 'Author's Note' to his *Being Pakeha Now* (1999), expressed the view that Maori rights issues had been so well met in recent times that it was now necessary to fight the Pakeha corner:

> When I wrote a book called *Being Pakeha* in the early 1980s it emerged from a very different social and cultural climate than that which exists in New Zealand on the cusp of the twenty-first century. Then, it seemed to me, the most important task facing a historian of my background was to make Maori preoccupations and expectations intelligible to Pakeha New Zealanders; to make it clear why I believed that Maori had every right to be Maori in their own country and to expect Pakeha to respect them.
>
> Two decades on, with the Maori renaissance and the Waitangi Tribunal process in full flow, that need has been met . . . What I am conscious of now is a rather different but equally pressing need. It is to explain Pakeha New Zealanders to Maori and to themselves; and to do this in terms of *their* right to live in this country, practise their values and culture and be themselves.[171]

The temper of the times made it politic to jettison 'Closing the Gaps'. A Treaty provision in the Public Health and Disability Act passed in the same year immediately prompted complaints from opposition members that this entailed special treatment or higher priority for Maori. In fact, the provision was to involve Maori in establishing the objectives and functions of district health boards (DHBs). To remove any suggestion that Maori might enjoy special privileges, a clause in the Act precluded preferential access to services on the basis of race.[172] The Act did recognise Maori as indigenous people, however, and DHBs were required under the Act to involve them in decision-making processes because of their rights and status under the Treaty.[173]

At the same time, many long-standing affirmative action measures designed to rectify Maori and Pasifika socio-economic disadvantage and assist development remained firmly in place. In the same year that 'Closing the Gaps' was shelved, the government began a review to clarify local government's relationship with the Treaty of Waitangi. The ensuing Local Government Act (2002) included, under several sections, provisions to foster Maori involvement in local government decision-making processes and to ensure that significant decisions about land or a body of water needed to take into account the relationship of Maori and their cultural traditions. It also provided local government with the power to establish Maori wards and constituencies.[174] In education, health and social welfare services, the Labour/Alliance government continued to fund capacity development to enable Maori providers to gain experience in contract management and delivery. Only the 'Closing the Gaps' rhetoric disappeared.

'The thin end of a wedge'

Maori disillusionment with Labour intensified in 2003 as a result of a heated controversy over who owned the foreshore and seabed. In June, the Court of Appeal ruled that Maori might have customary interests in the foreshore and seabed, which could potentially lead to private title being granted in the Maori Land Court. The issue arose in 1997 when eight Marlborough Sounds iwi, denied marine farming licences by the local council for years, wanted to clarify the nature of their customary rights to the seabed.[175]

Media discussion about the Court of Appeal ruling played on public anxieties about restricted access to the nation's beaches. In fact, little land adjacent to the foreshore remained in Maori hands. Where it did, as in Auckland's Okahu Bay, the public enjoyed unfettered access. The fact that local authorities routinely leased one third of the country's foreshore to private companies, and another third was already in private ownership, received little attention.[176]

Labour responded to the ruling by proposing legislation that declared the foreshore and seabed to be Crown land, and prevented any further judicial investigation of the issue. The government's stated objective in taking this stance was to preserve the foreshore and seabed for all New Zealanders. To give some semblance of credence to Maori interests, however, the proposed Bill provided for the Maori Land Court to regulate where customary interests were demonstrated to have been uninterrupted since 1840.[177]

The Bill attracted controversy from the outset. Several Maori MPs strongly opposed it, and in May 2004 Tariana Turia, Associate Minister of Maori Affairs, resigned over the issue. National objected to the Bill because of the consideration it accorded to uninterrupted customary right, which it perceived as giving special privilege to Maori. In January 2004, the party's leader Don Brash delivered a highly publicised speech to the Orewa Rotary Club, warning against racial separatism. Drawing on a long tradition of 'One New Zealand' discourse, Brash promised:

> We intend to remove divisive race-based features from legislation. The 'principles of the Treaty' — never clearly defined yet ever expanding — are the thin end of a wedge leading to a racially divided state and we want no part of that. There can be no basis for special privileges for any race, no basis for government funding based on race, no basis for introducing Maori wards in local body elections, and no obligation for local governments to consult Maori in preference to other New Zealanders. We will remove the anachronism of the Maori seats in Parliament ... Having done all that, we really will be one people — as Hobson declared us to be in 1840.[178]

National's flagging popularity soared in the immediate aftermath of this speech, gaining seventeen percentage points in a February 2004 Colmar Brunton poll.[179] Many New Zealanders apparently shared Brash's resentment about perceived special treatment and privileges for Maori, and were unhappy with policies based on Treaty rights.[180] This sentiment was especially prominent among people of Brash's age and gender.[181]

In April and May, some 15,000 people, united by a sense of injustice and angry at being denied the opportunity of a court hearing, marched against the Foreshore and Seabed Bill in a hikoi from Cape Reinga to Wellington. As race relations grew increasingly polarised, Labour, worried by National's sudden spurt in popularity, signalled a change in direction. Upon the conclusion of the hikoi in Wellington, for example, Clark refused to meet the marchers, having earlier dismissed them as 'haters and wreckers'.[182] An editorial in the *Herald* noted with some asperity: 'Helen Clark is willing to antagonise Maori, and risk losing another Maori MP, because she is more concerned about National's appeal to Pakeha. Indeed, she may welcome the chance the hikoi provides today to show the limits of her tolerance of Maori aspirations.'[183] Clark, noting that the government may have moved ahead of public opinion on Treaty issues,[184] created a new post, Minister of Race Relations. In July 2004, its first holder,

Prime Minister David Lange (left); Finance Minister Roger Douglas (centre) and Richard Prebble, Minister of Transport and of Railways, reveal the dire state of the economy at the 'Opening the Books' presentation, August 1984. *EP/1984/4089/24A, Dominion Post Collection, Alexander Turnbull Library*

MPs Anne Hercus (left) and Helen Clark (centre) and then-president Jim Anderton (right) at the 1983 Labour Party Conference. *John Miller*

After the bombing: police check for evidence on and around the *Rainbow Warrior*, Marsden Wharf, Auckland, July 1985. *Gil Hanly*

The Pramazons, a group of anti-nuclear women, walked from Whakatane to Gisborne in 1983 performing en route a show about colonisation and militarisation in the Pacific. *Gil Hanly*

Marchers in Taihape protest against the fourth Labour government's farm and economic policies, March 1988. *Fairfax New Zealand, EP-Protests-General-From-1986-001, Alexander Turnbull Library*

Comedian John Clark as farmer Fred Dagg, in trademark black singlet and gumboots, enjoying a contemplative moment. *Peter Bush*

During the stock market boom of the mid-1980s, towering corporate buildings quickly multiplied, particularly in Auckland. Under construction (centre) is the Fay Richwhite Building. In comparison, housing conditions among the Auckland poor were often crowded and dilapidated (opposite, below). *Gil Hanly*

Key ministers of the fourth National government field questions at a press conference after delivering the economic statement to Parliament on 20 December 1990. Left to right: Finance Minister Ruth Richardson, Prime Minister Jim Bolger, Bill Birch and Simon Upton. *EP/1990/4372/21, Dominion Post Collection, Alexander Turnbull Library, Wellington, New Zealand*

All Black great Jonah Lomu playing Wales at Wembley Stadium in 1997. Born in Auckland in 1975, of Tongan descent, he is one of New Zealand's many Pasifika sporting heroes. *Peter Bush*

New immigrants bring new leisure activities. An end-of-year celebratory game of kilikiti (a Samoan version of cricket) at Macalister Park, Berhampore, Wellington, in December 1996. *EP/1995/4667, Evening Post Collection, Alexander Turnbull Library*

A Chinese dragon is carried across a Wellington pedestrian crossing, September 1999.
EP1999/2748/17, Dominion Post Collection, Alexander Turnbull Library

Otara Market in South Auckland has, like the city, become increasingly multicultural, with a distinctive mix of Maori, Pakeha, Asian and Pacific Island produce and shoppers. *Gil Hanly*

Pacific Island church-
goers, Ponsonby Road,
Auckland, 1980s. *Gil Hanly*

Gay pride: partygoers
outside SPQR restaurant,
Ponsonby, Auckland, the
morning after the Hero
Parade. *Arno Gasteiger*

Trevor Mallard, a Pakeha, announced: 'Pakeha and Maori are both indigenous people to New Zealand now', and reassured the public that special privileges for Maori were no longer part of Labour policy.[185]

The Foreshore and Seabed Act passed in November 2004 with the help of New Zealand First (a narrow victory of 61 in favour, 59 against). It drew censure from several quarters: Maori were angry, the National Party thought it unfair, the Greens denounced it as an abrogation of Maori rights, and eminent legal scholars lent their voice to the chorus of disapproval.[186] A Waitangi Tribunal report in 2004 decried the Act as a clear breach of Treaty principles, and expressed dismay that 'polarised positions (not necessarily underpinned by good information) have quickly been adopted, and real understanding and communication have been largely absent'.[187] In 2005, the United Nations General Assembly unequivocally stated that the Foreshore and Seabed Act clearly discriminated against Maori.[188]

One important, unforeseen consequence of the controversy was the creation of the Maori Party. Formed in July 2004 by co-leaders Tariana Turia and Pita Sharples, this quickly established itself as a political force, winning four of the seven Maori seats in the 2005 election. Its leaders hoped it would prove a unifying force in Maoridom, providing a voice for important issues affecting all Maori.[189] After the 2008 election, the Maori Party supported National to form a coalition government together with ACT, New Zealand and United Future.[190]

In March 2011, John Key's National government repealed the Foreshore and Seabed Act and replaced it with the Marine and Coastal Area (Takutai Moana) Act. This legislation restored access to the courts to seek recognition of customary title and guaranteed the rights of all New Zealanders in the common marine and coastal area.[191] Hailed by Attorney-General Christopher Finlayson as 'a just and durable resolution to the issue', it evoked bitter controversy from some Maori. Green Party co-leader Metiria Turei, for example, denounced the Act as 'discriminatory', 'racist' and 'a very unjust outcome . . . The Maori Party have betrayed Maori voters and those who supported them in 2004'.[192] The activist and outspoken MP for Te Tai Tokerau Hone Harawira also took issue with the Maori Party's acceptance of the new legislation. In 2010, he denounced the Bill as 'a fraud' because '98 per cent of Maori will not be able to meet the threshold to claim customary title'.[193] In January 2011, after a disciplinary committee recommended his expulsion, he resigned from the Maori Party. By April, he had formed the Mana Party, which aims to give a voice to 'the poor, the powerless and the dispossessed'.[194] In the 2011 election, Harawira retained his Te Tai Tokerau seat by a comfortable majority, and although in opposition, occupies the front bench in Parliament as leader of Mana.

In 2012, the government's desire to sell assets — in this instance, shares in electricity generating and retailing company Mighty River Power — came into conflict, just as it did in 1987, with unresolved Maori rights issues. In September 2012, some 1000 Maori from iwi around the country met at a national hui convened by the Maori King Te Arikinui Tuheitia Paki at Ngaruawahia's Turangawaewae marae, and determined to work together to halt the share sale.[195] The Maori Council had earlier lodged a claim with the Waitangi Tribunal against the government's intended partial float. In August 2012, an interim Tribunal report ruled that the Crown would breach Treaty principles if it sold the shares without first providing Maori with remedy or rights recognition. After the government revealed it would ignore a 'shares plus' scheme proposed by the interim report (which would give iwi a say in how energy companies are run), in late October 2012 the Maori Council announced its intention to take the matter to the High Court.[196] In February 2013, however, the Supreme Court dismissed the appeal from the unsuccessful bid on the grounds that the government sale of the Mighty River Power shares was not in breach of the Tainui Waikato settlement. Chief Justice Dame Sian Elias in her ruling noted that the Court was not persuaded that a material impediment arose from the proposal, but added: 'While the appellants have ultimately failed as to the ultimate result, they nonetheless succeeded on an important point of principle, namely that the Crown was bound to comply with the principles of the Treaty of Waitangi before deciding to sell the shares.'[197]

Polarised responses

On 14 February 1998, the National Museum of New Zealand Te Papa Tongarewa opened in Wellington amidst great media fanfare and excited public anticipation. The new institution, which aimed to operate in a bicultural fashion and included a working marae, featured a display of 'monumental proportions' (650 square metres) devoted solely to the Treaty of Waitangi.[198] Visitors could hardly avoid the impression that the Treaty was central to New Zealand's national identity, prized as a taonga by Maori and celebrated as a founding document by Pakeha.

Yet the Treaty's increased prominence after 1984 produced, and continues to produce, polarised responses. In the same year that Te Papa opened, a survey of attitudes and values about politics and government found that 33.8 per cent of New Zealanders wanted the Treaty abolished altogether; 29.1 per cent believed there should be greater limits on Maori claims under the Treaty; 25 per cent thought the Treaty should be dealt with through the Waitangi Tribunal as at present; and only 5 per cent wanted the Treaty strengthened and given the force of law. Some two thirds strongly opposed giving Maori special land and fishing rights to make up for past injustices; almost 17 per cent were neither in favour nor against; and about 16 per cent favoured these rights.[199]

The long-term impacts of the claims process and the push for a more effective bicultural Treaty partnership after 1984 for Maori are difficult to accurately ascertain. In the early twenty-first century, long-standing 'gaps' between Maori and Pakeha have not closed, although there are some improving trends — in education especially.[200] Other developments attest to the ongoing strength of the Maori Renaissance, however, and to the effectiveness of policies designed to answer the Maori desire for tino rangatiratanga.[201] With a population of over half a million, Maoridom is more numerous and complex than ever before. Treaty settlements have facilitated iwi investment in their localities in the form of Maori-owned trusts, many of which exert an increasing influence over local and regional development.[202] Iwi deliver health, housing, youth, justice and social service programmes, and successfully (and sometimes unsuccessfully) engage in diverse commercial ventures.[203] Partnerships with the private sector and government allow tribes to devise their own education plans that incorporate distinctive aspirations within a state framework. Tuwharetoa, for example, has an extensive professional development programme for principals and literacy leaders, while the Ngati Porou East Coast partnership Whaia te iti Kahurangi focuses on professional development, community language and curriculum guidelines.[204] Non-iwi groups such as West Auckland's Te Whanau o Waipareira Trust continue to offer numerous health and social welfare services. In 2003, a national Urban Maori Authority formed to lobby for a greater share of Treaty resources for non-iwi.[205]

MMP and the advent of the Maori party have increased Maori political influence, while Maori culture and Maori writers, artists, entertainers and sportspeople continue to play a vital role on the national stage. In 2003, government launched the Te Rautaki Reo Maori strategy, with the aim of strengthening and revitalising te reo.[206] In the same year, the Maori Television Act ushered in a government-funded channel with a Maori language content of at least 50 per cent. Offering a wide range of programmes — from earnest and educational to entertaining and humorous — this has proved a hit with all New Zealanders.[207]

The Lange government's promise to honour the Treaty altered internal race relations and earned international recognition for New Zealand as a pioneer of reparative justice for its indigenous people. But the Treaty's increased status did not prove palatable to many New Zealanders. The line of thinking that perceived Maori rights guaranteed under Article 2 as iniquitous 'special privileges' entered mainstream politics. Two years before Don Brash's Orewa speech, the National Party's 2002 election manifesto proclaimed: 'too much about the Treaty of Waitangi divides us. It's time to move on.' In the same publication, National promised, if elected, to 'close the book on Treaty claims within our first twelve months'.[208] Although this did not eventuate, in 2006 an amendment to the Treaty of Waitangi Act stipulated that the Tribunal not be permitted to register new historical claims submitted on or after 2 September 2008.[209] In the months before this deadline, however, a significant number of new claims were lodged, so 'closing the book' will be a protracted process.[210]

In her speech during the 1990 sesquicentenary celebrations, Queen Elizabeth II referred to the Treaty as

> a guide for all New Zealanders of goodwill, to all those whose collective sense of justice, fairness, and tolerance will shape the future. Your Court of Appeal has declared that the obligation on Treaty partners is to show each other the utmost good faith. The many children here today, and the diversity of cultures they represent, remind us all of that obligation to them and their future.[211]

In the course of the sesquicentenary, a dominant refrain among media commentators and politicians was that celebrating the Treaty served to reinforce a sense of national unity. Whether this notion features in the Treaty's bicentenary in 2040 is difficult to predict. Contentious, and capable of numerous interpretations, the Treaty, like Maori culture, is unique to this country and has shaped its identity. Since 1984, ongoing opposition and disputes notwithstanding, it has played an increasing role in upholding the rights and mutual responsibilities of Maori and Pakeha, and all New Zealand citizens, old and new.

CHAPTER TWELVE

A Plaited Rope

IMMIGRATION AND ITS IMPACT

. . . the selection of new immigrants will be based on criteria of personal merit without discrimination on grounds of race, national or ethnic origin . . .

Immigrants will be encouraged to participate fully in New Zealand's multicultural society while being able to maintain valued elements in their own heritage.
— Department of Labour, 1986[1]

In 2004, the distinguished anthropologist Dame Joan Metge delivered a lecture in which she expressed excitement about the weaving together of cultural heritages in contemporary New Zealand.[2] She employed a metaphor much loved by Maori orators, that of 'he taura whiri', a plaited rope, which she hoped would inspire a new model of nation building:

> Such a model would begin with strands representing the two parties to the Treaty of Waitangi, Maori and Pakeha, splice in the diversity of other ethnic groups, and plait them all together into a strong and effective whole, creating a sense of belonging together, of national identity . . .[3]

After 1984, the fourth Labour government aimed to plait together not only a more equitable bicultural Treaty partnership but also a more multicultural society. The race relations and immigration policies implemented at this time exerted a profound impact on the economy, on national, regional and local communities, and on New Zealand culture generally. They also provoked considerable resistance and ongoing debate.

The more open immigration policies inaugurated by the 1987 Immigration Act resulted in a wave of primarily Asian immigrants, whose presence provoked periodic controversy. Braiding 'the rope of peoples' could prove a difficult task. Despite some occasional fraying around the edges, however, the process continued. In the early twenty-first century the various composite strands have inexorably altered and enlivened New Zealand society. In contrast to the ethnic homogeneity rigorously maintained for many decades, the underscoring ethos now draws its energy from a distinctive blend of biculturalism and multiculturalism. New Zealand's ethnic and cultural profile reflects its geographical status as a Pacific Rim nation. An integral part of 'Australasia', it is also an enthusiastic participant in an increasingly globalised world system.

Enriching the social fabric

In 1986, in keeping with its plans to restructure the economy and workforce, and concerned by net departures of 100,000 in the decade to 1986,[4] the Lange government commenced a major immigration policy review. Its stated objectives were: 'to enrich the multicultural social fabric of New Zealand society through the selection of new settlers principally on the strength of their potential personal contribution to the future wellbeing of New Zealand'; facilitate the reunion of family members; allow more refugees; and make the entry of visitors to New Zealand easier.[5]

With New Zealand's ties with Britain loosening and contact with Asia increasing, previously dominant views of the latter as 'extremely poor, uncivilised and populous' gave way to admiration for the programmes of rapid industrialisation that were raising millions out of poverty. With its vital and booming economy, Asia was now a 'place of miracles and tigers'.[6] In 1971, Norman Kirk expressed the view that 'New Zealand's future lay with Asia and the Pacific'. Immigration policy therefore needed to be based on equality and ignore 'questions of race, colour and religion'.[7] Changes to immigration and citizenship laws in the mid-1970s abolished the distinction between 'British' and 'foreign', but little had practically changed. New Zealand still favoured Northern European migrants over other sources of immigrants.[8] A decade later, this was no longer the case. The 1986 review led to the 1987 Immigration Act, which overturned previous immigrant selection criteria such as ease of assimilation into a white,

Anglo-centric culture. Now, all immigrants in possession of capital and skills deemed desirable to the new economy were welcome — their provenance no longer relevant. The government allowed permanent entry to those with family or close relatives already here and committed to accepting 800 more refugees annually.

In 1991, the National government conducted another immigration policy review. This resulted in points-based immigration selection criteria that took into account factors such as age, employability, educational qualifications and capital input. As a result, more tertiary educated and professional migrants became eligible. For example, between 1986 and 1991, the majority of Taiwanese immigrants qualified for entry under the business category; after 1991, they entered New Zealand as skilled immigrants.[9]

The 1987 law change and the 1991 amendment dramatically altered patterns of immigration and settlement. Between 1986 and 2006, New Zealand's overseas-born population increased by 558,000. In 1989, the proportion of immigrants from European and American countries fell from 54 to 29 per cent, Pasifika people rose from 22 to 37 per cent, and those from Asian countries reached 31 per cent,[10] up from 6 per cent in 1986.[11] African immigrants, in particular white South Africans, also began arriving in large numbers. Between 1992 and 1996, 10,175 South Africans, part of a post-apartheid diaspora spurred by rising crime and related security concerns in their home country, were approved for permanent immigration to New Zealand. Between 1 July 1996 and 30 June 2001, 18,534 applications from South Africans were approved for permanent residence, making South Africa either the second- or third-highest source of immigrants during those years.[12]

However, this second wave of non-European immigrants — the first was the influx of Pacific migrants from the mid-twentieth century — was dominated by Asians. 'The key regional driver of New Zealand's migration system has become Asia, especially the countries of China, India, Korea (ROK) and, since the mid-2000s, the Philippines.'[13] Until 1995, when the law changed again, the proportion of Asian immigrants continued to climb. Between 1991 and 1994, 54.2 per cent of New Zealand's 69,090 approved immigrants were of Asian birth.[14] Most were either young, educated, middle-class professionals, or 'urban entrepreneurs and technocrats' from Hong Kong, Taiwan, Malaysia and Singapore who, as business migrants, brought money and skills.[15] Writing in 1994, Prime Minister Bolger proclaimed: 'we are deliberately adding an Asian dimension to all our thinking. We are quite deliberately adding an Asian strand to our national identity.'[16] The momentum slowed down after a 1995 law change (see below) but picked up again in 2001, due to an easing of the 1995 restrictions. In 2002, 54 per cent of new resident approvals were for Asians, with a large majority from China (PRC) and India. At the same time, 64,000 temporary work permits and 78,000 student visas were approved, awarded mostly to Chinese or Indians. Between 2002 and 2009, Asian citizens accounted for over 900,000 (51 per cent) of all those approved for residence, study or work.[17]

About 80 per cent of immigrants settled in Auckland, reshaping the demographic profile and cultural geography of New Zealand's largest city.[18] In 2001, one in every eight Aucklanders was of Asian ethnicity. Eighty-one per cent of these populations were born overseas.[19] By 2006, Asian people made up 18.6 per cent of Auckland's population, compared to 9.0 per cent for the whole country.[20]

Initially, many of these asset-rich Chinese (mainly Taiwanese) migrants settled in affluent areas such as the North Shore, Epsom, Remuera and Pakuranga–Howick.[21] A 1996 *North & South* article by Nicola Legat captured the ambience of one of these new suburbs:

> ... there is an extraordinary new subdivision named Howick Park ... construction sites are bustling with New Zealand builders and tradesmen. The houses are colossal and almost exclusively built in a curious design hybrid which combines the 1950s brick and tile bungalow with the Southern antebellum mansion ... 75 percent of the buyers are Asian and all design-and-build houses are constructed according to the precepts of *feng shui* ...
>
> Also ... there is an extraordinary new shopping centre ... [where] the businesses ... are almost exclusively Asian ... The whole shopping centre is, in fact, like a slice of Hong Kong — newer, cleaner and more spacious certainly, but with the smells and sounds of Hong Kong nevertheless.[22]

As more, less affluent Asian immigrants arrived, they settled throughout Auckland, clustering in middle/lower-priced suburbs such as Mt Roskill, Mt Albert and North Shore City. Indians concentrated in Mt Albert and Mt Roskill, as well as around Manukau City, and large concentrations of Chinese (and some Indian) students resided in or near the central city, drawn by the proximity of the language schools and tertiary institutions.[23]

A new environment
Many immigrants, both skilled and unskilled, encountered (and continue to encounter) ongoing difficulties adjusting to their new environment and being

accepted by locals. A young Asian blogger living in Christchurch recently complained:

> People remind me I'm an outsider when they look at my skin colour and a) assume I'm illiterate or b) tell me to go home. A teacher of mine once asked my mother if she knew what algebra was. My mother is capable of teaching Year 13 calculus and that teacher had trouble with long division.[24]

Business migrants who came to New Zealand after the 1987 Immigration Act often found it difficult to set up the same profitable enterprises they ran in their home country. David Chen, a Taiwanese migrant to Wellington, commented that New Zealand government agencies were not forthcoming with information, even when asked: 'We knew little about New Zealand's business environment. Consequently, we encountered many problems in our first few years.' Although his business eventually succeeded, he noted this was not the case for many of his compatriots. Some became what was popularly known as 'astronauts', returning to their home countries to work while their families remained in New Zealand:

> Unfortunately, many were misinformed or received little information on the business and professional environment in New Zealand prior to their emigration. Hence when they arrived in New Zealand they were disillusioned by the lack of opportunities and the many barriers in their business or professional pursuit. It is often the last resort for them to leave their family behind and return to Taiwan to conduct their business or professional career.[25]

Highly qualified young Asians arrived in the country expecting to attain good jobs only to find their qualifications not recognised, or employers who asked for New Zealand experience. One young Indian immigrant reported:

> Many young well-educated Indians have come expecting to find jobs immediately and been disappointed . . . Some have gone back to India within a month because they are not able to handle the pressure and the feeling of rejection. They go and knock at every door and no one wants them.[26]

Getting interviewed often proved problematic. An American-trained senior banker reported that she would have been happy with 'a smaller job', but even that proved impossible to find: 'at first I thought it wouldn't be too difficult, to find just a small job, not a high-level one like the one I held in Taiwan . . . I didn't know that when they heard a foreign accent on the phone, they would refuse me right away.'[27] Employers were also apparently put off by a foreign-sounding name on a CV. Using a more English- or Kiwi-sounding name could work wonders. One young Asian woman recalled: 'I had always suspected there was a problem; but then I got my proof. I sent in two copies of my CV, one with my actual (very ethnic sounding) name and the other with the most typical kiwi [sic] name I could think of, Sarah Smith. Sarah Smith got short-listed almost every time, but I never got a call using my own name.'[28] After graduating from Auckland with a first-class Master's degree in Politics, and applying for 175 jobs, Malaysian-born New Zealand-educated Yik Kun Heng decided to go to Hong Kong. While all his classmates with English names secured jobs quickly, he received just three interviews, none of which resulted in work. Despite being counselled by a career advisor to change his name, he refused because:

> That's too much of an ask for anyone. It's almost like you have to give up your identity, everything you are as a person, your history, just to secure a job and pay cheque. No one should have to fight that hard to get a pay cheque, and that's just a job. To get a career, what am I going to have to do?[29]

As a result of these employment difficulties, young Asians, although possessing the highest tertiary qualifications, had (and continue to have) a higher unemployment rate than all other migrant groups entering New Zealand. They are 'repeatedly shown to be at a disadvantage in gaining employment compared with NZ-born job applicants'.[30] Although most eventually find employment, it is not always commensurate with qualifications and experience.[31]

While many Asian immigrants face difficulties on arrival — finding work, being accepted into a community, adapting to a different culture, becoming proficient in English — most eventually overcome these challenges. The Park family, for example, migrated to Christchurch from Seoul in 1993. After initially finding the city lonely and difficult, they finally landed good jobs and began to enjoy a busy social life in a supportive community. They credited their ability to 'settle into life' in their new country to 'the general friendliness and acceptance of New Zealanders'.[32] Kanchana (an IT specialist) and Shalini Wickramasinghe (a doctor) from Sri Lanka both quickly found good jobs, made friends and encountered no discrimination. Indeed, the hospital where Shalini works is multicultural, with 32 languages spoken among the staff, and 'everybody mixes easily'.[33] Even for those lucky migrants who experienced few difficulties finding a job or making new friends, however, immigrating to New Zealand involved a steep learning curve, adjusting to a new culture and way of life. In the mid-1990s, those newcomers suffering from feelings of displacement or alienation faced a new, overt level of discrimination, as some articles in the popular press began to take a critical view of Asian migrants. At the same time, the opposition to Asian immigration central to the political platform of New Zealand First leader, Winston Peters, began to attract both media attention and a receptive audience.

'Inv-Asian' backlash

In 1992, New Zealand polls started to show public attitudes about Asian immigration moving away from initial enthusiasm toward a more negative view. Opposition was particularly prominent among the less educated and older sections of the population.[34] In April 1993, the issue exploded into the public arena when a feature article entitled 'Inv-Asian' in Auckland's *Eastern Courier* proclaimed: 'whichever way you look at it, New Zealand has had/has got/will have problems of Asian migration . . .' The article proceeded to present a stereotypical view of Asian migrants: they were materialistic, lived in ostentatious houses, pushed up house prices in Auckland's eastern suburbs, drove fancy European cars, and educated their children at the New Zealand taxpayer's expense while intending to return to their country of origin. New Zealand was losing its British cultural and economic heritage and becoming an Asian country: 'What lies behind the image of crowds of Asian children coming out of the best schools, the buying of expensive homes, slow erratic drivers in big new Mercedes and migration figures which suggest Auckland is becoming the Taipei/HongKong/Seoul of the South Pacific?'[35]

A public debate ensued, which exposed some strong anti-Asian feelings, particularly in Auckland, where the majority of new immigrants settled. The Asian community responded with letters to the editor, opinion pieces and follow-up articles expressing hurt and dismay at the racism expressed. The Chinese in Auckland held a political rally requesting explanations from Members of Parliament, and laid a complaint with the Race Relations Conciliator.[36]

In the lead-up to the 1996 election, Winston Peters and the newly formed New Zealand First Party sensed an opportunity to tap into public concern about immigration, particularly from Asia. In February, he launched an attack in Howick, (nicknamed 'Chowick'), the heart of Auckland's Asian community. Peters criticised 'the rows of ostentatious homes in this very suburb, occupied in some cases by children whose parents have no ties to this country', and questioned the loyalty of immigrants who, after having 'milked New Zealand's resources' and educated their children here, returned home. Instead of the 50,000 plus (60 per cent of whom were of Asian origin) who entered New Zealand the previous year, New Zealand First promised to allow only 10,000 specially vetted immigrants annually.[37] Over the next months, Peters travelled the country expounding his 'shape up or ship out' immigration policy. He highlighted problems caused by Asian gangs, absent parents, language difficulties, lack of cultural assimilation, and Asians buying up New Zealand assets, promising: 'migrants who don't fulfil their commitments to this country will be sent home . . .'[38] The effect was immediate and augured electoral success for Peters. His party's popularity in the opinion polls skyrocketed from 6 per cent in January 1996 to 30 per cent in May.[39]

Several editorials, columns and feature articles criticised Peters' views and highlighted the positive aspects of Asian immigration. Some Maori, however, shared his belief that Asian immigration would depress their socio-economic position. Ranginui Walker, a senior University of Auckland academic and former chair of the New Zealand Maori Council (1974–1990), for example, predicted that New Zealand's 'policy of easy access'[40] would have a damaging impact on crime and Maori unemployment: '[Maori] will be even more marginalised by bringing in skilled and business immigrants. Working-class Pakeha will share the same fate.'[41] Walker depicted open immigration policies as part of a government plot to dilute Maori influence:

> Although its primary rationale is economic, the government's immigration policy must be seen for what it is, a covert strategy to suppress the counter-hegemonic struggle of the Maori by swamping them with outsiders who are not obligated to them by the treaty.[42]

News of New Zealand's anti-Asian sentiment featured in the international press. Under the title 'Barren Times for Race Relations', *Time* magazine wrote about the 'envy of the status and wealth of many of the migrants that is leading to friction in middle New Zealand'. The article also claimed that many New Zealanders found Asian students' high academic achievements threatening.[43] The *Wall Street Journal* devoted an editorial to this subject, describing Peters' policies as 'the modern face of anti-immigrant discrimination', while the *China Daily*, the *South China Morning Post* and the *Outlook* in India all criticised the formation of an anti-immigration, anti-Asian political party.[44]

Although support for New Zealand First had decreased to 14.4 per cent by the election, it won all the Maori seats, held the balance of power, and negotiated a coalition deal with Bolger's National Party.[45] The anti-Asian immigration issue died down after the election, however, because in 1995, before the election campaign, National announced a more restrictive immigration policy that included an English language bond requirement. As Asians constituted the majority of immigrants from non-English-speaking countries, their numbers fell significantly.[46]

For the many Asians already happily settled in New Zealand the racist views expressed during 1996 were troubling and hurtful. The Lin family, for example, who migrated to Christchurch in 1990, set up a successful business and worked hard to gain acceptance, found the onslaught from New Zealand First unsettling. In Grace Lin's view, Peters had awakened the prejudices of New Zealanders: 'I like it here but sometimes I am not very happy because I feel a lot of Kiwis are not kind or nice any more. The feeling was good before, but not now . . .'[47] Robert Hum, an LSE-trained accountant, responded to Peters' attacks by forming an ethnically based political party to contest the 1996 election. This stood eleven candidates and received 0.12 per cent of the vote.[48] Singapore hotel tycoon Ow Chio Kiat, whose company bought Auckland's Regent Hotel, declared he would not have made that investment had he known of Peters' views: 'If at any time I feel our presence is not welcome, we will be quite happy to pull out. I am taken aback that such views can be bandied around. Nowhere else in the world have I come across them.'[49] In fact, like Peters, the Australian Liberal politician Pauline Hanson was gaining media attention and a growing number of supporters at this time by raising objections both to immigration, particularly Asian, and to government support for aboriginal rights.

During the 2002 election campaign, Peters, whose popular support had withered in the intervening period, once again embraced an anti-immigration platform. Inveighing against policies that allowed 'any Tom, Dick, Harry, Mustaq or Bin Laden who wants to come here',[50] he accused immigrants of causing everything from traffic gridlocks to pushing up house prices and inflation, to bringing in AIDS and other infectious diseases.[51] He also claimed new migrants were pushing Maori to the bottom of the heap. His speech 'Immigration or You', delivered to Te Tai Tokerau Maori at Otiria marae at Moerewa, played on Maori fears of displacement:

In New Zealand we have to be careful to preserve our unique society . . . We place our country at risk by bringing in thousands of people whose views are formed by alien cultures and rigid religious practices . . . We also have to ask ourselves how our society will look in the future as a result of these policies and most of all, Maori — the first settlers of this country — have to ask themselves the hard question about where they will fit into the picture.[52]

Peters' 2002 anti-immigration campaign had two catalysts. First was what he described as 'the stupidity of Helen Clark taking more than 140 so-called refugees off the *Tampa*', a Norwegian fishing vessel carrying Afghani asylum seekers, after Australia denied it permission to enter her territorial waters in 2001.[53] The second was a recent surge in immigration from Asia. In 1998, in response to a sharp fall in the number of immigrants between 1996 and 1998, National again changed immigration criteria to attract skilled immigrants. As a result, residence approval (52,856) combined with student or temporary work visas saw immigration to New Zealand reach an unprecedented high in 2002 and 2003.[54]

This time, however, the media almost universally condemned Peters' anti-immigration stance, and his views did not translate into election success. He gained only 4.0 per cent of the vote, down 10.2 per cent from his 1999 result.[55] Since the 1996 election campaign, public attitudes towards Asians had generally grown more favourable. Media coverage became more balanced and nuanced, with reports, editorials and opinion pieces highlighting the Asian community's important contributions to New Zealand's economy and society.[56] There were a few exceptions to this more positive attitude, however, most notably a 2006 *North & South* article by Deborah Coddington, a former list MP for the conservative ACT Party.

This feature article, 'Asian Angst: Is it time to send some back?', maintained that 'the Asian menace has been steadily creeping up on us . . . In less than two decades criminal behaviour among Asian immigrants has gone from a few uppity wealthy boy racers to highly organised and ruthless criminals seemingly prepared to do anything for big profit.' Coddington claimed that Asian immigrants cheated New Zealand's health system, abused legal aid, and brought diseases such as TB into the country. Murders, domestic violence, student P pushers, kidnapping and violent robbery were all becoming almost daily events amongst the Asian community. Well-organised Asian gangs peddled drugs, poached paua, and ran prostitution, extortion, gambling, loan sharking and fraud operations, while Asian counterfeiters busily created false passports, immigration documents, diplomas, driver's licences, birth, marriage and divorce certificates, and 'even mobility parking permits . . . disquiet grows in heartland New Zealand about the quality of migrants we're letting through the door'.[57]

The piece evoked outraged responses from various correspondents, bloggers and academics, both Asian and European.[58] Grant Hannis (journalism lecturer, Massey University), Charles Mabbett (media advisor, Asia:NZ) and Tze Ming Mok and eighteen others (fifteen of whom were Asian) laid complaints with the Press Council criticising Coddington's selective use of statistics and her discriminatory language. Upholding the complaints, the Council deemed that Coddington had misused statistics and used 'emotionally loaded language'.[59]

The various Asian communities in New Zealand worked actively from the late twentieth century onwards to improve contemporary perceptions of Asia and Asian migrants. An increasing number of Asian MPs and journalists, as well as newspapers and proactive national and community organisational structures, all played a part in this process. In the 1990s (and since), several community organisations were founded to offer cultural, economic and social support to new immigrants. By facilitating integration, establishing links with non-Asian community groups, organising conferences to increase awareness of Asian issues among the wider public, and speaking out in the interests of their communities, these groups played, and still play, an important role in assimilating and raising the Asian profile within New Zealand.[60]

The government too, anxious to foster links with Asia, and to increase public understanding of its diverse cultures, set up the public–private Asia New Zealand Foundation (Asia:NZ) in 1994. With extensive offerings including conferences, seminars, educational programmes, internships, inter-country exchanges, special events, research, arts and community grants to individuals and community groups, along with the research and publication of articles, books and pamphlets, the Foundation helps New Zealanders to 'connect and forge links with Asian counterparts and wider Asian communities'.[61]

In the early years of the twenty-first century, New Zealand's Asian population continues to exert a significant cultural and economic impact.[62] New Zealanders' eating habits, for example, now reflect a strong Asian influence, with Asian restaurants, food retailers and supermarkets flourishing throughout the country. Sports popular among Asian communities, such as table tennis and badminton, are also thriving,[63] as are all manner of business, cultural, educational, trading, social and tourist links between Asia and New Zealand. In the 1940s, New Zealanders viewed Asia and Asians with suspicion; now more than 70 per cent of the public regard the Asian region as significant for the country's future.[64] New Zealand businesses realise the potential of establishing a presence in Asia, and Asian New Zealanders have developed profitable trading and investment links with their homelands. China is now the country's biggest trading partner and an important source of foreign investment, while Korea, Japan, Singapore Malaysia and Thailand are amongst its top ten trading partners.[65] Tourism from and to Asia expands yearly, and New Zealand has joined a growing number of pan-Asian economic and cultural organisations. The expanding New Zealand Asian population is predicted to reach 15.8 per cent of the total population by 2026.[66]

Polynesian explosion

As noted in earlier chapters, from the 1950s onwards, Pasifika people started migrating to New Zealand to fill the demand for semi- and unskilled labour in New Zealand's expanding secondary industries. Until the mid-1970s, when the economic boom slowed and unemployment grew, resulting in a government clampdown on immigration, the ethnic population from the Pacific Islands in New Zealand swelled. In 1945, it was 2159; by 1966, it was 29,000; by 1971, the figure was in excess of 40,000, half of whom were Samoan and 30 per cent from the Cook Islands.[67] Immigration virtually halted between the mid-1970s, and the early 1980s.[68] New Zealand's Pasifika population nevertheless continued to climb, largely due to a high fertility rate. Between 1984 and 1989, the total New Zealand population increased by 11 per cent, while the Pasifika population grew by 33 per cent from 167,070 to 231,798.[69] By 2001, the percentage of the population of Pacific descent in New Zealand was 6.46, up from 3.07 in 1981. With 60 per cent born here and a median age of 21 years as opposed to 35 years for the total population, the Pasifika population was both youthful and rapidly expanding. By 2006, it comprised 6.9 per cent of the total New Zealand population, with over two thirds (67 per cent) living in Auckland, giving that city the largest Pacific population in the world.[70] The resident Pacific community's impact on New Zealand's cultural, social and economic life, like its numbers, continues to expand.

Spiritual and social support: community churches

Pacific Island churches have played, and still play, a pivotal role in providing spiritual and social support to both recent immigrants and long-established Pasifika New Zealand families. For new immigrants, the church community replaced the old home village community, becoming the centre where old and young, new and established Pasifika people could meet and socialise, worship and seek advice and assistance in their own languages. For lonely newcomers especially, the local church eased the transition into an often-bewildering new society. Sarona Meata'a Aiono-Iosefa's family, for example, one of very few of Pacific Island descent in Christchurch in the late 1960s, found in their church a familiar and comforting support:

> For our secondary schooling we attended Burnside High School . . . My brother, sister and I made up one of the only two Samoan families at Burnside; the Siaves and the Aionos — that was us . . . Life for us, and other Pacific Island families in Christchurch at the time revolved around school and church. Today I can appreciate that the church was the support network that helped my dad through his mundane factory and cleaning jobs, and church helped Mum overcome suburban isolation.[71]

The seeds of the largest Pasifika church, The Pacific Islanders' Congregational Church (PICC), were sown in 1943, when a certain Reverend Walsh began to provide services for Cook Islanders and Niueans in the Beresford Street Congregational Church in Freemans Bay. From these small beginnings, the multi-ethnic, multicultural Pacific Islanders' Congregational Church grew, establishing congregations and forming parishes throughout New Zealand.[72] An associated theological college, established in 1951 in Auckland, trained Pacific Islanders to minister to Pacific settlements in towns, villages and rural areas such as Tokoroa, Mangakino, Rotorua, Porangahau, Hastings, Wellington and Christchurch. Services were first held in members' houses until congregation numbers expanded sufficiently to form parishes and hold formal church services.

Unlike the ethnic-specific churches that emerged later on, 'the PICC emphasis was on Pacific solidarity and the PIs working together . . . The PICC and other churches became the home, community, source of identity and solace for many PI families as they are today.'[73] (The only Pacific group not to join the PICC were the Tongans, as they formed their own Tongan Methodist Church.) Because the PICC expanded so quickly, the parent body, the Congregational Union of New Zealand (CUNZ), was unable to continue its support and assistance. Consequently, in 1972, the church merged with the much larger Presbyterian Church of New Zealand to become the Pacific Island Presbyterian Church (PIPC). Regardless of religious affiliation, the PICC church became the meeting place for new and old immigrants, in search of a social and spiritual life among fellow Pacific people. One young woman recounted:

We were Catholics but before the Samoan Catholic Chaplaincy in Auckland was formed, we had two choices. We could go to the local, mainly Palagi Catholic church where services were in English, or walk across town to the PICC where we found people we knew and services in our language. So, every Sunday we dressed and walked across town to the PICC and then turned around and walked home — high heels and all. It took most of the day but it was worth it to meet our own people and new arrivals who seemed to turn up every week.[74]

Within the church, each ethnic group operated more or less autonomously, retaining its own language and cultural traditions, holding services in its own language and later creating its own pre-school language nests. One Wellington PICC congregation member recollects: 'I remember PICC was Sundays spent listening to sermons first in English, then in Cook Island [sic] Maori and then sometimes in Samoan . . . long, long services.'[75]

The PICC, and the later established ethnically based Polynesian churches, all formed their own sports teams, counselling services, Bible classes, Sunday schools, youth groups, music groups, mothers' groups and social clubs which embraced the whole family. Public and religious holidays were celebrated with large gatherings which involved the whole community in a day of sports competitions, entertainment, socialising and eating: 'PICC was the New Year's day [sic] kilikiti match at Kilbirnie Park: teams of over 80, singing, dancing and whistle blasts, potato salad, hams, chicken and chop suey.'[76] Women's groups ran social services that included visiting the elderly and sick and supporting new immigrants with food, clothing and information.[77] Most churches also provided comprehensive advice and assistance on tax, employment, housing, budgeting and legal matters. Reverend Lagi Fatatoa Sipeli, born in Niue, described the role of a pastor in the PICC during the 1960s and 1970s:

In Niue, the role of the pastor is to perform the sacrament and to take other services. Here the role of the minister is much wider than that. He becomes a jack-of-all-trades, he looks after the social needs of the people. He helps people to get employment, he helps people to get transport from one point to another: all that is very important to a newcomer.[78]

As other denominations — such as Catholic, Mormon, and Seventh-day Adventists — established churches in New Zealand for their Pacific congregations, the growth of the PICC slowed, although it still retains the largest congregation.[79] In the 1960s, a group of Samoans, wanting to maintain the traditions and language of their homeland, and to 'preserve indigenous forms of Christianity', broke away from the PICC to form the Samoan Congregational Christian Church, which became known as Ekalesia Fa'apotopotoga Kerisiano Samoa (EFKS), or in English the CCCS. New congregations formed rapidly: by 1994, there were 51 EFKS churches dotted throughout New Zealand.[80] More recently, many younger New Zealand-born Pasifika people who find the values and practices preached by the traditional Pacific churches too prescriptive have switched to the Pentecostal charismatic movement. Academic Jemaima Tiatia, writing of the friction between the generations, has pointed out that 'the church itself has been an issue, where the youth find that the services are too monotonous and reflective of the ways of the "homeland". Whilst this primarily satisfies island-born members, it in turn alienates those who are born in New Zealand.'[81]

Breaking down fences: PACIFICA

Many Pacific Island women arrived in New Zealand in the 1960s and 1970s with little or no English, and little understanding or knowledge of the culture and ways of their new country. Having no social networks, they often became isolated in suburbs while their husbands went out to work and their children to school. Moreover, local bodies and governments made little or no provision to identify and include Pacific Island needs into health education and social policies. Aware of these problems, and keen to find a solution, in 1976 Samoan-born Eletino Paddy Walker launched PACIFICA, a national group to meet and promote the specific needs of Pacific women in New Zealand.[82] In the words of former PACIFICA national president, Tepaeru Tereora: 'We wanted to break down some of the invisible fences between us and create a rippling effect of friendship within the Pacific community.'[83] Jacinta Underhill, a founding member, remembers that when she and her husband Jack first arrived in Porirua in the 1960s, there were no community amenities, no churches, and few shops and schools: 'We PI families made our own community, and we had to start with quite basic things such as learning how to cook using an electric stove, how flush systems worked and what vegetables to grow.'[84]

PACIFICA also sought to create closer communication between Island and European women, and aimed to give Pacific women a voice, a sense of identity, and a forum in which to articulate and advance their needs. At the time of its launch in 1976, Paddy Walker explained: 'Our aim is to create opportunities for Pacific Island women so that they can play a more meaningful role in society. We want to become a more organised voice — for too long we have been left on the periphery.[85] Once the organisation was formally inaugurated in 1977, it grew quickly to 28 branches all over New Zealand. By 1992, it had 33 branches and 1000 members.[86] It set up play groups, health centres and advisory centres where families could find help with their problems — budgeting, housing, filling out forms, dealing with government departments and so on. Educational programmes and scholarships were progressively set up.[87] Politicians, belatedly recognising the need to involve Pacific peoples in the formation of policy formulation and implementation of policies concerning their welfare, started consulting with or co-opting members onto local health, education and social welfare boards. To ensure Pacific women's concerns were heard, and their programmes promoted, PACIFICA formed links with the Ministry of Pacific Island Affairs and the Ministry of Women's Affairs, along with several other national and international organisations.[88]

Young PACIFICA branches were started, and to give younger New Zealand-born Pacific women a voice, a young representative was appointed to the national council. As a result, the organisation has retained its strength and unity, with a large membership of Pacific women from all ages and walks of life. Samoan-born Agnes Mary Eti Ivala Laufiso (third national president of PACIFICA) believes that: '[PACIFICA] was one of the most encouraging developments for Pacific Islanders in New Zealand. Nowhere was there a place where Pacific Islanders could get together to discuss their lives and the things that were happening to their families in a way that was so positive.'[89] Unfortunately, despite the existence of such organisations, and the ongoing support and spiritual solace provided by various churches, the economic and social reforms of the 1980s and 1990s had a dramatic impact on the wellbeing of many Pasifika people in New Zealand.

Disadvantage, discrimination and identity

During the restructuring of the 1980s and 1990s, Maori and Pasifika people in semi- and unskilled labouring jobs were particularly vulnerable to restructuring and lay-offs. With larger families to feed, house and educate, as well as family and church obligations, many Pacific Island families struggled to survive the hard times. Between 1986 and 1991, their employment rate plummeted from 62 to 43 per cent.[90] By 2001, this rate had recovered to 55 per cent but still remained considerably lower than the 1986 rate. Unemployment rates remain higher than those for the total population. In 2010, for example, when national unemployment reached 6.8 per cent, the rate for Pasifika people rose to 14.1 per cent.[91] Although more Pasifika people are acquiring skills and tertiary qualifications, many still work in low-paid, unskilled labouring jobs and this leaves them vulnerable in times of economic downturn.[92]

The fact that, like Maori, the Pasifika population features disproportionately in crime statistics is linked to unemployment and economic disadvantage. Young Pasifika people, who are particularly affected by unemployment — their rate was 37.6 per cent for 15–19-year-olds and 21.5 per cent for 20–24-year-olds in 2001[93] — also feature strongly in crime statistics with higher rates of conviction and prosecution than the total population, particularly for violent offences.[94] Many disaffected Polynesian youths living in crowded conditions in poor neighbourhoods such as Otara and Mangere have joined gangs, which can often lead to involvement in crime. In the 1990s, South Auckland youth street gangs started to appear, modelled on and named after US street gangs such as the Crips and the Bloods. By 2006, there were about 73 such gangs in South Auckland.[95]

Counties Manukau has a youthful population, a high proportion of Maori and Pacific peoples, and areas of high economic deprivation. In Mangere, 56 per cent and in Otara, 69 per cent of residents identified themselves as Pacific people in the 2010 census. One of every three people living in Manukau City in 2001 lived in areas designated as decile 10 (the most deprived areas). In Otara, 94 per cent of people and in Mangere, 78 per cent of people are living in some of New Zealand's most deprived areas.[96]

Media have frequently dwelt on the criminal behaviour of new migrants from the Pacific Islands: negative or sensational media reports about 'overstayers' in the 1980s regularly featured Polynesians. At the same time, newspapers sometimes played a positive role, exposing discriminatory practices. In 1986, for example, the *Auckland Star* journalist David McLoughlin wrote a feature about racial discrimination in the Immigration Division of the Department of Labour. His findings, later verified by the Race Relations Office, revealed that although overstayers from other countries outnumbered those from the Pacific Islands, officials focused on the latter, who consequently comprised more than 80 per cent of those prosecuted. 'Pacific Islanders were one third of the average 10,000 overstayers in New Zealand, but 86 per cent of those prosecuted for overstaying.'[97] McLoughlin also criticised immigration officers' disrespectful attitudes when dealing with Pacific Islanders.[98]

In April of the same year a *Star* editorial asked: 'Does this country operate a clandestine "whites only" policy?' It went on to discuss the difficulties that an Indian and a Tongan family encountered trying to get visas to visit family in New Zealand, while those from Europe, the USA and Australia needed no visas. It concluded: 'Quite clearly the way we treat visitors depends very much on the country from which they come. The law may be equal but the policy is not.'[99] Writing in *North & South* in 1994, David McLoughlin again described the 'Immigration Service's shabby, racist treatment of Pacific Islanders and refugees . . . Immigrant applicants [from Pacific Island countries] are officially regarded as second-class human beings.' This article exposed a case where an alleged Samoan overstayer with six children, seven brothers and sisters and a mother living in New Zealand was detained for deportation. By contrast, a young German boy who stole from trampers in the Abel Tasman National Park was not deported. As the article pointed out: 'Almost every week the Immigration Service deports Samoans and Tongans who probably meet family and humanitarian criteria. If that happened to Britons or Americans or Germans, public opinion wouldn't stand for it.' On the other hand, the article described how easy it was for white South African immigrants to obtain residency visas. In comparison to Pacific Islanders and Asians, who often had to wait up to a year and undergo multiple interviews and checks, South Africans frequently gained approvals within a month with neither checks nor interviews. Moreover, they had the lowest rejection rate of any major immigrant group — only 6.7 per cent compared to 20 per cent for all immigrants.[100]

The print media's role in conveying negative stereotypes of Pacific people as 'criminals, overstayers, rapists, unemployed street brawlers' is illustrated by coverage of a murder in Otara on 30 April 1989. Initial newspaper reports about the incident, which involved Samoan youths killing a Tongan man and seriously injuring another, were inaccurate, and repeatedly highlighted the accused's ethnicity. Three days after the crime, Fetuli Ioane, a journalism trainee at Manukau Polytechnic, published an article entitled 'What Really Happened at Otara' disproving claims that the incident was a gang feud, or the consequence of a 'race war' between Samoans and Tongans.[101]

In response to yet another negative report written by the *Auckland Star* in April 1989, a young Pacific Islander wrote: 'We are doing well, we're not shouting about it. There are successful [Pacific Island] faces in New Zealand, faces white New Zealand won't always be able to ignore. These are the faces that will silence the generations, and yes, the racism.'[102] Media coverage frequently continued to emphasise the negative however. In 1989, the newly founded *Pasefika* magazine neatly summed up the situation: 'When the Pacific people have rejoiced, they have celebrated without a media presence; when they are sad, it has been at the centre of the public eye.'[103]

In contemporary New Zealand, while multiple articles highlight the growing social and health problems among the Polynesian community, few celebrate their successes, and those that do are generally about sports stars.[104] This negativity in the media influences public perceptions and attitudes towards Polynesian immigrants. Asian immigrants now receive less negative publicity than was the case in the 1990s, and public opinion toward them has accordingly grown more favourable. By contrast, public polls consistently show animosity toward Polynesian immigrants. Certain sectors of the public believe that Pasifika people have contributed to an increase in crime, are welfare dependents, abuse the health system, and are a drag on the economy.[105]

In response, Pasifika people in New Zealand are developing their own media and a growing number are training as journalists. Radio networks now transmit in various Pacific languages, and Radio New Zealand now has a number of weekly news/magazine programmes as well as daily news bulletins in several Pacific languages.[106] Pasifika faces appear more regularly on mainstream television, and the number of Pacific Island television programmes has also increased. Community newspapers, often running articles in several languages, have proliferated. The maxim 'We must bask in the glories of our children's achievements, we must celebrate the success of our brothers and sisters, and we must come together in times of sadness and be united', written by the magazine *Pasefika* in 1989, is being gradually more and more realised.[107]

Within Pasifika communities, difficulties often arise between the older generation, who continue to embrace traditional cultural values, and the younger New Zealand-born generation, whose values, identity and cultural preferences have been more influenced by their country of birth. Many young Pasifika people born in New Zealand no longer speak a Pacific language (53 per cent spoke one in 1996). Their church affiliation has fallen off, and they frequently challenge the influence and control of elders, as well as the traditional role of Pacific women. While Pacific Island parents often find they no longer enjoy the absolute control they had in their Island societies, many Pasifika people born in New Zealand struggle to find a cultural balance and sense of identity. Melani Anae's description of her identity struggles could apply to many New Zealand-born Pacific people:

I am — a Samoan, but not a Samoan . . .
To my 'aiga in Samoa, I am a *Palagi*,
I am — a New Zealander, but not a New Zealander . . .
To New Zealanders I am a 'bloody coconut' at worst, a 'Pacific Islander' at best
I am — to my Samoan parents, their child.[108]

Samoan lawyer Leatigagaeono Simative Perese attributes the high crime statistics to the real tensions many young 'PIs' feel between the traditional demands of their parents and contemporary New Zealand ways:

> The youth courts of New Zealand have become the coalface of PI young peoples' struggles with identity, poverty and a total lack of self-esteem and worth . . . I see conflicts of traditional versus contemporary, of self in a complex world and a conflict of membership . . . It is PIs' job as adults to help PIs believe in themselves, to inspire them with the vision that our early navigators instilled in us . . .[109]

A great many Pasifika people in New Zealand, however, have expressed their search for an identity through literature, music, art, theatre and film. The result has been an explosion of creativity over the last three decades.

A Pacific efflorescence

In the latter half of the twentieth century, a 'Pacific efflorescence'[110] put its stamp on New Zealand culture. Government, too, increasingly acknowledged the importance and potential of the country's young, expanding Pasifika population. In 1985, the Department of Internal Affairs established a Pacific Affairs Unit to monitor the handling of Pacific issues by other departments. In the same year, a Pacific Island Affairs Advisory Council was set up; and in 1990, a Ministry of Pacific Island Affairs was created to promote the cultural and economic development of Pacific peoples in New Zealand. By 2001, there were 84 early childhood centres teaching in a Pacific language throughout the country. Pacific/Polynesian studies formed part of school and tertiary curriculums, while Auckland's Pasifika Education Centre, operating since 1976, promoted learning for Pasifika people in the adult and community education sector. In 2004, the University of Auckland built a Fale Pasifika. A symbol of identity for Pasifika students and staff, it is the second-largest such structure in the world.

Members of New Zealand's Pasifika community are prominently involved in a wide range of contemporary artistic and cultural endeavours, from television and radio to literature, art and music. They have used these vehicles both to challenge the influence of traditional culture and to carve out new definitions of what it means to be Pasifika in New Zealand. Cluny Macpherson's description of how music has reflected and defined a distinctive Pasifika identity within New Zealand could apply to all the arts:

Music . . . allowed younger Pacific people to redefine what it meant to be a Pacific person in Aotearoa and to communicate these to large numbers of others in similar situations. They were able to reflect their urban, Pacific experience in Aotearoa in new musical forms and to communicate these to other young people in forms such as reggae and hip hop . . . the emergence of production companies, radio and television stations . . . ensured that their work was soon widely available. Many young Pacific people were able to listen to the music and to find in it confirmation that their experiences and feelings were shared by others.[111]

Popular musicians include (among many others) Scribe, Annie Crummer, Ardijah, Che Fu and Fat Freddy's Drop. In 1996, Teremoana Rapley, who is of Maori/Cook Islands/Kiribati descent, was voted the Recording Industry Association of New Zealand (RIANZ) top female vocalist. In 2009, Pasifika musicians scooped seven of the 22 awards at the Vodafone New Zealand Music Awards. Hip hop artists such as Dei Hamo, Ermehn, King Kapisi and Dawn Raid represent an 'urban Pasifika flavour'[112] that incorporates several ingredients, including Pacific history and culture and the hardships of contemporary life in urban Auckland. Hip hop artist King Kapisi, describing his rap album *Savage Thoughts* (2000), paid tribute to music's cultural and social importance:

Basically telling people not to forget their heritage and roots, and informing youths about the injustices done to our peoples. A nation's culture is being lost thru new influences. There needs to be more people that acknowledge our past.[113]

The hip hop impresario Phil Fuemana founded Urban Pacifika Records in 1990, the first record company owned and run by Pasifika people. Based in South Auckland and focusing on the Polynesian experience, it introduced the rest of New Zealand to the distinctive sound and character of Polynesian rap and R&B.

Urban Pacifika Records is based in the notorious badlands of Otara, in the heart of South Auckland . . . the Polynesian Capital of the World . . . The basic nature of determination against hardship is the spirit of Urban Pacifika Records . . .[114]

'How Bizarre', a song performed by the wittily named OTC (Otara Millionaires Club) with Phil's brother Pauly as lead singer, became not only the biggest-selling New Zealand record ever, but an international hit. Simon Grigg, who released the song, puts it success down to a distinct urban Pacific sound:

It's the classic Kiwi strum meets punk rock meets disco meets a South Pacific beach party meets classic soul meets reggae and everything in between. [Alan Jansson's] fusing of acoustic guitars with hip hop loops became a globally recognisable sound, and is quoted as an influence by a variety of artists around the world.[115]

Dawn Raid Entertainment, a Polynesian enterprise founded in Papatoetoe in 1996 by co-CEOs 'Brotha D' (Danny Leaoasavaii) and 'YDNA' (Andy Murnane) was named after the infamous dawn raids of the 1970s (see Chapter 8). For Brotha D, the name represented both a link with the past and a triumph over adversity:

Just a reminder to the younger generation, there was a time in our history this happened with the Muldoon government and all, we're survivors of the dawn raid days. We've all moved on . . . Look at us now. We're successful.[116]

The Dawn Raid label has signed some of the country's biggest-selling, award-winning hip hop, rap, R&B and soul artists including Savage, Aaradhna, Monsta, Deceptikonz, Adeaze, Mareko and others. It started its own clothing label and retail stores, and set up a musical educational pro-gramme in South Auckland through the Dawn Raid Community Trust. Its two 'StR8 from the Streetz' compilation albums showcased the musical talents of young South Auckland teens from disadvantaged backgrounds.[117] After some financial wobbles in 2007, John Barnett, of South Pacific Pictures, and Michael Stiassny bought the business and have continued to promote Polynesian talent throughout New Zealand and across the globe.[118]

Since the 1970s, Pasifika prose and poetry writers have created what Paul Millar has described as 'a vibrant new literature that more accurately represents New Zealand's position as a South Pacific Nation.'[119] In a series of poems entitled *Sanctuary of Spirits* (1963), Alistair Te Ariki Campbell, of Cook Islands Maori and European descent, was one of the first to 'breach the barrier' and explore his Polynesian culture and history.[120] In prose fiction, Albert Wendt's seminal *Sons for the Return Home* (1973) explored the complexities of the migrant Pasifika experience and search for identity in urban New Zealand. Questions of iden-tity also feature in the work of the celebrated Niuean artist, poet and novelist John Pule: 'My heart and thoughts were always on Niue. But here I was living in Aotearoa on someone else's land. Writing helped change me, painting helped change me . . . We go back home with our Nikes and our jeans and we think we know things. But the local people just think we're stupid.'[121] Pule published his first poetry collection *Sonnets to Van Gogh and Providence* in 1982 and his first novel *The Shark that Ate the Sun (Ko E Mago Ne Kai E La)* in 1992. Among contemporary Pasifika poets, one of the most acclaimed, Selina Tusitala Marsh, is of Samoan, Tuvalu, English and French descent. The first Pacific Islander to graduate with a doctorate of English from the University of Auckland, she is now an academic, a charismatic performance poet, and an important new voice in Pasifika literature. Her *Fast Talking PI* collection of poems won the 2010 NZSA Jessie Mackay Best First Book Award for Poetry in 2010.[122]

Theatre, film and television have also been important mediums for conveying Pasifika culture, social issues and life stories. In the last three decades, numerous plays have used both drama and humour to describe Pasifika experience in New Zealand. Many have toured the country and in the process raised public awareness about this aspect of the country's multicultural heritage.[123] Auckland's Pacific Theatre, established in 1987, provided fledgling Pasifika playwrights, actors and directors with an opportunity to prove their creative talents and gave Auckland audiences an insight into Pacific culture. In Christchurch, the Pacific Underground theatre group, established in 1994, helped foster the careers of some of New Zealand's most talented Pasifika actors and musicians. Among them is the actor, writer and comedian Oscar Kightley, who in 1996 wrote, with Simon Small, *Fresh off the Boat*. This play, which explored the dreams, challenges and realities of Samoan immigrants adjusting to life in urban New Zealand, performed to sell-out audiences in New Zealand, Samoa and Australia. In 1998, Kightley helped found the Naked Samoans comedy group, and in 2004 was one of the creators of the popular animated television series *bro'Town*, about young Pacific Island schoolboys growing up in Auckland. Kightley has also maintained a long association with Pacific Underground, which performs an extensive repertoire of 'original plays about the Pacific experience in New Zealand'.[124]

Another talented Samoan New Zealander, Makerita Urale, wrote the landmark play *Frangipani Perfume* in 1997. First performed at BATS Theatre in Wellington and featuring an all-female cast, it examined the lives of three vital, energetic Samoan sisters making their way in New Zealand. Toa Fraser, of Fijian and British parentage, moved to Auckland from Britain in 1989. His plays *Bare* (1998) and *No. 2* (1999) won multiple awards, toured Australia and were performed at the Edinburgh Festival. *No. 2* was made into a successful film in 2006. Fraser co-wrote the screenplay (with Vincent Ward) for the 2005 film *River Queen*, and directed the 2008 film *Dean Spanley*, which starred New Zealand actor Sam Neill and veteran British actor Peter O'Toole.

In 1995, veteran film-makers and artists Don Selwyn and Ruth Kaupua-Panapa created an opportunity for young Pacific Island writers, actors and directors by developing a series of short films entitled *Tala Pasifika*. These films focused on family dynamics and explored the tension between 'the cultural practices and values of one's homeland [and] the accommodations that adopted countries impose'.[125] In 1996, Sima Urale (sister of Makerita and of the musician King Kapisi), whose first short films formed part of the *Tala Pasifika* series, made a short film called *O Tamaiti*. This powerful examination of the struggles experienced by a Samoan immigrant family in New Zealand won international acclaim and awards. Urale also won awards for her 1997 documentary *Velvet Dreams* and her short film *Still Life* (2001). The year 2006 saw the release of the popular feature film *Sione's Wedding*, a comedy written by Oscar Kightley and James Griffin and directed with visual flair by Chris Graham, whose frenetic music videos defined the aesthetic of the New Zealand hip hop boom in the early 2000s. Focused on the misadventures of four Samoan friends in central Auckland, the film had both a light subject matter and touch. For New Zealand's large Pasifika community, seeing itself reflected in a feature film was an important touchstone of cultural confidence.

In the visual arts, Pasifika artists such as Lily Laita, Andy Leleisi'uao, Lonnie Hutchinson, Ani O'Neill, Fatu Feu'u, John Pule, Niki Hastings-McFall, Michael Tuffery and Edith Amituanai are among New Zealand's foremost practitioners today. Art historian Michael Dunn has described painter Lily Laita (of Maori and Samoan descent) as New Zealand's finest expressionist since Philip Clairmont.[126] These artists' work, which varies immensely, employs various mediums and reflects different themes. For some, art is one of the threads linking them back to their homeland; for others, it is an exploration of family issues and the complexities of maintaining a dual cultural identity in New Zealand. The architectural theorist Albert Refiti has observed: 'The question of Pacific identity is a reality for many Pacific artists in the diaspora . . . Home now for the Pacific diaspora is less about the homeland of our ancestors than about a meshwork of complex knotted sites where lives and routes intersect.'[127] Tongan stone-carving artist Filipe Tohi, who migrated to New Zealand in 1978, explained that art offered a means of connecting with the past: 'I work in stone because it keeps me thinking about the past. It makes me think about home, it connects me.'[128] In the 1990s, Michel Tuffery's works of performance art were inspired by Pacific stories and examined the challenges brought about by contesting cultural values:

You know there's some of us who do live in cities but we've adapted in a different way and taken on different attitudes, and then you've got the ones who were born in the Islands and they've got their own attitudes . . . Sometimes they actually clash. And this is what this whole performance piece is about, it's like the clashing of two cultures.[129]

Traditional Pacific Island art forms have been maintained in New Zealand, but have also evolved and adapted over time. Items crafted by women as presentation gifts at ceremonial events, for a young woman's trousseau, or as tokens of affection and friendship continued to be made after migrating to New Zealand.[130] Groups such as the Waitakere Pacific Living Arts Group and the Tufuga Mataponiu a Niue keep traditional weaving, knitting, and sewing skills alive and teach them to the younger generation. Many of these groups started as a means of bringing isolated Pasifika women together. Niuean Lineaha Lind, a Niuean community coordinator, explained:

There needs to be this sort of environment, or our women would stay at home otherwise. With the group they can get together and share activities, share materials and share knowledge . . . I remember my mother . . . after the kids left home she was on her own and told to lock the door and not to open it to anyone. So we need something for the elderly . . . to get together to share jokes, stories and their grievances from their families.[131]

For the older generation, such groups offer a link to their homeland, and provide an environment where they can speak their own language and 'interact in culturally meaningful ways'.[132] Many groups have also begun to experiment with new materials and ideas and now produce a variety of innovative work that sells in boutiques, airport shops, art galleries and stores throughout New Zealand. Weavers of Tongan tapa cloth for example, who struggled to obtain the traditional bark for making the cloth, now use different types of cloth, dyes and material more readily available in New Zealand, and incorporate new designs that reflect a changed environment.

In common with many Maori artists, Pasifika artists in New Zealand such as Fatu Feu'u integrate traditional motifs into their work, while New Zealand artist Lester Hall transforms tapa cloths from the markets into modern contemporary artworks. Tapa designs decorate a wide variety of articles — from lampshades and ceramics to greeting cards, commercially printed fabrics and clothes. Tapa maker and weaver Maile Drake believes that the popularity of these designs and products reflects a growing Pacific cultural influence throughout New Zealand.[133] Many artists also incorporate and adapt other traditional methods from their Pacific homelands — such as weaving, sewing, knitting and crocheting. Ani O'Neill, for example, has created artwork that comments on social and environmental issues in New Zealand and in her native Cook Islands using traditional Cook Islands weaving, quilting, embroidery and crochet traditions.

Dance, an integral part of Pacific culture, continues to play a significant role among Pasifika communities throughout New Zealand. The sheer size of Polynesian school dance festivals testifies to its popularity with all New Zealanders. The annual 'Polyfest' (ASB Auckland Secondary Schools Maori and Pacific Islands Cultural Festival) is the largest Pacific dance festival in the world, drawing over 8000 participants and nearly 100,000 spectators.[134] 'Tu Tangata', the Wellington secondary schools' Polynesian festival, is equally popular, as is the Polyfest in Dunedin for Otago pre- and primary school pupils.

Contemporary dance companies Black Grace, founded by Neil Ieremia, and Mau, established by Lemi Ponifasio, each combine European modern dance with Pacific indigenous dance forms. Ieremia's motivation in forming his company was

> to give voice to some Pacific Island stories, things that affected my island community in particular . . . Most New Zealand dance, prior to 1995, was largely done by European women living in New Zealand and a few European males . . . I wanted to make it something I could identify with.[135]

Pacific festivals that showcase Pacific peoples' diverse engagement with the arts have grown exponentially since the 1990s. Auckland's Pasifika Festival, the Christchurch Pacific Arts Festival and the Positively Pasifika Festival in Wellington run over several days and bring together performers, spectators and stallholders from all over the Pacific and New Zealand.[136] Smaller festivals in provincial towns, like their big-city counterparts, nurture and develop Pacific cultural practices and attract spectators and performers from far and wide.

These and other artistic endeavours receive support from local councils, local arts infrastructure and funding bodies. For example, the Pacific Arts Committee, a subcommittee of Creative New Zealand, funds a number of Pacific initiatives, from community-based projects to a writers' residency in Hawaii and artists' residencies in the Cook Islands and Samoa. Tautai Contemporary Pacific Arts Trust (1995) runs workshops, arranges visits by

Pacific artists to schools and tertiary institutions, and finds mentors for aspiring young artists. Fresh Gallery Otara opened in 2006 to showcase young South Auckland artists; and mainstream dealer galleries, and national and local public galleries, frequently feature artists of Polynesian descent.[137]

The creativity of Pacific peoples in New Zealand has been fuelled by the complexities and dilemmas of maintaining identity within a dominant culture. At the same time, the efflorescence of Pasifika art and culture in recent decades has helped to increase the public's understanding of immigrants' experiences, and to recognise and take pride in the fact that New Zealand is a Pacific country that is enlivened and enriched by people from the various Pacific cultures.

Sport and belonging

As Pasifika sportspeople have become increasingly visible in national teams and individual events, sport has functioned both as a means of integration, bridging white and brown cultures, and as an expression of cultural and religious affiliations. The first wave of Polynesian immigrants in the 1950s quickly formed their own sports clubs and associations, which were generally structured around a church community. In 1953, for example, Reverend Tariu Teaia, pastor of the Wellington PICC, and his wife Mama Tangimetua formed the Pacific Islands Congregational Basketball (now Netball) Club (PIC). In 1998, PIC produced a book celebrating its forty-fifth anniversary, and its website proudly explained the club's ethos: 'Like those Pacific pioneers the Club comes from humble beginnings where the priority was fellowship and a shared cultural understanding of the world and one's place in it . . . PIC has forged a path that leads to success, fostered by a living Pacific spirit . . . We have built and maintain a strong extended family environment for all our members.'[138]

By the mid-1970s, PIC netball teams were winning national competitions and attracting the notice of national coaches. In 1975, Cook Islander Margaret Matenga became the club's first Silver Fern; the first in a long line of members who went on to play, captain or coach the national netball team. Many others have represented Wellington, Samoa and the Cook Islands. Although the club has become more multicultural, it still retains its Pacific cultural and religious identity. Club member and former captain and current Silver Ferns coach Waimarama Taumaunu explained: 'This club takes pride in pursuing excellence in netball whilst always maintaining its very strong Pacific and Church origins, and embraces the cultures of all its members. So within PIC you will find a whole range of relationships: friends, family, and future family.'[139]

Administered, promoted, coached and managed by Pacific women, the PIC remains a strong force in New Zealand netball.[140]

Early sports clubs such as the PIC helped foster a sense of common identity and community among various Pasifika cultures. They frequently held competitions, tournaments and sports days, often in conjunction with a major festival or community day. By joining a club, new immigrants struggling to integrate encountered a familiar culture, made friends and learned about Palagi life.[141] Takau Ariki Taru, for example, an honorary life member of the PIC, remembers that shortly after arriving in New Zealand she was living in Karori. She learnt about the PIC while attending church and promptly joined. Her three daughters later also became members.[142] Today, Pacific Island group networks are maintained through such clubs and 'new generations of New Zealand-born players maintain the rivalries of their parents' villages' — even if they have never set foot there.[143]

Sport also offered opportunities for Pacific Islanders to integrate and develop connections with mainstream New Zealand life and culture. Until the 1970s, they played in their own ethnic teams, which competed successfully in national and provincial sporting competitions. In the 1960s, for example, the New Zealand Samoan Society netball team consistently won the Auckland netball championship, while in the 1970s the Samoan (Ponsonby) rugby team topped the competition table. From the 1970s, however, these formerly separate entities started to be incorporated into national, provincial and local sporting teams. In the 1970s, Samoan, Tongan and Cook Islands ethnic teams became affiliated to the Ponsonby Rugby Club. Sean Mallon has written about how this legendary club was responsible for involving Pacific Island players in New Zealand rugby, helping them in the process to integrate more fully into New Zealand society at large. The club helped Pacific Island migrants find jobs and houses, involved them in the club organisation, and included them in a very active social life in which all cultures mixed.[144]

When Samoan team member Bryan Williams was picked for the All Blacks in 1970, Ponsonby club member Tumanuvao Alfred Tupu remembers: 'The interest from then on in our club was great. Even the young boys who had never heard of him came around and joined the club.'[145] Since that time, the presence of Pacific players in provincial and national teams has steadily grown. The winning Super 12 Auckland team of 1996 included six Samoans, three Tongans and two Fijians, one of whom — Joeli Videri — was named Super 12 Player of the Year. Some of the most celebrated All Blacks in recent times — including Jonah Lomu, Michael Jones, Va'aiga Tuigamala (commonly known as 'Inga the Winger'), Tana Umaga (the first of several Pasifika players to captain the All Blacks) — are of Pacific Island descent. In addition to being role models for young New Zealanders of all ethnicities, these and numerous other outstanding players from the Pasifika community have both encouraged young Pacific Islanders to play rugby and simultaneously evoked a sense of both national and community pride.[146] For Va'aiga Tuigamala, pride in being selected as an All Black went hand in hand with a celebration of his ethnic identity: 'The pinnacle of my life was being selected to play for the All Blacks. Whether you are Samoan, Palagi or Tongan, that is what every rugby player in New Zealand dreams about. But that doesn't mean I am less Samoan. I am proud to be Samoan.'[147] New Zealand-born Tana Umaga, too, highlighted the duality of his identity: 'I'm a New Zealander with Samoan parents . . . I'll never forget my culture, or my parents' background, and I am proud of all of that. I'll never forget the Samoan part of me . . .'[148]

As with male rugby players, netballers have celebrated their sporting success both as Pacific people and New Zealanders. Former Silver Fern Rita Fatialofa observed: 'You play for New Zealand but you're not entirely a Kiwi because you're Samoan, and you're not entirely Samoan because you're born here. So I say I'm a New Zealander, but I am also very proud to be Samoan.'[149] Since the 1970s, when Margaret Matenga's success as a Silver Fern inspired generations of young Pasifika girls to take up netball, the presence of Pacific Island players in national and provincial netball teams has grown rapidly. By 1993, nine of the 24 players in the Silver Ferns training squad were of Pacific Polynesian descent. In 2012, eight out of the sixteen players were of Pasifika or Maori descent.[150]

Many members of New Zealand's Pasifika community have also attained national and international recognition in individual sporting codes. For example, internationally ranked boxing professionals Jimmy Peau and David Tua follow a long tradition of Pacific Islanders' participation and success in the sport. Beatrice Faumuina and Valerie Adams have also earned national and international fame in discus and shot put respectively, with multiple world titles and Olympic gold medals. Faumuina, a four-time Olympian and New Zealand flag-bearer and team captain at the 2004 Athens Olympics, was made an Officer of the New Zealand Order of Merit in 2005 in recognition of her services to sport. Valerie Adams, also an Olympic champion, has been named Halberg Sportswoman of the Year seven consecutive times: 2006 to 2012.[151]

Television has helped to turn New Zealand's Pasifika athletes into household names. These sportspeople have 'transcended ethnic identities' to become 'the national face of individual sporting codes and of the sporting nation.[152] Among their local and ethnic communities, their successes generate both pride and a feeling of national inclusiveness. Tasileta Te'evale has argued that the Pacific peoples' contribution and influence in New Zealand sport goes beyond athletic prowess to the culture surrounding sport. 'At national secondary school sports competitions, for instance, a team will often bellow out a Pacific chant for their team. Words of prayers will be said as part of the team talk, Pacific challenges will be laid to [the] opposing team.'[153] Until stopped by administrators, Cook Islands drumming became a regular feature of Auckland Warriors rugby league matches. Now the team's promotional material contains a distinctive Samoan warriors' cry, heard in ceremonial dances. Even young male Palagi fans have started making the cry.[154] The journalist Tom Hyde maintains that sport has helped to bring different social, cultural and ethnic identities together, and that where 'politicians and the law still fail to bring us together, sport may be one of our last hopes'.[155]

Transnationalism, multiculturalism, globalism

In the nineteenth and early twentieth century, New Zealand's economic inter-ests and sense of national identity evolved and flourished within the context of the transnational British Empire, which answered its defence and diplo-matic needs. Contemporary New Zealand, while still an active member of the Commonwealth, has become more attuned to its status as a Pacific nation, one that now enjoys the economic and cultural benefits of a 'transnationalism of Pacific and Asian communities'.[156] The appointment in 2006 of Sir Anand Satyanand, New Zealand's first Governor-General of Asian-Pacific heritage, symbolised this evolution, which commenced in the latter decades of the twen-tieth century.[157]

Increasing globalisation of labour and capital markets has witnessed a shift away from Anglo-centric immigration policies; as a consequence, New Zealand now has a more Asian-Pacific profile. Former Labour Minister for Immigration David Cunliffe explained in 2005 that New Zealand's economy needed skilled immigrants: 'in a global race for talent and we must win our share'.[158] The Immigration Department endorsed this sentiment in 2012 by making the entry criteria easier for family members: 'New Zealand faces growing global competition for migrants with the skills we need to grow our economy. Being able to sponsor your parents to live here is important to help attract and retain skilled migrants . . . This will give New Zealand a competitive advantage in the international hunt for these highly skilled workers.'[159]

Almost every aspect of society bears witness to this multicultural shift. Ethnic restaurants, sushi, noodle and karaoke bars abound; in some Auckland suburbs, road signs are in Asian and English. Supermarkets and speciality shops offer all manner of Asian and Pasifika food and consumer goods. There are bilingual Christian churches, Sikh, Hindu, and Buddhist temples along with Muslim mosques nationwide; Chinese, Indian and Pasifika radio and television channels; and at least 20 Asian- or Pacific-language newspapers, mostly free and produced in Auckland.[160] Some cinemas specialise in Bollywood films, and an annual Asian film festival is a popular event in several urban centres. The Hindu Diwali Festival of Lights, the Chinese New Year, Pasifika festivals showcasing Polynesian arts and crafts, culture, food, music and dance, attract thousands of people. Multi-racial street markets also add colour and interest to urban life. The Otara market, in South Auckland, for example, is 'the biggest Polynesian market in the world', where Pacific Islands, Maori, Asian and Pakeha stallholders compete for business side by side and 'Indian and Chinese food stalls compete with stands selling coconut and pineapple buns and hot rewena bread'.[161]

At the same time, in addition to high immigration, New Zealanders continue to emigrate. Some 800,000 New Zealanders live overseas — over half of this number in Australia.[162] (Maori Australians, who in 2008 numbered some 100,000, are sometimes referred to as 'Maussies'.)[163] There is periodic concern about this ongoing outflow, both to Australia and elsewhere, but

> New Zealand has recently come to see this diaspora as an asset . . . transnational links are seen as important to New Zealand's benefit . . . state-sponsored transnationalism . . . seeks to network certain New Zealanders, and the communities they have established elsewhere, with a New Zealand homeland.[164]

Transnationalism and multiculturalism are part of a globalised twenty-first-century New Zealand economy and culture. A great many New Zealanders, not least those from Pacific and Asian communities, live highly mobile, transnational lives.

Between 2001 and 2006, Pacific immigration to New Zealand once again increased to a net gain of 15,898, but many more Pasifika people came to study, to visit relatives, or for temporary or seasonal work.[165] After spending years in New Zealand, some Pasifika people return to the Islands to develop business opportunities, reclaim familial land, or to retire. Many come and go on a regular basis. It is not uncommon for New Zealand-born Pasifika people to return to their ancestral homeland to find their roots, and some choose to remain there. Albert Wendt has described this search for home:

> [W]hen you don't belong completely to any culture . . . you will always be an out-
> sider and suffer from a sense of unreality . . . I know I can't live away from Samoa for
> too long. I need a sense of roots, of home — a place where you live and die. I would
> die as a writer without roots; but when I go home I'm always reminded that I'm an
> outsider, palangified (sic) [Europeanised].[166]

Many Pasifika New Zealanders move not just to or from the Pacific Islands to New Zealand, but to other countries where educational or work prospects seem better. Professor Epeli Hau'ofa has argued that in undertaking these migrations, Pacific peoples are only doing what they have always done, as they move

> by the tens of thousands, doing what their ancestors did in earlier times: enlarging
> their world as they go, on a scale not possible before . . . they strike roots in new
> resource areas, securing employment and overseas family property, expanding
> kinship networks through which they circulate themselves, their relatives, their
> material goods, and their stories all across their ocean.[167]

Facilitated by new transport and communication technologies, there is there-fore a continuous flow of money, information, culture and skills around the Pacific Rim as transnational Pasifika people circulate among and communicate with their extended networks and families.

Most Asian immigrants also retain strong connections with their home countries. Many visit on a regular basis, some remit money to their families, others return to their home country to work or to retire, while large numbers spend either short or extended periods of time between the two countries. They come and go for a wide variety of reasons, from work to changing family needs. In the case of the People's Republic of China (PRC), for example, many have been drawn back by that country's proactive search for 'overseas talents'. Taiwan successfully undertook the same process (effectively a reverse brain drain) earlier. Even so, most retain strong links with New Zealand, keeping in touch by email, internet and frequent visits. Many others consider returning when it is time to educate their children. For example, one top professional who returned to China for cultural reasons wanted to come back to New Zealand later because: 'My children are born in China . . . I want them to be educated with New Zealand values. In New Zealand I learnt that one of the goals in life should be to live happily, not just fulfilling duties and making money.'[168] All this coming and going creates important economic and social links between Asian countries and New Zealand, and plays an important part both in boosting tourism and attracting overseas students. These connections have resulted in an increasing number of small and large businesses with links in both countries.[169]

As a result of opening up immigration policies after 1987, New Zealand has one of the highest proportions of overseas-born residents as a percentage of total population of any country in the world.[170] It is one of the most diverse societies in the OECD, with over 200 ethnicities recorded in the last census. Almost 23 per cent of people living in New Zealand were born elsewhere and over 17 per cent speak two or more languages.[171] Multiculturalism has helped introduce the country to new opportunities in education, tourism, trade and commerce, and facilitated engagement with the global community. In the latter half of the twentieth century, the 'rope of peoples'[172] acquired more strands, and in the process a society that had formerly been proudly homogenous grew more ethnically diverse. New Zealand no longer perceives itself as a 'Britain of the South'. In the early twenty-first century it is a country made up of people from diverse cultures, one that is both economically and culturally engaged with its neighbours in the Pacific and Asia and with an increasingly globalised world.

CONCLUSION

The 'Earthly Paradise' Transformed

Simply by sailing in a new direction
You could enlarge the world.
— Allen Curnow, 1942[1]

In 1953, a British reporter covering the royal tour wrote a piece for the *Otago Daily Times* extolling New Zealand as a rather dull but in many ways enviable 'earthly paradise': 'New Zealanders have all but achieved the sort of State for which undoctrinaire people who are insecure or subject to injustice or without hope have always yearned. And if the result is a little unexciting and complacent, permeated by a sort of pleasant tedium, that is the unvarying characteristic of earthly paradise.'[2] The complacency the reporter observed resulted from a prosperous, secure way of life. With a paternalistic state attending to their basic needs, New Zealanders in the 1950s enjoyed almost full employment, one of the highest standards of living in the world, and a largely shared set of community values and aspirations. Both major political parties agreed on the need for ample social welfare provisions and the importance of controlling and regulating the economy. The vast adoring crowds who greeted Queen Elizabeth

414

II during her 1953 tour testified to enduring emotional ties with the Mother Country. Economic links also remained strong, as Britain still purchased the lion's share of New Zealand's agricultural output. With the notable exception of the bitter 1951 waterfront dispute, the 'pleasant tedium' remained unruffled. The population boomed, as young couples married and raised children in newly created suburbs. Car ownership soared, and motorways, supermarkets and shopping malls proliferated.

New Zealand in its early twenty-first-century incarnation bears little resemblance to its post-war, statist, conservative, proudly monocultural self. Now one of the most deregulated free-market economies in the world, it is also one of the most multicultural and the most 'globalised'. Governments work actively to increase the country's profile and sell its 'brand' internationally. When, during her time as Prime Minister, Helen Clark's regular globetrotting attracted criticism, she remained unapologetic, observing that 'the world would get on quite well if we never existed at all, so it is an issue of New Zealand being relevant . . . we have to get out and sell our goods and it is about brand, profile and image'.[3] While keen to be part of the globalised cultural marketplace, the Clark government took several measures to further loosen ties with Britain. In its first term, it abolished the practice of granting imperial honours, and in its second introduced measures to remove the right to appeal to the Privy Council in London. Arguing for this change, Governor-General Dame Silvia Cartwright, in her speech on the opening of Parliament on 27 August 2002, described it as 'a crucial affirmation of New Zealand's sovereignty and self-identity and self-reliance'.[4]

Although New Zealand did not seem to relish the prospect of self-reliance after the war and moved away from the folds of empire reluctantly, new defence alliances and economic imperatives caused it to establish trade and diplomatic links around the globe: engagement with an increasingly globalised culture and economy crucially shaped the country's development after 1945. 'Globalisation' is often criticised for its propensity to homogenise culture and erode national distinctions, but for New Zealand after World War II, participating in an increasingly globalised economy and culture augmented a sense of independent nationalism. Paradoxically, this national identity was deeply indebted to international ideas, movements and events.

Prior to 1945, New Zealand's cultural, diplomatic and trade relations operated primarily within the traditional imperial networks. In the early twenty-first century, Australia, Asia and the Pacific countries are the primary source of military, economic and cultural ties. Australia and New Zealand, in particular, now occupy a 'common world'. In 1995, the two countries signed a Trans-Tasman Mutual Recognition Arrangement (TTMRA). The agreement allowed free movement of people and goods between the two countries.[5] Prime ministers, foreign, trade and defence ministers, as well as a raft of other officials, meet and consult on a regular basis; tourists, sportspeople, family and business visitors travel back and forth; and Australian and New Zealand citizens live and work freely in each other's countries. Over half of New Zealand visits overseas are to Australia, while Australians head the number of tourists to New Zealand.[6] The introduction, in 2005, of a combined New Zealand/Australia queue at New Zealand and Australian airports symbolises this close relationship.

At the same time, New Zealand's political and economic bonds with Britain, though diminished, still endure. The United Kingdom is the third-largest source of tourists and of migrants to New Zealand. Every year, large numbers of young New Zealanders continue to travel to Britain, settling in London in particular, to live and work as part of their OE ('overseas experience'). A 2011 survey of New Zealand expatriates found around 27 per cent resided in Britain.[7] Recent statistics show, however, that the number of young New Zealanders heading to the United Kingdom for their OE has declined. In 2012, only 13 per cent of long-term departures were headed for Britain. According to Statistics New Zealand, this was the lowest level in 30 years. In the same year, nearly 4 per cent of those embarking on their OE headed to China, an increase of more than 3000 per cent. Commenting on this phenomenon in the *New Zealand Herald*, journalist Simon Day wrote: 'It used to be a chip buttie and a pint in the East End — now it's yum char in Shanghai.'[8] Professor Paul Spoonley of Massey University attributed the trend towards OEs in Asia to the fact that: 'In a geopolitical sense, Asia is much more important to New Zealand. The second [factor] is that we have a much larger Asian population.' He went on to observe: 'The umbilical cord that we had with the UK, if it isn't gone, it is going . . . I think the Pacific and Asia is growing much more important.'[9] This cultural trend notwithstanding, popular affection for the Queen and the royal family within New Zealand remains strong: those who desire a republic are a minority, and British television, radio and news media outlets retain a strong presence in New Zealand.

The bond with Britain and the Commonwealth is one of several continuities that, despite over six decades of economic, cultural and technological transformation, link the New Zealand of the early twenty-first century with that of 1945. Although farming is now a more streamlined and technologically driven industry, the primary sector remains the country's biggest exporter. Where sheep once ruled supreme, now it is cows: dairy products make up one quarter of the country's exports and account for one third of the world's dairy trade. Fonterra, the world's fourth-largest dairy company, sells to over 100 countries, making it New Zealand's largest global company. Despite the fact that most New Zealanders live in cities, rural life is still a cultural touchstone.

In the 1940s, John Mulgan deemed rugby, racing and beer to be Kiwis' most favoured pastimes, and certainly the attractions of rugby (and of beer perhaps more than racing) remain undiminished. The All Blacks, formerly amateurs who took time off from their farms or salaried jobs to play, are now high-profile professionals whose skills (and formidable pre-game haka) inspire veneration at home and respect abroad. New Zealand sailors are also world-renowned, and highly sought after internationally. If the country has produced more than its share of world-class sporting heroes, this is perhaps because participating in sports, whether with competitive zeal and determination or in a more relaxed and sociable fashion, has long been a valued aspect of the national culture, popular with residents of tiny rural communities and cities alike. Cheering spouses and offspring from the sidelines remains an enjoyable, often time-consuming, aspect of New Zealand family life.

The nature of family life has altered significantly since the immediate post-war period, reflecting changes in social and moral norms. In 1945, politicians devised policies to support and assist young nuclear families. Women generally married young and promptly had children. For the baby-boom generation, expectations and norms about family life changed rapidly; types of families grew more diverse and this trend increased over time. Marriage rates dropped from an all-time high of 45.5 per 1000 in 1971 to 16.5 in 1996, to 13.5 in 2006, to 11.8 in 2011. Whereas in 1960 the median age of marriage was 22, by 2006 it had risen to 28.2. Although heterosexual couples with children are still the largest single category of family, the trend since 1945 has been towards varied family types, with those in de facto relationships, single-parent families, blended or stepfamilies, civil unions and same-sex relationships, as well as the proportion of people who never marry, increasing over time.[10]

Women's liberation played a role in transforming New Zealand family life, as more women participated in the labour market and accessed tertiary education. Working outside of the home and studying longer influenced decisions about when to start a family, as well as the number of children couples opted to have. In 1971, women comprised 30 per cent of university enrolments; by 1985, the figure was 49 per cent. Since the mid-1990s, women have been more likely than men to participate in tertiary education.[11] By 2007, women made up 47 per cent of the national workforce, and by 2010, New Zealand could boast two women governors-general, two women prime ministers, a female attorney-general and a Speaker of the House, as well as cabinet ministers, mayors and local politicians, bishops, professionals and business executives. In March 2013, the British magazine *The Economist*'s 'glass ceiling index' ranked New Zealand the best place in the world to be a working woman. The *New Zealand Herald* reported that this ranking was greeted with 'a degree of disbelief' on the paper's Facebook page, where numerous posted comments cited dire statistics about underrepresentation on company boards and in CEO positions.[12] New Zealand women still occupy lower-status and lower-paid jobs than men: in 2008, the average weekly income for New Zealand men was $976 and $657 for women.[13] Domestic violence towards women remains an ongoing problem: a 2004 study showed that 33 to 39 per cent of New Zealand women experience violence from an intimate partner in the course of their lifetime.[14] Women still assume responsibility for the large proportion of unpaid domestic work, from looking after children to running the house. News items and feature articles remind residents with depressing regularity that New Zealand has one of the worst rates of child abuse in the world. These sorts of problems and inequalities are of course not unique to New Zealand, but they offer an antidote to arguments that hold up the country's two women prime ministers and governors-general as further evidence of its 'exceptionalism'.

The state-supported New Zealand film industry is one particularly potent and widely publicised means of promoting the country's unique 'brand, profile and image'. The first instalment of director Peter Jackson's fantasy epic *The Lord of the Rings* trilogy, based on the books by J. R. R. Tolkien, was released in 2001. This series concluded in 2003 and was followed by a three-part adaptation of *The Hobbit*, beginning in 2012. The films simultaneously produced profits across several spheres, notably tourism, and are widely credited with raising global recognition of 'Brand New Zealand'.[15] Green, pristine, and it would sometimes seem, eerily uninhabited, New Zealand has long been emphasised in tourist marketing as a destination that offers both spectacular scenery and adventure: an authentic, '100% Pure' alternative to mundane working life in 'advanced' urban societies. Tourism in 2012 generated a direct contribution of $6.2 billion or 3.3 per cent of New Zealand's GDP.[16]

Attracting foreign investment and foreign capital is inextricably linked with advocating 'Brand New Zealand'. This process augments a sense of self-identity by drawing on those qualities that are perceived as attractive and distinctive, and marketing them to the rest of the world. At the same time, economic globalisation can imperil national independence, in particular by diminishing control over national resources. In recent years, a series of controversies have highlighted contradictory and simultaneous impulses for both liberalisation and protection among the New Zealand public. In 2010, for example, when a dispute with the actors' union threatened to stymie the local filming of the *Hobbit* movies, Prime Minister John Key persuaded Parliament to rewrite the national labour laws and pledged a substantial incentive package in production costs and $10 million to the Warner Bros. studio's marketing budget.[17] In the *New Zealand Herald* of 27 October 2010, columnist Brian Rudman lamented the way sections of the New Zealand public vilified both the actors' union and its spokespeople, local actresses Robyn Malcolm and Jennifer Ward-Lealand, during the dispute, commenting that: 'Samuel Parnell, the father of the eight-hour day, would have turned in his grave at the way the day set aside in his memory [25 October] was desecrated. Up and down the land, crowds marched and rallied to pledge to be servile to a Hollywood movie conglomerate.'[18]

The *Hobbit* controversy was followed by a different public response to international economic interests. The proposed sale of Crafar dairy farms (the country's largest family-owned dairy business, which went into receivership in 2009) to a Chinese conglomerate provoked sustained public outcries and organised opposition. Then in 2012–13, members of the public who oppose the Key government's agenda for strategic asset sales organised a series of public marches and launched a petition calling for a public referendum on the matter. The Crafar sale proceeded in November 2012, and, at the time of writing, in 2013, asset sales have commenced amidst ongoing protests. The critical response to these issues attests to a palpable public ambiguity concerning key developments in the country's recent past and its future direction. The tension is between those who advocate the benefits of a transnational globalised economy and culture and those who favour a more stable and protected but perhaps less dynamic one, owned and controlled by New Zealanders. Each approach, as the developments of the past few decades have illustrated, involves a set of distinctive benefits and drawbacks. Many of the heralded social and economic advances of the late twentieth century — the increasing diversity of New Zealand's population, the evolution of a dynamic, internationally competitive primary economy, increasing sophistication and declining cultural isolation — stemmed from the pronounced opening up of a previously rather staid and insular nation to global influences, human and capital flows. On the other hand, after 1984 in particular, many New Zealanders were made all too aware of the costs — human, social and economic — of liberalisation.

In 1945, the socially conservative loyal dominion followed a clear map of its future course and was confident in the values that would light the way. But before long the country and its people were navigating uncharted waters. As the twentieth century progressed, the 'pleasant tedium' and security of the 'earthly paradise' gave way to a more stimulating but often daunting set of challenges. Former certainties receded as, for good and for ill — sometimes simultaneously for both — New Zealand operated in a world in which the global and the local seemed ever less distinct. As the twentieth century ebbed and the twenty-first commenced, it became clear that the country's journey, in the words of Allen Curnow, 'was something different, something / Nobody counted on.'[19]

NOTES

INTRODUCTION Unforeseen Directions: After 1945

1 Leslie Lipson, *The Politics of Equality: New Zealand's Adventures in Democracy*, Chicago, Chicago University Press, 1948, pp. 367–8.
2 Ibid., p. 367.
3 Ibid., pp. 488, 493, 492.
4 See Margaret McClure, *A Civilised Community: A History of Social Security in New Zealand 1898–1998*, Auckland, Auckland University Press in association with the Historical Branch, Department of Internal Affairs, 1998, pp. 101–5.
5 For the American post-war domestic idyll see Lizabeth Cohen, *Consumer's Republic: The Politics of Mass Consumption in Post-war America*, New York, Alfred Knopf, 2003; for Australia see John Murphy, *Imagining the Fifties: Public Culture and Private Sentiment in Menzies' Australia*, Kensington, University of NSW Press, 2002.
6 Robert Semple, Labour's Minister of Works, used the phrase 'new born world' to describe this young and forward-looking society, *New Zealand Parliamentary Debates*, vol. 271, 1945, p. 202.
7 This phrase, commonly invoked to describe 1950s and early 1960s New Zealand, is from Bruce Mason's celebrated 1959 play, *The End of the Golden Weather: A Voyage into a New Zealand Childhood*, Wellington, New Zealand University Press and Price Milburn, 1962.
8 See Michael Bassett, *The State in New Zealand 1840–1984: Socialism without Doctrines?*, Auckland, Auckland University Press, 1998, pp. 253–4. For an overview of New Zealand's economic growth from 1950 see John Singleton, 'An Economic History of New Zealand in the Nineteenth and Twentieth Centuries', http://eh.net/encyclopedia/article/Singleton.NZ; Table 1, p. 1 shows per capita GDP in New Zealand compared with the United States and Australia.

9 John Mulgan, *Report on Experience*, London, Oxford University Press, 1947, p. 17.
10 Lipson, *The Politics of Equality*, p. 503.
11 This report, entitled 'Divided We Stand: Why Inequality Keeps Rising', appeared in December 2011 and New Zealand's ranking was widely reported in the media; TVNZ's *ONE News* of 7 December 2011, for example, described the findings as 'a huge wake-up call.' See tvnz.co.nz/national-news/nz-s-rich-and-poor-gap-huge-wake-up-call-expert-4608382.
12 Erik Olssen uses this phrase to describe New Zealand in the 1970s, after the economic recession and Britain's entry into the EEC, in his article 'New Zealand in the American Century', in Roberto Rabel (ed.), *The American Century? In Retrospect and Prospect*, Westport, Connecticut, Praeger, 2002, p. 185.

CHAPTER ONE On an Even Keel? Peace, Prosperity, Consensus

1 This vision of a future post-war New Zealand featured in Mulgan's memoir *Report on Experience*, written in 1945 and published posthumously. Cited from the London, Oxford University Press edition of 1947, p. 15.
2 Bill Pearson's essay 'Fretful Sleepers: A Sketch of New Zealand Behaviour and its Implications for the Artist' was first published in *Landfall* in 1952. This excerpt reproduced in Alex Calder (ed.), *The Writing of New Zealand: Inventions and Identities*, Auckland, Reed, 1993, p. 170.
3 'What does it mean to us?', *Evening Post*, 8 May 1945, p. 4.
4 'Wellington's Emotion: People in Jubilant Mood', *Taranaki Herald*, 10 May 1945, p. 2.
5 'Victory Day, New Plymouth Rejoices, Feelings of Relief', *Taranaki Herald*, 10 May 1945, p. 5.
6 Peter Fraser cited in Nancy M. Taylor, *The New Zealand People at War: The Home*

Front, Official History of New Zealand in the Second World War, 1939–1945, Wellington, Historical Publications Branch, Department of Internal Affairs, Government Printer, 1986, p. 1265.

7 This figure is from Commonwealth War Graves Commission data; New Zealand's deaths per capita were second only to those of the United Kingdom among Commonwealth nations. See www.cwgc.org.

8 Flo Small cited in Judith Fyfe, *War Stories Our Mothers Never Told Us*, Auckland, Penguin, 1995, pp. 112–13.

9 'Warriors Come Home: Maori Battalion Honoured', *Dominion*, 24 January 1946, reproduced in Agnes Broughton et al., *The Silent Migration, Ngāti Pōneke Young Māori Club 1937–1948: Stories of Urban Migration told to Patricia Grace, Irihapeti Ramsden and Jonathan Dennis*, Wellington, Huia, 2001, p. 213.

10 Mihipeka Edwards cited in Broughton et al., *The Silent Migration*, pp. 218–19.

11 Les Cleveland cited in Alison Parr, *Silent Casualties: New Zealand's Unspoken Legacy of the Second World War*, Auckland, Tandem Press, 1995, p. 154.

12 See Alison Parr, *Home: Civilian New Zealanders Remember the Second World War*, Auckland, Penguin, 2010, pp. 270–3. The phrase 'emotional anaesthetic' is from Parr, *Silent Casualties*, p. 147.

13 Parr, *Silent Casualties*, pp. 120–2, 129–33.

14 Ibid., pp. 136–40.

15 Taylor, *The New Zealand People at War*, p. 1270.

16 Ibid., p. 1276 re training centres, pp. 1278–9 re business loans and p. 1280 re housing loans.

17 Robert Chapman, 'Great Expectations: New Zealand Since the War', in *New Zealand Politics and Social Patterns: Selected Works*, edited and with an introduction by Elizabeth McLeay, Wellington, Victoria University Press, 1998, p. 74.

18 Taylor, *The New Zealand People at War*, p. 1281.

19 Nell Hartley, *Goodbye Yesterday*, Auckland, Lasting Memories, 2001, p. 74.

20 Ibid., pp. 74–75.

21 Keith Sinclair, *A History of New Zealand*, revised edn, Auckland, Penguin, 2000, p. 279.

22 Bronwyn Dalley, 'The Golden Weather, 1949–1965', Chapter 11 in Bronwyn Dalley and Gavin McLean (eds), *Frontier of Dreams: The Story of New Zealand*, Auckland, Hodder Moa, 2005, p. 304.

23 Labour had traditionally been anti-conscription and Peter Fraser himself had in 1916–17 served a prison term for protesting against it. But Fraser, convinced that Russian communism threatened world peace, felt New Zealand should be prepared for another war. After a narrowly won referendum, conscription was reintroduced, a move which alienated many traditional Labour supporters.

24 Barry Gustafson, *The First 50 Years: A History of the New Zealand National Party*, Auckland, Reed Methuen, 1986, p. 54.

25 Robert Chapman, 'From Labour to National', in Geoffrey W. Rice (ed.), *The Oxford History of New Zealand*, 2nd edn, Auckland, Oxford University Press, 1992, p. 372.

26 Ormond Wilson, 'A Future for Tweedle-dee?', in *Here & Now*, October 1953, p. 15.

27 Sinclair, *A History of New Zealand*, revised edn, p. 297.

28 Ibid., p. 300.

29 Michael Bassett, *The State in New Zealand 1840–1984: Socialism without Doctrines?*, Auckland, Auckland University Press, 1998, p. 13.

30 Ibid., pp. 14–16.

31 Gustafson, *The First 50 Years*, p. 47.

32 Barry Gustafson, *Kiwi Keith: A Biography of Keith Holyoake*, Auckland, Auckland University Press, 2007, p. 166.

33 Gustafson, *The First 50 Years*, p. 41.

34 Chapman, 'From Labour to National', in Rice (ed.), *The Oxford History of New Zealand*, 2nd edn, p. 373.

35 Gustafson, *The First 50 Years*, p. 69 and see Chapman, 'From Labour to National', in Rice (ed.), *The Oxford History of New Zealand*, 2nd edn, p. 378.

36 Gustafson, *The First 50 Years*, p. 78.

37 Keith Sinclair, *Walter Nash*, Auckland, Auckland University Press and Oxford University Press, 1976, p. 320.

38 Ibid., p. 302.

39 Ibid., p. 308.

40 Gustafson, *The First 50 Years*, p. 80.

41 Ibid., p. 75.

42 Gustafson, *Kiwi Keith*, p. 2.

43 Chapman, 'From Labour to National', in Rice (ed.), *The Oxford History of New Zealand*, 2nd edn, p. 381.

44 Gustafson, *Kiwi Keith*, p. 2.

45 Gustafson, *The First 50 Years*, p. 92.

46 Cited in Barry Gustafson, 'No Land is an Island: Twenty-first Century Politics', 2010 Robert Chapman Lecture, University of Auckland, p. 3.

47 Robert Chapman, 'From Labour to National', in Rice (ed.), *The Oxford History of New Zealand*, 2nd edn, p. 373.

48 Tom Brooking, *Milestones: Turning Points in New Zealand History*, Palmerston North, Dunmore Press, 1999, pp. 178–9.

49 'The Big Blue', *New Zealand Listener*, 17 February 2001, p. 34.

50 Cited in 'The Big Blue', ibid., p. 33.

51 The official forum of the international communist movement, founded in 1947 after the dissolution of the first forum, the Comintern, in 1943.

52 Holland, *Evening Post*, 23 February 1951.

53 Sinclair, *Walter Nash*, p. 283.

54 Quoted in Dick Scott, *151 Days: History of the Great Waterfront Lockout and Supporting Strikes, February 15–July 15, 1951*, Auckland, Southern Cross Books, 1954, p. 67.

55 Bill Sullivan cited in Sinclair, *Walter Nash*, p. 283 and 'Can we . . .?' query of 26 February 1951 cited in Michael Bassett, *Confrontation '51: The 1951 Waterfront Dispute*, Wellington, Reed, 1972, p. 90.

56 Jock Phillips, 'The '51 Lockout: The Last Hurrah', in David Grant (ed.), *The Big Blue: Snapshots of the 1951 Waterfront Lockout*, Christchurch, Canterbury University Press, 2004, p. 170.

57 Quoted in Scott, *151 Days*, p. 111.

58 Phillips, 'The '51 Lockout: The Last Hurrah', in Grant (ed.), *The Big Blue*, p. 164.

59 Ibid.

60 Cited in Bassett, *Confrontation '51*, p. 127.

61 Gustafson, *The First 50 Years*, p. 60.

62 *New Zealand Parliamentary Debates*, vol. 322, 8 July 1960, cited in Bassett, *Confrontation '51*, p. 237, fn. 52.

63 This phrase is from a National Party publicity pamphlet delivered to every home in the country. Gustafson, *The First 50 Years*, p. 60.

64 Cited in 'Chronology of Events', in Grant (ed.), *The Big Blue*, p. 188.

65 See Chapman, 'From Labour to National', in Rice (ed.), *The Oxford History of New Zealand*, 2nd edn, p. 376.

66 Margaret McClure, *A Civilised Community: A History of Social Security in New Zealand 1898–1998*, Auckland, Auckland University Press in association with the Historical Branch, Department of Internal Affairs, 1998, p. 106.

67 James Belich, *Paradise Reforged: A History of the New Zealanders from the 1880s to the Year 2000*, Auckland, Allen Lane/The Penguin Press, 2001, p. 492.

68 Melanie Nolan, *Breadwinning: New Zealand Women and the State*, Christchurch, Canterbury University Press, 2000, p. 212.

69 Mary Taylor, personal communication of 23 November 1996, cited in McClure, *A Civilised Community*, p. 109.

70 Graeme Dunstall, 'The Social Pattern', in Rice (ed.), *The Oxford History of New Zealand*, 2nd edn, p. 454.

71 J. V. Baker, 'Population', in A. H. McLintock, *An Encyclopaedia of New Zealand*, vol. 2, Wellington, Government Printer, 1966, p. 824.

72 Dalley, 'The Golden Weather, 1949–1965', in Dalley and McLean (eds), *Frontier of Dreams*, p. 308.

73 G. Brae, 'Birth Rates in New Zealand 1945–1965', in *New Zealand Economic Papers*, vol. 2, no. 1, Wellington, 1967, pp. 7–8.

74 Heather Knox, 'Feminism, Femininity and Motherhood in Post-World War II New Zealand', MA thesis, History, Palmerston North, Massey University, 1995, pp. 6–7.

75 Gustafson, *Kiwi Keith*, pp. 160–2.

76 Walter Nash, *New Zealand: A Working Democracy*, London, J. M. Dent & Sons, 1945, p. 211.

77 Mary Ratley, *You and Your Home*, Wellington, Reed, 1957, p. 13, quoted in Louise Shaw, 'A Woman's Place?', in Barbara Brookes (ed.), *At Home in New Zealand: History, Houses, People*, Wellington, Bridget Williams Books, 2000, p. 165.

78 Hamish Keith and Phillip Ridge, *A Lovely Day Tomorrow: New Zealand in the 1940s*, Auckland, Random Century, 1991, p. 24.

79 Gael Ferguson, *Building the New Zealand Dream*, Palmerston North, Dunmore Press, 1994, p. 160.

80 Ben Schrader, *We Call It Home: A History of State Housing in New Zealand*, Auckland, Reed, 2005, p. 139.

81 Ibid., pp. 48–51.

82 Shaw, 'A Woman's Place?', in Brookes (ed.), *At Home in New Zealand*, p. 166.

83 Quoted in Schrader, *We Call It Home*, p. 51.

84 Ferguson, *Building the New Zealand Dream*, p. 181.

85 Belich, *Paradise Reforged*, p. 493.

86 Ferguson, *Building the New Zealand Dream*, p. 177.

87 See T. G. McGee, 'The Social Ecology of New Zealand Cities', in John Forster (ed.), *Social Process in New Zealand: Readings in Sociology*, Longman Paul, Auckland, 1969, p. 149, Table 1.

88 Evelyn Stokes, *History of Tauranga County*, Palmerston North, Dunmore Press, 1980, p. 330.

89 Campbell James Gibson, 'Demographic History of New Zealand', PhD thesis, Demography, University of California, Berkeley, 1971, p. 73.

90 K. B. Cumberland, 'The Essential Nature of Auckland', in Graham Bush and Claudia Scott (eds), *Auckland at Full Stretch: Issues of the Seventies*, Auckland, Auckland City Council/Board of Urban Studies, University of Auckland, 1977, p. 20.

91 Dunstall, 'The Social Pattern', in Rice (ed.), *The Oxford History of New Zealand*, 2nd edn, p. 456.

92 Schrader, *We Call It Home*, p. 100. See also Mark Derby, 'Suburbs — New Suburbs, 1950s–1970s', *Te Ara — The Encyclopedia of New Zealand*, updated 28 September 2011, www.teara.govt.nz/en/suburbs/5.

93 Schrader, ibid., p. 180.

94 Professor Kenneth B. Cumberland, 'Living in New Zealand Cities', in *The Journal of the New Zealand Institute of Architects*, vol. 22, no. 5, June 1955, p. 96.

95 See Derby, 'Suburbs', www.teara.govt.nz/en/suburbs/page-5.

96 Ranginui Walker, *Ka Whawhai Tonu Matou: Struggle Without End*, Auckland, Penguin Books, 1990, pp. 199–201; Schrader, *We Call It Home*, pp. 186–7.

97 Schrader, *We Call It Home*, p. 181.

98 Lauren Quaintance, 'Porirua: An Unfortunate Experiment', in *North & South*, June 1998, p. 82.

99 Ibid., p. 82.

100 Schrader, *We Call It Home*, p. 182.

101 Quaintance, 'Porirua: An Unfortunate Experiment', p. 82.

102 Malcolm McKinnon (ed.), *New Zealand Historical Atlas/Ko Papatuanuku e Takoto Nei*, Auckland, David Bateman in association with the Historical Branch, Department of Internal Affairs, 1997, plate 96.

103 Cliff Irving to Ben Schrader, 30 June 2003, quoted in Schrader, *We Call It Home*, p. 188.

104 Don Borrie, 'The Truth About Porirua', letter in *North & South*, July 1998, p. 12; John Burke, 'Why Single out Porirua?', letter in *North & South*, August 1998, p. 13.

105 See David Pearson, *Johnsonville: Continuity and Change in a New Zealand Township*, Australia, George Allen & Unwin, 1980, pp. 27–28.

106 See Jenny Carlyon and Diana Morrow, *A Fine Prospect: A History of Remuera, Meadowbank and St Johns*, Auckland, Random House, 2011, pp. 117–20.

107 *New Zealand Official Yearbook*, 1966, pp. 61–62.

108 Dalley, 'The Golden Weather, 1949–1965', in Dalley and McLean (eds), *Frontier of Dreams*, p. 329.

109 *New Zealand Official Yearbook*, 1966, p. 62.

110 Gibson, 'Demographic History of New Zealand', p. 73.

111 Graham Hawkes, *On the Road: The Car in New Zealand*, Wellington, Government Print Books, 1990, p. 69.

112 G. T. Bloomfield, *New Zealand: A Handbook of Historical Statistics*, Boston, G. K. Hall, 1984, pp. 248–9.

113 *New Zealand Official Yearbook*, 1966, p. 320.

114 McGee, 'The Social Ecology of New Zealand Cities', in Forster (ed.), *Social Process in New Zealand*, p. 152.

115 Hawkes, *On the Road*, p. 80.

116 Keith and Ridge, *A Lovely Day Tomorrow*, p. 48.

117 Paul Smith, *Twist and Shout: New Zealand in the 1960s*, Auckland, Random House, 1991, p. 42.

118 See McKinnon (ed.), *New Zealand Historical Atlas*, plates 75 and 65 respectively.

119 Bloomfield, *New Zealand: A Handbook of Historical Statistics*, p. 182. The planes were flown by ex-air-force pilots.

120 See B. L. Evans, *A History of Agricultural Production and Marketing in New Zealand*, Palmerston North, Keeling and Mundy, 1969, pp. 199–219.

121 Bloomfield, *New Zealand: A Handbook of Historical Statistics*, p. 189.

122 *New Zealand Official Yearbook*, 1966, p. 636.

123 *New Zealand Official Yearbook*, 1953, p. 260. Wool alone accounted for 52% of the total value of merchandise exports in 1951.

124 *New Zealand Official Yearbook*, 1967, p. 641;

and also Evans, *A History of Agricultural Production and Marketing*, p. 145.

125 This phrase was used as late as 1962 by British Prime Minister Harold Macmillan; cited in John Singleton, 'Auckland Business: The National and International Context', in Ian Hunter and Diana Morrow (eds), *City of Enterprise: Perspectives on Auckland Business History*, Auckland, Auckland University Press, 2006, p. 8.

126 Dunstall, 'The Social Pattern', in Rice (ed.), *The Oxford History of New Zealand*, 2nd edn, p. 455.

127 H. C. D. Somerset, *Littledene: Patterns of Change*, Wellington, New Zealand Council for Educational Research, 1974, p. 119. The first study, in 1938, was entitled *Littledene: A New Zealand Rural Community* and was also published by the New Zealand Council for Educational Research.

128 David C. Thorns and Charles P. Sedgwick, *Understanding Aotearoa/New Zealand: Historical Statistics*, Palmerston North, Dunmore Press, 1997, p. 79.

129 Gary Hawke, 'Economic Trends and Economic Policy', in Rice (ed.), *The Oxford History of New Zealand*, 2nd edn, p. 423.

130 Tokoroa's population rose from several hundred in the early 1950s to 11,200 in 1966; Gibson, 'Demographic History of New Zealand', p. 73.

131 Cumberland, 'Living in New Zealand Cities', p. 95.

132 Thorns and Sedgwick, *Understanding Aotearoa/New Zealand*, pp. 78–83. By 2006, over 80% of the working population was employed in the tertiary sector while the manufacturing sector had dropped to 12% and the primary sector to 7%.

133 Hawke, 'Economic Trends and Economic Policy', in Rice (ed.), *The Oxford History of New Zealand*, 2nd edn, p. 426.

134 Ibid., p. 427.

135 Ibid., p. 431.

136 Dunstall, 'The Social Pattern', in Rice (ed.), *The Oxford History of New Zealand*, 2nd edn, p. 454.

137 Pamphlet issued by Department of Labour and Employment, Memo to Minister of Employment, 12 September 1946, National Archives, PM 20/21, pp. 11–12, quoted in Megan Hutching, *Long Journey for Sevenpence: Assisted Immigration to New Zealand from the United Kingdom 1947–1975*, Wellington, Victoria University Press, 1999, p. 49.

138 Tom Brooking and Roberto Rabel, 'Neither British nor Polynesian: A Brief History of New Zealand's Other Immigrants', in Stuart William Greif (ed.), *Immigration and National Identity in New Zealand: One People, Two People, Many Peoples?*, Palmerston North, Dunmore Press, 1995, p. 38.

139 Leslie Lipson, *The Politics of Equality: New Zealand's Adventures in Democracy*, Chicago, Chicago University Press, 1948, p. 487.

140 *Appendices to the Journals of the House of Representatives*, 1946, vol. 5, I-17, 'Report of the Dominion Population Committee', p. 99.

141 National Archives, L122/1/27, part 5, Memo for Minister of Employment from Director of Employment, 15 April 1948, quoted in Ann Beaglehole, *A Small Price to Pay: Refugees from Hitler in New Zealand, 1936–1946*, Wellington, Allen & Unwin and the Historical Branch, Department of Internal Affairs, 1988, pp. 5–6.

142 K. W. Thomson, 'The Dutch', in K. W. Thomson and A. D. Trlin (eds), *Immigrants in New Zealand*, Palmerston North, Massey University, 1970, pp. 153, 156.

143 Beaglehole, *A Small Price to Pay*, p. 21.

144 Official history of Canterbury College, quoted in Michael King, *The Penguin History of New Zealand*, Auckland, Penguin Books, 2003, p. 415. For a discussion of the cultural impact of these refugees, see King, ibid., pp. 416–18, and R. A. Lochore, *From Europe to New Zealand: An Account of our Continental European Settlers*, Wellington, Reed in conjunction with the New Zealand Institute of International Affairs, 1951, pp. 77–83.

145 Leonard Bell and Diana Morrow (eds), *Jewish Lives in New Zealand: A History*, Auckland, Godwit, 2012, pp. 353–4.

146 Manying Ip, *The Dragon and the Taniwha: Māori and Chinese in New Zealand*, Auckland, Auckland University Press, 2009, p. 99.

147 M. Taher, 'The Asians', in Thompson and Trlin (eds), *Immigrants in New Zealand*, p. 41.

148 Brooking and Rabel, 'Neither British nor Polynesian', in Greif (ed.), *Immigration and National Identity in New Zealand*, p. 39; see also Sean Brawley, '"No 'White Policy' in New Zealand": Fact and Fiction in New Zealand's Asian Immigration Record,

1946–1978', *New Zealand Journal of History*, vol. 27, no. 1, 1993, pp. 16–36.

149 One of the largest concentrations of Pacific Islanders outside Auckland was in Tokoroa where they made up 10% of the population. David Boardman, 'Polynesian Immigrants: Migration Process and Distribution in New Zealand', in Stephen D. Webb and John Collette (eds), *New Zealand Society: Contemporary Perspectives*, Sydney, Wiley, 1973, p. 321.

150 Kerry Howe, 'New Zealand's Twentieth-Century Pacifics: Memories and Reflections', *New Zealand Journal of History*, vol. 34, no. 1, 2000, p. 17.

151 Boardman, 'Polynesian Immigrants', in Webb and Collette (eds), *New Zealand Society: Contemporary Perspectives*, p. 322.

152 Brooking and Rabel, 'Neither British nor Polynesian', in Greif (ed.), *Immigration and National Identity in New Zealand*, p. 40.

153 Joan Metge, *A New Maori Migration: Rural and Urban Relations in Northern New Zealand*, London, Athlone Press, 1964, p. 128.

154 Ranginui Walker, 'The Social Adjustment of the Maori to Urban Living in Auckland', PhD thesis, Anthropology, Auckland, University of Auckland, 1970, p. 78.

155 Ibid., p. 197.

156 Paul Meredith, 'Urban Māori — Urbanisation', *Te Ara — The Encyclopedia of New Zealand*, updated 4 March 2009, www.teara.govt.nz/en/urban-maori/1.

157 D. T. Rowland, 'Maori Migration to Auckland', *New Zealand Geographer*, vol. 27, no. 1, 1971, p. 21.

158 Broughton et al., *The Silent Migration*, p. 46.

159 In *Te Whānau: A Celebration of Te Whānau o Waipareira*, Waitakere City, Te Whānau o Waipareira, 2001, p. 12, quoted in Paul Meredith, 'Urban Māori — Hopes and reality', *Te Ara — The Encyclopedia of New Zealand*, updated 4 March 2009, www.teara.govt.nz/en/urban-maori/2.

160 Walker, 'The Social Adjustment of the Maori', p. 502.

161 Ibid., p. 516.

162 Walker, *Ka Whawhai Tonu Matou*, p. 200.

163 Melissa Matutina Williams, '"Back-home" in the City: Maori Migration from Panguru to Auckland', PhD thesis, History, Auckland, University of Auckland, 2010, p. 115.

164 Ibid., p. 154.

165 Ibid., p. 115.

166 Ibid., pp. 104–8.

167 Walker, 'The Social Adjustment of the Maori', p. 347; see also John Rangihau, 'Being Maori', in Michael King (ed.), *Te Ao Hurihuri: Aspects of Maoritanga*, Auckland, Reed Books, 1992, pp. 184–5.

168 Williams, '"Back-home" in the City', pp. 165–7.

169 Ibid., p. 91.

170 Metge, *A New Maori Migration*, p. 209.

171 Ibid., p. 206.

172 R. J. Walker, 'Urbanisation and the Cultural Continuity of the Ethnic Minority: The Maori Case', in Paul Baxter and Basil Sansom, *Race and Social Difference: Selected Readings*, Harmondsworth, Penguin, 1972, p. 406.

173 See Chapter 4 for an examination of the Centre's cultural role during the 1950s and early 1960s.

174 Broughton et al., *The Silent Migration*, pp. 225–6. The quotes are from Paul Potiki, a long-time member of the club whose family was instrumental in setting it up.

175 Walker, 'Urbanisation and the Cultural Continuity of the Ethnic Minority', p. 404.

176 Ranginui Walker, 'The Maori People since 1950', in Rice (ed.), *The Oxford History of New Zealand*, 2nd edn, p. 504.

177 Ibid., p. 510.

178 Walker, 'Urbanisation and the Cultural Continuity of the Ethnic Minority', p. 408; see also Walker, 'The Maori People since 1950', in Rice (ed.), *The Oxford History of New Zealand*, 2nd edn, p. 509.

179 Walker, 'The Maori People since 1950', in Rice (ed.), *The Oxford History of New Zealand*, 2nd edn, p. 510.

180 Aroha Harris, 'Dancing with the State: Maori Creative Energy and the Politics of Integration 1945–1967', PhD thesis, History, Auckland, University of Auckland, 2007, p. 93.

181 Later Szászy; she served as League president from 1973 to 1977.

182 *Te Ao Hou*, Spring 1954, p. 9.

183 Harris, 'Dancing with the State', p. 94.

184 Ibid., p. 97.

185 Nolan, *Breadwinning: New Zealand Women and the State*, p. 204.

186 Harris, 'Dancing with the State', p. 102.

187 Schrader, *We Call It Home*, pp. 60–61, and Williams, '"Back-home" in the City', p. 85.

188 Nolan, *Breadwinning: New Zealand Women and the State*, p. 204.

189 Ferguson, *Building the New Zealand Dream*, p. 167.

190 Schrader, *We Call It Home*, p. 57.

191 Ferguson, *Building the New Zealand Dream*, p. 169.

192 Schrader, *We Call It Home*, p. 61.

193 Williams, '"Back-home" in the City', p. 124.

194 Walker, 'The Social Adjustment of the Maori', p. 66.

195 Harris, 'Dancing with the State', p. 83.

196 Michael King, *Whina: A Biography of Whina Cooper*, Auckland, Penguin Books, 1991, p. 184.

197 Harris, 'Dancing with the State', p. 99. 'Te reo me ona tikanga' means Maori language and culture.

198 This influential report, and the controversy it gave rise to, is considered more extensively in Chapter 8 within the context of race relations.

199 See Chapter 8.

200 See *Appendices to the Journals of the House of Representatives*, 1946, vol. 5, I-17, p. 3.

201 Ibid., 'Report of the Dominion Population Committee', p. 112.

202 McClure, *A Civilised Community*, p. 105.

203 Mary Wrigley writing in the *New Zealand Woman's Weekly*, cited in Helen May, *Minding Children, Managing Men: Conflict and Compromise in the Lives of Postwar Pakeha Women*, Wellington, Bridget Williams Books, 1992, p. 51.

204 Dr Reeve, Superintendent of the Services Hospital for Women in Rotorua, writing to the *New Zealand Woman's Weekly*, cited in May, *Minding Children, Managing Men*, p. 50.

205 Memo, Wellington District Officer to Minister of Labour, 29 August 1945, L4/5/766, quoted in Deborah Montgomery, *The Women's War: New Zealand Women 1939–1945*, Auckland, Auckland University Press, 2001, p. 177.

206 *Dominion*, 20 July 1954.

207 Helen May, 'Motherhood in the 1950s: An Experience of Contradiction', in Sue Middleton (ed.), *Women and Education in Aotearoa New Zealand*, Wellington, Allen & Unwin/Port Nicholson Press, 1988, p. 66.

208 Montgomery, *The Women's War*, p. 171.

209 Nolan, *Breadwinning: New Zealand Women and the State*, p. 205.

210 Eugenia Kaledin, *Mothers and More: American Women in the 1950s*, cited in Nolan, *Breadwinning: New Zealand Women and the State*, p. 206, fn. 71.

211 Phoebe Meikle writing as Leslie M. Hall in *Landfall*, vol. 45, March 1958, p. 48.

212 Dalley, 'The Golden Weather, 1949–1965', in Dalley and McLean (eds), *Frontier of Dreams*, p. 312.

213 Miriam Gilson, 'Women in Employment', in Forster (ed.), *Social Process in New Zealand*, pp. 190–1.

214 Prue Hyman, 'Trends in Female Labour Force Participation in New Zealand since 1945', in *New Zealand Economic Papers*, vol. 12, 1978, p. 157.

215 Ibid., pp. 157–8, 161.

216 Melanie Nolan, 'A Subversive State? Domesticity in Dispute in 1950s New Zealand', *Journal of Family History*, vol. 27, no. 1, January 2002, p. 67.

217 Nolan, *Breadwinning: New Zealand Women and the State*, p. 225.

218 Gilson, 'Women in Employment', in Forster (ed.), *Social Process in New Zealand*, p. 193.

219 Nolan, *Breadwinning: New Zealand Women and the State*, p. 223.

220 Ibid., p. 226.

221 Gilson, 'Women in Employment', in Forster (ed.), *Social Process in New Zealand*, p. 193.

222 Nolan, *Breadwinning: New Zealand Women and the State*, p. 229.

223 See ibid., pp. 192–229.

224 Taylor, *The New Zealand People at War*, pp. 1077–8. By 1971, women would constitute 31% of the permanent staff; see Nolan, *Breadwinning: New Zealand Women and the State*, p. 230.

225 Margaret Corner, *No Easy Victory: Towards Equal Pay for Women in the Government Service 1890–1960*, Wellington, New Zealand Public Service Association/Dan Long Trust, 1988, p. 49.

226 Cited in Corner, *No Easy Victory*, p. 56.

227 Cited in Corner, ibid., p. 70.

228 Ibid., pp. 76–77.

229 Margot Roth, 'Housewives or Human Beings?', *New Zealand Listener*, 20 November 1959, pp. 6–7.

230 *New Zealand Woman's Weekly*, 4 May 1950, p. 10.

231 *New Zealand Woman's Weekly*, 5 January 1959, pp. 35–36.

232 Sandra Coney, *Every Girl: A Social History of Women and the YWCA in Auckland*, Auckland, Auckland YWCA, 1986, p. 240.

233 May, *Minding Children, Managing Men*, p. 64.

234 Ibid.

CHAPTER TWO Loosening the Bonds:
New Friends, New Enemies

1 F. L. W. Wood, *This New Zealand*, Hamilton, Paul's Book Arcade, 1958 (first edn, 1952), p. 205.

2 George Laking cited in Malcolm Templeton (ed.), *An Eye, An Ear, and a Voice: 50 Years in New Zealand's External Relations 1943-1993*, Wellington, Ministry of Foreign Affairs and Trade, 1993, p. 29.

3 G. R. Hawke, *The Making of New Zealand: An Economic History*, Cambridge, Cambridge University Press, 1985, p. 127.

4 'What Does it Mean to Us?', *Evening Post*, 8 May 1945, p. 4.

5 Wood, *This New Zealand*, p. 205.

6 Ormond Wilson, *New Zealand Parliamentary Debates*, vol. 276, 8 July 1947, pp. 298-9.

7 Telegram from the Secretary of State for Dominion Affairs, London, to the High Commissioner for the United Kingdom, Wellington, 13 June 1940, quoted in W. David McIntyre and W. J. Gardner (eds), *Speeches and Documents on New Zealand History*, Oxford, Clarendon Press, 1971, p. 367.

8 David McIntyre, 'The Future of the New Zealand System of Alliances', in *Landfall*, vol. 21, no. 4, December 1967, pp. 327-45.

9 George Laking in Templeton (ed.), *An Eye, An Ear, and a Voice*, p. 37. George Laking became Secretary of Foreign Affairs in 1966.

10 Philippa Mein Smith, Peter Hempenstall and Shaun Goldfinch with Stuart McMillan and Rosemary Baird, *Remaking the Tasman World*, Christchurch, Canterbury University Press, 2008, p. 105.

11 Ian McGibbon (ed.), *Undiplomatic Dialogue: Letters between Carl Berendsen and Alister McIntosh, 1943-1953*, Auckland, Auckland University Press in association with the Ministry of Foreign Affairs and Trade, Historical Branch, Department of Internal Affairs, 1993, p. 7. Alister Donald McIntosh (1906-1978) was Secretary of External Affairs and Permanent Head of the Prime Minister's Department until his retirement in 1966.

12 Mary Boyd, 'New Zealand and the other Pacific Islands', in Keith Sinclair (ed.), *The Oxford Illustrated History of New Zealand*, 2nd edn, Auckland, Oxford University Press, 1997, pp. 295-322.

13 Denis McLean, *The Prickly Pair: Making Nationalism in Australia and New Zealand*, Dunedin, Otago University Press, 2003, p. 142.

14 *Hawera Star*, 30 January 1954, quoted in Jock Phillips, *Royal Summer: The Visit of Queen Elizabeth II and Prince Philip to New Zealand, 1953-54*, Wellington, Historical Branch, Department of Internal Affairs and Daphne Brasell Associates, 1993, p. 16.

15 These featured respectively in the *Auckland Star*, 11 June 1947, p. 4; *Zealandia*, 23 October 1947, vol. XIV, no. 25, p. 6; *New Zealand Herald*, 9 March 1947; all quoted in Maxine Anne Iversen, 'Inextricable Links: Pakeha Perceptions of Identity and their Relationships to Britain at the Time of the Statute of Westminster', MA thesis, History, Auckland, University of Auckland, 1996, p. 62.

16 Iversen, 'Inextricable Links', p. 64.

17 See ibid., pp. 60-71, for a detailed account of the Aid for Britain campaign and the extent to which the public participated.

18 Peter Lund, '"Independence Plus": New Zealand and the Commonwealth 1945-1950', MA thesis, History, Christchurch, University of Canterbury, 1985, p. 70.

19 *Auckland Star*, 25 March 1950, p. 2.

20 Iversen, 'Inextricable Links', p. 66.

21 *New Zealand Herald*, 2 April 1947, editorial, p. 6.

22 In 1931, the British Parliament passed the Statute of Westminster which gave full autonomy to Canada, Australia, South Africa, Newfoundland, the Irish Free State and New Zealand.

23 *New Zealand Parliamentary Debates*, vol. 279, 7 November 1947, pp. 535 and 549.

24 Ibid., 7 November 1947, p. 535.

25 See J. C. Beaglehole, 'The Development of New Zealand Nationality', in *Journal of World History*, vol. 2, no. 1, 1954, p. 119.

26 Hon. Mr Parry, Minister of Foreign Affairs, *New Zealand Parliamentary Debates*, vol. 281, 17 August 1948, p. 1520; Mr Doidge, National MP for Tauranga, p. 1542.

27 Leslie Lipson, *The Politics of Equality*, Chicago, University of Chicago Press, 1948, p. 497.

28 'Population Increase in New Zealand', 12 October 1949, PM 20.21, NZ, quoted in Iversen, 'Inextricable Links', p. 54.

29 See Tom Brooking and Roberto Rabel, 'Neither British nor Polynesian: A Brief History of New Zealand's Other Immigrants', in Stuart William Greif,

Immigration and National Identity in New Zealand: One People, Two Peoples, Many Peoples?, Palmerston North, Dunmore Press, 1995, p. 37.

30 Peter Downes and Peter Harcourt, *Voices in the Air: Radio Broadcasting in New Zealand*, Wellington, Methuen, 1976, p. 153.

31 *New Zealand Listener*, 29 May 1953, p. 4.

32 *New Zealand Observer*, Wednesday, 10 December 1953, p. 5.

33 *Rotorua Post*, 30 January 1954, quoted in Phillips, *Royal Summer*, p. 54.

34 By this time, New Zealand had experienced a boom in agricultural prices and demand and enjoyed the world's second highest standard of living.

35 *Hawera Star*, 30 January 1954, quoted in Phillips, *Royal Summer*, p. 16.

36 Tangiwai means 'weeping water' in Maori.

37 Phillips, *Royal Summer*, p. 22.

38 See ibid., p. 11.

39 *Otago Daily Times*, 26 January 1954, p. 1.

40 Ibid.

41 *New Zealand Parliamentary Debates*, vol. 277, 21 August 1947, p. 536.

42 *New Zealand Parliamentary Debates*, vol. 276, 11 July 1947, p. 456.

43 *New Zealand Official Yearbook*, 1966, p. 636: by 1965 that figure had dropped to 51 per cent.

44 James Belich, *Paradise Reforged: A History of the New Zealanders from the 1880s to the Year 2000*, Auckland, Allen Lane/The Penguin Press, 2001, p. 311, and see also J. D. Gould, *The Rake's Progress? The New Zealand Economy since 1945*, Hodder & Stoughton, Auckland, 1982, p. 65.

45 See Lund, '"Independence Plus"', pp. 49–69.

46 See Keith Sinclair, *A History of New Zealand*, revised edn, Auckland, Penguin, 2000, pp. 295–6.

47 George Laking in Malcolm Templeton (ed.), *An Eye, An Ear and a Voice*, p. 52. Laking replaced Alister McIntosh as Secretary of External Affairs in 1966.

48 Letter from Holland to his cabinet, 5 November 1956, cited in Malcolm Templeton, *Ties of Blood and Empire: New Zealand's Involvement in Middle East Defence and the Suez Crisis 1947–57*, Auckland, Auckland University Press in association with the New Zealand Institute of International Affairs, 1994, p. 224.

49 Barry Gustafson, *Kiwi Keith: A Biography of Keith Holyoake*, Auckland, Auckland University Press, 2007, p. 1.

50 Ian F. G. Milner, *New Zealand's Interests and Policies in the Far East*, New York, Institute of Pacific Relations, 1939, pp. 16 and 19.

51 Extracts from a statement by the Hon. F. W. Doidge in the House of Representatives, 5 September 1950, in *New Zealand Foreign Policy: Statements and Documents, 1943–57*, Wellington, Ministry of Foreign Affairs, 1972, pp. 217–20.

52 Michael Stenson, 'The Origins and Significance of "Forward Defence" in Asia', in Sir Alister McIntosh et al., *New Zealand in World Affairs: Volume I, 1945–1957*, Wellington, New Zealand Institute of International Affairs, 1977, pp. 182–3.

53 Ibid., p. 183.

54 Ian McGibbon, 'The Defence Dimension', in Anthony L. Smith (ed.), *Southeast Asia and New Zealand: A History of Regional and Bilateral Relations*, Wellington, New Zealand Institute of International Affairs and Victoria University Press, 2005, p. 12.

55 See I. C. McGibbon, 'The Defence of New Zealand 1945–1957', in McIntosh et al., *New Zealand in World Affairs: Volume I, 1945–1957*, pp. 154–7.

56 Extracts from a statement made in the House of Representatives by the Rt Hon. S. G. Holland, 24 March 1955, in *New Zealand Foreign Policy: Statements and Documents, 1943–57*, pp. 393–4.

57 Ibid., p. 394.

58 Speech made by Holland in the House, 24 March 1955, in McIntyre and Gardner (eds), *Speeches and Documents on New Zealand History*, p. 396.

59 McGibbon, 'The Defence Dimension', in Smith (ed.), *Southeast Asia and New Zealand*, p. 19.

60 Malaya united with Sabah, Sarawak and Singapore in 1963, creating Malaysia. In 1965, Singapore withdrew from the federation.

61 Extracts from a statement by the Hon. F. W. Doidge in the House of Representatives, 12 July 1950, in *New Zealand Foreign Policy: Statements and Documents, 1943–1957*, p. 209.

62 *New Zealand Parliamentary Debates*, vol. 304, 30 September 1954, p. 2102.

63 *The Colombo Plan at 50: A New Zealand Perspective, 50th Anniversary of the Colombo Plan, 1951–2001*, Wellington, Ministry of Foreign Affairs and Trade, 2001, n.p.

64 *The Colombo Plan at 50*, n.p.
65 The Hon. T. L. Macdonald, Minister of External Affairs, 'New Zealand's Foreign Policy', in *New Commonwealth*, 30 May 1955, pp. 515–16.
66 See Mark G. Rolls, 'Growing Apart: New Zealand and Malaysia', in Smith (ed.), *Southeast Asia and New Zealand*, p. 213.
67 Ann Trotter, 'New Zealand in World Affairs: Sir Carl Berendsen in Washington, 1944–1952', in *The International History Review*, vol. 12, no. 3, August 1990, p. 479.
68 See Ian McGibbon, 'New Zealand's Intervention in the Korean War, June–July 1950', in *The International History Review*, vol. 11, no. 2, May 1989, pp. 205–408, for a discussion on the background to the war.
69 *New Zealand Listener*, 28 July 1950, p. 4.
70 Malcolm McKinnon, *Independence and Foreign Policy: New Zealand in the World since 1935*, Auckland, Auckland University Press, 1993, p. 118.
71 See McGibbon, 'New Zealand's Intervention in the Korean War', pp. 278–9.
72 *Auckland Star*, 18 July 1950, editorial, p. 2. See also Ian McGibbon, *New Zealand and the Korean War*, Auckland, Oxford University Press, 1992, pp. 57–58, 73.
73 McGibbon, 'New Zealand's Intervention in the Korean War', p. 282.
74 Ibid., p. 286.
75 There were £46 million' worth of wool exports in 1949, which rose to over £74 million in 1950, £128 million in 1951 and £82 million in 1952; *New Zealand Official Yearbook*, 1953, p. 260.
76 Richard Kennaway, *New Zealand Foreign Policy, 1951–1971*, Wellington, Hicks Smith, 1972, p. 28.
77 Letter from Alister McIntosh, Secretary of External Affairs and Permanent Head of the Prime Minister's Department, to Carl Berendsen, New Zealand's ambassador in Washington, 12 April 1950, in McGibbon (ed.), *Undiplomatic Dialogue*, p. 225.
78 Quoted in Eric Olssen, 'The Origins of Anzus Reconsidered', in *Historical and Political Studies*, vol. 1, no. 2, December 1970, p. 107.
79 Ann Trotter, 'Sir Carl Berendsen in Washington', p. 481.
80 Trevor Richard Reese, *Australia, New Zealand and the United States: A Survey of International Relations, 1941–1968*, London, Oxford University Press, 1969, p. 157.
81 Letter from F. W. Doidge, Minister of External Affairs, to Sir Carl Berendsen, New Zealand Ambassador, Washington, 9 May 1950, in Robin Kay (ed.), *Documents on New Zealand External Relations, Volume III, The Anzus Pact and the Treaty of Peace with Japan*, Wellington, Historical Publications Branch, Department of Internal Affairs, V. R. Ward, Government Printer, 1985, p. 546. ANZUS stands for Australia, New Zealand and United States.
82 Comments made by Churchill when he returned to power in England towards the end of 1951; Reese, *Australia, New Zealand and the United States*, p. 128.
83 *New Zealand Parliamentary Debates*, vol. 295, 9 October 1951, p. 205; See also McKinnon, *Independence and Foreign Policy*, pp. 120–3.
84 Quoted in McKinnon, *Independence and Foreign Policy*, p. 120.
85 Letter, Holland to UKHC, Wellington (R. Price), 22 March 1951, in Kay (ed.), *Documents on New Zealand External Relations, Volume III, The Anzus Pact and the Treaty of Peace with Japan*, p. 674, quoted in Brook Barrington, 'New Zealand and the Search for Security 1944–1954: "A Modest and Moderate Collaboration"', PhD thesis, History, Auckland, University of Auckland, 1993, p. 202.
86 A. D. McIntosh, 'Administration of an Independent New Zealand Foreign Policy', in T. C. Larkin (ed.), *New Zealand's External Relations*, Wellington, New Zealand Institute of Public Administration, 1962, p. 31.
87 See F. L. W. Wood, 'The ANZAC Dilemma', *International Affairs*, vol. 29, April 1953, pp. 184–92.
88 R. R. Cunninghame, 'The Development of New Zealand's Foreign Policy and Political Alignments', in Larkin (ed.), *New Zealand's External Relations*, p. 26.
89 *Appendices to the Journals of the House of Representatives*, 1966, vol. 1, A-8, 'Review of Defence Policy 1966', pp. 5–6.
90 Some military historians have called this policy 'Forward Defence'. See, for example, Ian McGibbon, 'Forward Defence: The Southeast Asian Commitment', in Malcolm McKinnon (ed.), *New Zealand in World Affairs: Volume II, 1957–1972*, Wellington, New Zealand Institute of International Affairs, 1991, pp. 9–39.
91 Claire Loftus Nelson, *Long Time Passing: New Zealand Memories of the Vietnam*

War, Wellington, National Radio, 1990, p. 20.

92 *External Affairs Review*, vol. XIII, no. 6, June 1963, p. 27.

93 Minutes of Chiefs of Staff Committee, COS (61) M. 46, 14 December 1961, 478/4/6, quoted in Roberto Rabel, 'Vietnam and the Collapse of the Foreign Policy Consensus', in McKinnon (ed.), *New Zealand in World Affairs, Volume II, 1957–1972*, p. 44.

94 Quoted in Rabel, 'Vietnam and the Collapse of the Foreign Policy Consensus', in McKinnon (ed.), *New Zealand in World Affairs: Volume II, 1957–1972*, p. 45.

95 Roberto Rabel, *New Zealand and the Vietnam War: Politics and Diplomacy*, Auckland, Auckland University Press, 2005, p. 133.

96 Brief: 'Visit of Mr Cabot Lodge', April 1965, PM 478/4/I, quoted in Rabel, *New Zealand and the Vietnam War*, p. 93.

97 EA to PM, 1 May 1965, PM 478/4I, quoted in Rabel, *New Zealand and the Vietnam War*, p. 97.

98 Quoted in Nelson, *Long Time Passing*, p. 16.

99 *Dominion*, 14 May 1965, quoted in McKinnon, *Independence and Foreign Policy*, p. 158.

100 McGibbon in Smith (ed.), *Southeast Asia and New Zealand*, p. 13.

101 Gustafson, *Kiwi Keith*, p. 293. The EEC is now the European Union (EU).

102 Juliet Lodge, *The European Community and New Zealand*, London, Frances Pinter, 1982, p. 44.

103 Chris Nixon and John Yeabsley, *New Zealand's Trade Policy Odyssey: Ottawa, via Marrakech, and On*, Wellington, New Zealand Institute of Economic Research, 2002, p. 116, cited in Gustafson, *Kiwi Keith*, p. 300.

104 Sir Con O'Neill, Deputy Undersecretary of State in charge of EEC negotiations, cited in Gustafson, *Kiwi Keith*, p. 303.

105 Ibid.

106 Quoted in Con O'Neill, *Britain's Entry into the European Community*, London, Whitehall History Publications and Frank Cass, 2000, pp. 160–1, cited in Gustafson, *Kiwi Keith*, p. 303.

107 Record of meeting, 21 September 1970, CAB 164/463, British National Archives, cited in Gustafson, *Kiwi Keith*, pp. 304–5.

108 Gustafson, *Kiwi Keith*, p. 308.

109 *New Zealand Official Yearbook*, 1973, p. 614.

110 Derek Tonkin to K. W. Kelley, Foreign and Commonwealth Office, 12 November 1971, FCO 24/1258, British National Archives, in Gustafson, *Kiwi Keith*, p. 308.

111 Gary Hawke, 'Economic Trends and Economic Policy', in Rice (ed.), *The Oxford History of New Zealand*, 2nd edn, p. 424.

112 Geoff Bertram, 'The New Zealand Economy 1900–2000', Chapter 22 in Giselle Byrnes (ed.), *The New Oxford History of New Zealand*, Melbourne, Oxford University Press, 2009, p. 544.

113 Gustafson, *Kiwi Keith*, p. 319.

114 Gould, *The Rake's Progress?*, p. 102.

115 Kennaway, *New Zealand Foreign Policy, 1951–1971*, pp. 125–6.

116 McKinnon, *Independence and Foreign Policy*, p. 211.

117 Mein Smith et al., *Remaking the Tasman World*, p. 112.

118 Philippa Mein Smith, 'The Tasman World', in Byrnes (ed.), *The New Oxford History of New Zealand*, p. 313.

119 McKinnon, *Independence and Foreign Policy*, p. 220.

120 See Mein Smith et al., *Remaking the Tasman World*.

121 Kennaway, *New Zealand Foreign Policy, 1951–1971*, p. 118.

122 Ian McGibbon, 'From Anzac Pact to ANZAC Frigates: The Australia–New Zealand Defence Relationship since the Second World War', in *Australia–New Zealand: Aspects of a Relationship*, proceedings of the Stout Research Centre, Eighth Annual Conference, Victoria University of Wellington, 6–8 September 1991, Wellington, n.p.

123 Bruce Brown, '"Foreign Policy is Trade": Trade is Foreign Policy: Some Principal New Zealand Trade Policy Problems since the Second World War', in Ann Trotter (ed.), *Fifty Years of New Zealand Foreign Policy Making: Papers from the Twenty-eighth Foreign Policy School, 1993*, Dunedin, University of Otago Press, 1993, pp. 84–85.

124 Ibid., p. 85.

125 Boyd, 'New Zealand and the other Pacific Islands', in Sinclair (ed.), *The Oxford Illustrated History of New Zealand*, 2nd edn, p. 298.

126 Mein Smith et al., *Remaking the Tasman World*, p. 109.

127 McGibbon (ed.), *Undiplomatic Dialogue*, p. 107.

128 Ibid., p. 230.

129 Ibid., p. 181.

130 McGibbon, *New Zealand and the Korean War*, p. 99.

131 Gustafson, *Kiwi Keith*, p. 189.

132 Cited in Gustafson, ibid., p. 190.

133 I. M. R. McLennan to Commonwealth Relations Office, 21 August 1964, CAB 95/453, British National Archives, and Bruce Cumming to Commonwealth Relations Office, 4 July 1961, DO 169/38, British National Archives, cited in Gustafson, *Kiwi Keith*, p. 177.

134 Damon Salesa, 'New Zealand's Pacific', Chapter 7 in Byrnes (ed.), *The New Oxford History of New Zealand*, p. 167.

135 Boyd, 'New Zealand and the other Pacific Islands', in Sinclair (ed.), *The Oxford Illustrated History of New Zealand*, 2nd edn, pp. 310, 314.

136 Gustafson, *Kiwi Keith*, p. 177.

137 Ibid., p. 195.

138 Ibid., p. 193.

139 Boyd, 'New Zealand and the other Pacific Islands', in Sinclair (ed.), *The Oxford Illustrated History of New Zealand*, 2nd edn, p. 295.

CHAPTER THREE Creating New Zealand: Culture and Character

1 Charles Brasch, cited in *Thirty-seven New Zealand Paintings from the Collection of Charles Brasch and Rodney Kennedy*, Auckland, Auckland City Art Gallery, 1958, p. 6.

2 W. H. Oliver's chapter about New Zealand art and culture 1940–1980, in Geoffrey W. Rice (ed.), *The Oxford History of New Zealand*, 2nd edn, Auckland, Oxford University Press, 1992, pp. 539–70 was aptly entitled 'The Awakening Imagination'.

3 Francis Pound, *The Invention of New Zealand: Art & National Identity 1930–1970*, Auckland, Auckland University Press, 2009, p. 331.

4 Allen Curnow (ed.), *The Penguin Book of New Zealand Verse*, Auckland, published under licence from Penguin Books by Blackwood and Janet Paul, 1960, pp. 59–60.

5 See Pound, *The Invention of New Zealand*, pp. 330–3.

6 Ibid., p. 31.

7 Keith Sinclair, 'Memories of T. H. Scott (1918–60)', *Landfall*, vol. 14, no. 2, June 1960, p. 182.

8 Pound, *The Invention of New Zealand*, pp. 7 and 9.

9 C. K. Stead, *South-West of Eden: A Memoir, 1932–1956*, Auckland, Auckland University Press, 2010, p. 271.

10 Pound, *The Invention of New Zealand*, Chapter 1:2, pp. 14–25.

11 C. K. Stead, *In the Glass Case: Essays on New Zealand Literature*, Auckland, Auckland University Press/Oxford University Press, 1981, p. 1945.

12 Denis Glover, 'The Magpies', in Bill Manhire (ed.), *Selected Poems: Denis Glover*, Wellington, Victoria University Press, 1995, p. 32. This poem first appeared in Allen Curnow (ed.), *Recent Poems*, Christchurch, Caxton Press, 1941.

13 This continued until 1988, when the fund came under the responsibility of the New Zealand Arts Council, administered since 1994 by Creative New Zealand.

14 Oliver, 'The Awakening Imagination', in Rice (ed.), *The Oxford History of New Zealand*, 2nd edn, pp. 560–1.

15 Ibid., p. 560, and see Sarah Shieff, 'Nathan's Kin: Jews and Music in New Zealand', in Leonard Bell and Diana Morrow (eds), *Jewish Lives in New Zealand: A History*, Auckland, Random House, 2012, pp. 26–49.

16 Allen Curnow (ed.), Introduction, *A Book of New Zealand Verse 1923–45*, Christchurch, Caxton Press, 1945, p. 17.

17 Ibid., pp. 14–15.

18 Oliver, 'The Awakening Imagination', in Rice (ed.), *The Oxford History of New Zealand*, 2nd edn, p. 42.

19 Allen Curnow, 'New Zealand Literature: The Case for a Working Definition', in Allen Curnow, *Look Back Harder: Critical Writings 1935–1984*, ed. Peter Simpson, Auckland, Auckland University Press, 1987, p. 200.

20 See Stead, *South-West of Eden*, pp. 195–6.

21 Curnow (ed.), Introduction, *A Book of New Zealand Verse 1923–45*, p. 43.

22 Peter Simpson, 'Brasch, Charles (1909–73)', in Roger Robinson and Nelson Wattie (eds), *The Oxford Companion to New Zealand Literature*, Auckland, Oxford University Press, 1998, p. 68.

23 Charles Brasch, 'The Islands', in Curnow (ed.), *The Penguin Book of New Zealand Verse*, p. 178.

24 Quoted in Keith Sinclair, *Halfway Round the Harbour: An Autobiography*, Auckland, Penguin Books, 1993, p. 140.

25 John Geraets, 'Landfall Under Brasch: The

Humanizing Journey', PhD thesis, English, Auckland, University of Auckland, 1982, p. 55.

26 See Charles Brasch, 'Foreword', *Landfall Country: Work from Landfall ,1947–1961*, Christchurch, Caxton Press, 1962, p. 13.

27 Paula Green, 'The Fifties, Sixties and Seventies', in Paula Green and Harry Ricketts (eds), *99 Ways into New Zealand Poetry*, Auckland, Vintage Books, 2010, p. 150.

28 Alistair Campbell, 'At the great water's edge', in Alistair Campbell, *Mine Eyes Dazzle*, Christchurch, Pegasus Press, 1951, p. 24.

29 Green, 'The Fifties, Sixties and Seventies', in Green and Ricketts (eds), *99 Ways into New Zealand Poetry*, p. 151.

30 Kendrick Smithyman, *A Way of Saying: A Study of New Zealand Poetry*, Auckland, Collins, 1965, p. 46.

31 Charles Doyle, *Recent Poetry in New Zealand*, Auckland, Collins, 1965, p. 14.

32 Sinclair, *Halfway Round the Harbour*, p. 152.

33 Elizabeth Caffin, 'Romantics and Modernists, 1945–1960', in Terry Sturm (ed.), *The Oxford History of New Zealand Literature in English*, 2nd edn, Auckland, Oxford University Press, 1998, p. 474.

34 James K. Baxter, 'A Bucket of Blood for a Dollar (A conversation between Uncle Sam and the Rt Hon. Keith Holyoake, Prime Minister of New Zealand)', in John Weir (ed.), *James K. Baxter: Collected Poems*, Auckland, Oxford University Press, 1995, p. 320.

35 James K. Baxter, *Recent Trends in New Zealand Poetry*, Christchurch, Caxton Press, 1951, pp. 7–8.

36 Allen Curnow, 'The Skeleton of the Great Moa in the Canterbury Museum, Christchurch', in Allen Curnow, *Selected Poems*, Penguin, Auckland, 1982, p. 77.

37 Patrick Evans, *The Penguin History of New Zealand Literature*, Auckland, Penguin, 1990, p. 165.

38 Peter Simpson, Introduction to Curnow, *Look Back Harder*, p. xii.

39 Ibid., p. xiii.

40 Frank McKay, *James K. Baxter as Critic: A Selection from his Literary Criticism*, Auckland, Heinemann Educational, 1978, p. 77.

41 Ibid., p. 90.

42 Curnow (ed.), *The Penguin Book of New Zealand Verse*, p. 64.

43 MacDonald P. Jackson, Chapter 6, 'Poetry, Part One, Beginnings to 1945', in Sturm (ed.), *The Oxford History of New Zealand Literature in English*, 2nd edn, p. 430.

44 Mary Stanley, 'The Wife Speaks', in *Starveling Year and Other Poems*, Auckland, Auckland University Press, 1994, p. 23.

45 Allen Curnow, 'New Zealand Literature: The Case for a Definition', in Wystan Curnow (ed.), *Essays on New Zealand Literature*, Auckland, Heinemann Educational, 1973, p. 140.

46 Caffin, 'Romantics and Modernists, 1945–1960', in Sturm (ed.), *The Oxford History of New Zealand Literature in English*, 2nd edn, p. 467.

47 Green, 'The Fifties, Sixties and Seventies', in Green and Ricketts, *99 Ways into New Zealand Poetry*, p. 156.

48 Hone Tuwhare, 'That Morning Early', in Tuwhare, Hone, *Small Holes in the Silence: Collected Works*, Auckland, Random House, 2011, p. 24.

49 Terry Sturm, 'Tuwhare, Hone (1922–)', in Robinson and Wattie (eds), *The Oxford Companion to New Zealand Literature*, p. 550.

50 Allen Curnow, *Collected Poems, 1933–1973*, Wellington, A. H. & A. W. Reed, 1974, p. xiii.

51 J. C. Reid, *Creative Writing in New Zealand: A Brief Critical History*, Auckland, printed for the author by Whitcombe & Tombs, 1946, p. 8.

52 M. H. Holcroft, 'A Good Year for Books', *New Zealand Listener*, 16 December 1960, p. 10.

53 See Lawrence Jones, Chapter 3, 'The Novel', in Sturm (ed.), *The Oxford History of New Zealand Literature in English*, 2nd edn, pp. 120–78.

54 See C. K. Stead's analysis of *Man Alone* in 'John Mulgan: A Question of Identity', in *In the Glass Case*, pp. 67–99.

55 See ibid., p. 85, on Johnson's Kiwi qualities and his similarity to the soldiers described in *Report on Experience*.

56 Lawrence Jones, 'Ballantyne, David (1924–86)', in Robinson and Wattie (eds), *The Oxford Companion to New Zealand Literature*, p. 39.

57 Bill Pearson, 'Fretful Sleepers: A Sketch of New Zealand Behaviour and its Implications for the Artist', in *Fretful Sleepers and Other Essays*, London,

Heinemann Educational, 1974, pp. 1–32.

58 Ibid., p. 12.

59 Lawrence Jones, 'Courage, James (1905–63)' in Robinson and Wattie (eds), *The Oxford Companion to New Zealand Literature*, p. 113.

60 Frank Sargeson, *Sargeson*, Auckland, Penguin, 1981, p. 241.

61 See Janet Wilson (ed.), Introduction, *Frank Sargeson's Stories*, Auckland, Cape Catley, 2010, p. 12.

62 Quoted in R. A. Copland, *Frank Sargeson*, Wellington, Oxford University Press, 1976, pp. 9–10.

63 Joan Stevens, *The New Zealand Novel, 1860–1965*, 2nd edn, Wellington, A. H. & A. W. Reed, 1966, pp. 69–70.

64 Wilson (ed.), Introduction, *Frank Sargeson's Stories*, p. 12. Sargeson received a two-year suspended sentence for the homosexual offence, on the condition that he live with his uncle on his Okahukara farm.

65 Stead, *South-West of Eden*, p. 299.

66 'A Letter to Frank Sargeson', *Landfall*, vol. 7, no. 1, March 1953, p. 5.

67 See Wilson (ed.), Introduction, *Frank Sargeson's Stories*, p. 18.

68 See Frank Sargeson to Denis Glover, 26 January 1937, and Sargeson to Glover, 9 August 1937, in Sarah Shieff (ed.), *Letters of Frank Sargeson*, Auckland, Vintage/Random House, 2012, pp. 12 and 14.

69 Robert Chapman, 'Fiction and the Social Pattern', in Elizabeth McLeay (ed.), *New Zealand Politics and Social Patterns: Selected Works by Robert Chapman*, Wellington, Victoria University Press, 1999, p. 44. This essay, written in 1952, first appeared in *Landfall*, vol. 7, no. 1, March 1953.

70 Quoted in Heather Roberts, *Where Did She Come From? New Zealand Women Novelists 1862–1987*, Wellington, Allen & Unwin/Port Nicholson Press, 1989, p. 65.

71 The other three 'grande dames' were Margery Allingham, Agatha Christie and Dorothy L. Sayers. See Terry Sturm, 'Popular Fiction', in Sturm (ed.), *The Oxford History of New Zealand Literature in English*, 2nd edn, pp. 591–2.

72 Peter Simpson, *New Zealand Writers and their Work: Ronald Hugh Morrison*, Auckland, Oxford University Press, 1982, p. 12.

73 See Julia Millen's biography *Ronald Hugh Morrieson*, Auckland, David Ling, 1996, and her entry 'Morrieson, James Ronald Hugh (1922–1972)', in *Dictionary of New Zealand Biography, Te Ara — The Encyclopedia of New Zealand*, updated 1 September 2010, www.teara.govt.nz/en/biographies/5m57/morrieson-james-ronald-hugh.

74 Stead, *In the Glass Case*, p. 109.

75 Bill Manhire, *Maurice Gee*, Auckland, Oxford University Press, 1986, p. 5.

76 Interview by Peter Beatson, 'Noel Hilliard: The Public and Private Self', March 1988, n.p., www.massey.ac.nz/massey/fms/Colleges/College%20of%20Humanities%20and%20Social%20Sciences/PEP/PDF_documents/Sociology/Beatson/Noel%20Hilliard%20Interview.pdf.

77 Ibid.

78 H. Winston Rhodes, *New Zealand Fiction since 1945: A Critical Survey of Recent Novels and Short Stories*, Dunedin, J. McIndoe, 1968, p. 32.

79 Janet Wilson, 'Duckworth, Marilyn (1935–)', in Robinson and Wattie (eds), *The Oxford Companion to New Zealand Literature*, p. 148.

80 Evans, *The Penguin History of New Zealand Literature*, p. 197.

81 See, for example, the discussion by C. K. Stead, 'Sylvia Ashton-Warner', in *In the Glass Case*, pp. 51–66. In 1980, Warner's autobiography *I Passed This Way*, New York, Knopf, 1979, won the New Zealand Book Award for Non-Fiction.

82 Jones, 'The Novel', in Sturm (ed.), *The Oxford History of New Zealand Literature in English*, 2nd edn, p. 167.

83 J. C. Reid, 'Literature', in A. L. McLeod (ed.), *The Pattern of New Zealand Culture*, New York, Cornell University Press, 1968, p. 32.

84 Robin Hyde, letter in D. I. B. Smith (ed.), Introduction, *Passport to Hell*, Auckland, Auckland University Press, 1986, p. xviii.

85 Janet Frame, 'Beginnings', *Landfall*, vol. 19, no. 1, March 1965, p. 45.

86 Quoted in Jones, 'The Novel', in Sturm (ed.), *The Oxford History of New Zealand Literature in English*, 2nd edn, p. 181.

87 Rhodes, *New Zealand Fiction since 1945*, p. 47.

88 See, for example, Bill Pearson, 'A Mixed Performance', in Bill Pearson, *Fretful Sleepers and Other Essays*, pp. 73–79.

89   Sturm, 'Popular Fiction', in Sturm (ed.), *The Oxford History of New Zealand Literature in English*, 2nd edn, p. 610.

90   Ibid., p. 601.

91   Chapman, 'Fiction and the Social Pattern', in McLeay (ed.), *New Zealand Politics and Social Patterns*, p. 23.

92   Michael Beveridge, 'Conversation with Frank Sargeson: An Interview with Michael Beveridge', in Kevin Cunningham (ed.), *Conversation in a Train and other Critical Writing*, Auckland, Auckland University Press/Oxford University Press, 1983, p. 164.

93   Jones, 'The Novel', in Sturm (ed.), *The Oxford History of New Zealand Literature in English*, 2nd edn, p. 170.

94   Ian Cross, 'The God Boy', a lecture delivered to Stage 1 students at the University of Otago on 20 September 1962, in *Journal of New Zealand Literature*, no. 8, 1990, pp. 8–10.

95   Chapman, 'Fiction and the Social Pattern', in McLeay (ed.), *New Zealand Politics and Social Patterns*, p. 46.

96   See Peter Gibbons, 'From National Identity to Post-colonial Perspectives, 1930s–1990s', in Sturm (ed.), *The Oxford History of New Zealand Literature in English*, 2nd edn, pp. 72–73.

97   John Stenhouse, 'Religion and Society', in Giselle Byrnes (ed.), *The New Oxford History of New Zealand*, Melbourne, Oxford University Press, 2009, p. 353.

98   Sinclair, *Halfway Round the Harbour*, p. 82.

99   Dennis McEldowney, 'Publishing, Patronage, Literary Magazines', in Robinson and Wattie (eds), *The Oxford Companion to New Zealand Literature*, p. 655.

100 Noel Waite, 'Pegasus Press', ibid., p. 435.

101 David Blackwood Paul, 'Publishing and Bookselling', in A. H. McLintock (ed.), *An Encyclopaedia of New Zealand*, vol. 2, Wellington, R. E. Owen, Government Printer, 1966, p. 885.

102 'New Zealand Listener', in Robinson and Wattie (eds), *The Oxford Companion to New Zealand Literature*, p. 399.

103 The *Journal* was established in 1907. For a detailed history, see Gregory O'Brien, *A Nest of Singing Birds: 100 Years of the New Zealand School Journal*, Wellington, Learning Media Limited, 2007.

104 J. C. Beaglehole, 'A Small Bouquet for the Education Department', *Arts Year Book*, no.

7, 1951, Wellington, Wingfield Press, p. 124.

105 Quoted in O'Brien, ibid., p. 37.

106 Ibid., p. 7.

107 Chapman, 'Fiction and the Social Pattern', in McLeay (ed.), *New Zealand Politics and Social Patterns*, pp. 26, 46.

108 Beveridge, 'Conversation with Frank Sargeson', in Cunningham (ed.), *Conversation in a Train and other Critical Writing*, pp. 174–5.

109 Elizabeth Louise C'Ailceta Cooke, 'The Group 1927–1977: An Annotated Bibliography', Master of Library and Information Studies, Wellington, Victoria University, 1999, p. 8.

110 Gordon H. Brown and Hamish Keith, *An Introduction to New Zealand Painting 1839–1980*, 2nd edn, Auckland, Collins, 1982, p. 139.

111 Gordon H. Brown, *New Zealand Painting, 1920–1940: Adaptation and Nationalism*, Wellington, Queen Elizabeth II Arts Council of New Zealand, 1975, pp. 11 and 58.

112 Linda Gill, 'Hodgkins, Frances Mary (1869–1947)', *Dictionary of New Zealand Biography, Te Ara — The Encyclopedia of New Zealand*, updated 30 October 2012, www.teara.govt.nz/en/biographies/2h41/hodgkins-frances-mary.

113 A. H. McLintock (ed.), *National Centennial Exhibition of New Zealand Art: Catalogue*, Wellington, Department of Internal Affairs, 1940, pp. 15–16.

114 *The Studio*, vol. 135, no. 161, April 1948, p. 103.

115 P. A. Tomory, 'Looking at Art in New Zealand', *Landfall*, vol. 12, no. 2, June 1958, p. 167.

116 Charles Brasch, 'A Note on the Work of Colin McCahon', *Landfall*, vol. 4, no. 4, December 1950, p. 338.

117 See Brown and Keith, *An Introduction to New Zealand Painting*, pp. 100–2.

118 M. H. Holcroft, *Encircling Seas*, Christchurch, Caxton Press, 1946, p. 195.

119 Michael Dunn, *A Concise History of New Zealand Painting*, Auckland, David Bateman, 1991, p. 106.

120 Gordon H. Brown, *Colin McCahon: Artist*, 2nd edn, Wellington, Reed, 1993, p. 26.

121 Colin McCahon, 'Beginnings', *Landfall*, vol. 80, no. 4, December 1966, pp. 360–4.

122 P. A. Tomory, 'It Started in the Thirties', *New Zealand Listener*, 6 November 1964, p. 5.

123 Peter Tomory, 'The Visual Arts', in Keith Sinclair (ed.), *Distance Looks Our Way: The Effects of Remoteness on New Zealand*, Auckland, Paul's Book Arcade for the University of Auckland, 1961, p. 74.

124 Peter Simpson, 'Emerging Abstraction', in Ron Brownson (ed.), *Art Toi: New Zealand Art at Auckland Art Gallery Toi o Tāmaki*, Auckland, Auckland Art Gallery Toi o Tāmaki, Auckland 2011, p. 122.

125 Charles Brasch, 'The Group Show: Pictures from Two Decades', *Press*, 22 November 1947, p. 5.

126 M. T. Woollaston, *The Far-away Hills: A Meditation on New Zealand Landscape*, Auckland, Auckland Gallery Associates, 1962, p. 42.

127 Brown and Keith, *An Introduction to New Zealand Painting*, p. 143.

128 A. R. D. Fairburn, 'Art in Canterbury: Some Notes on the Group Show', *Landfall*, vol. 2, no. 1, March 1948, p. 50.

129 H. Wadman, *Yearbook of the Arts in New Zealand*, no. 3, 1947, p. 11.

130 Ron Brownson, 'Journey into New Zealand Art 1920–1965', in Brownson (ed.), *Art Toi*, p. 91.

131 E. H. McCormick, 'The Louise Henderson Exhibition: A Note in Retrospect', *Landfall*, vol. 8, no. 1, March 1954, p. 54.

132 Gordon H. Brown, *New Zealand Painting, 1940–1960: Conformity and Dissension*, Wellington, Queen Elizabeth II Arts Council of New Zealand, 1981, p. 84.

133 Gordon Walters, 'A Difficult Time for Artists', *Landfall*, 'The Fifties Issue', New Series, vol. 1, no. 1, April 1993, p. 22.

134 Alan Wright and Edward Hanfling, *Mrkusich: The Art of Transformation*, Auckland, Auckland University Press, 2009, p. 4.

135 Ibid., p. 2.

136 Peter Leech, 'Milan Mrkusich: The Architecture of the Painted Surface', *Art New Zealand*, no. 19, Autumn 1981, p. 37.

137 Michael Dunn and Petar Vuletic, *Milan Mrkusich: Paintings 1946–1972, Essay on Development*, Auckland, Auckland City Art Gallery, 1972, p. 8.

138 Michael Brett, 'Abstract Artists Come in from the Cold', *Auckland Star*, 9 April 1974, quoted in Wright and Hanfling, *Mrkusich*, p. 8.

139 'British Tachiste Painting "Not Worthy" of National Gallery', *Auckland Star*, 7 June 1958.

140 'Mr. Westbrook's Impression After Dominion Tour', *New Zealand Herald*, 10 December 1952.

141 Maria E. Brown, 'The History and Function of the Auckland City Art Gallery in Constructing a Canon of Modernist New Zealand Art', MA thesis, Art History, Auckland, University of Auckland, 1999, p. 56.

142 Brown, *New Zealand Painting, 1920–1940: Conformity and Dissension*, p. 89.

143 Brown and Keith, *An Introduction to New Zealand Painting*, p. 181.

144 John Summers, 'The Group Show', *Landfall*, vol. 3, no. 1, March 1949, p. 63.

145 Tony Green, 'Modernism and Modernization', in Mary Barr (ed.), *Headlands: Thinking Through New Zealand Art*, Sydney, Museum of Contemporary Art, 1992, p. 152.

146 Brown, *New Zealand Painting, 1940–1960: Conformity and Dissension*, p. 57.

147 D. P. Miller, 'Don Peebles Retrospective', Dowse Art Gallery, 1973, p. 4, quoted in Brown, ibid.

148 Brown, 'The History and Function of the Auckland City Art Gallery in Constructing a Canon of Modernist New Zealand Art', pp. 205–10.

149 See Brown and Keith, *An Introduction to New Zealand Painting*, pp. 133–47.

150 Peter Cape, *New Zealand Painting since 1960: A Study in Themes and Developments*, Auckland, Collins, 1979, p. 15. This was known as the Queen Elizabeth II Arts Council from 1963.

151 Walters, 'A Difficult Time for Artists', p. 22.

152 Stewart Bell Maclennan, 'Art in New Zealand: Survey, Trends and Influences, 1938 to Present', in A. H. McClintock (ed.), *An Encyclopedia of New Zealand*, vol. 1, Wellington, R. E. Owen, Government Printer, 1966, p. 87.

153 Arnold Wilson, 'Beginning to Bubble', *Landfall*, 'The Fifties Issue', New Series, vol. 1, no. 1, April 1993, p. 24.

154 Ibid., pp. 26–27.

155 Jonathan Mane-Wheoki, 'Modern Maori Art', in Brownson (ed.), *Art Toi*, p. 163.

156 Maclennan, 'Art in New Zealand', in McLintock (ed.), *An Encyclopedia of New Zealand*, vol. 1, p. 87.

157 Mane-Wheoki, 'Modern Maori Art', in Brownson (ed.), *Art Toi*, p. 168. Hotere was included in Gordon H. Brown and Hamish Keith's *An Introduction to New Zealand*

Painting 1839–1980, Auckland, William Collins, 1969, p. 177. Again he was the only Maori to be included in Gil Docking's *Two Hundred Years of New Zealand Painting*, Wellington, A. H. & A. W. Reed, 1971, p. 180.

158 Christina Barton, 'Post-Object Art: Ralph Hotere, Te Aupouri, born 1931', in Brownson (ed.), *Art Toi*, p. 256.

159 Roger Duff, 'Report on Native Rock Drawings of South Canterbury', 15 February 1946, pp. 1–2, Archives New Zealand, Wellington, microfilm 3564, quoted in Pound, *The Invention of New Zealand*, p. 286.

160 Theo Schoon, 'Maori Rock Drawings', Radio New Zealand Sound Archives, Theo Schoon and Roger Duff, introduced by Arnold Wall, 1952, quoted in Pound, *The Invention of New Zealand*, p. 283.

161 A. R. D. Fairburn, 'Polynesian Cave Drawings', in *Home and Building*, vol. XI, no. 6, June–July 1949, p. 63.

162 Pound, *The Invention of New Zealand*, p. 296.

163 Brownson in *Art Toi*, p. 93.

164 Oliver, 'The Awakening Imagination', in Rice (ed.), *The Oxford History of New Zealand*, 2nd edn, p. 581.

165 Paul Pascoe and Humphrey Hall, 'The Modern House' (1947), in Douglas Lloyd Jenkins (ed.), *New Dreamland: Writing New Zealand Architecture*, Auckland, Godwit, 2005, p. 136.

166 See Oliver, 'The Awakening Imagination', in Rice (ed.), *The Oxford History of New Zealand*, 2nd edn, p. 562.

167 Paul Pascoe, 'Houses', in *Making New Zealand*, no. 20, 1939, pp. 24–25.

168 Douglas Lloyd Jenkins, *At Home: A Century of New Zealand Design*, Auckland, Godwit, 2004, p. 92.

169 Vernon Brown quoted in Yvonne Chunn, 'Plainly, Vernon Brown', in *Thursday*, 23 January 1975, pp. 6–9.

170 Vernon Brown quoted in David Mitchell and Gillian Chaplin, *The Elegant Shed: New Zealand Architecture since 1945*, Auckland, Oxford University Press, 1984, p. 28. Arney Road is in the Auckland suburb of Remuera.

171 These publications included, among others, *Home and Building* (originally *Building Today*, which started in 1936), *Design Review Yearbook of the Arts* (1945) and *Landfall* (1947). Elements of these architects' houses were widely copied by New Zealand builders.

172 'On the Necessity for Architecture: The Manifesto of the Architectural Group' (1948), in Jenkins (ed.), *New Dreamland*, p. 142.

173 Julia Gatley (ed.), *Group Architects: Towards a New Zealand Architecture*, Auckland, Auckland University Press, 2010, p. 50.

174 *New Zealand Herald*, 11 May 1950.

175 Miles Warren, 'Style in New Zealand Architecture', in *New Zealand Architect*, no. 3, 1978, p. 2.

176 Jenkins, *At Home*, p. 119.

177 Peter Shaw, *A History of New Zealand Architecture*, 2nd edn, Auckland, Hodder Moa Beckett, 1997, pp. 147–50.

178 Ibid., p. 141.

179 Jenkins, *At Home*, p. 109.

180 See Linda Tyler, 'Plischke, Ernst Anton (1903–1992)', *Dictionary of New Zealand Biography*, Te Ara — The Encyclopedia of New Zealand, updated 1 September 2010, www.TeAra.govt.nz/en/biographies/5p31/1.

181 Jenkins, *At Home*, p. 134.

182 Ibid., p. 130.

183 Ibid., p. 128.

184 Mitchell and Chaplin, *The Elegant Shed*, pp. 67–71.

185 Ibid., pp. 65–71.

186 Shaw, *A History of New Zealand Architecture*, 2nd edn, p. 160.

187 Mitchell and Chaplin, *The Elegant Shed*, p. 53.

188 Jack Manning (then of Thorpe, Cutter, Pickmere and Douglas), quoted in Mitchell and Chaplin, ibid., p. 40.

189 Ibid., pp. 61, 63 and 64.

190 Shaw, *A History of New Zealand Architecture*, 2nd edn, p. 151.

191 Mitchell and Chaplin, *The Elegant Shed*, p. 40.

192 Ibid., p. 74.

193 See William H. Allington, 'Architecture', in Ian Wards (ed.), *Thirteen Facets: Essays to Celebrate the Silver Jubilee of Queen Elizabeth the Second, 1952–1977*, Wellington, E. C. Keating, Government Printer, 1978, p. 350.

194 Stead, *South-West of Eden*, p. 271.

195 R. M. Chapman, 'No Land is an Island: Twentieth Century Politics', in Sinclair (ed.), *Distance Looks Our Way*, p. 44. The title 'Distance Looks Our Way' is from Charles Brasch's poem 'The Islands'.

CHAPTER FOUR Leisure and Popular
Pastimes: Unsettling Influences

1 John Mulgan, *Report on Experience*,
London, Oxford University Press, 1947,
p. 6.
2 Keith Sinclair, *Walter Nash*, Auckland,
Auckland University Press/Oxford
University Press, 1976, p. 306.
3 See Roberto Rabel (ed.), *The American
Century? In Retrospect and Prospect*,
Westport, Connecticut, Praeger, 2002, p. 1.
4 *New Zealand Parliamentary Debates*, vol.
219, 18 September 1928, p. 324.
5 Geoff Lealand, *A Foreign Egg in Our
Nest? American Culture in New Zealand*,
Wellington, Victoria University Press, 1988,
p. 90.
6 Erik Olssen, 'New Zealand in the
American Century', Chapter 13 in Rabel
(ed.), *The American Century?*, p. 182.
7 Harry Bioletti, *The Yanks Are Coming:
The American Invasion of New Zealand,
1942–1944*, Auckland, Century Hutchinson,
1989, p. 75.
8 Ibid., pp. 64–69; for quote re jitterbugging,
see p. 64.
9 P. J. Downey, 'The Celluloid Jungle',
Landfall, vol. 7, no. 4, December 1953,
p. 282.
10 See Jock Phillips, 'The Influence of
American Culture on New Zealand since
the Second World War', in Anne Trotter
(ed.), *New Zealand, Canada and the United
States: The Papers of the Twenty-second
Foreign Policy School*, Dunedin, University
of Otago, University Extension, 1987,
pp. 38–39, for an account of Phillips's
survey of *Landfall* and the *New Zealand
Listener* in 1947.
11 Noel Hilliard, 'Preserving Culture from the
Vulture', *Here & Now*, July 1952, p. 17.
12 See Peter J. Read, 'Blue Suede Gumboots?
The Impact of Popular Culture on New
Zealand in the 1950s', MA thesis, History,
Dunedin, University of Otago, 1990, p. 15.
13 See *New Zealand Listener*, 31 January 1958,
p. 9.
14 Phillips, 'The Influence of American
Culture on New Zealand', in Trotter (ed.),
*New Zealand, Canada and the United
States*, p. 32.
15 See Read, 'Blue Suede Gumboots?',
pp. 28–31.
16 Phillips, 'The Influence of American

Culture on New Zealand', in Trotter (ed.),
*New Zealand, Canada and the United
States*, p. 29 re sports preferences, and p. 35
re the origin of television programmes; see
p. 34, Table 1 for the film screenings survey.
17 Erik Olssen, 'New Zealand in the
American Century', in Rabel (ed.), *The
American Century?*, p. 184.
18 Phillips, 'The Influence of American
Culture on New Zealand', in Trotter (ed.),
*New Zealand, Canada and the United
States*, p. 41.
19 Patrick Day, *The Radio Years: A History
of Broadcasting in New Zealand*, vol. 1,
Auckland, Auckland University Press in
association with the Broadcasting History
Trust, 1994, p. 321.
20 John Proudfoot quoted in Peter Downes
and Peter Harcourt, *Voices in the Air:
Radio Broadcasting in New Zealand,
A Documentary*, Wellington, Methuen/
Radio New Zealand, 1976, p. 99.
21 Day, *The Radio Years*, p. 280. This merger
was ostensibly as a wartime economy
measure.
22 See James E. Ritchie, *Television in New
Zealand Research and Development*,
Hamilton, University of Waikato, 1977,
Psychology Research Series, no. 7, p. 1.
23 Day, *The Radio Years*, p. 220. Shelley had
been Director of the National Broadcasting
Service since 1936.
24 Downes and Harcourt, *Voices in the Air*,
p. 104.
25 Ibid., p. 118.
26 Day, *The Radio Years*, p. 289.
27 Ibid., p. 290.
28 J. C. Reid, *Listening to Radio*, Wellington,
Department of Education, 1957, p. 25.
29 Day, *The Radio Years*, p. 208.
30 Ibid., p. 301.
31 Patrick Day, *Voice & Vision: A History
of Broadcasting in New Zealand*, vol. 2,
Auckland, Auckland University Press in
association with the Broadcasting History
Trust, 2000, p. 68.
32 Day, *The Radio Years*, p. 292.
33 *New Zealand Listener*, 1 July 1949, in Day,
The Radio Years, p. 292.
34 Brian Pauling, 'Seventy Years of Radio:
An Overview', in Helen Wilson (ed.), *Radio
Book 1994*, Christchurch, New Zealand
Broadcasting School, Christchurch
Polytechnic, 1994, p. 9.
35 Day, *Voice & Vision*, p. 98.
36 *Checkpoint* is still on air today, making

it New Zealand's longest-running news programme; see www.radionz.co.nz/national/programmes/checkpoint/about.

37 Chris Bourke, *Blue Smoke: The Lost Dawn of New Zealand Popular Music 1918–1964*, Auckland, Auckland University Press, 2010, p. 186.

38 Downes and Harcourt, *Voices in the Air*, p. 146.

39 Quoted in David McGill, *Kiwi Baby Boomers: Growing Up in New Zealand in the 40s, 50s and 60s*, Lower Hutt, Mills Publications, 1989, p. 120.

40 Hamish Keith, *Reader's Digest New Zealand Yesterdays*, 2nd edn, Auckland, David Bateman, 2001, p. 161.

41 McGill, *Kiwi Baby Boomers*, p. 114.

42 Day, *The Radio Years*, p. 306.

43 Hamish Keith and Phillip Ridge, *A Lovely Day Tomorrow: New Zealand in the 1940s*, Auckland, Random Century, 1991, p. 59.

44 Downes and Harcourt, *Voices in the Air*, p. 131.

45 See 'Basham, Maud Ruby, "Aunt Daisy", MBE', from A. H. McLintock (ed.), *An Encyclopaedia of New Zealand*, Wellington, R. E. Owen, Government Printer, 1966; *Te Ara — The Encyclopedia of New Zealand*, updated 22 April 2009, www.teara.govt.nz/en/1966/basham-maud-ruby-aunt-daisy-mbe.

46 Keith and Ridge, *A Lovely Day Tomorrow*, p. 59. Selwyn Featherston Toogood (1916–2001) was born in Wellington. In 1977, he was appointed to the Queen's Service Order for services to broadcasting.

47 Selwyn Toogood quoted in Downes and Harcourt, *Voices in the Air*, p. 139.

48 Selwyn Toogood, Obituary, *New Zealand Herald*, 28 February, 2001.

49 Keith and Ridge, *A Lovely Day Tomorrow*, p. 60.

50 McGill, *Kiwi Baby Boomers*, p. 116.

51 Bourke, *Blue Smoke*, p. 324.

52 Ibid., p. 323.

53 Cited in Bourke, *Blue Smoke*, p. 265.

54 David Paul Ausubel, *The Fern and the Tiki: An American View of New Zealand National Character, Social Attitudes, and Race Relations*, Massachusetts, Christopher Publishing House, 1977 edn, p. 131.

55 Middlebrow, 'On the Air', *New Zealand Truth*, 24 August 1955, p. 26.

56 Bourke, *Blue Smoke*, p. 265.

57 Ibid., p. 267.

58 Ibid., p. 324.

59 Downes and Harcourt, *Voices in the Air*, p. 164.

60 McGill, *Kiwi Baby Boomers*, p. 148.

61 Day, *The Radio Years*, p. 315.

62 Peter Graham, *So Brilliantly Clever: Parker, Hulme and the Murder that Shocked the World*, Wellington, Awa Press, 2011, pp. 159 and 198.

63 *Dominion*, 6 July 1954.

64 Redmer Yska, *All Shook Up: The Flash Bodgie and the Rise of the New Zealand Teenager in the Fifties*, Auckland, Penguin, 1993, p. 64.

65 Roy Shuker, Roger Openshaw and Janet Soler (eds), *Youth, Media and Moral Panic in New Zealand: From Hooligans to Video Nasties*, Palmerston North, Department of Education, Massey University, c. 1990, p. 21.

66 Yska, *All Shook Up*, p. 68.

67 *Dominion*, 1 September 1954.

68 *Evening Post*, 13 July 1954, quoted in Yska, *All Shook Up*, p. 68.

69 O. C. Mazengarb, 'Report of the Special Committee on Moral Delinquency in Children and Adolescents', Wellington, Government Print, 1954, p. 7.

70 Ibid., p. 34.

71 Ibid., p. 36.

72 Ibid., p. 41.

73 Ibid., p. 29.

74 Bronwyn Dalley, *Family Matters: Child Welfare in Twentieth-Century New Zealand*, Auckland, Auckland University Press with the Historical Branch, Department of Internal Affairs, 1998, pp. 179, 180–93.

75 Janet Madeline Soler, 'Drifting towards Moral Chaos: The 1954 Mazengarb Report: A Moral Panic over Juvenile Immorality', MPhil thesis, Education, Palmerston North, Massey University, 1988, p. 250.

76 Dalley, *Family Matters*, p. 196.

77 Keith Moore, *Bodgies, Widgies and Moral Panic in Australia 1955–1959*, Paper presented to the Social Change in the 21st Century Conference, Centre for Social Change Research, Queensland University of Technology, 29 October 2004, http://eprints.qut.edu.au/633/1/moore_keith.pdf.

78 Ausubel, *The Fern and the Tiki*, p. 129.

79 Shuker et al., *Youth, Media and Moral Panic*, p. 19.

80 Yska, *All Shook Up*, p. 56.

81 Dalley, *Family Matters*, p. 180.

82 Dorothy May Crowther, *Street Society*, Christchurch, Department of Psychology

and Sociology, University of Canterbury, 1955, p. 5.

83 Yska, *All Shook Up*, p. 144.

84 Crowther, *Street Society*, p. 5.

85 A. E. Manning, *The Bodgie: A Study in Abnormal Psychology*, Wellington, Reed, 1958, p. 9.

86 Yska, *All Shook Up*, p. 176.

87 Manning, *The Bodgie*, p. 9.

88 Jon Stratton, 'Bodgies and Widgies — Youth Cultures in the 1950s', *Journal of Australian Studies*, vol. 8, no. 15, 1984, p. 21.

89 See Yska, *All Shook Up*, p. 177; pp. 153–70 deals with the trial of Frederick Foster, and Chapter 8, pp. 171–94, with that of Paddy Black.

90 Ibid., p. 208.

91 Manning, *The Bodgie*, pp. 69–71, 84 and 86.

92 Yska, *All Shook Up*, p. 207.

93 Megan Ritchie, 'Shaken, But Not Stirred? Youth Cultures in 1950s Auckland', MA thesis, History, Auckland, University of Auckland, 1997, p. 15.

94 Ausubel, *The Fern and the Tiki*, p. 131.

95 McGill, *Kiwi Baby Boomers*, pp. 147 and 144.

96 The 'Must the Hooligan Take Control?' editorial featured in the *Evening Post* of 12 September 1960, E3. For politicians' references to the 'festering' problem and the 'canker in our midst' see *New Zealand Parliamentary Debates*, vol. 324, 30 August–October 1960, pp. 2401–11, 2245–57, 2367–99.

97 This phrase was used in the 'Must The Hooligan Take Control?' editorial of 12 September 1960, *Evening Post*, E3.

98 See Dalley, *Family Matters*, pp. 171–215.

99 Ibid., p. 196.

100 *New Zealand Herald*, 30 May 1955, in *Auckland Scrapbook*, 8, December 1952–July 1955, p. 285, cited in Ritchie, 'Shaken but not Stirred?', p. 22.

101 See Ritchie, 'Shaken, But Not Stirred?, p. 23 and 53.

102 See Bourke, *Blue Smoke*, p. 266.

103 John Dix, *Stranded in Paradise: New Zealand Rock and Roll, 1955 to the Modern Era*, Auckland, Penguin Books, 2005, p. 19. See also Bronwyn Dalley and Gavin McLean (eds), *Frontier of Dreams: The Story of New Zealand*, Auckland, Hodder Moa, 2005, p. 332.

104 Dix, *Stranded in Paradise*, p. 19.

105 Bourke, *Blue Smoke*, p. 277.

106 Suzanne Ormsby, 'Te Reo Puoro Maori

Mai I Mua Tae Noa Mai Ki Inaianei: The Voice of Maori Music, Past, Present, and Future: Maori Musicians of the 1960s', MA thesis, Education, Auckland, University of Auckland, 1996, p. 185.

107 Georgina White, *Light Fantastic: Dance Floor Courtship in New Zealand*, HarperCollins, Auckland, 2007, p. 160.

108 Bourke, *Blue Smoke*, p. 251.

109 Ormsby, 'Te Reo Puoro Maori', p. 126.

110 *Te Ao Hou*, no. 27, June 1959, p. 53.

111 Ormsby, 'Te Reo Puoro Maori', p. 77.

112 Bourke, *Blue Smoke*, p. 155.

113 Ormsby, 'Te Reo Puoro Maori', p. 107.

114 Ibid., p. 162.

115 Bourke, *Blue Smoke*, p. 331.

116 Rimini Paul, quoted in Ormsby, 'Te Reo Puoro Maori', pp. 107–9.

117 Dix, *Stranded in Paradise*, p. 39.

118 Bourke, *Blue Smoke*, p. 268.

119 Ibid., p. 281.

120 Neil McKelvie, *45 South in Concert*, Invercargill, Southland Musicians Club, 2006, p. 38.

121 Ibid., p. 71.

122 Bourke, *Blue Smoke*, p. 282.

123 Ibid., p. 272.

124 White, *Light Fantastic*, p. 170.

125 McKelvie, *45 South in Concert*, p. 159.

126 *Southern News*, October 1956, p. 5 quoted in Read, 'Blue Suede Gumboots?', p. 98.

127 Quoted in Bourke, *Blue Smoke*, p. 284.

128 *Otago Daily Times*, 20 March 1959, p. 2.

129 Ibid., 21 March 1959, p. 5.

130 Dix, *Stranded in Paradise*, p. 29.

131 Ibid., p. 48; Bourke, *Blue Smoke*, p. 345.

132 The Loxene Golden Disc Award for the year's best album was founded in 1965 by the NZBC and Reckitt & Coleman and named after one of their shampoos, Loxene; see www.nzhistory.net.nz/media/photo/loxene-golden-disc-awards.

133 Dix, *Stranded in Paradise*, p. 49.

134 Ibid., pp. 57–58.

135 Yska, *All Shook Up*, p. 42. Until 1953, records were 78s or the long-playing plastic 33⅓ rpm (revolutions per minute) discs. The arrival of the 45 rpm single in 1953 revolutionised the market.

136 Cited in Yska, *All Shook Up*, p. 142.

137 Bourke, *Blue Smoke*, p. 298.

138 Ibid., p. 299.

139 Ritchie, 'Shaken but not Stirred?', pp. 82–86.

140 White, *Light Fantastic*, p. 174.

141 McGill, *Kiwi Baby Boomers*, p. 153.

142 Quoted in Yska, *All Shook Up*, p. 56.
143 McGill, *Kiwi Baby Boomers*, p. 153.
144 Gordon Campbell, 'Rock Around the Two Half Hours', *New Zealand Listener*, 8 May 1982 p. 14.
145 Sam Elworthy, *Ritual Song of Defiance: A Social History of Students at the University of Otago*, Dunedin, Otago University Students' Association, 1990, p. 76.
146 *Critic*, 21 April 1954, p. 2 and 22 September 1960, p. 1 cited in Elworthy, *Ritual Song of Defiance*, p. 94.
147 Yska, *All Shook Up*, pp. 111–12.
148 Ibid., p. 122.
149 Geoffrey B. Churchman, *Celluloid Dreams: A Century of Film in New Zealand*, Wellington, IPL Books, 1997, p. 40.
150 Yska, *All Shook Up*, p. 109.
151 McGill, *Kiwi Baby Boomers*, p. 131.
152 Glenda Leader, 'Screening Rites', *New Zealand Listener*, July 1991, p. 20.
153 Keith, *Lovely Day*, p. 64.
154 Wayne Brittenden, *The Celluloid Circus: The Heyday of the New Zealand Picture Theatre, 1925–1970*, Auckland, Godwit, 2008, p. 21.
155 Lealand, *A Foreign Egg in Our Nest?*, p. 84.
156 Gordon Mirams, *Speaking Candidly: Films and People in New Zealand*, Hamilton, Paul's Book Arcade, 1945, p. 5.
157 Ibid., p. 25.
158 'Real Danger in Films', letter from Bill Pearson in *Here & Now*, June 1953, p. 34.
159 McGill, *Kiwi Baby Boomers*, p. 126.
160 Ibid., p. 130.
161 Churchman, *Celluloid Dreams*, p. 28.
162 See Jenny Carlyon and Diana Morrow, *A Fine Prospect: A History of Remuera, Meadowbank and St Johns*, Auckland, Random House, 2011, pp. 101–3.
163 McGill, *Kiwi Baby Boomers*, p. 126.
164 Lealand, *A Foreign Egg in Our Nest?*, p. 85.
165 Churchman, *Celluloid Dreams*, p. 29.
166 Ibid., p. 30.
167 Albert Abramson, 'The Invention of Television', Chapter 1 in Anthony Smith (ed.), *Television: An International History*, Oxford University Press, Oxford, 1998, pp. 18–19.
168 *New Zealand Listener*, 1 June 1985, p. 14.
169 Day, *Voice & Vision*, p. 33; and see 'Beginnings' by Graham Ford, *New Zealand Listener*, 1 June 1985, p. 15.
170 Day, *Voice & Vision*, p. 54.
171 *New Zealand Listener*, 1 June 1985, p. 15.
172 Laurence Simmons, 'Television Then', in Roger Horrocks and Nick Perry (eds), *Television in New Zealand: Programming the Nation*, Auckland, Oxford University Press, 2000, pp. 54 and 59.
173 Ibid., p. 62.
174 Day, *Voice & Vision*, p. 100.
175 Ibid., p. 101.
176 Simmons, 'Television Then', in Horrocks and Perry (eds), *Television in New Zealand: Programming the Nation*, p. 59.
177 See Day, *Voice & Vision*, pp. 57–58.
178 Robert Boyd Bell, *New Zealand Television: The First 25 Years*, Auckland, Reed Methuen, 1985, p. 119.
179 Ibid., p. 87.
180 Day, *Voice & Vision*, p. 56.
181 Ibid., p. 73.
182 Ibid., p. 55.
183 Barry Gustafson, 'The National Governments and Social Change, 1949–1972', in Keith Sinclair (ed.), *The Oxford Illustrated History of New Zealand*, 2nd edn, Auckland, Oxford University Press, 1997, p. 274.
184 See www.teara.govt.nz/en/olympic-and-commonwealth-games/page-9.
185 D. C. Pitts, 'The Joiners: Associations and Leisure in New Zealand', in Stephen D. Webb and John Collette (eds), *New Zealand Society: Contemporary Perspectives*, Sydney, Wiley, 1973, pp. 157–62.
186 Charlotte Macdonald, 'Ways of Belonging: Sporting Spaces in New Zealand History', in Giselle Byrnes (ed.), *The New Oxford History of New Zealand*, Melbourne, Oxford University Press, 2009, p. 289.
187 Ibid., p. 293.
188 Jock Phillips, *A Man's Country? The Image of the Pakeha Male: A History*, Auckland, Penguin Books, 1987, p. 88.
189 *New Zealand Official Yearbook*, 1990, p. 347.
190 Quoted in Piet de Jong, *Saturday's Warriors: The Building of a Rugby Stronghold*, Palmerston North, Department of Sociology, Massey University, 1991, p. 59.
191 De Jong, p. 56.
192 Phillips, *A Man's Country?*, p. 265.
193 McGill, *Kiwi Baby Boomers*, p. 48.
194 Ibid., p. 51.
195 He was named player of the century by the NZRU in 1999.
196 Alex Veysey, *Colin Meads: All Black*, Auckland, Collins, 1974, p. 13.
197 John Nauright and David Black, 'New Zealand and International Sport: The Case

of All Black–Springbok Rugby, Sanctions and Protest Against Apartheid 1959–1992', in John Nauright (ed.), *Sport, Power and Society in New Zealand: Historical and Contemporary Perspectives*, Sydney, Australian Society for Sports History, 1995, p. 71.

198 M. H. Pearson, 'Heads in the Sand: The 1956 Springbok Tour to New Zealand in Perspective', in Richard Cashman and Michael McKernan, *Sport in History: The Making of Modern Sporting History*, St Lucia, University of Queensland Press, 1979, p. 275.

199 Phillips, *A Man's Country?*, p. 264.

200 Trevor Richards, 'New Zealanders' Attitudes to Sport as Illustrated by Debate Over Rugby Contacts with South Africa', in Brad Patterson (ed.), *Sport, Society and Culture in New Zealand*, Wellington, Stout Research Centre, c. 1999, p. 44.

201 Nauright and Black, 'New Zealand and International Sport', in Patterson (ed.), *Sport, Power and Society in New Zealand*, p. 74.

202 Jock Phillips, 'Men Women and Leisure since the Second World War', in Caroline Daley and Deborah Montgomerie, *The Gendered Kiwi*, Auckland, Auckland University Press, 1999, p. 215.

203 See Jennifer Curtin, 'More than Male-Gazing: Reflections on Women's Engagement with Rugby Union in New Zealand', Chapter 1 in Robb Hess and Nikki Wedgwood (eds), *Women, Football and History*, Hawthorn, Victoria, Maribyrnong Press, [unpublished].

204 Macdonald, 'Ways of Belonging: Sporting Spaces in New Zealand History', in Byrnes (ed.), *The New Oxford History of New Zealand*, p. 286.

205 Daley and Montgomerie, *The Gendered Kiwi*, p. 217.

206 Murray Robb and Hilary Howorth, *New Zealand Recreation Survey: Preliminary Report*, Wellington, New Zealand Council for Recreation and Sport, 1977, pp. 12–13.

207 John Nauright and Jayne Broomhall, 'A Woman's Game: The Development of Netball and a Female Sporting Culture in New Zealand, 1906–70', in *The International Journal of the History of Sport*, vol. 2, no. 3, December 1994, p. 395.

208 *Wanganui Herald*, 19 May 1929, quoted in Nauright and Broomhall, 'A Woman's Game', p. 389.

209 *Christchurch Sun*, 28 August 1929, quoted in Nauright and Broomhall, ibid., p. 395.

210 Nauright and Broomhall, 'A Woman's Game', p. 389.

211 Macdonald, 'Ways of Belonging', in Byrnes (ed.), *The New Oxford History of New Zealand*, p. 288.

212 By 1977, this number had risen to over 6000, not including primary school teams. Sandra Coney, 'Physical Education in Girls' Secondary Schools, The Game for Game's Sake', in Sandra Coney (ed.), *Standing in the Sunshine: A History of New Zealand Women since They Won the Vote*, Auckland, Penguin Books, 1993, p. 243.

213 Nauright and Broomhall, 'A Woman's Game', p. 389.

214 Charlotte Macdonald, 'Putting Bodies on the Line: Marching Spaces in Cold War Culture', in Patricia Vertinsky and John Bale (eds), *Sites of Sport: Space, Place, Experience*, London, Routledge, 2004, p. 88.

215 Jill Williams, Val Browning and Charlotte Macdonald, 'New Zealand Marching Association, 1945–', in Anne Else, *Women Together: A History of Women's Organisations in New Zealand*, Daphne Brasell Associates Press with the Historical Branch, Department of Internal Affairs, 1993, p. 438.

216 A. R. D. Fairburn, 'Are Marching Girls Decadent?', *Here & Now*, July 1952, p. 9.

217 Quoted in Sandra Coney, 'Marching Girls in New Zealand: Military Precision, Chorus Line Glamour', in Coney (ed.), *Standing in the Sunshine*, p. 250.

218 Sir Peter Blake was, tragically, shot and killed by pirates in 2001. He was in South America, on an environmental mission.

219 See 'New Zealand — a sailing nation', www.newzealand.com/travel/media/features/recreation-&-sport/sailing_nz-sailing-na-tion_feature.cfm.

220 See Perrin Rowland, *A History of the Restaurant in New Zealand*, Auckland, Auckland University Press, 2010, p. 264, fn. 19.

221 Miles Fairburn, 'Is there a Good Case for New Zealand Exceptionalism?', Chapter 6 in Tony Ballantyne and Brian Moloughney (eds), *Disputed Histories: Imagining New Zealand's Pasts*, Dunedin, Otago University Press, 2006.

CHAPTER FIVE **In Ferment: Contested and Protested Values**

1 'Upsurge of Protest', *New Zealand Monthly Review*, May 1965, Notes and Comments, p. 1.

2 Holyoake, speech notes for 1971 National Party Conference, Holyoake Papers, 85-46, 2A, Alexander Turnbull Library, in Barry Gustafson, *Kiwi Keith: A Biography of Keith Holyoake*, Auckland, Auckland University Press, 2007, p. 346.

3 See Adrian Blackburn, *The Shoestring Pirates*, revised and expanded edn, Auckland, Hauraki Enterprises, 1988, pp. 1–97.

4 Ibid., p. 15.

5 This article of 1 May 1966 is reproduced in Blackburn, ibid., p. 25.

6 Government created the New Zealand Broadcasting Authority in 1968, which eventually issued the first commercial broadcasting licences to Radio Hauraki and Radio i on 24 March 1970. See M. W. Shanahan, 'The Impact of Deregulation on the Evolution of Commercial Radio', in Karen Neill and M. W. Shanahan (eds), *The Great New Zealand Radio Experiment*, Southbank, Victoria, Thomson/Dunmore Press, 2004, pp. 17–46.

7 Elsie K. Morton, 'City's First Flight Was a Sad Flop', *New Zealand Herald*, 29 January 1966, p. 11.

8 Ibid., p. 1.

9 Ibid. Prior to the creation of Auckland Airport, international air travel had been a minority activity, and flights of the 'short-hop' variety; see James Belich, *Paradise Reforged: A History of the New Zealanders from the 1880s to the Year 2000*, Auckland, Allen Lane/The Penguin Press, 2001, p. 427.

10 Graham Hutchins, *The Swinging Sixties: When New Zealand Changed Forever*, Auckland, HarperCollins, 2008, pp. 50–51, and Barry Gustafson, 'The National Governments and Social Change (1949–1972)', in Keith Sinclair (ed.), *The Oxford Illustrated History of New Zealand*, new edn, Auckland, Oxford University Press, 1999, pp. 280–1.

11 Hutchins, *The Swinging Sixties*, p. 50. Government bought the Australian and British shareholding in TEAL in 1961, and changed the name to Air New Zealand in 1965.

12 *New Zealand Official Yearbook*, 1978, p. 346.

13 Margaret McClure, *The Wonder Country: Making New Zealand Tourism*, Auckland, Auckland University Press, 2004, p. 212.

14 M. H. Holcroft, 'The Sound of Sunday', *New Zealand Listener*, 3 December 1965, p. 10.

15 *New Zealand Official Yearbook*, 1976, p. 83.

16 Steve Hoadley, 'Immigration Policy', in Raymond Miller (ed.), *New Zealand Government and Politics*, 3rd edn, Auckland, Oxford University Press, 2003, p. 525.

17 Figures from Graeme Dunstall, 'The Social Pattern', in Geoffrey W. Rice (ed.), *The Oxford History of New Zealand*, 2nd edn, Auckland, Oxford University Press, 1992, p. 462.

18 See 'Taming the Lightning (a New Zealand Perspective) — Milestones: A New Zealand Timeline of Communications and Computing', www.wordworx.co.nz/KiwitelcoTimeline.htm.

19 Ibid., and see 'The History of Computers', http://inventors.about.com/library/blcoindex.htm, re IBM's 1981 PC.

20 John Dix, *Stranded in Paradise: New Zealand Rock and Roll, 1955 to the Modern Era*, Auckland, Penguin Books, 2005, p. 214.

21 See Chapter 16, 'Bruno's Thing', in Dix, ibid., pp. 118–27.

22 Bill Pearson, 'Fretful Sleepers: A Sketch of New Zealand Behaviour and its Implications for the Artist' (1952), reproduced in Chapter 16 of Alex Calder (ed.), *The Writing of New Zealand: Inventions and Identities*, Auckland, Reed, 1993, pp. 169–70.

23 David C. Thorns and Charles P. Sedgwick, *Understanding Aotearoa/New Zealand: Historical Statistics*, Palmerston North, Dunmore Press, 1997, p. 144.

24 This letter by Anne McRae of Wellington appeared in the correspondence columns of the *New Zealand Listener*, 18 January 1975, p. 6 in response to an earlier (December 1974, p. 6) editorial by Ian Cross lamenting the lack of public profile of New Zealand intellectuals.

25 Tony Judt, *Postwar: A History of Europe since 1945*, London, Vintage Books, 2010, pp. 394–5.

26 Andrew Marr, *A History of Modern Britain*, London, Pan Books, 2007, p. 265.

27 This phrase is used by Gustafson in 'The National Governments and Social Change', in Sinclair (ed.), *The Oxford Illustrated History of New Zealand*, new edn, p. 294.

28 Suzanne Mackwell, 'Radical Politics and Ideology in the Coming of Post-Industrial Society: The Values Party in Perspective', MA thesis, Political Science, Christchurch, University of Canterbury, 1977, p. 40.

29 See Patrick Day, *Voice & Vision: A History of Broadcasting in New Zealand*, vol. 2, Auckland, Auckland University Press in association with the Broadcasting History Trust, 2000, p. 144. The NZBC made $1,100 from sale of the storm footage, which earned the corporation that year's World Newsfilm Award.

30 Brian Easton, 'The 1970s: The Way We Were', *New Zealand Listener*, 22 December 1979, p. 20.

31 Dix, *Stranded in Paradise*, p. 75.

32 Frank Stark, 'The Entertainers', *New Zealand Listener*, 1 June 1985, p. 23.

33 Cited in Gustafson, *Kiwi Keith*, p. 158.

34 R. D. Muldoon, *The Rise and Fall of a Young Turk*, Wellington, A. H. & A. W. Reed, 1974, p. 148.

35 Census figures cited in Laurie Guy, *Shaping Godzone: Public Issues and Church Voices in New Zealand 1840–2000*, Wellington, Victoria University Press, 2012, p. 362.

36 Census statistics cited in Belich, *Paradise Reforged*, p. 515. According to Belich, the figures relating to declining religious adherence 'would have been worse were it not for an inflow of Pacific Island immigrants, who were more religious than average'.

37 John Stenhouse, 'Religion and Society', Chapter 14 in Giselle Byrnes (ed.), *The New Oxford History of New Zealand*, Melbourne, Oxford University Press, 2009, p. 352.

38 Ibid.

39 Keith Sinclair, *A History of New Zealand*, revised edn, Auckland, Penguin, 2000, p. 309.

40 Tim Shadbolt, *A Mayor of Two Cities*, Auckland, Hodder Moa, 2008, p. 39. Shadbolt became a mayor, first of Waitemata (Waitakere) and then of Invercargill, in later life.

41 Helen May, *Minding Children, Managing Men: Conflict and Compromise in the Lives of Postwar Pakeha Women*, Wellington, Bridget Williams Books, 1991, p. 208.

42 M. H. Holcroft, 'After Liberation', *New Zealand Listener*, 16 July 1973, p. 5.

43 Guy, *Shaping Godzone*, p. 366.

44 Ibid., p. 367. The 1971 film *A Clockwork Orange* received the first ever R20 classification in 1972.

45 Ibid.

46 Bernard Orsman, Obituary, 'Patricia Bartlett', *New Zealand Herald*, 11 November 2000, n.p.

47 See Guy, *Shaping Godzone*, pp. 368–76 on this debate.

48 L. D. Guy, 'The Cinematograph Film Censorship Debate in New Zealand, 1965–1976', MA research essay, History, Auckland, University of Auckland, 1992, p. 34.

49 These figures and the grass-roots quote are from Brett Knowles, 'Into the Seventies: The Beginnings of Moralist Protest', http://webjournals.ac.edu.au/journals/ET/knowles-b-new-life-churches-phd-otago-1994/05-into-the-seventies-the-beginnings-of-moralist-p/, n.p.

50 Ibid.

51 Guy, *Shaping Godzone*, p. 276.

52 Roberto Rabel, *New Zealand and the Vietnam War: Politics and Diplomacy*, Auckland, Auckland University Press, 2005, p. 175.

53 This group, based on the English parent organisation, formed in 1959. Its membership was small but committed.

54 See Elsie Locke, *Peace People: A History of Peace Activities in New Zealand*, Christchurch, Hazard Press, 1992.

55 Cited in Claire Loftus Nelson, *Long Time Passing: New Zealand Memories of the Vietnam War*, Wellington, National Radio, 1990, p. 43.

56 Rabel, *New Zealand and the Vietnam War*, p. 360.

57 Ibid., p. 161.

58 Ibid., p. 243.

59 Ibid., p. 254.

60 Alister Taylor cited in Nelson, *Long Time Passing*, p. 42.

61 Rabel, *New Zealand and the Vietnam War*, p. 295.

62 Ibid., p. 296.

63 Ibid., p. 297.

64 *New Zealand Herald*, 17 January 1970, cited in Redmer Yska, *Truth: The Rise and Fall of the People's Paper*, Nelson, Craig Potton Publishing, 2010, p. 145.

65 'The Bombers', Comedia Pictures

Documentary Drama proposal/background research papers, courtesy Redmer Yska.

66 *New Zealand Monthly Review*, June 1970, p. 5.

67 Rabel, *New Zealand and the Vietnam War*, p. 304.

68 Ibid., p. 309.

69 Ibid., pp. 315 and 323.

70 Ibid., pp. 314–27.

71 Ibid., p. 361.

72 Cited in Nelson, *Long Time Passing*, p. 46.

73 Tim Shadbolt, *Bullshit & Jellybeans*, Wellington, Alister Taylor Publications, 1971, p. 37.

74 Ibid., p. 15.

75 Alexander MacLeod, 'Path of Protest', *New Zealand Listener* 14 February 1972, p. 45.

76 See Gabrielle M. Maxwell, 'Political Attitudes and Radical Youth Movements', in Stephen Levine (ed.), *New Zealand Politics: A Reader*, Melbourne, Cheshire, 1975, pp. 343–56.

77 Deborah Challinor, *Grey Ghosts: New Zealand Vietnam Vets talk about Their War*, Auckland, Hodder Moa Beckett, 1998, pp. 211–13.

78 Ibid., p. 208.

79 *Star* (Christchurch), 19 August 1971, PM 474/4/14, cited in Rabel, *New Zealand and the Vietnam War*, p. 317.

80 Quote from Marshall interview, featured in Part 1 of a three-part Television New Zealand videorecording entitled 'Vietnam, The New Zealand Story' made in 1982, cited in Rabel, *New Zealand and the Vietnam War*, p. 358.

81 Don Carson, anti-Vietnam War protester, quoted in Nelson, *Long Time Passing*, p. 45.

82 Neville Peat, *Manapouri Saved! New Zealand's First Great Conservation Success Story*, Dunedin, Guardians of Lakes Manapouri, Monowai and Te Anau, 1994, pp. 15–16.

83 Michael King, *The Penguin History of New Zealand*, Auckland, Penguin, 2003, pp. 439–40.

84 Peat, *Manapouri Saved!*, p. 44.

85 Ibid., p. 59.

86 Ibid., p. 60.

87 David Young, *Our Islands, Our Selves: A History of Conservation in New Zealand*, Dunedin, University of Otago Press, 2004, p. 173.

88 Nicola Wheen, 'A History of New Zealand Environmental Law', in Eric Pawson and Tom Brooking (eds), *Environmental Histories of New Zealand*, Auckland, Oxford University Press, 2002, p. 265.

89 This poster, devised by Bob Harvey, later a mayor of Waitakere City, is reproduced in Young, *Our Islands, Our Selves*, p. 177.

90 Preface to *Blueprint for New Zealand: An Alternative Future*, Wellington, New Zealand Values Party, 1972, p. 5.

91 Young, *Our Islands, Our Selves*, p. 176.

92 Preface to *Blueprint for New Zealand: An Alternative Future*, p. 1.

93 R. K. Dell, 'Fleming, Charles Alexander (1916–1987)', *Dictionary of New Zealand Biography*, Te Ara — The Encyclopedia of New Zealand, updated 30 October 2012, www.TeAra.govt.nz/en/biographies/5f9/fleming-charles-alexander; and Bing Lucas, Obituary, *New Zealand Herald*, 23 December 2000, www.nzherald.co.nz/nz/news/article.cfm?c_id=1&objectid=166169; and see Young, *Our Islands, Our Selves*, pp. 189–90 for a summary of Lucas's long and distinguished career.

94 Young, *Our Islands, Our Selves*, p. 179.

95 Ibid., p. 180.

96 Graham Searle, *Rush to Destruction*, Wellington, A. H. & A. W. Reed, 1975, p. 188.

97 Young, *Our Islands, Our Selves*, p. 181.

98 The Maruia Declaration is reproduced in Young, ibid., p. 182.

99 Guy Salmon's obituary of his father (written with 'grateful acknowledgment' to John Andrews, George Gibbs and Graham Ramsay) John Tenison Salmon (CBE, MSc DSc NZ, FRSNZ FRPS FRES, 1910–1999); see www.royalsociety.org.nz/publications/reports/yearbooks/year1999/obituaries/john-salmon/.

100 See Young, *Our Islands, Our Selves*, p. 181.

101 The latter (endearingly minute) species was reduced to one breeding pair in 1979. By the 1990s, thanks to fostering and manipulation of nesting behaviour, the robins were enjoying a demographic surge.

102 Young, *Our Islands, Our Selves*, pp. 187–93.

103 Ibid., p. 192.

104 Ibid., pp. 178–9.

105 See Rebecca Priestley, *Mad on Radium: New Zealand in the Atomic Age*, Auckland, Auckland University Press, 2012, especially Chapter 3, 'Cold War and Red-Hot Science: The Nuclear Age Comes to the Pacific', pp. 64–100.

106 Malcolm McKinnon, *Independence and*

Foreign Policy: New Zealand in the World since 1935, Auckland, Auckland University Press, 1993, p. 187.

107 Kevin Clements, *Back from the Brink: The Creation of a Nuclear-Free New Zealand*, Wellington, Allen & Unwin/Port Nicholson Press, 1988, p. 184. This was accepted by the US under 1974 legislation, though New Zealand still maintained its no-visit stance.

108 Ibid., p. 63.

109 Michael Szabo, *Making Waves: The Greenpeace New Zealand Story*, Auckland, Greenpeace New Zealand, 1991, pp. 14–15.

110 See Locke, *Peace People*, pp. 286–96.

111 Cited in Clements, *Back from the Brink*, p. 66.

112 Michael Bassett, 'Kirk, Norman Eric (1923–1974)', *Dictionary of New Zealand Biography, Te Ara — The Encyclopedia of New Zealand*, updated 30 October 2012, www.teara.govt.nz/en/biographies/5k12/kirk-norman-eric.

113 John Dunmore, *Norman Kirk: A Portrait*, Palmerston North, New Zealand Books, 1972, p. 100.

114 Norman Kirk, *Towards Nationhood: Selected Speeches of Norman Kirk*, Palmerston North, New Zealand Books, 1969.

115 Cited in Margaret Hayward, *Diary of the Kirk Years*, Wellington, A. H. & A. W. Reed, 1981, p. 147.

116 Cited in Hayward, ibid.

117 Ibid., p. 191.

118 Mary Boyd, 'New Zealand and the other Pacific Islands', in Sinclair (ed.), *The Oxford Illustrated History of New Zealand*, new edn, p. 321.

119 Bassett, 'Norman Kirk', *DNZB*.

120 Clements, *Back from the Brink*, p. 72.

121 Ibid., p. 78.

122 Later the *Canterbury* relieved the *Otago* and stayed in position at Mururoa until 6 August.

123 Norman Kirk cited in Clements, *Back from the Brink*, p. 80.

124 Jock Phillips, 'Generations, 1965–1984', in Bronwyn Dalley and Gavin McLean (eds), *Frontier of Dreams: The Story of New Zealand*, Auckland, Hodder Moa, 2005, p. 357.

125 This image is reproduced in Vincent O'Malley, Bruce Stirling and Wally Penetito (eds), *The Treaty of Waitangi Companion*, Auckland, Auckland University Press,

2010, p. 308. It appeared in the *New Zealand Herald* on 7 February 1973.

126 Peat, *Manapouri Saved!*, p. 9. From 1973, Environmental Protection and Enhancement Procedures required environmental impact assessments for all government works likely to have environmental effects.

127 Cited in Lucy Sargisson and Lymon Tower Sargent, *Living in Utopia: New Zealand's Intentional Communities*, Aldershot, Ashgate Publishing, 2004, p. 41.

128 Ibid., p. 42.

129 Hayward, *Diary of the Kirk Years*, p. 223.

130 Sargisson and Sargent, *Living in Utopia*, p. 45.

131 Cited in Michael Bassett, *The State in New Zealand 1840–1984: Socialism without Doctrines?*, Auckland, Auckland University Press, 1988, p. 329.

132 An Accident Compensation Commission was set up in 1974 to implement the regulations of the 1972 Accident Compensation Act. The architect of this scheme, regarded as one of the most significant legal reforms of the twentieth century, was Owen Woodhouse, later knighted for his achievement.

133 Belich, *Paradise Reforged*, p. 397.

134 Alan McRobie, 'The Politics of Volatility, 1972–1991', in Rice (ed.), *The Oxford History of New Zealand*, 2nd edn, p. 389.

135 Bassett, *The State in New Zealand*, p. 330. The level set for 1973 was 8.5%.

136 McRobie, 'The Politics of Volatility', in Rice (ed.), *The Oxford History of New Zealand*, 2nd edn, p. 389.

137 Minister of Trade and Industry Warren Freer's scheme prescribed maximum prices for retail goods, but it was difficult to administer, laden down with bureaucracy, and easy to evade.

138 *Evening Post*, 4 September 1974, p. 1.

139 Belich, *Paradise Reforged*, p. 405.

140 McRobie, 'The Politics of Volatility', in Rice (ed.), *The Oxford History of New Zealand*, 2nd edn, p. 390.

141 Sinclair, *A History of New Zealand*, revised edn, p. 322. The latter figure (18%) is from Dunstall, 'The Social Pattern', in Rice (ed.), *The Oxford History of New Zealand*, 2nd edn, p. 475.

142 See Redmer Yska, Chapter 9, 'Twilight Zone', in Yska, *Truth: The Rise and Fall of the People's Paper*, p. 162.

143 Ibid., p. 164.

144 This image is reproduced in Yska, ibid., p. 162.

145 Austin Mitchell, *The Half-Gallon Quarter-Acre Pavlova Paradise*, Christchurch, Whitcombe & Tombs, 1972, p. 11.

CHAPTER SIX Schisms: A Society Divided

1 Ian Johnstone, *Stand and Deliver*, Whatamango Bay, Cape Catley, 1998, p. 94.

2 Wellington anti-tour protester cited in Geoff Walker and Peter Beach (eds), *56 Days: A History of the Anti-Tour Movement in Wellington*, Wellington, Lindsay Wright on behalf of Citizens Opposed to the Springbok Tour (COST), 1982, p. 65.

3 Colin James, *Quiet Revolution: Turbulence and Transition in Contemporary New Zealand*, Wellington, Allen & Unwin/Port Nicholson Press, 1986, p. 89.

4 See Barry Gustafson, *His Way: A Biography of Robert Muldoon*, Auckland, Auckland University Press, 2000, p. 165.

5 Sinclair, *A History of New Zealand*, revised edn, Auckland, Penguin, 2000, p. 326.

6 Bob Jones, *Memories of Muldoon*, Christchurch, Canterbury University Press, 1997, p. 32.

7 Keith Sinclair, 'Hard Times', in Keith Sinclair (ed.), *The Oxford Illustrated History of New Zealand*, new edn, Auckland, Oxford University Press, 1999, p. 354.

8 Colin James in the *Sunday Times*, 9 August 1992, cited in Gustafson, *His Way*, p. 190.

9 See 'New Zealand's Place on the OECD Ladder', Figure 1, www.treasury.govt.nz/publications/research-policy/wp/2002/02-14/01.htm; using OECD data, it had fallen to seventeenth by 1976.

10 Gustafson, *His Way*, p. 251.

11 Sinclair, *A History of New Zealand*, revised edn, p. 324.

12 Jock Phillips, 'Generations: 1965–1984', in Bronwyn Dalley and Gavin McLean (eds), *Frontier of Dreams: The Story of New Zealand*, Auckland, Hodder Moa, 2005, p. 353.

13 Gustafson, *His Way*, p. 250.

14 Ibid., p. 243.

15 James, *Quiet Revolution*, p. 62.

16 Steve Hoadley, 'Immigration Policy', in Raymond Miller (ed.), *New Zealand Government and Politics*, 3rd edn, Auckland, Oxford University Press, 2003, p. 525.

17 Gustafson, *His Way*, pp. 250–1.

18 Ibid., p. 241.

19 Ibid., p. 215.

20 Ibid., p. 230.

21 Reverend Dr George Armstrong cited in Kevin Clements, *Back from the Brink: The Creation of a Nuclear-Free New Zealand*, Wellington, Allen & Unwin/Port Nicholson Press, 1988, p. 109.

22 Ibid., p. 110.

23 Ibid., p. 113.

24 Ibid., p. 113.

25 Michael Szabo, *Making Waves: The Greenpeace New Zealand Story*, Auckland, Greenpeace New Zealand, 1991, p. 75.

26 Szabo, *Making Waves*, p. 56.

27 Gustafson, *His Way*, p. 259.

28 James, *Quiet Revolution*, p. 113.

29 Gustafson, *His Way*, p. 259.

30 Clements, *Back from the Brink*, p. 114.

31 Ibid., p. 118.

32 By 1986, there were 104 local body nuclear weapons-free zones, encompassing over 72% of New Zealanders, or 2,190,151 people; see ibid., p. 116. The 57.4% opposed to entry of ships equipped with nuclear weapons into New Zealand waters is a statistic that emerged from a 1984 poll conducted by Charles Crothers and Georgina Murray. It contrasts with a 1979 poll conducted for the Foundation for Peace Studies, which indicated that 61.5% of the sample polled would be willing to allow visits by American ships armed with nuclear weapons to New Zealand territorial waters 'for all reasons or for good will'. See Clements, ibid., pp.120–21.

33 Nicola Wheen, 'A History of New Zealand Environmental Law', in Eric Pawson and Tom Brooking (eds), *Environmental Histories of New Zealand*, Auckland, Oxford University Press, 2002, p. 268.

34 Ibid., p. 268.

35 Tom Brooking, *The History of New Zealand*, Westport, Connecticut, Greenwood Press, 2004, p. 146.

36 Gustafson, *His Way*, p. 273.

37 See www.nzhistory.net.nz/carless-days for New Zealanders' reminiscences about carless days.

38 Michael Bassett, *The State in New Zealand 1840–1984, Socialism without Doctrines?*, Auckland, Auckland University Press, 1998, pp. 365–6.

39 Ibid., p. 366.

40 David Young, *Our Islands, Our Selves:*

A History of Conservation in New Zealand, Dunedin, University of Otago Press, 2004, p. 198.

41 Brian Easton, 'The 1970s: The Way We Were', *New Zealand Listener*, 22 December 1975, p. 20.

42 *New Zealand Herald*, 12 June 1978, cited in Young, *Our Islands, Our Selves*, p. 201.

43 Young, *Our Islands, Our Selves*, p. 202.

44 Ibid., p. 204.

45 Szabo, *Making Waves*, p. 63.

46 Ibid., p. 70.

47 See Peter Simpson, 'The Recognition of Difference', in Geoffrey W. Rice (ed.), *The Oxford History of New Zealand*, 2nd edn, Auckland, Oxford University Press, 1992, pp. 571–85. The phrase 'debate, diversity and difference' is found on p. 574.

48 James, *Quiet Revolution*, p. 42.

49 See W. O. Oliver, 'The Awakening Imagination', in Rice (ed.), *The Oxford History of New Zealand*, 2nd edn, pp. 562–3 for a discussion of writers' sense of assurance during the 1970s in dealing unselfconsciously with universal themes in a New Zealand setting.

50 Simpson, 'The Recognition of Difference', in Rice, ibid., p. 575.

51 John Dix, *Stranded in Paradise: New Zealand Rock and Roll, 1955 to the Modern Era*, Auckland, Penguin Books, 2005, p. 260.

52 Duncan Petrie and Duncan Stuart, *A Coming of Age: Thirty Years of New Zealand Film*, Auckland, Random House, 2008, p. 27.

53 Ibid., p. 28.

54 Sinclair, *A History of New Zealand*, revised edn, p. 332.

55 See Vincent O'Malley, Bruce Stirling and Wally Penetito (eds), *The Treaty of Waitangi Companion*, Auckland, Auckland University Press, 2010, pp. 338–41.

56 See Laurie Guy, *Shaping Godzone: Public Issues and Church Voices in New Zealand 1840–2000*, Wellington, Victoria University Press, 2012, pp. 304–5. After the National Council of Churches drew attention to the issue, universities, trade unions and the Maori community also expressed their opposition to the tour.

57 Trevor Richards, *Dancing on Our Bones: New Zealand, South Africa, Rugby and Racism*, Wellington, Bridget Williams Books, 1999, p. 34.

58 Ibid.

59 Polls showed that in 1971, 73% supported the Springboks playing in New Zealand and 16% were opposed; *Evening Post*, 26 October 1971, cited in Barry Gustafson, *Kiwi Keith: A Biography of Keith Holyoake*, Auckland, Auckland University Press, 2007, p. 202, text and fn. 70.

60 Richards, *Dancing on Our Bones*, p. 46.

61 Charlotte MacDonald, 'Ways of Belonging: Sporting Spaces in New Zealand History', Chapter 12 in Giselle Byrnes (ed.), *The New Oxford History of New Zealand*, Melbourne, Oxford University Press, 2009, p. 290; Malcolm McKinnon, *Independence and Foreign Policy: New Zealand in the World since 1935*, Auckland, Auckland University Press, 1993, p. 240.

62 McKinnon, *Independence and Foreign Policy*, p. 240.

63 Ibid., p. 241.

64 Ibid., p. 243.

65 Phillips, 'Generations: 1965–1984', in Dalley and McLean (eds), *Frontier of Dreams*, p. 357.

66 McKinnon, *Independence and Foreign Policy*, p. 243.

67 Ibid., p. 245.

68 Cited in McKinnon, ibid., p. 244.

69 Ibid.

70 Ibid., pp. 246–7.

71 Geoff Chapple, *1981: The Tour*, Wellington, Reed, 1984, p. 314.

72 See Peter King and Jock Phillips, 'A Social Analysis of the Springbok Tour Protesters', in David Mackay, Malcolm McKinnon, Peter McPhee and Jock Phillips (eds), *Counting the Cost: The 1981 Springbok Tour in Wellington*, Wellington, History Department, Victoria University, Occasional Papers No. 1, 1982, pp. 5–7.

73 Tom Newnham, *By Batons and Barbed Wire: A Response to the 1981 Springbok Tour of New Zealand*, Auckland, Real Pictures Ltd and Tom Newnham, 1981, p. 11.

74 This figure is from Newnham, *By Batons and Barbed Wire*, p. 17, but in Richards, *Dancing on Our Bones*, p. 222, the figure cited is 2500 media at the airport and 5000 protesters.

75 Newnham, *By Batons and Barbed Wire*, p. 17.

76 See Neil Reid, 'Arresting Times', *Sunday Star-Times*, 27 March 2011, p. C9, which focuses on activist Kevin Hague, now a Green MP.

77 Ross Meurant, *The Red Squad Story*, Auckland, Harland Publishing, 1982, p. 42.

78 Ibid., p. 43.

79 Unnamed officer cited in Louise Greig, 'The Police and the Tour', in Louise Greig and Rachel Barrowman, *The Police and the 1981 Tour*, Wellington, History Department, Victoria University, Occasional Papers No. 2, 1985, p. 12.

80 Jim McLay, *New Zealand Parliamentary Debates*, vol. 439, 28 July 1981, p. 2016, cited in Malcolm McKinnon, 'Resolution and Apprehension: The Parliamentary National Party and the 1981 Springbok Tour', in Mackay, McKinnon, McPhee and Phillips (eds), *Counting the Cost*, p. 23.

81 Aussie Malcolm, *New Zealand Parliamentary Debates*, vol. 439, 28 July 1981, p. 2026, cited in McKinnon, 'Resolution and Apprehension', in Mackay, McKinnon, McPhee and Phillips (eds), *Counting the Cost*, p. 31.

82 Statements from marchers collected by the Council for Civil Liberties in the week following Molesworth Street, cited in Rachel Barrowman, 'A Report on the Molesworth Street Incident', in Greig and Barrowman, *The Police and the 1981 Tour*, p. 26.

83 King and Phillips, 'A Social Analysis of the Springbok Tour Protesters', in Mackay, McKinnon, McPhee and Phillips (eds), *Counting the Cost*, p. 12.

84 Piet de Jong, *Saturday's Warriors: The Building of a Rugby Stronghold*, Palmerston North, Department of Sociology, Massey University, 1991, p. 60.

85 McKinnon, 'Resolution and Apprehension', in Mackay, McKinnon, McPhee and Phillips (eds), *Counting the Cost*, p. 36.

86 Cited in Walker and Beach (eds), *56 Days*, p. 23.

87 Ibid., p. 15.

88 See Guy, *Shaping Godzone*, p. 330.

89 Newnham, *By Batons and Barbed Wire*, p. 69.

90 There were three tests, on 15 August in Christchurch, 29 August in Wellington, and 12 September in Auckland.

91 Newnham, *By Batons and Barbed Wire*, p. 86.

92 Cited in Newnham, ibid., p. 89.

93 McKinnon, *Independence and Foreign Policy*, p. 248.

94 At the same time, several urban seats were lost to Labour. The election victory was a very near-run thing, with National enjoying a post-election majority of only one in the House and Labour garnering more of the popular vote. See McKinnon, 'Resolution and Apprehension', in Mackay, McKinnon, McPhee and Phillips (eds), *Counting the Cost*, p. 37.

95 This quote is from Peter Utting and Jeya Wilson, *Babes in Verwoerds: Two New Zealanders in South Africa*, Wellington, Price Milburn, 1982, p. 118, cited in Richards, *Dancing on Our Bones*, p. 230. The authors, who were in South Africa at the time, wrote in that book about the reaction of black Africans who approached them in the aftermath of the cancelled Waikato game.

96 'Tom Scott's Political Notebook', *New Zealand Listener*, 5 September 1981, p. 13.

97 Bruce Jesson, 'The Tour is Over', *New Zealand Listener*, 3 October 1981, p. 16.

98 Graeme Lay, 'Beyond the Paddock', *New Zealand Listener*, 26 September 1981, p. 21.

99 Peter Stevens, 'No Man's Time', *New Zealand Listener*, 3 October 1981, p. 10.

100 Roger Hall, 'The Tour is Over', *New Zealand Listener*, 3 October 1981, p. 15.

101 See ibid., p. 15.

102 Keith Sinclair, *Halfway Round the Harbour: An Autobiography*, Auckland, Penguin Books, 1993, p. 206.

103 Cited in Michael King, *After the War: New Zealand Since 1945*, Auckland, Hodder & Stoughton in association with Wilson & Horton, 1988, p. 180. See also Ben Schrader, 'Parades and Protest Marches — Protest Marches, 1980s to 2000s', *Te Ara — The Encyclopedia of New Zealand*, updated 13 July 2012, www.teara.govt.nz/en/parades-and-protest-marches/page-6.

104 James, *Quiet Revolution*, p. 101.

105 Ibid., pp. 100-1.

106 Gustafson, *His Way*, p. 352.

107 Ibid., p. 273.

108 Reports in the *Evening Post* of 2 May 1982 cited in McKinnon, *Independence and Foreign Policy*, p. 207.

109 Gustafson, *His Way*, p. 292.

110 Ibid., p. 359.

111 James, *Quiet Revolution*, p. 131.

112 Ibid., p. 130.

113 See Gustafson, *His Way*, pp. 370-5 for a detailed account of the dramatic events and decisions leading to the snap election.

114 Ibid., p. 382.

115 Muldoon made this statement during an interview with the journalist Ian Fraser on the current affairs programme *Seven Days* in July 1975.

116 Gustafson, *His Way*, p. 357.

117 Ibid., p. 379.

118 Chapter 6 of Colin James' *Quiet Revolution*, for example, is entitled 'An Unwiser Canute'.

CHAPTER SEVEN Feminism and Gay Rights: Liberation and its Legacy

1 Jocelyn, 1st Women's Liberation Orientation Course, June–August 1972, in 'An Introduction to Women's Liberation', Dunedin, Dunedin Collective for Woman, 1972, p. 3. Only authors' first names feature in this bound collection of papers written by members of the Dunedin Collective for Woman.

2 Sue Kedgley, Foreword to Sue Kedgley and Mary Varnham (eds), *Heading Nowhere in a Navy Blue Suit*, Wellington, Daphne Brasell Associates, 1993, p. 2.

3 See Helen May, *Minding Children, Managing Men: Conflict and Compromise in the Lives of Postwar Pakeha Women*, Bridget Williams Books, Wellington, 1992, p. 211.

4 Christine Dann, *Up from Under: Women and Liberation in New Zealand 1970–1985*, Wellington, Allen & Unwin/Port Nicholson Press, 1985, p. 5.

5 Ibid.

6 Sandra Coney, *Standing in the Sunshine: A History of New Zealand Women since They Won the Vote*, Auckland, Viking, 1993, p. 142.

7 Ibid.

8 Lauris Edmond, *An Autobiography*, Wellington, Bridget Williams Books, 1994, pp. 244–5.

9 See Chapter 1 of this book.

10 Joan Stacpoole, 'Women: There's a Long Way to Go', *New Zealand Listener*, 9 October 1972, p. 13.

11 Helen May, *Politics in the Playground: The World of Early Childhood in New Zealand*, Wellington, Bridget Williams Books and the New Zealand Council for Educational Research, 2001, p. 144. The percentage rise cited applies to the period 1971–1980.

12 Melanie Nolan, *Breadwinning: New Zealand Women and the State*, Christchurch, Canterbury University Press, 2000, p. 248.

13 Ibid., p. 249.

14 Coney, *Standing in the Sunshine*, p. 142.

15 Dann, *Up from Under*, p. 3.

16 Ibid.

17 Maud Cahill and Christine Dann (eds), *Changing Our Lives: Women Working in the Women's Liberation Movement 1970–1990*, Wellington, Bridget Williams Books, 1991, pp. 78–79.

18 See May, *Minding Children, Managing Men*, p. 212.

19 Jocelyn, 1st Women's Liberation Orientation Course, in 'An Introduction to Women's Liberation', p. 1.

20 Coney, *Standing in the Sunshine*, p. 142.

21 Mary Varnham, 'Who'll Marry Her Now?', in Kedgley and Varnham (eds), *Heading Nowhere*, pp. 109 and 113.

22 Fern Mercier, 'An Odyssey', in Cahill and Dan (eds), *Changing Our Lives*, p. 51.

23 Raewyn Dalziel, 'National Organisation for Women, 1972', in Anne Else (ed.), *Women Together: A History of Women's Organisations in New Zealand, Ngā Rōpū Wāhine o te Motu*, Wellington, Historical Branch, Department of Internal Affairs and Daphne Brasell Associates, 1993, pp. 98–99.

24 Joyce Herd, *Cracks in a Glass Ceiling: New Zealand Women 1975–2004*, Dunedin, New Zealand Federation of Graduate Women, 2005, p. 5.

25 *Up from Under*, a newspaper created by the Wellington Women's Liberation Movement in 1971, was another popular feminist publication.

26 Cited in Dann, *Up from Under*, p. 103.

27 Jocelyn, 1st Women's Liberation Orientation Course, in 'An Introduction to Women's Liberation', p. 3.

28 Allison Webber, 'All the Prejudice that's Fit to Print', in Kedgley and Varnham (eds), *Heading Nowhere*, p. 38.

29 Sandra Coney, *Stroppy Sheilas and Gutsy Girls: New Zealand Women of Dash and Daring*, Auckland, Tandem Press, 1998, p. 147.

30 Barbara L. Brookes, 'A Germaine Moment: Style, Language and Audience', Chapter 8 in Tony Ballantyne and Brian Moloughney (eds), *Disputed Histories: Imagining New Zealand's Pasts*, Dunedin, University of Otago Press, 2006, pp. 198 and 200. Ngahuia Volkerling, of Te Arawa, Waikato and Tuhoe descent, later returned to her original surname, Te Awekotuku. She is now Professor of Research at the School of Maori and Pacific Development, University of Waikato.

31 Ibid., p. 202.

32 Ibid., p. 206.

33 Ibid., pp. 204 and 209.

34 Ibid., p. 212.

35 Marilyn Duckworth, *Camping on the Faultline: A Memoir*, Auckland, Vintage, 2000, p. 208.

36 Sue Kedgley, talk presented to WEA Educational Association, 10 September 1972, in *New Zealand Listener*, 16 October 1972, p. 19.

37 Viv Walker, 'A Working-Class Woman Meets Feminism', in Cahill and Dann (eds), *Changing Our Lives*, pp. 101–2.

38 'The Convention and the Press', in Sandra Coney (ed.) assisted by Anne Parsons (et al.), *United Women's Convention 1973*, Auckland, September 1973, [bound booklet; no publisher], p. 55.

39 Cited in Coney (ed.), ibid., p. 54.

40 Christine Dann, 'Equal Pay: How the Bosses Cheat', *Broadsheet*, no. 50, June 1957, p. 15, cited in Melanie Nolan, *Breadwinning: New Zealand Women and the State*, Christchurch, Canterbury University Press, 2000, p. 254.

41 See ibid., pp. 251–4.

42 Dann, *Up from Under*, p. 66.

43 Nolan, *Breadwinning*, p. 296.

44 See Major Thelma Smith, *Parents Centres Bulletin*, no. 42, March 1970, cited in Nolan, ibid., p. 280.

45 Ibid., pp. 280–1.

46 Ibid., p. 282.

47 Ibid., pp. 278–88.

48 Laurie Guy, *Shaping Godzone: Public Issues and Church Voices in New Zealand 1840–2000*, Wellington, Victoria University Press, 2012, p. 395.

49 Coney, *Standing in the Sunshine*, pp. 140–1.

50 This book, as the subtitle proclaimed, was 'by and for women' and produced by the Boston Women's Health Book Collective, Boston. Published in 1973, it was an expanded version of a booklet originally produced in 1970 under a different title.

51 Dann, *Up from Under*, p. 129.

52 Pauline Ray, 'IWY — Where Next?', *New Zealand Listener*, 20 December 1975, p. 14.

53 Rae Julian, 'Women's Electoral Lobby of New Zealand, 1975', in Else (ed.), *Women Together*, p. 104.

54 Dawn Ibbotson cited in Herd, *Cracks in a Glass Ceiling*, p. 1.

55 Michael Dean, 'The Liberators', *New Zealand Listener*, 15 November 1975, p. 8.

56 Anne Else, 'Feminist Art Networkers 1982–1988', in Else (ed.), *Women Together*, p. 477.

57 Riemke Ensing (ed.), *Private Gardens: An Anthology of New Zealand Women Poets*, Dunedin, Caveman Press, 1977, with an Afterword by Vincent O'Sullivan.

58 See Margot Roth's editorial on this theme, *New Zealand Women's Studies Journal*, August 1984, pp. 3–5.

59 Dann, *Up from Under*, p. 118.

60 Cited in Karen Jackman, 'Film on women – by women', *New Zealand Listener*, 22 November 1975, p. 17.

61 Kedgley, Foreword to Kedgley and Varnham (eds), *Heading Nowhere*, p. 33.

62 In 1976, the *New Zealand Herald* noted that in 1971, 38% of the world's population lived in countries in which abortion was freely available; by 1976, that figure had increased to 64%. See Guy, *Shaping Godzone*, p. 393.

63 Barry Gustafson, *His Way: A Biography of Robert Muldoon*, Auckland, Auckland University Press, 2000, p. 161.

64 See Colin James, 'Social Credit and the National Party', in Howard R. Penniman (ed.), *New Zealand at the Polls: The General Election of 1978*, Washington, DC, American Enterprise Institute for Public Policy Research, 1980, p. 165.

65 Coney, *Standing in the Sunshine*, p. 141.

66 Guy, *Shaping Godzone*, p. 414.

67 D. P. Kennedy to A. N. V. Dobbs, 8 March 1972, ABQU 632 W4452 35/14/2, Family Life 1971–85, Archives New Zealand, Wellington, cited in Claire Gooder, 'A History of Sex Education in New Zealand, 1939–1985', PhD thesis, History, Auckland, University of Auckland, 2010, p. 212. The full title of the Ross Report (named after J. A. Ross, Superintendent of Curriculum Development for the Education Department) was 'Human Development and Relationships in the School Curriculum'; see Gooder, 'A History of Sex Education', p. 215.

68 Ibid., p. 194.

69 Allanah Ryan, 'Remoralising Politics', in Bruce Jesson, Allanah Ryan and Paul Spoonley (eds), *Revival of the Right: New Zealand Politics in the 1980s*, Auckland, Heinemann Reed, 1988, p. 59.

70 Gooder, 'A History of Sex Education', p. 222. The Johnson Committee, from which the Johnson Report ensued, was created under the Department of Education during Labour's term in office but its report

and recommendations were produced under a more conservative National government.

71 Ibid., p. 253.

72 See Webber, 'All the Prejudice That's Fit to Print', in Kedgley and Varnham (eds), *Heading Nowhere*, p. 43.

73 Sandra Coney, 'Why the Women's Movement Ran out of Steam', in Kedgley and Varnham (eds), *Heading Nowhere*, pp. 59–60.

74 Ibid., pp. 68–73.

75 There is some ambiguity about the locale of the attack, with *Broadsheet* (see following note) naming Western Park and another source Auckland Domain (Kai Jensen, *Whole Men: The Masculine Tradition in New Zealand Literature*, Auckland, Auckland University Press, 1996, p. 1). Thompson himself told a *Metro* journalist that he was taken to a deserted spot near Auckland Zoo ('*Another Life*, excerpts from Mervyn Thompson's autobiography', *Metro*, December 1986, p. 206).

76 Kathleen Ryan, 'Rape Fight Back', *Broadsheet*, no. 119, May 1984, p. 10.

77 The 1977 Human Rights Commission Act outlawed discrimination on the basis of sex, race and religion.

78 *All About Women in New Zealand*, Wellington, Statistics New Zealand, 1993, pp. 19–21.

79 M. Gilson, 'Women in Employment', in John Forster (ed.), *Social Process in New Zealand: Readings in Sociology*, Auckland, Longman Paul, 1969, p. 192, Table 6.

80 Coney, *Standing in the Sunshine*, p. 237.

81 Dann, *Up from Under*, p. 177.

82 Penny Jamieson cited in Herd, *Cracks in a Glass Ceiling*, p. 4.

83 Mary O'Regan, 'Radicalised by the System', in Cahill and Dann (eds), *Changing Our Lives*, pp. 162 and 164.

84 *Women in New Zealand*, Wellington, Department of Statistics Te Tari Tatau/ Ministry of Women's Affairs, 1990, pp. 47 and 52.

85 'Cheryl' in Rosemary Barrington and Alison Gray, *The Smith Women: 100 New Zealand Women Talk About their Lives*, Wellington, Reed, 1981, p. 195. The women's first names were altered to protect anonymity.

86 'Sarah' in Barrington and Gray, ibid., p. 197, 'Melissa', p. 199 and 'Alma', p. 195.

87 Jock Phillips, 'Generations: 1965–1984',

in Bronwyn Dalley and Gavin McLean (eds), *Frontier of Dreams: The Story of New Zealand*, Auckland, Hodder Moa, 2005, p. 351.

88 Nolan, *Breadwinning*, pp. 261–5.

89 May, *Politics in the Playground*, p. 144.

90 *Auckland Star* and *Evening Post*, 15 October, cited in May, ibid., p. 146. Although Wall was reported as using the phrase 'dumping ground' in both the *Auckland Star* and *Evening Post* of 15 October, his statement as recorded in the *Parliamentary Debates* was actually: 'He was not concerned about the requirements of the affluent, educated woman who wanted to dump her responsibilities to her children.' *New Zealand Parliamentary Debates*, vol. 234, 14 October 1980, p. 4163.

91 Ibid. This quote is from Sonja Davies' summary of the Christian argument in her article 'What Price Equality?', *Early Childhood Quarterly*, vol. 3, no. 2, pp. 3–5.

92 Ibid., p. 145.

93 Ibid., p. 144.

94 Guy, *Shaping Godzone*, pp. 436–8.

95 Dolores Janiewski and Paul Morris, *New Rights, New Zealand: Myths, Moralities and Markets*, Auckland, Auckland University Press, 2005, p. 122. The 'Women Who Want to be Women' group had links to the American anti-feminist organisation Eagle Forum.

96 Guy, *Shaping Godzone*, p. 437.

97 May, *Minding Children, Managing Men*, p. 275.

98 Jenny Phillips, *Mothers Matter Too: A Handbook for Women at Home*, Wellington, Reed, 1983.

99 James Belich, *Paradise Reforged: A History of the New Zealanders from the 1880s to the Year 2000*, Auckland, Allen Lane/The Penguin Press, 2001, p. 504.

100 Gordon McLauchlan, *The Passionless People*, Auckland, Cassell, 1976, pp. 135–6.

101 Helen Paske, 'Unmoulding Men', *New Zealand Listener*, 27 January 1979, p. 22.

102 See Jock Phillips, *A Man's Country? The Image of the Pakeha Male: A History*, Auckland, Penguin Books, 1987, p. 284.

103 'Ross' in Alison Gray, *The Jones Men: 100 New Zealand Men Talk About their Lives*, Wellington, Reed, 1983, p. 69.

104 'Brad' in Gray, ibid., p. 84.

105 See 'The family connection', in Gray, ibid., pp. 132–4, and 'What's the best thing that happened to you?', pp. 142–3.

106 Lois Cox, 'That's What I am: I'm a Lesbian', in Alison J. Laurie and Linda Evans (eds), *Outlines: Lesbian and Gay Histories of Aotearoa*, Lesbian and Gay Archives New Zealand (LAGANZ), Wellington, 2005, p. 68.

107 Paul Millar, *No Fretful Sleeper: A Life of Bill Pearson*, Auckland, Auckland University Press, 2010, p. 210.

108 Laurie Guy, *Worlds in Collision: The Gay Debate in New Zealand, 1960–1986*, Wellington, Victoria University Press, 2002, pp. 38–39.

109 Maurice Gee, *Plumb*, Auckland, Penguin, 1978, p. 200.

110 Alison Laurie, 'Filthiness Became a Theory: An Overview of Homosexual and Lesbian Organising from Nineteenth Century Europe to Seventies New Zealand', in Laurie and Evans (eds), *Outlines*, p. 13.

111 Tighe Instone cited in Valda Edyvane, Tighe Instone and Porlene Simmonds, 'Wasted Days and Wasted Nights? Lesbian Socialising in Wellington from the Late 1960s', in Laurie and Evans (eds), ibid., p. 77.

112 Laurie, 'Filthiness Became a Theory', in Laurie and Evans (eds), ibid., p. 15.

113 Lindsay Taylor cited in Chris Brickell, *Mates and Lovers: A History of Gay New Zealand*, Auckland, Godwit, 2008, p. 294.

114 Guy, *Worlds in Collision*, p. 103.

115 Murray Edmond, 'Poetics of the Impossible', in Alan Brunton, Murray Edmond and Michele Leggott (eds), *Big Smoke: New Zealand Poems 1960–1975*, Auckland, Auckland University Press, 2000, p. 28.

116 Ngahuia Te Awekotuku, Shirley Tamihana, Julie Glamuzina and Alison Laurie, 'Lesbian Organising', in Else (ed.), *Women Together*, p. 550. By 1989, the Maori word takatapui or takatapuhi (beloved and intimate friend of the same gender) was used by Maori lesbians and gays.

117 Brickell, *Mates and Lovers*, p. 341.

118 John Croskey in Brickell, ibid., p. 301.

119 Ibid., p. 335.

120 Gustafson, *His Way*, pp. 161–2.

121 The front page in question is reproduced in Redmer Yska's *Truth: The Rise and Fall of the People's Paper*, Nelson, Craig Potton Publishing, 2010, p. 174.

122 Laurie, 'Filthiness Became a Theory', in Laurie and Evans (eds), *Outlines*, p. 16.

123 Brickell, *Mates and Lovers*, p. 308.

124 Concerned Parents Association newsletter, September 1985, cited in Ryan, 'Remoralising Politics', in Jesson, Ryan and Spoonley (eds), *Revival of the Right*, p. 76. See also Guy, *Worlds in Collision*, Chapter 5, pp. 123–87.

125 Cited in Ryan, 'Remoralising Politics', in Jesson, Ryan and Spoonley (eds), *Revival of the Right*, p. 64. The coalition included groups such as Women for Life, the Concerned Parents Association, the Society for the Promotion of Community Standards, Credo and SPUC.

126 Janiewski and Morris, *New Rights, New Zealand*, p. 123.

127 See Selwyn Dawson, 'God's Bullies', *Metro*, July 1985, pp. 170–6.

128 The first HIV AIDS case in New Zealand was reported in 1984.

129 Guy, *Worlds in Collision*, p. 125.

130 John Stenhouse, 'Religion and Society', in Giselle Byrnes (ed.), *The New Oxford History of New Zealand*, Melbourne, Oxford University Press, 2009, p. 355.

131 Isaac Davison, 'Same-sex marriage law passed', 17 April 2013, http://www.nzherald.co.nz/nz/news/article.cfm?c_id=1&objectid=10878200.

CHAPTER EIGHT Race Relations: Renaissance and Reassessment

1 C. K. Stead, *South-West of Eden: A Memoir, 1932–1956*, Auckland, Auckland University Press, 2010, p. 11.

2 K. C. McDonald, *Our Country's Story: An Illustrated History*, Christchurch, Whitcombe & Tombs, 1963, p. 148.

3 Race Relations Conciliator, *Race Against Time*, Wellington, Human Rights Commission, 1982, p. 12.

4 Ernest and Pearl Beaglehole, *Some Modern Maoris*, New Zealand Council for Educational Research, Educational Research Series No. 25, Wellington, Whitcombe & Tombs/Oxford University Press, 1946. A separate survey by the Beagleholes of 57 Pakeha tertiary students, mentioned in the book within the context of a discussion about mixed marriage, found only 33% of females and 42% of males did not reject the idea of marrying a Maori; 'rather less than 20 per cent' of their parents or families would approve of intermarriage; see section entitled

'Intermarriage', pp. 55–62. The poster for *Broken Barrier* is reproduced in Duncan Petrie and Duncan Stuart, *A Coming of Age: Thirty Years of New Zealand Film*, Auckland, Random House, 2008, p. 20.

5   This poem, originally published in the *New Zealand Herald* in February 1959 under Curnow's pen-name 'Whim Wham' and entitled 'A Private Bar?', is reproduced in Terry Sturm (ed.), *Whim Wham's New Zealand: The Best of Whim Wham 1937–1988*, Auckland, Vintage, 2005, pp. 132–3.

6   See David Ausubel's *The Fern and the Tiki*, Angus & Robertson, Sydney, 1960, p. 155, on New Zealanders' unwillingness to accept that race relations in their country were anything but harmonious.

7   Stead, *South-West of Eden*, p. 11.

8   M. P. K. Sorrenson, 'Modern Maori: The Young Maori Party to Mana Motuhake', in Keith Sinclair (ed.), *The Oxford Illustrated History of New Zealand*, new edn, Auckland, Oxford University Press, 1999, p. 345.

9   In 1960, there were twelve members of the Commonwealth; by 1972, membership had risen to 31. The majority of the new Commonwealth countries were located in Africa, Asia and the Caribbean. The African nations were particularly concerned about anti-colonialism and anti-racism, and 'white supremacy became a target' in both the Commonwealth and the UN; see Barry Gustafson, *Kiwi Keith: A Biography of Keith Holyoake*, Auckland, Auckland University Press, 2007, p. 189.

10 Jack K. Hunn, 'Report on the Department of Maori Affairs: With Statistical Supplement', Wellington, *Appendices to the Journals of the House of Representatives*, 1961, vol. 2, G-10: infant mortality statistic, p. 20; unemployment, p. 28; crime, p. 32 (the Maori crime rate rose 50% in four years (1954–1958) whereas the European rate remained static); bath in home, p. 36; education, p. 25. The report noted that if Maori continued schooling at the same rate as other children, there would have been 890 in the sixth form as opposed to 125.

11 Ibid., pp. 63–87.

12 Ibid., p. 15.

13 Vincent O'Malley, Bruce Stirling, and Wally Penetito (eds), *The Treaty of Waitangi Companion*, Auckland, Auckland University Press, 2010, p. 280.

14 Presbyterian Church of New Zealand Maori Synod, *A Maori View of the Hunn Report*, Christchurch, 1961, p. 8. The old Maori story about the shark and the kahawai involved the friendly shark inviting the smaller fish to swim together with him; but this was a means to an end, and the big fish swallowed the smaller.

15 Cited in O'Malley et al. (eds), *The Treaty of Waitangi Companion*, p. 281.

16 Maori Synod, *A Maori View*, p. 10.

17 See Chapter 6 of this book for a more extensive treatment of this subject.

18 Gustafson, *Kiwi Keith*, p. 197.

19 Auckland businessman and CARE chairman Harold Innes cited in Trevor Richards, *Dancing on Our Bones: New Zealand, South Africa, Rugby and Racism*, Wellington, Bridget Williams Books, 1999, p. 31.

20 Cited in Richards, ibid., p. 31.

21 Gustafson, *Kiwi Keith*, pp. 202–3.

22 Ibid., p. 203.

23 See below re Nga Tamatoa and the Polynesian Panthers.

24 Richards, *Dancing on Our Bones*, p. 53.

25 R. G. Lawson, 'Race Relations and the Law', in Graham Vaughn (ed.), *Racial Issues in New Zealand*, Auckland, Akarana Press, 1972, p. 103. The Race Relations Act came into effect in 1972.

26 The individuals whose names are associated with this report were Judge Ivor Prichard and Department of Maori Affairs official Hemi Tono Waetford.

27 See Richard Boast, 'Te Tango Whenua — Maori Land Alienation — 20th-Century Developments, Conversion', *Te Ara — The Encyclopedia of New Zealand*, updated 22 September 2012, http://www.teara.govt.nz/en/te-tango-whenua-maori-land-alienation-/page-9.

28 Ranginui Walker, *Ka Whawhai Tonu Matou: Struggle Without End*, Auckland, Penguin Books, 1990, pp. 139 and 207, and O'Malley et al. (eds), *The Treaty of Waitangi Companion*, pp. 284–5.

29 Walker, *Ka Whawhai Tonu Matou*, p. 207.

30 Cited in O'Malley et al. (eds), *The Treaty of Waitangi Companion*, p. 288.

31 Iriaka Ratana, MP for Western Maori, *New Zealand Parliamentary Debates*, vol. 354, 7 November 1967, p. 4017, cited in O'Malley et al. (eds), *The Treaty of Waitangi Companion*, p. 288.

32 Richard S. Hill, *Maori and the State:*

Crown–Maori Relations in New Zealand/ Aotearoa, 1950–2000, Wellington, Victoria University Press, 2009, p. 159.

33 Ibid., p. 160. The curriculum of 'Native Schools' (founded in 1867) had a vocational focus, training Maori boys to become labourers and the girls to become housewives. English was the sole language. By contrast, private schools such as Te Aute College had high academic standards and produced many outstanding Maori leaders.

34 Ibid.

35 Ranginui Walker, 'The Maori People since 1950', in Geoffrey W. Rice (ed.), *The Oxford History of New Zealand*, 2nd edn, Auckland, Oxford University Press, 1992, p. 512, and Paul Spoonley, *Racism and Ethnicity*, Auckland, Oxford University Press, 1988, pp. 46–47.

36 Kaumatua are respected tribal elders.

37 Walker, *Ka Whawhai Tonu Matou*, p. 210.

38 Sandra Coney, *Standing in the Sunshine: A History of New Zealand Women since They Won the Vote*, Auckland, Viking, 1993, p. 144.

39 Walker, 'The Maori People since 1950', in Rice (ed.), *The Oxford History of New Zealand*, 2nd edn, p. 509.

40 There had been a Maori Studies section in the Anthropology Department at the University of Auckland since 1952. In the late 1960s, Maori Studies at the University of Waikato was set up and operated along with a German programme. In 1972, however, Waikato established a separate Centre for Maori Studies and Research, and in the same year Massey created a Chair of Social Anthropology and Maori Studies. A year later, Victoria University established a Chair in Maori Studies. See Steven Webster, *Patrons of Maori Culture: Power, Theory, and Ideology in the Maori Renaissance*, Dunedin, University of Otago Press, 1998, p. 157.

41 Statistics re enrolment are cited in Webster, *Patrons of Maori Culture*, p. 14; the quote re liberal intellectual guilt is on p. 158.

42 Andrew Sharp, *Justice and the Māori: Māori Claims in New Zealand Political Argument in the 1980s*, Auckland, Oxford University Press, 1990, p. 187.

43 'Noisy Protesters Disrupt Waitangi Event', *New Zealand Herald*, 8 February 1971, p. 3.

44 Editorial, ibid., p. 6.

45 *New Zealand Herald*, 16 February 1971, p. 6, cited in Miranda Johnson, '"Land of the

Wrong White Crowd": Pakeha Anti-racist Organisations and Identity Politics in Auckland, 1964–1981', MA thesis, History, Auckland, University of Auckland, 2002, p. 50.

46 *Sunday Times* editorial of 10 June 1973, reproduced in *CARE* magazine, no. 5, July 1973, p. 15.

47 See Coney, *Standing in the Sunshine*, pp. 144–5. Sir Kingi Ihaka, for example, rebuked the women of Nga Tamatoa on one occasion, claiming that their ancestors would be disgusted by their behaviour.

48 W. H. Oliver, 'The Awakening Imagination, 1940–1980', in Rice (ed.), *The Oxford History of New Zealand*, 2nd edn, p. 569.

49 James K. Baxter, 'In My View', *New Zealand Listener*, 24 January 1969, p. 10.

50 Miranda Johnson, '"The Land of the Wrong White Crowd": Anti-racist Organizations and Pakeha Identity Politics in the 1970s', *New Zealand Journal of History*, vol. 39, no. 2, 2005, p. 141.

51 Joan Metge, *The Maoris of New Zealand*, revised edn, London, Routledge & Kegan Paul, 1976, p. 178.

52 Interestingly, his attempt to augment national unity by renaming Waitangi Day 'New Zealand Day' proved unpopular with Pakeha and Maori alike and was reversed by National in 1976.

53 *New Zealand Herald*, 2 April 1974, cited in Sharp, *Justice and the Māori*, p. 206.

54 Prime Minister Norman Kirk, *New Zealand Parliamentary Debates*, vol. 391, 5 July 1974, p. 2691, cited in O'Malley et al. (eds), *The Treaty of Waitangi Companion*, p. 284.

55 G. V. Butterworth and H. R. Young, *Maori Affairs: A Department and the People Who Made It*, Wellington, Iwi Transition Agency/GP Books, 1990, p. 108.

56 Section 31(g).

57 The figure fell from 23,984 acres in 1970 to 6532 in 1976. See Butterworth and Young, *Maori Affairs*, p. 109.

58 Cited in Hill, *Maori and the State*, p. 163.

59 John Harré, 'Maori–Pakeha Intermarriage', in Erik Schwimmer (ed.), *The Maori People in the Nineteen-Sixties*, Auckland, Blackwood and Janet Paul, 1968, pp. 118–19.

60 Walker, 'The Maori People since 1950', in Rice (ed.), *The Oxford History of New Zealand*, 2nd edn, p. 511. And see Noel Harrison's *Graham Latimer: A Biography*, Wellington, Huia, 2002.

61 Michael King's entry 'Cooper, Whina (1895–1994)' in *Dictionary of New Zealand Biography, Te Ara — The Encyclopedia of New Zealand*, updated 1 September 2010, http://teara.govt.nz/en/biographies/5c32/cooper-whina, describes Whina as 'Te Rarawa woman of mana, teacher, store-keeper, community leader'.

62 Michael King, *Whina*, Auckland, Hodder & Stoughton, 1983, p. 207.

63 In addition to the aforementioned 1967 Maori Affairs Amendment Act, there were two other bitterly resented acts: the 1967 Rating Act, which gave the government the power to compel land sales to recover unpaid rates, and the 1953 Town and Country Planning Act, which placed restrictions on land and resource use.

64 See Sharp, *Justice and the Māori*, p. 8.

65 King, *Whina*, p. 272.

66 'Land March Not in Vain Says PM', *New Zealand Herald*, 13 October 1975, p. 1.

67 The idea of a tent embassy at Parliament was not unprecedented; in 1972, Aboriginal Australians set up a tent embassy in Canberra as part of a campaign for equal rights and recognition of past injustices.

68 Walker, 'The Maori People since 1950', in Rice (ed.), *The Oxford History of New Zealand*, 2nd edn, p. 513.

69 Sharp, *Justice and the Māori*, pp. 74–75.

70 See, for example, *In re the Bed of the Wanganui River* [1962] NZLR 600 and *In re the Ninety Mile Beach* [1963] NZLR 461, cited in Claudia Orange, *The Treaty of Waitangi*, Wellington, Allen & Unwin/Port Nicholson Press, with assistance from Historic Publications Branch, Department of Internal Affairs, 1987, pp. 245, fn. 59 and 296.

71 Sharp, *Justice and the Māori*, p. 89 states that despite contempt for the Treaty by some activists in the early 1970s, and the fact that important tribes such as Tuwharetoa and the Te Arawa confederation never actually signed it, the Treaty was by the early 1980s generally accepted as the reference point for injustice — that is, it was failure to honour the Treaty that was at fault rather than the document itself.

72 See Ruth Ross, 'Te Tiriti o Waitangi, Texts and Translations', *New Zealand Journal of History*, vol. 6, no. 2, 1972, pp. 129–54.

73 Metge, *The Maoris of New Zealand*, p. 331.

74 Orange, *The Treaty of Waitangi*, p. 247.

75 See David C. Thorns and Charles P.

Sedgwick, *Understanding Aotearoa/New Zealand: Historical Statistics*, Palmerston North, Dunmore Press, 1997, Table 2.10, p. 55. Quote re mean-mindedness from James Belich, *Paradise Reforged: A History of the New Zealanders from the 1880s to the Year 2000*, Auckland, Allen Lane/The Penguin Press, 2001, p. 532.

76 Duncan MacIntyre, Minister of Maori Affairs, in *Te Maori*, vol. 1, no. 4, May–June 1970, p. 54, cited in Johnson, '"Land of the Wrong White Crowd"', MA thesis, p. 33.

77 This phrase is used in Sorrenson, 'Modern Maori', in Sinclair (ed.), *The Oxford Illustrated History of New Zealand*, new edn, p. 345.

78 Melani Anae, Lautofa (Ta) Iuli and Leilani Burgoyne (eds), *The Polynesian Panthers 1971–1974: The Crucible Years*, Auckland, Reed, 2006.

79 Ta'afuli Andrew Fiu, *Purple Heart*, Auckland, Random House, 2006, pp. 12–13. The street in question was Summer Street, Ponsonby, Auckland.

80 Wayne Toleafoa cited in Anae et al. (eds), *The Polynesian Panthers*, p. 61.

81 Anae et al. (eds), ibid., p. 8.

82 Joris de Bres interviewed on the documentary *Dawn Raids*, TVNZ, Isola Productions, 2005, cited in Melani Anae, 'All Power to the People: Overstayers, Dawn Raids and the Polynesian Panthers', in Sean Mallon, Kolokesa Mahina-Tuai and Damon Salesa (eds), *Tangata Ole Moana: New Zealand and the People of the Pacific*, Wellington, Te Papa Press, 2012, p. 228.

83 *Zealandia*, 31 March 1974, cited in Anae, 'All Power to the People', in Mallon, Mahina-Tuai and Salesa (eds), *Tangata Ole Moana*, p. 228.

84 Anae, 'All Power to the People', in Mallon, Mahina-Tuai and Salesa (eds), *Tangata Ole Moana*, p. 230.

85 Barry Gustafson, *His Way: A Biography of Robert Muldoon*, Auckland, Auckland University Press, 2000, p. 161.

86 Belich, *Paradise Reforged*, p. 535.

87 See *New Zealand Truth*, 30 September 1975, p. 6.

88 'Immigration Fears', *Auckland Star*, 23 January 1975, p. 9. This inflow was described as 'putting undue strain on the economy'.

89 'New Zealand Can't Stop Influx from Some Islands', *Auckland Star*, 23 January 1975, p. 3.

90 Anae, 'All Power to the People', in Mallon, Mahina-Tuai and Salesa (eds), *Tangata Ole Moana*, p. 230.

91 Fiu, *Purple Heart*, pp. 23–24.

92 Mary Boyd, 'New Zealand and the other Pacific Islands', in Sinclair (ed.), *The Oxford Illustrated History of New Zealand*, new edn, p. 316.

93 Sharon Liava'a, 'Dawn Raids: When Pacific Islanders Were Forced to Go "Home"', MA dissertation, History, Auckland, University of Auckland, 1998, pp. 32–33, cited in Anae, 'All Power to the People', in Mallon, Mahina-Tuai and Salesa (eds), *Tangata Ole Moana*, p. 233.

94 Susan Butterworth, *More Than Law and Order: Policing a Changing Society 1945–92*, Dunedin, University of Otago Press, 2005, p. 193.

95 *City News*, 28 August 1974, p. 1 quotes extensively from this report. The headline reads: 'Task Force? Task Farce!'

96 'Task Force Honoured', *Auckland Star*, 12 July 1975, p. 2.

97 'Discrimination Complaints Up', *New Zealand Herald*, 9 October 1975, p. 5.

98 Most notably Karangahape Road, a centre for Pacific Island retail.

99 Accounts of the operation in the *Auckland Star*, 22 October 1976, p. 2 contain references to Maori being approached and asked for documentation.

100 *Auckland Star*, 22 October 1976, p. 1.

101 David Lange (elected Labour Prime Minister in 1984) cited in 'Carry Your Passport', *Auckland Star*, 22 October 1976, p. 2.

102 Eleanor Moyles made the latter comparison in a letter to the *Auckland Star*, 25 October 1976, p. 8.

103 'Bad Days', *Auckland Star*, 25 October 1976, p. 8.

104 See '"Checking" is All PM Says', *Auckland Star*, 28 October 1976, p. 1.

105 Butterworth, *More Than Law and Order*, p. 194.

106 *The April Report: Report of the Royal Commission on Social Policy*, Wellington, The Commission, 1988, vol. 1, p. 82.

107 Dansey was a former journalist, an author, and a member of the Arawa and Ngati Tuwharetoa tribes.

108 Peter Trickett, 'A Country for All Its Citizens', *New Zealand Listener*, 14 January 1978, p. 17.

109 Margaret McClure, *The Wonder Country:* *Making New Zealand Tourism*, Auckland, Auckland University Press, 2004, p. 217. Around this time, Rotorua boasted Maori meter maids, dressed in traditional costume.

110 Ibid., p. 221.

111 Among the 200 people who attended that first hui were Selwyn Muru, Para Matchitt, Ralph Hotere, Katarina Mataira, Rowley Habib, Witi Ihimaera, Buck Nin, Donna Awatere, Cliff Whiting and Charles Bennett. See Averil Herbert, 'Te Moana: Nga Puna Waihanga Annual Hui: Te Rua Tekau Tau, 1973–1993', Whanganui, Nga Puna Waihanga, 1993.

112 Bill Pearson, 'The Maori and Literature 1938–1965', in Schwimmer (ed.), *The Maori People in the Nineteen-Sixties*, p. 256.

113 Jill McCracken, 'Family', *New Zealand Listener*, 7 December 1974, p. 38.

114 Teacher and sculptor Arnold Manaaki Wilson created the 'Pateaka', a programme in the late 1970s. Its objective was for students to produce an artwork while living according to Maori values and experiencing a Maori approach to learning and development. See Janinka Greenwood and Arnold Manaaki Wilson, *Te Mauri Pakeaka*, Auckland, Auckland University Press, 2006.

115 See 'A New Face of Maori Fashion' in Lucy Hammonds, Douglas Lloyd Jenkins and Claire Regnault, *The Dress Circle: New Zealand Fashion Design since 1940*, Auckland, Random House, 2010, p. 212.

116 Harry Dansey, *Te Raukura: The Feathers of the Albatross*, Auckland, Longman Paul, 1974, p. 1, cited in Johnson, '"Land of the Wrong White Crowd"', MA thesis, p. 83.

117 Some of King's publications include *Moko Maori* (1972); *Face Value: A Study in Maori Portraiture* (1975); *Te Puea* (1977); *Tihe Mauriora: Aspects of Maoritanga* (1978); *Being Maori* (1981); *Whina: A Biography of Whina Cooper* (1983); and *Being Pakeha* (1985).

118 Jock Phillips, 'Vision and Fulfilment', *New Zealand Listener*, 21 January 1978, p. 42.

119 See Michael King's favourable review of the new edition entitled 'Victim's Story' in *New Zealand Listener*, 22 March 1975, p. 33.

120 This column originated in 1970 when its author was Graham Butterworth. Syd Jackson took over for a short time before Walker commenced in 1973.

121 W. D. Farmer (Wellington), letter to editor

of 8 March 1975, *New Zealand Listener*, p. 6.

122 David Young, 'Maori TV: A Presence for a People', *New Zealand Listener*, 1 July 1978, pp. 22–23.

123 Matt Elliott, *Billy T: The Life and Times of Billy T James*, Auckland, HarperCollins, 2009, p. 60.

124 'Radio's Role: Still a Long Way to Go', *New Zealand Listener*, 1 July 1978, pp. 22–23.

125 Ibid., p. 23.

126 A film version of the novel, made in 1979, directed by Paul Maunder, starred Fiona Lindsay as Sarah and Uelese Petaia as Sione.

127 Jill McCracken, 'Let's Come Together', *New Zealand Listener*, 1 March 1975, p. 13. Ihaka was perhaps presciently anticipating the vibrant Pasifika Festival, which commenced in 1993 in Western Springs, one of the most popular events in Auckland's social calendar, and a visually spectacular celebration of the diversity and vitality of Pacific Island culture in New Zealand.

128 'Unique Community Arts Festival', *New Zealand Listener*, 20 March 1976, p. 23.

129 Waitangi Tribunal, *Report of the Waitangi Tribunal on the Orakei Claim*, Wai-9, (*Orakei Report*), p. 103. The aim was to subdivide and build houses on 17 acres, dedicate 1 acre to a Youthline Hostel, and add another 22.5 acres to the Council Parks. The balance of 19 acres around Kitemoana Street would be 'subject to further investigation'.

130 Mike Rameka, 'Report to the Orakei Maori Committee', 13 May 1977, in Ranginui Walker, 'Bastion Point documents', Auckland University Library, n.p.

131 Father Terry Dibble, cited in *Orakei Report*, p. 153.

132 'Report to the Orakei Maori Committee', 13 May 1977, in Walker, 'Bastion Point documents', n.p.

133 Gustafson, *His Way*, p. 205.

134 For example: 'History may yet be made at Bastion Point. Let it be remembered not as a battleground, like "Wounded Knee", but as a Treaty Ground, where amends were clearly made for a clearly proven record of "sad, sorry and shameful" dealings', letter to newspaper by Gerhard Rosenberg, cited in J. P. Hawke, 'Report to the Orakei Maori Committee', 13 April 1977, p. 2, in Walker, 'Bastion Point documents'.

135 Gustafson, *His Way*, p. 205. Under the Orakei Block (Vesting and Use) Act 1978, a Ngati Whatua Trust Board was created.

For $257,000 (loaned by the Maori Trustee) it received 11.6 hectares of land for Maori residential use; 12.5 hectares was set aside for a recreation reserve and 1.7 hectares was vested in the Housing Corporation. This settlement, which included some 33 state houses in Kitemoana Street, was worth some $2 million dollars. Muldoon believed it was generous; while acceptable to the Ngati Whatua elders, it was rejected by the protesters.

136 'Peace Prevails as Protest Ends After 17 Months', *New Zealand Herald*, 26 May 1978, p. 5.

137 *Orakei Report*, p. 165.

138 'Left Without a Choice', *New Zealand Herald* editorial, 26 May 1978, p. 6.

139 Cited in 'Maori MP on "Sad Episode"', *New Zealand Herald*, 26 May 1978, p. 5.

140 Matiu Rata, *New Zealand Parliamentary Debates*, vol. 417, 1978, p. 322.

141 'Left Without a Choice', *New Zealand Herald* editorial, 26 May 1978, p. 6.

142 As the 1987 Waitangi Tribunal report on Orakei later observed: 'it was only after "Bastion Point" that a new caution was apparent in the Crown's dealing with Maori land throughout the country and there was an awareness that something had to be done about old claims if only to properly research them before things got out of hand'; *Orakei Report*, p. 107.

143 Gustafson, *His Way*, p. 206.

144 *Auckland Star*, 1 May 1979, cited in O'Malley et al. (eds), *The Treaty of Waitangi Companion*, p. 298.

145 Tony Reid, 'Mocking the Maori', editorial, *New Zealand Listener*, 26 May 1979, p. 6.

146 Walker, *Ka Whawhai Tonu Matou*, pp. 224 and 225.

147 When Auckland District Council chairman Ranginui Walker filed separate complaints against the students with the Race Relations Conciliator after the trial, the 'enormous public response' to the complaint resulted in a digest, published by the Conciliator, of the more than 300 submissions for and against the actions of Te Haua. See O'Malley et al. (eds), *The Treaty of Waitangi Companion*, p. 297. This was the genesis of the 1982 Human Rights Commission report *Race Against Time*, which included these views in summary form but extended the brief to incorporate a broader assessment of contemporary New Zealand race relations.

148 Hill, *Maori and State*, p. 197. These
initiatives for more Maori self-reliance
were aligned with international agreements; in 1978, for example, New Zealand
had become a signatory to the UN's
International Covenant on Civil and
Political Rights, the first article of which
was people's right to self-determination.

149 Butterworth and Young, *Maori Affairs*,
pp. 113–14.

150 Ranginui Walker, 'The Maori People since
1950', in Rice (ed.), *The Oxford History of
New Zealand*, 2nd edn, p. 515.

151 Walker, *Ka Whawhai Tonu Matou*, p. 237.

152 Ibid., p. 247.

153 Derek Dow, 'Driving Their Own Health
Canoe', in Bronwyn Dalley and Margaret
Tennant (eds), *Past Judgement: Social
Policy in New Zealand History*, Dunedin,
University of Otago Press, 2004, p. 102.

154 Peter Tapsell, 'Maori Health — The
Push for Parity', *New Zealand Listener*, 8
December 1979, p. 40.

155 J. D. K. North, Chairman, Forward
Planning Committee, Medical Research
Council, preface to Eru W. Pomare, 'Maori
Standards of Health: A Study of the 20-year
Period 1955–1975', Wellington, Medical
Research Council of New Zealand, 1980,
n.p.

156 Pomare, *Maori Standards of Health*,
pp. 40–41.

157 Mason Durie, *Whaiora: Maori Health
Development*, Auckland, Oxford University
Press, 1994, p. 71. See http://www.
health.govt.nz/our-work/populations/
maori-health/maori-health-models for
a graphic illustration of the four cor-
nerstones of Maori health that together
comprise Te Whare Tapa Whā.

158 Durie, *Whaiora*, p. 134.

159 Ibid., p. 67.

160 Sorrenson, 'Modern Maori', in Sinclair
(ed.), *The Oxford Illustrated History of New
Zealand*, new edn, p. 345.

161 Ibid.

162 'Grieving Father Slams Violence', *Auckland
Star*, 7 January 1976, p. 1; McReady is
quoted in 'Gang Violence Vow: 'I'll Put an
End to it', *Auckland Star*, 8 January 1976,
p. 1.

163 See Pip Desmond, *Trust: A True Story of
Women and Gangs*, Auckland, Random
House, 2009, for an insight into one of
these schemes, aimed at women involved
with Maori gang members.

164 As his biographer has noted, Muldoon
had 'a rather strange personal relationship'
with Maori gangs which resulted in several
unlikely social encounters; see Gustafson,
His Way, p. 207.

165 Butterworth, *More Than Law and Order*,
p. 198. This baton was a move towards
'semi-armed' policing.

166 This (difficult to translate) term denotes
Maori self-reliance, self-determination,
and/or sovereignty; Paul Spoonley defines
it as Maori sovereignty in *Race and
Ethnicity*, Auckland, Oxford University
Press, 1993, p. 49.

167 Walker, *Ka Whawhai Tonu Matou*, pp. 228
and 244.

168 Donna Huata Awatere, *Maori Sovereignty*,
Auckland, Broadsheet, 1984, p. 10.
Awatere's series of 'Maori Sovereignty'
articles appeared in *Broadsheet* in three
parts: in no. 100, June 1982, pp. 38–42;
no. 103, October 1982, pp. 24–29; and no.
106, January–February 1983, pp. 12–21.
An additional part, 'Exodus', was written
for the 1984 book.

169 See, for example, the *Auckland Star* of 5
February 1985, p. 4.

170 See, for example 'Treatment of Dead
Shocks Maoris', *New Zealand Times*, 27
March 1983, and 'Courtesy, Custom, Death,
Protest', in *Auckland Star*, 12 April 1983,
both in Ranginui Walker, 'Race Relations,
1979–1983', bound newspaper clippings,
University of Auckland Library, p. 51.

171 'Souvenirs Insulting', *Auckland Star*, 2 June
1983, in Walker, ibid., p. 60.

172 'Souvenirs Go Too Far', *Auckland Star*, 3
June 1983, in Walker, ibid., p. 60.

173 *New Zealand Herald*, 14 June 1982, cited in
Sharp, *Justice and the Māori*, p. 203.

174 *Dominion Sunday Times*, 11 January 1981,
cited in Sharp, *Justice and the Māori*, p. 203.

175 'Warning on racism in nurse training',
Auckland Star, 26 July 1983, in Walker, 'Race
Relations, 1979–1983', p. 62. The member
in question who made the comparison to
apartheid was Mrs Frances Miller.

176 Cited in Walker, *Ka Whawhai Tonu Matou*,
p. 236.

177 Ibid., pp. 231–6. Arrests rose from eight in
1981, to 27 in 1982, to 99 in 1983 — the latter
following a pre-emptive police strike.

178 Figures vary from 1000 to 3000.

179 *New Zealand Herald*, 7 February 1984, 'Sir
David in Vain Wait for Hikoi Delegation', in
Walker, 'Race Relations, 1979–1983', p. 71.

180 Sir James Henare, for example, a member of the Maori Trust Board for the past 44 years, publicly apologised about what he perceived as a grave discourtesy 'contrary to Maori etiquette and good manners'. 'Peace Walk Apology', *New Zealand Herald*, 11 February, 1984, in Walker, ibid., p. 72.

181 'Open Letter to Sir David Conveys Regret, Gratitude, Hope', *New Zealand Herald*, 11 February 1984, in Walker, ibid., p. 72.

182 'Waitangi Walkers Put Case', *New Zealand Herald*, 11 February 1984, in Walker, ibid., p. 72.

183 Michael King, 'The Past Repeopled', *New Zealand Listener*, 8 December 1979, p. 10.

184 Jack K. Hunn, 'Report on the Department of Maori Affairs: With Statistical Supplement', *Appendices to the Journals of the House of Representatives*, 1961, vol. 2, G-10, p. 15.

185 See 'Left Without a Choice', *New Zealand Herald*, 26 May 1978, p. 6.

186 Hilda Phillips, one of the most vocal advocates of this notion, waged an irate campaign throughout the 1970s and 1980s insisting that any form of legal differentiation between races militated against New Zealanders' common shared humanity. See her feature article 'Can Discrimination Achieve Racial Equality?' in the *New Zealand Listener*, 19 April 1975, p. 9.

187 As Andrew Sharp has observed: 'it [multiculturalism] drowned them in the clamour of others'; *Justice and the Māori*, p. 215. For many anti-racist activists, multiculturalism and biculturalism were not necessarily opposed, as the Race Relations Conciliator advised in *Race Against Time*, 1982, p. 51: 'The first step towards a multi-cultural society is the deliberate development of a bi-cultural New Zealand.'

CHAPTER NINE **Transformations: Doing the Impossible**

1 Margaret Wilson, 'Oh What a Party', in Margaret Clark (ed.), *For the Record: Lange and the Fourth Labour Government*, Wellington, Dunmore Publishing, 2005, p. 29.

2 See Colin James, *The Quiet Revolution*, Wellington, Allen & Unwin/Port Nicholson Press, 1986, pp. 142–6 for a discussion about the new Labour leaders.

3 Geoff Bertram, 'The New Zealand Economy, 1900–2000', in Giselle Byrnes (ed.), *The New Oxford History of New Zealand*, Melbourne, Oxford University Press, 2009, p. 559.

4 Tony Judt, *Postwar: A History of Europe since 1945*, London, William Heinemann, 2005, p. 540.

5 Martin Holland and Jonathan Boston (eds), *The Fourth Labour Government: Politics and Policy in New Zealand*, 2nd edn, Oxford, Oxford University Press, 1990, p. 2.

6 Keith Sinclair, 'Hard Times (1972–1990)', in Keith Sinclair (ed.), *The Oxford Illustrated History of New Zealand*, 2nd edn, Auckland, Oxford University Press, 1997, p. 362.

7 Douglas, *There's Got to be a Better Way! A Practical ABC to Solving New Zealand's Major Problems*, Wellington, Fourth Estate Books, 1980, p. 75.

8 Barry Gustafson, 'No Land is an Island: Twenty-first Century Politics', Chapman Lecture, University of Auckland, 2010, p. 7.

9 Brian Easton, *In Stormy Seas: The Post-War New Zealand Economy*, Dunedin, University of Otago Press, 1997, p. 226.

10 Michael Bassett, *The State in New Zealand 1840–1984: Socialism without Doctrines?*, Auckland, Auckland University Press, 1998, p. 375.

11 Barry Gustafson, 'The Labour Party', in Hyam Gold (ed.), *New Zealand Politics in Perspective*, Auckland, Longman Paul, 1985, p. 151.

12 Jim Bolger, 'Lange and Parliament', in Clark (ed.), *For the Record*, p. 31.

13 David Lange, *My Life*, Auckland, Viking, 2005, p. 151.

14 Douglas, *There's Got to be a Better Way*, p. 9.

15 Bassett, *The State in New Zealand*, p. 369.

16 Douglas, *There's Got to be a Better Way*, p. 75.

17 'The Changing Face of New Zealand Capitalism', *New Republic*, March 1986, in Bruce Jesson, *To Build a Nation: Collected Writings 1975–1999*, ed. Andrew Sharp, Auckland, Penguin, 2005, p. 173.

18 This phrase is used in Sinclair, *A History of New Zealand*, revised edn, Auckland, Penguin, 2000, p. 358 to describe the protected New Zealand economy, prior to the post-1984 reforms.

19 Denis Welch, 'Bank on the Run', *New Zealand Listener*, 27 October 1984, p. 13.

20 Quoted in Marcia Russell, *Revolution: New Zealand from Fortress to Free Market*, Auckland, Hodder Moa Beckett, 1996, p. 67.

21 Lange, *My Life*, p. 176.

22 Quoted in Colin James, *New Territory: The Transformation of New Zealand 1984–92*, Wellington, Bridget Williams Books, 1992, p. 149.

23 Quoted in Russell, *Revolution*, p. 69.

24 Roger Douglas in Russell, ibid., p. 80.

25 Geoffrey Palmer cited in Margaret McClure, *A Civilised Community: A History of Social Security in New Zealand 1898–1998*, Auckland, Auckland University Press in association with the Historical Branch, Department of Internal Affairs, 1998, p. 214.

26 Letter in *North & South*, March 1987, p. 17.

27 http://www.greypower.co.nz/.

28 'Group Power', *New Zealand Herald*, 10 September 1993, Section 3, p. 3.

29 This phrase is used by Bronwyn Dalley and Gavin McLean in 'Breaking Free, 1984–2005', in Bronwyn Dalley and Gavin McLean (eds), *Frontier of Dreams: The Story of New Zealand*, Auckland, Hodder Moa, 2005, p. 367.

30 Gerald Hensley, *Friendly Fire: Nuclear Politics and the Collapse of ANZUS, 1984–1987*, Auckland, Auckland University Press, 2013, p. x.

31 Ibid., p. xi.

32 Malcolm McKinnon, *Independence and Foreign Policy: New Zealand in the World since 1935*, Auckland, Auckland University Press, 1993, p. 286.

33 Cited in Michael Szabo, *Making Waves: The Greenpeace New Zealand Story*, Auckland, Reed, 1991, p. 132.

34 John Dyson (with Joseph Fitchett), *Sink the Rainbow! An Enquiry into the 'Greenpeace Affair'*, Auckland, Reed Methuen, 1986, p. 9.

35 Szabo, *Making Waves*, p. 134.

36 W. D. McIntyre, 'From Dual Dependency to Nuclear Free', in Geoffrey W. Rice (ed.), *The Oxford History of New Zealand*, 2nd edn, Auckland, Oxford University Press, 1992, p. 535.

37 Hensley, *Friendly Fire*, p. 267.

38 See Hensley, *Friendly Fire*, pp. 279 and 306.

39 James Belich, *Paradise Reforged: A History of the New Zealanders from the 1880s to the Year 2000*, Auckland, Allen Lane/The Penguin Press, 2001, p. 439.

40 Michael Williams, 'The Political Economy of Privatization', in Holland and Boston (eds), *The Fourth Labour Government*, 2nd edn, p. 141.

41 Russell, *Revolution*, p. 111. Rod Deane was a prominent economist and former Deputy Governor of the Reserve Bank.

42 Ibid., p. 109.

43 Alan Bollard and David Mayes, *Corporatisation and Privatisation in New Zealand*, Wellington, New Zealand Institute of Economic Research, 1991, p. 28.

44 Craig Howie and Claire Ramsay, *The Reforms, Riding the Rollercoaster: A Summary of New Zealand's Economic and Social Reforms, 1984–1998*, Dunedin, Otago Daily Times, 1998, p. 32.

45 Quoted in Russell, *Revolution*, p. 110.

46 John Martin, 'Remaking the State Services', in Holland and Boston (eds), *The Fourth Labour Government*, 2nd edn, p. 125.

47 *Press*, 17 February 1988.

48 Colin James, 'Breaking the Mould', in Colin James and Alan McRobie, *Turning Point: The 1993 Election and Beyond*, Wellington, Bridget Williams Books, 1993, p. 16.

49 Russell, *Revolution*, p. 119.

50 Howie and Ramsay, *The Reforms*, p. 34.

51 Bollard and Mayes, *Corporatisation and Privatisation in New Zealand*, p. 28.

52 Quoted in Russell, *Revolution*, p. 126.

53 Paul Goldsmith, *Serious Fun: The Life and Times of Alan Gibbs*, Auckland, Random House, 2012, p. 152.

54 Ibid. The programme 'Hard Arts' screened on 17 August 2006.

55 Richard Prebble, *I've Been Thinking*, Auckland, Sentra, 1996, p. 27.

56 Ibid., p. 42.

57 Ibid., p. 35 described New Zealand as 'the Poland of the South Pacific'; the phrase 'a paradise for free marketeers' appears in Jane Kelsey, *The New Zealand Experiment: A World Model for Structural Adjustment?*, Auckland, Auckland University Press, 1995, p. 8.

58 Richard Le Heron, 'Manufacturing, Services and Tourism', in Steve Britton, Richard Le Heron and Eric Pawson (eds), *Changing Places in New Zealand: A Geography of Restructuring*, Christchurch, New Zealand Geographical Society, 1993, p. 126.

59 Ibid., pp. 129–35.

60 James, *New Territory*, p. 179.

61 Labour Market Statistics, Department of Statistics, Wellington, 1996, p. 67.

62 Ibid.

63 Stephen Harris, 'So, Where are the New Jobs to Come From? Looking for the Sunrise Industries', in *New Zealand Outlook*, May 1987, p. 52.

64 Selwyn Parker, 'Living in Hope in Hastings', *North & South*, September 1990, pp. 58–67.

65 Quoted in Russell, *Revolution*, pp. 124–5.

66 Catherine Watson, 'No Jobs, No Hope', *New Zealand Listener*, 17 February 1992, pp. 22–27.

67 Russell, *Revolution*, p. 127.

68 *Press*, 16 February 1988.

69 Ibid., 9 February 1988.

70 Ibid., 10 February 1988.

71 Vangelis Vitalis, 'Trade, Innovation and Growth: The Case of the New Zealand Agriculture Sector', Paper presented to the OECD Global Trade Forum on Trade, Innovation and Growth, 14–15 October 2007, Paris, OECD, p. 12.

72 Stephen Harris, 'Out in a Colder World: Farming Reaches a Crucial Turning Point', *New Zealand Outlook*, May–June 1986, p. 41.

73 Vitalis, 'Trade, Innovation and Growth', p. 13.

74 Russell, *Revolution*, p. 105.

75 Howie and Ramsay, *The Reforms*, p. 25.

76 Quoted in Russell, *Revolution*, p. 130.

77 Quoted in Russell, ibid., p. 102.

78 Russell, *Revolution*, p. 103.

79 Neil G. Gow, 'Farmer Entrepreneurship in New Zealand: Some Observations from Case Studies', 15th Congress — Developing Entrepreneurship Abilities to Feed the World in a Sustainable Way, 14–19 August 2005, Campinas, São Paulo, Brazil, p. 290.

80 Harris, 'Out in a Colder World', pp. 44 and 45.

81 Keith Ovenden, 'Elworthy: Farming's Embattled Leader', *North & South*, July 1986, p. 23.

82 Vitalis, 'Trade, Innovation and Growth', p. 15.

83 Angus Gordon, *In the Shadow of the Cape: A History of the Gordon Family of Clifton*, Waipukurau, CHB Print, 2004, p. 173.

84 Vitalis, 'Trade, Innovation and Growth', p. 15.

85 Ibid.

86 Ibid., pp. 15–16.

87 Gow, 'Farmer Entrepreneurship in New Zealand', pp. 290 and 291.

88 Vitalis, 'Trade, Innovation and Growth', p. 18.

89 Ibid., p. 21. And see http://www.agritour. co.nz.

90 Gordon, *In the Shadow of the Cape*, p. 165.

91 James Russell, personal (email) communication with the author, 30 November 2012.

92 Cited in Russell, *Revolution*, p. 106.

93 Cited in Russell, ibid., p. 105.

94 Cited in Russell, ibid., p. 106.

95 Cited in Russell, ibid., p. 107.

96 Sinclair, 'Hard Times (1972–1990)', in Sinclair (ed.), *The Oxford Illustrated History of New Zealand*, 2nd edn, p. 364.

97 Olly Newland quoted in Russell, *Revolution*, p. 84.

98 Kelsey, *The New Zealand Experiment*, p. 89.

99 Ibid.

100 David Grant, *Bulls, Bears and Elephants: A History of the New Zealand Stock Exchange*, Wellington, Victoria University Press, 1997, p. 306.

101 Olly Newland, *Lost Property: The Crash of 1987 . . . and the Aftershock*, Auckland, HarperCollins, 1994, p. 47.

102 Grant, *Bulls, Bears and Elephants*, p. 284.

103 Ibid.

104 Quoted in Russell, *Revolution*, p. 150.

105 James, *New Territory*, p. 174.

106 Ibid.

107 Olly Newland, *Lost Property, The Crash of 1987 . . . and the Aftershock*, 20th anniversary edn, Auckland, Empower Leaders Publishing, p. 88.

108 Graeme Hunt, *Hustlers, Rogues & Bubble Boys: White-Collar Mischief in New Zealand*, Auckland, Reed, 2001, p. 89.

109 Grant, *Bulls, Bears and Elephants*, p. 345.

110 Russell, *Revolution*, p. 152.

111 Grant, *Bulls, Bears and Elephants*, p. 308.

112 Ibid., p. 285.

113 Ibid., p. 345.

114 Ibid., p. 356.

115 James, *New Territory*, p. 178.

116 Selwyn Parker, 'After the Crash: Who's Hurting?', *North & South*, July 1988, pp. 83–91.

117 Quoted in Russell, *Revolution*, p. 154.

118 Watson, 'No Jobs, No Hope', p. 23.

119 Parker, 'After the Crash', p. 89.

120 Michael Cullen, Opening remarks, in Clark (ed.), *For the Record*, p. 10.

121 James, *New Territory*, p. 179.

122 Ibid., p. 181.

123 See Hunt, *Hustlers, Rogues & Bubble Boys*, pp. 88–89.

124 Smith sold his former company, Auckland Coin and Bullion, to Goldcorp. See ibid.,

Hustlers, Rogues & Bubble Boys, p. 88.

125 Ibid., pp. 88–91.

126 Ibid., p. 83.

127 Denise McNab, 'Equiticorp — The Longest Goodbye', *New Zealand Herald*, 15 November 2010, http://www.nzherald.co.nz.

128 Hunt, *Hustlers, Rogues & Bubble Boys*, p. 83.

129 'NZ's most notorious white collar crime', copyright Fairfax NZ News, updated 29 October 2008, http://www.stuff.co.nz/business/695065/NZs-most-notorious-white-collar-crime.

130 Hunt, *Hustlers, Rogues & Bubble Boys*, p. 84.

131 Cited in Hunt, ibid.

132 Cited in Simon Louisson, '"The Hawk" Who Soared Then Fell from Grace', *New Zealand Herald*, 20 October 2007, http://www.nzherald.co.nz/news/print.cfm?objectid=10470980.

133 Hunt, *Hustlers, Rogues & Bubble Boys*, p. 84.

134 This phrase is TV critic Diana Wichtel describing the ethos behind the *Gloss* series, cited in Paul Stanley Ward, 22 September 2008, '*Gloss* — Episode One — A Perspective', http://www.nzonscreen.com/title/gloss---episode-one-1987/background.

135 Stanley Ward, ibid.

136 Ibid.

137 Professor Roger Openshaw, 'Examining Education Reform and Tomorrow's Schools', http://www.massey.ac.nz/massey/about-massey/news/article.cfm?mnarticle_uuid=B7017EC1-96BF-57FE-AA3F-1588D2C4F394.

138 Geoffrey W. Rice, 'A Revolution in Social Policy, 1981–1991', in Rice (ed.), *The Oxford History of New Zealand*, 2nd edn, p. 491.

139 David Lange, 'Tomorrow's Schools', August 1988, quoted in 'Tomorrow's Schools: Yesterday's Mistake?', A paper to the PPTA Annual Conference from the Executive, Wellington, 30 September–2 October 2008, http://www.parliament.nz/NR/rdonlyres/937BC6FE-EEBF-4369-8623-5C61FA85D4A6/166118/49SCES_EVI_00DBHOH_BILL9112_1_A30267_NewZealandPos.pdf.

140 See also Cathy Wylie, 'The Impact of Tomorrow's Schools in Primary Schools and Intermediates: 1991 Survey Report', Wellington, New Zealand Council for Educational Research, 1992, p. 143, http://www.nzcer.org.nz/system/files/271.pdf.

141 P. Burke, 'Membership, Motivation and Perceptions of Power', Paper presented to the New Zealand Association for Research in Education (NZARE) Conference, December 2000, Hamilton, quoted in Robyn Baker, 'Parental and Community Involvement in Schools: Opportunities and Challenges for School Change', 12 March 2002, http://www.nzcer.org.nz/research/publications/parental-and-community-involvement-schools-opportunities-and-challenges-school.

142 http://schools.reap.org.nz/tanui/Jubileepages/Tomorrows%20Schools.htm.

143 Robin Gauld, 'Health Policy and the Health System', in Raymond Miller (ed.), *New Zealand Government and Politics*, 4th edn, Melbourne, Oxford University Press, 2006, p. 618.

144 Rice, 'A Revolution in Social Policy, 1981–1991', in Rice (ed.), *The Oxford History of New Zealand*, 2nd edn, p. 489.

145 H. Clark, 'A New Relationship: Introducing the New Interface Between the Government and the Public Health Sector', Wellington, Department of Health, 1989, http://www.moh.govt.nz/notebook/nbbooks.nsf/0/1DF75C37B5FDC9AB-4C2565D700186C3F.

146 Robin Gauld, *Revolving Doors: New Zealand's Health Reforms*, Wellington, Institute of Policy Studies, Victoria University, 2001, p. 68.

147 Graham Bush, 'The Historic Reorganization of Local Government', in Holland and Boston (eds), *The Fourth Labour Government*, 2nd edn, p. 235.

148 Michael Bassett, *Working With David: Inside the Lange Cabinet*, Hodder Moa, Auckland, 2008, p. 491.

149 Bush, 'The Historic Reorganization of Local Government', in Holland and Boston (eds), *The Fourth Labour Government*, 2nd edn, p. 238.

150 Bassett, *Working With David*, p. 41.

151 McClure, *A Civilised Community*, p. 211.

152 Rice, 'A Revolution in Social Policy, 1981–1991', in Rice (ed.), *The Oxford History of New Zealand*, 2nd edn, p. 488.

153 James, *New Territory*, p. 75.

154 Rice, 'A Revolution in Social Policy, 1981–1991', in Rice (ed.), *The Oxford History of New Zealand*, 2nd edn, p. 488; Margaret McClure, 'A Badge of Poverty or

a Symbol of Citizenship? Needs, Rights and Social Security, 1935–2000', in Bronwyn Dalley and Margaret Tennant (eds), *Past Judgement: Social Policy in New Zealand History*, Dunedin, University of Otago Press, 2004, pp. 151–2.

155 David Lange, interview with Margaret McClure, 31 August 1995, in McClure, *A Civilised Community*, p. 226.

156 Royal Commission on Social Policy, *The April Report, Vol. 1, New Zealand Today*, Wellington, 1988, p. v, quoted in McClure, *A Civilised Community*, p. 226.

157 McClure, *A Civilised Community*, p. 227.

158 Quoted in Murray McLaughlin, 'Master Plan', *New Zealand Listener*, 19 December 1987, p. 22.

159 McClure, *A Civilised Community*, p. 228.

160 Bassett, *Working With David*, p. 243.

161 Russell, *Revolution*, p. 131

162 Lange, *My Life*, p. 261.

163 Russell, *Revolution*, p. 135.

164 Lange, *My Life*, p. 237.

165 Ibid., p. 244.

166 Ibid., p. 247.

167 Ibid., p. 243.

168 Bassett *Working With David*, pp. 297 and 286.

169 Lange, *My Life*, p. 352.

170 Russell, *Revolution*, p. 166.

171 Margaret Pope, *At the Turning Point: My Political Life with David Lange*, Auckland, AM Publishing, 2011, pp. 243–4.

172 Quoted in Bassett, *Working With David*, p. 458.

173 Michael Cullen's speech 'Reflecting on the Fourth Labour Government' was first delivered at the Stout Research Centre at Victoria University of Wellington and reproduced in the *New Zealand Herald* of 1 May 2004; see http://www.nzherald. co.nz/nz/news/article.cfm?c_id=1&objec- tid=3563691, p. 1.

174 The term 'New Zealand Experiment', used in the media and elsewhere to describe New Zealand's far-ranging and compre- hensive neo-liberal economic and social policy reforms, features in the title of Jane Kelsey's critical analysis of the reforms, *The New Zealand Experiment: A World Model for Structural Adjustment?*. The phrase 'the most ambitious and comprehensive structural reforms undertaken by any OECD country' is from a 1994 report on New Zealand by Moody's Investors Service, cited in Kelsey, *The New Zealand Experiment*, p. 7.

CHAPTER TEN 'Focused by Events': A Second Wave of Reform

1 Cited in Marcia Russell, *Revolution: New Zealand from Fortress to Free Market*, Auckland, Hodder Moa Beckett, 1996, p. 215.

2 Colin James, 'Rogernomics-plus with Ruth', in Colin James and Alan McRobie, *Turning Point: The 1993 Election and Beyond*, Wellington, Bridget Williams Books Limited, 1993, p. 32.

3 Ruth Richardson, 'The Fortunes and Fates of Reformers', in Margaret Clark (ed.), *The Bolger Years: 1990–1997*, Wellington, Dunmore Press, 2008, p. 142.

4 Quoted in Russell, *Revolution*, p. 215.

5 Richardson, 'The Fortunes and Fates of Reformers', in Clark (ed.), *The Bolger Years*, p. 145.

6 Howard Fancy and Graham Scott, 'The Treasury and the Government', in Clark (ed.), *The Bolger Years*, p. 63.

7 Ibid., pp. 62–64.

8 Quoted in Russell, *Revolution*, pp. 219–20.

9 Statement by the Prime Minister, the Hon. J. B. Bolger, in 'Economic and social initiative, December 1990: Statements to the House of Representatives/ J.B. Bolger, Ruth Richardson, W.F. Birch', Wellington, The Government, 1990, pp. 9–10.

10 Geoffrey Rice, 'A Revolution in Social Policy', in Geoffrey W. Rice (ed.), *The Oxford History of New Zealand*, 2nd edn, Auckland, Oxford University Press, 1992, p. 493.

11 Ruth Richardson, *Making a Difference*, Christchurch, Shoal Bay Press, 1995, p. 84.

12 Bolger, *Economic and social initiative*, p. 9.

13 Richardson, *Making a Difference*, pp. 64–65.

14 Mark Prebble, 'Critical New Elements in Government Thinking', in G. R. Hawke (ed.), *A Modest Safety Net? The Future of the Welfare State*, Wellington, Institute of Policy Studies, Victoria University, 1991, p. 4.

15 *Dominion*, 20 December 1990, p. 1.

16 Ibid., p. 8.

17 David McLoughlin, 'The Welfare Burden', *North & South*, June 1991, pp. 42–55.

18 *Dominion*, 21 December 1990.

19 Ibid., 24 December 1990.

20 Ibid., 22 February 1991.

21 Jenny Shipley with Simon Upton,

Lockwood Smith and John Luxton, 'Social Assistance: Welfare that Works: A Statement of Government Policy on Social Assistance', Wellington, Department of Social Welfare, 1991, p. 13.

22 Catherine Goodyear, director of the Anglican–Methodist Family Care Centre, Dunedin, quoted in Craig Howie and Claire Ramsay, *The Reforms, Riding the Rollercoaster: A Summary of New Zealand's Economic and Social Reforms, 1984–1998*, Dunedin, Otago Daily Times, 1998, p. 47.

23 *New Zealand Herald*, 3 August 1991, p. 1.

24 Ibid., p. 8.

25 George Drain, quoted in Joanna Wane, 'Greys Are Great', *New Zealand Listener*, 24 October 1992, pp. 21–22.

26 Margaret McClure, 'A Badge of Poverty or a Symbol of Citizenship? Needs, Rights and Social Security, 1935–2000', in Bronwyn Dalley and Margaret Tennant (eds), *Past Judgement: Social Policy in New Zealand History*, Dunedin, University of Otago Press, 2004, p. 153. The Alliance Party, formed in 1991, represented an alliance between the New Labour Party, the Democratic Party, Mana Motuhake and the Greens, an environmental party.

27 McClure, *A Civilised Community: A History of Social Security in New Zealand 1898–1998*, Auckland, Auckland University Press in association with the Historical Branch, Department of Internal Affairs, 1998, p. 254.

28 Jane Clifton, 'Oldies with "Battle Shields" Go Marching', *Dominion*, 4 March 1994, p. 2.

29 Omar Hamed, 'A Social Movement History of Public Opposition to New Zealand's Health Reforms, 1988–1999', draft PhD thesis, History, Auckland, University of Auckland, 2013, pp. 187–207.

30 See Statement by the Minister of Labour and State Services, Bill Birch, *Economic and social initiative*, pp. 37–45.

31 Brian Gaynor, 'A Belfast in New Zealand?', *New Zealand Outlook*, April 1987, p. 65.

32 Hon. W. F. Birch (Minister of Labour) moving to introduce the Employment Contracts Bill, *New Zealand Parliamentary Debates*, vol. 511, 19 December 1990, p. 478.

33 Jim Bolger, *A View from the Top: My Seven Years as Prime Minister*, Auckland, Viking, 1998, pp. 52–56.

34 Russell, *Revolution*, p. 221; See also, for example, Pat Walsh, 'The Employment Contracts Act', in Jonathan Boston and Paul Dalziel, *The Decent Society? Essays in Response to National's Economic and Social Policies*, Auckland, Oxford University Press, 1992, pp. 59–76.

35 See, for example, Alan Gibbs and Douglas Myers in Russell, *Revolution*, pp. 223–4.

36 Brian S Roper, *Prosperity for All? Economic, Social and Political Change in New Zealand since 1935*, Southbank, Victoria, Thomson Learning/Dunmore Press, 2005, p. 112.

37 *Otago Daily Times*, 8 April 1991.

38 Neil Lunt, Mike O'Brien and Robert Stephens, *New Zealand, New Welfare: New Developments in Welfare and Work*, Australia, Cengage Learning, 2008, p. 15.

39 'Report of the Labour Committee on the Inquiry into the Effects of the Employment Contracts Act 1991 on the New Zealand Labour Market', Second Session, 43rd Parliament, Mr Max Bradford, Chairman, *Appendices to the Journals of the House of Representatives*, vol. 24, 1991–1993, I-9D, item 2.1, 'Effect of the Act on Workplace Relations', p. 19.

40 Ibid., item 6, 'Effect of the Act on Productivity', p. 35.

41 Ibid., item 9, 'Effect of the Act on International Competitiveness', p. 38.

42 Ibid., item 3.4, 'Undue Influence/Freedom of Association', p. 26.

43 Ibid., item 4.2, 'Effect on Youth Workers', p. 30. The suggestion re youth rates legislation was implemented in 1994.

44 This organisation comprised about 50 chief executives of the larger business sector in New Zealand.

45 This publication is cited but not named in A. J. Geare, 'A Review of the New Zealand Employment Contracts Act 1991', Dunedin, Foundation for Industrial Relations Research and Education NZ, 1993, p. i.

46 Anne Knowles, Employers' Federation, interview of 17 August 1993, in Sarah Heal, 'The Struggle For and Against the Employment Contracts Act, 1987–1991', MA thesis, Political Studies, Dunedin, University of Otago, 1994, Appendix, p. 186.

47 Ibid.

48 Ashley Rush, interview of 19 August 1993, in Heal, ibid., Appendix, p. 165.

49 Steph Breen, interview of 17 August 1993, in Heal, ibid., Appendix, pp. 172 and 173.

50 Mark McLaughlan, 'What's so Awful about the Employment Contracts Act?', *North & South*, February 1996, p. 102.

51 Ibid., p. 99.

52 Kerr and Ryan both cited in McLaughlan, ibid., p. 102.

53 Cited in McLaughlan, ibid., p. 104.

54 Cited in McLaughlan, ibid., p. 105.

55 Ibid., p. 106.

56 Andrew Morrison, 'The Employment Contracts Act and its Economic Impact', Parliamentary Library Background Paper No. 16, November 1996, Executive Summary, p. 4.

57 Ibid., Conclusion, p. 14.

58 Ibid., pp. 9 and 14.

59 See Alan Gibbs cited in Chapter 20, 'Mother's Medicine', Russell (ed.), *Revolution*, p. 223.

60 Myers in Russell, *Revolution*, pp. 223–4.

61 Douglas in Russell, ibid., p. 222.

62 This quote is from a letter Conway wrote in response to the McLaughlan article in *North & South*. It was published, along with two other lengthy letters opposed to the ECA and its impacts, in the 'Write of Reply' column of that magazine, March 1996, p. 28.

63 Robin Gauld, 'Health Policy and the Health System', in Raymond Miller (ed.), *New Zealand Government and Politics*, 4th edn, Melbourne, Oxford University Press, 2006, p. 618.

64 Ibid.

65 Shipley et al., *Welfare that Works*, p. 60.

66 See Hamed, 'A Social Movement History of Public Opposition to New Zealand's Health Reforms, 1888–1988', for a full discussion of the public criticism and outrage at the introduction of hospital charges, pp. 16–47.

67 Communist Party of New Zealand, 'Fight Until We've Won', *Worker's Voice*, 25 February 1992, p. 17, quoted in Hamed, 'A Social Movement History of Public Opposition to New Zealand's Health Reforms', p. 35.

68 Hamed, 'A Social Movement History of Public Opposition to New Zealand's Health Reforms', p. 46.

69 *Dominion*, 18 February 1991.

70 Naomi Gilling and Tamara Pitelen, 'Thousands rally against health cuts', *Press*, 26 October 1993, p. 1.

71 NZPA, '3000 Join Protest Against Health Cuts', *Dominion*, 12 December 1994, p. 9.

72 'Far North Protest Pays Off', *New Zealand Herald*, 24 March 1995. See Hamed, 'A Social Movement History of Public Opposition to New Zealand's Health Reforms', pp. 47–84.

73 Noel O'Hare, 'Fighting for their Health: Small-town Hospital Services are Back Under the Knife', *New Zealand Listener*, 19 July 1994, pp. 18–24.

74 O'Hare, 'Fighting for their Health', p. 21.

75 H. R. McGuigan, 'The Big Chop', letter in *North & South*, October 1994, p. 37.

76 See, for example, Rachel Eyre and Robin Gauld, 'Community participation in a rural community health trust: the case of Lawrence, New Zealand', *Health Promotion International*, vol. 18, no. 3, September 2003, pp. 189–97, http://www.ncbi.nlm.nih.gov/pubmed/12920139.

77 Robin Gauld, 'Health Policy and the Ever-Changing Health Care System', in Raymond Miller (ed.), *New Zealand Government and Politics*, 3rd edn, Melbourne, Oxford University Press, 2003, p. 442.

78 Joanna Manning, 'Report Summary: The Cartwright Report's Findings and Recommendations', in Joanna Manning (ed.), *The Cartwright Papers: Essays on the Cervical Cancer Inquiry 1987–88*, Wellington, Bridget Williams Books, 2009, pp. 27–44, nn. 53 and 54.

79 Ibid., pp. 36–39.

80 Ibid., p. 42.

81 http://www.justice.govt.nz/publications/global-publications/d/directory-of-official-information-archive/directory-of-official-information-december-2009/alphabetical-list-of-entries-1/h/health-and-disability-commissioner.

82 Joanna Manning and Ron Paterson, 'New Zealand's Code of Patients' Rights', in Manning (ed.), *The Cartwright Papers*, p. 176.

83 Sandra Coney (ed.), *Unfinished Business: What Happened to the Cartwright Report?*, Auckland, Women's Health Action, 1993, p. 48.

84 Richard Shaw and Chris Eichbaum, *Public Policy in New Zealand: Institutions, Processes and Outcomes*, 2nd edn, Auckland, Pearson Education, 2008, p. 248.

85 Howie and Ramsay, *Riding the Rollercoaster*, p. 44.

86 McClure, *A Civilised Community*, p. 242.

87 Charles Waldegrave, Robert Stephens and Peter King, New Zealand Poverty Measurement Project, 'Assessing the Progress on Poverty Reduction', *Social Policy Journal of New Zealand*, issue 20, June 2003, p. 199, http://www.msd.govt.nz/

about-msd-and-our-work/publications-resources/journals-and-magazines/social-policy-journal/spj20/assessing-the-progress-on-poverty-reduction-20-pages197-222.html.

88 Kate McPherson, 'Food Insecurity and the Food Bank Industry: Political, Individual and Environmental Factors Contributing to Food Bank Use in Christchurch', MA thesis, Geography, Christchurch, University of Canterbury, 2006, p. 12.

89 Labour Market Statistics, Wellington, Department of Statistics, 1996, p. 67.

90 McPherson, 'Food Insecurity and the Food Bank Industry', p. 13.

91 McClure, *A Civilised Community*, p. 244.

92 Bob Stephens, 'Budgeting with the Benefit Cuts', in Jonathan Boston and Paul Dalziel, *The Decent Society: Essays in Response to National's Economic and Social Policies*, Auckland, Oxford University Press, 1992, p. 111.

93 McClure, *A Civilised Community*, p. 246.

94 McPherson, 'Food Insecurity and the Food Bank Industry', p. 36.

95 Ibid., p. 35.

96 Howie and Ramsay, *Riding the Rollercoaster*, p. 46.

97 Laurence Murphy, 'Housing Policy', in Jonathan Boston, Paul Dalziel and Susan St John, *Redesigning the Welfare State in New Zealand: Problems, Policies, Prospects*, Auckland, Oxford University Press, 1999, p. 227.

98 Waldegrave et al., 'Assessing the Progress on Poverty Reduction', p. 209.

99 M. Mowbray, *Distributions and Disparity: New Zealand Household Incomes*, Wellington, Ministry of Social Policy, 2001, p. 54.

100 Laurence Murphy, 'Housing Policy', in Boston et al., *Redesigning the Welfare State in New Zealand*, p. 227.

101 Quoted in Ben Schrader, *We Call It Home: A History of State Housing in New Zealand*, Auckland, Reed, 2005, p. 72.

102 Ibid., p. 70.

103 Ibid.

104 Charles Waldegrave, 'Assessing the Social Impacts of the New Zealand Housing Reforms during the 1990s', The Family Centre Social Policy Research Unit, A paper for the Ministry of Social Policy Seminar Series, 25 October 2000, p. 15.

105 Housing New Zealand Annual Report, 1996/97, p. 5. For the origins of New Zealand First, see page 336, this chapter.

106 'The Royal Commission — The Road to MMP', http://www.nzhistory.net.nz/politics/fpp-to-mmp/royal-commission, (Ministry for Culture and Heritage), updated 2 November 2011.

107 Jack Vowles et al., *Proportional Representation on Trial: The 1999 New Zealand General Election and the Fate of MMP*, Auckland, Auckland University Press, 2002, p. 2.

108 Bronwyn Dalley and Gavin McLean (eds), *Frontier of Dreams: The Story of New Zealand*, Auckland, Hodder Moa, 2005, p. 379.

109 Jack Vowles et al, *Towards Consensus? The 1993 General Election and Referendum in New Zealand and the Transition to Proportional Representation*, Auckland, Auckland University Press, 1995, p. 8.

110 Bolger, *A View from the Top*, p. 194.

111 Quoted in Russell, *Revolution*, pp. 242–3.

112 Richardson, *Making a Difference*, p. 181.

113 Ibid., pp. 188–91 Aghast at the lack of fiscal transparency which had allowed the Labour government to hide the true state of the economy in 1990, the National government developed the Fiscal Responsibility Act which required all governments to be honest and transparent with the accounts and to give public updates of the state of the economy every few months.

114 David McLoughlin, 'What Have We Got to Lose?', *North & South*, October 1996, pp. 69–83.

115 Labour Market Statistics, Wellington, Statistics New Zealand, 2006, p. 129.

116 OECD, *Employment Outlook 2005: How Does France Compare?*, http://www.oecd.org/els/employmentpoliciesand-data/35050668.pdf.

117 Bruce Jesson, 'Now is the Time to Organise an Opposition', *The Republican*, no. 63, January 1988, in *To Build a Nation: Collected Writings 1975–1999*, ed. Andrew Sharp, Auckland, Penguin, 2005, p. 201.

118 Peter Aimer and Raymond Miller, 'New Zealand Politics in the 1990s', in Vowles et al., *Proportional Representation on Trial*, p. 2.

119 James Belich, *Paradise Reforged: A History of the New Zealanders from the 1880s to the Year 2000*, Auckland, Allen Lane/The Penguin Press, 2001, p. 408.

120 Raymond Miller, 'Preparing for MMP: 1993–1996', in Raymond Miller (ed.), *New*

Zealand Politics in Transition, Auckland, Oxford University Press, 1997, p. 37.

121 Aimer and Miller, 'New Zealand Politics in the 1990s', in Vowles et al., *Proportional Representation on Trial*, p. 7.

122 Ian Grant, *Public Lives: New Zealand's Premiers and Prime Ministers, 1856–2003*, Wellington, New Zealand Cartoon Archive, 2003, p. 185.

123 Colin James, 'Politician of the Year', *New Zealand Herald*, 22 December 1999, http://www.colinjames.co.nz/herald/Herald_1999/Herald_column_Dec_22_99.htm.

124 Grant, *Public Lives*, p. 189.

125 Roper, *Prosperity for All?*, p. 220.

126 Waldegrave et al., 'Assessing the Progress on Poverty Reduction', p. 209.

127 Gauld, 'Health Policy and the Ever-Changing Health Care System', in Miller (ed.), *New Zealand Government and Politics*, 3rd edn, p. 444.

128 Michael O'Brien, *Poverty, Policy and the State: Social Security Reform in New Zealand*, Bristol, The Policy Press, 2008, p. 199.

129 Helen Clark, September 2001, quoted in David Choat, 'Was Helen Clark a "third way" Prime Minister?', http://www.policyprogress.org.nz/2010/11/was-helen-clark-a-third-way-prime-minister/.

130 See Ministry of Social Development website for the history of the changes in the various social departments, http://www.msd.govt.nz/about-msd-and-our-work/about-msd/history/index.html.

131 New Zealand Government, 2006, quoted in Louise Humpage, 'Working for New Zealand: A Background Paper on Recent and Proposed Welfare Reforms in New Zealand', Auckland, Public Policy Group, University of Auckland, March 2007, p. 1, http://www.artsfaculty.auckland.ac.nz/images/cms/files/LHumpage/Humpage%20Welfare%20forum%20background%20paper%20Mar%2007.pdf.

132 O'Brien, *Poverty, Policy and the State*, p. 212.

133 Steve Maharey, 'Benefits and Super Rise, Work-for-the-dole Abolished', 1 April 2001, http://www.beehive.govt.nz/node/10143.

134 O'Brien, *Poverty, Policy and the State*, pp. 215–18.

135 Shaw and Eichbaum, *Public Policy in New Zealand*, 2nd edn, p. 272.

136 Susan St John and Keith Rankin, 'Escaping the Welfare Mess?', Auckland, Department of Economics, Auckland Business School, Working Paper No. 267, revised December 2009, p. 9, http://pol-econ.com/EWM/EscapingWelfareMessWP267.pdf.

137 Ibid., p. 11.

138 'Working for Families: A Benefit Cut', Wellington, Wellington People's Centre, March 2006, http://www.cpag.org.nz/assets/Wgtn%20People%27s%20Centre.pdf.

139 Simon Collins, 'Stings in the Tail of Beneficiaries Bill', *New Zealand Herald*, 1 March 2007.

140 Louise Humpage and Susan St John, 'A Bill the Poor Will Pay for', *New Zealand Herald*, 11 June 2007.

141 Quoted in Collins, 'Stings in the Tail of Beneficiaries Bill'.

142 Charles Waldegrave and Bob Stephens, 'Counting the True Costs of Poverty Trap', *New Zealand Herald*, 29 November 2012, p. A38.

143 Ibid.

144 Michael Cullen, 'Reflecting on the Fourth Labour Government', *New Zealand Herald*, 1 May 2004, http://www.nzherald.co.nz/nz/news/article.cfm?c_id=1&objectid=3563691.

145 Paul Dalziel, 'New Zealand's Economic Reforms: An Assessment', *Review of Political Economy*, vol. 14, no. 1, 2002, pp. 44–45.

146 Lewis Evans, Arthur Grimes, Bryce Wilkinson and David Teece, 'Economic Reform in New Zealand 1984–95: The Pursuit of Efficiency', *Journal of Economic Literature*, vol. 34, December 1996; quotes from pp. 1893, 1856 and 1895.

147 Roderick Deane, email sent to authors, December 2012.

148 Paul Perry and Alan Webster, *New Zealand Politics at the Turn of the Millennium: Attitudes and Values about Politics and Government, The Political Report of the Third New Zealand Study of Values*, Auckland, Alpha Publications, 1999, p. 1.

149 See Richard Le Heron, 'Manufacturing, Services and Tourism', in Steve Britton, Richard Le Heron and Eric Pawson (eds), *Changing Places in New Zealand: A Geography of Restructuring*, Christchurch, New Zealand Geographical Society, 1993, p. 127.

150 *New Zealand Official Yearbook*, 2010, p. 272.

151 See Raewyn Dalziel, 'A Modern Revolution', in Keith Sinclair, *A History of New Zealand*, revised edn, Auckland, Penguin, 2000, p. 345.

152 Perry and Webster, *New Zealand Politics at the Turn of the Millennium*, Section 2B, p. 71.

CHAPTER ELEVEN Shifting Tides: Maori, Pakeha and the Treaty after 1984

1 Chief Justice Sir James Prendergast famously referred to the Treaty of Waitangi as a 'simple nullity' in the case of *Wi Parata v Bishop of Wellington* (1877) 3 NZ Jur. (NS) (Supreme Court) 72.

2 This complex, much-debated term can be defined as self-determination, or chieftainship; for some Maori, it implies absolute sovereignty.

3 See Richard S. Hill, *Maori and the State: Crown–Maori Relations in New Zealand/Aotearoa, 1950–2000*, Wellington, Victoria University Press, 2009, p. 200.

4 Cited in Nick Ventnor, 'A Maori Agenda', *Dominion Post*, 26 February 2005, in Hill, ibid., p. 203.

5 Mason Durie, *Te Mana, Te Kāwanatanga: The Politics of Māori Self-Determination*, Auckland, Oxford University Press, 1998, p. 6.

6 Submission no. 30, 'Tribal Development', presented by Dan Te Kanawa of Ngati Maniapoto, *Maori Economic Development Summit Conference: Conference Proceedings*, Wellington, Ministry of Maori Affairs, 1984, p. 2.

7 Andrew Sharp, *Justice and the Māori: The Philosophy and Practice of Māori Claims in New Zealand since the 1970s*, 2nd edn, Auckland, Oxford University Press, 1997, p. 191.

8 Hill, *Maori and the State*, p. 205.

9 G. V. Butterworth and H. R. Young, *Maori Affairs: A Department and the People Who Made It*, Wellington, Iwi Transition Agency/GP Books, 1990, p. 119.

10 *New Zealand Official Yearbook*, 2000, p. 140.

11 Michael King, *Being Pakeha: An Encounter with New Zealand and the Maori Renaissance*, Auckland, Hodder & Stoughton, 1985, pp. 173 and 175.

12 James Belich, *The New Zealand Wars and the Victorian Interpretation of Racial Conflict*, Auckland, Auckland University Press, 1986, and Claudia Orange, *The Treaty of Waitangi*, Wellington, Allen & Unwin, with assistance from the Historical Branch, Department of Internal Affairs, 1987.

13 Cited in Nicola Legat, 'Taha Maori — Why All the Fuss?', *Metro*, September 1986, p. 85.

14 Durie, *Te Mana, Te Kāwanatanga*, p. 62.

15 Jane Kelsey, *A Question of Honour? Labour and the Treaty 1984–1989*, Wellington, Allen & Unwin, 1990, p. 72.

16 Ranginui Walker, 'The Maori People since 1950', in Geoffrey W. Rice (ed.), *The Oxford History of New Zealand*, 2nd edn, Auckland, Oxford University Press, 1992, p. 516. The official title of the case was *New Zealand Maori Council v Attorney General* [1987] 1 NZLR 641 (Court of Appeal).

17 The Court also ruled that the Treaty of Waitangi (State Enterprises Act) 1988 applied to interests in land represented by coal-mining leases in the Crown's agreement with Coalcorp issued March 1988; see Walker in Rice (ed.), ibid., p. 517.

18 Ibid.

19 Durie, *Te Mana, Te Kāwanatanga* , p. 155.

20 The reference to the 'juggernaut' of Rogernomics is from Kelsey, *A Question of Honour?*, p. 77. David Lange also used this expression when describing his split with Roger Douglas.

21 See Hill, *Maori and the State*, pp. 224–5. Sir Robin Cooke, president of the Court of Appeal, used the expression '. . . with the utmost good faith' in his judgment on the Lands case. On a more practical level, the new Treaty partnership found expression in the creation of the Crown Forestry Rental Trust in 1989. See Alan Ward, *An Unsettled History: Treaty Claims in New Zealand Today*, Wellington, Bridget Williams Books, 1999, pp. 38–40.

22 Ranginui Walker, *Ka Whawhai Tonu Matou: Struggle Without End*, Auckland, Penguin Books, 1990, p. 279.

23 'Puao-Te Ata-Tu (Day Break): The Report of the Ministerial Advisory Committee on a Maori Perspective for the Department of Social Welfare', Wellington, The Committee, 1 July 1986, Appendix, p. 26.

24 Ibid.

25 Walker, *Ka Whawhai Tonu Matou*, p. 281.

26 Hill, *Maori and the State*, p. 237.

27 Walker, *Ka Whawhai Tonu Matou*, p. 281.

28 Walker, ibid., p. 272.

29 'The Curriculum Review: The Report of the Committee to Review the Curriculum for Schools', Wellington, Department of Education, 1987, excerpt reproduced in Project Waitangi, 'School Charters and the Treaty: A Guide for Trustees from a Pakeha Perspective', Auckland, Race Relations Office, 1988, p. 10.

30 Project Waitangi, ibid., p. 6.

31 Ibid., p. 7.

32 In 1999, the Education (Te Aho Matua) Act made it a requirement that kura kaupapa adhere to the principles of Te Aho Matua — the principles, beliefs, values and customs that essentially define the schools.

33 Walker, 'The Maori People since 1950', in Rice (ed.), *The Oxford History of New Zealand*, 2nd edn, p. 515.

34 Mason Durie, *Ngā Tai Matatū: Tides of Māori Endurance*, Auckland, Oxford University Press, 2005, p. 50. Two other wananga have subsequently been established: Te Wananga o Aotearoa (1983) and Te Whare Wananga o Awanuiarangi (1990).

35 Mason Durie, *Mauri Ora: The Dynamics of Māori Health*, Auckland, Oxford University Press, 2001, p. 53.

36 Durie, *Ngā Tai Matatū*, p. 51.

37 See Edgar Rout cited in 'Report of the Committee of Inquiry into Procedures Used in Certain Psychiatric Hospitals in Relation to Admission, Discharge or Release on Leave of Certain Classes of Patients', Wellington, The Committee, August 1988, p. 171.

38 In 1988, when Harawira and four of her staff were charged with intent to injure and eventually convicted, she was also found guilty on a separate charge of threatening to kill, and ended up serving nine months; See *Report of the Committee of Inquiry into Procedures Used in Certain Psychiatric Hospitals*, pp. 175-6.

39 'Harawira Attack Vicious, Violent', *New Zealand Herald*, 26 April 1989, p. A3.

40 Hill, *Maori and the State*, p. 212.

41 Graham Bush, 'The Historic Reorganisation of Local Government', in M. Holland and J. Boston (eds), *The Fourth Labour Government: Politics and Policy in New Zealand*, 2nd edn, Auckland, Oxford University Press, 1990, p. 238.

42 Janine Hayward, 'Is Local Government a Treaty Partner?', in Janine Hayward (ed.), *Local Government and the Treaty of Waitangi*, Melbourne/Auckland, Oxford University Press, 2003, p. 8.

43 Ibid., pp. 7-8.

44 Cited in Sharp, *Justice and the Māori*, p. 234.

45 Hayward, 'Is Local Government a Treaty Partner?', in Hayward (ed.), *Local Government*, p. 8.

46 Ibid., p. 10.

47 Ibid., pp. 3-7.

48 Ibid., p. 10.

49 Speech at Waitangi, 6 February 1989, cited in Vincent O'Malley, Bruce Stirling, and Wally Penetito (eds), *The Treaty of Waitangi Companion*, Auckland, Auckland University Press, 2010, p. 361. The epigraph on page 344 is also from this speech.

50 *New Zealand Herald*, 27 November 1987, cited in Walker, *Ka Whawhai Tonu Matou*, p. 283.

51 *New Zealand Herald*, 4 December 1987, cited in Walker, ibid.

52 Martin Hames, *Winston First: The Unauthorised Account of Winston Peters' Career*, Auckland, Random House, 1995, p. 65 gives Peters the credit for coining the phrase 'sickly white liberal'.

53 Ibid., p. 81.

54 Ward, *An Unsettled History*, p. 35.

55 *New Zealand Herald*, 25 January 1988, p. 8 and 27 January 1988, p. 3.

56 *New Zealand Herald*, 1 July 1988, cited in Sharp, *Justice and the Māori*, p. 119.

57 *Sunday Star*, 13 November 1988, cited in Sharp, ibid., p. 119.

58 Pat Booth, 'Learning to Live with the Waitangi Tribunal: The Facts without Fear', *North & South*, June 1988, p. 78.

59 Angus Gillies, *Ngati Dread: Footsteps of Fire*, vol. 1, Auckland, Rogue Monster Books, 2008, p. 6. Gillies published two further books about the Ruatoria troubles: *No Dreadlocks No Cry* (2009) and *Revelations* (2011).

60 Jarrod Gilbert, *Patched: The History of Gangs in New Zealand*, Auckland, Auckland University Press, 2013, p. 184. The 10 per cent unemployment rate in the Gisborne and Bay of Plenty regions reflected national trends.

61 Liz Janis and Louise Wright, 'Kill a White', *Sunday Star*, 20 March 1988, cited in O'Malley et al. (eds), *The Treaty of Waitangi Companion*, p. 370.

62 Sonya Haggie, 'I Just Want to Clear My Name', *New Zealand Woman's Weekly*,

18 July 1988, p. 11, cited in O'Malley et al. (eds), ibid. And see Chris Daniels, 'Maoridom Mourns Top Activist', *New Zealand Herald*, 12 October 1999, www.nzherald.co.nz/nz/news/article.cfm?c_id=1&objectid=15781.

63 Carroll Wall, 'Te Pakeha: The Search for White Identity', *Metro*, November 1986, pp. 36 and 44.

64 Rosemary McLeod, 'Bleeding White, Middle Class and Carrying the Can', *North & South*, November 1988, p. 49.

65 C. K. Stead, 'The New Victorians', *Metro*, February 1989, p. 124.

66 Ibid., p. 123.

67 Ibid.

68 Hyam Gold and Alan Webster, *New Zealand Values Today: The Popular Report of the November 1989 New Zealand Study of Values*, Palmerston North, Alpha Publications, 1989, pp. 30–31.

69 Ibid., p. 34. A *Metro* readers' poll, conducted in the same year, showed 76% believed there should be less emphasis on things Maori in national life; 65% wanted the Maori seats, the Maori football team and the Maori Education Foundation abolished. See 'At the End of the Eighties: Your Mood', *Metro*, October 1989, pp. 71–72.

70 Sharp, *Justice and the Māori*, p. 198. Issues surrounding Maori fishing rights were in fact then still in the process of being determined.

71 Ibid., p. 199. This attitude was not unique to New Zealand. In 1996, Australian Liberal Pauline Hanson won what was assumed to be a safe Labor seat by making remarks about Aboriginal people being 'looked after too much by government bureaucrats'; cited in Ken Gelder and Jane Jacobs, *Uncanny Australia: Sacredness and Identity in a Postcolonial Nation*, Carlton South, Victoria, Melbourne University Press, 1998, p. 14.

72 Cited in Hiwi Tauroa, *Healing the Breach: One Maori's Perspective on the Treaty of Waitangi*, Auckland, Collins, 1989, p. 122.

73 Durie, *Te Mana, Te Kāwanatanga*, p. 188.

74 See Kelsey, *A Question of Honour?*, pp. 51–56.

75 Hill, *Maori and the State*, p. 239.

76 *The Treaty of Waitangi, The Symbol of Our Life Together as a Nation*, Wellington, New Zealand 1990 Commission, 1989, cited in Hill, ibid., p. 240.

77 Sue Abel, *Shaping the News: Waitangi Day on Television*, Auckland, Auckland University Press, 1997, p. 30. One notable feature about the 1990 commemorative events was the coming together, several days before Waitangi Day, of various tribal groups supporting their respective waka.

78 Andrew Mason, editorial of 5 February 1990, *New Zealand Listener*, cited in Abel, ibid., p. 31.

79 Abel, ibid., p. 30.

80 Cited in Abel, ibid., p. 56.

81 Bishop Vercoe's speech on Waitangi Day 1990, *New Zealand Herald*, 7 February 1990, in O'Malley et al. (eds), *The Treaty of Waitangi Companion*, p. 383.

82 See Abel, *Shaping the News*, pp. 109–18. The *Holmes* show edited Vercoe's speech to accord with a celebratory note; see p. 111.

83 Richard Long reporting from Waitangi for TV ONE, cited in Abel, ibid., p. 100.

84 Butterworth and Young, *Maori Affairs*, p. 121.

85 Alex Frame, 'Te Heu Heu Tukino VII, Hepi Hoani (1919–1997)', *Dictionary of New Zealand Biography*, Te Ara — *The Encyclopedia of New Zealand*, updated 30 October 2012, www.teara.govt.nz/en/biographies/5t8/te-heuheu-tukino-vii-hepi-hoani.

86 Hill, *Maori and the State*, p. 242.

87 Ibid.

88 Ibid., p. 248.

89 Pat Booth, 'Winston Peters: The Man YOU Want as Prime Minister', *North & South*, July 1990, p. 41.

90 Hames, *Winston First*, p. 117.

91 See Hill, *Maori and the State*, p. 250.

92 Douglas Graham, *Trick or Treaty?*, Wellington, Institute of Policy Studies, Victoria University, 1997, p. 50.

93 Ann Sullivan, 'Maori Politics and Government Policies', in Raymond Miller (ed.), *New Zealand Politics in Transition*, 3rd edn, Auckland, Oxford University Press, 2003, p. 364.

94 David McLoughlin, 'The Maori Burden', *North & South*, November 1993, p. 61.

95 Sullivan, 'Maori Politics and Government Policies', in Miller (ed.), *New Zealand Politics in Transition*, 3rd edn, p. 364.

96 Robin Mitchell, *The Treaty & the Act: The Treaty of Waitangi (1840) and the Treaty of Waitangi Act (1975)*, Christchurch, Cadsonbury Publications, 1990, p. 100.

97 Stuart C. Scott, *Travesty after Travesty*, Christchurch, Certes Press, 1996, p. 7. Scott,

a successful businessman and one-time president of the New Zealand Chamber of Commerce (1968–69), served as Honorary Danish Vice-Consul then Honorary Consul in Dunedin for more than 30 years.

98 Ibid., p. 8; quote re 'advances of Maori influence' features in the Preface.

99 Irihapeti Ramsden and Paul Spoonley, 'The Cultural Safety Debate in Nursing Education in Aotearoa', *New Zealand Annual Review of Education/Te Arotake a Tau o Te Ao o te Mataurangi i Aotearoa*, vol. 3, 1993, p. 163.

100 Carroll du Chateau, 'Culture Shock', *Metro*, June 1992, p. 96.

101 Ibid., pp. 97 and 102.

102 Elaine Papps and Irihapeti Ramsden, 'Cultural Safety in Nursing: The New Zealand Experience', *International Journal for Quality in Health Care*, vol. 8, no. 5, 1996, p. 492.

103 *Dominion* editorials of 27 July and 6 August, cited in Ramsden and Spoonley, 'The Cultural Safety Debate', p. 167.

104 Bruce Ansley, 'Anna and the Rednecks', *New Zealand Listener*, 14 August 1993, pp. 22–23.

105 Cate Brett, 'Putting Penn to Paper: The Whole Story about Christchurch Polytechnic and Cultural Safety', *North & South*, October 1993, p. 68.

106 Ibid., p. 77.

107 See Brian Stabb, 'How I Became Culturally Unsafe', *Evening Post*, 29 May 1995, pp. 4–5.

108 The report included eight recommendations made by a Nursing Council Review Committee charged with investigating the teaching of cultural safety. The Nursing Council's *New Zealand Draft Guidelines for the Cultural Safety Component in Nursing and Midwifery* was produced in March 1996.

109 Walter Christie cited in Richard Hill, *Anti-Treatyism and Anti-Scholarship*, TOWRU Occasional Papers No. 8, 2002, p. 5. Yet some anti-Treaty writers were teachers themselves; see David Round, *Truth or Treaty? Commonsense Questions about the Treaty of Waitangi*, Christchurch, Canterbury University Press, 1998.

110 Alan Duff, *Once Were Warriors*, Auckland, Tandem Press, 1990.

111 Emiel Martens, *Once Were Warriors, The Aftermath: The Controversy of OWW in Aotearoa New Zealand*, Amsterdam, Aksant, 2007, p. 26.

112 Cited in Martens, ibid., p. 136.

113 See, for example, Ranginui Walker's critique of Duff's biological determinism, in 'Te Karenga: Getting Real', *Metro*, August, 1995, p. 134, cited in Christina Stachurski, *Reading Pakeha? Fiction and Identity in Aotearoa New Zealand*, New York, Rodopi, 2009, p. 137.

114 See Stachurski, ibid., pp. 138–45 for a discussion of Duff and libertarianism.

115 Alan Duff, *Maori: The Crisis and the Challenge*, Auckland, HarperCollins, 1993, p. 112.

116 See Martens, *Once Were Warriors, The Aftermath*, p. 99.

117 Two prominent Maori critics of the film, Sue Sarich and academic and film-maker Leonie Pihama, were concerned about its lack of historical context and perpetuation of negative stereotypes. Although Duff's ideas about a 'warrior' gene reached a wider audience through the film, his prescriptions were altered. In contrast to the book, the movie ends with Beth moving to the country and reconnecting with a traditional marae. For Duff, however: 'Tribalism kills every nation which practises it as Maori do'; Duff, *Maori: The Crisis and the Challenge*, p. 116.

118 In 2006, for example, Prime Minister Helen Clark referred to the family of two murdered Maori babies Chris and Cru Kahui as a '*Once Were Warriors*-type family' in a television programme; Clark cited in Martens, *Once Were Warriors, The Aftermath*, p. 146.

119 In 1995, with Christine Fernyhough, he founded the Alan Duff Charitable Association, better known as the Duffy Books in Home scheme, to provide low-cost books to underprivileged children and encourage them to read.

120 Hill, *Maori and the State*, p. 253. A separate Treaty Negotiations portfolio was added to Graham's ministerial positions in 1993.

121 Graham, *Trick or Treaty?*, p. 43.

122 Ibid., pp. 43–44.

123 The Sealords deal was unique because most settlements involved a tribe or tribal confederation and land. In 1991, following the Waitangi Tribunal's Ngai Tahu Report, the Crown commenced some preliminary direct negotiations with that tribe, the first step on a long and often arduous path. A 'landbank' to hold surplus Crown land that might be used in future reparations

proved a positive innovation, used successfully in other negotiations.

124 Hill, *Maori and the State*, pp. 254–5.

125 See Durie, *Te Mana, Te Kāwanatanga*, pp. 157–61 for an extensive examination of the Maori dissent over the Sealords deal, and the various court cases and appeals that followed in its wake.

126 For the particulars of this complex case and decision see Durie, ibid., p. 96.

127 Hill, *Maori and the State*, p. 255.

128 Durie, *Te Mana, Te Kāwanatanga*, p. 169.

129 Hill, *Maori and the State*, p. 259.

130 Waikato Raupatu Claims Settlement Act 1995, section 6, cited in Sharp, *Justice and the Māori*, p. 300.

131 Durie, *Mauri Ora*, p. 52.

132 Te Ture Whenua Maori Act 1993, section 2(2), cited in Hill, *Maori and the State*, p. 258.

133 Durie, *Mauri Ora*, p. 52.

134 Christine Cheyne, Mike O'Brien and Michael Belgrave (eds), *Social Policy in Aotearoa New Zealand: A Critical Introduction*, 3rd edn, Auckland, Oxford University Press, 2005, p. 157.

135 Hill, *Maori and the State*, p. 263.

136 Abel, *Shaping the News*, p. 153.

137 Russell Brown, 'The confused New Zealander's guide to Moutoa', *New Zealand Listener*, 22 April, 1995, p. 20.

138 Durie, *Te Mana, Te Kāwanatanga*, p. 128. Te Ahi Ka, a group of radical activists, took responsibility for Ballance's decapitation. A pumpkin was then placed on his shoulders.

139 Ibid.

140 Ibid.

141 Tom Scott, 'Corridors of Power', *New Zealand Listener*, 22 April 1995, p. 19.

142 Ibid., p. 18.

143 Contents pages of Hineani Melbourne (ed.), *Maori Sovereignty: The Maori Perspective*, Hodder Moa Beckett, Auckland, 1995.

144 Contents pages of Carol Archie (ed.), *Maori Sovereignty: The Pakeha Perspective*, Hodder Moa Beckett, Auckland, 1995.

145 Cited in Durie, *Te Mana, Te Kāwanatanga*, p. 235.

146 Sullivan, 'Maori Politics and Government Policies', in Miller (ed.), *New Zealand Politics in Transition*, 3rd edn, pp. 366–7. In the course of 1995, representatives of the Nga Iwi Katoa Trust who occupied the former Tamaki Girls' College were

eventually served trespass notices. In Rotorua, the Whakarewarewa Maori Arts and Crafts Institute was occupied by Te Roopu a Te Pohuta; student protesters organised an occupation at the University of Waikato; and the old Patea Courthouse was taken possession of by Taranaki Maori.

147 Sharp, *Justice and the Māori*, pp. 309 and 311.

148 Hill, *Maori and the State*, p. 257. A 'partnership experiment' between the Crown and the National Maori Congress in the early 1990s had resulted in a Crown–Congress Joint Working Party to examine the issue of surplus railway lands, but this, according to Hill, 'produced few tangible results'.

149 See Richard T. Price, 'The Politics of Modern History-making: The 1990s Negotiations of the Ngai Tahu Tribe with the Crown to Achieve a Treaty of Waitangi Claims Settlement', Christchurch, Macmillan Brown Centre for Pacific Studies, University of Canterbury, Macmillan Brown Working Paper Series No. 7, 2001, p. 30.

150 Cate Brett, 'Who Are the Ngai Tahu and What Do They Really Want?', *North & South*, November 1992, p. 58.

151 As Charles Croft (Kaiwhakahaere of Te Runanga o Ngai Tahu) noted in the tribe's 1996 Annual Report: 'A major component of the decision of negotiators to close a Heads of Agreement with the Crown prior to the election was a judgment call on the likely effects of the election and the shape and character of the new MMP Parliament. It is too early yet to assess whether the judgment call was the right one'; cited in Price, p. 26.

152 Durie, *Ngā Tai Matatū*, p. 217.

153 Ibid.

154 Margaret Kiri Joiner, 'The Life-cycle of a Small Political Party: The Case of New Zealand First', MA thesis, Political Science, Auckland, University of Auckland, 2010, p. 63. Older people figured prominently (32% of supporters were over 65), as did Maori (over 20% of the total Maori vote across all Maori electorates went to New Zealand First). Eighty per cent of the party vote derived from those in the lowest income (less than $30,000 per annum) bracket.

155 Durie, *Ngā Tai Matatū*, p. 217.

156 See below within the context of the 'Closing the Gaps' policy.

157 Durie, *Ngā Tai Matatū*, p. 219.
158 Sullivan, 'Maori Politics and Government Policies', in Miller (ed.), *New Zealand Politics in Transition*, 3rd edn, p. 368.
159 Durie, *Mauri Ora*, pp. 9–10.
160 Laurie Guy, *Shaping Godzone: Public Issues and Church Voices in New Zealand 1840–2000*, Wellington, Victoria University Press, 2012, p. 475.
161 Ibid., p. 476.
162 *New Zealand Listener*, 17 October 1998, p. 17, cited in Guy, ibid., p. 477.
163 Gordon Campbell, *New Zealand Listener*, 26 December 1998, p. 24, cited in Guy, ibid., p. 476. The phrase 'Enough is enough' was raised by Sir Paul Reeves at Parliament, where the hikoi ended.
164 For a detailed account of the meeting and its impact, see Chapter 23 of Guy, *Shaping Godzone*, pp. 463–80.
165 Te Puni Kokiri, 'Progress towards Closing Social and Economic Gaps between Maori and Non-Maori: A Report to the Minister of Maori Affairs', Wellington, Te Puni Kokiri (Ministry of Maori Development), 1998, p. 6.
166 Wyatt Creech reported in *Dominion*, 16 July 1998, cited in Green, 'Maori and Pakeha 1900–2000', p. 59.
167 'He Putahitanga Hou: Labour on Maori Development', 16 October 1999, p. 2, cited in Terence Green, 'Maori and Pakeha 1960–2000: The Justice of Positive Discrimination', MA thesis, Political Science, Auckland, University of Auckland, 2002, p. 59.
168 See S. Chapple, 'Maori Socio-economic Disparity', *Political Science*, vol. 52, no. 2, December 2000, pp. 101–15. In particular, the 1998 statistics relied on a volatile definition of ethnicity. Cheyne, et al. (eds), *Social Policy in Aotearoa New Zealand*, later summarised the problem: 'Statistics New Zealand changed the format of census questions census by census, responding to Maori demands to have iwi-status recognised, but in doing so making it almost impossible to compare Maori at one point in time with the same group five or ten years later. Comparing policy outcomes for Maori over time presented major difficulties'; 3rd edn, p. 153.
169 *Sunday Star-Times*, 10 December 2000, cited in Green, 'Maori and Pakeha 1900–2000', p. 62.
170 *Evening Post*, 2nd edn, 12 December 2000,

cited in Green, ibid., p. 63.
171 Michael King, *Being Pakeha Now: Reflections and Recollections of a White Native*, Auckland, Penguin Books, 1999, p. 9.
172 Durie, *Ngā Tai Matatū*, p. 196.
173 Ibid., p. 228.
174 See Local Government Act 2002, sections 14, 77 and 81.
175 Durie, *Ngā Tai Matatū*, p. 101.
176 Ann Sullivan, 'Maori Politics and Government Policies', in Raymond Miller (ed.), *New Zealand Government and Politics*, 4th edn, Auckland, Oxford University Press, 2006, p. 610.
177 Durie, *Ngā Tai Matatū*, pp. 101–2.
178 'Nationhood', an address by Don Brash, Leader of the National Party, to the Orewa Rotary Club, 27 January 2004, www.national.org.nz/files/orewarotaryclub_27jan.pdf.
179 'Poll Puts National Ahead of Labour', *New Zealand Herald*, 15 February 2004. The poll was conducted for Television New Zealand.
180 These ideas were enthusiastically endorsed when espoused by Brash, yet the One New Zealand Party, founded by Walter Christie in 1999 and based on the slogan 'One Law, One People, One New Zealand', did not receive much publicity, even in 2002, when minor parties were prominent; see Hill, *Anti-Treatyism and Anti-Scholarship*, p. 55.
181 According to Jon Johansson: 'Polling showed that Brash resonated most strongly with people of his own age and gender'; see Johansson, 'Orewa and the Rhetoric of Illusion', *Political Science*, vol. 56, no. 2, 2004, pp. 124–5, cited in O'Malley et al. (eds), *The Treaty of Waitangi Companion*, p. 396.
182 'Call for Peaceful Protest', *New Zealand Herald*, 5 May 2004, p. A2, and also the editorial 'Shifting Sand Causes PM to Behave Oddly', p. A18, which noted that Clark appeared to be 'throwing caution to the winds' in making these remarks.
183 'Shifting Sand Causes PM to Behave Oddly', *New Zealand Herald*, 5 May 2004, p. A18, www.nzherald.co.nz/nz/news/article.cfm?c_id=1&objectid=3564434.
184 Evan Te Ahu Poata-Smith, 'Ka Tika A Muri, Ka Tika A Mua? Māori Protest Politics and the Treaty of Waitangi Settlement Process', in Paul Spoonley, Cluny Macpherson and David Pearson

(eds), *Tangata Tangata: The Changing Ethnic Contours of New Zealand*, Southbank, Victoria, Dunmore Press, 2004, p. 80.

185 'Mallard Stakes Treaty Position', *Dominion Post*, 29 July 2004, cited in Durie, *Ngā Tai Matatū*, p. 224.

186 Durie, *Ngā Tai Matatū*, p. 105. For the legal scholars' views, see F. M. Brookfield, 'Maori Claims and the "Special" Juridical Nature of the Foreshore and Seabed', *New Zealand Law Review*, vol. 2, 2005, and P. G. McHugh, 'Aboriginal Title in New Zealand: A Retrospect and Prospect', *New Zealand Journal of Public and International Law*, vol. 2, 2004.

187 Wai 1071, www.waitangi-tribunal.govt.nz/reports/summary.asp?reportid={838C5579-36C3-4CE2-A444-E6CFB1D4FA01}.

188 United Nations General Assembly 2005, Decision 1 (66), New Zealand Foreshore and Seabed Act 2004, United Nations, Geneva.

189 Another organisation aiming to foster Maori unity formed in 2005 when the first Iwi Chairs Forum convened at Takahanga marae in Kaikoura. Since that time, the Forum has met at four hui per year at different marae around the country to share knowledge and information between iwi.

190 Sharples became Minister of Maori Affairs, Associate Minister of Corrections and Associate Minister of Education, and Turia became Minister for the Community and Voluntary Sector, Associate Minister of Health and Associate Minister for Social Development and Employment.

191 This common area has no fee simple and cannot be sold.

192 TVNZ, 'New Foreshore Bill Passed', *ONE News*, 24 March 2011, http://tvnz.co.nz/politics-news/new-foreshore-bill-passed-4082232.

193 Hone Harawira cited in 'Foreshore Replacement Bill "a fraud"', *New Zealand Herald*, 6 December 2010, www.nzherald.co.nz/nz/news/article.cfm?c_id=1&objectid=10692490.

194 http://mana.net.nz/wp-content/uploads/2011/10/MANA_pamphlet_web.pdf.

195 Danya Levy, 'Iwi "more united than ever" on Water Rights', *Dominion Post*, 24 August 2012, www.stuffco.nz/dominion-post/news/politics/7676605/Iwi-more-united-than-ever-on-water-rights.

196 Kate Chapman, 'Waitangi Tribunal: Asset Sales Must Halt', *Dominion Post*, 24 August 2012, www.stuff.co.nz/dominion-post/news/7543278/Waitangi-Tribunal-Asset-sales-must-halt.

197 Cited in Tracy Watkins, 'Challenge to SOE Sale Dismissed', 27 February 2013, www.stuff.co.nz/national/politics/8358532/Challenge-to-SOE-sale-dismissed.

198 Pete Bossley, 'The Treaty: The Genesis and Importance of the Treaty of Waitangi Exhibit', *Architecture New Zealand, special edition, The Designing of Te Papa*, February 1998, p. 64.

199 See 'Views on the Treaty', in Paul Perry and Alan Webster, *New Zealand Politics at the Turn of the Millennium: Attitudes and Values about Politics and Government, The Political Report of the Third New Zealand Study of Values*, Auckland, Alpha Publications, 1999, pp. 73–76. This was the third such survey undertaken through the Sociology Department at Massey University — the first two being in 1985 and 1989. Using self-identified class and ethnicity variables, those wanting the present process to continue were Maori, Pasifika peoples and those in the lower socio-economic class; those more wanting to see the Treaty abolished were Pakeha, Europeans, lower middle class and working class; p. 75.

200 By 2003, for example, more than 85% of Maori children entering school had attended early childhood education, and Maori had the highest rate of increase in achieving NCEA Level 1, with an increase of 17% compared to 10% for non-Maori; Durie, *Ngā Tai Matatū*, pp. 39 and 231.

201 See Durie, *Ngā Tai Matatū*, pp. 37–44 for a summary of socio-economic disparities, and observations about the relative roles of material circumstances and ethnicity, and also p. 44, Durie's observation: 'Benchmarking Maori performance solely against non-Maori progress often misses the essence of being Maori and can devalue the significance of indigeneity. Best outcomes for Maori therefore need to be measured not only against individual performance in health or education or employment, but also against the level of participation in te ao Maori — the Maori world.'

202 Sullivan, 'Maori Politics and Government Policies', in Miller (ed.), *New Zealand Government and Politics*, 4th edn, p. 613.

203 By 2003, for example, Ngai Tahu was involved in environmental management, social development in the form of health, education and welfare programmes, te reo teaching, and several businesses including tourism, fishing, property, and health care for the elderly; Durie, *Ngā Tai Matatū*, p. 51.

204 Durie, ibid.

205 Hill, *Maori and the State*, p. 270.

206 A national census in 2006 stated there were 157,000 te reo speakers in New Zealand — some 4% of the total population; see www.maorilanguage.info/mao_lang_faq.html.

207 Durie, *Ngā Tai Matatū*, p. 49. In September 2004, its total audience of 351,000 included 71% non-Maori, while its Maori audience of 142,000 represented 35% of the Maori population.

208 'Close the Book on Treaty Claims', *National Times 2002*, (party manifesto May 2002), Wellington, 2002, n.p.

209 Treaty of Waitangi Act 1975, section 6AA, see www.legislation.govt.nz/act/public/1975/0114/latest/DLM435534.html. (This applied to new historical claims or historical amendments to contemporary claims; new contemporary claims could still be lodged however.)

210 See www.raineycollins.co.nz/_r/uploads/2010/03/maori-issues-summer-2008.pdf, which refers to some 2000 new claims lodged before the September 2008 deadline.

211 Queen Elizabeth II, Waitangi Day speech, 1990, *New Zealand Herald*, 7 February 1990, cited in O'Malley et al. (eds), *The Treaty of Waitangi Companion*, p. 381.

CHAPTER TWELVE **A Plaited Rope: Immigration and its Impact**

1 *Immigration and New Zealand: A Statement of Current Immigration Policy*, 4th edn, Wellington, Department of Labour, February 1986, cited in Andrew Trlin and Paul Spoonley (eds) *New Zealand and International Migration: A Digest and Bibliography, Number 2*, Palmerston North, Massey University, 1992, p. 3.

2 Joan Metge, 'He Taura Whiri: The Treaty Our Guide', Chapter 2 in Joan Metge, *Tuamaka: The Challenge of Difference in Aotearoa New Zealand*, Auckland, Auckland University Press, 2010, p. 26.

3 Ibid., p. 11.

4 *New Zealand Official Yearbook*, 2010, p. 101.

5 R. D. Bedford, R. S. J. Farmer and A. D. Trlin, 'The Immigration Policy Review, 1986: a review', in *New Zealand Population Review*, vol. 13, no. 1, May 1987, pp. 50–51.

6 Tim Beal and Farib Sos, *Astronauts from Taiwan: Taiwanese Immigration to Australia and New Zealand*, Wellington, Asia Pacific Research Institute, 1999, p. 52.

7 Quoted in Tom Brooking and Roberto Rabel, 'Neither British nor Polynesian: A Brief History of New Zealand's Other Immigrants', in Stuart William Greif (ed.), *Immigration and National Identity in New Zealand: One People, Two Peoples, Many Peoples?*, Palmerston North, Dunmore Press, 1995, p. 43.

8 Malcolm McKinnon, *Immigrants and Citizens: New Zealanders and Asian Immigration in Historical Context*, Wellington, Institute of Policy Studies, Victoria University, 1996, pp. 42–45.

9 Manying Ip, 'Seeking the Last Utopia: The Taiwanese in New Zealand', in Manying Ip (ed.), *Unfolding History, Evolving Identity: The Chinese in New Zealand*, Auckland, Auckland University Press, 2003, pp. 194–5. See also Anne Henderson, 'Untapped Talents: The Employment and Settlement Experiences of Skilled Chinese in New Zealand', in Ip (ed.), ibid., pp. 143–4.

10 *New Zealand Herald*, 8 November 1989, quoted in McKinnon, *Immigrants and Citizens*, p. 46.

11 Paul Spoonley and Richard Bedford, *Welcome to Our World? Immigration and the Reshaping of New Zealand*, Auckland, Dunmore Publishing, 2012, p. 84.

12 Richard Bedford, 'Out of Africa . . . New Migrations to Aotearoa', in Geoff Kearsley and Blair Fitzharris (eds), *Glimpses of a Gaian World: Essays in Honour of Peter Holland*, Dunedin, University of Otago, 2004, p. 363.

13 Richard Bedford, Paul Callister and Robert Didham, 'Arrivals, Departures and Net Migration, 2001/02–2008/09', in Andrew Trlin, Paul Spoonley and Richard Bedford (eds), *New Zealand and International Migration: A Digest and Bibliography, Number 5*, Palmerston North, Massey

University, 2010, p. 77. New Zealand is not alone. Other cities around the Pacific Rim such as Los Angeles, Sydney, Vancouver and Brisbane have all experienced large waves of Asian immigration.

14 Brooking and Rabel, 'Neither British nor Polynesian', in Greif (ed.), *Immigration and National Identity*, p. 46.

15 Henderson, 'Untapped Talents', in Ip (ed.), *Unfolding History, Evolving Identity*, p. 143. See also Manying Ip, 'Chinese New Zealanders', in Greif (ed.), *Immigration and National Identity*, pp. 192–3.

16 'The Pacific Community? The Next Steps', 9 November 1994, cited in Foreword to McKinnon, *Immigrants and Citizens*, p. i.

17 Spoonley and Bedford, *Welcome to Our World?*, p. 91. In the year to June 2012, Chinese immigrants totalled 7991, Indian 7141, and those from all other Asian countries 13,359. See Rodney Dickens, 'A Range of Migration and Population Growth Insights', Strategic Risk Analysis Limited, October 2012, p. 2, www.sra.co.nz/ pdf/MigrationOct12.pdf.

18 Brooking and Rabel, 'Neither British nor Polynesian', in Greif (ed.), *Immigration and National Identity*, p. 46.

19 Statistics New Zealand, 2002, quoted in Raymond Chui, 'Auckland's "Economic Immigrants" from Asia', in Ian Carter, David Craig and Steve Matthewman (eds), *Almighty Auckland?*, Palmerston North, Dunmore Press, 2004, p. 111.

20 QuickStats about Auckland Region, Cultural Diversity, www.stats.govt. nz/Census/2006CensusHomePage/ Quickstats.

21 Henderson, 'Untapped Talents', in Ip (ed.), *Unfolding History, Evolving Identity*, p. 143.

22 Nicola Legat, 'Immigration: What Have We Got to Fear?', *North & South*, June 1996, pp. 48–63.

23 Jing Xue, Wardlow Friesen and David Sullivan, 'Diversity in Chinese Auckland: Hypothesising Multiple Ethnoburbs', in *Population, Space and Place*, vol. 18, issue 5, 2012, pp. 579–95, published online 26 August 2011 in Wiley Online Library, http://onlinelibrary.wiley.com/doi/10.1002/ psp.688/pdf.

24 http://emigratetonewzealand.word-press.com/migrant-stories/chapter-7/ immigrant-kid/.

25 Quoted in Beal and Sos, *Astronauts from Taiwan*, p. 107.

26 Janet McAllister, 'Passages From India', *Metro*, November 2002, pp. 66–73.

27 Mrs J., 1994, personal communication with Manying Ip, quoted in Ip, 'Seeking the Last Utopia', in Ip (ed.), *Unfolding History, Evolving Identity*, p. 199.

28 Marie Gee Wilson, Priyanka Gahlout, Lucia Liu and Suchitra Mouly, 'A Rose by Any Other Name: The Effect of Ethnicity and Name on Access to Employment', *University of Auckland Business Review*, vol. 7, no. 2, 2005, p. 65, www.uabr. auckland.ac.nz/files/articles/Volume11/ v11i2-a-rose-by-any-other-name.pdf.

29 'Auckland Bosses Accused of Racism', *Auckland Now*, 25 March 2012, p. 1, www. stuff.co.nz/auckland/local-news/6633681/ Auckland-bosses-accused-of-racism.

30 Adrienne N. Girling, James H. Liu and Colleen Ward, 'Confident, equal and proud? A Discussion Paper on the Barriers Asians Face to Equality in New Zealand', Centre for Applied Cross-cultural Research, Victoria University, for the Human Rights Commission, August 2010, pp. 10–11, http://cacr.victoria.ac.nz/__data/ assets/pdf_file/0017/4085/Barriers-to-Asian-Equality-Discussion-Paper.pdf; see also Henderson, 'Untapped Talents', in Ip (ed.), *Unfolding History, Evolving Identity*, pp. 141–64.

31 See Henderson, 'Untapped Talents', in Ip (ed.), *Unfolding History, Evolving Identity*, pp. 150–8, and Spoonley and Bedford, *Welcome to Our World?*, pp. 188–95.

32 Hannah Brown, 'An Asian at My Table', *North & South*, May 2003, p. 56.

33 Ibid., p. 52.

34 Andrew Trlin, Anne Henderson and Regina Pernice, 'Asian Immigration, Public Attitudes and Immigration Policy: Patterns and Responses in New Zealand', in Eleanor Laquian, Aprodicio Laquian and Terry McGee (eds), *The Silent Debate: Asian Immigration and Racism in Canada*, Vancouver, Institute of Asian Research, 1998, pp. 228–30.

35 'Inv-Asian', *Eastern Courier*, 16 April 1993, pp. 6–7, Special feature part 1; 23 April 1993, pp. 6–7, part 2.

36 Kate McMillan, 'Immigration, Nationalism, and Citizenship Debates in the 1990s', in Andrew Trlin, Paul Spoonley and Noel Watts (eds), *New Zealand and International Migration: A Digest and*

Bibliography, Number 4, Palmerston North, Massey University, 2005, pp. 70–85.

37 *New Zealand Herald*, 14 February 1996.
38 Ibid., 30 March 1996.
39 Paul Spoonley and Andrew Trlin, *Immigration, Immigrants and the Media: Making Sense of Multicultural New Zealand*, Palmerston North, New Settlers Programme, Massey University, 2004, p. 26.
40 Ranginui Walker, 'Immigration Policy and the Political Economy of New Zealand', in Greif (ed.), *Immigration and National Identity*, p. 300.
41 Ibid., p. 302.
42 Ibid., p. 292.
43 *Time* magazine, 17 May 1993, pp. 40–41.
44 All quoted in Graeme Hunt, 'Asia Takes Note of Rising NZ Xenophobia', in *New Zealand Business Review*, 17 May 1996, p. 12.
45 McMillan, 'Immigration, Nationalism, and Citizenship Debates', in Trlin, Spoonley and Watts (eds), *New Zealand and International Migration: A Digest and Bibliography, Number 4*, p. 76.
46 See Elsie Ho and Richard Bedford, 'The Asian Crisis and Migrant Entrepreneurs in New Zealand: Some Reactions and Reflections', *New Zealand Population Review*, vol. 24, 1998, pp. 72–81.
47 Grace Lin cited in Legat, 'Immigration: What Have We Got to Fear?', p. 53.
48 In 1997 this party merged with the United Party.
49 David McLoughlin, 'New Zealand at the Crossroads', *North & South*, July 1996, p. 43.
50 *New Zealand Listener*, 20 September 2002, p. 21.
51 *New Zealand Herald*, 26 June and 1 July 2002. See also David Fickling, 'Not-so-nice New Zealand', *Guardian*, 15 December 2003, www.guardian.co.uk/world/2003/dec/15/worlddispatch.australia.
52 Quoted in Tony Ballantyne, 'Writing out Asia: Race, Colonialism and Chinese Migration in New Zealand History', in Charles Ferrall, Paul Millar and Keren Smith (eds), *East by South: China in the Australasian Imagination*, Wellington, Victoria University Press, 2005, p. 90.
53 *New Zealand Herald*, 26 June 2002.
54 Richard Bedford, Jacqueline Lidgard and Elsie Ho, 'Arrivals, Departures and Net Migration 1996/97–2002/03', in Trlin, Spoonley and Watts (eds), *New Zealand*

and International Migration: A Digest and Bibliography, Number 4, p. 48.

55 Raymond Miller, 'New Zealand First', in Raymond Miller (ed.), *New Zealand Government and Politics*, 4th edn, Melbourne, Oxford University Press, 2006, p. 379.
56 Andrew Butcher and Paul Spoonley, 'Inv-Asian: Print Media Constructions of Asians and Asian Immigration', in Paola Voci and Jacqueline Leckie (eds), *Localizing Asia in Aotearoa*, Wellington, Dunmore Publishing, 2011, pp. 106–9.
57 Deborah Coddington, 'Asian Angst: Is it Time to Send Some Back?', *North & South*, December 2006, pp. 37–47.
58 See 'Write of reply' column in *North & South*, January 2007, pp. 12–14, February 2007, pp. 15–19, March 2007, pp. 14 and 17.
59 See Butcher and Spoonley, 'Inv-Asian', in Voci and Leckie (eds), *Localizing Asia in Aotearoa*, pp. 109–11.
60 See Spoonley and Bedford, *Welcome to Our World?*, pp. 115–16.
61 Asia New Zealand Foundation, 'Building New Zealand's Links with Asia', www.asianz.org.nz/sites/asianz.org.nz/files/files/Asia%20NZ%20Profile%202011.pdf.
62 See John Bryant, Murat Genç and David Law, 'Trade and Migration to New Zealand', New Zealand Treasury Working Paper 04/18, September 2004, www.treasury.govt.nz/publications/research-policy/wp/2004/04-18/twp04-18.pdf.
63 See a discussion in Spoonley and Bedford, *Welcome to Our World?*, pp. 249–60.
64 Mervin Singham, Director, Office of Ethnic Affairs Te Tari Matawaka, 'Sharing a Patch of Earth', in Edwina Pio, *Longing & Belonging: Asian, Middle Eastern, Latin American and African peoples in New Zealand*, Wellington, Dunmore Publishing, 2010, p. 19.
65 *New Zealand Herald*, 26 April 2013, www.nzherald.co.nz/business/news/article.cfm?c_id=3&objectid=10879910.
66 Statistics New Zealand, 'National Ethnic Population Projections: 2006 (base) — 2026 update', p. 5, hwww.stats.govt.nz/browse_for_stats/population/estimates_and_projections/national-ethnic-population-projections-info-releases.aspx.
67 Spoonley and Bedford, *Welcome to Our World?*, pp. 123 and 129–31.
68 From 1 April 1971 to 31 March 1981 New

Zealand experienced a total net migration loss of 102,000. See Spoonley and Bedford, ibid., p. 131.

69 Cluny Macpherson, 'From Pacific Islanders to Pacific People and Beyond', in Paul Spoonley, Cluny Macpherson and David Pearson (eds), *Tangata Tangata: The Changing Ethnic Contours of New Zealand*, Southbank, Victoria, Dunmore Press, 2004, p. 136.

70 Ministry of Pacific Island Affairs, 'About Pacific Peoples in New Zealand', www.mpia.govt.nz/demograph-ic-fact-sheet/and www.mpia.govt.nz/pacific-peoples-in-new-zealand/.

71 Sarona Meata'a Aiono-Iosefa, 'Shifting Sands', in Peggy Fairbairn-Dunlop and Gabrielle Makisi (eds), *Making Our Place: Growing up PI in New Zealand*, Palmerston North, Dunmore Press, 2003, p. 109.

72 See Cluny Macpherson, 'Empowering Pacific Peoples: Community Organisations in New Zealand', in Sean Mallon, Kolokesa Mahina-Tuai and Damon Salesa (eds), *Tangata Ole Moana: New Zealand and the People of the Pacific*, Wellington, Te Papa Press, 2012, pp. 186–92.

73 Peggy Fairbairn-Dunlop, 'Some Markers on the Journey', in Fairbairn-Dunlop and Makisi (eds), *Making Our Place*, p. 26.

74 Quoted in Macpherson, 'Empowering Pacific Peoples', in Mallon, Mahina-Tuai and Salesa (eds), *Tangata Ole Moana*, p. 192.

75 Fairbairn-Dunlop, 'Some Markers on the Journey', in Fairbairn-Dunlop and Makisi (eds), *Making Our Place*, pp. 27–28.

76 Ibid.

77 Statistics New Zealand, 'Pacific Progress: A Report on the Economic Status of Pacific Peoples in New Zealand', 2002, p. 30, www.stats.govt.nz/browse_for_stats/people_and_communities/pacific_peoples/pacific-progress.aspx.

78 Macpherson, 'Empowering Pacific Peoples', in Mallon, Mahina-Tuai and Salesa (eds), *Tangata Ole Moana*, p. 193.

79 The 1991 census showed that there were Pacific Island congregations attached to 24 different religious denominations. See Feiloaiga Taule'ale'ausumai, 'New Religions, New Identities: The Changing Contours of Religious Commitment', in Cluny Macpherson, Paul Spoonley and Melani Anae (eds), *Tangata O Te Moana Nui: The Evolving Identities of Pacific Peoples in*

Aotearoa/New Zealand, Palmerston North, Dunmore Press, 2001, p. 188.

80 Taule'ale'ausumai, 'New Religions, New Identities', in Macpherson, Spoonley and Anae (eds), *Tangata O Te Moana Nui*, p. 184.

81 J. Tiatia, *Caught Between Cultures: A New Zealand-Born Pacific Island Perspective*, Auckland, Christian Research Association, 1998, p. 15, quoted in Taule'ale'ausumai, 'New Religions, New Identities', in Macpherson, Spoonley and Anae (eds), *Tangata O Te Moana Nui*, p. 181.

82 Paddy Walker (1917–), of mixed Cook Islands and New Zealand heritage, was born in Samoa and came to New Zealand for her education in 1927. She married Bill Walker, and settled in Auckland. She has been extremely active in civic affairs, working to help women and children of the Pacific Islands. She has been appointed an Officer of the Order of the British Empire for her work. When her husband Bill died in the 1990s, she returned to live in Rarotonga, where she has continued her work.

83 Fairbairn-Dunlop, 'Some Markers on the Journey', in Fairbairn-Dunlop and Makisi (eds), *Making Our Place*, p. 30.

84 Quoted in Fairbairn-Dunlop and Makisi (eds), ibid., p. 31.

85 'Pacific Women Getting Together', *Evening Post*, 28 February, 1976, p. 16, quoted in Macpherson, 'Empowering Pacific Peoples', in Mallon, Mahina-Tuai and Salesa (eds), *Tangata Ole Moana*, p. 194.

86 Ibid., p. 195.

87 Fairbairn-Dunlop, 'Some Markers on the Journey', in Fairbairn-Dunlop and Makisi (eds), *Making Our Place*, p. 32.

88 Macpherson, 'Empowering Pacific Peoples', in Mallon, Mahina-Tuai and Salesa (eds), *Tangata Ole Moana*, p. 195.

89 Quoted in Mallon, Mahina-Tuai and Salesa (eds), ibid., p. 197.

90 Statistics New Zealand, 'Pacific Progress', p. 47.

91 Winnie Laban, 'Pacific Island Unemployment Remains Twice the National Average', 5 August 2010, www.labour.org.nz/news/pacific-island-unemployment-remains-twice-the-national-average.

92 Statistics New Zealand, 'Pacific Progress', p. 51.

93 Ibid., p. 58.

94 Ibid., p. 37.
95 Ministry of Social Development, 'From Wannabes to Youth Offenders: Youth Gangs in Counties Manukau — Research Report', Auckland, Centre for Social Research and Evaluation Te Pokapū Rangahau Arotake Hapori, September 2006, pp. 4–7 and 13, www.msd.govt.nz/about-msd-and-our-work/publications-resources/research/youth-gangs-counties-manukau/index.html.
96 Ibid., pp. 4–7.
97 *Auckland Star*, 12 August 1986, p. 1.
98 See Prue Toft, 'Overstayers: A Case of Exaggeration', Chapter 15 in Paul Spoonley and Walter Hirsch (eds), *Between the Lines: Racism and the New Zealand Media*, Auckland, Heinemann Reid, 1990, p. 114. McLoughlin's report appeared in the *Sunday Star* of 23 March 1986. On 12 August the *Auckland Star* ran a front-page story under the title 'Race Conciliator Backs Our Story'.
99 *Auckland Star*, 15 April 1986, p. A6.
100 David McLoughlin, 'Immigration out of Control', *North & South*, May 1994, pp. 44–54.
101 Finau Kolo, 'An Incident in Otara: The Media and Pacific Island Communities', Chapter 17 in Spoonley and Hirsch (eds), *Between the Lines*, p. 121.
102 Quoted in Samson Samasoni, 'Pacific Island Responses to Our Monocultural Media', Chapter 20 in Spoonley and Hirsch (eds), ibid., p. 134.
103 Quoted in Spoonley and Hirsch (eds), ibid., p. 135.
104 See Robert Loto et al., 'Pasifika in the News: The Portrayal of Pacific Peoples in the New Zealand Press', *Journal of Community and Applied Social Psychology*, vol. 16, issue 2, 2006, pp. 105–8 for a discussion on negative and positive news reports.
105 See Spoonley and Bedford, *Welcome to Our World?*, pp. 225–7.
106 See www.radionz.co.nz/genre/maori,pacific.
107 Samasoni, 'Pacific Island Responses to Our Monocultural Media', in Spoonley and Hirsch (eds), *Between the Lines*, pp. 135–7.
108 Melani Anae, 'O A'u/I — My Identity Journey', in Fairbairn-Dunlop and Makisi (eds), *Making Our Place*, p. 89.
109 Fairbairn-Dunlop, 'Some Markers on the Journey', in Fairbairn-Dunlop and Makisi (eds), ibid., p. 41.
110 Teresia Teaiwa and Sean Mallon, 'Ambivalent Kinships? Pacific People in New Zealand', in James H. Liu, Tim McCreanor, Tracey McIntosh and Teresia Teaiwa (eds), *New Zealand Identities: Departures and Destinations*, Wellington, Victoria University Press, 2005, p. 210.
111 Cluny Macpherson, 'One Trunk Sends out Many Branches: Pacific Cultures and Cultural Identities', in Macpherson, Spoonley and Anae (eds), *Tangata O Te Moana Nui*, pp. 77–78.
112 Kirsten Zemke-White, 'Rap Music and Pacific Identity in Aotearoa: Popular Music and the Politics of Opposition', in Macpherson, Spoonley and Anae (eds), ibid., pp. 228–42.
113 'King Kapisi's Savage Thoughts', *New Zealand Musician*, vol. 9, no. 2, October/November 2000, p. 55.
114 Quoted in Zemke-White, 'Rap Music and Pacific Identity in Aotearoa', in Macpherson, Spoonley and Anae (eds), *Tangata O Te Moana Nui*, p. 235.
115 'How bizarre: New Zealand's Most Successful Music Single', www.nzhistory.net.nz/media/video/how-bizzare, (Ministry for Culture and Heritage), updated 30 August 2012.
116 Quoted in Alexander Bisley, 'Brotha D, Godfather of New Zealand Hip-Hop', *Salient*, http://salient.org.nz/features/brotha-d-godfather-of-new-zealand-hip-hop, posted 26 April 2004.
117 Ibid.
118 Dawn Raid Entertainment, www.dawnraid.co.nz/about.html. See also Fulimalo Pereira, 'Arts Specific: Pacific Peoples and New Zealand's Arts', in Mallon, Mahina-Tuai and Salesa (eds), *Tangata Ole Moana*, p. 322.
119 Paul Millar, 'So Dazzling a Creature: Pacific Island Writers in New Zealand Literature', in Sean Mallon and Pandora Fulimalo Pereira (eds), *Pacific Art Niu Sila: The Pacific Dimension of Contemporary New Zealand Art*, Wellington, Te Papa Press, 2002, p. 161.
120 Pereira, 'Arts Specific', in Mallon, Mahina-Tuai and Salesa (eds), *Tangata Ole Moana*, pp. 306–7.
121 Scott Whitney, 'The Bifocal World of John Pule: This Niuean Writer and Painter is Still Searching for a Place to Call Home', *Pacific Magazine*, 1 July 2002, http://factualworld.com/article/John_Pule.

122 Selina Tusitala Marsh, *Fast Talking PI*, Auckland, Auckland University Press, 2009.

123 Pereira, 'Arts Specific', in Mallon, Mahina-Tuai and Salesa (eds), *Tangata Ole Moana*, p. 322.

124 Teaiwa and Mallon, 'Ambivalent Kinships?', in Liu, McCreanor, McIntosh and Teaiwa (eds), *New Zealand Identities*, p. 220.

125 Sarina Pearson, 'Film and Photography: Picturing New Zealand as a Pacific Place', in Mallon and Pereira (eds), *Pacific Art Niu Sila*, pp. 179–80.

126 Pereira, 'Arts Specific', in Mallon, Mahina-Tuai and Salesa (eds), *Tangata Ole Moana*, p. 326.

127 Albert L. Refiti, 'Building the House of Noa Noa and Lave Lave: A Possible Theory of Pacific Art', in Ron Brownson et al., *Home ALK: Artists of Pacific Heritage in Auckland*, Auckland, Auckland Art Gallery Toi o Tāmaki, 2012, p. 12.

128 Pacific Artspace website, www.pacific_art-space.com/artists/filipe/filipe/htm, quoted in Caroline Vercoe, 'Art Niu Sila: Contemporary Pacific Art in New Zealand', in Mallon and Pereira (eds), *Pacific Art Niu Sila*, p. 193.

129 See arTok: Pacific Arts Online, www.abc.net.au/arts/artok/festival/default.htm, quoted in Vercoe, ibid., p. 199.

130 Pereira, 'Arts Specific', in Mallon, Mahina-Tuai and Salesa (eds), *Tangata Ole Moana*, pp. 312–13.

131 Lineahi Lund, quoted in Pandora Fulimalo Pereira, 'Lalaga: Weaving Connections in Pacific Fibre', in Mallon and Pereira (eds), *Pacific Art Niu Sila*, p. 81.

132 Ibid., p. 89.

133 Maile Drake, 'Ngatu Pepa: Making Tongan Tapa in New Zealand', in Mallon and Pereira (eds), ibid., pp. 53–63.

134 Pereira, 'Arts Specific', in Mallon, Mahina-Tuai and Salesa (eds), *Tangata Ole Moana*, p. 319.

135 Quoted in Mallon, Mahina-Tuai and Salesa (eds), ibid.

136 Ibid., p. 320.

137 See ibid., p. 333.

138 See PIC Netball Club, '45 Years of PIC Netball', http://pipcnewtown.wellington.net.nz/sports-recreation/pic-netball-club/.

139 Ibid., pp. 5–6.

140 See Tasileta Te'evale, 'We Are What We Play: Pacific Peoples, Sport and Identity in Aotearoa', in Macpherson, Spoonley and Anae (eds), *Tangata O Te Moana Nui*, p. 217.

141 Palagi means westerners or Caucasians in Samoan.

142 PIC Netball Club, '45 Years of PIC Netball', p. 3.

143 Sean Mallon, 'Conspicuous Selections: Pacific Islanders in New Zealand Sport', in Mallon, Mahina-Tuai and Salesa (eds), *Tangata Ole Moana*, p. 293.

144 Ibid., p. 290.

145 Ibid.

146 Since Umaga's captaincy in 2004/5, Rodney So'oialo, Malili 'Mils' Muliaina, Keven Mealamu and Jerry Collins, all of Samoan descent, have been captains. See Mallon, ibid., p. 298.

147 Va'aiga Tuigamala, 'Inga the Winga', in Fairbairn-Dunlop and Makisi (eds), *Making Our Place*, p. 232.

148 Colleen Ward and En-Yi Lin, 'Immigration, Acculturation and National Identity in New Zealand', in Liu, McCreanor, McIntosh and Teaiwa (eds), *New Zealand Identities*, p. 159.

149 Tom Hyde, 'White Men Can't Jump', *Metro*, September 1993, p. 67.

150 Figures from Netball New Zealand, personal communication, 17.11.2012.

151 See '2013 Westpac Halberg Awards', *ONE Sports News*, http://tvnz/othersports-news/happened-2013-westpac-halberg-awards-5341791.

152 Mallon, 'Conspicuous Selections', in Mallon, Mahina-Tuai and Salesa (eds), *Tangata Ole Moana*, p. 296.

153 Te'evale, 'We Are What We Play', in Macpherson, Spoonley and Anae (eds), *Tangata O Te Moana Nui*, p. 226.

154 Mallon, 'Conspicuous Selections', in Mallon, Mahina-Tuai and Salesa (eds), *Tangata Ole Moana*, p. 298.

155 Hyde, 'White Men Can't Jump', p. 69.

156 Paul Spoonley and Cluny Macpherson, 'Transnational New Zealand: Immigrants and Cross-Border Connections and Activities', in Spoonley, Macpherson and Pearson (eds), *Tangata Tangata*, p. 190.

157 Anand Satyanand was born in New Zealand to Fijian Indian parents. He studied law at Auckland University, was made a judge in 1982, and in 1995 was appointed as an ombudsman, serving two five-year terms before becoming Governor-General in 2006.

158 Kate McMillan, 'Immigration Policy' in

Miller (ed.), *New Zealand Government and Politics*, 4th edn, p. 644.

159 Immigration New Zealand, 'Changes to immigration family residence categories', press release of 10 May 2012, www.immigration.govt.nz/migrant/general/generalinformation/news/familycategorychanges.htm.

160 Wardlow Friesen, 'Diverse Auckland: The Face of New Zealand in the 21st Century', *Outlook*, edition 06, Wellington, Asia New Zealand Foundation, April 2008, p. 15.

161 *New Zealand Herald*, 23 October, 2010.

162 Spoonley and Macpherson, 'Transnational New Zealand', in Spoonley, Macpherson and Pearson (eds), *Tangata Tangata*, p. 190. This figure is an extrapolation — see www.stats.govt.nz/browse_for_stats/population/mythbusters/1million-kiwis-live-overseas.aspx, which examines the oft-cited myth that over one million New Zealanders live overseas.

163 See Carl Walrond, 'Māori Overseas — Settling in Australia', *Te Ara — The Encyclopedia of New Zealand*, updated 22 September 2012, www.teara.govt.nz/en/maori-overseas/page-3.

164 Spoonley and Macpherson, 'Transnational New Zealand', in Spoonley, Macpherson and Pearson (eds), *Tangata Tangata*, p. 190.

165 Richard Bedford, 'Pasifika Mobility: Pathways, Circuits, and Challenges in the 21st Century', in Alastair Bisley (ed.), *Pacific Interactions: Pasifika in New Zealand — New Zealand in Pasifika*, Wellington, Institute of Policy Studies, Victoria University, 2008, p. 93, http://ips.ac.nz/publications/files/f8e7a96f573.pdf.

166 Ibid., p. 127.

167 Quoted in Bisley (ed.), ibid., p. 88.

168 Quoted in Manying Ip, 'Returnees and Transnationals: Evolving Identities of Chinese (PRC) Immigrants in New Zealand', *Journal of Population Studies*, vol. 33, December 2006, p. 98.

169 See Manying Ip, 'Here, There, and Back Again: A New Zealand Case Study of Chinese Circulatory Transmigration', January 2012, www.migrationinformation.org/Feature/display.cfm?id=878.

170 McMillan, 'Immigration Policy', in Miller (ed.), *New Zealand Government and Politics*, 4th edn, p. 644.

171 Pio, *Longing & Belonging*, p. 16.

172 Metge, 'He Taura Whiri', in Metge, *Tuamaka*, p. 11. 'The Rope of Peoples' is the name of a drawing by Cliff Whiting that featured on the cover of the Historic Places Trust Annual Report of 1990.

CONCLUSION **The 'Earthly Paradise' Transformed**

1 From 'Landfall in Unknown Seas', in *Early Days Yet: New and Collected Poems 1941–1997*, Auckland, Auckland University Press, 1997, p. 226.

2 Patrick O'Donovan, 'Land of Content: New Zealand Permeated by a Pleasant Tedium', *Otago Daily Times*, 5 February 1954, p. 4.

3 Cited in Robert Patman and Chris Rudd (eds), *Sovereignty under Siege? Globalization and New Zealand*, Aldershot, Ashgate Publishing, 2005, p. 18.

4 Her Excellency the Governor-General of New Zealand, 'Speech from the Throne', Opening of the 47th Parliament, 27 August 2002, www.scoop.co.nz/stories/PA0208/S00234.htm.

5 Philippa Mein Smith, *A Concise History of New Zealand*, Port Melbourne, Victoria, Cambridge University Press, 2011, p. 209 re 'a common world', and p. 305 re TTMRA.

6 Ibid., p. 319.

7 Felicity Barnes, *New Zealand's London: A Colony and its Metropolis*, Auckland, Auckland University Press, p. 275, fn. 3.

8 Simon Day, 'Go East, Young Men (and Women)', *New Zealand Herald*, 17 March 2013, p. A9.

9 Professor Paul Spoonley cited in Day, ibid.

10 *The Kiwi Nest: 60 Years of Change in New Zealand Families*, Wellington, Families Commission, Research Report No. 3/08, June 2008, pp. 20, 27 and 34. Marriage rate per 1000 statistic for 2011 from Demographic Trends: 2012, Marriage, civil union, and divorce, www.stats.govt.nz/browse_for_stats/population/estimates_and_projections/demographic-trends-2012/marriage%20civil%20union%20and%20divorce.aspx.

11 Ibid., p. 34.

12 Nicholas Jones, 'It's a Start: New Zealand Women Get Ahead', *New Zealand Herald*, 9 March 2013, p. 6. In 2011, the '25 Per Cent Group', made up of CEOs and chairs from public, private and multinational companies, formed with the aim of achieving 25% female participation on New Zealand corporate boards by 2015.

13 Justice Susan Glazebrook, New Zealand Court of Appeal, 'Gender Equality in the Workforce: A Work in Progress', 22 October 2009, p. 6, http://papers.ssrn.com/sol3/papers.cfm?abstract_id=1556764.

14 J. Fanslow and E. Robinson, 'Violence against Women in New Zealand: Prevalence and Health Consequences', *New Zealand Medical Journal*, vol. 117, no. 1206, 2004, cited on womensrefuge.org.nz website.

15 Jennifer Lawn, 'Creativity Inc.: Globalizing the Cultural Imaginary in New Zealand', www.massey.ac.nz/massey/fms/Colleges/College%20of%20Humanities%20and%20Social%20Sciences/EMS/Creativity.pdf, p. 9.

16 www.stats.govt.nz/browse_for_stats/industry_sectors/Tourism/tourism-satellite-account-2012/summary-results.aspx.

17 Michael Cieply and Brooks Barnes, 'New Zealand Wants a Hollywood Put on its Map', *New York Times*, 23 November 2012, www.nytimes.com/2012/11/24/business/media/new-zealand-wants-a-hollywood-put-on-its-map.html?pagewanted=all&_r=1&.

18 Brian Rudman, 'Hobbit Folk Grovel to Feudal Movie Lords', *New Zealand Herald*, 27 October 2010, www.nzherald.co.nz/business/news/article.cfm?c_id=3&objectid=10683203.

19 'The Unhistoric Story', in *Early Days Yet*, p. 235.

SELECT BIBLIOGRAPHY

Abel, Sue, *Shaping the News: Waitangi Day on Television*, Auckland, Auckland University Press, 1997

Anae, Melani, Iuli, Lautofa (Ta) and Burgoyne, Leilani (eds), *The Polynesian Panthers 1971–1974: The Crucible Years*, Auckland, Reed, 2006

Archie, Carol (ed.), *Maori Sovereignty: The Pakeha Perspective*, Hodder Moa Beckett, Auckland, 1995

Auckland City Art Gallery, *Thirty-Seven New Zealand Paintings from the Collection of Charles Brasch and Rodney Kennedy*, Auckland, Auckland City Art Gallery, 1958

Ausubel, David Paul, *The Fern and the Tiki: An American View of New Zealand National Character, Social Attitudes, and Race Relations*, Angus & Robertson, Sydney, 1960; North Quincy, Massachusetts, Christopher Publishing House, 1977

Ballantyne, Tony and Moloughney, Brian (eds), *Disputed Histories: Imagining New Zealand's Pasts*, Dunedin, Otago University Press, 2006

Barr, Mary (ed.), *Headlands: Thinking Through New Zealand Art*, Sydney, Museum of Contemporary Art, 1992

Barrington, Brook, 'New Zealand and the Search for Security 1944–1954: "A Modest and Moderate Collaboration"', PhD thesis, History, Auckland, University of Auckland, 1993

Barrington, Rosemary and Gray, Alison, *The Smith Women: 100 New Zealand Women Talk About their Lives*, Wellington, Reed, 1981

Bassett, Michael, *Confrontation '51: The 1951 Waterfront Dispute*, Wellington, Reed, 1972

——, *The State in New Zealand 1840–1984: Socialism without Doctrines?*, Auckland, Auckland University Press, 1998

——, *Working With David: Inside the Lange Cabinet*, Auckland, Hodder Moa, 2008

Baxter, James K., *Recent Trends in New Zealand Poetry*, Christchurch, Caxton Press, 1951

Baxter, Paul and Sansom, Basil, *Race and Social Difference: Selected Readings*, Harmondsworth, Penguin, 1972

Beaglehole, Ann, *A Small Price to Pay: Refugees from Hitler in New Zealand, 1936–1946*, Wellington, Allen & Unwin and the Historical Branch, Department of Internal Affairs, 1988

Beaglehole, Ernest and Pearl, *Some Modern Maoris*, Christchurch, Whitcombe & Tombs, 1946

Beaglehole, J. C., 'The Development of New Zealand Nationality', *Journal of World History*, vol. 2, no. 1, 1954

Beal, Tim and Sos, Farib, *Astronauts from Taiwan: Taiwanese Immigration to Australia and New Zealand*, Wellington, Asia Pacific Research Institute, 1999

Bedford, R. D., Farmer, R. S. J. and Trlin, A. D., 'The Immigration Policy Review, 1986: a review', *New Zealand Population Review*, vol. 13, no. 1, May 1987

Belich, James, *Paradise Reforged: A History of the New Zealanders from the 1880s to the Year 2000*, Auckland, Allen Lane/The Penguin Press, 2001

Bell, Leonard and Morrow, Diana (eds), *Jewish Lives in New Zealand: A History*, Auckland, Godwit, 2012

Bioletti, Harry, *The Yanks Are Coming: The American Invasion of New Zealand, 1942–1944*, Auckland, Century Hutchinson, 1989

Blackburn, Adrian, *The Shoestring Pirates*, revised and expanded edn, Auckland, Hauraki Enterprises, 1988

Bloomfeld, G. T., *New Zealand: A Handbook of Historical Statistics*, Boston, G. K. Hall, 1984

Bolger, Jim, *A View From the Top: My Seven Years as Prime Minister*, Auckland, Viking, 1998

Bollard, Alan and Mayes, David, *Corporatisation and Privatisation in New Zealand*, Wellington, New Zealand Institute of Economic Research, 1991

Booth, Pat, 'Learning to Live with the Waitangi Tribunal: The Facts without Fear', *North & South*, June 1988

Boston, Jonathan and Dalziel, Paul, *The Decent Society? Essays in Response to National's Economic and Social Policies*, Auckland, Oxford University Press, 1992

Boston, Jonathan and St John, Susan, *Redesigning the Welfare State in New Zealand: Problems, Policies, Prospects*, Auckland, Oxford University Press, 1999

Bourke, Chris, *Blue Smoke: The Lost Dawn of New Zealand Popular Music 1918–1964*, Auckland, Auckland University Press, 2010

Brash, Don, 'Nationhood', Orewa Rotary Club, 27 January 2004, http://www.national.org.nz/files/orewarotaryclub_27jan.pdf

Brickell, Chris, *Mates and Lovers: A History of Gay New Zealand*, Auckland, Godwit, 2008

Brittenden, Wayne, *The Celluloid Circus: The Heyday of the New Zealand Picture Theatre, 1925–1970*, Auckland, Godwit, 2008

Britton, Steve, Le Heron, Richard and Pawson, Eric, *Changing Places in New Zealand: A Geography of Restructuring*, Christchurch, New Zealand Geographical Society, 1993

Brookes, Barbara (ed.), *At Home in New Zealand: History, Houses, People*, Wellington, Bridget Williams Books, 2000

Broughton, Agnes et al., *The Silent Migration, Ngāti Pōneke Young Māori Club 1937–1948: Stories of Urban Migration told to Patricia Grace, Irihapeti Ramsden and Jonathan Dennis*, Wellington, Huia, 2001

Brown, Gordon H., *New Zealand Painting 1920–1940: Adaptation and Nationalism*, Wellington, Queen Elizabeth II Arts Council of New Zealand, 1975

——, *New Zealand Painting, 1940–1960: Conformity and Dissension*, Wellington, Queen Elizabeth II Arts Council of New Zealand, 1981

——, *Colin McCahon: Artist*, 2nd edn, Wellington, Reed, 1993

Brown, Gordon H. and Keith, Hamish, *An Introduction to New Zealand Painting 1839–1980*, 2nd edn, Auckland, Collins, 1982

Brownson, Ron (ed.), *Art Toi: New Zealand Art at Auckland Art Gallery: Toi o Tāmaki*, Auckland Art Gallery, Toi o Tāmaki, Auckland 2011

—— et al., *Home ALK: Artists of Pacific Heritage in Auckland*, Auckland Art Gallery, Toi o Tāmaki, 2012

Bryant, John, Murat, Genç and Law, David, 'Trade and Migration to New Zealand', New Zealand Treasury Working Paper 04/18, http://www.treasury.govt.nz/publications/research-policy/wp/2004/04-18/twp04-18.pdf

Bush, Graham and Scott, Claudia (eds), *Auckland at Full Stretch: Issues of the Seventies*, Auckland, Auckland City Council/Board of Urban Studies, University of Auckland, 1977

Butterworth, G. V. and Young, H. R., *Maori Affairs: A Department and the People Who Made It*, Wellington, Iwi Transition Agency/GP Books, 1990

Butterworth, Susan, *More than Law and Order: Policing a Changing Society 1945–92*, Dunedin, University of Otago Press, 2005

Cahill, Maud and Dann, Christine (eds), *Women Working in the Women's Liberation Movement 1970–1990*, Wellington, Bridget Williams Books, 1991

Byrnes, Giselle (ed.), *The New Oxford History of New Zealand*, Melbourne, Oxford University Press, 2009

Calder, Alex (ed.), *The Writing of New Zealand: Inventions and Identities*, Auckland, Reed, 1993

Campbell, Alistair, *Mine Eyes Dazzle*, Christchurch, Pegasus Press, 1951

Cape, Peter, *New Zealand Painting since 1960: A Study in Themes and Developments*, Auckland, Collins, 1979

Carlyon, Jenny and Morrow, Diana, *A Fine Prospect: A History of Remuera, Meadowbank and St Johns*, Auckland, Random House, 2011

Carter, Ian, Craig, David and Matthewman, Steve (eds), *Almighty Auckland?*, Palmerston North, Dunmore Press, 2004

Cashman, Richard and McKernan, Michael, *Sport in History: The Making of Modern Sporting History*, St Lucia, University of Queensland Press, 1979

Challinor, Deborah, *Grey Ghosts: New Zealand Vietnam Vets talk about their War*, Auckland, Hodder Moa Beckett, 1998

Chapman, Robert, *New Zealand Politics and Social Patterns: Selected Works*, edited and with an introduction by Elizabeth McLeay, Wellington, Victoria University Press, 1998

Cheyne, Christine, O'Brien, Mike and Belgrave, Michael (eds), *Social Policy in Aotearoa New Zealand: A Critical Introduction*, 3rd edn, Auckland, Oxford University Press, 2005

Churchman, Geoffrey B., *Celluloid Dreams: A Century of Film in New Zealand*, Wellington, IPL Books, 1997

Clark, Margaret (ed.), *For the Record: Lange and the Fourth Labour Government*, Wellington, Dunmore Publishing, 2005

—— (ed.), *The Bolger Years: 1990–1997*, Wellington, Dunmore Press, 2008

Clements, Kevin, *Back from the Brink: The Creation of a Nuclear-Free New Zealand*, Wellington, Allen & Unwin/Port Nicholson Press, 1988

Coddington, Deborah, 'Asian Angst: Is It Time to Send Some Back?', *North & South*, December 2006

Coney, Sandra (ed.), *Standing in the Sunshine: A History of New Zealand Women since They Won the Vote*, Auckland, Penguin Books, 1993

—— (ed.), *Unfinished Business: What Happened to the Cartwright Report?*, Auckland, Women's Health Action, 1993

Copland, R. A., *Frank Sargeson*, Wellington, Oxford University Press, 1976

Corner, Margaret, *No Easy Victory: Towards Equal Pay for Women in the Government Service 1890–1960*, Wellington, New Zealand Public Service Association/Dan Long Trust, 1988

Crowther, Dorothy May, *Street Society*, Christchurch, Department of Psychology and Sociology, University of Canterbury, 1955

Cullen, Michael, 'Reflecting on the Fourth Labour Government', *New Zealand Herald*, 1 May 2004, http://www.nzherald.co.nz/nz/news/article.cfm?c_id=1&objectid=3563691

Cumberland, Kenneth B., 'Living in New Zealand Cities', *The Journal of the New Zealand Institute of Architects*, vol. 22, no. 5, June 1955

Cunningham, Kevin (ed.), *Conversation in a Train and other Critical Writing*, Auckland, Auckland University Press/Oxford University Press, 1983

Curnow, Allen, *Collected Poems, 1933–1973*, Wellington, A. H. & A. W. Reed, 1974

—— *Look Back Harder: Critical Writings 1935–1984*, ed. Peter Simpson, Auckland, Auckland University Press, 1987

——, *Selected Poems*, Auckland, Penguin, 1982

—— (ed.), *A Book of New Zealand Verse 1923–45*, Christchurch, Caxton Press, 1945

—— (ed.), *The Penguin Book of New Zealand Verse*, Auckland, (1960), published under licence from Penguin Books by Blackwood and Janet Paul, 1966

Curnow, Wystan (ed.), *Essays on New Zealand Literature*, Auckland, Heinemann Educational, 1973

Daley, Caroline and Montgomerie, Deborah, *The Gendered Kiwi*, Auckland, Auckland University Press, 1999

Dalley, Bronwyn, *Family Matters: Child Welfare in Twentieth-Century New Zealand*, Auckland, Auckland University Press with the Historical Branch, Department of Internal Affairs, 1998

—— and McLean, Gavin (eds), *Frontier of Dreams: The Story of New Zealand*, Auckland, Hodder Moa, 2005

—— and Tennant, Margaret (eds), *Past Judgment: Social Policy in New Zealand History*, Dunedin, University of Otago Press, 2004

Dalziel, Paul, 'New Zealand's Economic Reforms: An Assessment', *Review of Political Economy*, vol. 14, no. 1, 2002

Dann, Christine, *Up from Under: Women and Liberation in New Zealand 1970–1985*, Wellington, Allen & Unwin/Port Nicholson Press, 1985

Day, Patrick, *The Radio Years: A History of Broadcasting in New Zealand*, vol. 1, Auckland, Auckland University Press in association with the Broadcasting History Trust, 1994

——, *Voice & Vision: The History of Broadcasting in New Zealand*, vol. 2, Auckland, Auckland University Press in association with the Broadcasting History Trust, 2000

de Jong, Piet, *Saturday's Warriors: The Building of a Rugby Stronghold*, Palmerston North, Department of Sociology, Massey University, 1991

Dix, John, *Stranded in Paradise: New Zealand Rock and Roll, 1955 to the Modern Era*, Auckland, Penguin Books, 2005

Douglas, Roger, *There's Got to be a Better Way! A Practical ABC to Solving New Zealand's Major Problems*, Wellington, Fourth Estate Books, 1980

Downes, Peter and Harcourt, Peter, *Voices in the Air: Radio Broadcasting in New Zealand*, Wellington, Methuen, 1976

Duckworth, Marilyn, *Camping on the Faultline: A Memoir*, Auckland, Vintage, 2000

Duff, Alan, *Once Were Warriors*, Auckland, Tandem Press, 1990

——, *Maori: The Crisis and the Challenge*, Auckland, HarperCollins, 1993

Dunn, Michael, *Milan Mrkusich: Paintings 1946–1972, Essay on Development*, Auckland, Auckland City Art Gallery, 1972

——, *A Concise History of New Zealand Painting*, Auckland, David Bateman, 1991

Durie, Mason, *Whaiora: Maori Health Development*, Auckland, Oxford University Press, 1994

——, *Te Mana, Te Kāwanatanga: The Politics of Māori Self-Determination*, Auckland, Oxford University Press, 1998

——, *Mauri Ora: The Dynamics of Māori Health*, Auckland, Oxford University Press, 2001

——, *Ngā Tai Matatū: Tides of Māori Endurance*, Auckland, Oxford University Press, 2005

Dyson, John (with Fitchett, Joseph), *Sink the Rainbow! An Enquiry into the 'Greenpeace Affair'*, Auckland, Reed Methuen, 1986

Easton, Brian, *In Stormy Seas: The Post-War New Zealand Economy*, Dunedin, University of Otago Press, 1997

Edmond, Lauris, *An Autobiography*, Wellington, Bridget Williams Books, 1994

Else, Anne, *Women Together: A History of Women's Organisations in New Zealand*, Daphne Brasell Associates Press with the Historical Branch, Department of Internal Affairs, 1993

Elworthy, Sam, *Ritual Song of Defiance: A Social History of Students at the University of Otago*, Dunedin, Otago University Students' Association, 1990

Evans, B. L., *A History of Agricultural Production and Marketing in New Zealand*, Palmerston North, Keeling and Mundy, 1969

Evans, Lewis, Grimes, Arthur, Wilkinson, Bryce and Treece, David, 'Economic Reform in New Zealand 1984–95: The Pursuit of Efficiency', *Journal of Economic Literature*, vol. 34, December 1996

Evans, Patrick, *The Penguin History of New Zealand Literature*, Auckland, Penguin, 1990

Fairbairn-Dunlop, Peggy and Makisi, Gabrielle, *Making Our Place: Growing up PI in New Zealand*, Palmerston North, Dunmore Press, 2003

Fairburn, A. R. D., 'Are Marching Girls Decadent?', *Here & Now*, July 1952

Ferguson, Gael, *Building the New Zealand Dream*, Palmerston North, Dunmore Press, 1994

Ferrall, Charles, Millar, Paul and Smith, Keren (eds), *East by South: China in the Australasian Imagination*, Wellington, Victoria University Press, 2005

Fiu, Ta'afuli Andrew, *Purple Heart*, Auckland, Random House, 2006

Fyfe, Judith, *War Stories Our Mothers Never Told Us*, Auckland, Penguin, 1995

Gatley, Julia (ed.), *Group Architects: Towards A New Zealand Architecture*, Auckland, Auckland University Press, 2010

Gauld, Robin, *Revolving Doors: New Zealand's Health Reforms*, Wellington, Institute of Policy Studies, Victoria University, 2001

Geare, A. J., *A Review of the New Zealand Employment Contracts Act 1991*, Dunedin, Foundation for Industrial Relations Research and Education NZ, 1993

Gee, Maurice, *Plumb*, Auckland, Penguin, 1978

Geraets, John, 'Landfall Under Brasch: The Humanizing Journey', PhD thesis, English, Auckland, University of Auckland, 1982

Gibson, Campbell James, 'Demographic History of New Zealand', PhD thesis, Demography, University of California, Berkeley, 1971

Gilbert, Jarrod, *Patched: The History of Gangs in New Zealand*, Auckland, Auckland University Press, 2013

Gillies, Angus, *Ngati Dread: Footsteps of Fire*, vol. 1, Auckland, Rogue Monster Books, 2008

Gold, Hyam (ed.), *New Zealand Politics in Perspective*, Auckland, Longman Paul, 1985

Gold, Hyam and Webster, Alan, *New Zealand Values Today: The Popular Report of the November 1989 New Zealand Study of Values*, Palmerston North, Alpha Publications, 1989

Goldsmith, Paul, *Serious Fun: The Life and Times of Alan Gibbs*, Auckland, Random House, 2012

Gooder, Claire, 'A History of Sex Education in New Zealand, 1939–1985', PhD thesis, History, Auckland, University of Auckland, 2010

Gordon, Angus, *In the Shadow of the Cape: A History of the Gordon Family of Clifton*, Waipukurau, CHB Print, 2004

Gould, J. D., *The Rake's Progress? The New Zealand Economy since 1945*, Auckland, Hodder & Stoughton, 1982

Gow, Neil G., 'Farmer Entrepreneurship in New Zealand: Some Observations from Case Studies', 15th Congress — Developing Entrepreneurship Abilities to Feed the World in a Sustainable Way, 14–19 August 2005, Campinas, São Paulo, Brazil

Graham, Douglas, *Trick or Treaty?*, Wellington, Institute of Policy Studies, Victoria University, 1997

Graham, Peter, *So Brilliantly Clever: Parker, Hulme and the Murder that Shocked the World*, Wellington, Awa Press, 2011

Grant, David, *Bulls, Bears and Elephants: A History of the New Zealand Stock Exchange*, Wellington, Victoria University Press, 1997

—— (ed.), *The Big Blue: Snapshots of the 1951 Waterfront Lockout*, Christchurch, Canterbury University Press, 2004

Grant, Ian, *Public Lives: New Zealand's Premiers and Prime Ministers, 1856–2003*, Wellington, New Zealand Cartoon Archive, 2003

Gray, Alison, *The Jones Men: 100 New Zealand Men Talk About Their Lives*, Wellington, Reed, 1983

Green, Paula and Ricketts, Harry (eds), *99 Ways into New Zealand Poetry*, Auckland, Vintage Books, 2010

Green, Terence, 'Maori and Pakeha 1960–2000: The Justice of Positive Discrimination', MA thesis, Political Science, Auckland, University of Auckland, 2002

Greif, Stuart (ed.), *Immigration and National Identity in New Zealand: One People, Two People, Many Peoples?*, Palmerston North, Dunmore Press, 1996

Gustafson, Barry, *The First 50 Years: A History of the New Zealand National Party*, Auckland, Reed Methuen, 1986

——, *His Way: A Biography of Robert Muldoon*, Auckland, Auckland University Press, 2000

——, *Kiwi Keith: A Biography of Keith Holyoake*, Auckland, Auckland University Press, 2007

——, 'No Land is an Island: Twenty-first Century Politics', 2010 Robert Chapman Lecture, University of Auckland

Guy, Laurie, 'The Cinematograph Film Censorship Debate in New Zealand, 1965–1976', MA research essay, History, Auckland, University of Auckland, 1992

——, *Worlds in Collision: The Gay Debate in New Zealand, 1960–1986*, Wellington, Victoria University Press, 2002

——, *Shaping Godzone: Public Issues and Church Voices in New Zealand 1840–2000*, Wellington, Victoria University Press, 2012

Hammonds, Lucy, Jenkins, Douglas Lloyd and Regnault, Claire, *The Dress Circle: New Zealand Fashion Design since 1940*, Auckland, Random House, 2010

Harris, Aroha, *Hīkoi: Forty Years of Māori Protest*, Wellington, Huia, 2004

——, 'Dancing with the State: Maori Creative Energy and the Politics of Integration 1945–1967', PhD thesis, History, Auckland, University of Auckland, 2007

Hartley, Nell, *Goodbye Yesterday*, Auckland, Lasting Memories, 2001

Hawke, G. R., *The Making of New Zealand: An Economic History*, Cambridge, Cambridge University Press, 1985

—— (ed.), *A Modest Safety Net? The Future of the Welfare State*, Wellington, Institute of Policy Studies, Victoria University, 1991

Hawkes, Graham, *On the Road: The Car in New Zealand*, Wellington, Government Print Books, 1990

Hayward, Janine (ed.), *Local Government and the Treaty of Waitangi*, Melbourne/Auckland, Oxford University Press, 2003

Hayward, Margaret, *Diary of the Kirk Years*, Wellington, A. H. & A.W. Reed, 1981

Heal, Sarah, 'The Struggle For and Against the Employment Contracts Act, 1987–1991', MA thesis, Political Studies, Dunedin, University of Otago, 1994

Hensley, Gerald, *Friendly Fire: Nuclear Politics and the Collapse of ANZUS, 1984–1987*, Auckland, Auckland University Press, 2013

Herbert, Averil, *Te Moana: Nga Puna Waihanga Annual Hui: Te Rua Tekau Tau, 1973–1993*, Whanganui, Nga Puna Waihanga, 1993

Herd, Joyce, *Cracks in a Glass Ceiling: New Zealand Women 1975–2004*, Dunedin, New Zealand Federation of Graduate Women, 2005

Hill, Richard S., *Anti-Treatyism and Anti-Scholarship*, TOWRU Occasional Papers No. 8, 2002

——, *Maori and the State: Crown–Maori Relations in New Zealand/Aotearoa, 1950–2000*, Wellington, Victoria University Press, 2009

Ho, Elsie and Bedford, Richard, 'The Asian Crisis and Migrant Entrepreneurs in New Zealand: Some Reactions and Reflections', *New Zealand Population Review*, vol. 24, 1998

Holcroft, M. H., *Encircling Seas*, Christchurch, Caxton Press, 1946

Holland, Martin and Boston, Jonathan (eds), *The Fourth Labour Government: Politics and Policy in New Zealand*, 2nd edn, Oxford, Oxford University Press, 1990

Horrocks, Roger and Perry, Nick (eds), *Television in New Zealand: Programming the Nation*, Auckland, Oxford University Press, 2000

Howie, Craig and Ramsay, Claire, *The Reforms, Riding the Rollercoaster: A Summary of New Zealand's Economic and Social Reforms, 1984–1998*, Dunedin, Otago Daily Times, 1998

Humpage, Louise, 'Working For New Zealand: A Background Paper on Recent and Proposed Welfare Reforms in New Zealand', Auckland, Public Policy Group, University of Auckland, March 2007, http://www.artsfaculty.auckland.ac.nz/images/cms/files/LHumpage/Humpage%20 Welfare%20forum%20background%20paper%20Mar%2007.pdf

Hunn, Jack K., 'Report on the Department of Maori Affairs: With Statistical Supplement', Wellington, *Appendices to the Journals of the House of Representatives*, 1961, vol. 2, G-10

Hunt, Graeme, *Hustlers, Rogues & Bubble Boys: White-Collar Mischief in New Zealand*, Auckland, Reed, 2001

Hunter, Ian and Morrow, Diana (eds), *City of Enterprise: Perspectives on Auckland Business History*, Auckland, Auckland University Press, 2006

Hutching, Megan, *Long Journey for Sevenpence: Assisted Immigration to New Zealand from the United Kingdom 1947–1975*, Wellington, Victoria University Press, 1999

Hutchins, Graham, *The Swinging Sixties: When New Zealand Changed Forever*, Auckland, HarperCollins, 2008

Hyman, Prue, 'Trends in Female Labour Force Participation in New Zealand since 1945', *New Zealand Economic Papers*, vol. 12, 1978

Ip, Manying, *The Dragon and the Taniwha: Māori and Chinese in New Zealand*, Auckland, Auckland University Press, 2009

——, 'Here, There, and Back Again: A New Zealand Case Study of Chinese Circulatory Trans-migration', January 2012, http://www.migrationinformation.org/Feature/display.cfm?id=878

—— (ed.), *Unfolding History, Evolving Identity: The Chinese in New Zealand*, Auckland, Auckland University Press, 2003

Iversen, Maxine Anne, 'Inextricable Links: Pakeha Perceptions of Identity and their Relationships to Britain at the Time of the Statute of Westminster', MA thesis, History, Auckland, University of Auckland, 1996

James, Colin, *Quiet Revolution: Turbulence and Transition in Contemporary New Zealand*, Wellington, Allen & Unwin/Port Nicholson Press, 1986

——, *New Territory: The Transformation of New Zealand 1984–92*, Wellington, Bridget Williams Books, 1992

—— and McRobie, Alan, *Turning Point: The 1993 Election and Beyond*, Wellington, Bridget Williams Books, 1993

Janiewski, Dolores and Morris, Paul, *New Rights, New Zealand: Myths, Moralities and Markets*, Auckland, Auckland University Press, 2005

Jesson, Bruce, *To Build a Nation: Collected Writings 1975–1999*, ed. Andrew Sharp, Auckland, Penguin, 2005

Jesson, Bruce, Ryan, Allanah and Spoonley, Paul (eds), *Revival of the Right: New Zealand Politics in the 1980s*, Auckland, Heinemann Reed, 1988

Jing Xue, Wardlow, Friesen and Sullivan, David, 'Diversity in Chinese Auckland: Hypothesising Multiple Ethnoburbs', *Population, Space and Place*, vol. 18, issue 5, 2012, published online 26 August 2011 in Wiley Online Library, http://onlinelibrary.wiley.com/doi/10.1002/psp.688/pdf

Johnson, Miranda, '"Land of the Wrong White Crowd": Pakeha Anti-racist Organisations and Identity Politics in Auckland, 1964–1981', MA thesis, History, Auckland, University of Auckland, 2002

——, '"The Land of the Wrong White Crowd": Anti-racist Organizations and Pakeha Identity Politics in the 1970s', *New Zealand Journal of History*, vol. 39, no. 2, 2005

Johnstone, Ian, *Stand and Deliver*, Whatamango Bay, Cape Catley, 1998

Joiner, Margaret Kiri, 'The Life-cycle of a Small Political Party: The Case of New Zealand First', MA thesis, Political Science, Auckland, University of Auckland, 2010

Judt, Tony, *Postwar: A History of Europe since 1945*, London, Vintage Books, 2010

Kay, Robin (ed.), *Documents on New Zealand External Relations, Volume III, The Anzus Pact and the Treaty of Peace with Japan*, Wellington, Historical Publications Branch, Department of Internal Affairs, V. R. Ward, Government Printer, 1985

Kearsley, Geoff and Fitzharris, Blair, *Glimpses of a Gaian World: Essays in Honour of Peter Holland*, Dunedin, University of Otago, 2004

Kedgley, Sue and Varnham, Mary (eds), *Heading Nowhere in a Navy Blue Suit*, Wellington, Daphne Brasell Associates, 1993

Keith, Hamish and Ridge, Phillip, *A Lovely Day Tomorrow: New Zealand in the 1940s*, Auckland, Random Century, 1991

Kelsey, Jane, *A Question of Honour? Labour and the Treaty 1984–1989*, Wellington, Allen & Unwin, 1990

——, *The New Zealand Experiment: A World Model for Structural Adjustment?*, Auckland, Auckland University Press, 1995

Kennaway, Richard, *New Zealand Foreign Policy, 1951–1971*, Wellington, Hicks Smith, 1972

King, Michael, *Being Pakeha: An Encounter with New Zealand and the Maori Renaissance*, Auckland, Hodder & Stoughton, 1985

——, *Whina: A Biography of Whina Cooper*, Auckland, Penguin Books, 1991

——, *Frank Sargeson: A Life*, Auckland, Viking, 1995

——, *Being Pakeha Now: Reflections and Recollections of a White Native*, Auckland, Penguin, 1999

Knox, Heather, 'Feminism, Femininity and Motherhood in Post-World War II New Zealand', MA thesis, History, Palmerston North, Massey University, 1995

Laquian, Eleanor, Laquian, Aprodicio and McGee, Terry (eds), *The Silent Debate: Asian Immigration and Racism in Canada*, Vancouver, Institute of Asian Research, 1998

Larkin, T. C. (ed.), *New Zealand's External Relations*, Wellington, New Zealand Institute of Public Administration, 1962

Laurie, Alison J. and Evans, Linda (eds), *Outlines: Lesbian and Gay Histories of Aotearoa*, Wellington, Lesbian and Gay Archives New Zealand (LAGANZ), 2005

Lealand, Geoff, *A Foreign Egg in Our Nest? American Culture in New Zealand*, Wellington, Victoria University Press, 1988

Lipson, Leslie, *The Politics of Equality: New Zealand's Adventures in Democracy*, Chicago, University of Chicago Press, 1948

Liu, James H., McCreanor, Tim, McIntosh Tracey and Teaiwa, Teresia (eds), *New Zealand Identities: Departures and Destinations*, Wellington, Victoria University Press, 2005

Lloyd Jenkins, Douglas, *At Home: A Century of New Zealand Design*, Auckland, Godwit, 2004

—— (ed.), *New Dreamland: Writing New Zealand Architecture*, Auckland, Godwit, 2005

Locke, Elsie, *Peace People: A History of Peace Activities in New Zealand*, Christchurch, Hazard Press, 1992

Lodge, Juliet, *The European Community and New Zealand*, London, Frances Pinter, 1982

Loto, Robert et al., 'Pasifika in the News: The Portrayal of Pacific Peoples in the New Zealand Press', *Journal of Community and Applied Social Psychology*, vol. 16, issue 2, 2006

Lund, Peter, '"Independence Plus": New Zealand and the Commonwealth 1945–1950', MA thesis, History, Christchurch, University of Canterbury, 1985

Lunt, Neil, O'Brien Mike and Stephens, Robert, *New Zealand, New Welfare: New Developments in Welfare and Work*, Australia, Cengage Learning, 2008

McClure, Margaret, *A Civilised Community: A History of Social Security in New Zealand 1898–1998*, Auckland, Auckland University Press in association with the Historical Branch, Department of Internal Affairs, 1998

McClure, Margaret, *The Wonder Country: Making New Zealand Tourism*, Auckland, Auckland University Press, 2004

McGibbon, Ian C., 'The Defence of New Zealand 1945–1957', in Sir Alister McIntosh et al., *New Zealand in World Affairs: Volume I, 1945–1957*, Wellington, New Zealand Institute of International Affairs, 1977

——, 'New Zealand's Intervention in the Korean War, June–July 1950', *The International History Review*, vol. 11, no. 2, May 1989

——, *New Zealand and the Korean War*, Auckland, Oxford University Press, 1992

—— (ed.), *Undiplomatic Dialogue: Letters between Carl Berendsen and Alister McIntosh, 1943–1953*, Auckland, Auckland University Press in association with the Ministry of Foreign Affairs and Trade, Historical Branch, Department of Internal Affairs, 1993

McGill, David, *Kiwi Baby Boomers: Growing Up in New Zealand in the 40s, 50s and 60s*, Lower Hutt, Mills Publications, 1989

McIntyre, W. David, 'The Future of the New Zealand System of Alliances', *Landfall*, vol. 21, no. 4, December 1967

—— and Gardner, W. J. (eds), *Speeches and Documents on New Zealand History*, Oxford, Clarendon Press, 1971

Mackay, David, McKinnon, Malcolm, McPhee, Peter and Phillips, Jock (eds), 'Counting the Cost: The 1981 Springbok Tour in Wellington', Wellington, History Department, Victoria University, Occasional Papers No. 1, 1982

McKay, Frank, *James K. Baxter as Critic: A Selection from his Literary Criticism*, Auckland, Heinemann Educational, 1978

McKinnon, Malcolm, *Independence and Foreign Policy: New Zealand in the World since 1935*, Auckland, Auckland University Press, 1993

——, *Immigrants and Citizens: New Zealanders and Asian Immigration in Historical Context*, Wellington, Institute of Policy Studies, Victoria University, 1996

—— (ed.), *New Zealand in World Affairs: Volume II, 1957–1972*, Wellington, New Zealand Institute of International Affairs, 1991

McLauchlan, Gordon, *The Passionless People*, Auckland, Cassell, 1976

McLaughlan, Mark, 'What's So Awful about the Employment Contracts Act?', *North & South*, February 1996

McLean, Denis, *The Prickly Pair: Making Nationalism in Australia and New Zealand*, Dunedin, Otago University Press, 2003

McLeay, Elizabeth (ed.), *New Zealand Politics and Social Patterns: Selected Works by Robert Chapman*, Wellington, Victoria University Press, 1999

McLeod, A. L. (ed.), *The Pattern of New Zealand Culture*, New York, Cornell University Press, 1968

McLeod, Rosemary, 'Bleeding White, Middle Class and Carrying the Can', *North & South*, November 1988

McLintock, A. H., *An Encyclopaedia of New Zealand*, Wellington, Government Printer, 1966

McLoughlin, David, 'The Welfare Burden', *North & South*, June 1991

——, 'What Have We Got to Lose?', *North & South*, October 1996

Macpherson, Cluny, Spoonley, Paul and Anae, Melani, *Tangata O Te Moana Nui: The Evolving Identities of Pacific Peoples in Aotearoa/New Zealand*, Palmerston North, Dunmore Press, 2001

McPherson, Kate, 'Food Insecurity and the Food Bank Industry: Political, Individual and Environmental Factors Contributing to Food Bank use in Christchurch', MA thesis, Geography, Christchurch, University of Canterbury, 2006

Mackwell, Suzanne, 'Radical Politics and Ideology in the Coming of Post-Industrial Society: The Values Party in Perspective', MA thesis, Political Science, Christchurch, University of Canterbury, 1977

Maharey, Steve, 'Benefits and Super Rise, Work-for-the-dole Abolished', 1 April 2001, http://www.beehive.govt.nz/node/10143

Mallon, Sean and Pereira, Pandora Fulimalo (eds), *Pacific Art Niu Sila: The Pacific Dimension of Contemporary New Zealand Art*, Wellington, Te Papa Press, 2002

Mallon, Sean, Mahina-Tuai, Kolokesa and Salesa, Damon (eds), *Tangata Ole Moana: New Zealand and the People of the Pacific*, Wellington, Te Papa Press, 2012

Manhire, Bill, *Maurice Gee*, Auckland, Oxford University Press, 1986

Manhire, Bill (ed.), *Selected Poems: Denis Glover*, Wellington, Victoria University Press, 1995

Manning, A. E., *The Bodgie: A Study in Abnormal Psychology*, Wellington, Reed, 1958

Manning, Joanna (ed.), *The Cartwright Papers: Essays on the Cervical Cancer Inquiry 1987–88*, Wellington, Bridget Williams Books, 2009

Maori Economic Conference Proceedings, Wellington, 1984

Marr, Andrew, *A History of Modern Britain*, London, Pan Books, 2007

Martens, Emiel, *Once Were Warriors, The Aftermath: The Controversy of OWW in Aotearoa New Zealand*, Amsterdam, Aksant, 2007

May, Helen, *Minding Children, Managing Men: Conflict and Compromise in the Lives of Postwar Pakeha Women*, Wellington, Bridget Williams Books, 1992

——, *Politics in the Playground: The World of Early Childhood in New Zealand*, Wellington, Bridget Williams Books and the New Zealand Council for Educational Research, 2001

Mazengarb, O. C., *Report of the Special Committee on Moral Delinquency in Children and Adolescents*, Wellington, Government Print, 1954

Mein Smith, Philippa, Hempenstall, Peter and Goldfinch Shaun with McMillan, Stuart and Baird, Rosemary, *Remaking the Tasman World*, Christchurch, Canterbury University Press, 2008

Melbourne, Hineani (ed.), *Maori Sovereignty: The Maori Perspective*, Hodder Moa Beckett, Auckland, 1995

Metge, Joan, *A New Maori Migration: Rural and Urban Relations in Northern New Zealand*, London, Athlone Press, 1964

——, *The Maoris of New Zealand*, revised edn, London, Routledge & Kegan Paul, 1976

——, *Tuamaka: The Challenge of Difference in Aotearoa New Zealand*, Auckland, Auckland University Press, 2010

Meurant, Ross, *The Red Squad Story*, Auckland, Harland Publishing, 1982

Middleton, Sue (ed.), *Women and Education in Aotearoa New Zealand*, Wellington, Allen & Unwin/ Port Nicholson Press, 1988

Millar, Paul, *No Fretful Sleeper: A Life of Bill Pearson*, Auckland, Auckland University Press, 2010

Millen, Julia, *Ronald Hugh Morrieson*, Auckland, David Ling, 1996

Miller, Raymond (ed.), *New Zealand Government and Politics*, 3rd edn, Auckland, Oxford University Press, 2003; 4th edn, Melbourne, Oxford University Press, 2006

Milner, Ian F. G., *New Zealand's Interests and Policies in the Far East*, New York, Institute of Pacific Relations, 1939

Ministry of Social Development, 'From Wannabes to Youth Offenders: Youth Gangs in Counties Manukau — Research Report', Auckland, Centre for Social Research and Evaluation Te Pokapū Rangahau Arotake Hapori, Auckland, September 2006, http://www.msd.govt.nz/ about-msd-and-our-work/publications-resources/research/youth-gangs-counties-manukau/ index.html

Mirams, Gordon, *Speaking Candidly: Films and People in New Zealand*, Hamilton, Paul's Book Arcade, 1945

Mitchell, Austin, *The Half-Gallon Quarter-Acre Pavlova Paradise*, Christchurch, Whitcombe & Tombs, 1972

Mitchell, David and Chaplin, Gillian, *The Elegant Shed: New Zealand Architecture since 1945*, Auckland, Oxford University Press, 1984

Mitchell, Robin, *The Treaty & the Act: The Treaty of Waitangi (1840) and the Treaty of Waitangi Act (1975)*, Christchurch, Cadsonbury Publications, 1990

Montgomery, Deborah, *The Women's War: New Zealand Women 1939–1945*, Auckland, Auckland University Press, 2001

Moore, Keith, *Bodgies, Widgies and Moral Panic in Australia 1955–1959*, Paper presented to the Social Change in the 21st Century Conference, Centre for Social Change Research, Queensland University of Technology, 29 October 2004, http://eprints.qut.edu.au/633/1/moore_keith.pdf

Morrison, Andrew, 'The Employment Contracts Act and its Economic Impact', Parliamentary Library Background Paper No. 16, November 1996

Muldoon, R. D., *The Rise and Fall of a Young Turk*, Wellington, A. H. & A. W. Reed, 1974

Mulgan, John, *Report on Experience*, London, Oxford University Press, 1947

Nauright, John (ed.), *Sport, Power and Society in New Zealand: Historical and Contemporary Perspectives*, Sydney, Australian Society for Sports History, 1995

Nauright, John and Broomhall, Jayne, 'A Woman's Game: The Development of Netball and a Female Sporting Culture in New Zealand, 1906–70', *The International Journal of the History of Sport*, vol. 2, no. 3, December 1994

Neill, Karen and Shanahan, M. W. (eds), *The Great New Zealand Radio Experiment*, Southbank, Victoria, Thomson/Dunmore Press, 2004

Nelson, Claire Loftus, *Long Time Passing: New Zealand Memories of the Vietnam War*, Wellington, National Radio, 1990

Newland, Olly, *Lost Property: The Crash of 1987 . . . and the Aftershock*, Auckland, HarperCollins, 1994

Newnham, Tom, *By Batons and Barbed Wire: A Response to the 1981 Springbok Tour of New Zealand*, Auckland, Real Pictures Ltd and Tom Newnham, 1981

Nixon, Chris and Yeabsley, John, *New Zealand's Trade Policy Odyssey: Ottawa, via Marrakech, and On*, Wellington, New Zealand Institute of Economic Research, 2002

Nolan, Melanie, *Breadwinning: New Zealand Women and the State*, Christchurch, Canterbury University Press, 2000

——, 'A Subversive State? Domesticity in Dispute in 1950s New Zealand', *Journal of Family History*, vol. 27, no. 1, January 2002

O'Brien, Gregory, *A Nest of Singing Birds: 100 Years of the New Zealand School Journal*, Wellington, Learning Media Limited, 2007

O'Brien, Michael, *Poverty, Policy and the State: Social Security Reform in New Zealand*, Bristol, The Policy Press, 2008

O'Hare, Noel, 'Fighting for their Health: Small-town Hospital Services Are Back under the Knife', *New Zealand Listener*, 19 July 1994

O'Malley, Vincent, Stirling, Bruce and Penetito, Wally (eds), *The Treaty of Waitangi Companion*, Auckland, Auckland University Press, 2010

OECD, *Employment Outlook 2005: How Does France Compare?*, http://www.oecd.org/els/employmentpoliciesanddata/35050668.pdf

Olssen, Eric, 'The Origins of Anzus Reconsidered', *Historical and Political Studies*, vol. 1, no. 2, December 1970

Ormsby, Suzanne, 'Te Reo Puoro Maori Mai I Mua Tae Noa Mai Ki Inaianei: The Voice of Maori Music, Past, Present and Future: Maori Musicians of the 1960s', MA thesis, Education, Auckland, University of Auckland, 1996

Papps, Elaine and Ramsden, Irihapeti, 'Cultural Safety in Nursing: The New Zealand Experience', *International Journal for Quality in Health Care*, vol. 8, no. 5, 1996

Parr, Alison, *Silent Casualties: New Zealand's Unspoken Legacy of the Second World War*, Auckland, Tandem Press, 1995

——, *Home: Civilian New Zealanders Remember the Second World War*, Auckland, Penguin, 2010

Patterson, Brad (ed.), *Sport, Society and Culture in New Zealand*, Wellington, Stout Research Centre, c. 1999

Pawson, Eric and Brooking Tom (eds), *Environmental Histories of New Zealand*, Auckland, Oxford University Press, 2002

Pearson, Bill, *Fretful Sleepers and Other Essays*, London, Heinemann Educational, 1974

Pearson, David, *Johnsonville: Continuity and Change in a New Zealand Township*, Australia, George Allen & Unwin, 1980

Peat, Neville, *Manapouri Saved! New Zealand's First Great Conservation Success Story*, Dunedin, Guardians of Lakes Manapouri, Monowai and Te Anau, 1994

Perry, Paul and Webster, Alan, *New Zealand Politics at the Turn of the Millennium: Attitudes and Values about Politics and Government, The Political Report of the Third New Zealand Study of Values*, Auckland, Alpha Publications, 1999

Petrie, Duncan and Stuart, Duncan, *A Coming of Age: Thirty Years of New Zealand Film*, Auckland, Random House, 2008

Phillips, Jock, *A Man's Country? The Image of the Pakeha Male: A History*, Auckland, Penguin Books, 1987

——, *Royal Summer: The Visit of Queen Elizabeth II and Prince Philip to New Zealand, 1953–54*, Wellington, Historical Branch, Department of Internal Affairs and Daphne Brasell Associates, 1993

Pio, Edwina, *Longing & Belonging: Asian, Middle Eastern, Latin American and African Peoples in New Zealand*, Wellington, Dunmore Publishing, 2010

Pomare, Eru W., 'Maori Standards of Health: A Study of the 20-year Period 1955–1975', Wellington, Medical Research Council of New Zealand, 1980

Pound, Francis, *The Space Between: Pakeha Use of Maori Motifs in Modernist New Zealand Art*, Auckland, Workshop Press, 1994

——, *The Invention of New Zealand: Art & National Identity 1930–1970*, Auckland, Auckland University Press, 2009

Prebble, Richard, *I've Been Thinking*, Auckland, Sentra, 1996

Presbyterian Church of New Zealand Maori Synod, *A Maori View of the Hunn Report*, Christchurch, 1961

Price, Richard T., 'The Politics of Modern History-making: The 1990s Negotiations of the Ngai Tahu Tribe with the Crown to Achieve a Treaty of Waitangi Claims Settlement', Christchurch, Macmillan Brown Centre for Pacific Studies, University of Canterbury, Macmillan Brown Working Paper Series No. 7, 2001

Priestley, Rebecca, *Mad on Radium: New Zealand in the Atomic Age*, Auckland, Auckland University Press, 2012

'Progress towards Closing Social and Economic Gaps between Maori and Non-Maori: A Report to the Minister of Maori Affairs', Wellington, Te Puni Kokiri (Ministry of Maori Development), 1998

'Puao-Te Ata-Tu (Day Break): The Report of the Ministerial Advisory Committee on a Maori Perspective for the Department of Social Welfare', Wellington, The Committee, 1 July 1986

Rabel, Roberto, *New Zealand and the Vietnam War: Politics and Diplomacy*, Auckland University Press, Auckland, 2005

—— (ed.), *The American Century? In Retrospect and Prospect*, Westport, Connecticut, Praeger, 2002

Race Relations Conciliator, *Race Against Time*, Wellington, Human Rights Commission, 1982

Ramsden, Irihapeti and Spoonley, Paul, 'The Cultural Safety Debate in Nursing Education in Aotearoa', *New Zealand Annual Review of Education/Te Arotake a Tau o Te Ao o te Mataurangi i Aotearoa*, vol. 3, 1993

Read, Peter J., 'Blue Suede Gumboots? The Impact of Popular Culture on New Zealand in the 1950s', MA thesis, History, Dunedin, University of Otago, 1990

Reid, J. C., *Creative Writing in New Zealand: A Brief Critical History*, Auckland, printed for the author by Whitcombe & Tombs, 1946

'Report of the Committee of Inquiry into Procedures Used in Certain Psychiatric Hospitals in Relation to Admission, Discharge or Release on Leave of Certain Classes of Patients', Wellington, The Committee, August 1988

'Report of the Labour Committee on the Inquiry into the Effects of the Employment Contracts Act 1991 on the New Zealand Labour Market', Second Session, 43rd Parliament, Mr Max Bradford, Chairman, *Appendices to the Journals of the House of Representatives*, vol. 24, 1991–1993, I.9D, item 2.1, 'Effect of the Act on Workplace Relations'

Rice, Geoffrey W. (ed.), *The Oxford History of New Zealand*, 2nd edn, Auckland, Oxford University Press, 1992

Richards, Trevor, *Dancing on Our Bones: New Zealand, South Africa, Rugby and Racism*, Wellington, Bridget Williams Books, 1999

Richardson, Ruth, *Making a Difference*, Christchurch, Shoal Bay Press, 1995

Ritchie, Megan, 'Shaken, But Not Stirred? Youth Cultures in 1950s Auckland', MA thesis, History, Auckland, University of Auckland, 1997

Robb, Murray and Howorth, Hilary, *New Zealand Recreation Survey: Preliminary Report*, Wellington, New Zealand Council for Recreation and Sport, 1977

Robinson, Roger and Wattie, Nelson (eds), *The Oxford Companion to New Zealand Literature*, Auckland, Oxford University Press, 1998

Roper, Brian S., *Prosperity for All? Economic, Social and Political Change in New Zealand since 1935*, Southbank, Victoria, Thomson/Dunmore Press, 2005

Ross, Ruth, 'Te Tiriti o Waitangi, Texts and Translations', *New Zealand Journal of History*, vol. 6, no. 2, 1972

Rowland, Perrin, *A History of the Restaurant in New Zealand*, Auckland, Auckland University Press, 2010

Russell, Marcia, *Revolution: New Zealand from Fortress to Free Market*, Auckland, Hodder Moa Beckett, 1996

Sargisson, Lucy and Sargent, Lymon Tower, *Living in Utopia: New Zealand's Intentional Communities*, Aldershot, Ashgate Publishing, 2004

Schrader, Ben, *We Call It Home: A History of State Housing in New Zealand*, Auckland, Reed, 2005

Scott, Dick, *151 Days: History of the Great Waterfront Lockout and Supporting Strikes, February 15–July 15, 1951*, Auckland, Southern Cross Books, 1954

Scott, Stuart C., *Travesty after Travesty*, Christchurch, Certes Press, 1996

Searle, Graham, *Rush to Destruction*, Wellington, A. H. & A. W. Reed, 1975

Shadbolt, Tim, *Bullshit & Jellybeans*, Wellington, Alister Taylor Publications, 1971

——, *A Mayor of Two Cities*, Auckland, Hodder Moa, 2008

Sharp, Andrew, *Justice and the Māori, Māori Claims in New Zealand Political Argument in the 1980s*, Auckland, Oxford University Press, 1990

Shaw, Peter, *A History of New Zealand Architecture*, 2nd edn, Auckland, Hodder Moa Beckett, 1997

Shaw, Richard and Eichbaum, Chris, *Public Policy in New Zealand: Institutions, Processes and Outcomes*, 2nd edn, Auckland, Pearson Education, 2008

Shieff, Sarah (ed.), *Letters of Frank Sargeson*, Auckland, Vintage/Random House, 2012

Shipley, Jenny with Upton, Simon, Smith, Lockwood and Luxton, John, 'Social Assistance: Welfare that Works: A Statement of Government Policy on Social Assistance', Wellington, Department of Social Welfare, 1991

Shuker, Roy, Openshaw, Roger and Soler, Janet (eds), *Youth, Media and Moral Panic in New Zealand: From Hooligans to Video Nasties*, Palmerston North, Department of Education, Massey University, c. 1990

Simpson, Peter, *New Zealand Writers and their Work: Ronald Hugh Morrieson*, Auckland, Oxford University Press, 1982

Sinclair, Keith, 'Memories of T. H. Scott (1918–60)', *Landfall*, vol. 14, no. 2, June 1960

——, *Walter Nash*, Auckland, Auckland University Press and Oxford University Press, 1976

——, *Halfway Round the Harbour: An Autobiography*, Auckland, Penguin Books, 1993

——, *A History of New Zealand*, Auckland, Penguin, revised edn, 2000

—— (ed.), *Distance Looks Our Way: The Effects of Remoteness on New Zealand*, Auckland, Paul's Book Arcade for the University of Auckland, 1961

—— (ed.), *The Oxford Illustrated History of New Zealand*, 2nd edn, Auckland, Oxford University Press, 1997; new edn, 1999

Smith, Anthony L. (ed.), *Southeast Asia and New Zealand: A History of Regional and Bilateral Relations*, Wellington, New Zealand Institute of International Affairs and Victoria University Press, 2005

Smith, Paul, *Twist and Shout: New Zealand in the 1960s*, Auckland, Random House, 1991

Smithyman, Kendrick, *A Way of Saying: A Study of New Zealand Poetry*, Auckland, Collins, 1965

Soler, Janet Madeline, 'Drifting towards Moral Chaos: The 1954 Mazengarb Report: A Moral Panic over Juvenile Immorality', MPhil thesis, Education, Palmerston North, Massey University, 1988

Somerset, H. C. D., *Littledene: Patterns of Change*, Wellington, New Zealand Council for Educational Research, 1974

Spoonley, Paul, *Racism and Ethnicity*, Auckland, Oxford University Press, 1988

Spoonley, Paul and Bedford, Richard, *Welcome to Our World? Immigration and the Reshaping of New Zealand*, Auckland, Dunmore Publishing, 2012

Spoonley, Paul and Hirsch, Walter (eds), *Between the Lines: Racism and the New Zealand Media*, Auckland, Heinemann Reid, 1990

Spoonley, Paul, Macpherson, Cluny and Pearson, David (eds), *Tangata Tangata: The Changing Ethnic Contours of New Zealand*, Southbank, Victoria, Thomson/Dunmore Press, 2004

Spoonley, Paul and Trlin, Andrew, *Immigration, Immigrants and the Media: Making Sense of Multi-cultural New Zealand*, Palmerston North, New Settlers Programme, Massey University, 2004

St John, Susan and Rankin, Keith, 'Escaping the Welfare Mess?', Auckland, Department of Economics, Auckland Business School, Working Paper No. 267, revised December 2009, http://pol-econ.com/EWM/EscapingWelfareMessWP267.pdf

Stachurski, Christina, *Reading Pakeha? Fiction and Identity in Aotearoa New Zealand*, New York, Rodopi, 2009

Stanley, Mary, *Starveling Year and Other Poems*, Auckland, Auckland University Press, 1994

Statistics New Zealand, 'Pacific Progress: A Report on the Economic Status of Pacific Peoples in New Zealand', 2002, http://www.stats.govt.nz/browse_for_stats/people_and_communities/pacific_peoples/pacific-progress.aspx

Stead, C. K., *In the Glass Case: Essays on New Zealand Literature*, Auckland, Auckland University Press/Oxford University Press, 1981

——, 'The New Victorians', *Metro*, February 1989

——, *South-West of Eden, A Memoir 1932–1956*, Auckland, Auckland University Press, 2010

Stenson, Michael, 'The Origins and Significance of "Forward Defence" in Asia', in Sir Alister McIntosh et al., *New Zealand in World Affairs: Volume I, 1945–1957*, Wellington, New Zealand Institute of International Affairs, 1977

Stevens, Joan, *The New Zealand Novel, 1860–1965*, 2nd edn, Wellington, A. H. & A. W. Reed, 1966

Stokes, Evelyn, *History of Tauranga County*, Palmerston North, Dunmore Press, 1980

Stratton, Jon, 'Bodgies and Widgies — Youth Cultures in the 1950s', *Journal of Australian Studies*, vol. 8, no. 15, 1984

Sturm, Terry (ed.), *The Oxford History of New Zealand Literature in English*, 2nd edn, Auckland, Oxford University Press, 1998

—— (ed.), *Whim Wham's New Zealand: The Best of Whim Wham 1937–1988*, Auckland, Vintage, 2005

Szabo, Michael, *Making Waves: The Greenpeace New Zealand Story*, Auckland, Greenpeace New Zealand, 1991

Tauroa, Hiwi, *Healing the Breach: One Maori's Perspective on the Treaty of Waitangi*, Auckland, Collins, 1989

Taylor, Nancy M., *The New Zealand People at War: The Home Front, Official History of New Zealand in the Second World War, 1939–1945*, Wellington, Historical Publications Branch, Department of Internal Affairs, Government Printer, 1986

Templeton, Malcolm, *Ties of Blood and Empire: New Zealand's Involvement in Middle East Defence and the Suez Crisis 1947–57*, Auckland, Auckland University Press in association with the New Zealand Institute of International Affairs, 1994

—— (ed.), *An Eye, An Ear, and a Voice: 50 Years in New Zealand's External Relations 1943–1993*, Wellington, Ministry of Foreign Affairs and Trade, 1993

The April Report: Report of the Royal Commission on Social Policy, Wellington, The Commission, 1988, vol. 1

The Police and the 1981 Tour, Wellington, History Department, Victoria University, Occasional Papers No. 2, 1985

Thomson, K. W. and Trlin, A. D. (eds), *Immigrants in New Zealand*, Palmerston North, Massey University, 1970

Thorns, David and Sedgwick, Charles, *Understanding Aotearoa/New Zealand: Historical Statistics*, Palmerston North, Dunmore Press, 1997

'Tomorrow's Schools', http://schools.reap.org.nz/tanui/Jubileepages/Tomorrows%20Schools.htm

Tomory, P. A., 'Looking at Art in New Zealand', *Landfall*, vol. 12, no. 2, June 1958

Trlin, Andrew and Spoonley, Paul (eds), *New Zealand and International Migration: A Digest and Bibliography, Number 2*, Palmerston North, Massey University, 1992

Trlin, Andrew, Spoonley, Paul and Watts, Noel (eds), *New Zealand and International Migration: A Digest and Bibliography*, Number 4, Palmerston North, Massey University, 2005

Trlin, Andrew, Spoonley, Paul and Bedford, Richard (eds), *New Zealand and International Migration: A Digest and Bibliography, Number 5*, Palmerston North, Massey University, 2010

Trotter, Ann, 'New Zealand in World Affairs: Sir Carl Berendsen in Washington, 1944–1952', *The International History Review*, vol. 12, no. 3, August 1990

—— (ed.), *New Zealand, Canada and the United States: The Papers of the Twenty-second Foreign Policy School*, Dunedin, University of Otago, University Extension, 1987

—— (ed.), *Fifty Years of New Zealand Foreign Policy Making: Papers from the Twenty-eighth Foreign Policy School, 1993*, Dunedin, University of Otago Press, 1993

Tuwhare, Hone, *Small Holes in the Silence: Collected Works*, Auckland, Random House, 2011

Vaughn, Graham (ed.), *Racial Issues in New Zealand*, Auckland, Akarana Press, 1972

Vertinsky, Patricia and Bale, John (eds), *Sites of Sport: Space, Place, Experience*, London, Routledge, 2004

Veysey, Alex, *Colin Meads: All Black*, Auckland, Collins, 1974

Vitalis, Vangelis, 'Trade, Innovation and Growth: The Case of the New Zealand Agriculture Sector', Paper presented to the OECD Global Trade Forum on Trade, Innovation and Growth, 14–15 October 2007, Paris, OECD

Voci, Paola and Leckie, Jacqueline (eds), *Localizing Asia in Aotearoa*, Wellington, Dunmore Publishing, 2011

Vowles, Jack et al., *Towards Consensus? The 1993 General Election and Referendum in New Zealand and the Transition to Proportional Representation*, Auckland, Auckland University Press, 1995

—— et al., *Proportional Representation on Trial: The 1999 New Zealand General Election and the Fate of MMP*, Auckland, Auckland University Press, 2002

Waitangi Tribunal, *Report of the Waitangi Tribunal on the Orakei Claim*, Wai-9, (*Orakei Report*)

Walker, Geoff and Beach Peter (eds), *56 Days: A History of the Anti-Tour Movement in Wellington*, Wellington, Lindsay Wright on behalf of Citizens Opposed to the Springbok Tour (COST), 1982

Walker, Ranginui, 'The Social Adjustment of the Maori to Urban Living in Auckland', PhD thesis, Anthropology, Auckland, University of Auckland, 1970

——, *Ka Whawhai Tonu Matou: Struggle Without End*, Auckland, Penguin Books, 1990

Wall, Carroll, 'Te Pakeha: The Search for White Identity', *Metro*, November 1986

Ward, Alan, *An Unsettled History: Treaty Claims in New Zealand Today*, Wellington, Bridget Williams Books, 1999

Wards, Ian (ed.), *Thirteen Facets: Essays to Celebrate the Silver Jubilee of Queen Elizabeth the Second, 1952–1977*, Wellington, E. C. Keating, Government Printer, 1978

Webster, Steven, *Patrons of Maori Culture: Power, Theory, and Ideology in the Maori Renaissance*, Dunedin, University of Otago Press, 1998

Weir, John (ed.), *James K. Baxter: Collected Poems*, Auckland, Oxford University Press, 1995

White, Georgina, *Light Fantastic: Dance Floor Courtship in New Zealand*, HarperCollins, Auckland, 2007

Williams, Melissa Matutina, '"Back-home" in the City: Maori Migration from Panguru to Auckland', Phd thesis, History, Auckland, University of Auckland, 2010

Wilson, Janet (ed.), *Frank Sargeson's Stories*, Auckland, Cape Catley, 2010

Wilson, Marie Gee, Gahlout, Priyanka, Liu, Lucia and Mouly, Suchitra, 'A Rose by Any Other Name: The Effect of Ethnicity and Name on Access to Employment', *University of Auckland Business Review*, vol. 7, no. 2, 2005, http://www.uabr.auckland.ac.nz/files/articles/Volume11/v11i2-a-rose-by-any-other-name.pdf

'Women in New Zealand', Wellington, Department of Statistics Te Tari Tatau/Ministry of Women's Affairs, 1990

Wood, F. L. W., *The ANZAC Dilemma*, International Affairs, vol. 29, April 1953

——, *This New Zealand*, Hamilton, Paul's Book Arcade, 1958, (first edn, 1952)

Woollaston, M. T., *The Far-away Hills: A Meditation on New Zealand Landscape*, Auckland, Auckland Gallery Associates, 1962

'Working for Families: A Benefit Cut', Wellington, Wellington People's Centre, March 2006, http://www.cpag.org.nz/assets/Wgtn%20People%27s%20Centre.pdf

Wright, Alan and Hanfling, Edward, *Mrkusich: The Art of Transformation*, Auckland, Auckland University Press, 2009

Young, David, *Our Islands, Our Selves: A History of Conservation in New Zealand*, Dunedin, University of Otago Press, 2004

Yska, Redmer, *All Shook Up: The Flash Bodgie and the Rise of the New Zealand Teenager in the Fifties*, Auckland, Penguin, 1993

——, *Truth: The Rise and Fall of the People's Paper*, Nelson, Craig Potton Publishing, 2010

INDEX